INTRODUCTION TO REFERENCE WORK

VOLUME I   *Basic Information Services*

INTRODUCTION TO REFERENCE WORK

Volume I **Basic Information Services**

Eighth Edition

William A. Katz
State University of New York at Albany

Boston   Burr Ridge, IL   Dubuque, IA   Madison, WI   New York
San Francisco   St. Louis   Bangkok   Bogotá   Caracas   Kuala Lumpur
Lisbon   London   Madrid   Mexico City   Milan   Montreal   New Delhi
Santiago   Seoul   Singapore   Sydney   Taipei   Toronto

McGraw-Hill Higher Education

A Division of The **McGraw-Hill** Companies

INTRODUCTION TO REFERENCE WORK, VOLUME I
Published by McGraw-Hill, an imprint of The McGraw-Hill Companies, Inc. 1221 Avenue of the Americas, New York, NY, 10020. Copyright © 2002, 1997, 1992, 1987, 1982, 1978, 1974, 1969 by The McGraw-Hill Companies, Inc. All rights reserved. No part of this publication may be reproduced or distributed in any form or by any means, or stored in a data base or retrieval system, without the prior written consent of The McGraw-Hill Companies, Inc., including, but not limited to, in any network or other electronic storage or transmission, or broadcast for distance learning.

Some ancillaries, including electronic and print components, may not be available to customers outside the United States.

This book is printed on acid-free paper.

domestic   3 4 5 6 7 8 9 0 DOC/DOC 0 9 8 7 6 5 4 3
international   1 2 3 4 5 6 7 8 9 0 DOC/DOC 0 9 0 9 8 7 6 5 4 3 2 1

ISBN 0-07-244107-0

Editorial director: *Phillip A. Butcher*
Sponsoring editor: *Valerie Raymond*
Project manager: *Diane M. Folliard*
Production supervisor: *Heather Burbridge*
Designer: *Gino Cieslik*
Producer, Media technology: *Lance Gerhart*
Compositor: *Electronic Publishing Services Inc., NYC*
Typeface: *10/12 Baskerville*
Printer: *R. R. Donnelley & Sons Company, Crawfordsville*

Library of Congress Cataloging-in-Publication Data

Katz, William A., 1924–
    Introduction to reference work / William A. Katz.—8th ed.
        p. cm.
    Includes bibliographical references and index.
    Contents: v. 1. Basic information services—v. 2. Reference services and reference processes.
    ISBN 0-07-244107-0 (v. 1) — ISBN 0-07-244143-7 (v. 2)
    1. Reference services (Libraries) 2. Reference books—Bibliography. I. Title.

Z711.K32 2002
025.5'52—dc21

                                                                                                    00-069536

INTERNATIONAL EDITION ISBN 0-07-112074-2
Copyright © 2002. Exclusive rights by The McGraw-Hill Companies, Inc. for manufacture and export.
This book cannot be re-exported from the country to which it is sold by McGraw-Hill. The International Edition is not available in North America.

www.mhhe.com

ABOUT THE AUTHOR

WILLIAM A. KATZ is a professor at the School of Information Science and Policy, State University of New York at Albany. He was a librarian at the King County (Washington) Library for four years and worked in the editiorial department of the American Library Association. He received his Ph.D. from the University of Chicago and has been the editor of *RQ,* the journal of the Reference and Adult Services Division of the American Library Association, and the *Journal of Education for Librarianship.* Professor Katz is now editor of *The Reference Librarian,* a quarterly devoted to issues in modern reference and information services, and *The Acquisitions Librarian,* concerned with collection development. He is the editor of *Magazines for Libraries* and has compiled a second edition of *The Columbia Granger's Guide to Poetry Anthologies.* He is editor of a series on the history of the book for Scarecrow Press including his *A History of Book Illustration* and *Dahl's History of the Book.* Presently, he is writing a cultural history of reference books.

CONTENTS

PREFACE

As in previous editions, this eighth edition of *Introduction to Reference Work: Volume I, Basic Information Services* is virtually rewritten. It is the author's conviction that the ongoing revolution in reference sources and the reference process requires such complete revision.

NEW TO THIS EDITION

Since the previous edition of this text, which offers an overview of reference services for curious students, the computer revolution has become an intransigent part of the library. What was radical is now an acceptable, expected part of daily library reference work. The revolution sped from agitation to acceptance in less than a decade. This is not to say the shape and methodology of reference service is now established. Change and motion is built into the electronic miracle and it continues to transform itself. Reference can be summarized in the words of the immortal Monty Python: "Now, for something completely different." Not a month goes by that somebody, somewhere discovers a new method of finding answers to questions. And it normally is tied closely to a computer.

Today reference libraries turn to indexes, encyclopedias, or directories for the same type of information as they did decades ago. The essential difference is threefold.

- First, one may use not only a print source, but also an electronic database, usually online and easily accessible on the Internet. CD-ROMs, too, are popular.

- Second, the library offers access not only to local resources, but also to all that has been published since the beginning of printing. There is little information that is not within the reach of a computer keyboard in almost every library in the United States and Canada.

- Third, the reference librarian uses traditional basic reference works and now acts as mediator as well, a middle person between masses of information and the user who is unable to discriminate the good from the poor, the best from the better. More and more the reference librarian has become the key professional information expert. Today he or she is necessary to filter the mass of undifferentiated information that flows over national and international networks.

Other trends in this revision are based upon probable reference services in the next decade. The changes represent a consensus among working reference librarians:

1. The Internet and its numerous configurations and promises is the basic carrier for information. In a short time it will replace standard print and CD-ROM formats.

2. The information highway is filled with ruts, bumps, and numerous hazards which few laypersons can avoid. The trained reference librarian not only bypasses such dangers but takes the user from beginning to end of a search with a minimum of difficulty.

3. Thanks to government intervention which ensures cheap access to the Internet, coupled with a growing trend towards literally giving away hardware in order to persuade people to use the Internet, all libraries will have Internet services available free to the public.

4. At the same time, standard information sources will remain as they are today, slightly to wildly expensive. As truly refined information databases become increasingly available, the library equally is increasingly important to ensure information's free access to the public.

5. Public, school, and academic libraries will make more databases available. The reference librarians will be called upon to solve problems as they arise for individual users.

6. The new technologies will increase the amount of reference services.

7. Thanks to constant changes in technology and resources, the librarian will have to continually renew, sharpen, and master new skills.

8. Subject expertise is increasingly important, particularly as the number of reference sources become more specific and the users more sophisticated.

9. Demand for instruction in the use of everything from computers to networks to pamphlets and, more particularly, online CD-ROM searching will continue to grow.

This first volume is by way of a training manual. No one can move into the finer points of reference services (present and future) without an understanding and mastery of basic reference forms, no matter what packages they are delivered in. The primary purpose, as in past editions, is to offer a lucid, accurate description of standard reference sources.

PLAN OF THE BOOK

The organization is much the same as in all editions. There is no reason to change since the text is dealing with fundamentals which, no matter what the information highway looks like or where it wanders, are essential to information understanding.

The first section considers the reference services process. Chapter 1 and Chapter 2 cover the parameters and meaning of the electronic library. Both chapters are expanded over the previous edition. The initial chapters serve as an explanation to two vital areas of reference services—the community served and the technologies employed in service.

As in the previous edition, Part II, Information: Control and Access, is concerned with bibliography and indexes. At this point, though, the basic layout changes. There is first an online format for a reference work, followed by a CD-ROM version, and last by the usually initial printed book.

The format pattern (throughout both the first and second volume) for reference works is shown below:

Online: Title of the reference source/publisher when it began publication/frequency — and usually with a URL, i.e., an Internet address. As all major reference sources are for a fee, the Internet address is not the actual address of the database (which requires a password), but the address of the publisher and background information on the source. Turn to your library's Web page to find the actual reference source online. If there, use the link to the online source. If not available from the library, turn to another library and/or use the publisher's URL given here as many for-fee databases allow a limited free search, which is ideal for students.

CD-ROM: Title and publisher not given as the same as for online. Note, though, where title of CD-ROM differs from the online version, this title is given when it began publication/frequency/price where this is known.

Print: Title, which often differs from the online and/or CD-ROM when it began publication/frequency/price (usually, let it be noted, much earlier than the electronic formats).

It is important to recognize that prices and bibliographical data changes. Even titles and publishers are subject to revision. Still, the basic information given here remains much the same from year to year.

Bibliographical data is based on publishers' catalogs, *Books In Print, Gale Directory of Database,* and examination of the titles. Online and

CD-ROM titles, for the most part, have been used at a computer terminal. Also, the author has turned to excellent reviews for support and assistance—particularly those in the *Library Journal, Booklist, Online, Database,* and *Choice.* The information is applicable as of 2000 and, like price, is subject to change.

Emphasis is on form, not on specific titles. Each form, from bibliographies to biographies, is discussed. Examples are given of titles—and particularly those titles likely to be found in most public, academic, or school libraries.

In describing each reference title the primary focus is on content, and how that content differs from, say, similar titles. The use of the reference work is indicated.

No exhaustive effort is made to show how to search X or Y database. Basic search patterns, especially where they are found in similar databases, are considered, but sophisticated searching is not discussed. Why? First, most schools and libraries have separate, necessary courses on database searching. Second, software (in which the search is found) is as likely to change as rapidly as the means of delivery of information. What may be a valid explanation of a search today may be nothing but history tomorrow. On the other hand, the basic content, the basic search approach, is not likely to change. And that is why both are stressed.

Part III, Sources of Information, follows the pattern of previous editions. Again, entries are as they were outlined for the first section. Here, though, the focus is on using "one-stop" information sources and how they fit into the average reference services arrangement.

ONLINE VERSION OF THE TEXT AND UPDATES

This text, and its companion volume, can be purchased in electronic format. Contact either your McGraw-Hill sales representative or visit www.mhhe.com/primis/online for more information.

Updates to the text will be available on an accompanying website: www.mhhe.com/katz.

SUGGESTED READING

In both volumes, suggested readings are found in the footnotes and at the end of each chapter. When a publication is cited in a footnote, the reference is rarely duplicated in the "Suggested Reading" section. For the most part, these readings are limited to publications issued since 1998. In addition to providing readers with current thinking, the more recent citations have the added bonus of making it easier for the student to locate the readings. It is beyond argument, of course, that *all* readings need not necessarily be current. Many older articles and books are as valuable today as they were when first published. Thanks to teachers who have retained earlier editions of this text it is possible to have a bibliography of previous readings.

Two points about Internet readings. Material on the Internet dates the moment it is published, whether in print or online. What is listed here is considered basic, if only for a few years. Second point: *Books in Print* from year to year has from 550 to 650 "Internet Guides." Most of these are so ephemeral to be worthless, but an effort has been made to pick a few that deserve a longer life and are likely to be of most value to beginners.

ACKNOWLEDGMENTS

Thanks are due to the reviewers who critiqued this book: Lesley Farmer, California State University, Long Beach; Judith V. Lechner, Auburn University; Ketty Rodriguez, University of Southern Mississippi; Gail M. Staines, University of Buffalo; Ibrahim M. Stwodah, Longwood College.

Thanks are also due to the editors for this volume, Valerie Raymond and Amy Shaffer, as well as thanks also to the indexer, Kelly Lutz.

William A. Katz

INTRODUCTION TO REFERENCE WORK

VOLUME I *Basic Information Services*

PART I
INTRODUCTION

CHAPTER ONE
REFERENCE LIBRARIANS ON THE
INFORMATION HIGHWAY

Since the first reference librarian rolled out of bed in Sumeria about 5,000 years ago, the day's activities have been shaped by questions. The librarian, who flourishes under scores of designations, from the early "keeper of tablets" to the modern "information scientists,"[1] is expected to come up with precise answers to sometimes sloppy queries.

In the beginning, replies were drawn from memory. There was not that much to remember. A wise person could say he or she knew all there was to know. In small communities older people were respected (and needed) because the memory of the old preserved the history and the day by day working information required for existence—whether it be avoiding marauders or knowing where to go in a period of little food. By the 16th century "as parish registers became more systematized and printing was more widespread, the old were gradually stripped of their role as the community's memory."[2]

With the Dark Ages (c. 410–800) and through the Medieval period and early Renaissance (c. 800–1500) the average library had a dozen or so volumes and a large library might boast no more than 100 to 500 tomes. The limited amount of reading matter explains the comforting notion of an educated reader that all that was to be known was available.

---

[1]Heard now and then in place of the descriptor "reference librarian" is "knowledge manager." This has numerous definitions, but "the basic elements include accessing, evaluating, managing, organizing, filtering and distributing information." Essentially, of course, it is the same definition of "reference librarian." For a less sanguine view of this development see Ernest Perez, "Knowledge Management…." *Database*, April/May, 1999, p. 75–77.

[2]George Minois, *History of Old Age*. Chicago, IL: University of Chicago Press, 1989, p. 248.

The invention of printing in the mid-15th century, the wide distribution of books by the 16th century, the growth of literacy among the middle classes in the 17th and 18th century, and the 19th century's mass education movement increased both the amount and the demand for information. As early as the mid–18th century, people were complaining there simply was too much to read, too much to know. Here, for example, is the writer Laurence Sterne in 1760 discussing an early version of the information explosion:

> Thus my fellow labourers and associates in this great harvest of our learning, now ripening before our eyes; thus it is, by slow steps of casual increase, that our knowledge physical, metaphysical, physiological, polemical, nautical, mathematical, enigmatical, technical, biographical, romantical, chemical, and obstetrical, with fifty other branches of it, (most of 'em ending, as these do, in *ical*) have...gradually been creeping upwards.[3]

More books are published each year trying to analyze today's information explosion than were found in monastic libraries from the fall of Rome to the invention of printing. The claim is not as ridiculous as it may seem. In 1400 years (i.e., c. 100–1500) the amount of information had only doubled. Today information doubles several times each year.

The growth of learning today no longer can be termed "gradual." Increasingly it is apparent that finding specific bits of data among the mass of undifferentiated information is the great challenge. And who meets that challenge? Well, for one, reference librarians.

INFORMATION SOURCES

Less than a decade ago information sources were synonymous with the printed book. Today the definition is turned on its electronic head. There are one to three billion online websites which may (or may not) contain useful information. Despite the development, librarians and wise laypeople rely on specific information sources rather than undifferentiated websites.

Basic reference sources are available online or as CD-ROMs, or DVDs. It is unusual to use only printed reference works unless one is seeking information before the early 1980s. Few electronic sources are retrospective. Slightly after the turn of the century all major information

[3]Laurence Sterne, *Tristram Shandy*. New York, NY: Modern Library, 1928, Book 1, Chapter 21, p. 56. Literature has numerous examples about the mass of information and difficulties of retrieving what is wanted, e.g., see for example the by now classic story *The Library of Babel* by Jorge Luis Borges. Here people have access to a library which contains answers to everything, including future events. Joy turns to despair as users realize the library is so big they are unable to find the answers they are looking for.

sources, and particularly those used daily by reference librarians, will be in digital form. Many, in fact, will not be available in print.

Be that as it may, the content, if not methods of retrieval, remains the same no matter what format the publisher chooses. It is essential that the professional librarian be able to turn to X or Y source for the proper answer to X or Y question. How many titles should the new librarian be familiar with when taking over a reference position?

The guides, directories, and bibliographies of reference sources—such as *Guide to Reference Books* or *Gale Directory of Databases*—list and annotate from close to 10,000 databases to 15,000 printed reference books. Selected guidelines for a given subject or size of library may range in number from a few hundred to about 2000. "Best Reference Books of…," a regular annual selection in *Library Journal*, normally selects 30 to 40 titles as the "best" of the year.

Surveys, formal and informal, constantly check to see what reference sources are used in a typical library. Today, that is expanded to include in what formats—print or digital. Answers represent as much habit as considered selection, as much personal favorites as the sum total of the library staff's choices. Much depends, too, on what question is asked, how it is phrased, and how it is interpreted by the individual librarian. Within a single day the same query might be fielded in several different fashions by as many librarians. As long as the answer(s) is correct, it matters not, at least if about the same amount of time and effort was spent on the query.

With all those variables, skepticism is in order for any except of the in-house survey of "best" and "better" reference sources. Generalizations are the result of even the most careful study. The generalizations often add up to much of the same. For example, inevitably when asked what is the single most-used source for reference questions the catalog comes first followed by such standards as a periodical index, the *World Almanac, Statistical Abstract of the United States* and a dozen other much used sources.[4]

[4]For example: Nancy Henry et al., "Scaling the Pyramids: Building a Collection of Basic Foundations," *Reference & User Services Quarterly*, Spring 2000, pp. 229–232. "What are the five print reference books that you can't work without?" A consensus includes: *World Almanac, World Book, Encyclopedia of Association, Random House Unabridged Dictionary*, 2nd ed.,*Britannica, Statistical Abstracts*, and the local, regional and major city phone books (p. 235). Online databases considered as basic: Gale Group's InfoTrac indexes; Phone disc or similar products; American Business Disk; Electric Library; Amazon.com and the related *Books in Print Plus*. In other places, other libraries, the list is much the same. See Carol Tenopir, "Reference Use Statistics," *Library Journal*, May 1, 1998, pp. 32, 34. In a survey of 44 university libraries, the author found "a library's online catalog answer the largest percentage of reference questions…followed closely by print reference books." OCLC, a bibliographic network, found that among the books most widely held by its over 32,000 library members there were a few reference titles. In order of most found in libraries they were: Turabian's *A Manual For Writers; Bartlett's Familiar Quotations; The New York Public Library Desk Reference; The Chicago Manual of Style; The Random House Dictionary;* and about six more including the librarian's own *Guide to Reference Books. OCLC Newsletter*, July/August, 1999, pp. 19–21.

The most popular "reference book" in America is the Bible. It is found in 93 percent of homes, primarily because 96 percent of Americans believe in God. One-third of Americans claim to read the Bible once a week, but as with other works of reference (in and out of libraries) retention of information is not a strong point. The response of regular Bible readers to a quiz shows the percentage who:

Can't name the authors of the four Gospels: 54%.

Don't know what a Gospel is: 63%.

Can't name five of the Ten Commandments: 58%.

Think Joan of Arc was Noah's wife: 10%.[5]

How many reference titles in print, CD-ROM, online, and in yet-to-be-revealed formats should the student master? There is no single answer. There are numerous variables. Also, each library has its own "core" collection, its own "canon." In this text about 400 to 500 titles are considered basic. At the other extreme in his *Distinguished Classics of Reference Publishing* (Phoenix, AZ: Oryx Press, 1992) which moves from quotations to encyclopedias, James Rettig and friends agree that there are at least 31 "major reference works" which anyone worthy of the name of reference librarian should know. As a rule of thumb, the beginner should be familiar with the much-used titles, from bibliography and indexes to encyclopedias and almanacs, found in every library. This amounts to mastering between 100 to 300 reference works. Beyond that is the universe of 15,000-plus titles.

All major print reference works are now online (and/or on CD-ROM). While the format differs the use and content of the reference book is the same online or off. Also there are now scores to thousands of websites which are unique to the Internet which from time to time may be useful in reference. Fortunately, knowledge of the basic titles is enough—at least for beginners.

Struggling to keep up with the latest information sources may not only be stressful, it can be a danger to your health. A published study found that "stress can shrink the part of the brain that stores memories." And another, a year later, found that "surfing can be particularly dangerous because it tends to be a leisure activity and people are less aware of their posture and hands." People of all ages often find themselves with computer aches and pains.[6]

---

[5]Russell Shorto, "Belief by the Numbers," *The New York Times Magazine*, December 7, 1997, p. 60–61.

[6]*The New York Times*, March 28, 1998, p. WK4; August 5, 1999, p. G3.

The Control–Access–Directional Type of Source

The first broad class or form of reference sources is the bibliography. This form is variously defined, but in its most general sense it is a systematically produced descriptive list of records.

Control. The bibliography serves as a control device, a kind of checklist. It inventories what is produced from day to day and year to year in such a way as to enable both the compiler and the user to feel they have a control, through organization, of the steady flow of knowledge. The bibliography is prepared through research (finding the specific source), identification, description, and classification.

Access. Once the items are controlled, the individual items are organized for easy access to facilitate intellectual work. All the access types of reference works can be broadly defined as bibliographies, but they may be subdivided as follows:

1. Bibliographies of reference sources and the literature of a field, of either a general or a subject nature, for example, *Guide to Reference Books* or *The Information Sources of Political Science.*

2. The library catalog or the catalogs of numerous libraries arranged for easy access at a computer. Technically, these are not bibliographies but are often used in the same manner.

3. General bibliographies, which include various subject forms of bibliography, for example, *The National Union Catalog.*

4. Indexes and abstracts, which are usually treated separately from bibliographies but are considered bibliographical aids—systematic listings which help identify and trace materials. Indexes to the contents of magazines and newspapers are the most frequently used types in the reference situation. Examples: *The Readers' Guide to Periodical Literature* and *The New York Times Index.*

Direction. Bibliographies themselves normally do not give definitive answers, but serve to direct users to the sources of answers. For their effective use, the items listed must be either in the library or available from another library system.

These days most access and control sources of reference works are available in digital form. Few remain only in print.

Source Type

Works of source type usually suffice in themselves to give the answers. Unlike the access type of reference work, they are synoptic.

Encyclopedias. The single most-used sources are encyclopedias; they may be defined as works containing informational articles on subjects in every field of knowledge, usually arranged in alphabetical order. They are used to answer specific questions about X topic or Y person or general queries which may begin with "I want something about Z." Examples: *Encyclopaedia Britannica; World Book Encyclopedia.* Today, all are available in print, online, and on CD-ROMs.

Fact Sources. Yearbooks, almanacs, handbooks, manuals, and directories are included in this category. All have different qualities, but they share one common element: They are used to look up factual material for quick reference. Together, they cover many facets of human knowledge. Examples: *World Almanac; Statesman's Year Book.*

Dictionaries. Sources that deal primarily with all aspects of words, from proper definitions to spelling, are classified as dictionaries. Examples: *Webster's Third New International Dictionary; Dictionary of American Slang.*

Biographical Sources. The self-evident sources of information on people distinguished in some particular field of interest are known as biographical sources. Examples: *Who's Who; Current Biography.*

Geographical Sources. The best-known forms are the atlases, which not only show given countries but may illustrate themes such as historical development, social development, and scientific centers. Geographical sources also include gazetteers, dictionaries of place names, and guidebooks. Example: *The Times Atlas of the World.*

Government Documents

Government documents are official publications ordered and normally published by federal, state, and local governments. Since they may include directional and source works, their separation into a particular unit is more for convenience and organization than for different reference use. Examples: *Monthly Catalog of United States Government Publications* (access type); *United States Government Manual* (source type).

The neat categorization of reference types by access and by source is not always distinct in an actual situation. A bibliography may be the only source required if the question is merely one of verification or of trying to complete a bibliographical citation. Conversely, the bibliography at the end of an encyclopedia article or a statement in that article may direct the patron to another source. In general, the two main categories—access and source—serve to differentiate among the principal types of reference works.

ELECTRONIC SOURCES

The "information highway," "information superhighway," "information infra-structure," and "communications network" are a few descriptors indicative of change and confusion. Whatever it may be called, the necessary approach requires a vast amount of technology. And that's what drives many reference librarians to the tea room. The constant change and shift in technology and of carriers of information is not only confusing but expensive. The time taken to master the forms and keep the library sources current is frightening. By not keeping up, today's modern librarian can be tomorrow's antique.

As a brief reminder: a *CD-ROM* ("compact disc-read-only memory") appears to be a CD from which one plays music. It holds up to 250,000 pages of text. Also, if "multimedia" programmed, it can hold pictures, sound, music, and so on."[7] *DVD*: Originally DVD stood for "digital video disk." The acronym remains, but the name was abandoned when producers realized the discs would be used for other purposes. The primary commercial use remains for television because the discs offer higher resolution pictures and better sound than a VCR tape.[8]

Online refers to information gathering from a server or mainframe computer's "database."[9] This, too, may have multimedia features, and these will become more sophisticated. There are two major divisions online, for–fee and free. Commercial online vendors and publishers (i.e., data dealers) expect payment for what is online. Their products, from indexes to encyclopedias, require that the library pay for information retrieval, by the hour, and subscribe or otherwise reach some type of monetary agreement with the publisher. (The jargon "gated content" means the information is paid for by the user to the commercial firm, or the "gate.") The second division is typified by the Internet World Wide Web which, for the most part, offers free information and entertainment.[10]

[7]Many believe, including the author of this text, that CD-ROMs will disappear. They will give way to online—at least for reference work. In terms of entertainment, the CD-ROMs may be about for many years to come. See: Peter Jacso, "Know When to Hold 'em…" *Computers in Libraries*, March, 1999, pp. 38–42. He, too, supports the notion that the CD is doomed for reference services.

[8]DVD developments have a major interest for librarians. In time DVD-ROM (or similar technology with perhaps another name) will replace CD-ROMs as carriers because of its superior storage capabilities, seven or more times greater than CDs. Images and sound, too, are superior. Paul Nicholls, "DVD is Coming" *Computers in Libraries*, May, 1999, p. 57.

[9]A "database" is an electronic form of data, i.e., in this text, the contents of what a few years ago would be found in a reference book. Normally the database is stored in a computer file or on a CD-ROM. It can be text or numerical, or both and usually includes multimedia features from sound to visuals.

[10]The for-fee, or free designation may disappear. All information may be free when and if new methods of gaining online profit become available, i.e., advertising or similar techniques which brings America free information on the radio and TV. Many, including this author think the general for-fee databases may give this up to reach a wider audience.

Why Electronic?

Until a few years ago if you wanted to read a page from the *Oxford English Dictionary*, which traces the history of words, you had to pull the heavy volume from the shelf, hunt up the information, and possibly copy it down or photocopy the page. If you were in a library without this reference work, it was necessary to have the page sent, or go to a library that had the set. There were other problems. The volume you needed might be missing, the page you needed might be torn out, and so on. Enter the electronic OED (*Oxford English Dictionary*) in a digitized form. Now one may search for the same word at a computer terminal. Furthermore, it is possible to do such things as search for your word in the millions of quotations in the complete set. There are numerous other points of data one may extract electronically in seconds. Using the print version the same quest might take hours, even months. Similar shortcuts are now possible with countless reference works.

Electronic databases, online or CD-ROM, are practical. The advantage to looking up an encyclopedia article in digital form is that it simultaneously offers text, illustrations, possibly sound effects, and a video of whatever the subject from bird life to Chaucer. Scholars can now examine archives, manuscripts, and rare book texts.

Why do publishers and reference publishers specifically prefer electronic to print? There are several basic reasons. First, it is much less expensive than print. Also, there are no major packaging and mailing costs. Second, the data online can be updated by the minute, which increases the use (and text sales) of the reference work. Third, some, but not all, encourage interactivity which allows the users to send questions or feedback. Four, there is promise of multimedia features from video to sound.

There is no question about the future of digitized information. In 2000 approximately 80 percent of American libraries, regardless of type or size, have some type of electronic reference work, usually an encyclopedia and/or an index. The larger and richer the library, the more evidence there is of electronic forms of information. Even with Internet access, small- to medium-sized libraries still rely primarily on printed reference works. Why? Because they can't afford the more expensive for-fee reference works online. All reference sections rely on some printed materials. Most retrospective reference questions are answered from such works. The electronic databases rarely cover data published before the mid-1980s.

In another decade or so print reference works will disappear entirely, particularly when retrospective indexes are put online. Note, though, this does not mean all print, but primarily reference works which are much easier to use online.

Database Knowledge

The librarian must have a thorough knowledge of the electronic database, and must be able to quickly ascertain such things as period of coverage, type of materials considered, and frequency of updating.

There are about a dozen widely used databases out of a possible choice of over 6,000. Public and academic reference librarians are more likely to search (in rough order of such use): *Psychological Abstracts, ERIC, ABI/Inform, MLA* (Modern Language Association), *MEDLINE, Dissertation Abstracts International, Social Sciences Citation Index, PAIS, Newspaper Abstracts* and the *GPO Monthly Catalog.* Clients, on the other hand, are likely to confine searches to much more general databases such as those offered by EBSCO, UMI, IAC, or the H. W. Wilson Company. And where available they will use OCLC's *First Search* choices such as *ArticlesFirst* and the numerous catalogs.

Various systems and software allow the searcher to: (1) search databases within a given large subject area and (2) find out how many times a key word(s) appear in each of the databases. Many systems permit the user to type in the key word and see how often it appears in 20, or fewer, related databases.

There are useful mnemonic devices for the trained searcher, but of limited use of laypersons. First one must choose the proper broad subject area, which is not all that difficult; but then one must decide which databases to search. Only the person familiar with the databases can choose wisely. For example, is it better to use a database with 3,026 entries for "nuclear waste" or one with 30 or 3? It depends on what is indexed, the situation, and, more importantly how familiar the searcher is with the given database(s).

WHO USES REFERENCE SERVICES

Where do the majority of people seek information? These days the majority turn to the Internet, particularly at home. Other than from the Internet, or from friends and working colleagues, studies find that about 50 percent turn to a library. Close behind is perusal of their own magazines and newspapers, as well as the home print library. The alarming note for parents, teachers, and librarians is that teenagers now prefer the Internet to the library, even though it may take them hours to find what they might find in minutes in a library. Working at home they are not forced to ask for help or work out the structure of library organized information.

Patrons, clients, users—the people who wander in and out of libraries and reference sections—generally are of three or four basic types. A small percentage, probably under one percent in academic libraries and negligible in public libraries, are researchers who are seeking raw data. Other than the need to be pointed in the direction of what they are looking for or to find quickly what they require, they generally fall outside the working circle of the average reference librarian.

The next large group are those seeking specific answers (resources to short facts) to equally specific questions. This is the primary audience for the reference librarian as mediator. Most of these people know little or nothing about the library and are interested only in the response, which should be precise, brief, and right on target. Again, this is probably no more than 5 to 10 percent of the users, at least in academic and special libraries. Public librarians will find a smaller percentage of such types, but these normally can be categorized as involved in business.

The largest group who need the reference librarians are those who have an undifferentiated requirement for information. They may range from the student who has to write a paper on the hobbies of Lincoln to the doctor who may be looking for hobbies to take his mind off medicine. Neither requires specific answers. Both want a variety of material, at various levels of depth and sophistication. The danger here is that the reference librarian will see these people as those who should be finding the information on their own, who should, at best, be turned over to someone in the general reading room. The librarian, then, has given up a process of information mediation where it may be needed the most. The student and the layperson not only want to know what to read, but what not to read. They both require an analysis that some reference librarians might consider not really part of their professional job.

It's difficult to categorize people who turn to reference librarians for assistance. One group, though, is the cause of more headaches than another. There are the "don't know and don't care" types. They are pushed into a library by parents and/or necessity to squeak through a course. This slice of the American public has become progressively less informed on current events, history, geography and just about anything.

> I teach an undergraduate class on public opinion at the University of Michigan, and at the beginning of every semester for the past 10 years, students in this class—mostly juniors and seniors—have taken a brief quiz on assorted historical facts. This semester's results especially concerned me. Only seven percent of my students could name this state's two United States senators, for example, and barely one-third could name the Secretary of State. Fewer than half could say when World War II began and ended.[11]

[11]Richard Craig. "Don't Know Much About History," *The New York Times,* December 8, 1997, p. A25. A Washington-based nonprofit academic organization asked 556 seniors at 55 leading colleges and universities (including Ivy League schools) 34 high school-level questions about history. The average score: only 53 percent of the questions were answered correctly. And none of the questions were above the standard high school History 101 course. *The New York Times,* July 2, 2000, p. WK7.

There are numerous explanations from lack of interest in anything which does not further a career to lack of an international enemy which requires global awareness. Others say too much television, or Internet, or poor schools, or lack of motivation, or...fill in your own explanation. A more optimistic reference librarian will encourage the half awake, half asleep to appreciate, if not entirely enjoy learning.

What It Takes

Will you be a good reference librarian?

The answer depends as much upon the library as the individual. On a large staff someone who delights in technology will find a position assisting with computer searches as well as keeping others advised of the best hardware, software, and the twists, turns, and off- and on-ramps of the information highway. Where the librarian is the only professional within four towns, the opportunities to master technological skills are checked by lack of money, lack of space, lack of time, and lack of the luxury of concentration on reference work. More likely, the average reference librarians is somewhere in between.

Reference librarians are unanimous about what the successful librarian needs: (1) Subject area knowledge (i.e., what is available in print, online, from other resources, etc.). This means not only having a skilled appreciation of reference sources in general, but understanding better than anyone else how to dig out data from a given subject field. A generalist with a particular expertise is much sought after. (2) Conversational skills. This means an ability to talk to all types of people, to find out what they need. Furthermore, one should know whether a formal reference interview is required or whether it is easier to simply find the citation or answer. (3) Competence in selecting and acquiring materials—from databases to print almanacs and biographical sources.

Public service is one of the most pleasurable aspects of the profession. There are drawbacks.[12] Sometimes the questions asked will be repetitive, dull, or simple, although important to the person asking. Not everyone wants to know either the meaning of art or the best approach to ending the drug problem. In fact, the majority of reference queries are of a ready-reference type which require a quick, fact answer.

Is the reference librarian a generalist? Is she as comfortable with Einstein as with T.S. Eliot? A few years ago the answer was a resounding "yes." Books and articles supported the librarian in this role. Gradually, thanks as much to electronic advances as to increased fragmented infor-

---

[12]Each year there are countless surveys to determine job satisfaction among librarians. There is a consensus that librarianship is equivalent to other professions. Some 54 percent would recommend librarianship as a career. Rachel Gordon and Sarah Nesbeitt, "Who We Are..." *Library Journal*, May 15, 1999, pp. 36–39.

mation sources, the proud designation disappeared. Now it is the specialist, at least in libraries where there is more than one professional about. The librarian, sometimes with two masters degrees, not only is comfortable following the generalist lines, but when called upon answers problems in the role of a bibliographer, expert in 19th–century literature or sciences. Ironically these same hard–edged experts are cheerfully building software to replace them, much as IBM pushed the world's chess champion out of first place with a decisive win. Most librarians, though, still look to the printed book not the computer.[13]

What should one learn in basic training for reference work or, for that matter, the profession as a whole? Getting to feel at home in a reference section requires that the beginner master reference works. One must be comfortable at a computer terminal as well as talking with a less-than-verbal user who is looking for a jam recipe or a way to get through to the next day.

In time the beginner becomes a veteran. And veteran librarians never quit, or are fired, or die. They simply gain fame as being among the wisest people in the world. A psychologist suggests "a steady diet of simple pleasures will keep you [happy]." Add to this the delights of being a reference librarian. There is the zest for life formula.[14]

REFERENCE SERVICE GUIDELINES

The Reference and Adult Services Division of the American Library Association offers reference librarians a set of guidelines which help both to define their work and chart, if only in a tentative way, a philosophy of service. The guidelines are called "Information Services for Information Consumers: Guidelines for Providers" and "Guidelines for Behavioral Performance of Reference and Information Services Professionals."[15] Directed to all those who have any responsibility for providing reference and information services, the guidelines' most valuable contributions are the succinct description of a reference librarian's duties.

The guidelines address information services from six points of view: services, resources, access, personnel, evaluation, and ethics. The primary service is "to provide an end product: the information sought by the user."

[13]Gordon and Nesbeitt, *op. cit.* Only 20 of 391 respondents chose librarianship as a career because they enjoy work with technology/computers. The majority close it as a career because they love books and reading.

[14]*Harper's Magazine*, November, 1997, p. 32.

[15]"Information Services for Information Consumers: Guidelines for Providers," *RQ,* Winter 1990, pp. 262–265. "Guidelines for Behavioral Performance of Reference and Information Services Professionals," *RQ,* No. 2, 1996, pp. 200–203. These frequently are updated.

Teaching people how to find information is a second important duty. "Such instruction can range from the individual explanation of information sources or creation of guides and appropriate media to formal assistance." There is a stress on the need for current, accurate resources as well as easy access to those sources and the reference librarian. A section on personnel underlines the importance of being "thoroughly familiar with and competent in using information sources." There is much more, but the statement concludes with an emphasis on the American Library Association's Code of Ethics which "governs the conduct of all staff members."

The ethics code leads to the next set of guidelines on evaluation of reference librarians and their services. In order to ensure "we collectively succeed" in the highly complex reference process, the "Behavioral Guidelines" urge librarians: (1) *Be approachable.* "The initial verbal and non-verbal responses of the librarian will influence the depth and level of the interaction between the librarian and the patron." (2) *Show interest.* "A successful librarian must demonstrate a high degree of interest in the reference transaction." (3) *Conduct a reference interview.* Here behavioral attributes which lead to a good interview are noted as well as methods of clarifying the patron's question. (4) *Conduct a search.* Again behavioral measures to aid in the search are listed, because "without an effective search, accurate information is unlikely to be found." (5) *Follow up.* "The reference transaction does not end when the librarian walks away from the patron. The librarian is responsible for determining if the patron is satisfied with the results of the search."

QUESTIONS AND SEARCHES

There are two or three traditional library approaches to analyzing reference questions. The usual is to count how many questions are asked, and how long it takes to give an answer. This is noted for statistical reports and, not incidentally, to rationalize need for more money and personnel. The practice continues today, but there is equal focus on types of questions. Not that categorization is easy. Given access to users of electronic searches, it is difficult at times to determine what kind of questions they are asking. Still, where analysis is employed the framework for queries remains much the same. This can be divided into two general types:

1. *The user asks for a known item.* The request is usually for a specific document, book, article, film, or other item, which can be identified by citing certain features such as an author, a title, or a source. The librarian has only to locate the needed item through the catalog, an index, a bibliography, or a similar source—and, often, all are searchable at a computer terminal.

2. *The user asks for information without any knowledge of a specific source.* Such a query triggers the reference interview—an important consideration in reference services discussed throughout this text and most particularly in the second volume. Most reference questions are of a general type, particularly those in school and public libraries where the average user has little or no knowledge of the reference services available.

Handling the two broad types of questions may not be as easy as it seems. For example, the person who asks for a specific book by author may (1) have the wrong author, (2) actually want a different book by that author, (3) discover that the wanted book is not the one required (for either information or pleasure), or (4) ask the librarian to obtain the book on interlibrary loan and then fail to appear when the book is received. All this leads most experienced reference librarians to qualify the "known–item" type of question. The assumption made by the librarian is usually correct, and the user really needs more information or help than indicated. Therefore, librarians tend to ask enough questions to clarify the real needs of the user rather than accept what may be only a weak signal for help.

A more finely drawn categorization of reference questions can be divided into four types:

1. *Direction.* "Where is the catalog?" "Where are the indexes?" "Where is the telephone?" The general information or directional question is of the information booth variety, and the answer rarely requires more than geographical knowledge of key locations. The time required to answer such questions is negligible, but directional queries can account for 30 to 50 percent of the questions put to a librarian in any day. The percentage given here and in what follows are relative and may vary from library to library.

2. *Ready reference.* "What is the name of the governor of Alaska?" "How long is the Amazon River?" "Who is the world's tallest person?" These are the typical ready-reference or data queries that require only a single, usually uncomplicated, straightforward answer. The requested information is normally found without difficulty in standard reference works, ranging from encyclopedias to almanacs and indexes. Many of these may be accessed at a computer terminal.

Ready-reference queries may be divided and subdivided in many ways. Crossing almost all subject lines, one can construct a classification scheme similar to the news reporter's five W's. These are *(a) Who?* Who is...; Who said...; Who won...; and so forth. *(b) What?* What does coreopsis look like? *(c) Where?* Where is the center of the United States? Where is the earth's core? *(d) Why?* Why does water boil? Why, why, why...almost anything. (This, the favored beginning of all children's queries, continues with most of us through life.) *(e) When?* When was *Coriolanus* written? When was the automobile invented? Most of these queries require only a specific piece of data. Also, many might be modified or rephrased in such a way as to get a yes, no, or maybe answer: Is aspirin harmful? Was America discovered in 1492?

It usually takes more than a minute or two to answer this type of question. The catch is that while 90 percent of such queries are simple to answer, another 5 to 10 percent may take hours of research because no standard reference source in the library will yield the necessary data. Apparently simple questions are sometimes complicated, such as "What are the dates of National Cat Week?" (Answer: Flexible, but usually in early November.) "When and where was Russian roulette first played?" (Answer: Cambridge University in 1801. Lord Byron describes the incident in his memoirs.)

The percentage of ready-reference questions will differ from library to library, but about 50 to 60 percent of the questions asked in a public library are of the ready-reference type. Public libraries, which may have a well-developed phone service for reference questions as well as a high percentage of adult users, tend to attract the ready-reference question. Requests for background information make up the other 40 to 50 percent or so of the queries.

In academic, school, and special libraries, specific-search questions account for a larger percentage of the total.

3. *Specific-search questions.* "Where can I find information on sexism in business?" "What is the difference between the conservative and the liberal views on inflation and unemployment?" "Do you have anything on the history of atomic energy?" "I have to write a paper on penguins for my science class. What do you have?" The essential difference between the specific-search and the ready-reference question is important. Ready-reference queries usually can be answered with data, normally short answers from reference sources. Specific-search answers almost always take the form of giving the user a document, a list of citations, a book, a report, an Internet site, etc.

More information is required for the user who is writing a school paper, is preparing a speech, or is simply interested in learning as much about a subject as necessary for his or her needs. This query often is called a *bibliographical inquiry*, because the questioner is referred to a bibliographical aid such as the catalog, an index, or a bibliography. Most of these, even in small libraries, are available on CD-ROM or online, and makes searching much easier—*if*, and the "if" should be stressed, the user knows how to get information from the electronic database. At this point the librarian may have to step in to offer help.

Of course, not all specific-search questions involve bibliographies. At a less sophisticated level, the librarian may merely direct the user to an article in an encyclopedia, to a given section of the book collection, or to a digital newspaper index.

The time it takes to answer a user's question depends not only on what is available, but also on the librarian. If the librarian offers a considerable amount of help, the search can take from 10 minutes to an hour or more. Conversely, a less helpful or busier librarian may turn the question into a two-second directional one by simply pointing the user to the catalog or the computer.

Some types of specific-search questions are treated by librarians as reader advisory problems. These are questions that, in essence, ask "What is the best source of information for my needs?" Questioners may be seeking everything from fiction and poetry to hobby magazines. Depending on the size and the organizational pattern of the library, their queries may be handled by subject or reader advisory librarians or by reference librarians. In a small library these are one and the same person.

4. *Research.* Almost any of the types of questions described in the "specific-search" section above may be turned into research questions. A research query is usually identified as that coming from an adult specialist who is seeking detailed information to assist in specific work. The request may be from a professor, a business executive, a scientist, or other person who needs data for a decision or additional information about a problem. With the exception of some academic and special libraries, this type of inquiry is a negligible part of the total reference pattern in libraries.

Ready-reference and specific-search queries presuppose specific answers and specific sources, which, with practice, the librarian usually can locate quickly. Research questions differ from other inquiries in that most involve trial-and-error searching or browsing, primarily because *(a)* the average researcher may have a vague notion of the question but usually cannot be specific; *(b)* the answer to the yet-to-be-completely formulated question depends on what the researcher is able to find (or not find). The researcher recognizes a problem, identifies the area that is likely to cover the problem, and then attempts to find what has been written about the problem.

The difficulty with the categorization of reference questions is that few are that easy to label. True, when someone asks for the bathroom, this is a simple directional query. True, when another person needs material on the salmon, this is a specific-search question. At the same time, a directional question may turn into a ready-reference query, and a specific-search need may develop into research.

For example, the young person who asks for material on the salmon actually may be interested in knowing where one can catch salmon in the immediate area. Hence a supposed search question is really a ready-reference query. Conversely, someone may ask where to catch salmon, although that person really wants to know about fishing conservation. A ready-reference question has been turned inside out into a search or even a research problem.

What type of information do people seek in a public library? Divorced of school assignments, which make up a large proportion of the queries, the subject questions most likely to surface are: first, medical and health problems, including fitness; second, computers and related technology; third, personal financial problems; and fourth and fifth, travel and business. Near the bottom of the list are questions about: literature and writers; bibliography and publishing; and the social sciences. While the results are only general, and subject to massive variations depending on the community involved, the findings at least indicate basic interests near the turn of the century. They can, of course, change quickly.[16]

REFERENCE INTERVIEW AND SEARCH

The common complaint heard among reference librarians about their work is that few people know how to ask reference questions. There are many reasons why the public may not appreciate the need for clarity at the reference desk, and these reasons are considered throughout this text. One way to clarify the individual's need is to launch the reference interview which may take only a minute or become quite involved.

The reference interview has several objectives. The first is to find out what and how much data the user needs. This should be simplicity itself, except that most people do not know how to frame questions. The child looking for information on horses may be interested in pictures, an encyclopedia article, or possibly a book on riding. No matter what the scope of the query, it probably will come out as "Do you have anything on horses?"

The adult has some notion of what is wanted, both in terms of quantity and quality. Yet, that same user may be vague about whether or not an article should be used from a particular journal. The qualifications of the author and publisher are better known to the librarian than to the average reader. For example, in a string of 10 citations about solar energy, would a high school senior, a college senior, or a layper-

[16]Norman Oder, "What Does the Public Want to Know," *Library Journal*, November 15, 1997, p. S4–S6.

son be happier with citations from *Time, Reader's Digest,* and *Newsweek,* or from the *Monthly Energy Review, EPRI Journal,* and *Solar Energy?* These fundamental decisions of the librarian will be of great help to the average person.

The reference interview often, all too often, is short-circuited by lack of interest on the part of the librarian, lack of knowledge of such help by the user, and lack of patience by user or librarian as the interview begins. This, to say the least, tends to discourage both children and adults from approaching the librarian. No wonder in a situation like this that the average teenager is happier finding his or her own answers at the computer.

Both teenagers and adults who have become acquainted with the ease of searching at a library computer terminal, often will avoid the librarian. Type in a few key words, a personal name, a subject heading, and if the database matches the query, four or five citations come up on the screen. That's quite enough for the average student or layperson who believes this is the end of the quest. It may be only the beginning or a total dead end, and it is here, or better, before the search begins, that the interview is extremely useful.

Not too many years ago, most reference librarians agreed they should never interpret or analyze information, only help people to find what they needed. There still is some grumbling about reference librarians even indicating what is a good, mediocre or even bad website. Won't do! Today the primary professional duty of any reference librarian is to sift through the masses of information available, on or off the Web, and indicate what is suitable for a particular question, a particular person. Simply to hand an individual *The Physicians Desk Reference* without explaining what it does or does not do, is not enough.

The layperson looks at the reference librarian as an expert who knows as much about information as a doctor about medicine or the mechanic about a gearbox. It is a professional duty to offer opinion and discrimination—opinion about what is best and discrimination at what intellectual level. The Editor-in-Chief of *Library Journal* sums it up:

> The lawyer tells us what is legal and who to sue and why. Even the travel agent guarantees the best routes and lowest fares. If we aspire to be as "professional" as these others, we must be willing to risk giving the kind of value judgments they make and the advice they deliver. If we aspire to survive in this new age of easy access to all kinds of information, we have no choice but to elevate ourselves and our service to this crucially needed but high-risk role of information advisor. If we don't offer that kind of professional information service, who needs us?[17]

[17]John Berry, "Risking Relevant Reference Work," *Library Journal,* May 15, 1998, p. 6.

Much of the change has occurred, if more by necessity than design. Electronic resources force reference librarians to at least indicate how they are used and, in the process, which ones to consult for a given query. Along the way navigational problems inevitably arise which lead the librarian to give advice which usually becomes an informal reference interview. The librarian of today is more mobile, spends less time at a desk and more time giving aid to baffled users cruising the Web or the reference book stacks.

Who Is to Answer?

The fascinating result of analyses of types of questions is that (1) the majority of queries are directional or ready-reference pure and simple; (2) generally, the queries and sources used are basic and easy to understand; and (3) most questions, therefore, could be answered by a well-trained person with a bachelor's degree.

But that does not necessarily mean that the trained nonprofessional can or should replace the professional librarian for the purpose of answering directional and ready-reference queries. Often the simple questions can develop into complex ones requiring professional aid. Even where nonprofessionals are used sparingly, the average library can depend on nonreference librarians to help at the reference desk.

Does it make any difference whether a professional librarian or a clerk answers a reference question? No—if the question is answered to the satisfaction of the user. Yes—if either the clerk or the librarian fails to follow through with enough of the right information, or totally strikes out. If the clerk is better-educated, more personable and, yes, more experienced than the librarian, it may be that the clerk scores higher. Odds are, though, that the professional will do better because of superior knowledge. In fact, professionals score higher because they know what and how much is needed for individual requests.

Typically under-financed and with increasing demand for more sophisticated electronic reference sources, how does the average medium to large reference library withstand the pressure? Some answer, "they don't," and throw up their hands. More likely, though, the administration while cutting back sometimes on professional staff (usually to put aside money for those same electronic reference works) increase the number of paraprofessionals. A computer skilled non-librarian can do much with helping a user on the Web or with complicated databases. Another non-degree individual may be a whiz in answering ready-reference questions. Following channels, the usual process is to turn to the professional librarian only when there is a real problem, a question which can't be answered. There is much debate about this "solution" but it does help spread limited personnel and resources. "Reference departments must be careful, however, and not succumb to the HMO trend of severely limiting the time a doctor is allowed to spend with a patient. Most librarians surveyed enjoy their jobs in this electronic age precisely because of the new challenges and enhanced chance of getting a correct answer to difficult questions.[18]

Searching

In any search several steps are taken, sometimes almost subconsciously: (1) The question is clarified so it is as precise as possible. (2) The question is linked to a particular reference source. (3) The methods of searching are employed to narrow or expand the quest.

The problem is there is too much of everything. The tricks of the fast, efficient search vary from question to question, situation to situation. Still there are relatively simple search techniques. Most of these are as applicable to print as online. Search patterns are of one of two broad types. The most efficient is to go directly to the precise source. For example: a phone number to a phone book; a word's meaning to a dictionary; a statistic to a statistical handbook; a background question on art to an encyclopedia. The simple, direct match of question and source is not always that simple, or direct. The second more common approach is to go through a number of steps which will make the relationship between query and source more obvious. Basic steps to finding a correct answer follow several well-known routes:

1. The first step is to understand the question, whether it be a simple fact query (i.e., What is the population of Seattle?) or a search question (What are the arguments pro and con for gun control?), or a research query (Which are the best solutions to be sure the country enjoys economic growth through the next 50 years?) Each of these types calls for different search patterns. The simple fact question can be answered in a single reference source. Here the trick is to know which source to consult. The search question requires more information, usually found in an encyclopedia (for background and history) and updated in an index (for current thoughts and arguments). Someone leisurely searching for knowledge about this or that subject follows much the same pattern. The research problem calls into play the whole library and not one or two reference sources, but perhaps scores both on and off the Internet.

2. When the question is clarified one further modifies the question by turning to key words, phrases, and subject headings which best describe what one hopes to find. Actually, in refining and defining the subject the searcher is likely to have used key words or phrases, and these

---

[18]Carol Tenopir, "Reference Use Statistics," *Library Journal*, May 1, 1998, p. 34.

can be then used for the actual search. Someone wants information on English renaissance architecture. He may begin with a general notion about "architecture," narrow it down to "England" and then decide to make it even more narrow by confining it to the "renaissance period." All of the quoted words are key words that may be used in the search.

The key words should be as specific as possible. For example, "English renaissance architecture" sets the place, the time, and the subject. The query could be made even more specific by adding or substituting "London" for "England." The narrower, the more specific the search key words, the easier it is to find material. If it becomes too confined, then one may broaden it by adding other words and phrases.

3. If in a quandary as to what words or phrases to employ try one or two things: *(a)* Go to an index that is close to the subject of interest and see what subject headings they employ. Note, too, the *see* and *see also* references to find specific subject words and to find matching subject terms. *(b)* Consult standard works such as the *Library of Congress Subject Headings*, a multi-volume work that gives subjects in alphabetical order (See p. 137).

4. Once the topic and key words are isolated, one must know where to go to find the information. A basic decision concerns whether it should be print or online.

At this point there are at least three methods open for someone looking for information on the aforementioned topic "English renaissance architecture." *(a)* Consult the online catalog of the library and see if there are any books on the subject. *(b)* Consult an index of periodicals that is concerned primarily with architecture and/or art. In this case it would be *Art Index* or *Architectural Index*. Another possibility would be any general online index which would bring up less technical articles. The search would be done by entering the key words, or the subject headings used in the library catalog. *(c)* Go to the Internet and search out art and architectural sources such as "Art on the Net" which is a virtual gallery of artists and some architecture; or the University of California's "Architecture Slide Library."

There are many other methods to find what is needed. For example, a well-known English renaissance architect's name is a springboard into data possibly not covered in the initial search. One can turn to information on a famous cathedral and seek information on the specific place of worship. In other words, there is no limit to attacking the problem other than the searcher's imagination.

5. Keep an ongoing record of the information journey, at least for questions that require no more than a few minutes to answer. When an important site on the Internet has been found, bookmark it for future references. If X or Y index seems useful, and you may wish to come back to it, make a note of its name and what years it covered as well as subject headings employed.

6. All of the steps to find data turn on where to begin the search. Should it be the catalog, an index, or is a dictionary or biographical source better? Which index, or which biographical source? The secret of economical efficient reference is to know precisely where to go. Focus is all because there are many possibilities for wasting time, floating around in cyberspace, and failing to connect with what is required.

Search Summary

In terms of where does the reference librarian find answers there are three paths:

1. If a specific title, author, or subject consult the library catalog for a book.

2. If a specific source for a subject, person or whatever, go directly to that source (i.e., dictionary for a definition; atlas for a map; biographical reference work for a person's biography, etc.).

3. Lacking either of the above, which is most often the case, try to match the question with a reference form. Can the information be found more efficiently in an encyclopedia, in an index, or a biographical source? Once the form is isolated turn to print, online, CD-ROM, or the Internet for the handiest, most efficient entry into that dictionary or index, or other reference work.

Reference Librarian's Role

The hero of the library is the reference librarian who confidently can tie sources to answers, without even so much as a nervous tick. Where, for example, is the biographical source which will tell me the names of the three sons of Noah? (Shem, Ham, and Japheth); or what science encyclopedia is likely to answer an anxious reader's "What is the difference in the genetic makeup of me and Joe?" (We each share more than 99.8 percent of the same genetic makeup. The difference is less than .2 percent—which explains why you are handsome and Joe is a slob.)

Experienced librarians come up with correct answers through memory and considerable appreciation of reference sources. The latter is the jurisdiction of this text.

The superior reference librarian has other claims to fame besides a passable memory. Logic helps. The ability to take a jumbled query, sort it out, reword it, and feed it back to the person who put the ques-

[handwritten: workers in conversation]

tion as if it was his or hers is the skill of the reference interviewer. Other desirable attributes include appearing wise, affable, and sympathetic when someone asks you: "What is love?" or "What is the cure for the cold?" or "How can I get an A on my paper?"

The path to success is a calm Zen-like attitude. This is based as much upon a good disposition as confidence in when to say, ever so politely "Let's see what we can find." Work in a reference area will point the way. Reference sources inevitably will disclose answers to even the most remote, difficult query. And if not a precise response, at least it will be a reply which will satisfy.

Reference Service and the Library

The reference librarian does not function alone in a library, but is part of a larger unit, a larger mission. Today the library is considerably more than a warehouse.

Most libraries now have replaced or augmented the familiar card catalog with an online public access catalog. This is constantly referred to in the literature as OPAC (Online Public Access Catalog). Today these catalogs often carry other data and are among the first facilities to be included in local or international networks. Most of the large 225 academic library catalogs in 10 countries are accessible through Internet and other linking devices. The librarian, or user, sits down before a computer terminal, types in a few key letters or parts of words, and is given immediate access to the holdings of the library or other libraries—often with additional data.

Technology. The rapid development of new technologies in information storage and retrieval has meant that larger libraries often have a special office, division, or section devoted to (1) keeping the administration and librarians advised of developments from new methods of networking to improved computer screens; (2) evaluating hardware, software, and other components of the modern information systems; and, in many cases, (3) determining what to buy, what to avoid, and how to work within a given budget.

Reader Services: Circulation. Circulation is one of the two primary public service points in the library. After a book has been acquired and prepared for easy access, the circulation department is concerned with (1) checking out the material to the reader, (2) receiving it on return, and (3) returning it to its proper location.

Adult Services: Reference. An important component of reference service is adult services, often used as a synonym for "adult education."

This is a specialized area, although in daily work the average reference librarian will be involved in a range of adult services such as giving assistance with job and occupational information or providing service for the handicapped.

EVALUATION OF REFERENCE SOURCES

With more and more reference sources, evaluation is all. The librarian must keep up with the proliferation of information sources, but more important must be able to judge what is needed for the library and its particular audiences.

How does the librarian know whether a reference source is good, bad, or indifferent? A more detailed answer will be found throughout each of the chapters in this volume. Simply stated, however, a good reference source is one that answers questions, and a poor reference source is one that fails to answer questions. Constant use in practice will help in identifying any source, (whether a book or a database) with one of these two categories.

Because of the expense of most reference sources, the typical practice is to read one or more reviews before deciding whether to buy or lease. Databases available online require a similar decision.

Large libraries usually request, or automatically receive examination copies of print reference works before purchase. Similar arrangements for trials online, CD-ROMs, tapes, vendors, and so forth, may be arranged as well. Ideally, the reference source should be examined by a trained reference librarian before it is incorporated into the collection. No reviewer, review, or review medium is infallible. Smaller libraries usually have no choice but to accept the word of the reviewer.

Digital Evaluation

Effective evaluation of the content of digital databases depends on methods similar to those employed for evaluating the content of printed works. Purpose, authority, and scope are to be tested.

There are additional considerations. One must evaluate the various formats: How is the data accessed? Does it meet the specific needs of the average user? How is the work to be updated and how often? What software is necessary to make use of the database to its fullest? Is the search easy or difficult for a beginner, for a trained librarian? Is there documentation, that is, manuals, and so on? Is someone on call when help is needed?

One must also size up the comparative costs of the different vendors, various formats, and individual database charges against the speed and efficiency of the computer search. One should also scrutinize pricing policies.

Evaluative measures are considered throughout the text as each database or group of databases is examined. Whether in print or an electronic database, there are basic evaluative points concerning the all-important content. Sometimes in the love affair with electronic databases and technology, the librarian (and, more likely the public) forgets the only real purpose of the passable reference work is its content. The navigational tools, the bells and whistles, the low price, the thrill of the new— all are of major or minor importance. Only ease of use comes close to the content in importance. In the language of the clothing trade—even the best designed suit won't turn John or Joan into winning personalities unless they have inner substance. Obvious, of course, but sometimes forgotten by overzealous reference work publishers.

In a random sampling of 61 public libraries that provide online access to databases it was found that: "Nearly 87% of all respondents rated usefulness of content as of great importance and three-fourths said the same for quality of content. For small libraries with limited collections, usefulness of content is especially vital." At the same time, right behind subject coverage was ease of use—"the most common reason public library patrons use an online database."[19]

Aside from content the librarian must ask at least four basic questions about a reference work: What is its purpose? Its authority? Its scope? Its proposed audience? Finally, the format of the work must be considered for print and the navigational tools for electronic databases. These questions are as applicable to the *World Almanac* in print as the online index, *ABI/Inform.*

Note that even expert evaluation may miss the obvious. Error is perpetuated in the best of reference works. Mozart was *not* buried in a pauper's grave *nor* did Wellington say the Battle of Waterloo was won on the playing fields of Eton. These and scores of other notions of fact are found often in otherwise excellent reference sources from print to the Internet.

Primary Evaluative Criteria

1. *Purpose.* The purpose of a reference work should be evident from the title or form. The evaluative question must be posed: Has the author or compiler fulfilled the purpose? In an encyclopedia of dance, for example, has the purpose of capturing essential information about the dance been achieved? But immediately the librarian must ask other

---

[19]Carol Tenopir, "Influencing Database Use in Public Libraries," *Library Journal,* June 1, 1999, p. 40.

questions: What kind of dance and for what period? For what age group, experience, or sophistication in dance? For what countries? Is the emphasis on history, biography, practical application, or some other element?

The clues to purpose are found in:

a. The contents

b. The introduction or preface, which should give details about what the author or compiler expects this work to accomplish

c. The index, the sampling of which will tell what subjects are covered

A printed reference book without an index is usually of little or no value. Exceptions are dictionaries, indexes, directories, and other titles where the index is built into an alphabetical arrangement. This system is suitable for the data type of reference work, but not for running prose, where an index is absolutely essential.

Other hints about the purpose of a specific work are often given in the publisher's catalog, in advance notices received in the mail, and in the copy on the jacket or cover of the book. Such descriptions may help to indicate purpose and even relative usefulness, but are understandably less than objective.

1. *Electronic Databases.* Purpose clearly is stated by commercial database publishers. In digital format one will rely more on the publisher's or vendor's descriptive material than on actual examination. Here, particularly because of high cost and lack of immediate access, reviews are of major importance. On the Internet World Wide Web it may be difficult to ascertain purpose. One may look for the purpose on the home page or near the top of the first page, but this may or may not be included. A good sign the information is questionable is the lack of any statement of purpose, scope, or authority by the producer of the site page.

A reference work is only as good as its index. A truism, but is this applicable to electronic databases? Yes. Indexing might not seem important, since every search can be done word by word, phrase by phrase. Yet, in order to find what is needed, in order to avoid too many hits, each database must be properly "tagged" (i.e., a type of indexing usually done in a program language). If this is not done properly, much information is lost both to the search machine and to the individual searcher.

2. *Scope and Currentness.* Other questions of major importance in selecting a reference work: Will this be a real addition to our collection, and if so, what exactly will it add? The publisher usually will state the scope of the book in the publicity blurb or in the preface, but the librarian should be cautious. The author may or may not have achieved the scope claimed. For example, the publisher may claim that a historical atlas covers all nations and all periods. The librarian may check the scope of the new historical atlas by comparing it against standard works. Does the new work actually include *all* nations and *all* periods, or does it exclude material found in the standard works? If an index claims to cover all major articles in certain periodicals, a simple check of the periodicals' articles against the index will reveal the actual scope of the index.

In evaluating scope, consider what the author has contributed that cannot be found in other bibliographies, indexes, handbooks, almanacs, atlases, dictionaries, and so on. If the work is comprehensive within a narrow subject field, one may easily check it against other sources. For example, a who's who of education which limits itself to educators in the major colleges and universities in the Northeast may easily be checked for scope by comparing the current college catalog of P & Q University against the new who's who. If a number of faculty members are missing from the new work, one may safely conclude that the scope is not what is claimed. How current is the material? Is it updated daily (usually via online), weekly, monthly, or how often? Is the update thorough, or are only highlights of the service considered? The question of frequency of update is important for all reference works, but particularly indexes where there is a running record of sometimes daily activities. On the other hand, an encyclopedia of art or music might not require a revision more than every four or five years, or longer. Most reference works contain some dated information.[20] The best method of ascertaining whether the dated material is of value and of checking the regency factor is to sample the work. This is a matter of looking for names currently in the news, population figures, geographical boundaries, records of achievement, news events, and almost any other recent fact consistent with the purpose and scope of the work. It is important to remember that no reference work should be accepted or rejected after sampling only one or two items.

If the work purports to be a new edition the extent of claimed revisions should be carefully evaluated. This can easily be done by

---

[20]Online databases, which can be updated by the minute, are more current than their printed or CD-ROM equivalents. The latter have to be formatted and mailed before they can be used in the library. Online takes no more than a touch of a key. With that, though, there are examples where the online actually is not as current as the conventional reference sources. The librarian should be familiar with these time differences, especially where a given source is used frequently. (They are mentioned, where pertinent, throughout this text in discussion of different formats of information databases). Usually the online introductory screen, or database banner will give the name of the database and inclusive dates, including the date of the latest issue. Note, though, that the same database carried by different hosts— from OCLC to DIALOG—may have different updates. For a discussion of this see Peter Jacso "New Bottles? The Currency of Databases" *Online*, March/April, 1997, pp. 69–72.

checking the work against the earlier edition (disc) or by noting any great discrepancy between the dates of the cited materials and the date of publication.

The copyright date (usually found on the verso of the title page or at the bottom of the initial online page) represents two important checks on a reference work. First, the date gives an idea when the material was put in print or online, and when it was updated. More importantly, if the work no longer is in legal copyright, i.e., is at least 50 years old (and sometimes older), has any effort been made to bring it up-to-date, or is it simply a version of what for all but historical purposes is of little value to today's average searcher.

Electronic Databases. Online databases have made current data a reality. No longer does one have to wait for a printed index to reach the library to find out what happened a week or month ago. Cruise the Internet and usually the answer can be found in minutes, if not seconds. (This, to be sure, depends on knowing reliable, authoritative sites).

A major benefit of the Internet, as well as some commercial online databases, is that it allows material to be updated by the minute. Of course, few informational sites are that current, but the majority tend to stress up-to-date data. Many sites indicate when they were last updated. This may not be important for historical data, but quite another matter for yesterday's events. Always check the date. If for nothing else, it indicates ongoing or loss of interest by the sponsor.

3. *Audience.* With the exception of juvenile encyclopedias, most reference works regardless of format are prepared for adults. When considering the question of audience (in print or online) the librarian must ask one major question: Is this work for the scholar or student of the subject, or is it for the layperson with little or no knowledge? For example, in the field of organic chemistry, Beilstein's *Handbuch der Organischen Chemie* is as well known to chemists as the "top 10" tunes are to music fans. It is decidedly for the student with some basic knowledge of chemistry. Often the distinction in terms of audience is not so clear-cut.

A useful method of checking the reading level of a given reference work is for the librarian to examine a subject well known to him or her and then turn to one that is not so well understood. If both are comprehended, if the language is equally free of jargon and technical terminology, if the style is informative yet lively, the librarian can be reasonably certain the work is for the layperson. Of course, if the total work is beyond the subject competency of the librarian, advice should be sought from a subject expert. Still, this is an unlikely situation, since reference librarians tend to be experts in fields within which they operate.

Other Evaluation Factors

Beyond the basic evaluation of content, no matter what the format, there are other major evaluative points to consider. Briefly, they include:

1. *Cost.* A major factor of frustration in the evaluation and purchase of reference works is the expense involved. This is particularly true of the ubiquitous electronic reference sources whose price and cost patterns seem to be constantly in flux. The only thing certain is that they often cost as much if not more than print, at least at the present. In fact, some prices are astronomical. *Psycinfo*, the online database of the American Psychological Association (and discussed elsewhere in this text) costs $26,000 a year for large four-year colleges. The same index is about half as much for smaller libraries. The *Lexis-Nexis* index can run to well over $100,000 a year for large institutions. Actually, costs for the same two databases may be more when additional branches use the services, e.g., Florida's 10 state university campuses pay $157,000 for *PsycInfo*. Note: All figures as of late 2000.

In time this will change and digital prices will drop or disappear. Meanwhile many of the new technologies are often quite beyond the budget of underfinanced libraries. Budget, rather than client need, may determine whether a particular work is purchased.

Reference service, even on a minimum scale, can be a luxury. Approximately 80 percent of the public libraries in the United States serve a population of under 25,000. Although not all rural communities are financially starved, the majority are poor. Most libraries in these areas, with or without state or federal aid, suffer from a lack of reference materials, and 75 percent lack any user education in reference services.

2. *Searches.* One of the most meaningful questions about printed works concerns arrangement, treated here as part of the format. Arrangement is of major importance for print reference works. In electronic databases, which can be searched by the user, the arrangement *per se* is of no real importance. How to search the database, however, is of major concern.

Even the most carefully designed print work can be a nuisance if it is bound so that the pages do not lie flat or if it makes no clear distinction between headings on a page and subheads within the page. The apparatuses of abbreviation, typography, symbol, and indication of cross-reference must be clear and in keeping with what the user is likely to recognize. The use of offset printing from computerized materials has resulted in some disturbing complexities of format. For example, it may be impossible to tell West Virginia, when abbreviated, from western Virginia. Uniform lowercase letters would be equally confusing. Lack of spacing between lines, poor paper, little or no margins, and other hindrances to reading are all too evident even in some standard reference works.

A word regarding illustrations: When photographs, charts, tables, and diagrams are used, they should be current, clear, and related to the text. They should be adjacent to the material under discussion or at least clearly identified.

Electronic Databases. Obviously even the best commercial online or Internet site can be near worthless if it is difficult to search, if it fails to employ specific features. Major points of evaluation here include: *(a) Design.* Are the graphics useful or only glitz? Are the pictures clear and large enough? When moving from one area to another are there easy to understand navigational aids? Is the whole page layout suitable for the type of information supplied? Is there an overuse of color that makes it difficult to read the text? *(b) Multimedia.* Are there multimedia components and do they increase understanding, or are they only there for amusement? If audio, is it closely related to the text? If visual, how much and what is its relationship to the whole? *(c) Navigation.* How easy is it to find what is wanted? Can Boolean logic be employed? Are the links useful and valid to the main site's purpose? Are instructions clear and easy to follow? Indeed, are there any instructions? Is there key word searching, index updating, easy search tools? *(d) Organization.* Is the material organized in a logical way, and are the links set up to follow one after the other in a practical form?

The last word on evaluation may sound as cynical or as simplistic as the reader cares to interpret it, but it is this: Trust no one. The reviewer, the publisher, and the author do make mistakes, sometimes of horrendous proportions. The librarian who evaluates reference sources with constant suspicion is less likely to be the victim of those mistakes. Whenever possible examine and use the work in question. Make your own evaluation!

As with printed books there are now scores of accurate reviews of Internet databases. These are discussed throughout the text. A good general introduction to such evaluation will be found in Shirley Kennedy's *Best Bet Internet: Reference and Research When You Don't Have Time to Mess Around* (Chicago, IL: American Library Association, 1998). The close to 200 pages offers a concise method of evaluation and, more importantly, useful hints about the best sites and the superior ways of searching.

Publishers–Vendors–Data Dealers

An evaluative method that is rarely considered is a totally effective one. It is the refusal of a publisher to proceed with a reference work that is found wanting. Essentially the decision to publish a particular text is one of determining whether a market for the title exists and whether there is duplication of the proposed effort in another published work. Perhaps because the market for reference titles is largely institutional and libraries are the primary buyers, publishers field-test ideas with librarians. If little or no market seems possible, the idea, no matter how useful it may be to a few librarians, is dropped.

The publisher, again, is the filter between worth and garbage in commercial electronic databases. On the Internet it is another matter entirely. The marvel of the Internet is that anyone can go online with a message. No one stands between the message and its distribution. There need be no publisher, no editor, no evaluation at all. As pointed out earlier, this is jolly as long as the message is of any worth. Lacking the publisher filter, all too often so called reliable reference materials are no more than casual opinion supported only by bias, a hunch and a place on the Web.

A major publisher of reference works includes better trade publishers from Oxford University Press to Random House. Few librarians have difficulty identifying these well-known names. Beyond them are the more closely reference identified publishers. Here their almost entire list consists of reference works, both print and digital. The majors are: The H. W. Wilson Company, best known for *The Readers Guide to Periodical Literature; Reed/Bowker*, a truly international firm with such titles as *Books in Print* and *Ulrich's International Periodical Directory;* The Gale Group, a conglomerate controlled by the Thompson Corporation. In this group are Gale Research; IAC, the indexing firm; and Primary Source Media. LEXIS-NEXIS, the combination general-legal indexing service; Bell & Howell, who took over University Microfilms and fly under the name of ProQuest.

Certain types of reference works are closely identified with certain publishers, (e.g., abstracts and indexes where one thinks immediately of the Wilson Company, UMI, Gale and Ebsco). Scribner's, for another example, is considered a highly reliable source of scholarly subject encyclopedias. And so it goes, not only for print editions, but for digital works as well. A well known, reliable publisher usually is tantamount to an acceptable reference work.

In the United States, the major commercial vendor (or data dealer) for general reference services is DIALOG who, with a new owner, was undergoing a name change in mid-2000. (Throughout this text DIALOG primarily is used, although it may be renamed numerous times).[21] About

---

[21]The problem is that the online publishers constantly change names, e.g., see Carol Tenopir, "A Name (Un)like Any Other Name," *Library Journal,* June 1, 2000, pp. 36–38. She points out that what was once Dow Jones & Company and Reuters Group indexing system is now "Factiva." UMI became Bell & Howell Information and Learning, and in June, 2000 adopted a new name: ProQuest. As Tenopir points out, "With the accelerated pace of mergers, acquisitions, and joint ventures, even more name changes can be expected."

850 other players are listed in the "Online Services" section of the *Gale Directory of Databases*. (The major vendors in terms of library use, aside from DIALOG, would include OCLC's First Search; and Ovid (technology and medical-scientific). The same directory lists well over 2,000 database and CD-ROM publishers and producers.

Generally, the publisher or producer is the one who gathers the information and publishes it (online, on a CD-ROM, in print, on a magnetic tape, or a combination of these). The vendors, who may be the publishers as well, make the material available to libraries. Sometimes confusion arises about who is doing what. The H. W. Wilson Company, both on CD-ROM and online, distributed the *MLA Bibliography*, published by the Modern Language Association. Wilson is a publisher, a vendor, and a sales point for CD-ROMs. Therefore, the producer, the vendor, and the distributor may be the same, or they may differ. (Later, Silver Platter, who simply produces other people's information on CD-ROMs, took over the *MLA Bibliography*.)

1. *Authority/Objectivity*. The most important evaluative point is to test the authority and objectivity of the information given, particularly online.

2. *Objectivity*. Objectivity and fairness of a work are considerations, particularly in reference works that rely on prose rather than simple statistics or collections of facts. Does the author have a bias about politics, religion, race, sex, or the proper type of color to paint a study? No one is totally objective, but those who write reference books must indicate the worth of both sides when there is a matter of controversy.

In certain areas accuracy is more opinion. "Advice to the public about what to eat, what medicines to take and, basically, how to live, seems to do an about-face every time a new study is published in a medical journal...eager to benefit...the public may not recognize that science is essentially a work in progress, and the latest word is rarely the last one."[22]

Electronic Databases. A major value of a standard, traditional reference work is that the publisher stands behind the facts. True, the emphasis sometimes is wrong, the scope is too much or too little, but the basic data is reliable. Readers come to accept this as a truth—a truth that no longer is always the case on the Internet. There may be no evident cen-

---

[22]"It's Good. No, It's Bad," *The New York Times*, March 28, 1998, p. WK4. Examples given here show the march of scientific information often is in retreat: "Margarine has long been thought to contain a safer type of fat than butter, but it turns out it is just as bad for arteries." And "salad is good for you in every way—except that more and more causes of food poisoning are being blamed on fresh fruit and vegetables that have been contaminated with bacteria." Yogurt is supposed to increase age span, but a report from a 121-year-old Azerbaijani man notes he never touches the stuff.

tral control, no editor, no staff, no review methods, or anything associated with the average print/CD-ROM reference title.[23] Where the reference work online does not give information about itself, it is rarely worth consulting, at least for reference purposes.

An Internet critic puts it this way:

> We will use common sense when reading anything on the Net, and we will teach our children to apply the same.
>
> Both you and your children are going to need excellent B.S. detectors to make it in the twenty-first century. Better get started. You cannot Make Money Fast on the Net. Your teenage son is not in chat with Tyra Banks. The Good Times virus doesn't exist. And just as you looked up dirty words in the dictionary, your kids are going to sneak a peek at some spicy stuff, with probably the same life-changing results.[24]

The Web notoriously lacks authority because it not only represents work of experienced, standard publishers, but embraces individual efforts. Democratic? Yes. Advisable? Yes, but not where an individual refuses to identify the source of data.

The primary question is who stands behind the data on the Internet. There are several basic leads to authority: *(a)* If the reference source is found on one of the 3,000 or so library home pages, it is most likely it has been checked out and is to be trusted. It may not be the best, but at least if certified on a home page it is likely to be reliable. *(b)* Check the domain suffix in the site's address (i.e., the sponsor of the data may not give a name, but the address at least indicates authority). The most common tipoffs for reliability: *.edu* means that it has an educational sponsor; *.gov* a government sponsor; *.org* a noncommercial not-for-profit organization. The one to watch is *.com*, as this is a commercial group and may or may not be more involved with selling, advertising, and downright propaganda than objective information. *(c)* The person or company behind the Web page should be easy to identify (e.g., is there an address, a name, a phone number?). [Note: an e-mail address by itself is hardly enough, although too often this is the only verification given.] Also, is it clear where the facts were gathered, or is it just plain opinion, and so labeled. *(d)* If there is advertising, it should be separate from the text and multimedia so the user knows where the plugs begin and the information ends.

---

[23]Kurt Vonnegut's Massachusetts Institute of Technology 1997 commencement speech is an amusing, yet typical example of a prominent Internet error, hoax, or innocent mistake. Mr. Vonnegut had never been the commencement speaker. The speech began with the stirring words: "If I could offer you only one tip for the future, sunscreen would be it." It moved around the world via e-mail. The problem: the speech was never really a speech at all. It was a newspaper column in *The Chicago Tribune* (June 1, 1997). The e-mail "pass it along" false speech reached hundreds of thousands of people before its true author was discovered.

[24]Angela Gunn, "Balancing Acts," *Yahoo*, September, 1998, p. 68.

There are two primary sources of information online. The first is free and put online from everyone from the federal government to a concerned vegetarian. While the government material is authoritative, although often controversial, the work of an individual or small group may or may not be all that reliable.

Reliability, on the other hand, usually is assured when, unfortunately perhaps, the library or the individual pays for the information. This is similar to purchasing a reference book or a CD-ROM. What some have come to call "data dealers" are the equivalent (and often the same) as reference book publishers. These major sources of online and other forms of electronic data offer reference sources which are discussed in every chapter of this text. Among the best known: R.R. Bowker, OCLC, EBSCO, Gale Group, UMI, Wilson and Lexis-Nexis.

When an online source—particularly on the Web—is *not* free, but only available for a fee, and when the company asking for a fee is a known, reliable data dealer, the librarian can be relatively sure the source is authoritative. Conversely, when the information is given away, then one must consider what follows.

A reliable way of finding answers to authority, is to read the website's home page, or equivalent source of background information. This side of the home page, look for: *(a)* a description of scope and authority at the top or beginning of the page; *(b)* "help" files which may or may not have the information; *(c)* FAQs (Frequently Asked Questions) which may include what is needed; *(d)* examine the contents for dates, material such as books, and periodicals covered, etc. The problem is that this takes time, too much time. As a rule of thumb, avoid any site where this kind of "digging" is necessary.[25]

SUGGESTED READING

Eberhard, George, ed., *The Whole Library Handbook*, 3rd ed. Chicago, IL: American Library Association, 2000. Under ten subject headings, from library literature to trivia and back, this light-hearted guide covers almost all aspects of library education, history, and working in a library. As entertaining as it is factual, this is a splendid introduction for the student.

[25] This text is involved with reference questions and answers—answers which are expected to be authoritative. It is not concerned with online personal opinion which may or may not be authoritative. Opinion is the democratic glory of the Internet World Wide Web, but a headache for reference services. Reva Basch sums it up: "Manufactured consent (i.e., mainstream media reports from newspapers and television to magazines and, yes, reference works) is impossible online. The medium is incapable of consensus. It rejects authority...the Net has produced no digital-era Walter Cronkite, no universally respected dispenser of wisdom. Everyone is a reporter, a critic, and a commentator." "Reva's Wrap," *Online*, September/October, 1998, p. 96.

Hoffert, Barbara, "Book Report 2000," *Library Journal*, February 15, 2000, pp. 130–132. In this annual report, the *Library Journal* Book Review editor examines book budgets and what is spent on what. Allocations of funds are examined. See, too, "subject spendings" which indicate what people do or do not want by way of reading and reference materials in the library. This is both a profile of library purchases and the various public served. Check each year, near mid-February, for an update.

Lipow, Anne Grodzins, "In Your Face Reference Service," *Library Journal*, August, 1999, pp. 50–52. Here a working librarian calls for "librarians on call," i.e., available for questions at any time, any place on the Internet. While she admits that "currently the technology is too awkward to make a fully functioning interactive remote service possible," the author points out the need for planning such a service now. See, too, the supporting editorial by John Berry on p. 6 of the same issue.

Mangan, Katherine, "In Revamped Library Schools, Information Trumps Books," *The Chronicle of Higher Education*, April 7, 2000, p. 1+. A study of how library schools, and the country's employers, have changed in order to meet the needs of the new economy and the new information age.

Mendelsohn, Jennifer, "Learning Electronic Reference Resources: A Team Learning Project for Reference Staff," *College & Research Libraries*, July, 1999, pp. 372–383. It is not only a matter of memory when the librarian tackles the problem of keeping up with changes in reference sources. It equally is a matter of teaching as well as learning, and in the process one becomes familiar with new approaches, and new sources. One such effort is explained in detail here. It will do much to calm the reader who feels overwhelmed by the mass of information.

Quinn, Brian, "A Multi-model Approach to Enhancing Memory in Reference Service," *Reference & User Services Quarterly*, Spring, 1999, pp. 257–266. How does the average reference librarian remember what reference work (print to online) best answers a given question? No one really knows. Some excel, others stumble. Still, a working librarian offers a practical approach to the memory problem. He draws upon numerous studies and experience. May not solve your problem, but the hints are useful.

Retting, James and Cheryl LaGuardia, "Beyond 'Beyond Cool' Reviewing Web Resources," *Online*, July/August, 1999. Two of the country's best reviewers of reference works discuss "a standard list of criteria against which we, and other users, can measure the effectiveness of Web resources." In addition there are online and other sources given which will help in evaluation. A first choice for anyone, at any level, who is looking for practical guidance in the selection of databases. Highly recommended.

Spence, John and Lucene Dorsey, "Assessing Time Spent on Reference Questions at an Urban University Library," *The Journal of Academic Librarianship*, July 1998, pp. 290–294. Some 70 percent of questions asked at Arizona State University West take less than five minutes to answer. Longer questions take "a disproportionate amount of time." Questions over 11 minutes to answer take up only about 8 percent of the total time.

Tyckson, David, "What's Right with Reference," *American Libraries*, No. 5, 1999, pp. 57–63. An experienced reference librarian discusses reference service and the new technology. He views day-to-day work in terms of real life rather than as considered by "experts" in the literature more in love with jargon and hazy thinking than reference service as it is practiced. A nice balance of worthwhile praise for innovation and reservations about other approaches.

Vavrek, Bernard, "Is the American Public Library Part of Everyone's Life," *American Libraries*, January, 2000, pp. 60–64. One of the world's leading experts on libraries finds that for at least half the American public, the library offers "significant services and resources." Many depend on the library for most reference queries and a significant number access the library resources from their home computers.

White, Herbert, "Public Library Reference Service—Expectation and Reality," *Library Journal*, June 15, 1999, pp. 56, 58. The Voltaire of library services, explains that this is not the best of possible worlds for reference librarians unless they come to terms with what is provided and what should be provided. What can be done? The article gives a few practical solutions.

Zlatos, Christy, ed., "Coming of Age in Reference Services: A Case History of the Washington State University Libraries," *The Reference Librarian*, No. 64, 1999. Want to know how an academic reference service operates—in reality, not in theory? Interested in the history of developing such a service? Wonder about how working librarians see the future of reference services? All these and many other practical questions are answered in Ms. Zlatos' overview of a superior, yet typical reference situation.

CHAPTER TWO
THE ELECTRONIC LIBRARY

The electronic library is here. Just what is it? It is a library where information is stored electronically online as well as on CD-ROMs and DVDs. The Internet is the major carrier. The data may or may not be unique in an electronic format, i.e., some, if not much of it is duplicated in print. Certainly, too, the electronic data may be printed out at the computer.[1]

Anyone who wanders into a library has access to the Net, and most importantly, the guidance of reference librarians. It is the same in business, government, and other organizations where there is free, open Net access usually shepherded by a librarian. The Web is part of the daily work and leisure pattern of most Americans.

Library access, as well as at home, is made easier by inexpensive hardware and software. Libraries have the benefit of local, state, and federally supported access to the Web.

Usually access at home is via an Internet Service Provider (ISP) service such as America Online, and costs about $20 a month.[2] Internet

---

[1]Another descriptor in special libraries: "intelligence analyst." See Bonnie Hohhof and Lera Chitwood, "Crossroads," *Information Outlook*, February 2000, pp. 22–25. There are numerous other terms for the library with electronic technology: "digital library" or "electronic library" or "virtual library," often used as synonyms. There are at least two dozen or more definitions of these terms. By now this is of interest only to those still counting angels on the head of a pin. Common use of technology in the library has made definitions irrelevant. Most simply call it "the library" and let it go at that, with the assurance it will contain electronic databases as possibly printed 17th century books.

[2]"Free" computers are offered to anyone who will sign for a Net service such as CompuServe, e.g., the computer comes free if the user agrees to a given length of time on a given Net vendor. Other companies have similar agreements. The obvious plan is to make up the

access by cable, among the fastest of general services, is around $40 a month. Today the Internet is as common in American homes as television and ice cream. By 2000 an estimated 60 to 70 percent of American homes had a computer, and 45 to 50 percent had access to the Net and information sources found there. And the number grows each day. What does all of this mean to reference librarians?

Information no longer is the monopoly of libraries, television, radio, newspapers, and magazines. The floodgates have opened and there are now over one billion pages of data on the Net. (Some estimates are that by 2004 there will be 13 billion pages.) Reference librarians are needed to pull out of the Net relevant data for particular questions. Search engines can't do it because they cover only about 16 to 20 percent of the pages. Reference librarians are the Lewis and Clark of the vast Net territory.

CAST THE NET

By 2000 the Net became an integral part of American's way of living. "The way they buy everything from cars to airline tickets, and the way they communicate, invest, work and learn, is being fundamentally transformed by the Web. But it has come so fast that people are feeling overwhelmed by it." Despite obvious advantages, there are drawbacks: The Net "is totally open, interactive technology—but with no built-in editor, publisher, censor, or even filters. With one mouse click you can wander into a Nazi beer hall or a pornographer's library...or roam the Sorbonne library, and no one is there to stop or direct you...."[3]

A cursory surf of the Net makes two points obvious: (1) Many net sites are not well organized. It may take many minutes to find in a Net-only encyclopedia what is available in seconds in print. (2) The reliability of data found at reference sites on the Net often is below what one might expect from a standard print reference source. In time the Net will be as orderly as Melvil Dewey at breakfast, but for the time being consider the drawbacks.

The library groups similar books with similar books, similar periodicals with similar periodicals, etc. This is accomplished, usually, by employ-

---

cost by subjecting the user to heavy advertising. Note, too, that in many urban centers, in America and around the world, there are public computers open for use at a modest fee for anyone. Of course, much the same offer is made by a library. Here it is free.

[3]See Gregory Crawford "Internet Issues" *Public Libraries,* May/June 2000 for a discussion of children on the Net and filters. Thomas A. Friedman, "Are You Ready," *The New York Times,* June 1, 1999, p. A33. Here the author addresses problems faced by parents with "Net" children.

ing the Dewey Decimal system or, in larger, more specialized libraries the Library of Congress Subject Headings. For example, most (if not all) of books on "art" and about "artists" are in the same row of shelves.

There is no inherent order in the Net. There is no umbrella that serves to unite all subjects in one or two places. Instead the Net is a challenge where one must locate a given subject among thousands, if not hundreds of thousands of places. Take "art" for example. Simply using the term "art" the poor searcher will come up with thousands of possibilities for browsing. While one may soon isolate given areas of art on the bookshelves (thanks to subject classifications) this is not the case on the Net.[4]

The various websites, home pages, and search engines, etc., attempt to isolate, order, and otherwise apply a type of loose classification scheme to subject areas. This is of help and, in fact, may solve the problem of Net anarchy, if the user knows which site to select, which list to choose.

The electronic search has its problems, particularly for reference librarians who seek efficient, precise responses. For example, having spent over two hours trying to find suitable material on the Algonquin crafts for a fourth grader via Microsoft's encyclopedia *Encarta* and later through various websites, a parent commented: "So what was the biggest difference between old-fashioned library research and computer research? The odds. At the library, we would have found information in some children's reference book or another.... Using the computer, however, was an all-or-nothing experience."[5]

A reference librarian could have narrowed the odds by first helping the child to find the material needed in a book or periodical an/or by knowing precisely where to turn via the computer. Precision narrows the odds and, in fact, serves to strike the happy balance of when to turn to digital or print information. The librarian saves valuable time by finding specific data in the ocean of information and garbage.

The public knows the library is the best access point for reliable Internet information, e.g., public libraries head the list of locations for public access to the Net. Furthermore, in primary and secondary schools as well as colleges and universities the Net is an integral part of the library system.

The vital question for librarians is where to find the funds to connect the superhighway with schools, libraries, and other centers that are badly underfinanced and unable to even keep up with print materials.

[4]There are many other subtle drawbacks to Net reference searching. Professor Robert Darnton ("No Computer Can Hold the Past, *The New York Times,* June 12, 1999, p. A15) offers three cheers for cyberspace research. At the same time he warns it requires more than the Net "for students to understand the nature of historical knowledge."

[5]*The New York Times,* November 19, 1998, p. G11.

Even large, relatively well-financed libraries are torn between spending more and more on electronic sources and less and less on printed materials from journals to books.

It Is More than an Information Highway

Even the obtuse recognizes there is more to the Internet than a handy information retrieval system. Whether it be stock news for day traders[6] or cut-rate books online, the Net is by now ubiquitous. Information, at least in the sense of a reference librarian, is only part of a system. The Net is more involved with commerce and entertainment than fact finding. The countless facets of the Net are indicated throughout this text. For now it is worth emphasizing: (1) The Net is in the process of drastically changing not only the United States, but the rest of the world. In countries where computers are scarce, ruling parties have found that only one computer in a small community can undermine, even destroy totalitarian rule. It is a major propaganda source for politicians, advertisers, and low budget civic groups involved in everything from the environment to cleaning up city hall. (2) The Net is an ever-growing presence in the economy, which continues to shift from the industrial to the service. (3) The Net has the power to change behavior, from self-education to buying habits.

The Net is much more. One way or another it involves everyone in Western countries and in many other nations as well. Information is a major ingredient, but only one of many.

BIBLIOGRAPHIC NETWORKS

In addition to the Internet, there are major bibliographic networks in the United States and worldwide which use the Net as carriers as well as their own direct online services. These are well known to all reference librarians and usually referred to only by their initials.

The major nonprofit networks in the United States (and used, too, throughout much of the world) include: (1) OCLC—the Online Computer Library Center in Dublin, Ohio (http://www.oclc.org) which opens access to books, films, reports, etc. (2) RLIN (Research Libraries Information Network) (http://www.rlg.org) with books and related items online for use, primarily although not exclusively, by research libraries.

They are noteworthy, too, as all of them are for fee, i.e., they charge for almost all information found via their network. Little is free on these

---

[6]"Regulators who have examined the books of day-trading firms say that more than 9 out of 10 traders wind up losing money." "Day Trading's Underbelly," *The New York Times*, August 1, 1999, p. BU1.

networks and, in fact, the cost of using them runs into the thousands to hundreds of thousands of dollars each year. As carriers of information they are far superior to most of the free data on the Net. Confusion may arise as all of the bibliographic for fee networks do use the Net as a carrier. This does not mean, though, that the casual user may use the networks unless he or she has access to them via a library.

Note: Throughout this text the reader often will find reference to DIALOG or OCLC which is an automatic signal the described information source is for a fee. (The exception: a few government databases carried by these networks).

Online (through OCLC, RLIN, etc.), it is possible to literally view the holdings of thousands of libraries from the United States to Australia. The proliferation of information and the ability to locate and acquire such data through bibliography is impressive.

OCLC

The Online Computer Library Center (OCLC) has the greatest number of members, from all types and sizes of libraries, than any of the bibliographical networks. By 2000 OCLC claimed over 34,000 member libraries throughout the world, although most are in the United States and Canada.

The system supports a database of books, films, reports, or monographs derived from the Library of Congress and merged catalogs of the member libraries. It grows each year, month, and day. Approximately 2 million records a year are added. In 2000 the system contained over 23 million books, 1.5 million serials, and 700,000 audiovisual media, as well as 600,000 recordings.

Moving into other areas of information, OCLC introduced *First Search* in the mid–1990s. Here OCLC acts as a vendor of databases, in addition to its vast catalog. The user will find in *First Search* up to 60 electronic databases, from indexes to standard bibliographies, e.g., ERIC, PAIS, MEDLINE, and ABI/INFORM (all discussed in subsequent chapters). In 2000 OCLC reported over 2000 libraries had signed on for *First Search*. More than 45,000 to 50,000 searches online are done each day.

RLIN

Located in Mountain View, California, *RLIN* (Research Libraries Information Network) is the up-market bibliographical network. In addition to the records of the "ivy league" universities, it includes records from the major research centers.

While the membership is limited, the actual number of records is over 40 million. The small homogeneous membership has two things in common: (1) huge collections of materials, often of esoteric data; and (2) comparably large staffs in reference, acquisitions, and cataloging.

CitaDel is the RLIN equivalent of OCLC's *First Search* in that it is a package of databases from ABI/INFORM to *Newspaper & Periodical Abstracts.* As of the year 2000, the number of databases available was considerably less than from OCLC.

Commercial Networks

There are other sources of bibliographic databases, which usually are searched by librarians for users rather than the users having access to them. They are expensive and include the following:

1. DIALOG (http://www.dialog.com) is part of the DIALOG Corporation which includes numerous online services such as CARL, most used for its document delivery system. DIALOG has more than 500 databases available online, with particular strengths in technical and scientific information. The other emphasis is on business, news, and law.

2. OVID (http://www.ovid.com) formerly known as BRS, has a strong hand in medical technology, and related databases. It functions much like DIALOG in that it is more specialized than the general indexes and is used almost exclusively by librarians and experienced searchers.

3. Large commercial indexing companies by 2000 began to move in on the database networks. Working with one another they now offer not only indexes, but related information services such as government databases, bibliographic data, and health sources. Among the more prominent of such firms: EBSCO, Gale Group, Bell Howell and the H. W. Wilson company (see the chapter on general indexes for a discussion of each). All of this represents a bonus for libraries in that competition will not only increase the efficiency of online searching, but possibly make it less expensive.

REFERENCE ON THE INTERNET

What reference works are on the Internet?

Basically there are two types: for free and for fee.

The for free include most government databases as well as institutional and organizational information sources such as the 1,500 plus online public access catalogs (OPACs) from the United States and worldwide. Add to this 900 million or so free Web pages. These cover everything from astrology to physics. The amount of free data is overwhelming.

The for fee is qualitatively more impressive. It is easier to use than most of the free sources. Here are the professional, commercial sponsored databases and websites. Among these are OCLC First Search, DIALOG, LexisNexis, and scores of others discussed throughout this text.[7] (Note: There will come a time, possibly in the next few years, when present commercial databases will be offered free to users. It will come about when it is possible to make a profit other than through direct charges, i.e., via advertising, government support, etc.) Once the for free/for fee is appreciated, experience shows the reference librarian that there are numerous, specific areas in which the Web excels for reference service:

1. *Current Events:* A good number of people, particularly the better educated and those under 30 years of age, turn to the Net for information and news. In 1995 the percentage of adults who used the Net for news was a mere 4 percent. By mid–2000 the number had risen to 25 percent and was going higher. Aside from fast-breaking headline stories, the Net newshounds are looking for practical information. Hobbies, movies, and restaurants top the list with an 82 percent audience. Another 64 percent turn to science and health, while technology (usually computers) comes in at 60 percent and finance at 52 percent.

The news is free. The 800 to 900 daily newspapers, both American and international, give away their columns in the hope of attracting advertising. Only the *Wall Street Journal* charges a modest $59 a year to its 200,000 plus subscribers. *The New York Times,* with about 4 million foreign and domestic registered users, does not charge. By 2000, though, the ~~but~~ newspapers saw a source of income in libraries. Over 100 now charge to use their archives, or back files. Today's news is free but yesterday's are for a fee.

The Net is superior for what is going on today, or what is scheduled for tomorrow (from civic events to concerts and museum shows and baseball games). It is a time waster when one is seeking retrospective data. Lacking an index, and more importantly, lacking back issues for more than a few years, most print to Web current sources are impossible to search for older information. In another decade this will change, and most archives will be online. But for now it is a real problem for libraries. (Note: There are exceptions, for example, *The Christian Science Monitor* has online files, which can be searched by keywords back to 1980.)

---

[7]The fee is paid by the library, or in other situations by the business (such as a law firm) organization, government agency, etc. In almost all cases, from the person who comes into a public library to the undergraduate university student, the use of fee-based databases is free in the library. The library or organization, of course, absorbs the cost. Given that, most laypersons find it difficult to differentiate between free and for fee—and understandably so.

drawback of Web — currently difficult to research older data

2. *Popular events and personalities.* Between home pages, commercial plugs, and ongoing hype about popular culture, the Net is a gold mine for current data. The easiest approach is to enter a name or phrases in the search engine query box and await the results. Television and movie celebrities, otherwise hard to find in even the best newspaper and magazine indexes, will dominate pages and pages on the Net. Conversely, it is a time consuming, controversial place to look for data on historical figures. See the Biography chapter for a discussion of this point.

3. *Government.* The most reliable, usually current data on the Internet is from the federal government with less assured results from state and urban governments. Here, though, one tends to think in terms of specific needs, not "government" *per se.* For example, someone looking for material on secondary schools thinks of ERIC (the government online database), not government and then ERIC. The exception: information about the three branches of government and specific agencies.

4. *Travel.* There are numerous places to find everything about a point of travel from airline fares to the weather to historical sites to visit (or avoid during high tourism season). Once again, though, it may be faster to simply check into a guidebook—particularly for accurate information on hotels and sites. The Web is better, of course, for current weather conditions, current costs of travel, and so forth.

Other reference areas are discussed throughout this text. Still the four listed here are among the most popular and, if nothing else, indicate the information paths followed by reference librarians most frequently on the Internet, or at least over its toll–free highways.

Who and For What: Popular Sites

The aforementioned categories hardly begin to cover Net possibilities. Business on the Net, for example, is favored and much used by librarians in and out of a business section. Shopping, chat groups, and related "let's have fun and spend money" sites attract a huge number of laypeople.

The majority considers the Net an entertainment point more than a source of solid information. As such, the Net attracts a wide variety of people.

What are people doing on the Internet? Each month the magazine *Yahoo! Internet Life* lists the most popular websites. Inevitably entertainment, super personalities, and sports top the lists. Leading sites: Disney Online, The Weather Channel, CBS Sports, CNN, USA Today, and Warner Bros. If one turns to "What you're searching for" the leading search words vary with what is in the news and the time of year. A typical list for any given March: Easter, March (March Madness), NCAA tournament, Oscar, and St. Patrick. The leading chat groups inevitably focus on personalities.

The format for the *Yahoo!* page, as well as its name, changes frequently, but it is a good place to trace popular culture and its role on the Net.

One critic puts it this way: The Internet is "a refuge for conspiracy theorists, bigots, and perverts, but look at the bright side: It also preoccupies jokesters and assorted knuckleheads with entirely too much time on their hands…On the Internet, truth needn't take precedence over humor."[8]

Websites

A Web "page" is a fundamental unit, which may be one, or scores of "pages" in length, but can be read continuously without shifting to another point. Conversely a "website" is a series of Web pages, which may cover different areas, but can be reached at the same address. An "address" is the Uniform Resource Locator (URL). A "home page" is the Web page accessed by the basic URL. In library terms the home page is the link between the user and the library as well as other libraries, and information points on the Web which the librarians believe of interest.

In an analysis of Web sites: (1) Some 65 percent of the sites are public, i.e., provide unrestricted access to content. Only about 2 percent are private, while a good 27 percent are inactive and have no useable content. (2) Of the public sites, 20 percent are in languages other than English; and over half are in North America. This is likely to increase with time, but as English is an international language, not by that much. (3) The majority of sites, about 70 percent, describe the corporation or individual who put up the site, and, in many cases, extend this to online sales. The percentage indicates the primary goal of Web servers is to sell, much like today's television shopping channels. (4) About 11 percent of the sites are

---

[8]Tom Kuntz, "The Information Age is Here. Ah-ha-ha-ha-ha-ha-ha!" *The New York Times,* July 3, 1998, p. WK7. Among the humorous stories quoted by Tom Kuntz is the apocrypha story of an "actual radio conversation between a U.S. naval ship and Canadian authorities off the coast of Newfoundland." This was sent by e-mail by and down the North American continent.

Canadians: Please divert your course 15 degrees to the south to avoid a collision.

Americans: Recommend you divert your course 15 degrees to the north to avoid a collision.

Canadians: Negative. You will have to divert your course 15 degrees to the south to avoid a collision.

Americans: This is the Captain of a U.S. Navy ship. I say again, divert YOUR course.

Canadians: No. I say again, you divert YOUR course.

Americans: This the aircraft carrier U.S.S. Lincoln, the second-largest ship in the United States' Atlantic fleet. We are accompanied by three destroyers, three cruisers and numerous support vessels. I demand that you change your course 15 degrees north. I say again that's one five degrees north, or counter-measure will be undertaken to ensure the safety of this ship.

Canadians: This is a lighthouse. Your call.

American arrogance. ha ha ha

of value to libraries in that they actually provide information other than about the sponsor, i.e., news, online database reference works, collections of links to resources, etc.

Almost all medium to large libraries now have a page on the Web. Thanks to numerous computer programs it is not all that technically difficult to establish such a site. The problems arise with content, presentation, and arrangement. Few individuals can speak for the library so that numerous committee meetings seem necessary to arrive at even a partial consensus. Inevitably the reference librarian(s) should have a major voice in determining what is to be included and, equally important, what links to much used reference aids are to be included.

URLs. There are only a handful of signs in the URL address which indicate the initial source. These are restricted by the government and clearly indicate the sponsor of a site. The major domains: "edu" for use by schools and universities; "gov" is available only to governments; "org" is for nonprofit organizations, although this is too broadly interpreted; "mil" is for the military; and "net" for network type organizations such as a business serving providers and sites for networking. The most common, best known and most often used is "com" which indicates a business interest.

In 2000 additional top level domains found their way into addresses. This improves the target, if only what to avoid when one of these appears. The late entries: "rec" for recreation or entertainment; "firm" for businesses; "store" for someone selling goods; "web" for Web news and activities about the Web; "nom" for personal addresses. Reference librarians will want to look for information sites likely to be found under the new domains: "info" providing information services, although these can be, are likely to be commercial ventures; "arts" with an emphasis on the arts and culture.

Web addresses are a major business—just the name, nothing else. The owner of "www.drugs.com" sold the name for close to $900,000. And all you need to secure a home page on the Web is $70 and an unclaimed name with no more than 22 characters. That is not easy, as all the "good" names are taken, and numerous combinations are being snapped up each day.[9]

> **Searching the Web** If the Worldwide Web ever adopted a theme song, it could do worse than picking "I Still Haven't Found What I'm Looking For." Searching the Web is the most popular on-line activity—and often the most frustrating. More than half of the top 10 most visited domains were [search engines] according to an Internet metering service Media Metrix. But how many of the people visiting those sites found what they were looking for right away?[10]

[9]"First out of the starting gate," *New York Times,* August 23, 1999, p. C3. This is one of numerous articles on the Internet naming business. See, too: Ellen Rony, *The Domain Name Handbook* (New York: R&D Books, 1999).

[10]Matt Lake, "Desperately Seeking Susan or Suzie NOT Sushi," *The New York Times,* September 3, 1998, p. G1.

It appears simple enough. Someone looking for Lincoln's Gettysburg address enters those three words in the search engine box. The assumption is it is somewhere among the tens of millions of pages on the Net. The search engine may not necessarily find it, but come up with information on vacations in Gettysburg, places called Lincoln and news about the Lincoln Continental. Yes, there is a direct method of getting the specific speech, but not one often followed by beginners.

In any medium to large size library, students and laypersons are found clustered around one area of the reference section—the computer terminal. Most believe this is the place to find what is needed. Most have little or no searching skill other than an ability to manipulate digital forms of data for games.

Given a problem, other than where to locate the library bathroom or exit, the unskilled layperson turns to the computer, enters a word or two, and waits for results. True, she or he must first find a database, but this has become almost automatic in libraries where menus indicate one should turn to X or Y database for questions about large categories from "science" to "humanities." Experienced hands realize one of countless fast approaches is to use OCLC's *ArticleFirst* where there are some 17,000 periodicals with possible answers. Others may choose the *Expanded Academic Index*, with some 1,500 periodicals, or a related type of mass coverage index.

As there are so many magazines and journals inevitably even the most obtuse or difficult word or phrase will be matched with an article or two. Actually, the results are more likely to number 10 to 100 articles. The citations are printed out and the layperson or student then moves to the periodical section to find the material. (More sophisticated systems indicate if the library has the periodical. Many, too, offer abstracts or full text of the article online, which makes the searcher's quest even easier). If the printer has not jammed and the computer has not gone mad, the searcher walks away happy and convinced the quest is a success. Few laypeople have any concept of whether or not the articles truly will be useful.

Librarian as Mediator

One observer notes "reading on the Net has been famously likened to drinking from a fire-hose. Already there's more stuff out there than any human being could absorb in a lifetime. Faced with the cornucopia, there are basically only two survival strategies. One is to be ruthlessly selective...The other is to rely on others to do the filtering for you."[11]

---

[11]John Naughton, "Internet," *Observer* (London), January 10, 1999, p. 6.

> The Web is the online resource base of choice today for librarians…and end users…. The library (or librarian) as pivot point remains crucial in helping to shape the amorphous Web into a useful tool. The Web is too big and too pervasive to be the exclusive domain of any one group of professionals or any one approach to organization. Librarians bring knowledge to their user groups and evaluation skills that can help shape the Web into more of a digital library as we'd like it and less of a mere conglomeration of cool stuff.[12]

High-speed, efficient globalwide networks are the key to reference services. The role of the reference librarian in this new and ever-changing environment is both traditional and innovative. As in the past, the reference librarian must find answers to questions and will use the Internet and related networks for that purpose. Because of the vast areas of possibilities the librarian must, as mediator, be able to pick what is precisely needed.

The library in the community is where users will find the latest electronic and printed resources for gaining information. More importantly, it must be where users can turn for current, accurate, and friendly help in mastering their own navigational routes on the information highway. Librarians must not only promote the Internet, they must map it for users.

The reference librarian is the personal voice in the sea of computers and digitalized responses. Here a dialog replaces the infuriating, "push button 1." The reference expert does everything from actually showing someone how to use the Internet to advising which databases (paid or free) to use for a particular question. Primarily the librarian serves to reduce frustration by precise on target advice about the best places to turn to find an answer to a question.

How good is the final response from the Net? The librarian is there to suggest methods of analysis and evaluation of information to ensure the user has what is needed in a reliable form.

Some innocent users believe the Net is the beginning and end of information. The librarian must help determine when it really serves that purpose and when it is better, certainly less frustrating to use other sources. For example, someone seeking a quotation, background on an individual, or historical facts might be better off going to a book of quotations, a biographical source, or an encyclopedia either in print or in electronic format. If one wishes to find the amount of water in Zambia's Lake Kariba, one finds over 500 "Kariba" listings on the Net (2000). It can take from a minute to a half-hour to find the amount of water in Lake Kariba, but only a moment to discover the same information in the *Britannica*.

The challenge is to integrate the Internet into the total library information system. The key is to guide users in such a way that they know when to turn to an online commercial database, a CD-ROM, a book, or the Net.

---

[12]Carol Tenopir, "Shaping the Web," *Library Journal,* March 1, 1999, p. 36.

The best way today, although somewhat crude in that it is constantly being expanded, is to provide links to information from the library web page. The choices normally consider all information sources, not just the Net.

Library instruction has taken on a new meaning. In the old days it was no more than a matter of pointing out the catalog and where to find a few reference books. Now it is complicated and time consuming. For example, in a study of 68 university libraries it was found that nearly all offer onsite Internet training, while over half also offer training assistance for remote users. More than 95 percent are teaching as the person searches for the answer to a question.[13] Special librarians, serving a select group of users spend, "close to thirty percent of their time conducting research or assisting end-users with research related tasks. Another thirty-seven percent of their time...is dedicated to various administrative duties...The remaining twenty-eight percent...is spent on more strategic activities, such as planning, training and product or service development."[14]

SEARCH ENGINES

The search engine, or as some now call it, a "portal" is a rough service reference librarian. The idea is simple enough. Search the contents of Web pages, read the keywords on a page, and pick out what is relevant for a particular search. There are scores of configurations to this formula, but the computer sweep of the Net is much the same.[15]

The engines may be divided in several ways, but the key word index is basic. It accepts key words and coughs up broad results, often with sites numbering in the hundreds. Results usually are graded in some way so

[13]Carol Tenopir, "Reference Use Statistics," *Library Journal,* May 1, 1998, p. 32.

[14]Doug Church, "Breaking Free of the Reference Shackles," *Information Outlook,* March 1999, p. 19.

[15]"Web Search Engines" is the major topic of the May/June 1999 issues of *Online.* And other journals, such as *Choice* at least once a year devote much space to the search engine's development. For a rundown of specific features of the major search engines see Amelia Kassel, "Internet Power Searching..." *Information Outlook,* April, 1999, pp. 29–32. See p. 32, "Keeping Up" for a list of online sources which update and evaluate search engines and websites. See: Michael Specter, "Search and Deploy," *The New Yorker,* May 29, 2000, pp. 88–100. After an introduction in which he discusses search engines and their general problems (and victories), Specter turns to his main theme: the development of the search engine Google at Stanford University. He considers the project, how it started and who is involved. Along the way he suggests why Google is such a superior search engine and how it will be improved. Unusually good writing and a clear presentation makes this a must for any student.

A regular feature, "Internet Search Engine Updates" is useful to try to keep abreast of frequent changes in the basic search engines. This news is found in each issue of *Online* and is by far the best for current information. Even a cursory glance at the major periodicals covering the Net will show constant and current evaluation of the search engines.

[handwritten: Search tips for search engines]

that the major sites which fit the words entered by the user come first in the lineup. The catch is that unless the user is skilled, the massive results are likely to be overwhelming.

There are some basic rules for both librarians and laypersons seeking data via a search engine on the Net: *(a)* When possible use the search engine's "advanced" search, or whatever it may be called. *(b)* Search for phrases and place the phrase in quotes to limit the search to those specific words. *(c)* With even the most direct "crude" search, use several words rather than one or two. Exception: a proper noun, which should be put in quotes. (d) Have a list of synonyms ready in case the major word search fails.

Other search tips: (1) Read the search engine's help files to find out basics from the syntax to the use of plus and minus signs to include or exclude words. (2) Use limits, i.e., if the engine provides for it be sure to limit the search to English, to newsletters, to periodicals, to...well, to anything which targets the query. (3) Where several hundred or more results appear, it rarely is worth going beyond the first 10 or 20. Better to try another combination of words, phrases, etc. in a second search of the same topic. And be sure that words with double meanings are qualified with synonyms.

One peculiar notion is that the search engine, with its countless possible places to search, all neatly graded in terms of probable match of query with answer, are going to replace reference librarians. Hah! Anyone who has spent more than an hour or two trying to find an answer to a complex question via a search engine realizes they are not only fallible, but stupid. Even the best, and some are rather good, require considerable more effort to fathom than putting the question to a reference librarian, a human being.

Until such time as searching on the Net is more refined than it is today, the reference librarian will be spending an inordinate amount of time augmenting the search engine's efforts. In fact, as more data floods the Net, it is likely that the reference librarian will be more important as a mediator between individual and information.[16] So what is wrong?

Two points: The search engines are good to excellent and improving all of the time, but they rely on expert searchers. They are poor for the average person who only enters a keyword. Someone who puts in "war" or "peace" is going to be flooded with data. The wise librarian, the skilled

---

[16]Greg R. Notess, "The Never Ending Quest," *Online*, May/June 2000, pp. 27–34. In mid-2000 the relative newcomer search engine FAST claimed to index more than 300 million pages of about one billion on the Net. Other engines, from AltaVista to Yahoo! and Google claim about the same number. The problem is that the Web is expected to grow to over 13 billion pages by 2004. Can the engines keep up? Probably not.

searcher knows how to use Boolean logic and other qualifiers to limit the search to 10 or 20 items which zero in on specifics of war or peace.

The Net offers an information paradox. "Whole categories of publications never enter our lives, unless we intentionally propel ourselves into an unaccustomed aisle of the bookstore. Web browsers are capable of bringing anybody into contact with anything on little notice." This is convenient, but can be overwhelming. "The Internet's ability to establish arbitrary connections instantly is proving a bit much."[17]

Stripped of jargon and added commercial hopes, the search engine is a type of index or catalog that classifies millions of pages of the Worldwide Web. No two search engines are exactly alike although they all share three things in common: *(a)* An index of Web sites or Web pages, which searches roots for the key elements. *(b)* Each engine collects data, but updates it differently. *(c)* Each sorts out results and grades them according to relative value, but, again, each does this in a different fashion. They come in various shapes and forms, but are of two basic types. The first creates its own index. The second (often called megasearch engines) search existing indexes of other search engines.

Further categories would include: (1) Keyword indexes such as AltaVista and Lycos. Here the engine reads the first 200 to 300 words or so on a Web site page. After elimination of such words as "and," "the," and "for" it alphabetizes the words and puts them in an index. Word placement and frequency helps to determine ranking for a particular search. This approach is fast and general. (2) Subject directories such as Yahoo! have assigned specific subject headings, much as a library catalog, to the websites. This type is more specific than the keyword index, but does not generate as many possibilities as subject headings are assigned.

Each of the two basic methods has its problems. So in an effort to incorporate the best of both worlds, enter the metasearch engine that searches a number of databases and engines simultaneously. Another method is to launch the viewer into other major machines within the machine being searched. For example, Yahoo! offers access to AltaVista and similar keyword services.

A third effort to throttle back the chaos is the subject search machine. Rather than cover the whole net, the mechanism concentrates on a single subject area. The branded sites can be extremely narrow or cover a whole area of interests.

What makes it difficult is that search engines do not clearly explain how they differ one from the other. Yahoo!, for example, is not technically a search engine but a group of websites under subject headings. The oth-

---

[17]Philip Agre, "Yesterday's Tomorrow," *The Times Literary Supplement,* July 3, 1998, p. 4.

ers, from Hotbot to AltaVista, use software agents (i.e., crawlers or spiders) which automatically index page content and follow links to similar pages.

There are numerous other refinements, all of which are outlined in countless articles. For an update online see:

Search Engine Watch (http://www.searchenginewatch.com) serves two purposes. Edited by Greg Notess first and foremost it provides links to current news about search engines, e.g., "see what's new" or "search engine headlines," etc. Second, it regularly reviews and rates the engines side by side: "Read comparison reviews, see which search engines are most popular, and check out various tests and statistics." Numerous other features including a "search engine newsletter" make this a valuable place for a wide coverage of the subject.

Search Engine Showdown (http://www.searchengineshowdown.com) calls itself "the user's guide to Web searching" and carries a broad coverage of current activities in the field. Edited by Danny Sullivan there is a search engine chart by features, statistical summaries, search strategies, a subject directory, e-mail lists, and other features. It seems to be updated daily and is the best single place to find out what just happened.

Portals

Search engines have expanded to "portals" and many of them now wish to be known as portals rather than search engines. Take it or define it, the portal is simply an expanded version of the search engine. The portal is a large search engine that offers access not only to searching, but to e-mail, chat groups, and other services. Also, a portal can be a group of search engines, usually second rank, who group together to form a mega-website in order to survive.

The portal has not only directory duties but added features that make it more attractive to users—and investors. If you can put enough services and content into a single Web address you can bring in a lot more people with disparate interests and needs to the same place. This means the ability to sell more advertising based on a certain dollar amount for every 1,000 pages visited. Incidentally, only America Online and Yahoo, the two largest portals, seem to make a profit.

The portal notion can be a problem for reference librarians. While search engines are supposed to help people find what they want, the portal has something else in mind. It sends users to destinations as before. The catch: now the destination may be owned by the portal or by advertisers. Once the portal is an advertising captive it has the potential of being less than reliable as an objective information guide.

Best Search Engines

What are the best search engines beginners and would-be experts use for gathering information? Generally, those easiest to use and with the most specific results. Most engines cover from 200 to 300 million full text Web pages. The number is less important than how the search is refined.

Some of the basic search engines in order of preference by many librarians, although certainly not by all, would include as of mid 2000:

1. *Google* (http://www.google.com) is the work of researches at Stanford University who struck on the idea of determining the value of a particular website by the sheer number and quality of other sites that link back to it. In numerous ways it is the most efficient of the group in that it pinpoints rather than using a shotgun. Note: "I'm feeling lucky," is an option that takes the searcher directly to Google's single top site for the topic. A great time saver.

Size does matter when it comes to what is or is not located by a search engine. None keeps up with the one billion plus Web pages available, but a contender is Google. It claims by early 2001 to be able to search close to 600 million fully indexed Web pages, plus about 500 million partially indexed URLs, i.e., addresses online.

Google is an example of a search machine reaching out to non-English speakers by enabling searchers to use their native language online. Users can search for content in a specific language. By 2001 this meant service in 15 different languages from French and German to Japanese and Chinese. Obviously choices are fewer than in English. There are approximately 40 million Japanese language Web pages—as compared to well over 1 billion in English.

2. *Fast* (www.alltheweb.com) is the work of another group of academics, this time in Norway. It is one of the largest search engines about, with over 300 million sites. The problem here is that there is much duplication and while it has the benefit of covering more areas than most search engines, it is not all that subtle in its results. In time, though, it is likely to improve.

3. *Northern Light* (http://www.northernlight.com). This is both a general and specific search engine, and provides access to specialized fee-based materials. An agreement with Bell & Howell's/UMI "ProQuest Direct" allows Northern Light to provide access to full text articles from over 5,400 journals as well as from some books. While the customer pays for this full–text service, most of the searches are free. (See, too, the discussion of Northern Light's Usgovsearch search engine in the Government Documents chapter of this text.)

4. *Yahoo!* (http://www.yahoo.com). Best for searching broad, general topics. Technically this is a directory wedded to a search engine, but the results are much the same as for the other engines. The tremendous advantage over the others is that this is a listing of more than 350,000 sites, newsgroups, etc., which are evaluated by *Yahoo!*. In other words, rather than search all that is out there, they only search hand-picked information points. The result is that this tends to be more narrow, yet more reliable. There is a sophisticated subject and keyword searching mechanism that makes this extremely easy to use. Often is ranked "best" by reference librarians, followed by *AltaVista*.

5. *AltaVista Network* (http://www.altaista.com). Best for precise searches. Thanks to a sophisticated search system that equally is easy to use, *AltaVista Network* pinpoints more relevant places to turn for specific answers than any of the others. They, as other search engines, rank data in order of how likely it is to meet the needs of the person putting the query. The ranks are not always that accurate, but more searching normally will overcome the problem. A "live topics" feature allows the user to enter keywords and when the "live topic" is clicked on a page of possible related keywords, which can be used for additional searching, are shown. Clicking on one and rejecting another will narrow or broaden the search. One can search for graphics by using the word "image as a prefix for a search." Searches can be made of sites in 25 languages, i.e., if the users ask *AltaVista Network* to return results in French and German or Italian, then only material in those languages will be seen.

6. *Lycos* (http://www.lycos.com). Best for advanced, specific searches. Beginners should start with the home page where there are a number of easy-to-use links. Advance searches should turn to "Lycos Pro."

7. *Hot Bot* (http://www.hotbot.com). A part of Lycos, for both beginning and advanced searching. This is for the expert or beginning searcher who has patience. It offers the most aids for complicated quests for information. There are screens that allow the searcher to expand or broaden the search by data, location, organization, and the like. A beginner must follow these cues carefully, but it will be worth the time.

8. *Go* (http://www.go.com). Best for searching current events. It is a fast, efficient search engine that is easy to use and current. The search patterns particularly are good for ranking relevant sites and for being more on target with the search words entered. The problem is it has a limited number of sites in its index.

Metasearch Services[18]

There are quick ways of searching more than one service. The so called "metasearch services" don't do their own searching, but turn to existing engines. Two good examples: (1) *Copernic* (http://www.copernic.com) is one of the most inclusive of the search machines. It takes in a good dozen or more of the basic search aids from Yahoo! to AltaVista. One enters the term(s) and the dozen engines are searched at once. The resulting display, in order of importance, gives a sweep found in no other service, particularly one which is free. (2) *Metacrawler* (http://www.metacrawler.com). This searches a number of search engines and, unlike some of its competitors, it removes duplicate pages and offers scores, which indicate possible relevance. The catch: it has little Boolean logic. There are numerous other multi-engines, e.g., *Profusion* (http://www.profusion.com) which searches up to nine engines and then sorts out the results, removes duplicates, and ends up with a single list of sites.

Savvy-Search (http://www.savvysearch.com) is considered by some reference librarians to be the best of the metasearch machines. Why? Because it can be used for both narrow (i.e., specific subject/names etc. or broad searches—and in so doing limits which search engines it goes to for data. This in itself saves much time in staying close to what is relevant. It also allows storage of profile searches which may be done over and over again.

There is no one search engine, no single search pattern which will cover all possibilities. A comprehensive quest for information must not only consider various avenues followed by search engines but print, CD-ROMs and other formats.

Multi–searches

Most of the larger vendors, from DIALOG to SilverPlatter, offer an option to simultaneously search not one but several databases at the same time. While this is the similar technique for all search engines, here it is more refined (being limited to only a small group of professional databases) and sophisticated (with extremely fine-tuning for searchers). For example, DIALOG's "Major Papers" allows the user to search the contents of 16 papers at the same time. A general search engine might search up to 400 papers, but with little or no discrimination.

---

[18]For a clear explanation and comparison of the various metasearch services see: "Judi Repman and Randal Carlson, "Surviving the Storm: Using Metasearch Engines Effectively," *Computers in Libraries*, May, 1999, pp. 50–56.

"WebSPIRS," from SilverPlatter is a common gateway interface for use with the company's reference works (primarily indexes) carried via the Internet. One may first choose the indexes for searching or enter key words and let the system indicate how often those words, phrases or subject headings appear in related indexes. A search can then be made in one or a dozen indexes for the term or terms. The obvious advantage is that hard to find, hard to locate items are quickly located. Overuse, too, is apparent. Search for a common term and the system will spew forth thousands of possibilities. Used judiciously, these multisearch systems are a great time saver.

SEARCHING THE WEB

There are three basic types of searches at a computer terminal. The first is to enter a few words in the search engine box, primarily for the familiar ready-reference type or one or two-source quest. (What is the population of India? When was John Doe born? Where is Albany, New York in relation to New York City? Who is the Prime Minister of England?) Thanks to simplified search patterns, the average layperson may find what is needed without too much difficulty. The information may not always be the best, but at least it is something.

The second is the search or research query. One may use the search engine box, but considerably more than entering keywords is necessary. At this point one moves into expert, sophisticated searching which every reference librarian must know. This requires a good deal of skill on the part of the librarian. Here one may be looking, say, for everything on radon gas published over the past six months, only in the United States, or only by the government; or for radon gas in residential communities, and so on. Use of print sources is difficult enough, but to search online requires added ability.

The typical point of entry into any printed reference work is usually (but not always) subject, author, or, less frequently, title. Not so with a computer-assisted search. Here one may search by all of these, *plus*. The plus is important because the computer allows one to look for a key word in the text of an abstract, in a title, or even in the full text of the article or book.

For example, a cataloger gives only one subject heading to the article on the history of women in Rome. (The title of the article is "The Mother in Rome as a Manager.") The computer permits one to search the title by key words such as "women," "Rome," "mother," "manager," and any other important word that may be found in the title or any major word in the text of the article itself. All the points of entry ensure that one is no longer confined to a single subject heading, as valuable as that may be, or the author or title. Other tags or points of departure can be language, date, publication, and so forth. Finally, one can combine these to limit or expand a search.

The third, and by far the most efficient method, is to have the URL, i.e., the address of the Web page or site. This is similar to looking up a book by a precise author's name or title. It saves mucking about with subject headings and cross-references. Wherever possible, of course, the URL is the preferable first and possibly only step necessary for a successful search.

Today all medium to large libraries have their own Web page with specific links to equally specific online reference sources, i.e., URLs. These tend to be a mixture of free and for fee sources usually listed under broad categories from catalogs to indexes to encyclopedias, etc. As this website is not only specific but selective of the best in terms of what the library user needs, it is the first place to turn for more than simple searches. It is, too, an mnemonic aid. For example, the State University of New York at Albany library Web page (http://www.albany.edu/library) lists in alphabetical order all indexes it has access to online. If one can't recall if there is a Web index for anthropology, turn here for a reminder as well as a direct link to the index or abstracting services. (For a detailed discussion of library and related information websites see the section on "library websites" elsewhere in this text.)

For Free or For Fee Searches

Aside from ease of use, the tremendous advantage of the for fee reference source is that it is specific. One may move from the general index or encyclopedia to the specific dictionary or bibliography at a for fee site. As with print, the librarian simply lines up the question with the likely available source rather than wading around in the for free sea on the Net. Looking for material on Picasso? Turn to *Art Index*, a for fee index available on the Net. Trying to find background material on the Spanish-American War? Turn to the *Brittanica* online—and particularly the for fee version which has more material than the free work. The *Business Index* will instantly give information on the past month's stock market activities. The answer can be found, too, in free sites, but with considerably more work.

Of course there are scores, if not hundreds of free websites which are equally specific in given subject areas from weather and travel to data on a popular singer. Most of these tend to be scattered and unless one has the URL (again, check out the library's own Web page for help) it can take hours to find what might easily be discovered in minutes in a well-known for fee reference source—online or off.

Note, too, that the government sites are free and equally as valuable as many commercial websites. Still, these tend to be used much less until the librarian is familiar with the numerous possibilities. Newspapers, too, are free online, if only for a few days to a few years. But, again, they often are too broad for many specific questions, at least other than about current events. Also, most lack adequate online indexing or retrieval systems.

While the free/for fee method of selecting reference aids is a trifle arbitrary, it is at least a general guide for the reference librarian. Equally important is knowledge of reference forms, i.e., the ability to distinguish an index from a standard bibliography or an encyclopedia. Why bother? Because such knowledge makes it relatively easy to match the question with the likely source. Without such divisions of reference information, it is decidedly more difficult to find answers rapidly both online and in print.

The understanding of reference forms, free vs. for fee, and the ability to quickly hitch a query to a specific source is the mark of the professional. Anyone can enter a few keywords into a search engine's system and come up with something. As stressed in this text over and over again—that's not enough. The librarian, as the doctor, mechanic, and cook must know the tools of the trade or go down into a mass of ignominious questions without proper answers.

Frustrated Searching

Nothing better illustrates the potential problems of online searching than the experience of the average student. The pattern of student searches is by now a cliché among librarians. The standard approach is to enter one or two key words in a query box and hope for the best. The word by word search is typical of almost any library Net fan. Only one in nine users consider using Boolean logic, and not one in a thousand can conduct a sophisticated quest for hard to find data.

Most naive or optimistic students believe: (1) The Internet or any database which is accessed via a computer screen must have the answer. The response may be to any question from the progress of a bill through Congress, to "The Old Bill," an English singing group. (2) A typical search pattern is to type in a key word. In this case "bill." The answer appears on the screen. (3) Rarely is the citation read. The student prints out or downloads the first five to ten replies, and leaves content in the knowledge all is well.

There is the experience of one mother who employed two search engines: "I conducted searches on both sites to try to answer my seven-year-old daughter's question about the average life span of a house cat, and the results indicated that the technology still has a long way to go. It took me about 10 minutes of clicking on unlikely search results to learn that the answer is probably 15 years (according to a source who identified herself only as Cat Lady in a message she posted on the cat health bulletin board of Acme Pet.)"[19]

The mother's frustration is common. Here, for example, is a study by experts of how a typical user seeks Net data: Typically, retrieval of Web information is done by key word. The user types one or more key words into a search engine, which then returns all known resources containing those words. However, this approach can inundate the user with a plethora of irrelevant resources. Suppose, for example, we are interested in some basic information on the Grand Canyon (e.g., how deep it is). Typing "Grand Canyon" into the AltaVista search engine returns over 20,000 hits. The first nine hits were:

1. Web page for an inn near the Grand Canyon
2. Collection of photos of the Grand Canyon
3. Information on Arizona, "The Grand Canyon State"
4. Web page for an inn near the Grand Canyon
5. Narrative about a trip through the Grand Canyon
6. Advertisement for a cross-stitch set featuring an image of the Grand Canyon
7. Guide to Grand Canyon travel and lodging, and Grand Canyon statistics
8. Account of a trip through the Grand Canyon
9. Fact Sheet about the Grand Canyon

Out of the first nine hits, only the seventh and ninth hits appear to be directly relevant to our inquiry.[20]

There are two responses to the situation:

1. Librarians, as emphasized over and over again in this text, must be mediators between the individual and the Net. This seems particularly true for people who only understand the buckshot search for information.

2. As there is no evidence the average person will change the word by word search pattern, commercial data handlers are desperately trying to improve search techniques. This may help, but it won't be more than a patch work job. Nothing, at least for the next few decades, is likely to replace the knowledge and intuitive skills of the trained searcher. There are numerous reasons for this, but essentially it is the same old story—too much information. No sooner has a search engine found a method of sorting out a few facts when a mass more of data is put online.

---

[19]Michelle Slatalla, "Digital Bread Crumbs..." *The New York Times,* July 2, 1998, p. G8.
[20]*OCLC Newsletter,* November/December, 1997, p. 22.

Enter the Librarian

In one sense the student search is complete, and usually without much help from the librarian. The question here is whether or not the search is merely a representation of a search. The quality and the result of the quest lead the searcher to two conclusions: *(a)* there is more to information than most people appreciate; *(b)* if people are to be truly informed they more and more need the assistance of the librarian. This aid requires an interview and a well-planned search, not simply someone pointing the student to the computer terminals. If the librarian is to continue as a professional, interview and search are absolutely necessary to master, to understand, and, above all, to use in day to day service.

In some libraries when the decision is made to employ a serious, detailed online search, librarians ask the individual to fill out a preliminary form on which the question is stated. Sometimes this is done simply, but other times it is suggested that the user write a brief "narrative" in which the question is framed. For example, in one model of the form the following is requested: name and address of the user, title and purpose of the search, terms and the synonyms likely to be used in connection with the topic, list of important people in the field, and, sometimes, a note on maximum cost.

The use of the preliminary interview–search form is almost universal, simply because it saves valuable time. The form forces the user to consider the question and to be precise in its formulation. A similar form for any reference interview would no doubt improve all types of searches. The form also serves as a good departure point in formulating and negotiating new vocabulary as the librarian and patron work together.

Sometimes a research "expert" will present the librarian with a list of key words rather than the hoped–for "narrative." One problem with the list of key words is that the words may not be acceptable to the system. Often they do not take into account the interactive features of the computer search. It is always best to have a broad understanding of what is needed, not simply what the user sees as the major and minor terms. At the same time one does not want to dismiss this kind of assistance. It is better to have a user who is interested than one who expects the searcher to do everything.

Online searching is improved—if only in cutting the length of time needed to search—when there is a separate and quiet section for the interview and the search itself. Even though a ready-reference search may take no more than a minute or two, and can be done in a typical, busy reference situation, the in-depth online quest may run from 50 to 70 minutes. One can imagine how much longer this can take when it is done in the middle of the normal chaos at the reference desk.

The average user is going to crash, time and time again. What may be worse, the same user will walk away from the wreck convinced that there has been no accident, that the drive for information was a complete success. Experts and people wise enough to understand the complexities of information will usually want the assistance of a librarian. Furthermore, they may need help not only with databases, but also with the various technologies involved.

Perhaps all of this will resolve itself when the masses of information overwhelm even the most confident of the uninitiated. But for now the reference librarian must at least offer to be a mediator.

Search Techniques

When reference librarians speak of navigating the Web, they have two or three distinct paths to follow. First and foremost they tend to use for fee subscription paid databases, i.e., sources that are commercially produced for a profit. Examples are any of the indexes from UMI, EBSCO, the H. W. Wilson Company, etc. As indicated throughout this text, these tend to be better organized, certainly more rewarding in terms of current, reliable information than the "free" sites. Second, and most often for ready-reference queries, librarians turn to the same place most laypersons go—the millions of Web pages which offer free data on everything from ant hills to zesty librarians. And third, they may simply abandon the Web for easier to use, more familiar printed sources. This latter decision may seem simple enough, yet it is unusual for the average layperson to even consider an alternative to the Web—a fatal error in terms of time and frustration.

Given the librarian is familiar with the technology involved, which is not inconsiderate even in these days of simplification, the search may begin...always though built on the base of experience and knowledge as suggested in the previous pages of this chapter.

A commercial search expert, Mary McCarty, suggests what she calls the 5–4–3–2–1 approach to online searching:

(5) apply to Web resources the same five criteria used to evaluate print resources (currency, authority, scope/intended audience, tone, and ease of use); (4) try at least four search engines for every search, because the top search engines have little overlap and each includes only a small percentage of the total Web; (3) "triangulate—use three sources to verify suspicious Internet information" and use Web pages created by librarians to get higher quality information; (2) cost and speed are the two factors most important to employers; and (1) always go back to the one original source if a Web source refers to other information or is a reposting.[21]

[21]"Shaping the Web," *Library Journal,* March 1, 1999, p. 36 (McCarty is quoted by Carol Tenopir in her column, "Online Databases").

Expert Search Devices

Experienced online searches have individual approaches, but most agree there are several devices that speed the search and cut costs. While they follow the steps just outlined, they may do it in an abbreviated fashion.

At this point searchers turn to the computer for what is known as a "quick and dirty search."

1. Compose a "quick and dirty" search with a few terms, the logical operators, and no more than one adjacency operator. This "brief search" format has been useful for intermediaries and offers the advantage of using a small number of terms and operators. It is important that the user/searcher understand that this is a *trial* search. He/she is to use the information he/she finds to modify this search effectively.

2. Display results in a trial format for evaluation. Most database systems offer a format which provides some evaluative information (titles, lead paragraphs, index terms). Users should be instructed about using this information to determine how well they are doing, and they should also be taught how to modify their searches.

3. Modify the search with one or two simple changes. Limit the modifications to the following: adding terms to represent a concept, using another form of the terms for a concept (index phrases), or eliminating or intersecting a concept. Other changes may be necessary, but these three should be enough for the user to handle initially.

4. Print final results in a format containing all the necessary fields.

Most experts use Boolean logic, but with differences. The two major approaches: (1) Instead of using "and," use a plus sign +. (2) Employ "near," i.e., house near apartment. This should be used in search engines such as AltaVista instead of the usual "and" between key words. (3) Use double quotations to limit the search to a given subject or proper name, e.g., "Napoleon" or "French Revolution."

An important point about Web searches is made by Laura Cohen in her "hot tips for cool Web searches": She strongly advises the librarian to "read the help files available at most search engines' sites" first and always. Also, "search entries...often use different rules for each interface. Understand the difference and use the interface that is appropriate for your query."[22]

Confusion arises when one turns from a manual to a computer-assisted search. Some common problems: (1) The subject headings may not be the same in the printed and the machine-readable version. (2)

[22]Laura Cohen, "Searching for Quality..." *Choice,* Supplement, August, 1998, p. 21. This set of rules and suggestions is invaluable for reference librarians.

Dates of coverage differ, with the printed work normally going back many more years than the computer database. Most databases, for example, are retrospective only to the mid–1980s, although the printed index may go back twenty or more years beyond the computer cutoff. (3) The online search will likely have more current materials available than the printed source. (4) A number of search strategies are available with a computer, but with printed work the search is normally confined to a specific time period, and then by author or by subject.

Which type of search provides the best results for the user? There are so many variables that it is difficult to come to any general conclusion. First and foremost, the skill of the reference person is a major factor. An expert reference librarian will outperform the beginning computer searcher.

Boolean Logic

The key to subtle online searching is *Boolean logic.* This allows one to combine words and phrases to either limit or expand the search. Boolean logic is a synonym for sophisticated digital searching patterns. Normally, it is a part of almost all online searching patterns and is built into the search engine. It is not necessarily a part, though, of the for fee reference databases online—and here one must understand its more efficient use.

The primary method is to string a group of words together in such a way that it either widens or narrows the search. This is done by operators:

1. "And" connects two or more words which must be in the results. Example: Tom AND Jerry. This narrows the search in that both words must be in the item before it appears on the screen. A similar command is the "+" sign rather than "and." (Note: Most search engines now automatically include the "and" in their search so it is not necessary to normally use this command.)

2. "Or" narrows the search by telling the computer that it wants anything which has either X or Y in the topic. Example: Tom OR Jerry. This widens the search, as the searcher is calling for anything with either Tom or Jerry, not the two together.

3. "Not" is a more specific operator. It excludes the word after it from the resulting search. Example: Tom NOT Cat. The result is obvious. In a computer search one may use "–" instead of "not."

4. " " Quotation marks enclose words when one wants to find a specific phrase, name, object, etc. Example: "Encyclopaedia Britannica," which limits the search to this one set and not to every site or page with "encyclopedia" or "Britannica" present. Results will not be perfect, but at least better than without the limiting quotations.

In sophisticated searches, the librarian may string together a group of words and operators which narrow or broaden the search, but in any case makes it considerably more specific. Example: "Tom AND Jerry NOT Drink NOT Cats."

The ideal system should allow the user to (1) enter a command at any time; (2) retrieve data by date, language, geographical location, or other qualifiers; (3) have unrestricted use of Boolean operators and a number of search items; (4) link search statements and words; (5) query the material in the database by typing in terms which are as natural as possible; and (6) have the use of a thesaurus or dictionary.

The patterns of search are important because most laypersons who use electronic sources prefer the simple, direct route. The librarians, conversely, prefer the more sophisticated paths such as those provided by Boolean logic and its cousins. At any rate, it is of major importance in evaluating an online index whether it allows the use of Boolean logic or is more simplified in its approach.

FUTURE OF REFERENCE SERVICES

Reference librarians do a number of things besides mastering electronic formats. They are experts on acquisition of information sources; and are equally skilled in knowing what should be discarded from the collection. From day to day they take part in countless meetings and often act as administrators. Then there are the nitty-gritty aspects of the profession. Fixing the jammed printer next to the computer terminal or putting more paper in the copy machine may take as much time as attending meetings. There are times when librarians wonder why it is necessary to answer the telephone when there are 10 or more people waiting about for service.

Go to any library, public, academic, or school and for five or ten minutes watch what is going on in the reference area. Inevitably, the librarian is not only answering standard questions, but spending a considerable amount of the time teaching electronic searching skills to people.

There is a notion about, fed by advertising and optimistic ideas of the future, that it won't be long before Joe and his friends will be able to converse with a computer, i.e., Hal (of Kubrick's film "2001") without Hal's built in murderous paranoia. Put a question and Hal will give an instant accurate reply. It will be in a flat, noncommittal voice. Unlike a few rogue reference librarians, the voice inflections will not sound utter disdain for the person's ignorance. So long reference librarians, hello Hal.

Eventually this may come about, or as Dorothy Parker put it: "Oh, life is a glorious cycle of song, A medley of extreme paranoia; And love is a thing that can never go wrong; And I am Marie of Roumania." The reference room around the computers is filled with Kings and Queens of Roumania who believe by entering a word or two into an electronic database that the answer to their query will pop up on the screen, whether it be the population of New York City or the meaning of life. Lacking experience, the same innocent admits the response is not always exactly right, or even close. Still, give the computer time.

Meanwhile, while waiting, it is a safe guess that you, the reference librarian, will be about for a few more minutes. So, no, your studying reference sources is not likely to be an entire waste of time. Hal is still out there in space—with the Queen of Roumania.

Imagination and knowledge of public need will keep the reference librarian about for generations to come. It is not enough to simply have a warehouse of print or digital information. It requires that the librarian literally reach out to the person with a question, whether he or she be in the library or at home. Examples: (1) Provide answers to questions via e-mail (and/or fax). This may be actual reference questions or queries on how to find material on the Internet. (2) Provide library home pages with links to valuable information with notes on what has to be used in the library and what can be used at home. (3) Provide built-in questions to the user of a digital index. At the end of the search ask if the search has been a success or if the user needs help. (4) Provide one-to-one reference service online as one has in the past over the telephone. (5) And update telephone service so it is more than answering a few ready-reference queries.

There are scores of other ideas, both in practice and being worked out by librarians. These services keep reference librarians several jumps ahead of user needs. The primary point, and one which should be stressed over and over again by reference librarians, is that they offer personal, professional information at no cost to the user. No other information source (this side of the government and a few venturesome capitalists who are likely to switch to fees soon) can make that claim. The best information about at no fee is likely to win friends—and influence taxpayers at budget time.[23]

---

[23]Pilgrims pushing the delights of computers are less sanguine about the future of reference librarians and, in fact, seem to take delight in the notion they may disappear under a mass of digital databases. While calling for more "inventive" approaches to services, these librarians are suggesting the library, if not finished, is about to be so drastically changed as to no longer need traditional reference services. Give or take a few hundred years and they may be correct, but even that is a long bet. For a more typical, sensible, yet watch out for doomsday approach see: Gail Schlachter, "Clinging to Traditional Reference Services," *Reference & User Services Quarterly*, Spring 2000, pp. 223–228. Michael Schuyler, "Prognostications on Technology Unbound, or The Library to Come," *Computers in Libraries*, May 1999, pp. 30.

The Net's Future[24]

The year is 2020. Where will the computer fit in this postmillennial reference world?

There are as many responses as would-be experts. All are likely to be proven wrong. Still, it's gratifying to consider the delights and nightmares in store.

1. Data on the Net, or some other yet unforeseen information carrier, includes the sum total of human experience on this planet, the collective knowledge of over 5,000 years of recorded history.

2. There are even more people with access to electronic information than there are now to telephones. The use of the Net has spread worldwide and is pretty much equally divided among people.

3. Technology has reduced the size of microchip components so it is now possible to think about building robots which have common sense, can understand human knowledge, and, yes, can file all of the world's known information.

4. *Internet 2* is a much advanced edition of the older network. Allegedly 1,000 times faster, the claim is that the contents of the entire *Encyclopaedia Brittanica* could be delivered in a single second. The network is scheduled to be functional by mid–2000. It is financed primarily by the Department of Defense.

5. E-mail, one of the more popular features on today's computer, remains much the same. The differences: You can pay bills by simply inserting your smart credit card into the computer. The same channel may be used for shopping a virtual mall where exact pictures of sweaters to swatches of carpet are shown, and ordered.

The true answer about the future of electronic reference work and services is that no one really knows.

SUGGESTED READING

Borgman, Christine, "What are Digital Libraries? Comparing the Visions." *Information Processing & Management,* vol. 35, no. 3, 1999, pp. 227–243. The author explores the various definitions of "digital library" and explains why there is so much difference in both the definition and content of such a library. The conclusion is apparent—the old–fashioned book–oriented library will give way to the digital version.

---

[24]For an online discussion of the Future of the Net, and the progress on the second internet see: (http://K20.internetZ.edu).

Brandt, D. Scott, "Deconstructing Internet Searching," *Online & CD-ROM Review,* vol. 23, no. 4, 1999, pp. 206–207 A perceptive approach to searching in terms of "the big picture behind information retrieval." In a few pages the author has numerous useful tips on practical online searches—both for laypersons and librarians.

Brandt, D. Scott, "Do You Have an Ear for Searching," *Computers in Libraries,* May, 1999, pp. 42–44. A plea for different approaches to searches. "If someone is a different kind of searcher than you and I, it doesn't mean he or she is a candidate for correction or change therapy." Along the way the author gives some useful hints on the art.

Chun, Tham Yoke, "Worldwide Web Robots: An Overview," *Online & CD-ROM Review,* vol. 23, no. 3, 1999, pp. 135–142. Just how well do worldwide Web robots function? The author focuses on AltaVista and Excite to find the answer. A thorough, relatively easy to understand discussion of a sometimes complicated topic.

Fichter, Darlene, "Search Master: A New Role for Information Professionals," *Online,* March/April 2000, pp. 76–78. Exploring the notion that most people think all answers can be found at a computer terminal, the author suggests the librarian should move into the role of "search master." Briefly, this means an understanding of search engines, users, and how to wed the two to come up with satisfactory answers. One may argue with the terminology, but the argument about the need to master online searching is convincing.

Holland, William, *Teaching the Internet to Library Staff and Users.* New York: Neal-Schuman, 1999. This is a series of ready-to-use workshop plans for training both librarian staff and users. The sessions of 60 to 90 minutes are interested in covering basics. The organization of such speedy introductions is important—and here a success. Primarily for librarians concerned with the early stages of Internet training programs. Note: The author is a trained librarian on the staff of Microsoft.

Jacso, Peter, "Savvy Searching Starts With Browsing," *Online & CD-ROM Review,* vol. 23, no. 3, 1999, pp. 169–172. Tips on how to search based primarily on browsing the "indexes to explore the variations in the spelling of search terms." Indications of how to handle short cuts in searches are given throughout.

Jacso, Peter, "Savvy Searching," *Online & CD-ROM Review,* various issues. This is a regular column, and one of the best, by a member of the University of Hawaii faculty. Easy to understand tips and advice are given along with specific examples. Highly recommended for both beginner and expert.

Jansen, Bernard et al., "Real Life, Real Users, and Real Needs; A Study and Analysis of User Queries on the Web," *Information Processing and Management,* no. 36, 2000, pp. 207–227. The authors analyze the transaction logs of some 51,473 queries posed by 18,113 users at a major Internet search service. They show the various steps in refining the search as well as what constitutes a success or a failure. The main conclusion: There is a need to study more about how people (and librarians) seek information on the Web.

Kennedy, L. et al., "The False Focus on Online Searching," *Reference & User Services Quarterly,* Spring, 1999, pp. 1–12. Employing a specific case of searching for material, the authors explain the false starts and how they can be avoided in almost any search on the Web. While a trifle technical, it will be of value to anyone with more than a few days' experience in Net searches.

Kennedy, Lynn et al., "The False Focus on Online Searching," *Reference & User Services Quarterly,* Spring, 1999, pp. 267–273. Why do so many students and laypersons have difficulty with online searches? Kennedy and other research experts explain it is a matter of "false focus," which is another way of saying the average user wants an answer quickly and does not want to go through the logical, sometimes tedious but necessary steps of searching so familiar to librarians.

Klopper, Susan, "Finding a New Search Rhythm," *Online,* September/October, 1999, pp. 38–42. Using the metaphor of the old and the new dance steps, the author points out the delights and the problems of searching on traditional online databases vs. searches on the Web. The change to Web–based searches is applauded...but with some reservations.

Knopper, Steve, "The Early Bird Catches the Word," *Yahoo! Internet Life,* February 2000, pp. 128–132. The whole question of domain name registration on the Net is examined, particularly in view of 1999–2000 Congressional legislation. The focus is on "cybersquatting" and people who register Net addresses and names in the hopes of selling them later at a huge profit.

Latham, Joyce, "The World Online: IT Skills for the Practical Professional," *American Libraries,* March 2000, pp. 40–42. It's not just enough to understand reference sources, the appreciation of everything from the use of e–mail to Web browsers is necessary for the modern reference librarian. "We have to climb ladders of technical literacy that stand...between us and the viability of our profession." Just how to do this is explained by the director of automation at the Chicago Public Library.

Lawrence, John and Mary Ross, "Internet Reference: Boon or Bane?" *American Libraries,* May, 1999, pp. 74–78. A beginner asks an expert about the good/bad points of Internet reference. In his responses, Lawrence touches on everything from search engines to authority. And to answer the question: both, with reservations, think the Net is all for the good.

Linden, Julie, "The Library's Website is the Library" *C&RL News,* February 2000, pp. 99–101. A discussion of one aspect of the library website—distant learners. The author suggests an outline of a Web page which will meet their needs. In so doing she outlines the problems of any library Web page.

"Millenium Special: 2000 and Beyond," *Yahoo!,* December 1999, pp. 89–206. Most of the issue is given over to comments, opinions, and interviews with experts in dozens of fields. Each has a notion of what the Net means in terms of improving society. Topics move from a view of the future by eight prominent science fiction writers to other experts discussing entertainment and the outlook for computers. Take it or leave it, but an A+ for imagination.

"Navigating the Web," *Consumer Reports,* February, 1999, p. 63. A one-page guide for laypersons on how to get the most out of the Web in terms of information. The explanation is clear and concise—and one the librarian might wish to give to anyone who plans to seek data on the Web.

Negrino, Tom, "The Macworld Web Searcher's Companion," *Macworld,* pp. 1–76, May, 2000. A simplified guide for not only Mac users, but for all, to the skill of searching for information on the Web. Precise step-by-step suggestions are made, along with what to avoid. Excellent treatment for beginners.

O'Leary, Mick, "Web Personalization Does it Your Way," *Online,* March/April, 1999, p. 79–80. A regular columnist for this well-known magazine explains how business people get people to come to their site time after time. He calls it "personalization" and shows how the term is an umbrella not only for commercial searches but for the traditional current awareness service.

Proper, H.A. and P.D. Bruza, "What Is Information Discovery About," *Journal of the American Society for Information Science,* vol. 50, no. 9, 1999, pp. 737–750. The plethora of search engines has not solved the problem of searching on the Net for what is relevant. "The aim of this article is to provide a logic–based framework for information discovery, and relate this to the traditional field of information retrieval." And the authors succeed in explaining, in relatively jargon-free language, the key to the information framework.

Tennant, Roy, "Determining Our Digital Destiny," *American Libraries,* January 2000, pp. 54–58. Beyond the use of digital information and reference services, the librarian must master other electronic innovations from wedding various formats to the query to appreciating the delights of video or audio conferencing technologies. As the author says, "the game has changed and if libraries still want to play they'll have to invent their own future."

Timmons, Mary E., ed. *The Internet and Acquisitions* in *The Acquisitions Librarian,* no. 23, 2000. A good half dozen articles explore various aspects of the Net and how they may be used in acquisitions and reference services. Specific sites are given and evaluated from reader's advisory sites to those devoted to authors. Electronic resources are shown to be of value when limited to the best and better.

Vidmar, Dale, "Darwin on the Web: The Evolution of Search Tools," *Computers in Libraries,* May, 1999, pp. 23–28. Both a short history and a practical list of suggestions of how to search on the Web and what tools help or hinder. The author quotes and evaluates various search machines. His conclusion: "Different tools producing varying results may be essential to the future growth of the Worldwide Web."

PART II
INFORMATION: CONTROL AND ACCESS

CHAPTER THREE
BIBLIOGRAPHY

W here can I find a Web page on Catherine Wheels? Is there a book about inner tube collecting? How many novels by Nabokov are still available in bookstores? Where can I find reliable information about the American Civil War on the Internet? When was the recently television-reviewed book *Fat Boy* published, and by whom? How much will it cost me to buy an audiotape of exercises? And which one is best? Does the library have Singer's *The Slave*? No, well can I borrow it from another library?

These are familiar reference questions. In one form or another they are expected to be answered promptly and accurately because the librarian knows about books, Web pages, and related media. Thanks to bibliographies the librarian can meet the public's expectations.

The Net-wise layperson is likely to turn to a search engine for a reply to the queries. All well and good, but this is going to take much time, and more than a bit of luck. It is considerably less frustrating to know where to go, to know which website to call-up rather than to feed in a general query. Again and again it must be stressed that working on the Net is a superior vehicle for answering questions. The vital factor, though, is knowing specifically a reference source, not fishing around in an ocean of Web pages.

Knowledge of bibliographies, of the URLs for those bibliographies (or whether they are available only in print, and for what period of time, etc.) is a mark of the professional librarian. There are many definitions of bibliography, but no single definition is suitable for all situations. To most people, a bibliography is "a list of books." Experts give it a different meaning: the critical and historical study of printed books. In France, particularly during the late eighteenth century, the term emerged as a form of library science, that is, the knowledge and the theory of book lists. The Americans and the British now tend to divide it into "analytical," and "textual," as differentiated from a simple listing.[1]

Enumerative (i.e., a list) bibliography tells, among other things, who is the author of a book, who published it and where, when it was published, and how much it will cost to purchase, in either hardback, paperbound, or another form. Bibliographies are not necessarily confined to books. They may list other forms of communication from websites, films and recordings to photographs. A bibliography of, say, railroads could well include books, railroad websites, as well as films and photographs of railroads.

Once an item is located in a bibliography, the user wants to know (1) whether it is in the library and available to be read or (2) if not in the library, whether it is on order or can be obtained; (3) or a for fee website where the library offers access to the material online. If free, the question might be whether or not there are similar free sites online. The ideal library catalog or library Web page answers all of these queries.

SYSTEMATIC ENUMERATIVE BIBLIOGRAPHY

An effective enumerative bibliography needs several elements if it is to adequately meet the need for control and access.

Completeness. Through either a single bibliography or a combination of bibliographies, the librarian should have access to the complete records of all areas of interest, not only what is now available, but also what has been published in the past, what is being published today, and what is proposed for publication tomorrow. Also, the ideal bibliography should include the world, not only one nation's works.

---

[1]Analytical bibliography is concerned with the physical description of the book. Textual bibliography goes a step further and highlights certain textual variations between a manuscript and the printed book or among various editions.

Often the two are combined into one scientific or art form. This type of research is designed to discover everything possible about the author's ultimate intentions; the goal is to recover the exact words that the author intended in expressing his or her work. This is done by comparing different editions of the same work in a quest for large and small differences between the two or more volumes. Collating at this level is an effort to find the true, original work as prepared by the author, not by sometimes careless printers. One group of bibliographers may be experts in nineteenth-century printing practices and bookbinding and another group in paper watermarks or title pages. There are differences between analytical and textual bibliographies. Analytical bibliography is more concerned with the physical aspects of the book and textual bibliography with the author's words, that is, the exact text as the author meant it to appear in printed form.

Access to Part. Normally the librarian is apt to think of bibliographies in terms of the whole unit—a book, periodical, website, CD-ROM, manuscript, or the like. But an ideal bibliography should also be analytical, allowing the librarian to approach the specific unit in terms of the smallest part of a work, such as by subject, author, publisher, etc.

Various Forms. A comprehensive bibliographical tool will include all forms of published communication from reports and documents to the various types of electronic databases.

Day-to-Day Use

How does the reference librarian use bibliographies on a day-to-day basis? A bibliography is used for three basic purposes: (1) to identify and verify, (2) to locate, and (3) to select.

1. *Identification and verification.* The usual bibliographic citation gives standard information similar to that found in most catalogs: author, title, edition (if other than a first edition), place of publication, a collation (i.e., number of pages, illustrations, size), and price. Another element added to many bibliographies is the International Standard Book Number, abbreviated as ISBN or simply SBN, which is employed by publishers to distinguish one title from another. The ISBN number usually is on the verso of the title page. A similar system, the International Standard Serial Number (ISSN) is employed to identify serials. Electronic formats follow much the same pattern, but have additions from the type of hardware needed to availability on the Net.

In seeking to identify or verify any of these elements, a librarian will turn to the proper bibliography, usually beginning with the general source, such as *Books in Print* or *The National Union Catalog,* and moving to the particular, such as a bibliography in a narrow subject area.

2. *Location.* Location may be in terms of where the book is published, where it can be found in a library, or where it can be purchased. An online website or database will be located via its address online.

3. *Selection.* The primary aim of a library is to build a useful collection to serve users. This objective presupposes selection from a vast number of possibilities. In order to assist the librarian, certain bibliographies indicate what is available in a given subject area, by a given author, in a given form, or in a form suitable for certain groups of readers. A bibliography may give an estimate of the potential use of the particular work for the needs of a reader.

Experts and laypersons who know a subject well look up X or Y in a bibliography by its title or by the author's name. Those who are not experts tend to use subject headings. The more sophisticated and knowledgeable a person is in any field (whether it be automobiles or psychology), the more likely the individual is to try to search a bibliography by author. This is a very precise approach because one does not have to guess the subject headings in the bibliography. For example, is automobile under "Automobiles" or "Cars" or "Transportation"? The most complex search is a subject search. This equally is true of online searches. It is efficient to have a specific online address rather than try to find the material via a subject.

Future

Bibliographies and other reference works may be accessed in print and online. Today the online approach is favored. It will lead to two results:

1. By early in this century (i.e., 2000 plus) few national or general bibliographies will be available in print. The majority will be accessible only in an electronic form. This is less expensive, allows for faster updating of material, and is easier for searching.

2. There will, however, be "esoteric" printed bibliographies. These will be detailed scholarly works dealing with a specific subject. It is unlikely that these bibliographies will be limited to electronic access because they are not often used and as of now are less costly to produce in print form.

Meanwhile, one must learn about the scope of bibliographies. Why? Although the form may be transferred to an electronic system, the content is similar. The method of compilation and the problems involved are the same. The basic theory behind the intellectual approach to bibliography content does not differ with format.

National Bibliography

A bibliography such as our United States *National Union Catalog*, lists all works which are cataloged by the Library of Congress and other member libraries of the system. A bibliography of this type normally has many books *not* published in the country of origin. The NUC, for example, lists Chinese, French, Russian, and other foreign language titles as long as they have been cataloged.

National library catalogs are not limited by time, territory, language, subject, or forms of communication. Combined they come close to the ideal universal bibliography. And although none claim to be universal in scope, collectively they do offer a relatively comprehensive record of international publishing.

The Library of Congress *National Union Catalog* has materials from around the world, and a good proportion of its holdings consists of books, magazines, music, and the like from international publishers. Numerically, an idea of the scope of the Library of Congress holdings may be gathered from the fact that the Library contains more than 20 million books and 100 million discrete items. About five to six million new items are added each year. Comparatively speaking, the average number of books published in America each year hovers around 40,000 to 50,000 titles, a small part of the overall annual acquisitions of the Library of Congress net, which sweeps close to works by over one million authors. Quite similar figures apply to all national libraries.[2]

In order to be properly qualified as a national bibliography, the system must have two elements: (1) It needs a legal deposit system which ensures that the national library receives a copy of everything published in the bibliography's country of origin; and (2) the records must be from direct examination of the materials, not from the publisher or author. Most western countries now have depository and direct examination as a foundation for national bibliography.

Trade Bibliographies[3]

Trade bibliographies are limited to materials published within a given country. They may be further narrowed to a section of the country, a city, or even a hamlet. For ease of use such bibliographies are divided by time, form, and origin.

Time. This is a matter of listing works previously published, works being published, or works to be published. Such bibliographies are normally labeled as either retrospective or current.

Form. This classification may be in terms of bibliographical form: collections of works, monographs, components (e.g., essays, periodical

[2]One may claim that universal bibliography is a reality today, only to be frustrated by a country, region, or individual who refuses to methodically list what is issued. Eventually, most of the world will recognize standard bibliographical procedures to allow for universal bibliography, but that probability is far in the future.

[3]*Trade* bibliography is often used synonymously with national bibliography. *Trade bibliography* refers to a bibliography issued for and usually by the booksellers and publishers of a particular nation. The emphasis of a trade bibliography is on basic purchasing data. Information for a trade bibliography is gathered from the publishers, and the individual item listed is *not* examined by the compiler of the trade bibliography. A *national bibliography*, which includes additional information (often complete cataloging data), is compiled by librarians. The data are taken directly from the item which is examined by the cataloger. Result: National bibliographies are more complete and more accurate than trade bibliographies.

articles, poems); physical form (books, databases, recordings, pamphlets, microfilm) or published and unpublished works (manuscripts, dissertations).

A typical trade bibliography will set itself limits of time, form, and, obviously, origin. For example, *Books in Print* is limited to books available for purchase (time); it includes only printed books, both hardbound and paperback, and some monographs and series (form); and it is a trade bibliography, that is, issued by a commercial organization (origin).

EVALUATION OF BIBLIOGRAPHY

When considering the relative merits of a bibliography, one applies the general criteria used for evaluation of all reference works: purpose, authority, scope, etc. (See the discussion on "Evaluating Reference Sources" in Chapter One). Beyond the general considerations, one should evaluate a bibliography in the following manner:

1. *Purpose.* It is important that the bibliography fill a real need and that it not be a repetition of another work or so esoteric that it is of little or no value. The subject is stated clearly in the title and well defined in the preface.

2. *Scope.* The bibliography should be as complete as possible within its stated purpose. For example, a bibliography of books and periodical articles about nineteenth-century American railroads will include contemporary magazine reports about the construction of railroads. Reliable websites, too, are likely to be listed as are related CDs, recordings, etc. Where there are different forms, these must be clearly identified.

3. *Methodology.* The method of compiling the bibliography should be straightforward and should make clear that the compiler has examined all material listed. The items are to be described in a standard bibliographic style, and include the basic elements of a bibliographical entry.

4. *Organization.* The bibliography should be organized in a clear, easy-to-use fashion, and indexes (from subject and author to geographical location) should be included where multiple access is desirable. At the same time, look for material arranged in a logical fashion so that it is not always necessary to use the index, for example, alphabetical by author, by date, by subject, and so forth. The author must offer a clear explanation of how to use the work as well as definitions, a key to abbreviations, and the like. Online, the software should be sophisticated enough that one may do an equal type of search with entry points where needed.

5. *Annotations and abstracts.* Where descriptive and critical notes are used for entries, these should be clear, succinct, and informative.

6. *Bibliographical form.* This is a standard entry with the information one needs to identify and locate the item.

7. *Current.* The material should be current, at least where this is the purpose of the bibliography. It is conceivable that one would list only eighteenth- or nineteenth-century publications, and in such a case timeliness would not be a factor. Again, the great advantage of online bibliographies is they may be updated regularly, e.g., see *Books in Print* for an example.

8. *Accuracy.* It goes without saying that the material must be accurate. There should be some arrangement, if possible, for corrections to be made after publication, should the need arise.

GUIDE TO REFERENCE SOURCES

Note: Here, as throughout this chapter and in the text as a whole, the addresses for subscription (i.e., for a fee) online databases are that of the publisher, not of the actual database. To find for-a-fee databases (indicated by subscription price): *(a)* Turn to your library's Web page. The database usually is listed there with a link to the Web site. *(b)* Try another library in your area which offers users free access to for fee databases. *(c)* Use the publisher's online address given here. You may have to search for the specific title in the publisher's online catalog or search system. Once found the publisher may offer a free hour or two for sample searches.

Go directly to the address for free databases, i.e., those with "free" shown.

Print: Balay, Robert, *Guide to Reference Books,* 11th ed. Chicago: American Library Association, 1996, 2040 pp. $275.[4]

Online: *Walford, Albert John.* Walford's Guide to Reference Material, *London. The Library Association, 2000 to date, quarterly. (URL to be announced) Rate varies.*
Print: The Library Association, 1959 to date, annual, 3 vols. $195 to $225 each.

Print: Wynar, Bohdan. *American Reference Books Annual.* Englewood, CO: Libraries Unlimited, Inc., 1970 to date, annual. $110.

The basic purpose of a bibliographical guide to reference material is to introduce the user to (1) general reference sources for assistance in research in all fields and (2) specific reference sources which help in research in particular fields. The guides take a number of forms,

---

[4]Shortly the guide should be available via the Net. As of 2000 it was only in the print format.

but primarily are either (1) annotated lists of titles with brief introductory remarks before each section or chapter or (2) handbooks which not only list and annotate basic sources, but also introduce the user to investigative tools in a discursive, almost textbook like, approach.

There are several basic guides helpful in the selection and use of reference books.

1. *Guide to Reference Books* lists and annotates some 16,000 titles considered basic for the large library. Titles are arranged under main sections, from the social sciences to the humanities. It boasts an excellent 400-page index. The *Guide,* as its English cousin, begins with a broad subject and then subdivides it by more specific subjects and by forms. For example, there is a section on economics under the social sciences. This is subdivided by forms: guides, bibliographies, periodicals, dissertations, indexes and abstract journals, dictionaries and encyclopedias, atlases, handbooks, and so on. The economics section is later broken down into even more specific subjects and often, within the subject entry, a further division is made by country, as, for example, in the political science section. *Guide to Reference Materials* subdivides economics by bibliographies, thesauruses, encyclopedias and dictionaries, dissertations, and so on, generally following the Balay pattern. In practice, the arrangement is not really important. Each volume has an excellent title, author, and subject index.

Both guides include limited information on electronic reference sources, clearly indicating what is available in various formats. Attention to electronic databases has grown considerably and the guides offer sound advice as to which format(s) are best.

The problem with *Guide to Reference Books* is the lack of current material. The cutoff date for the 1996 edition is the start of 1994, or titles that are a good two years behind publication of the 11th edition. The promised new edition for 2001 is under the editorship of Robert Kief (head librarian at Harverford College in Pennsylvania), Balay having stepped down. It equally is likely to be dated before publication. It is hoped that the work will become available online to make it more current and, indeed, more useful. See the January issue of *College & Research Libraries* (Chicago: American Library Association) "Selected Reference Books." The 50 to 75 titles are carefully selected, annotated, and arranged by broad subject. This helps update the previous edition of *Guide to Reference Books.*

2. The British *Guide to Reference Material* (or "Walford") is more current than its American cousin and is therefore favored in many larger libraries. The three volumes are under constant revision and are published on a three-year schedule. Beginning in 2000 the three volumes became available on the Web. According to the publisher each volume will be updated electronically every three months. The print versions will continue to be issued as new editions at the rate of one a year, or the three over three years.

Guide to Reference Material follows the same procedure as its American counterpart, although since the bibliography is in three volumes the total number of titles is at least one-third or more greater than in *Guide to Reference Books*. There are often citations to reviews with judicious quotations from those reviews. The focus is more involved with England and the European Union.

Walford's three volumes, issued once every year with the process starting again when the third volume is published, cover science and technology, social sciences, and the humanities. (Vol. 1: *Science and Technology*; Vol. 2: *Social and Historical Sciences, Philosophy and Religion*; Vol. 3: *Generalia, Language and Literature, the Arts*). The organizational pattern follows the UDC, that is, Universal Decimal Classification. (This means, for example, the science volume includes anthropology which is not found under science in the American work.)

The high point of the three-volume work is the annotation style. The critical notes are written with a flair that made Walford famous. They are not only descriptive, but include well-directed barbs and praise when necessary. Most are a delight to read. Prior to his death in 2000, Walford turned over the volumes to a group of editors who continue with his fine writing style. (His name continues on as part of the title.)

While much of the focus in Walford's guide is on British and European Union works, it is broad enough to include the basic American titles as well. This is evident in the second volume covering the social sciences, philosophy, and religion which offers a fine selection of international reference works.

3. *American Reference Books Annual* (usually cited as ARBA) differs from both *Guide to Reference Books* and *Guide to Reference Materials* in three important respects: (1) It is limited to reference titles published or distributed in the United States and Canada; (2) it is comprehensive for a given year and makes no effort to be selective; (3) the annotations are written by more than 350 subject experts and are both more critical and more expository than those found in Balay or Walford. Depending on the extent of American publishing, the annual volume, usually available in March or April of the year following the year covered in the text, analyzes some 1,800 separate reference titles. The work is well organized and well indexed. Every five years the publisher issues a cumulative index to the set.

Recommended Reference Books for Small and Medium Sized Libraries and Media Centers (Englewood, CO: Libraries Unlimited, 1980 to date) is a cut-down version of the same publisher's *American Reference Books Annual*. The reviews are under major subject categories, and codes indicate use by academic, public, or school libraries. It includes from 500 to 550 reference works published the previous year which meet the needs of the smaller- to medium-sized reference collection.

    4. *Canadian Reference Sources: An Annotated Bibliography* (Vancouver, University of British Columbia, 1997. 1076 pp. $225.) The Canadian cousin to *Guide to Reference Books,* this lists about 4,000 reference sources of primary interest to Canadian librarians. Arrangement is similar to the American and English works. An essential difference: the work is bilingual, i.e., French/English. The guide was put together by Mary Bond and Martine Caron of the National Library of Canada. Note: Although the publication date is 1997, most sources are published before 1996.

Guides for Smaller Libraries

Most libraries are in the small- to medium-size category. The larger guides are too inclusive. A small library needs works that are considerably less exhaustive. Edited by Scott Kennedy, *Reference Sources for Small and Medium Sized Libraries* 6th ed. (Chicago: American Library Association, 1999) affords a useful list of some 2,000 basic titles. The descriptive/evaluative annotations are excellent and enough information is given to help the librarian decide whether or not purchase of the reference work is required. The standard titles, from dictionaries to indexes, remain much the same as in *Guide to Reference Books.* Electronic formats are included.

    Considerably more ambitious, the American Library Association's *Guide to Information Access* (1994) considers some 3,000 of "the best standard and electronic sources in the 36 most researched subject categories." Ably edited by Sandy Whiteley, the ALA guide is primarily an annotated listing of titles under subjects from "general reference sources" to "writing." The first 90 or so pages offer an introduction to research and electronic databases. Each of the numerous contributors is an expert in a field. The guide may be used by both librarians and laypersons.

Subject Bibliographies

A cursory glance at any subject area in either *Guide to Reference Books* or *Guides to Reference Materials* will reveal hundreds of subject bibliographies. Most of these follow the same pattern of organization and presentation, but are for a particular area of interest. The various disciplines and large areas of knowledge have their own bibliographies, their own versions of *Guide to Reference Books.*

    Some examples of subject bibliographies indicate the wide field— name a subject and inevitably there will be from one to 100 bibliographies concerning works in areas of interest. At random, here are a few subject guides which have explanatory titles: C.D. Hirt, *Information Sources in Science & Technology*, 3rd ed. (Englewood, CO: Libraries Unlimited, 1998); William Johnson, *Recent Reference Books in Religion*. (New York: Dearborn, 1999).

Turn to the Web for both "static" and ongoing bibliographies in almost any field. These are under various subject headings, but in a general way entrance is made possible by "bibliographies–medieval" or "bibliography–railroads," etc.

Static bibliographies are ones with a limited amount, if any at all, of new entries, e.g., *Literature in English*, www.library.yale.edu/humanities/.

English/englit offers guides, handbooks, encyclopedias and other related sources which constitute "a select bibliography of reference sources" in English. More likely, though, the site will be in a constant state of construction.

Bibliography of Bibliographies

Print: Bibliographic Index. New York: H. W. Wilson Company 1984 to date. Service.

A bibliography of bibliographies is, as the name suggests, a listing of bibliographies. One may find a bibliography on dogs at the end of an article in a periodical, at the conclusion of an essay in an encyclopedia, or as part of a book on pets. If one lists these three bibliographies and adds from a dozen to a thousand more on dogs, one has a bibliography of bibliographies about dogs.

The primary example of a bibliography of bibliographies is *Bibliographic Index*. Under numerous headings, one may find bibliographies about subjects, persons, and places. The entries represent (1) separate published books and pamphlets that are normally bibliographies in a specific subject area, for example, *East European and Soviet Economic Affairs: A Bibliography...;* (2) bibliographies that are parts of books and pamphlets, such as the bibliography which appears at the end of David Kunzle's book *The Early Comic Strip;* and (3) bibliographies published separately or in articles in approximately 3,000 English and foreign language periodicals. Emphasis is on American publications and a bibliography must contain more than 50 citations to be listed.

The inevitable catch to many reference works is applicable here: (1) The bibliographies are not listed until six months to a year after they are published, and (2) although books, and to a lesser degree pamphlets, are well covered, the index cannot be trusted to include many periodical bibliographies. Why? Because over 120,000 periodicals are issued, often with bibliographies, and the index includes analysis of only 3,000. Furthermore the bibliography must include a minimum of 50 citations or it is not listed.

CURRENT SELECTION AIDS

Online: Books in Print With Book Reviews. New York: R.R. Bowker, 1992 to date, monthly, www.booksinprint.com. Free. DIALOG file 470, $30 per hour. Rate varies. OCLC and other carriers.
Books in Print With Book Reviews on Disc, *1992 to date, monthly. $1,600.*

Online: Booklist ("Reference Book Bulletin"), Chicago: American Library Association, 1997 to date, semimonthly, www.ala.org/booklist/index). Free.

Print: 1905 to date, semimonthly. $56.*Online: Library Journal,* New York: R. R. Bowker, 1997 to date, semimonthly, www.libraryjournal.com. Free.
Print: 1876 to date, semimonthly. $79.

Online: Choice, Chicago: American Library Association, 1988 to date, monthly, www.ala.org/acrl/choice/home. Rate varies.
Print: 1964 to date, monthly. $200.

Online: Reference & User Services Quarterly (formerly RQ) Chicago: American Library Association, www.ala.org/rusa/rusq. Free.
Print: 1960 to date, quarterly. $50 (free to members).

The selection of reference sources is a major skill of the trained reference librarian who will spend a good deal of time picking just the right works for the needs of the audience served. And those needs vary from library to library. The first and most important selection is to recognize both known and anticipated requirements of the users.

How is a satisfactory selection policy reached? There must be a librarian who has subject competence; that is, one who knows the basic literature of a field, or several fields, including not only the reference works but also the philosophy, jargon, ideas, ideals, and problems that make up that field. There is no substitute for substantive knowledge. The librarian must have in-depth awareness of the type of writing and publishing done in that special field. Where is there likely to be the best review? Who are the outstanding authors, publishers, and editors in this field? What can and cannot be answered readily?

Selection is charted, rather than dictated, by the following:

1. Knowing as much as possible about the needs of those who use the reference collection.

2. Calling upon expert advice. In a school situation the expert may be the teacher who is knowledgeable in a certain area. In a public library it may be the layperson, skilled practitioner, or subject specialist who uses the library. Most people are flattered by a

request that draws upon their experience and knowledge, and one of the best resources of reference materials is the informed user.

3. Keeping a record of questions. This is done to determine not only what materials the library has but what it does not have. Most important, a record of *unanswered* queries will often be the basis for an evaluation of the reference collection.

4. Knowing what other libraries have, and what resources are available. For example, the small library contemplating the purchase of an expensive run of periodicals or a bibliography would certainly first check to see whether the same materials may be readily available in a nearby library.

These four points only begin to suggest the complexity of selection. Many libraries have detailed selection policy statements that consider in depth the necessary administrative steps which are merely hinted at here.

Formats, and particularly Internet sites, present another set of problems for selection. As indicated throughout this guide, one must first and always ask questions about the content, its reliability, its suitability for the library audience, etc. The Net requires evaluation in terms of accuracy, authority and how much information is given or withheld. The frequency of updates is of great importance as well. And where there are links to other sites, the essential query is: "How reliable are the link sites, and why were they chosen?" Beyond that are technical queries about the electronic versions. For both online and CD-ROM, the quality and the skill of the presentation, as well as navigation and media aids are of major importance.

All of the basic sources of reference reviews cited here now examine electronic media as well as print. In fact, as the importance of digital sources becomes increasingly important in reference services, the time will come when the electronic sections devoted to reference works will be larger than those given over to print.

The problem with some electronic format reviewers, though, is they put emphasis on technology rather than content. There is more concern with navigation than what is actually in the reference work. A glance, for example, at the excellent reference reviews in *Choice* magazine will make the point. Coming at the front of each issue they represent the opinions primarily of teachers and librarians. Most reviewers appreciate the importance of content.

Basic questions about selection remain, no matter what the format. On the Web:

> We need to answer the essential questions: Who is the progenitor of this information? Upon what authority is it presented? What is the expertise of the providers? How accurate, in-depth, comprehensive, and up-to-date

is it? Who is its audience? We'll be adding new evaluative criteria as well. What does it deliver in terms of its medium? Is it cheaper, easier, faster, user-friendly? How does it compare to its print or CD-ROM version or to similar products in the same or other formats?[5]

Books in Print with Book Reviews

Most libraries, regardless of size, will subscribe to at least two or three of the standard review journals. Larger libraries will have reviews available as part of larger electronic databases. *Books in Print With Book Reviews* includes *Booklist, Library Journal,* and *Choice,* as well as related and useful journals: *Publishers Weekly, Kirkus, BIOSIS, School Library Journal, Reference and Research Book News, University Press Book News, Sci-Tech Book News,* and a half dozen others. (For descriptions of the major review sources, see below.) There are close to 400,000 book reviews (not all of them of reference works by any means) available on this single megasource. None of the journals is entirely satisfactory in the reviews of online offerings, but at least they cover the basics of interest to the majority of libraries—and certainly to students.

Standard Reviews

"Reference Books Bulletin," a section in the twice-a-month issue *of The Booklist,* is the single most important place for a librarian to turn for accurate, current, and in-depth reviews of general reference works. Each section is prefaced by a series of notes about publishing, reference services, and new works. This is followed by unsigned reviews. The names of the members who write the reviews and serve on the committee (librarians and teachers) are given in each issue.

In the course of a year, the service reviews about 100 to 150 major works, and about double that number of more conventional, less expensive titles. From time to time a whole issue, or a good part of an issue, is dedicated to an overview of encyclopedias, dictionaries, children's reference works, and the like. The reviews are cumulated in a separate publication each year. Reviews appear no more than six months after publication of the reviewed book, and sometimes even sooner. There are detailed reviews of CD-ROM and online databases most likely to be used in the average library. The analysis is useful particularly for the layperson who wishes to learn the good and bad points about searching for the layperson. In fact, the reviews of databases are among the best now available. Note: *Booklist* is available free on the Net. The online reviews are updated regularly and there is a limited archive of back reviews.

[5]Francine Fialkoff, "Reviewing Electronic Media," *Library Journal,* January, 1999, p. 73.

Other current reviews of reference books and information sources include:

1. *Choice.* While specifically geared to college libraries, this professional journal evaluates a number of reference titles of value to all libraries. These are listed under "Reference." *Choice* reviews electronic databases in each issue. Nonreference databases are scattered throughout the various subject areas. Also, from time to time bibliographical essays in the front of the magazine highlight reference titles. There are approximately 6,800 reviews a year, of which about 500 cover reference books. The reviews are usually 120 to 500 words in length and are signed. Almost all reviewers make an effort to compare the title under review with previously published titles in the same subject area, a feature which is particularly useful but rarely found in the other reviews. When budgets are tight, when choices must be made, it is of great importance that comparisons are available.

The August number, "special supplement" is an annual summary of the best reference/subject resources available on the Internet. It is an excellent guide to current reference Net sources. Most of these are taken from previous issues. There are special features, such as those on the Net by Laura Cohen, which make this considerably more than a collection of past reviews. Basic for both public and college libraries.

While more expensive online than in print, the *Choice* reviews in this format have the usual added features of electronic data. The features are similar for the other online reviews, e.g., ability to search not only by author and title, but by key words, date, readership level, etc. Also, reviews often appear before they are in print.

2. *Library Journal.* Again, the general book review section leads off with "Reference." There are about 450 reference reviews each year. These are 100 to 150 words long, usually written by librarians or teachers, and all are signed. Also, *School Library Journal* includes reviews of reference titles.

Some of the best reviews of electronic databases for reference purposes are found in *Library Journal.* Cheryl LaGuardia of Harvard evaluates both CD-ROMs and online databases in her "Database and Disc Reviews." In her methodical systematic way she points out the good and bad points of each and ends by suggesting the "best" for a given reference situation. The column alone is enough for most librarians to make decisions about electronic reference titles.

Other columns cover current websites (e.g., "Web Watch") as well as the latest in computer technology.

Note: The *Library Journal* is available, in an abridged form, on the Net for free. Not all reviews are online. An added service, *Academic*

Newswire (www.bookwire.com/ljdigital/newswire/newswire.htm) has news from over 100 correspondents on campus as well as book reports.

3. *Reference & User Services Quarterly.* The last section of this quarterly is given over entirely to the review of reference books. A few other related titles are considered, but, unlike *Library Journal* and *Choice,* this makes no effort to review general books. About 300 reference titles are considered each year. Reviews average about 200 words each.

In addition to the section on "Reference Books," electronic databases are evaluated. These are excellent, critical reviews which consider the most often used online services. Finally, under "Professional Materials," about 10 to 12 books are usually considered for librarians involved in reference work. According to the editor the purposes of the website is "to serve as both an early alert system and a reference to the content of past issues."

4. *American Libraries,* the monthly magazine of the American Library Association, does not regularly review reference books, but it does have an annual feature of interest: The "Outstanding Reference Sources of [year]," appearing in the May issue, is a compilation of the best reference titles of the year selected by the Reference Sources Committee of the ALA. Choice is based on quality and suitability for small- to medium-sized libraries. Selection includes digital sources. Some 35 to 45 titles are selected, and the results, usually with each work annotated, appears in various other library publications. The *Library Journal* offers a competitor, "Reference Books of [the year]," with titles selected by its book review editors. This appears in the April 15 issue which is devoted almost entirely to reference services.

5. "Selected Reference Books of [year]," appears in the March issue of *Colleges and Research Libraries.* This is a carefully chosen list of titles likely to supplement the next edition of *Guide to Reference Books.* And while of primary value to academic libraries, it is a handy checklist for all types and sizes of libraries.

Reviews of sites on the Internet and Web pages are regular features of the basic general reference sources just discussed. In addition, throughout this guide, there are suggested Net sources for reviews. And hardly a week goes by that this or that publisher does not offer a guide to the best and better Internet resources, if not always for reference, at least for the general public's information needs. Note: The paradox is that almost all of the guides are in print, not in electronic formats.

There are other approaches to reference works and news of the reference and information services field. One leader is *Reference Services Review* (Ann Arbor, MI: Pierian Press, 1972 to date, quarterly). This does not so much review new books as offer a dozen or more bibliographies.

These may include an annotated listing on AIDS or one on the joys of mountain climbing. All the authors or compilers are experts in their respective fields. From time to time, too, there are general overviews of reference services.

While there are no reviews, *The Reference Librarian* (New York: Haworth Press, 1981 to date, semi-annual) features 15 to 25 articles on a single subject of interest to reference librarians. The topics may range from online searching, to ethics, to distance learning. The authors are working librarians who offer a unique approach to various subject interests.

INDEXES TO REVIEWS

Online: Book Review Digest. New York: H. W. Wilson Company, 1984 to date, weekly, www.hwwilson.com. $25 to $40 per hour. OCLC and other vendors.
CD: 1983 to date, quarterly. $1,095.
Print: 1905 to date, monthly. Service.

Online: Book Review Index. Detroit: Gale Group, 1969 to date, 3 times a year, www.gale.com. Rate varies. DIALOG file 137, $57 per hour.
CD: Book Review Index on CD-ROM, 1965 to date, annual. $1,250. Annual update, $495.
Print: 1965 to date, bimonthly. $215. Cumulations 1965 to date. Price varies.

The titles considered here are specialized. Their sole purpose is to list book reviews. They are used by students and others seeking background material on a given work as well as by the reference librarian on the lookout for notices about specific reference books. The reviews are *limited* to printed books. With few exceptions, electronic formats are not considered. Note: Sources of reviews of electronic sources will be found in another section of this text.

The long-standing, well-known *Book Review Digest* is a place where experienced librarians look first for reviews—at least if the book is by a well-known or controversial writer. Lesser known authors rarely are found here because the publisher requires (1) that at least four reviews of a novel are published before the novel is listed and (2) that a minimum of two reviews of nonfiction are published before inclusion. This solves the problem of space, at least in print, but poses the difficulty—rarely is a first novel reviewed. Much the same is true of important but less-than-popular nonfiction titles.

Still, if the book is relatively noticed, then the *Book Review Digest* is an ideal source. Why? Because it gives a brief summary of the content of the reviewed title and, more important, it gives enough of an excerpt from a review for the reader usually to know whether the book is worth considering. This type of annotation saves much looking up of the original review(s). Another distinct advantage is that the print work goes back to 1905, thus giving the researcher an important resource for contemporary reviews of many titles which by now have become classics. Also, there is a subject approach to many of the titles reviewed. This can be valuable when someone is looking for a book, say, on pirates and has no idea of the author or title.

The librarian must know the approximate date that the book was published. The fastest method is simply to search the cumulative or the annual index volumes, from 1983, the CD-ROM or online service. If the date cannot be found in these indexes, the librarian should turn to the catalog where the title may be entered or to one of the national or trade bibliographies such as *Books in Print*. Another possibility is to search for a title by using a bibliographic network, such as OCLC.

Book Review Index covers reviews in more than 900 periodicals from 1965 to date. The publisher claims over 3 million citations for some 1.5 million separate titles. Unlike the *Book Review Digest,* there is only a citation to the review, not a summary of the review's content. Therefore, the user must hunt down the review before any decision may be made about the quality and desirability of the book. On the other hand there are many more sources than found in *Book Review Digest* (900 vs. *BRD's* 100). It is the first place to turn for titles which may be noticed in only one or two periodicals.

The print reviews are listed in two sections; the first by author, and the second by title. Unfortunately, there is no subject approach. On an average, about 75,000 books are covered each year, with about one to two reviews per title. This contrasts sharply with the other basic key to reviews, *The Book Review Digest*. Here one finds only about 6,000 titles considered.

A useful feature of the index for the reference librarians is that all reference works are marked with an "r." Thus one can look through the bimonthly issues for updated information on new works otherwise missed. Other codes include a "p" for a periodical review; and a "c" and a "y" for children and young people.

The electronic version, obviously a better buy than the print cumulations, offers a straightforward method of searching from 1965 or 1969 to the present. Points of entry include, of course, the author and the title; but in addition one may select a search by periodical where the review appeared, publication year and the like. Also, unlike the print version, here one may search by subject as well as key words in titles.

Modest reference budgets will dictate the *Book Review Digest* as a first choice. Larger libraries will have both the review services.

The majority of periodical and newspaper indexes, discussed in Chapter 4, include citations to reviews of books. When one is looking for a review, say, of a current best seller a general magazine index, particularly online, would be a first place to turn.

ELECTRONIC DATABASES

Online: Gale Directory of Databases. Farmington Hills, MI: Gale Group, 1994
to date, semiannual, (September, March), www.gale.com. Rate
varies. Also DIALOG file 230, which includes *Cyberbound's Guide to
Internet Databases* (discussed later in this text).
CD: 1993 to date, semiannual. $390.
Print: 1993 to date, semiannual, 2 vols. $340.

The single best guide to electronic databases, from CD-ROMs and
online services to magnetic tape is the comprehensive *Gale Directory of
Databases.* There is nothing quite like it, and it is a necessary purchase for
any library where there are questions about the content and availability
of electronic databases. More than 14,000 sources are described in detail.

An important point: This is a bibliography of current databases. It
lists what is available. It is nonevaluative, and can't be used for "best" or
"better" anymore than one could turn to *Books in Print* for such help.
To determine which is the most useful database for a given library
requires reading in other places, and more particularly evaluations found
in periodicals discussed throughout this text.

The print version consists of two volumes. The first covers about
7,500 online databases only. The second primarily is made up of about
6,500 CD-ROMs, with other sections on diskettes, magnetic tape, hand-
held products, and batch-access items. In both volumes there are three
helpful indexes: Database producers (about 4,000) with their names and
addresses and all of their products which, in turn, are numbered and
refer to the first part of the guide. Online services (some 2,500) which
is primarily a listing of vendors, and a geographic index. A subject index
is a bit too broad, but is of some aid. Finally the complete master index
covers everything in the book(s).

An introductory essay (repeated in each volume) gives an overview
of the state of the art of databases for the previous year. This should be
required reading. Often written by the expert of experts, Martha
Williams, it highlights quantity and quality in electronic information
sources. See too Williams's "New Database Products" which appears twice
per year in the journal *Online & CD-ROM Review.*

Within each volume there are individual entries for the titles
arranged in alphabetical order. A systematic approach gives similar basic
information for each item. There are 21 different pieces of data from the
address and fax and phone number of the producer to "alternate electronic formats" for the product when available. The heart of the infor-

mation is the "content" note which gives precise information on what is included in the database. Years of coverage, frequency, price, and other information are part of each descriptive entry.

The online and CD-ROM versions are, of course, much easier to search than the two print volumes; but the information in both is much the same. At any rate, the reference guide is likely to be used as much by laypersons as librarians, and, in whatever form, it should be found in most libraries.

BIBLIOGRAPHIES: NONPRINT MATERIALS

The previous discussion has been limited to guides and indexes to print and electronic bibliographies. There is another large group of reference works called "nonprint." Under this less-than-precise umbrella term one finds two universally familiar formats: (1) Motion pictures, whether they be animation or videos or part of hypertext CD-ROMs; (2) Sound, from music on CDs to voice-overs on DVDs. Aside from the two nonprint communication sources, there are items such as globes, overhead projector materials to models. These and the more traditional nonprint materials are an essential part of a reference service, particularly in school libraries or, as they are called, "school media centers" or "learning centers."

When working with resources other than books, the reference librarian functions much as she or he would when working with the traditional media:

1. In schools, universities, and colleges, the librarian will be called upon by the classroom teacher for information on media that are available in the library and may be ordered, or even borrowed, from other libraries.

2. The students will want information and advice about multimedia for the primary learning process.

3. The layperson's needs will be somewhat similar, although here most of the emphasis is likely to center on advice about the library's videos, recordings, and so on, which may extend knowledge (or recreational interests) beyond the traditional book.

The reference librarian should be conversant with at least the basic bibliographies and control devices for the media. Knowledge of bibliographies and sources is important for answering questions dealing directly with audiovisual materials: "Where can I find [such and such], a catalog of films, records, tapes?" "Do you have anything on video that will illustrate this or that?" "What do you have on recordings or video pertaining to local history?" In large libraries, such questions might be referred to the proper department, but in small and medium-size libraries, the questions usually will have to be answered by the reference librarian.

Guides and Bibliographies

Online: A–V Online, Norwood, MA: Silver Platter, 1998 to date, quarterly, www.silverplatter.com. Rates vary. DIALOG file 46, $30 per hour.
CD: NICEM Reference CD-ROM, 1999 to date. Rates vary.
Print: NICEM Media Indexes. Albuquerque, NM: NICEM (National Information Center for Educational Media), 1964—no longer in print. Rates vary.

There are no entirely satisfactory bibliographies for nonprint materials. There is nothing which gives an overview of the material as found in *Books in Print* or *Guide to Reference Books* for printed materials. Lacking overall bibliographical control, the materials are difficult to track. The lack of such tools accounts in no small way for the development of media experts who are familiar with the many access routes.

The closest thing to *Books in Print* for audiovisual materials is *A-V Online.* (In print this was the *NICEM Media Indexes.*) The purpose of *A-V Online* is to provide noncritical information on what is available in nonprint materials. And, although directed at elementary and secondary school needs, a good deal of the data is applicable to other types of libraries. Hence, they can be used to answer such queries as "What transparencies are available for geography?" "What educational films are there on animals?" "On environmental studies?" And so on. Essentially the database contains more than 455,000 records, often with abstracts, to educational materials. "Educational" must be stressed. There is nothing here which would pass, say, for a standard grade-B motion picture. The database includes: 16- and 35-millimeter filmstrips; transparencies; audio and video tapes; records, from early presses to advanced CDs; slides, 8-millimeter motion picture cartridges, CD-ROMs and software are indexed, too, but not thoroughly.

The *NICEM Print Indexes* (now out-of-print) were a series of individual indexes, *not* a single work. Each item is briefly annotated, but only a description, not evaluation. Full information is given as to cost, rental (when available), and necessary bibliographical information for identification and order.

Books in Print (see the next chapter) is a source of A-V material, but these are limited by type. BIP offers the *Complete Video Directory* (1991 to date, quarterly) which covers not only educational but popular entertainment from exercise videos to movies. See, too, their self explanatory *Words on Cassette* (1994 to date, annual) which gives all the vital information on audiobooks. Both of these are part of the digital *Books in Print.* Another useful bibliographic guide is OCLC's *World Cat,* discussed later, which often will supply more A-V records than the *A-V Online.*

Index to Media Reviews

CD-ROM: Media Review Digest. Ann Arbor, MI: The Pierian Press, 1989
to date, annual. $395 to $600.
Print: 1970 to date, annual. $250.

Media Review Digest indexes reviews of media which have appeared
in over 150 periodicals. The 20,000 or so indexed reviews each year
include full citations by type of medium. Some excerpts from reviews
are given and an evaluative sign shows whether the comments were favorable or not. A librarian can use it in almost the same way as the indexes
to book reviews, that is, to check reviews, probably for purposes of buying or renting a given item. The information provided is full, and often
includes descriptions of the material as well as cataloging information.

The electronic format not only has the reviews, but provides links
to about 300,000 reviews on the Net.

Again, as with book reviews, the librarian may turn to a periodical
index, preferably one online for current reviews of media from videos
to films and CDs.

Precision One MediaSource (Williamsport, PA: Brodart Automation,
1994 to date, annual, $395) is a CD-ROM which gives the user access to
thousands of media items from CD-ROMs and videos to films and recordings. These represent the holdings and the efforts of the Consortium
of College & University Media Centers who worked with Brodart to produce the database. Full bibliographic information is given for each as well
as information on what it costs to purchase or rent. The bibliography may
be accessed via title, subject, run time, producer and the like. More limited than the other sources noted here, it serves a useful purpose for identification and verification.

Microform

Print: Guide to Microforms in Print: Author–Title. New Providence, NJ: R.
R. Bowker, 1961 to date, annual, 2 vols. $430.

While there is every reason to believe that in a decade or so microform will be entirely replaced by full texts in digital form (online, CD-
ROM, etc.), today it remains an important part of many library
collections.[6] Microform is used in libraries to preserve space, to keep bibliographies and other reference aids relatively current, and to provide
easy access to users.

[6]Undermining the future of microfilm is the primary producer, Bell Howell. Their "Digital
Vault Initiative" (a euphemism for near death to microfilm) ultimately will provide 5.5
billion pages of what is now on microfilm in digital form which can be read at a computer.
Another player, Chadwyck-Healey, offers 3,500 journals and other printed materials back
to the late-18th century.

Microform exists in two formats: the roll and the flat transparency or card. The familiar 35-millimeter reel or roll has been in libraries for so long that many librarians and users think only of this form when microform is mentioned. The flat microform comes in several basic varieties: (1) Microfiche, or fiche, is available in different sizes, but the favored is the standard 4 by 6 inches, with an average of 98 pages per sheet. Various reductions may either increase or decrease the number of pages on a sheet. (2) Ultrafiche, as the name implies, is an ultrafine reduction, usually on a 4- by 6-inch transparency. One card may contain 3,000 to 5,000 pages. (3) Micropoint is a 6- by 9-inch card which contains up to 100 pages of text in 10 rows and 10 columns.

For purposes of storage and convenience, most librarians with substantial holdings in periodicals and newspapers store them on microform. Books, particularly those hard to locate or out of print, are on microform as are various other printed works, from reports to government documents.

The equivalent of *Books in Print* for microform is the ever-expanding *Guide to Microforms in Print*. It lists alphabetically over 100,000 titles from some 500 publishers, including international firms. Arranged by title and author in one alphabetical listing, the guide lists books, journals, newspapers, government publications, and related materials. Sixteen different types of microform are considered, and the types, with explanation, are listed in the preface. This is a partner with *Subject Guide to Microforms in Print* (2 volumes, $430) which lists the same titles under about 400 subject headings. A third volume is a supplement which is published six months after the main set and adds around 2,500 titles.

SUGGESTED READING

Bordeianua, Sever et al., "Delivering the Electronic Resources with Web OPACs...". *Reference Services Review*, Spring 2000, pp. 111–118. The authors describe Web-based online public access catalogs (OPACS) which are a vital link in the bibliographic chain. The literature is examined and the authors come up with several suggestions on how to improve the service. Other Web-based entries to the library holdings are considered.

Harmon, Robert, *Elements of Bibliography*. Metuchen, NJ: Scarecrow Press, 1989. This is a basic guide to the fundamentals of bibliography for beginners. It is particularly good in its discussion of the often-used enumerative bibliographies. Some attention is given to the electronic forms of bibliography.

Jordy, Matthew et al., "Book Reviews as a Tool for Assessing Publisher Reputation," *College & Research Libraries*, March, 1999, pp. 132–142. Discernible variations in usually positive reviews allow the careful reader to ascertain which are the best and better publishers. The in depth study makes this clear as it does the various relationships between price and quality—not always related. Also, there is a concentrated look at *Choice* as a review source. Mattos, Jodie and Joseph Yue, "Saving Money by Using Online Bookstores,"

Computers in Libraries, May 2000, pp. 42–47. While the focus is on the services and promises of Amazon.com, the various uses of online bookstores for bibliographic purposes will interest many reference librarians.

Stokes, Roy, *A Bibliographical Companion.* Metuchen, NJ: Scarecrow Press, 1989. A dictionary of terms employed in bibliography. The descriptions, terminology, and general approach are as literate as they are a delight to read. Highly recommended for both beginners and would-be experts.

Studies in Bibliography. Charlottesville, VA: University of Virginia, various dates. Published for the Bibliographic Society of the University of Virginia, this annual publication contains articles of particular interest to textual and analytical bibliographers. A cursory glance at any of the contributions will give the student an excellent idea of what the process is about. Besides that, many of the pieces are fine reading in themselves.

Zalewski, Daniel, "Through The Looking Glass," *Lingua Franca,* June/July, 1997, pp. 6–7. A description of the use of the McLeod Portable Collator, a handmade contraption which allows analytical and textual bibliographers to compare different editions of the same book. In describing the modest machine the author points out the joys and delights of looking for discrepancies, large and small, in different variations of a similar title.

CHAPTER FOUR
NATIONAL AND TRADE
BIBLIOGRAPHIES

"What is available on harpoon guns and whaling?" asks a recent convert to *Moby Dick*. There are as many ways to answer that question as latter day Ahabs. One sound approach, particularly for the person who wants as much material as is available, (or thinks he or she does) is to consult a national and/or trade bibliography.

Yes, the query could be fed into a Net search engine. Yes, results would be found there. The problem with this approach, as emphasized throughout the text, is that it is similar to using a shotgun to hit a distant bull's-eye. It is much more efficient, time saving, and certainly accurate to take up a rifle, or a bow and arrow. Not to overwork the metaphor, but a bibliography gives the librarian the correct weapon to find what is needed without futile shots on the Net.

The primary difference between a trade and national bibliography, as defined in the previous chapter, is that the former limits itself to works published or which originate in a given country. National bibliography moves beyond national boundaries to take in whatever worldwide will be of value.

Numerous national bibliographies such as the Library of Congress *National Union Catalog* have "union" in their title. Why? Well, not only does the catalog reveal all about a given publication—from author to publisher and when it was first made available—but it tells where the librarian may find X or Y item.

Beyond pinpointing the attributes of an item, a union catalog indicates who has what. A fuller, often-repeated definition is this: A union catalog is an inventory common to several libraries; it lists some or all of their publications maintained in one or more libraries. The user turns to a union list to locate a given book, CD-ROM, periodical, or newspaper in another library, which may be in the same city or thousands of miles away. Given the location and the operation of an interlibrary loan, copying process, or online services, the user can then have the particular book or item borrowed from the holding library.

In an electronic age are such catalogs useful? Indeed they are. If nothing else, they help to narrow the search to relevant, specific items. Such aids will continue, on and offline, for generations.

NATIONAL UNION CATALOG (MARC)[1]

Online: Library of Congress Catalogs. Washington, DC: U.S. Library of Congress, 1968 to date, weekly. DIALOG file 426, $30 per hour. OCLC, RLIN, plus other carriers.

CD: CDMARC Bibliographic, 1968 to date, quarterly. $1,200. *Online: Library of Congress Online Catalog,* http://1cweb.loc.gov/catalog. Free.

The *National Union Catalog,* or *NUC* as it is often called, is a bibliography that is frequently consulted. Today the *NUC* is as much a part of online searches as any reference work in the library. Except for unusual cases, the microfiche or the printed volumes (which were used before electronic databases) are not used. The microfiche is, to say the least, awkward and cumbersome as a cursory glance at the instructions issued by the Library of Congress will show.

Today libraries and individuals consult the *NUC* as part of a larger bibliographic system such as OCLC. One looks for a book by Amy Cruse on the Net via OCLC. It is in the majority of cases an *NUC* record. One may take a further step and see which libraries have the book. Inevitably, the Library of Congress symbol pops up as does symbols for libraries in various sections of the country, and sometimes abroad.

The point here, and it is worth emphasis: these days few librarians go directly to the *NUC.* They use it as part of a larger, for fee bibliographic service. The joy here, though, is that laypersons seeking free information may

[1]Note: Here as throughout this chapter and in the text as a whole the addresses for subscription (i.e., for a fee) online databases is that of the publisher, not of the actual database. To find for fee databases (indicated by subscription price): *(a)* Turn to your library's Web page. The database usually is listed there with a link to free access to for fee databases. *(b)* Use the publisher's online address given here. You may have to search for the specific title in the publisher's online catalog or search system. Once found the publisher may offer a free hour or two for sample searches. Go directly to the address for free databases, i.e., those with "free" shown.

search the abbreviated *NUC* directly via the *Library of Congress Online Catalog*. This is possible as all government databases are free to the public.

Anyone looking for a book (by author, by subject, or by title) in the local online library catalog can understand the scope and purpose of the *National Union Catalog*. The *NUC* is a vastly expanded version of your university, public, or school library catalog.

Background

The National Union Catalog began in card form in 1901. By 1926, the *NUC* had over two million cards, physically located in the Library of Congress. Anyone who wanted to consult the *NUC* had to query the Library of Congress or go there in person. The problem was solved, or so it was thought, by sending duplicate cards of the *NUC* to key research libraries throughout the United States. This procedure proved as costly as it was inefficient. Beginning therefore, in the early 1940s, work started on the printed–book catalog. The individual cards were reproduced in the familiar *NUC* book form instead of being sent to libraries card by card. However, it was not decided until January 1, 1956, that the book catalogs should be expanded to include not only Library of Congress holdings but also the imprints of other libraries.

What was to be done with *The National Union Catalog* prior to 1956, that is, with the card catalog in the Library of Congress which was not in book form? The answer came in 1968 when *The National Union Catalog: Pre-1956 Imprints* began to be published.

The *Pre-1956 Imprints* (London: Mansell, 1968–1981, 754 vols., $35,000. Microform: $11,750) is a cumulative *National Union Catalog*. The more than 11 million entries represent the *NUC* holdings prior to 1956. The rapid development of technology, from microfiche to online catalogs, makes it unlikely that there will ever be another printed bibliography of this size. (Balanced one upon the other, the 13.6-inch-tall volumes in a single set would stack higher than the Pan American Building in New York.) With all of this, the turn came to electronic formats in the mid-1980s. Heretofore print and microfiche and microfilm formats disappeared in most libraries. Their place has been taken by the *NUC* online.

Scope

What is the scope of today's *NUC*?

At a computer terminal one may call up the full bibliographical description of material, most of which is in the Library of Congress and has been cataloged since the founding of the collection. At the same time one is able to find titles unique to one or more of the 1,500 other libraries who feed information into the *NUC*. Essentially, the scope is wide enough to include virtually every book published from the first printing press in the Colonies to the present. It is much wider in that it includes, too, titles from around the world.

In addition to some four million books, there are items in different formats, from maps and periodicals to manuscripts and recordings. All may be located through the same *NUC*. These are available online as part of the LCMARC family, that is, after *LCMARC: Books All,* there are *LCMARC: Maps* (with close to 150,000 maps); music (110,000 or so printed music and manuscript music); serials (700,000 plus serials); and visual materials (140,000 available items).

Generally, the *National Union Catalog* offers the average individual all the bibliographical information needed. Still, there comes a time when more detail is required, when an item is so scarce, so elusive, and so esoteric that it may not be fully described (particularly in terms of its importance in the development of a subject) in *NUC*. At this point the search leads toward one of numerous retrospective, enumerative, analytical, or textual bibliographies. The basic bibliographies of this type are dutifully listed in both *Guide to Reference Books* and *Guide to Reference Materials,* as well as in specialized bibliographies dealing with everything from the history of printing to the history of medicine.

Use

How is *The National Union Catalog (NUC)* used in reference work? (What follows relates in particular to the printed format, but content is the same in the digitized forms.)

1. Since this is a union catalog that shows not only the holdings of the Library of Congress but also titles in over 1,500 other libraries, it allows the reference librarian to locate a given title quickly. Hence users who need a work that is not in their library may find the nearest location in *The National Union Catalog.* For example, the first edition of *I Remember,* by J. Henry Harper, is identified as being in eight other libraries. Location symbols for the eight are: OOxM, TxU, OCU, OCL, MnU, NIC, ViBibV, and WU. The initials stand for libraries in various parts of the country and are explained in the front of cumulative volumes and online. Depending on the policy of the holding library, the librarian may or may not be able to borrow the title on interlibrary loan. Failing a loan, it may be possible to get sections copied. All titles without indication of a contributing library are held by the Library of Congress. (The symbol of the Library is DLC.)

2. *The National Union Catalog* amounts to virtually a basic, full author bibliography. Anyone wanting to know every book (mag-

azine articles and other such items aside) that author X has published has only to consult the author's name.[2]

3. There is no end of the subject search possibilities, particularly of the digital databases where it is possible to search not only for assigned Library of Congress subject headings, but key words in the title and descriptive matter. Unless it is an extremely esoteric subject the librarian inevitably will need to modify by place, time, and so forth, or be swamped with too much material.[3]

4. The *NUC* gives details on a book (e.g., when it was published, by whom, and where) and helps the reference librarian to verify that it exists—an important matter when there is a question as to whether a particular publisher actually did publish this or that. Verification, however, is even more important when the reference librarian is attempting to straighten out the misspelling of a title or an author's name. In other words, the *NUC* sets the record straight when there is doubt about the validity of a given bit of information.

5. In terms of acquisitions, particularly of expensive or rare items, *NUC* permits a library to concentrate in subject areas with the assurance that the less-developed areas may be augmented by interlibrary loan from other libraries.

6. In terms of cataloging (which is basic to reference service), the *NUC* offers a number of advantages. The primary asset is central cataloging, which should limit the amount of original cataloging necessary.

7. The seventh advantage of *The National Union Catalog* is as much psychological as it is real. Its very existence gives the librarian (and more–involved lay users) a sense of order and control which would otherwise be lacking in a world that cries for some type of order.

[2]The *NUC* is referred to online in two parts: (1) MARC, an acronym for *machine-readable cataloging*, has reference to the *NUC* from 1968 through today, and now consists of over three million records. It is updated monthly with about 15,000 new records a month. (2) REMARC, an acronym for *retrospective machine-readable cataloging*, or retrospective MARC has reference primarily, although not exclusively, to many of the records in the *Pre-1956 Imprints* set. For a detailed, yet easy to follow explanation of MARC, see: *Understanding MARC Bibliographic* (Washington, DC: The Library of Congress). Frequently updated, the 30 pages is free to libraries. The OCLC *WorldCat* (of which the *NUC* is the core) reported in the *OCLC Newsletter* (November, 1997, p. 13) that William Shakespeare heads the list of the top 100 authors with the most entries (31,187) in the catalog. A little more than one-half as many (14,118) are found under Charles Dickens, followed by Goethe (10,323), Sir Walter Scott (9,733) and Martin Luther (8,332).

[3]Subject headings come from the *Library of Congress Subject Headings*, discussed in the chapter on indexes.

One may use the online version of the *NUC* (1) by accessing it through an OCLC or RLIN, (2) by the individual library which has *NUC* as part of the online library catalog, or (3) by simply buying the CD-ROMs or tapes as issued by the Library of Congress for various uses, private, and public.

On the Web

The *NUC* available on the Web, as part of larger bibliographic utility, such as OCLC, is by subscription, i.e., for a fee.

Another version of the *NUC* is free, but it is limited to books only cataloged by the Library of Congress and not those found in *NUC* libraries. This is the *Library of Congress Online Catalog*. Having located a title in this catalog, the user may determine if it is available in X or Y library by consulting "Search Other Catalogs," a feature of the *LC Online Catalog*.

The free online catalog from LC claims about 12 million records—from books to films. Comparatively, the *NUC* has over 100 million records. Still, 12 million is enough for most searches, e.g., *Books in Print* has only 3 million plus titles, limited, to be sure, to books.

All the standard search methods are available from author and subject to title and call number. A typical search will turn up a half dozen items for more esoteric subjects, and screen after screen for general topics, or well-known writers. The bibliographic information is full. If more details are necessary there is provisions for turning to standard MARC or printed LC cataloging. There are sophisticated methods of searching, (basic, advanced, number, browse) particularly when one is uncertain of spelling the precise way to put a subject, dates, etc. Equally important, one may limit the search by date, language, etc.

Archives on the Web

Researchers working with archives have a useful aid in *Archives USA* (www.chadwyck.com) an online site (London: Chadwyck-Healey, 1998 to date, quarterly, rate varies). This offers each access to close to 5,000 archive collections which house about 110,000 subjects by name. There are some 1,000 links to repository home pages as well as about the same number of links to online finding aids for archives. The usual searching patterns are followed and the results are as full as made available by the individual archive.

The database includes and updates: (1) *The Directory of Archives and Manuscript Repositories in the United States,* which was published in 1988. (2) *The National Union Catalogue of Manuscript Collections,* from the Library of Congress. (3) And about 44,000 additional collections published separately from (1) and (2).

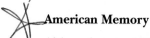

American Memory

Although not a bibliography as such, there is one section of the Library of Congress system which has gained wide popularity. This is: Library of Congress. *National Digital Library Project American Memory* (www.loc.gov) or (http://rs6.loc.gov/amhome.html). The Digital Library's purpose is to preserve major American historical documents in digital form. This will allow use of the documents without danger to damaging the originals. Furthermore, it opens up the material to libraries throughout the world, as well as to individuals who no longer have to make expensive trips to the library holding the documents.

So far [2000] about 300,000 items (out of over 70 to 80 million) are available, grouped in 17 collections under the name of *American Memory*, including photographs documenting life during the Depression, theatrical memorabilia…African American pamphlets, and films of the San Francisco earthquake. The site attracts more than 20 million hits each month.

Internet/OPAC

The *NUC* and local library catalogs are available through other channels on the Internet. Many people these days simply want to find out what is in their own library catalog, known as the "online public access catalog," or OPAC. There are now over 1,500 online catalogs from libraries around the world. All large institutions feature an OPAC which can be accessed, among other places, free on the Net.[4] Most library Web pages give links to basic catalogs in other libraries.

A single example of a library catalog to search would include the great research collection at the New York Public Library:

The New York Public Library Catalog: CATNYP (www.nypl.org/catalogs/catalogs). The *CATNYP* (Catalog of the New York Public Library) represents "the holdings of The Research Libraries, which do not circulate. Included are books, periodicals, manuscripts, maps, microfilms, music scores, prints, photographs and other material cataloged since 1971." Search is by subject, title, author, call number, etc. The local catalog (Leo: Library Entrance Online) requires Telnet.

Using bibliography formatting software (such as "End Note" and "End Link") one may build a file of up to 32,000 or more references. For example, one might tap into the University of California's Online Cat-

---

[4]*OPAC Directory* (Medford, NJ: Information Today, 1995 to date, annual) lists addresses of over 1,500 online public access catalogs in the U.S. and abroad. Aside from basic information on address, dial up instructions, etc. there usually is data on the subject strengths of the library. Inevitably, though, the local library Web page—and certainly *NUC*—will have links to most of the OPACs listed in the Directory.

alog *MELVIL* and tag records for a bibliography on the environment or
Jack London or whatever was needed. Records are displayed, the user tags
what is wanted (and can even specify what to include or exclude from the
record, such as a call number). The completed bibliography may then be
downloaded or sent from the *MELVIL* by e-mail.

NATIONAL BIBLIOGRAPHIES OUTSIDE THE UNITED STATES[5]

European national libraries follow much the same pattern as the Library
of Congress. Each nation has its own bibliography. These are listed in
detail in the *Guide to Reference Books,* and can only be suggested here.
Today all are in several forms from the traditional printed book to online.

   More important, all are linked to a bibliographical utility such as
OCLC and RLIN. Both of these have many of the millions of titles listed
in the foreign national bibliographies. Americans turn to European and
other national bibliographies only when they have exhausted the content
of OCLC and RLIN.

   Meanwhile, the Canadian and the British national bibliographies
are put to great use. The reason, of course, is that they are primarily
concerned with books in the English language.

National Bibliography in Canada

CD: CD-CATSS. Etobicoke, ON: ISM Library Information Services, 1983
   to date, quarterly. $2,532.

Online: National Library of Canada Catalogue. Ottawa, ON: National Library
   of Canada, 1951 to date, weekly, http://bibcat.gallery.ca/ or
   www.nlc-bnc.ca/canlib/eindex.htm)Free.
   Print: Canadiana: Canada's National Bibliography. Ottawa: National
   Library of Canada, 1867 to date, monthly, annual. Price varies.
   (Available on microfiche.)

   The Canadian equivalent of the NUC online LCMARC series, the
National Library of Canada Catalogue has more than nine million bibliographic records. Only part of these are found in either the magnetic tape
format or the print version. In other words, this is the first, the best, and
for some, the only place to turn for titles found in the National Library
of Canada as well as in about 1,000 cooperating libraries. Some 45,000 serials are in the social sciences and humanities, as well as close to 70,000 in
the sciences. A wide variety of other materials are dutifully cataloged. One

[5]There are numerous lists/links of national catalogs on the Internet, and many library home
pages feature such links.

may search the files in the standard way, as well as by Library of Congress numbers. Much of the material is a repetition of what is found in the Library of Congress records and is available, too, through OCLC and RLIN.

The Canadian cousin to OCLC/RLIN is the *ISM Library Information Services* (formerly *UTLAS International Canada*) or, as it is called more specifically, the *CATSS* (Catalogue Support System) which has 60 million records from the National Library of Canada, the Library of Congress, the British Library and all major national libraries. Updated daily, it is an excellent service which is used by many larger American libraries as well as most Canadian libraries.

Some retrospective and most ongoing records from the online bibliographical utility are available on CD-ROM as CD-CATSS. This contains about two million (vs. nine-plus million) online records and is updated quarterly. It serves the purpose of the ongoing LCMARC database in the United States.

National Bibliography in Britain

Online: "Blaise" British Library Catalogue, Boston Spa: British Library, 1980 to date, monthly, http://blaiseweb.bl.uk. Rates vary. Annual registration $170. After 1976: "OPAC 97" (http://opac97.bl.uk). Free on the Internet.
CD: BLGC on CD-ROM. 1991. Not updated. $18,500.
Print: The British Library General Catalogue of Printed Books. London: Bingley, 1980–87. 360 vols. 1975 (after 1975 supplements bring the set up to date. Price varies.

The *British Library General Catalogue,* like the *National Union Catalog,* covers various types of materials with separate databases for print, music, maps, and so on. Online they may be searched as a single unit. The basic *Catalogue* contains citations to items in what was known as the *British Museum Department of Printed Books.* There are about 3.8 million titles acquired to 1976. After that the *Catalogue* is supplemented, both in print and online, by current acquisitions. In total there are well over 19 million citations.

The CD-ROM version, which is not updated, has about 8.5 million citations representing the majority of material acquired by the Library before 1976. It serves primarily as a resource for those who do not wish to turn to the more comprehensive, updated version online.

The *British Catalogue,* just as the *National Union Catalog,* is offered in part, and free, on the Internet. The online free OPAC 97 has books catalogued from 1980; reference works from 1975; and serials and periodicals from 1900. The limited chronological span is no problem for anyone working with current titles, but is a headache for the person seeking, say, commentary on the novel before the mid 1970s.[6] Here one turns to Blaise.

Blaise is the for fee online *British Library General Catalogue of Printed Books* from the beginning to where OPAC picks up in 1976. It includes the online *Library of Congress NUC Catalog* from 1968. This offers access to over 19 million bibliographic records from "materials collected worldwide by the Library on a variety of subjects." Blaise also includes 21 catalogs. A sample: *British National Bibliography*, 1950 to date; *British Library General Catalogue of Printed Books, Books at Boston Spa*, 1980 to date; and others. Also, there are specialized bibliographies on Blaise such as *The English Short Title Catalogue*, a record of holdings in some 1500 worldwide libraries from the fifteenth through the eighteenth century. Available, too on CD-ROM from Primary Source Media for $2,295.

Note: By early 2000 there was discussion about putting most of the British Library catalog online free, i.e., as does the United States for the abbreviated *National Union Catalog*.

How much duplication is there between the massive British catalog and *The National Union Catalog?* Walford did a sampling and found that 75 to 80 percent of the titles in the British work are not in the American equivalent, and for titles published before 1800 that number increases to 90 percent. Some experts estimate that there are from 900,000 to over 1 million titles in the British Library catalog not found in other national bibliographies. With increased interest in capturing worldwide titles in *The National Union Catalog*, the amount of duplication will increase in the years ahead.

TRADE BIBLIOGRAPHY

Most of the enumerative bibliographies found in libraries can be classified as national or trade bibliographies. The American trade bibliography is a primary control device for bringing some order to the books published in the United States each year, not to mention pamphlets, reports, recordings, films, and other items. The pragmatic function of a trade bibliography is to tell the librarian what was, what is, and what will be available primarily from American publishers. (Other nations have similar bibliographies.) The bibliographies give necessary information (e.g., publisher, price, author, subject area, and Library of Congress or

[6]See the British Library home page (The British Library Portico: http://portico.bl.uk) for access to "information about all aspects of the services and collections of the United Kingdom's national library." An end run around the problem of lack of much retrospective material on the Internet *British Library Catalogue* is to turn to COPAC http://curlopac.ac.uk/copac) which provides "unified access to the online catalogues of some of the largest university research libraries in the UK and Ireland."

Dewey numbers), which is used for a number of purposes ranging from clarifying proper spelling to locating an item by subject area. (Electronic databases tend to be listed separately in separate bibliographies. These are discussed later.)

The process of compiling trade bibliographies differs from country to country, but there is a basic pattern. An initial effort is made to give a current listing of titles published the previous week, month, or quarter. This information is then cumulated for the annual breakdown of titles published and beyond that, those which are in print, those which are out of print, and those which are going to be published. (The same process applies to forms other than books.)

Thanks to electronic databases online and on CD-ROMs, the whole process has been speeded up as well as made easier for the user. A single keyboard and monitor may be used to search countless possibilities for a given title, author, subject and the like. This not only improves searching, but lowers the price of those searches. All of this is illustrated by the Reed Reference Publishing (i.e., the R.R. Bowker Company) series which is the heart of American trade bibliography.[7]

United States Trade Bibliography

All titles listed below are published by the R. R. Bowker Company, a subsidiary of Reed Elsevier Publishing, and are available online from Bowker as well as other vendors. Note: Bowker, as the other major bibliographic publishers, was switching from the initial CD-ROM format in early 2000 to almost exclusive use of online, and to a lesser extent standard print. A CD-ROM format in this edition of the text may well have disappeared by the next edition.

Online: Books in Print. 1991 to date, weekly, www.booksinprint.com. $1,850. Also, DIALOG file 470, $30 per hour. OCLC, OVID, and other carriers.[8]

CD: Books in Print on Disc, 1986 to date, monthly. $1,155. (Lower rates for quarterly, semiannual or annual CD).

Print: Books in Print, 1948 to date, annual. 9 vols. $550; *Supplement,* 1973 to date, 3 vols., annual;

---

[7]As the primary trade bibliography publisher, R.R. Bowker is part of the conglomerate, Reed Elsevier, Inc. of England, the United States, and Europe. Reed controls other reference companies, e.g., LEXIS-NEXIS; *Marquis Who's Who* series; Martindale Hubbell, and the publisher of *Library Journal* and *Publishers Weekly*...to name only a few.

[8]The initial *Books in Print* was published first in 1880 by Frederick Leypoldt who hired Richard Rogers Bowker to help. With 70,000 titles, *Books in Print* was first called the *American Catalogue.* The first edition of *Books in Print* (with that name) consisted of a single volume of 85,000 titles from about 400 publishers. Some 50 years later the 9 volumes has more than 3 million titles.

Print: Subject Guide to Books in Print, 1957 to date, annual, 5 vols. $370.

The two titles below are part of the online and CDROM above. Also published separately.

Print: Forthcoming Books, 1966 to date, bimonthly.

Print: Paperbound Books in Print, 1955 to date, biannual, 3 vols.

The most frequently consulted trade bibliography title is *Books in Print (BIP)* and the *Subject Guide to Books in Print.* [9] More than three million in-print books of all kinds (hardbounds, paperbacks, trade books, textbooks, adult titles, juveniles) are indexed by author and by title in *Books in Print.* (*In print* is a term which indicates the book is still available from a publisher. If not available, it is called "out of print.") The set is in four parts: (1) authors, (2) titles, (3) O. P. (out of print) and O.S. (out of stock), and (4) publishers. Actually the last volume may be used independently, as noted later, as a handy guide to publishers.

Besides telling the user whether the book can be purchased, from whom, and at what price, the trade bibliography also answers such questions as: "What books by William Faulkner are in print, including both hardbound and paperbound editions at various prices?" "Who is the publisher of *The Old Patagonian Express?*" "Is John Irving's first novel still in print?"

Almost every entry in *BIP* includes the author, co-author (if any), editor, price, publisher, year of publication, number of volumes, Library of Congress card number, and the International Standard Book Numbers (ISBN).

The majority of titles listed in *BIP* are similarly found in *Subject Guide to Books in Print.* In the subject approach, no entries are made for fiction, poetry, or bibles. (Note, though, that the guide does list books *about* fiction under the name of the author of the fiction; criticism of the works of Henry James, for example, is found under James.) The use of the subject guide, which virtually rearranges *BIP* under 77,000 Library of Congress subject headings, is self-evident. [10] It not only locates books

[9]Online bookstores are a quick way of checking information on print titles. The two largest stores virtually have *Books in Print* online. Amazon www.amazon.com) claims information available on 2.5 million titles, including thousands of out-of-print titles. Its primary rival Barnes and Noble (www.barnesandnoble.com) has more than 1.5 million titles in its catalogue. Book jobbers, such as Baker & Taylor virtually have *Books in Print* online for customers. In addition, they usually offer table of contents of more popular works as well as annotations. See, for example, Baker & Taylor's service at (www.btebis.com).

[10]Library of Congress subject cataloging is used only as a guide, and Bowker or the publisher frequently assigns modified Library of Congress headings. This, coupled with only about 1.1 subject headings per book, results in less than satisfactory retrieval. Often, too, a vast number of titles may be assigned under a heading so broad that a search is almost impossible. The solution is the digital *BIP* database which allows for both subject and keyword searching.

about a given subject but may also be used to help expand the library's collection in given areas. If, for example, books about veterinarians are in great demand, the guide gives a complete list of those available from American publishers. An important point: The list is inclusive, not selective. No warning sign differentiates the world's most misleading book about veterinarians from the best among, say, 20 titles listed. The librarian must turn to other bibliographies and reviews for judgments and evaluations of titles in any subject area. A fifth volume lists and cross-references all headings from the *Subject Guide.* The fact that sometimes the inquiry cannot be answered is not always the fault of the questioner's incorrect spelling of the title or of the author's name. *Books in Print,* through either filing errors or misinformation from the publishers, may fail to guide a user to a title which the user knows to be correct.

Issued in September of each year, *Books in Print* is supplemented by three volumes in March of the following year. Publishers list some newly published titles, price changes, as well as titles that are out of print or are to be issued before the next annual *BIP* volumes. These listings are arranged by author and by title as well as by subject; thus the *Books in Print Supplement* is also a supplement to *Subject Guide to Books in Print.* The *Supplement* includes an updated list of all publishers, with any address changes. For normal purposes, *BIP* is enough for most questions. When the original publishing date is more than one or two years old, when there has been a spurt of inflation, or when the librarian cannot find a title, a double check in the *Books in Print Supplement* is wise. As the online *BIP* is updated constantly, any library which uses this work extensively should use online rather than print, thus saving much double checking.

A definitive approach to what is going to be published is found in *Forthcoming Books.* This is likely to be of more value to acquisitions and cataloging personnel than to reference, but it does answer queries about a new book or possibly about a book the patron may have heard discussed on a radio or television program before it is actually published. The bimonthly lists books due to be published within the next five months by author and by title. Each issue of some 75,000 titles includes a separate subject guide.

Paperbound Books in Print, takes the paperbound titles out of *Books in Print* and, again, arranges them by author, title, and subject. The end result is a separate work with about 500,000 in-print titles. It has two distinct advantages over its parent volumes: (1) It is updated twice each year, spring and fall. The spring update includes about 25,000 new titles, plus 100,000 entry updates. (2) It is limited to paperbacks and therefore removes any confusion about the various forms in which the title may appear.

As in the *Books in Print* series, all western countries have much the same system for keeping track of titles published and in print. In England, for example, there is the well-known *Whitaker's Cumulative Book*

List (London: Whitaker, 1924 to date, quarterly), which is then cumulated annually. The annual volume has about 600,000 titles arranged in one alphabet, by author, title, and subject.

For Canada there is *Canadian Books in Print* (Downsview, ON.: University of Toronto Press, 1967 to date, annual). This is in two volumes. The first covers author and title; the second, subjects. A microfiche edition of the author/title volume is issued each quarter. *Books in Print Plus— Canadian Edition* provides information on 1.6 million Canadian titles and follows the same pattern as *Books in Print Plus,* discussed below.

Online and CD-ROM

The four basic trade bibliographies—*Books in Print, Books in Print Supplement, Subject Guide to Books in Print;* and *Forthcoming Books*—are grouped together on a CD-ROM as *Books in Print On Disc* (or, online *Books in Print*). The various versions of *Books In Print* now include audiobooks and videos, as well as the past 10 years of *Books Out of Print.* Videos may be searched by title, director, actors, etc. while the audiobooks include a search by the name of the narrator(s). The electronic *Books in Print* includes the complete text of book reviews from a dozen sources such as *Library Journal, Publishers Weekly* and *School Library Journal.* By mid-2000 there were close to 400,000 full text reviews, and the number grows each week. In addition, the system boasts: data on over 165,000 publishers, distributors, etc.; author biographies; bestseller lists; etc.

Thanks to a series of easy-to-follow menus which appear on the computer screen, one may search the file with a minimum of difficulty. Standard search patterns are followed. One may locate a title by one of the primary elements in the printed work such as author, title, publishing date, or ISBN. Possibly the greatest advantage for the reference librarian is the ability to search online by key words, in terms of author, subject, and title. Thus, someone with only a vague notion of the name of a book may be satisfied by being offered not one, but sometimes a half dozen or more closely related titles for consideration. Specifics are imperative. If one only enters basic words such as *economics,* the search result may show 3,000 or more such works used in a title. This problem can be overcome by using multiword search terms. One can modify the quest by stipulating a given price, audience, with or without illustrations, date of publication, and the like.

There are spin-offs from the basic *Books in Print.* These are found in some libraries as separate bound volumes. They are: *Scientific and Technical Books & Serials in Print, Medical and Health Care Books & Serials in Print,* and *Children's Books in Print.* Libraries that have purchased these, rather than the full *Books in Print,* continue to do so, but a much wiser move is simply to take the electronic format which includes all these titles, and forget the individual spin-offs.

The digital access helps to speed book orders. Many book jobbers (Baker & Taylor, Ingram Book Company, Brodart, etc.) allow the library to transmit information found in *Books in Print* directly to them. With typing a few computer keys, the order is electronically moved from the library to the book wholesaler. This saves the laborious typing of multi-form order slips and is much faster and likely to be more accurate.

PUBLISHING AND LIBRARIES

All titles below are published by R.R. Bowker Company and can be found online via (www.bowker.com/main/home).

Online and CD: Publishing Market Place Reference. 1994 to date. Price varies.

Online: Publishers, Distributors and Wholesalers of the United States. 1990 to date, monthly. DIALOG file 450. $60 per hour.

  Print: Publishers, Distributors and Wholesalers of the United States. 1988 to date, annual, 2 vols. $185.

  Print: American Book Trade Directory. 1915 to date, annual. $250.

  Print: Bowker Annual Library and Book Trade Almanac. 1965 to date, annual. $185.

Online: LMP (Literary Market Place) Online, 1998 to date, annual. $216.

  CD: Literary Market Place on Disc, 1996 to date, annual. $290.

  Print: 1940 to date, annual, pap. $190.

Online: American Library Directory. 1991 to date, annual. DIALOG file 460, $30 per hour.

  CD: 1998 to date, annual, price varies starting at $260.

  Print: 1923 to date, annual, 2 vols. $260.

  Print: World Guide to Libraries. 1983 to date, annual. $350.

Note: *The American Library Directory* and the *American Book Trade Directory* also are issued together on a single CD-ROM (1998 to date, annual, $395).

Those seeking a quick answer to the address or phone number of a publisher or name of an editor need only turn to several print sources. The most logical one for basic information is the last volume of *Books In Print* which includes distributors and publishers. There are numerous other sources, but the overall umbrella for such information is the *Publishing Market Place,* discussed later in this section. Here are grouped together basic sources of directory-type information on publishers, libraries, suppliers, and booksellers. The online and disc version contain the following, which are found, too, in individual print volumes:

1. *Publishers, Distributors and Wholesalers of the United States* offers convenient access to publishing companies in one alphabet. Basic data include names of primary personnel, telephone number, address, as well as names of subsidiaries, various divisions, and imprints. The ISBN prefixes assigned the publisher are indicated as are any acronyms or abbreviations. The service is preferable online where being current is important. Here the information is updated each month.

2. *American Book Trade Directory* lists booksellers, wholesalers, and publishers state by state and city by city, with added information on Canada, the United Kingdom, and Ireland. The average edition includes over 31,000 retail book dealers and wholesalers.

3. *The Bowker Annual: Library and Book Trade Almanac* is a related work which includes basic information on publishers and publishing. It is particularly valuable for the statistics on publishing for the previous year. In addition, as the title suggests, there are review articles and summaries of the past year's activities in various types of libraries. Other information includes updates on salaries of librarians, organization reports, product and supply directories, networks and consortia, award winners, and news. Again, statistical data are supplied.

4. *Literary Market Place* gives directory-type information on over 12,000 firms directly or indirectly involved with publishing in the United States (about 4,250 publishers are listed). It furnishes a partial answer to a frequently heard question at the reference desk: "Where can I get my novel [poem, biography, or other work] published?" Also, it is of considerable help to acquisition librarians, as it gives fuller information on publishers than do bibliographies such as *Books in Print*. Approximately 500 major, small-press publishers are included, that is, those who issue no more than three titles a year. Standard data, from address and fax number to names of primary personnel, are given for each publisher. It also has sections on marketing and publicity, book manufacturing, and sales and distribution.

The *Literary Market Place* includes names of agents whom the writer might wish to contact. However, it presupposes some knowledge of the publisher and fails to answer directly the question: "Does this publishing house publish fiction, or poetry, or other things?" For this, the beginner should turn to several much-used titles such as *Writer's Market* (Cincinnati, Ohio: Writer's Digest, 1929 to date, annual). This has a section on book publishers with paragraphs on types of materials wanted, royalties paid, and the manner in which copy is to be submitted. The remainder of the two-volume directory gives similar information for thousands of periodical publishers to whom freelance writers may submit material. *The Writer's Handbook* (Boston: The Writer, Inc., 1936 to date, annual) gives some of the same information, but at least one-half of each annual volume is devoted to articles on how to write, and its listings are not as complete as those in *Writer's Market*. Writers who wish information on small presses should consult the *International Directory of Little Magazines and Small Presses* (Paradise, CA: Dustbooks, 1965 to date, annual).

5. *The International Literary Market Place* is a simple broadening of the scope of the original *LMP*. Here one finds over 10,000 publishers listed from 170 countries, as well as another 18,000 distributors, suppliers, and so forth. Two indexes—subject and types of publications—knit the work together. Short informative essays cover such things as copyright, literary prizes, and the ISBN. This is available online as part of *Literary Market Place*. Obviously, for only a few dollars more, the online versions of these two works are preferable to the print—if nothing else they take up no space and have the advantage of advanced search techniques. Again, this is only one example of why both librarians and publishers are rushing to directory type reference works online.

6. The *American Library Directory* is included here to indicate that there are directories for virtually every profession. Published since 1923, it provides basic information on 37,500 public, academic, and special libraries in the United States, Canada, and Mexico. Arranged by state and city or town, the listings include names of personnel, library address and phone number, book budgets, number of volumes, special collections, salaries, subject interests, and so on. It has many uses, from seeking addresses for a survey or for potential book purchasers to providing necessary data for those seeking positions in a given library. (Information, for example, on the size of collections and salaries will sometimes tell the job seekers more than can be found in an advertisement.) Unfortunately, all versions are updated only once each year. Which format should the library buy? Again, it depends primarily on the amount of use. If there is little call for the work, online is most economical. If there is much need for printout, for locating odd bits of data, then online will be useful.

7. *The World Guide to Libraries* lists 40,000 libraries in 167 countries, including many school institutions. Arranged by continent, country, city, and type of library, the directory includes basic information, but not as much as found in its American counterpart.

The digital *Publishing Market Place* (which includes most of the above titles) follows the same search pattern as the earlier discussed *Books in Print On Disc*—a real plus if the library is likely to have both systems. One may search for a specific bit of information across the whole range of directories and guides. There are additions not found in the individual print versions: (1) Some 100,000 addresses for school and service organizations allow mailing-label capabilities. This is a plus for marketing people, but of little real value to librarians. (2) A "U.S. and international services and supplies" directory which gives 16,000 records for publishers and related corporations.

As a running record of what is going on in publishing, *Publishers Weekly* (New York: R. R. Bowker Company, 1872 to date) is required reading for reference librarians. This is the trade magazine of American publishers and, in addition, often contains articles, features, and news items of value to librarians. It is difficult to imagine an involved reference librarian not at least thumbing through the weekly issues, if only for the "*PW* Forecasts." Here the critical annotations on approximately 50 to 100 titles gives the reader a notion of what to expect in the popular fiction and nonfiction to be published in the next month or so.

Other Guides

Special libraries receive much more detailed treatment in the *Directory of Special Libraries and Information Centers* (Farmington Hills, MI: Gale Group, annual.

CD-ROM: Price varies. *Print:* 1963 to date, biennial, 3 vols., $360 to $435 per vol.).

This work lists over 22,000 units which are either special libraries or ones with special collections, including a number of public and university libraries. Arrangement is alphabetical by name, with a not-very-satisfactory subject index. (Subject headings are furnished by the libraries, and as there is no one standard listing, it tends to be erratic.) The second volume is the geographic/personnel index, and the third is a periodic supplement covering new material between editions. A spin-off of the basic set is the *Subject Directory of Special Libraries,* a three-volume work which simply rearranges the material in the basic set by subject area.

Many special libraries which do not appear in the two basic directories will be found in the print *Directory of Federal Libraries* (Phoenix, AZ: Oryx Press, 1987 to date, irregular). In the second edition (1993) there are over 2,500 listings, not only in the United States, but throughout the world. Indexes cover location, subject, and type of library.

BIBLIOGRAPHIES: PERIODICALS AND NEWSPAPERS

Online: Ulrich's International Periodicals Directory. New York: R.R. Bowker, 1991 to date, monthly, www.ulrichesweb.com. Rate varies. Also: DIALOG file 480, $15 per hour. OVID: Rate negotiated by site.
CD: Ulrich's On Disc. 1994 to date, quarterly. $595.
Print: 1932 to date, annual, 5 vols. $459. Includes semi-annual updates.

Online: EBSCONET, Ipswitch, MA: EBSCO Publishing, 1997 to date, monthly, EBSCO, www.ebsco.com. Rate varies.
CD; The Serials Directory, 1988 to date, quarterly. $525.
Print: 1986 to date, annual, 3 vols. $349.

Online: Magazines for Libraries. New York: R.R. Bowker, 1995 to date, biannual. [In *Ulrich's International Periodicals Directory Online.*]
CD: 1995 to date, biannual. Price varies.
Print: 1969 to date, biannual, 1,500 pp. $185.

When librarians talk about magazines, they usually refer to them as part of a larger family of serials. A *serial* may be defined in numerous ways, but at its most basic it is a publication issued in parts (e.g., a magazine which comes out weekly) over an indefinite period (i.e., the magazines will be published as long as possible; there is no cutoff date). Serials may be divided in several ways, for example: (1) Irregular serials: There are many types of these, such as proceedings of meetings which may come out only every third or fourth year. "Irregular" refers to the fact there is no fixed publishing date. (2) Periodicals: (a) journals, from the scholarly and scientific to the professional; (b) magazines, such as those found on most newsstands; and newspapers. Some would not subdivide journals and magazines, while others would offer more esoteric subdivisions.

Ulrich's International Periodicals Directory is a guide to periodicals from the United States and all global points.[11] It comes in five volumes and includes about 250,000 titles, including 7,400 daily and weekly newspapers (in the fifth volume) published in the United States. Periodicals are arranged under approximately 600 broad subject headings, and there is a title index. "International" is a true indication of content in that the 70,000 publishers are from 200 countries.

It is extremely easy to use. Say, for instance, one looks up a periodical under the subject of architecture. One finds the title and basic bibliographical information from the year it was first published as well as the frequency of publication (monthly, quarterly, etc.) and price. The address of the publisher is given, as is the name of the editor, and there are often indications of content in a 10- to 20-word descriptive line for about 12,000 of the more popular titles.

Of particular interest to reference librarians: (1) The primary places where a periodical is indexed are given. (2) There is often a circulation figure which is a rough idea of popularity. (3) Enough bibliographical information is given to allow either the librarian or the

---

[11]This usually is referred to by reference librarians simply as "Ulrich's" after the name of the woman who compiled the guide originally. Several other basic, long-lived reference works are referred to only by the author's/compiler's name, e.g., Webster's, Brewer's, Fowler, Chambers', Pears (an English encyclopedia), Wisden, Debrett's, Burke's, etc.

layperson to verify and order the periodical from a dealer. (4) Periodicals available online or in CD-ROM are listed.

The online version consists of the main work, plus related titles with self-explanatory names: *Magazines for Libraries; Irregular Serials and Annuals* (which includes numerous annual reference works), *The Bowker International Serials Database Update*, and *Sources of Serials*. The same data is on the online version.

Online, the service is updated monthly, the CD-ROM, quarterly, while the print volumes come out only once each year. (There is a free supplement issued twice a year, but this is difficult to use and it's a headache to have to refer back to for information not in the annual set.) The obvious advantage of the electronic formats is frequency and, to be sure, ease of searching. There are 23 points of entry including circulation and editor. And while the print volumes are fine for the average small- to medium-sized library, larger institutions that have considerable work with serials will need the electronic version(s).

Once again the digital reference version is preferable where more than routine serials work is involved. Why? Aside from additional entries and titles: (1) The librarian may locate a specific serial when only some of the data are known about the work, such as a key word in the title. (2) One may quickly verify a publisher's name, find an address, phone number, and so on. (3) The librarian can generate lists of journals, not only by subject, but by publisher, comparative prices, and the like. Referenced journals in a given subject field may be isolated. (4) Document delivery services, where available, are linked to a particular title or titles so the librarian may order from the UnCover, Faxon, UMI, British Library Document SupplyCentre, and so forth.

Publist.com (www.publist.com) is primarily a free online abbreviated version of *Ulrich's*. While there are several of the *Ulrich's* search options, numerous description fields are missing, from subscription price to date first started to other editor's name, etc. The only value of the site is to check the publisher's address, the title of the periodical and, where appropriate, the web site URL. Too much is lacking to make it of use for reference questions.

The nation's largest vendor of periodicals, EBSCO, publishes *The Serials Directory*. This was developed out of the firm's list of periodicals which it sells, as a vendor, to libraries, bookstores, and corporations. Although not all the titles in the EBSCO *Directory* are available from the firm, most can be ordered from them. How does it differ from *Ulrich's*? The number of titles (256,000) listed is about the same, so there is no real difference. The type of material (from irregular serials to popular magazines) is the same, as is the basic subject approach with a title index. Actually, then, the differences are quite small. The *Directory* indicates major indexing services for each title, but adds dates of coverage of the particular item, although hardly for all entries. It has a listing of 6,000 newspapers from around the world, and sometimes the brief descriptions are fuller than in *Ulrich's*.

Given two reference works that are almost identical in purpose and scope, a judgment has to be made about other elements. First and foremost is the matter of accuracy and complete coverage. Here *Ulrich's* is ahead, possibly for no other reason than that it has been around longer and therefore has a considerably more experienced staff. At any rate, the detailed information in *Ulrich's* tends to be more current, more thorough, and more complete in details.

Magazines for Libraries

The serial guides are similar to *Books in Print* in that they list what is available, *not* what is best or better. In order to determine that, the librarian should turn to *Magazines for Libraries*. The tenth edition, (2000) as those before it, lists and annotates about 8,000 magazines considered the best of their type. Online versions of all titles are given with their URLs. In addition, magazines available only online are listed separately at the end of each subject section. Selection is made by 180-plus subject experts. The international recommended titles are listed by subject from "advertising" to "women." There is a title index, as well as a separate subject index. What makes this work different is that, in addition to full bibliographic data for each title, each title has both a descriptive and evaluative summary of 100 to 200 words. The result is an invaluable guide for the librarian or layperson who must decide whether to select or drop a magazine. New editions are published every two years.

There are now some 6,000 small presses and almost as many little magazines published in the United States, Canada, and other English language countries. These are dutifully listed in alphabetical order by title in Len Fulton's *International Directory of Little Magazines & Small Presses* (Paradise, CA: Dustbooks, 1963 to date, annual, $30). For each title there is a 50 to 300 word nonevaluative description of the magazine or the press. Basic information is given as to what type of manuscripts are required, subscription prices, frequency of publication, and the like.

A common reference problem concerns the meaning of a particular set of initials or abbreviations used in footnotes for a periodical title. Abbreviations are far from standard, and it just may be that an author has a vital bit of information hidden away under a periodical abbreviation which puzzles everyone. The solution is found, in at least 99 percent of the cases, in *Periodical Title Abbreviations* (Farmington Hills, MI: Gale Group, 1976 to date, irregular). This guide includes close to 145,000 abbreviations. The first volume lists the abbreviation and the full title. The second volume reverses the process.

Another pressing question these days is "How do you know if X or Y periodical is available online?" This question can be broken down into two parts: (1) "Which magazine is indexed or abstracted online?" (2) "Which magazine is online in full text so that the total contents of the magazine may be printed out at will or the text may be searched for key words which lead one to the article or section of the article of interest?"

Ulrich's includes a section of periodicals online in alphabetical order by title. In *Magazines for Libraries* all of the periodicals listed which are online are indicated in the individual bibliographic data. In addition, see below.

Electronic Journal and Newspaper Directories

Online: Electronic Journal Access. Colorado Alliance of Research Libraries, www.coaliance.org/ejournal/. Free.

Print: Directory of Electronic Journals: Newsletters and Academic Discussion Lists. Washington, DC: Association of Research Libraries, 1991 to date.

Note: Free on the Internet for those who purchase print volume, www.arl.org/scomm/edir. Characteristics of today's e-journal may be summarized briefly: (1) It is a relatively new medium. Experiments with the form were made as early as the 1970s, but they only became a reality in the early 1990s. Quantitatively, about six new periodicals are added to the Internet each week. By the end of the century the total was somewhere between 4,000 and 5,000. (2) E-journals generally are divided by format: *(a)* print titles available both in print and in electronic form, or *(b)* titles only in electronic form without a print equivalent. The majority of scholarly and major popular titles are little more than electronic "full text" versions of the print title. They are available online (i.e., via the Internet, or a commercial service such as DIALOG, NEXIS or a document delivery organization such as UnCover). Archives and backfiles tend to be on CD-ROMs. There is a charge for using the electronic versions of most scholarly print journals. (3) The true e-journal has no print equivalent and is available only online, usually via the Internet. Some are multimedia, i.e., include not only print, but sound, videos, etc. There is no charge for nine out of ten of the "pure" e-journals. The majority of only online titles are one or two person efforts (primarily zines) with little or no editorial supervision. The real hope for the future is to broaden the online-only e-journal to include academic disciplines as well as popular interests. To date, the highest number of online-only e-journals are found in the sciences and education. In a decade or so their number is likely to grow as will popular titles online.

Electronic Journal Access is the first place to turn for both specific and general information on electronic journals. There are links to over 2,000 serials (including newsletters, zines, newspapers, etc.). In almost all cases one may read the current, and often past issues of the e-journal online at no cost. More important, this has the most exhaustive subject index of any e-journal site on the Net. Employing Library of Congress subject headings, the system allows the user to choose the first letter of a subject and then search. Those seeking a given subject may seek specific titles, or key words in the tables of contents, abstracts, etc. Also, there is an alphabetical title listing.

Another directory online is *NewJour* (University of California: San Diego and Yale University & University of Pennsylvania, http://gort. ucsd.edu/newjour). The most sophisticated of the source directories, *NewJour* has over 4,000 titles available (includes newsletters as well as periodicals). The system began in 1993, and has gained international fame not only for current listings of new e-journals (hence the title *New Jour,* i.e., new journals). About 2,500 readers view *NewJour* each day—explained by the fact it is such an excellent system as well as by the policy of updating material twice each day. Periodicals, too, may be searched alphabetically by title. The title search is two steps, i.e., the first step includes full bibliographic information about the periodicals, as well as the online address. As in other e-journal systems one may move from the bibliographic data to the full text of the online journal. Most have archives for past issues. And almost all are free.

The best single source of information on the online journal is in the annual *Directory of Electronic Journals.* This includes full bibliographic information (when available) as well as the address online of the title. It is a mixture of journals and newsletters available only online and print journals which have migrated to online. The former are normally free, the latter inevitably charge a fee. Those who purchase the print volume are given a password to use the same material free online.

In addition to the 4,000 or so periodicals, there are some 4,000 academic discussion and news groups listed with an explanation of their purpose. The list is selective and drawn from a much larger list. See, too, the introduction for an excellent overview of the electronic periodical and its future. A plus is the Alliance newsletter, "DataLink," which keeps the reader advised not only of progress on the project but of news about electronic journals throughout the world. It is well written, current and wide in scope.

There are, too, background articles on the subject as well as helpful "other directories of electronic journals." Of special interest is the "directory of major publishers of electronic journals" which updates information on who is doing what online.

Books and Periodicals Online (Washington, DC: Library Technology Alliance, 1995 to date, annual, 2 vols., $325) is an alphabetical listing by title of "more than 97,000 separate sources published in over 200 coun-

tries." In addition to the title each entry includes who carries the publication online, and whether it is full text or only a citation and abstract
of articles. Three indexes: vendor, publisher, former names. At a fee, of
course, the same directory is available on the Net (www.periodicals.net).

  Net Journal Directory. (Hillsdale, NJ: Hermograph, 1997 to date, semiannual, $220) is the most detailed listing of periodicals available on the
Web. The first issue listed some 9,500 titles, but by 2000 it was well over
11,000. Newspapers are included as well as magazines and journals. A typical entry includes the URL, data on format, price (if any), and dates
of coverage. There is a somewhat sketchy subject index. There is little
duplication here with other broader services.

  There are scores of guides to e-journals on the Net. A typical example: *Ejournal SiteGuide: a MetaSource* (www.library.ubc.ca/ejour). Produced
by Joseph Jones of the University of British Columbia library, this is a
"selected and noted set of links to sites for e-journals, which in turn provide links to individual titles...."

  Finally, the large serials vendors, such as EBSCO and Faxon, offer
access to information on electronic journals. Both services list in some
detail those journals which can be purchased via them. Note, though, that
the majority in each case are only those which charge for online reading matter. Free titles, covered in the other sources, rarely are listed.

Newspapers

On the Net newspapers primarily are turned to for daily information. The
weather is the most popular, followed by the front page and sports. In
terms of research, a good daily newspaper is invaluable. It hardly need be
explained that there is no better source of current news and cultural
events than found in a national newspaper, i.e., *The New York Times* to
The Los Angeles Times.

  But there are problems with newspapers on the Net.

  There are over 800 newspapers available, and only one (*The Wall
Street Journal*) by 2000 charges. It is true, too, that one may browse major
newsstand, popular magazines on the Net for free; although this is rarely
the case for academic journals that charge a high fee. There rarely are
substantial backfiles or indexes (at least free indexes) to search these
same free newspapers and magazines. This may change as by 2001. Some
100 newspapers are developing archives of back issues with online search
methods for digging up data. The catch—most will charge a fee for back
issue searching.

  It comes down to a simple equation. Daily, weekly, or monthly periodicals and newspapers—free to search contents. Backfiles, archives of
those same periodicals, and newspapers—one pays. No matter the cost,

no online index or abstracting service at this time offers full retrospective searching. Most backfiles begin in the mid-1980s or early 1990s. If the student is looking for newspaper articles before, say the mid-1980s, the best, and one of the only places to turn is *The New York Times Index*. Now available only in print this goes back to 1851. (See the chapter on indexes.)

This side of current newspapers, there are numerous sources of backfiles of older publications. These are used primarily by historians. An example: *Historical Newspapers Online* (London: Chadwyck-Healey, price varies, www.chadwyck.com). *Historical Newspaper Online* offers both the index and full text of *The Times* of London from 1970 to the early 1970s; as well as the index to *The New York Times* (1851–1923).

The majority of individual library Web pages have links to useful electronic journals and newspapers. Many of the journals cost the library a considerable amount of money but are made available, via the home page or other reference systems, for free to the public. This fact is worth advertising widely, particularly among students and teachers.

Newspapers, Radio, and Television

Online: Gale Database of Publications and Broadcast Media. Farmington Hills, MI: Gale Group, 1995 to date, semi-annual, http://www.gale.com. Rate varies.
Print: 1969 to date, annual, 3 vols. $395.

Newspapers are listed in *Ulrich's* and *The Serials Directory* and are found in the other guides as well. Still, for more complete information, arranged in a standard format, the *Gale Directory* is the best. As such, it is a standard item in most reference libraries. Material is arranged by state (and by province in Canada) and then by city and community. Under city, there are three basic subdivisions—newspapers, magazines, and radio and television. Basic data are given about each of 8,000 newspapers, whether daily, weekly, or monthly. The data include the paper's name, date of establishment, frequency of publication, political bias, circulation, names of primary staff members, and information on advertising rates. A supplement and an updating service are issued during the year.

In addition to newspapers, the guide includes 11,000 periodicals dutifully listed under place of publication. The information is about the same as that given for the newspapers, but considerably more limited than what is found in *Ulrich's* or the other standard bibliographies. Therefore, while the *Gale Directory* is useful in spotting, for example, how many magazines are published in Albany, New York, it fails to give the detailed information required by most librarians.

Maps are in the third volume with one map of each of the states and Canadian provinces, as well as one for Puerto Rico. This section is followed by telephone numbers and addresses for feature editors. The bulk of the third volume consists of a number of indexes to material found in the first two volumes.

The basic information for television and radio stations, as well as cable systems, is similar to the newspaper data. But there are vital additions such as call letters, channel numbers, network affiliations, wattages, areas of influence of the station, operating hours and the like. Advertising rates are included. It is hard to find more complete coverage of radio and television, at least in a general reference work such as this.

The online version has the same material as in the print volume, but differs in that: it is updated twice a year instead of once a year; and includes 11,000 newsletters in print as well as 15,500 directories in print.[12]

Working Press of the Nation (New York: R.R. Bowker, 1924 to date, 3 vols., $395) is a rival to Gale, and covers much the same material. The first volume covers newspapers; the second lists about 5,500 magazines and 1,600 newsletters (hardly a drop in the proverbial bucket compared to the same publisher's *Ulrich's* and *Magazine for Libraries*; and volume 3 includes television and radio.

Which one is best? It depends on what area is consulted. Gale is superior in its listing of magazines and television, while Bowker has an edge with newspapers. For most libraries, though, either will do nicely.

Serials: Union Lists

"Which library has X newspapers or Y periodicals?" The question is asked when the librarian or user finds just the right article in a magazine or newspaper, but then discovers that the library does not have the item. Usually it can be ordered on interlibrary loan or faxed. Also, it just may be that the full text of the magazine article is online, too. At any rate, faxing and the online route are expensive methods, and most people use the standard interlibrary approach.

Although there are now numerous printed union lists of serials, most larger libraries depend on what they find online, usually through OCLC, RLIN, and other networks.[13] Here one simply types in the name of the required serial and the standard information is forthcoming, from basic publishing data to, most important, the location of the title. The publishing data usually refers primarily to the first issue and are as com-

---

[12]The online version includes the *Directory of Publications,* plus what is found in the print versions: *Directories in Print* and Newsletters in Print.

[13]The online Union List of Periodicals maintained as part of the National Union Catalog offers locations of more than 800,000 serials as well as basic bibliographic data for each serial. The list is updated semiannually primarily from holdings of contributing libraries.

plete or as thorough as that found in the periodical directories. Online one may find records of at least 55,000 U.S. newspapers. The file continues to grow, and eventually will include almost all American papers, plus selected foreign titles.

Beyond online and the printed bibliographies, one must remember that most state and local libraries maintain records of their own regional and city or town newspapers. These usually become part of the online record, but much information is printed in more detail in state or local bibliographies of holdings. The programs to store these data often are federally funded and develop into the base of repository collections.

READER'S ADVISORY SERVICES

Reader's advisory services are common in public libraries and are often a part of reference services. They are defined succinctly by the Free Library of Philadelphia as "reading guidance, selection of materials to meet a particular interest or need, aid in identifying the best sources of information for a given purpose, instruction in the use of the library or a particular book, seeking an answer from or referral to other agencies or information sources outside the library." Actually, most libraries are somewhat more limited in their definition, and define "reading guidance" as helping people find books they wish to read, as well as assisting in the purchase of those books.

In one sense, the reference librarian is constantly serving as a guide to readers in the choice of materials, either specific or general. This is particularly true as an adjunct to the search-and-research type of question. Here the librarian will help the reader to find a material outside the reference collection.

At an informal stage, particularly in small and medium-sized libraries with limited staff, the reference librarian may help a patron select a "good read." For example, someone may wander into the reference room looking for a historical novel or a nonfiction work on the siege of Troy. The reference staff member as much for lack of support staff as his or her own interest may assist in finding the desired book, usually in the general collection.

Of lists there is no end, and one of the more popular types centers on "best" books for a given library situation. The lists, despite certain definite drawbacks, are useful for the following:

1. Evaluating a collection. A normal method of evaluating the relative worth of a library collection is to check the collection at random or in depth by the lists noted here.

2. Building a collection. Where a library begins without a book but with a reasonable budget, many of these lists serve as the key to purchasing the core collection.

3. Helping a patron find a particular work in a subject area. Most of the lists are arranged by some type of subject approach, and as the "best" of their kind, they frequently serve to help the user find material on a desired topic.

The advantage of a list is that it is compiled by a group of experts. Usually there is an editor and an authority, or several authorities, assisting in each of the major subject fields. However, one disadvantage of this committee approach is that mediocrity tends to rule, and the book exceptional for a daring stand, in either content or style, may not be included.

Used wisely, a "best" bibliography is a guide; it should be no more than that. The librarian has to form the necessary conclusions about what should or should not be included in the collection. If unable to do this, the librarian had better turn in his or her library school degree and call it quits before destroying a library collection. When any group of librarians discuss the pros and cons of best-book lists, the overriding opinion expressed is that such lists are "nice," but highly dubious crutches.

Another obvious flaw is that a list is normally tailored for a particular audience. Finally, despite efforts to keep the lists current (and here Wilson's policy of issuing frequent supplements is a great aid), many of them simply cannot keep up with the rate of book production. No sooner is the list of "best" books in anthropology out when a scholar publishes the definitive work in one area that makes the others historically interesting but not particularly pertinent for current needs.

Reader's Advisory Aids

CD: The Reader's Adviser on CD-ROM. 15th ed. New York: R.R. Bowker, 1996. $400.
Print: The Reader's Adviser. 1996, 6 vols. $350.

Online: NoveList. Ipswitch, MA: EBSCO, www.epnet.com, 1996 to date. $500.
CD: Good Reads. Provo, UT: Retro Link Associates, 1996 to date, quarterly. $500.

Print: Fiction Catalog, 13th ed. New York: H.W. Wilson Company, 1995–1999, with four annual supplements. $80.

Print: Public Library Catalog, 10th ed. New York: H.W. Wilson Company, 1993–1997, with four annual supplements. $180.

The Reader's Adviser is a standard among scores of general listings of "best" books. Planned originally for the bookseller seeking to build a basic stock, the six-volume set is now used extensively in libraries. Close to 55,000 titles are listed.

Arrangement in each work follows a set plan. First there is a general introduction to the topic, then an annotated listing of basic reference works for that subject, and, finally, biographies and bibliographies for individual authors within the given area. The five volumes move from "the best in American and British fiction, poetry, essays, literary biography, bibliography and reference" in Volume 1 to "the best in the literature of science, technology, and medicine" in the fifth volume. Each section is compiled by a subject expert, and the work is fundamental for anyone seeking basic titles.

The CD of the *Reader's Advisor* has all the data in the print set, but, unfortunately, has a complicated search system. It often is easier to turn to one of the six print volumes. (Obviously lacking a sense of humor, the publisher issues a close to 70-page manual to indicate, among other things, how to find on the CD the works of Mark Twain or something on adventure stories. By the time one has carefully studied the manual, Twain could have written Tom Sawyer.)

Prepared both by experts for laypersons and librarians, the CD-ROM *NoveList* and *Good Reads* services offer subject, author, title, or genre approaches to the "best" book for a particular situation, or a particular reader. In this respect they are similar to the print version; but part ways on two counts other than format. First, the hypertext links similar books which is a great aid for the reader advisor faced with the query, "Can you find me a book like the last one?" Second, there is a much wider subject approach than found in print guides.

NoveList has the advantage of including 75,000 titles, plus fiction, with some 30,000 full text reviews from *Booklist, Kirkus, Library Journal,* and *Publishers Weekly* since 1996. New titles and reviews are added each quarter. One can approach the listings by either subject or keyword(s), as well as by title and author. A nice added feature: links to author home pages and fiction related websites. There are full text feature articles on books as well as related topics. A "match a novel" option allows the user to "use a book you've read to find new titles." There are other guides such as "describe a plot" and "explore fiction types" as well as lists of prize-winning titles. Also, one may limit the search by age and reading levels.

Good Reads has a basic database of 10,000 novels, with new titles added each quarter. When a particular title is found there is a brief description of the plot and lead characters.

For a number of years the Wilson Company, with the aid of qualified consultants, has been providing lists of selected books for the school and public library. The consultants who determine which titles will be included are normally drawn from various divisions of the American

Library Association. Consequently, from the point of view of authority and reliability, the Wilson lists are considered basic for most library collection purposes.

There are five titles in what has come to be known as the Wilson Standard Catalog Series.[14] They follow more or less the same organization, differing primarily in scope and evident from the title, for example, *Children's Catalog, Middle and Junior High School Library Catalog, Senior High School Library Catalog,* and *Public Library Catalog.* The *Fiction Catalog* crosses almost all age groups, although it essentially supplements the *Public Library Catalog,* which does not list fiction. All the other catalogs have fiction entries.

Typical of the group, the *Public Library Catalog* begins with a classified arrangement of some 7,500 nonfiction works. Each title is listed under the author's name. Complete bibliographical information is given as well as an informative annotation. Except for an occasional few words of description added by the compilers, the majority of the annotations are quotations from one or more reviews. The reviews are noted by name, that is, *Choice, Library Journal,* and so forth, but there is no further citation to year, month, or page. Quotations are selected to indicate both content and value, but the latter is anticipated in that only the "best" books are chosen for inclusion.

From the point of view of partial reference need, the librarian may make a selection of a title by reading the annotation, or may invite the inquisitive reader to glance at the description. Further access is provided by a detailed title, author, and subject index.

In order to keep the service updated, a softcover annual volume of new selections is published each year until the next edition is issued. This method of updating is employed by Wilson in all of the standard catalog series.

The *Fiction Catalog* follows the same format as the public library aid. In it there are about 5,000 titles with critical annotations. An additional 2,000 titles will be included in the supplements. It is particularly useful for the detailed subject index, which lists books under not only one area, but numerous related subject areas. Furthermore, broad subjects are subdivided by geographical and historical area, and novelettes and composite works are analyzed by each distinctive part. Most of the titles are in print and anyone who has tried to advise a user about the "best," or even any, title in a given subject area will find this work of extreme value.

---

[14]Beginning in late 2000 with the 17th edition of the *Children's Catalog,* H. W. Wilson began a systematic program to put all of their collection development catalogs online. The Net version will include the annual four supplements between editions of the catalogs. Both the print and online 18th edition of the *Children's Catalog* will be available in mid-2001.

The obvious problems with *The Reader's Adviser* and the other guides is their expense and bulk. For individuals, nothing quite measures up to *Good Reading*, 23rd ed. (New York, R. R. Bowker, 1990). This reading list is familiar to many laypersons as it is limited to 2,500 of the "best" books arranged by broad subject. Each is annotated briefly, and the work covers all possible topics, including fiction from the Sumerians to modern times. Selection and notes are by 34 experts. And each section opens with a brief introduction. The style is commendable as are most of the choices. It is an ideal list for the would-be well-read individual. The guide is $44. That's not inexpensive, but it is less costly than the others.

Rapidly publishers are issuing similar lists for both CD-ROMs and online sites. These are mentioned throughout the text. The focus tends to be on information sources, not the stuff of the aforementioned booklists. This may change scope when and if people turn to the Web for recreational reading as well as reference data.

Buying Books on the Web

All types of books, as well as other media, may be purchased at the computer. Almost a household word to new books, *Amazon.com* (www.amazon.com) leads the way in acquiring wanted titles via the Internet Web. It is followed by *Barnes and Noble* (www.barnesandnoble.com) and *Borders* (www.borders.com). Book wholesalers, such as *Baker & Taylor*, offer services but limit it to libraries and related organizations.

Reference librarians are inclined to channel purchases to the library acquisitions section, but from time to time it is useful to recognize titles can be speeded along by using commercial sources and in the case of out-of-profit books turning to several sources of used and antiquarian titles.

Bookwire (www.bookwire.com) is useful in that it lists hundreds of dealers. Among the best bookstores for finding *older* reference works: *Powell's Books* (www.powells.com); *Bookfinder.com* (www.bookfinder.com); *Alibris* (www.alibris.com), and *ABE/Advanced Book Exchange* (www.abebooks.com). There are scores of others, but these tend to have the widest choices. There are numerous other sources for books. Choice depends as much upon service as what is offered. Reference librarians soon learn which online sources are the best for their particular needs.

Note: Elsewhere in this text there is a detailed discussion about the publication of books online and downloaded into a special reader. Here the concern is only with how to find the best of printed works.

SUGGESTED READING

Baker, Nicholson, "The Author vs. The Library," *New Yorker,* October 14, 1996, pp. 50–62. The champion of the card catalog and the foe of the then reorganized San Francisco Public Library explains in this influential article why readers should come first and technology second. He is opposed to "telecommunications enthusiasts who take over big old research libraries and attempt to remake them...as high traffic showplaces for information technology."

Balas, Jant, "Make New Friends..." *Computers in Libraries,* April, 1999, pp. 38–40. A discussion of online book services, both for new and older titles. Examples with URLs cited. See, too: "Buying Used books," *Yahoo! Internet Life,* March, 1999, p. 122; and "On the Street—Out-of-Print Searching..." *Against the Grain,* April, 1999, pp. 62–64.

Dilevko, Juris and Moya Mason, "Why You Should Read the Papers," *Public Libraries,* March/April 2000, pp. 85–87. Don't just find newspaper articles for readers, read the papers regularly yourself. This is the plea in an article dedicated to the premise that reference service can be improved when the librarians regularly read newspapers. Unfortunately, staff who do not pay attention to current events may "be providing a level of service that is not as good as it could be."

Pack, Thomas, "New Stream," *Online,* January/February 2000, pp. 17–24. Several companies now offer a combination of newspapers, reports, government documents, etc. to provide ongoing information to corporations. The author examines two of these (Wavo and NewsEdge). While the library might wish to subscribe to one or both, the primary delight of the article is that it gives librarians some practical ideas on how to present current business information.

CHAPTER FIVE
INDEXING AND ABSTRACTING SERVICES: GENERAL AND COLLECTIONS

The magazine index is the place to find information about everything and everybody. Given luck, a bit of experience, and help offered by the librarians, the searcher will find at least one article, possibly scores, to meet the need of a paper, speech, personal question, or plain curiosity.

Until the early 1990s the reference librarian turned to print indexes. Today, except to search for articles published before the mid-1980s, the librarian almost exclusively uses digital indexes. The catch: they are expensive. A digital index can cost dozens of times more than the old fashion print version. On the other hand, there often is no choice. Most of the general indexes are available only online.

Why are online indexes so popular? Essentially it is a matter of convenience. When one wants to search over any period of time, from months to years, several issues of the print index must be scanned—a time-consuming business, particularly when someone else is fingering the index issue the user needs. At a computer the complete index may be searched immediately.

Print indexes, as digital indexes, refer the user to an article which must then be found in the library. On the Internet many indexes not only give the citation but add the text of the full article as well. The librarian can find a citation to an article and read it online in a matter of minutes. Where print is employed it may take five to six times as long to find precisely the same material.

Today, despite fond memories of print indexes, no one from the amateur to the expert researcher wants to return to an antiquated system which takes more time, if not more patience, than the electronic carried message. Laypeople hardly care about formats—a notion which librarians sometimes forget. They do care, though, when they discover it difficult to find what they want because the online directions, search patterns, and paths are puzzling.

Print

At least for the next few years print indexes cannot be avoided. They are the only indexes available for most retrospective searching, and in smaller- to medium-sized libraries may be the only additional indexes to a single electronic alternative. The problem today is that students and laypersons, used to the computer, go to a library (or through their home PCs) to find electronic indexes. If the library has a superior print index for their needs, either through ignorance or choice, they will prefer to use the less precise online index. At this point, it is a wise idea for the librarian to explain what is available other than online.

INDEX SCOPE AND CONTENT

In the rush to find the best access ramp to the information highway, it may be forgotten that the essentials never change. From the first indexer to the last computer, content is first and foremost in importance. Today's reference librarian must be able to locate the right entrance ramp and map out the road for the individual user. This requires a sophisticated understanding of specifics regarding content.

1. *Periodicals*
    a. General indexes cover many periodicals in a broad or specific subject field. *The Readers' Guide to Periodical Literature* was the most widely known of this type of index. Today it is challenged by more massive indexes from EBSCO, Bell-Howell, IAC, etc. All are discussed in this chapter.
    b. Subject indexes cover not only several periodicals but also other material found in new books, pamphlets, reports, and government documents. The purpose is to index material in a narrow subject field. Examples of this type of index are the *Applied Science & Technology Index* and *Library Literature*.
2. *Newspapers.* There are numerous newspaper indexes in the United States. The best known is *The New York Times Index.* Today, there are many services which offer indexes to several newspapers. For example, *The National Newspaper Index,* as other larger general online indexes, routinely carry from two months to a year

or more of indexing to major newspapers, e.g., *The New York Times, The Wall Street Journal* and *The Christian Science Monitor.*

3. *Serials.* There are indexes to reports, both published and unpublished; government documents; proceedings of conferences and congresses as well as continuations; and other materials defined as serials, that is, any publication issued in parts over an indefinite period of time.

4. *Media.* Indexes help the user locate every form of the media from graphics and films to art reproductions.

5. *Book Indexes.* Book indexes rarely are used by reference librarians. They will point out to a reader where he or she may find books on their particular subject. At this point it is expected the reader is wise enough to consult the individual book indexes.[1] Note: Gradually online indexes are incorporating selected book indexes into their services, although usually this is in highly specialized subject areas. How far this will go is hard to say.

Abstract Services

An abstract offers an objective analysis of what a given article, book, film, and so forth contains. The informative abstract summarizes enough of the data to give the user an accurate idea of content. An abstract is never evaluative, at least by intent. It is purely descriptive. A typical abstract is from 100 to 300 words, but may be shorter or longer depending on the particular indexing service.

Users prefer, even demand indexes that include abstracts, because a well-written abstract allows the user to: (1) Decide whether or not it is worth the effort to locate the article, book, document, or other source. (2) Decide whether to simply use the information in the abstract.

The increased demand, even insistence, for abstracts has forced all general indexing firms to include them in recent years. A general service without abstracts should be avoided. This is true for subject indexes. The obvious catch is that many smaller indexes have no competition and must be in the library with or without abstracts.

[1]One can "read" a book index. For example, see the index in Mark Amory's *Life of Lord Berners* (London, 1998). Under "Berners" in the index one finds a type of short story: "Relations with mother...lacks friends in boyhood...juvenile ballet scores...homosexuality... depressions and melancholy...swims Hellespont...dilettantism...influenza... clavichord in car...Diaghilev commissions ballet from...supposed meeting with Hitler...spoof poem on noses and roses...teases Walton...takes snuff...offends Nancy Astor...sex urge dies... supposed cocaine-taking...declines occupational therapy...in Richmond nursing home." Berners (1883–1950) was not only a Baron with a fascinating life history, but a composer.

Which Index?

Which index should one turn to for the answer to a particular question? One turns to the general indexes for typical student and layperson queries; and for more detailed questions, one consults a subject index. Most indexes indicate their scope in the title. It is easy to imagine the contents of *Art Index*. At a more complex level, the librarian becomes familiar with several subject fields and is able to quickly call up names of highly specialized indexes within the subject area. If memory fails, then turn to *Guide to Reference Books, American Reference Books Annual, Magazines for Libraries* and other similar guides where basic indexes are arranged under subjects.

Where Is It Indexed?

One wants to know where a popular periodical is indexed. Simply consult a general index that covers popular periodicals—from the *Readers' Guide to Expanded Academic Index*—and you are likely to find your title indexed in that service. Obviously a popular subject journal will be found in an equally popular subject index from *General Science Index* to *ERIC*.

There are times when the periodical is esoteric and the title reveals little of content. Then it is much quicker to find the same information by consulting one or two sources: (1) *Ulrich's International Periodical Directory*, indicates one to a dozen particular places where a particular periodical is indexed. Look up the name of the magazine, and there is complete information including indexes that regularly analyze the title. (2) Another basic source of information is *Magazines for Libraries*. Each of the approximately 8,000 basic titles includes information concerning where a title is indexed. Also, the first section is an annotated listing of over 250 basic indexes and abstracting services. Both guides indicate what indexes are available in print, online, on CD-ROM, and in other formats.

The most sophisticated on target approach to matching an index to a given periodical is found in *Periodical Titles in OCLC FirstSearch*. Despite the awkward title, this service is an online method whereby the user enters the name of the periodical and the service shows where it is indexed and abstracted. It covers all the major and many minor indexes and includes over 120,000 periodical titles. Also, a subject or a name can be entered and the screen shows one to three dozen or more periodicals which cover that area. Another path is to type in the name of the index. One can ask for all titles in indexes, or only the full-text titles in indexes. For each entry there is the name of the periodical, the ISSN number, the beginning date of indexing in the service as well as the month the full text—if available—began. The problem here is that to see all of the periodicals indexed in ABI/INFORM one must examine 74 screens.

SEARCHING AN INDEX

Index services pride themselves on the various paths to successful searching.

The average user, including many a librarian, is not impressed. Familiar with the massive guidebooks (in print) to equally behemoth computer programs, the layperson looks for shortcuts to avoid memorizing the computer software maps. This is much the same with indexes, and particularly involved subject services. A casual observer of daily life at a reference point—in a school, public or academic setting—realizes how even the most sophisticated index is searched by the average citizen—with an ax.

Given an assignment inquest of a bit of information on travel or searching for the meaning of life, the average person only wants one thing: a fast, easy-to-use way to dig up an article or two about the subject. In the hope they have some understanding of a computer, the librarian leads them to a screen, perhaps calls up an index after a short reference interview, and leaves them to find what is needed.

And how does John or Mary "where is the article" person do? It depends on luck. They know a one way path to information. Type in a key word or a group of key words, or even a sentence, sit back and see what happens. If the gods are with them, two or three articles appear which have some semblance to what is needed.

Full text online has increased the delight of the average searcher. No more do they even have to decide whether the library has the magazine in which the article(s) appear. An icon flashes on to inform them they can download or print out the article without bothering to read the abstract, or even the title.

Only in rare cases—usually when the printer and the computer crash together—do they complain anymore about not finding anything. Almost all are happy with the new technology, with their spin down the information highway.

Experienced reference librarians may moan and groan about the lack of enthusiasm for the finer points of indexing by the layperson. On the other hand, things have not changed that much. A few years ago the father or sister of that same person would have thumbed through a few print issues of *Readers' Guide to Periodical Literature,* found (under a subject heading) a few likely articles, pinned down the magazine, Xeroxed some pages and would have left the library exhausted but pleased. The path to the process is now faster, more efficient and kinder to the user, but really no different.

As indicated throughout this text, many younger people (from early high school through college or university) have abandoned print reference sources entirely. They rely completely on the computer and more often than not are totally unaware of the existence of indexes online, much less how to use them. A primary role of today's librarian is to educate them, if only in a most simple way, about what can and can't be found online. There are two answers besides ubiquitous "education" to the less than satisfactory approach to indexes by laypersons: (1) The librarian might consider making the searches for the individual...a point which is discussed elsewhere. (2) The indexing publishers and vendors gradually are simplifying their programs to make them understandable to the average citizen.

There should be one lifeguard about when the public is drowning in information, or going mad trying to find what is needed. The librarian must understand the use of indexes, the intricacies of particular systems, and the best method of searching.

The Search and Subject Headings

There is a consensus that the best way to search an index is via an assigned subject heading. Usually an indexer looks at the article, determines subjects covered, and then assigns the subject headings. Online search engines do much the same thing—either via a computer or by real, live people—and cough-up many choices in order of preference. Of the two systems, the first, i.e., the considered assigned subject heading is by far the most accurate, the most time saving, the least frustrating.

In searching printed indexes, the librarian has to match the search subject or concept with the term used by the indexer. This is equally true for electronic searching, particularly where precision is necessary.

If the indexer uses the term *dwelling,* the user will find nothing if a search is made for *home,* although in many cases there may be a cross-reference under the listing "Home" which states, "see Dwelling." If there were enough cross-references, there would be no real problem, but there would be a gigantic online or print index. The solution has been to compromise. The indexer scans the text and then tries to assign subject headings most likely to be used by a majority of users.

Where do the indexers get these terms? They come directly from what is known as "controlled" subject-heading lists. These can be useful to the reference librarian seeking a specific subject term:

1. *The subject-heading list.* Most indexes employ some form of controlled vocabulary. The subject headings are predetermined, and the article is matched against an authoritative list of subject headings. The indexer selects one to three, or even more, terms from the list that best

describe the article's contents. The two basic lists of subject headings consulted by reference librarians and catalogers are:

a. *Library of Congress Subject Headings* (Washington, DC: Library of Congress, various dates). This is the familiar, fat multi-volume set, usually bound in red (hence, often called the *red books*). The set lists the standard Library of Congress subject headings in alphabetical order. If one wishes to see how they list the history of England, one turns to the entry "England" and finds the reference "see Great Britain—History." That one step gives the user a specific subject heading and saves much time churning about the online or print index looking for nonexistent English history books, at least under that subject heading, and covering all the land area of Great Britain. There are cross-references, synonyms, and other bits of advice and help which assist the user in finding the proper subject heading. (See the explanation of symbols, organization, etc., at the beginning of the first volume.)

The Library of Congress list is updated by new editions and, between editions, by additions and changes in the *Cataloging Service Bulletin*. As more than one critic has observed, the subject headings are a profile of our times, particularly in the past few years as the subject heading experts became more sympathetic with change.[2]

b. *Sears List of Subject Headings* (New York: the H. W. Wilson Company, various dates). This is the rough equivalent of the *Library of Congress Subject Headings* for smaller libraries. There are fewer subject headings. Sears represents a much-abridged edition, with changes suitable for smaller collections than the Library of Congress.

An end run around the assigned subject heading is provided with the computer search. Generally most databases have assigned subject headings. In this respect they follow the lead offered by their printed versions. At the same time there are numerous other entry points. Thanks to the ability of the computer to search out key words, the opportunities to find a needed piece of information are vastly increased. The computer search allows rapid access to new terms, to new and different ways of examining a subject.

Using an electronic search, one is not tied to the vagaries of subject headings assigned by someone who may not fully appreciate how people seek information. Keep in mind, though, that the use of subject headings almost always improves the ease and the accuracy of searches.

[2]The Library of Congress is aware of the responsibility—as well as numerous critics, chief of whom has been Sandy Berman. Nevertheless there is an ongoing debate between librarians and the Library of Congress about addition of new terminology (from in-line skating to additions of Islamic religion headings). In a fast-moving media world, LC finds it difficult to keep up with the terminology of television, the Internet, and the street corner.

2. *The thesaurus.* The thesaurus is similar to the subject heading list in that it is a list of terms used for indexing and for searching. It is a frequent companion for anyone doing a search. Unlike someone reading the text and deciding on what subject headings to use, the thesaurus simply draws upon key words from the documents themselves, or from similar documents in the subject area. Typically, the thesaurus is used in specific subject fields. It is not suitable for general periodical indexes.

The thesaurus shows relationships between terms. One may look up what amounts to broader and narrower concepts within a hierarchical structure built on one or more basic term categories. A term family in *reference services,* for example, could include terms for different kinds of services. Here one might find the term *reference interview* with the broader term, *information search,* and the narrower term, *verbal cues.* It is desirable to have the thesaurus available in print and online. Taking time to consult it, no matter in what format, will make the search more precise and usually much faster. Assigned subject headings, the subject thesaurus and common sense about likely terms an indexer might use helps to ensure a quick, easy search.

Veteran reference librarians more than appreciate the precision of assigned subject headings and a thesaurus. Unfortunately, few laypeople understand (or, for that matter, seem to care) about such matters. The result is the average library user, without assistance from a librarian, enters key words and hopes in time to find what is needed. The difference between the two approaches is like using a giant magnet to find a needle in a haystack, vs. tossing hay aside time and time again in hopes of locating the object.

FULL-TEXT AVAILABILITY

Why does a reference librarian select one index or abstracting service rather than another? As one might expect, it is the database with the appropriate content for the question. And where more than one index is available for the query, it is the one which is the easiest to use. A third factor deciding choice is full-text availability, which is cited as the number one reason for selecting X over Y indexing or abstracting service. "End users want full text," a librarian explains, "preferably with graphics, and they want it delivered over a Web interface that provides the flexibility for a variety of output and access options."[3]

[3]Carol Tenopir, "Database Use in Academic Libraries," *Library Journal,* May 1, 1999, p. 38. And more than full article text is now wanted. Publishers and indexers promise the user will be able to move easily from a citation in a journal article to the content of a footnote with a click or two of the mouse. *The New York Times,* November 18, 1999, p. G3. In 2000, for example, Academic Press began collaboration with 12 major scientific and scholarly

Most of the problems with "Where is the article?" have been solved by the simple practice of putting the article online. One finds a citation, uses a handy icon and the article appears on the screen to be downloaded, printed out or simply read.[4] All general indexes and many subject indexes have full-text articles. The indexing service, which is going to supply the full text of a magazine, contracts with the publisher to pay X cents or dollars to said publisher each time someone out there calls up the complete text from the publisher's magazine. The indexer, then, passes on this cost to the library.

While an added expense for the library, full text online is ideal for readers. The only problem is that not everything indexed is available in this fashion. One day, and in the not too distant future, all, or at least 99 percent of the articles will be in full text at the computer terminal. Meanwhile, there are several ways around the no text online problem. (1) Use the old fashioned method of taking down the citation and tracking through the library to find the magazine.[5] (2) If the magazine is not in the library, ordering the article on interlibrary loan and/or via other methods from asking for a fax copy to having it sent via e-mail, or online.

Searching Full Text

Having the full text available has added benefits besides convenience. The search is expanded from key words in the title or abstract or assigned subject heading to words in the text. The drawback, though, is obvious: too much of everything unless the searcher is quite specific. Looking for "dog" in an animal care magazine will result in pages and pages of undifferentiated material. Conversely, looking for the rare breed of dog, such as a Tibetan-Chinese Poodle, will find what the standard indexing practices might have skipped.

Another useful search feature, under different names and icons by the rival services, is the ability to offer subdivisions of the subject being

---

publishers to allow researchers to read the content of footnotes. By mid-2000 about 3 million articles across thousands of journals are linked by this service.

[4]For example, IAC's InfoTrac system employs the icon of a page, i.e.,"indicates that full text is available for printing or delivery." An open book icon "indicates that no text is available for printing or delivery, but the full content of the record (i.e., the magazine and the article) is held by your library." A sealed envelope "indicates that neither full content nor full text is available, but that you can send the record...to an electronic mail address."

[5]Most electronic indexing services allow the library to show holding notes on each record. The note indicates whether or not the journal (with the article) is available in the library; usually gives the holding dates, that is, 1973 to date, 1993 to 2000, and so on. Also, one may enter a negative note such as "Not available in this library. Ask the reference librarian for assistance."

investigated. For example: "illustration of books" is broken down into dozens of subheadings from period (16th century) to "themes, motives." Related to this is to "view other articles linked to these subjects." In this case five items appear from book jackets to the illustrated novels of F. Scott Fitzgerald.

Searching Paths and Techniques

How does one learn the finer points of searching a digital index? Experience. Beyond that it is crucial to read the instructions (print or in digital form or both) which accompany indexes. Here are the hints to a successful search. Check out, too, the frequent articles which appear in journals from *Online* to *Computers in Libraries*. (The major ones are listed and annotated in the "library periodicals" section of *Magazines for Libraries*).

The point is that almost anyone can find something from a digital index without any knowledge of searching. On the other hand why invest in a high powered car to go from home to the grocery store one block away. There is much data out there, but it requires skilled searching to find precisely what is needed rather than everything with the same general descriptor that is not needed.

In this text the indexes primarily are described in terms of how they are used, not how they are searched. This would require much space and, besides, the searching patterns tend to change almost from year to year, and certainly from index to index. Suffice it to say, though, that simply to describe what an index contains is hardly enough. It is an essential first step, but the next mile must be run by the attentive student who takes the time to study the searching patterns.

INDEX EVALUATION[6]

There are two basic decisions a reference librarian must make about an index.

First, which of the general indexing companies has the best index for the average user? The service must fit the budget, periodical holdings and mission of the library.

Second, which of thousands of subject indexes—indexing from agriculture to zoology journals—should the library consider? Here the

---

[6]David R. Majke, "Remote Host Databases: Issues and Content," *Reference Services Review,* Fall/Winter, 1997, pp. 23–35. This is an excellent still-current analysis of the basic, general indexes. More important the reference librarian offers a practical overview of the fluid situation and how to evaluate the various indexes. A quite superior, practical view.

choices are limited. Rarely is there more than one index covering a specific, narrow subject such as library literature or children's magazines.

Numerous factors shade the acquisition decisions. An index represents an analysis, usually by name and by subject, of a document. Since most books, magazines, reports, and other sources deal with content that is varied, the indexer must select key terms likely to be of most value to the user. (The noun *index* is derived from the stem of the Latin verb *dicare* which means literally to show.) A good index provides enough access points, from author and title to subject to publisher, to allow the user to find precisely what is needed. The index should be current and should be accessed in such a way that it does not take a four-week course of instruction to discover how to find material.

The basic evaluation of information sources is much the same whether they are in print or in electronic format. Essentially the librarian must have the same knowledge of the database as the printed version, although there are more details to remember. One, after all, can look at the printed *Psychological Abstracts* and, through trial and error, discover the pattern of presentation. Online that is possible but more difficult.

In an analysis of indexes, 10 basic points should be considered. Many are expanded in this section and in later discussion of the individual indexes.

1. The number of periodicals indexed and how many are available in full text. Electronic indexes have concentrated on expanding the number of indexed titles. The majority index from 1,200 to 2,000 titles with usually one-half to two-thirds of those indexed available with the full text online. Print tends to be more concerned with core titles, i.e., from 180 to 600. Unfortunately, many smaller libraries can only afford print, even in this age of cheap computers. They are lucky to have more than one online index. And as they depend on print, the user's horizons are limited by the number of periodicals not only indexed but readily available. In time, let's hope, this will change and the whole world of periodicals and indexes will be open to all libraries and to all of the public.[7]

2. If X number of periodicals are indexed, how many are available in the library? If not in the library, are they available in full text

---

[7]One might ask why in a country which puts so much stress on information, education, and the glories of the family and business, a library in a low-income area should have access only to articles from 350 magazines, while one in a high-income area can offer users anything they need from ten times that number of periodicals? This question, which the casual observer will note is raised over and over again in different forms throughout this text, is the jagged rip in the silver lining of American information systems.

with the service, or can individual articles be ordered easily and quickly from the indexing service—and at a reasonable price? If not, does the library have access to efficient interlibrary loan and/or documents from other outlets?

3. Precisely what is or is not indexed in a given journal? Some services, for example, index only primary articles; others index virtually the whole periodical.

4. The type of documents—from periodicals and reports to books and proceedings—which are included or excluded?

5. Which years are covered? Digital files begin primarily with the 1980s, a few with the 1970s, and only a handful in the 1960s. The emphasis for electronic databases is on recent articles, i.e., one to four years. Printed version begins with the first issue of ten, twenty, or even 100 years ago.

6. How often the database is updated—daily, weekly, or quarterly?

7. The subjects and subtopics covered, and what related fields are likely to be a concern to the service.

8. What is the indexing lag between the time the magazine is published, it is indexed, and it appears in the standard index? The lag may be a few days, a few weeks, or even months.

9. What provision is made for archives, i.e., how far back does the index go and may searches be formed which take in only a given number of years?

10. What's the price? This is difficult to ascertain as the services have numerous packages with as many prices based on such things as the number of periodicals indexed, full texts available, library budget, etc.

Searching Points

Searching is governed by other considerations. First and foremost, the software should be thorough and easy to understand. Also:

1. How effective are the access points that are provided? One would like to know the best access terms (subject, titles, abstracts, key words, codes, etc.) for a particular service. Also, one may compare similar services, although at this point the quality and type of indexing vary so much from service to service that a valid comparison is difficult.

2. Are there assigned subject headings, and, more important, just how much effort is given to assigning such headings? Is a thesaurus available? How frequently is the thesaurus (or word list) updated?

3. The types of concepts to search for when there is no thesaurus and the vocabulary is uncontrolled.

4. The relationship between the controlled and uncontrolled vocabularies where the database allows for both.

5. The codes or keys that may be used to shorten the search.

6. Does the publisher provide a "hot line" so searchers can call for assistance with difficult searches? Does the publisher send out a newsletter or other periodic update to inform users of changes? Does the publisher provide the means for users to suggest changes or to make complaints about features of the databases?

A considerable amount of time and effort is required to evaluate an index. Consequently, the majority of librarians rely on reviews or the advice of experts, or both, particularly when considering a specialized service. The advantages of learning evaluation techniques are as much to show the librarian how indexes or abstracts are (or should be) constructed and searched as to reveal points for acceptance or rejection.

Guides

If an electronic database requires a manual of 50 pages or more, which is not always that unusual, either it is a splendid example of sophisticated searching possibilities or a confusion of impossibilities. Unfortunately, too many tend to be the latter, and resemble nothing so much as the typical VCR guide or the how-to-do-it book which comes with a desktop computer. Length is not the only quick evaluative check of database guides. There are others:

1. *Jargon.* The guide should be in language comprehensible to the average layperson. While "interface" and "media toolbar" may be plain English to hackers, they are meaningless to beginners. Also, anyone who requires jargon to explain the operation of a CD-ROM is likely to have a product beyond the reach of the person to whom it is directed.

2. *Tutorial programs.* The directions should be straightforward. Few people want to march through a tutorial program that will train them in every aspect of searching.

3. *Illustrations.* Illustrations, graphs, charts, and the like are useful as long as they (1) can be understood without reference to another manual and (2) are not repeating everything on the disc itself, usually as part of the menu.

4. *Well-written directions.* Finally, the overall set of directions should be logical, well written, and easy to understand. Again, "easy to understand" by the beginner, not by the dedicated computer fan.

EVALUATION PROBLEMS AND COST

When one speaks of an index "online" this means the index is: *(a)* Directly from the publisher and is available on the Internet, usually at a substantial fee. The fee is paid by the library and the Net service is made available in the library and/or at the home of the student or faculty member. *(b)* From a standard vendor such as DIALOG or OCLC. Again a fee, again picked up by the library. The vendor may offer the index over the vendor's wire, or more likely via the Internet.

The publisher's databases are not only distributed directly by them, e.g., the H. W. Wilson Company, but by most of the major vendors. DIALOG, the largest of the group, offers something like 500 databases, the majority of which are indexes. OCLC, the nonprofit bibliographic service, via its "First Search" has around 100 databases available. The commercial Internet vendor, *America Online,* has only a handful, and none is a major indexing service. Other networks and services from RLIN to OVID have similar arrangements. Libraries decide which one of these carriers to use, if any, based upon price structure, speed of service, and, well just about all the points outlined in the previous evaluative scale.

The large bibliographic networks carry, among other services, individual indexes and full text capacity. One, for example: *OCLC: Electronic Collections Online.* This offers links from indexes available via OCLC's First Search to full text of articles.[8]

In describing, evaluating and comparing the various online indexes (as well as to a lesser extent their CD-ROM cousins), there are other problems which will not go away soon. They are of interest to students. No sooner has a description been given in detail of an index, when there is a change. For example, this month a publisher may index X number of titles and offer Y number in full text. Next week, next month the number increases and/or certain of the basic list titles are dropped. This year there are four subdivisions of a basic index. Next year the number has been increased or decreased and, to make it more interesting, names are changed. Prices for various systems are difficult enough to come by, but they change rapidly, too.

Fee Structures

Figuring electronic database fees is by and large one of the most difficult aspect of electronic index reference services. There are as many different variables and pricing options as publishers and vendors. The H.

---

[8]The cost of this to libraries is relatively low, but require a maze of accounting such as subscribing to individual journals before using them online. This promises to be simplified.

W. Wilson Company databases are offered at a single price for one or a group of databases (with variation depending on number of users). OCLC's *First Search* permits the library users to search as long as they want and display as many records as needed for a flat fee. Unfortunately, the OCLC fee has numerous footnotes. DIALOG initiated a flat fee subscription in the late 1990s. An involved plan establishes the fee, although customers may purchase access to all of the DIALOG databases or various subject area indexes. Government DIALOG indexes such as ERIC are free on the Net.

As of 2001, there are no substantial indexes on the Net, other than government or educational sponsored, which are free. This is a major point and one which both librarians and laypersons should understand, particularly the latter who tries to search without an index or thinks the library indexing services are not paid for by the library. Much public relations work is needed here.

Licensing is an important factor in determining cost. Each vendor, publisher, and producer varies in the approach to how much the library is charged for X number of users accessing a database, where they are located, how they are using the system, and so on. There are twists beyond the number and cost of stations. Does, for example, the producer allow the library to keep old CD-ROM discs, or must they be returned? If online searching involves X amount of time is the rate lower than when only Y amount of time is used? Is there a different rate for the librarian, the student, the faculty member, the layperson? Flexible pricing for various situations is required. Some libraries join consortiums to negotiate better prices, others do it on their own. In any case careful comparison should be made with similar libraries to compare prices.

GENERAL PERIODICAL INDEXES[9]

A "general" index is one that indexes magazines and newspapers in all subject fields and is not aimed at one particular interest. These are the products primarily of five large publishers: EBSCO; the Gale Group's Information Access Co. (IAC); Bell-Howell; the H. W. Wilson Company; and LEXIS-NEXIS, which is both a legal and general publisher of indexing and related services. They all serve libraries. Their indexes share two things in common: (1) They cover magazines most likely to be requested in public, academic or school libraries. Several firms have special indexes for distinct types of libraries, although at the core of most are

[9]In the jargon, which changes from year to year, many of these major indexing services are labeled "remote hot databases" and "fulfillment centers." The latter is a nice George Orwellian touch which seems to escape the public relations people hired by the services.

the same 100 to 1,000 titles. (2) Backfiles are available, but for a limited period—primarily from the mid–1980s to early–1990s.

While only the major, much-used general indexing systems are discussed in this chapter, the reader should be aware there are scores more available, e.g., see the list of possibilities in the *Gale Directory of Databases.*

The general index is the ideal place to turn to answer questions which are indefinite. The person is not quite sure how broad or narrow the topic may be, and in what areas to search. Beyond that broad reason, it is a place to turn when the question: *(a)* requires current material; *(b)* requires more than one opinion, one view of a topic; *(c)* requires more material than found in the average reference works; *(d)* requires data on a new subject area not likely to be found in standard reference aids.

All general indexes share several points in common:

1. In addition to the citation, (i.e., the author, name of the article, and where the article appeared), the services have 100 to 150 word abstracts which tell the content of the article.

2. They offer from one-third to one-half or more of the titles indexed in full text. One finds a citation and rather than hunt about the library for the article, simply moves the cursor to an icon and up pops the full article.

3. In addition to periodicals, most of the services offer limited indexing of *The New York Times,* as well as *The Wall Street Journal* and *The Christian Science Monitor.*

4. None has impressive retrospective archives or files. This means the service is fine for searching last month's or last year's periodicals, but not usually more than four to ten years earlier than that. Furthermore, several indexers have a system whereby every month they add the current month and eliminate the same month, say, three years ago. Only the print version of the *Readers' Guide* allows the user to delve into general periodicals before the 1970s.

5. All have various search systems, but basically allow for key word searches and for the use of Boolean logic. Many, too, allow one to limit a search by years, peer-reviewed articles, language, etc. Each has its own search software, although through vendors it is possible to standardize searches.

6. Prices vary wildly. Some include hardware and software in the cost, some include partial full text, and others have different charges for various numbers of users, stations, magnetic tape, and so forth.

In a successful effort to broaden their appeal (and profit margin) the general indexing systems have branched out. They now all offer more than their own indexing products. What started out as a single index service is now a supermarket of multiple services. It is a well-trod information path. Earlier, online hosts from OCLC to DIALOG and LEXIS-NEXIS had the same idea and became giants in the supply of data from various databases. The game is familiar to anyone who follows the stock market: buyout, merge, and add to build as large a corporation as possible.

EBSCO, for example, has a series of other indexes available from other publishers. They range across the subject field, e.g., PsycInfo *(Psychological Abstracts)* to ERIC.

Eventually one or two of the five will merge with their competitors. The fear is that eventually a single giant firm will not only control indexes, but many of the channels down which information flows.

Other than an understanding of the basic patterns of often similar indexes, it is important to understand what X or Y company can deliver in terms of rapid, efficient service. As this changes, and is relative to the library in question, let it be enough for the student and librarian to learn the obvious rule about the indexes: Try 'em, test 'em, price 'em before you sign. Ask other librarians in similar situations what they think, what they have learned.

H. W. Wilson Indexes

All below published by: *H. W. Wilson Company* (New York, NY: www.hw wilson.com[10]) on WilsonWeb.

Online: Readers' Guide Abstracts, 1984 to date, weekly. $1,995. OCLC as well. CD: *WilsonDisc: Readers' Guide Abstracts.* 1984 to date, monthly. $1,500. *Print: Readers' Guide to Periodical Literature,* 1900 to date, 17 per year. $220.

Online: Wilson's OmniFile and Select Full Text Plus, 1998 to date, monthly. Price varies. OCLC as well.

The H. W. Wilson Company is known best for one index: *The Readers' Guide to Periodical Literature.* (Online and CD-ROM called *Readers' Guide Abstracts.*) It is found in most libraries because of its low cost and reputation. It particularly is the choice of small to medium sized libraries with limited budgets. Wilson groups its numerous online indexes under "WilsonWeb" to indicate one or all of them are available online from Wilson via the Internet. These indexes range from a coverage of art to science to the *Readers' Guide.*

---

[10]Here as throughout this chapter and in the text as a whole, the addresses for subscription (i.e.. for a fee) online databases are that of the publisher, not of the actual database. To find for fee databases (indicated by subscription price): *(a)* Turn to your library's Web page. The database usually is listed there with a link to the website. *(b)* Try another library in your area which offers users free access to for fee databases. *(c)* Use the publisher's online address given here. You may have to search for the specific title in the publisher's online catalog or search system. Once found, the publisher may offer a free hour or two for sample searches. Go directly to the address for free databases, i.e., those with "Free" shown.

Most general indexing services were founded in the mid 1980s. The H. W. Wilson Company can trace its beginnings a century earlier to 1898. It is by far the best known, and many librarians think the best indexing service about. It has more than 40 indexes available with full text and abstracts—in the basic formats: print, online, CD-ROM, magnetic tape.

The Wilson Company can boast it has: (1) Better in-depth indexing than its rivals. (2) Full texts, when offered, are complete and represent the whole of what is indexed. (Not always the case with other services.) (3) The number of periodicals indexed may be less than others, and this is the important consideration, the choices are carefully made to reflect the basic needs of libraries. Also, the limited number indexed more or less ensures the magazine will be available—often many years back—in the library.

Searching Patterns

Searching Wilson electronic indexes is a simple matter. Particular care has been taken to make them easy to use for the general public. The H. W. Wilson Company searching pattern is typical of many general indexes. The Wilson pattern of searching can be applied in a general way to almost all online index searches. For that reason it is a good idea to become thoroughly familiar with the Wilson method.

Wilson follows basic searching patterns for its digital services. There are different search modes: The simple, beginner mode is where the user types a key word or subject which brings up an index of headings or, more likely, articles which contain the key word. One may go on to browse for the correct related topics even when the subject heading entered by the user was close, but not precisely the same heading employed by the publisher. One may find the correct spelling, or broader or narrower terms within the onscreen index.

Beyond the ubiquitous "browse," found as the first step in almost all online search systems, the publisher offers more sophisticated, detailed search patterns. Similar search patterns are found among its competitors, although specifics differ. If anything is apparent, it is that the companies are anxious to devise systems that can be searched easily by the layperson.

The second mode is for the individual with some knowledge of the system, as well as of searching online. Here the prompter on the screen offers several avenues of search from the author's name, to subject words, title words, key words in the abstracts, and so on. Boolean logic may be used for subject and title searching. This system is quite easy to master, and equally easy to understand. Often it is preferred even by beginners as it is quicker and more precise than the sometimes laborious "browse" mode.

The third level of searching is used more by experts. Here sophistication and experience is the key to success. Not only is basic Boolean logic employed, but numerous qualifications are possible from "nesting" to searching for a physical feature such as a graph or illustration as part of the desired article.

It is worth emphasis: these same beginner to sophisticated steps in searching are followed by almost all indexing services online. Some are better. Some are bad. Most follow the Wilson indexes pattern.

The Readers' Guide[11]

The *Readers' Guide* indexes and abstracts 240 of the most popular magazines in the United States and Canada, including *The New York Times.* Many of these are found on newsstands and can be purchased by subscription. The range is wide, from *Consumer Reports* to *Foreign Affairs,* and the service delivers a good cross section of public opinion at various reading levels. In print, the *Readers' Guide* goes back to 1900, while the digital versions are only from 1984. The service is updated every two weeks, compared to weekly online, but only once a month on CD-ROM. Excellent abstracts (from 50 to 150 words in length) and superior indexing, particularly in assignment of subject headings, explains why the Wilson service is considered first by many librarians.

The *Readers' Guide Abstracts Full Text* (at $2,795) includes the full text of periodicals. A mini edition (at $1,095) includes fewer full-text magazines. And there are other configurations for various types and sizes of libraries, but only the *Readers' Guide Abstracts,* and if possible with full text, is recommended. No matter the avenue of the search, one is presented a list of articles which indicate they at least have some of the key words (subjects, etc.) indicated by the person making the search. The short entry gives the source and date, as well as the title of the article. One then calls up the specific article with a detailed abstract plus related subject headings which the diligent searcher may use to find related pieces.

Tabs give information about "libraries with item," or "get/display item" (used only when the full text is available) or "e-mail record." Other methods to "get item" are given from fax to interlibrary loan, often with prices.

All the digital Wilson indexes follow this basic pattern—as do most of the other indexes with variations as to how the material is presented to the searcher as well as symbols indicating what is or is not available in full text online.

---

[11]Since 1994 the *Readers' Guide for Young People* has been available online. It is for K–8 and designed to assist children with learning to master electronic indexes and other reference sources. The site includes basic magazines as well as biographies, book reviews, and music and movie reviews. Some abstracts and full-text articles.

Wilson's *OmniFile* and *Select Plus*

Unlike its rivals, until 1997 the H. W. Wilson Company had no massive database of periodicals and various priced subdivisions. Rather it offered separate indexes by broad subject, e.g., *Humanities Index, Social Sciences Index,* and *Applied Science and Technology Index.* In a wise move, the company decided in the late 1990s to combine several of its better known subject indexes. The combined, single file contains indexing for over 2,220 periodicals. This puts it in the running with the other large indexing companies. In addition to the 2,220 titles indexed, there are some 830 in full text available via *Wilson Select Full Text Plus.* The "OmniFile" compares favorably with the offerings of Wilson's rivals. Here subject indexes come together including: *Readers' Guide Abstracts Full Text, Social Sciences Abstracts Full Text, Wilson Business Abstracts Full Text, General Science Abstracts Full Text, Humanities Abstracts Full Text,* and *Educational Abstracts Full Text.* Also, about 180 select titles from the other Wilson indexes are added. In effect the user searches the contents of all of these indexes in one search, eliminating the need to search them one by one and establishing at the same time a large general online index.

Wilson has a number of other similar "OmniFiles" for the various disciplines and various sized libraries. All of this, of course, to tailor packages which libraries both need and can afford.[12]

Beyond this, the company is contracting out many of its indexes to select vendors such as OCLC and Bell-Howell. For example, Bell-Howell has a contractual agreement with Wilson to carry as part of its ProQuest Direct Online service the majority of Wilson indexes, e.g., *Social Science Plus Text* (400 periodicals with about half in full text); *General Science Plus Text* (169/one-third full text); *Education Plus Index* (427/about one-third full text) and so on through related reference such as *Current Biography* and *World Authors,* discussed in the chapter on bibliography in this text. Wilson indexes are available also via what the company calls other "information partners," such as OVID, DIALOG and Westlaw.

EBSCO

EBSCO Information Services (Ipswitch, MA: www.epnet.com).

Online: EBSCO Online *Academic Abstracts Full Text Elite,* 1984 to date, weekly. Price varies.

CD: Academic Abstracts, 1984 to date, monthly. Price varies.[13]

---

[12]There are five or more OmniFiles.

[13]There are variations of this for smaller libraries, e.g., MAS *(Magazine Article Summaries)* draws upon the same basic Masterfile of 3,200 titles and subdivides them for school and public libraries. The indexes (again with the premier, elite, and select subtitles) are at various prices depending on how many titles are indexed and how many are in full text.

EBSCO is now the largest subscription service in the United States (i.e., the library orders periodicals from EBSCO rather than from the individual publishers). Entering the online index field in the early 1990s it manages its own publishing and computer to which customers connect direct. For the time being it continues to offer CD-ROM versions of the online index.

It has a single "masterfile" (i.e., similar to Wilson's OmniFiles) which indexes about 3,200 to 4,000 periodicals—with up to 1,800 available in full text. This is of mid-2000. The number will grow each year, as it will for its competitors. This exceeds the offerings of any other general index and supports the boast of the company that it is "the largest information consortium in the world."

EBSCOhost, the umbrella term for the various EBSCO online services, has at its heart serials from 1993, although some are earlier and others are later.[14] Also several versions include *The New York Times* from 1989, *The Wall Street Journal* from 1993 and *The Christian Science Monitor* from 1995. Titles are available in full text from about 1984 or 1990 to the present.

As of 2000 EBSCO gave libraries an opportunity to purchase online, or in some cases CD-ROM, but not a print index *Academic Abstracts Full Text Elite* (940 or so indexed/abstracted journals/of which 160 are in full text); *Academic Abstracts Full Text Ultra* (940/470 full text); *Academic Search Select* (3,000/600 full text); *Academic Search Plus* (3,000/840); *Academic Search Elite* (3,000/1,200 full text); *Academic Search International* (870/620). All of EBSCOhost is offered at a high price in one index. Whittle down the database selection and the price can be lowered for libraries with different needs and budgets.

A characteristic of all the services is that each tailors a basic collection of periodicals and indexes to various types and sizes of libraries. Essentially there are different indexes with the same base for academic, public, and school libraries. For example, *Middle Search Plus* is tailored online for middle schools and high schools with special features for this group. There are 170 titles indexed, of which about 55 are in full text. In addition, and in view of the audience, the service adds an encyclopedia, documents of historical interest, and a full-text search of over 100 pamphlets.

EBSCO branches out into numerous subject indexes, many of which are discussed throughout this text. Examples, with self explanatory titles: *Business Source, Health Source,* and *Newspaper Source.*

With that, EBSCO adds outside databases (from *Books in Print* and *ERIC* to *PAIS*) to give the library a complete indexing package, even of

---

[14]Also, the firm plays about with "EBSCO Online" in their advertisements, as well as "EBSCO Host." No matter: EBSCO is the key identifier.

titles not directly under their control or editing. The hope here, as with competitors, is that the library will have to turn to only one source for basic general and subject indexes.

And just to make things as confusing as possible, the company, again, as its competitors, has a jolly habit of changing names of the services as well as adding or deleting titles indexed, as well as those in full text. Along the way the prices go up, sometimes down, and often sideways to accommodate as many customers as possible.

Searching Patterns

EBSCO searches follow a standard pattern, i.e., the user may look for material by key word or employ Boolean logic. There is, too, aids like "find more like" and "find best part" to narrow or widen the search. Results of the latter two methods are then ranked by relevancy. Natural word searching allows the user to put in key words, phrases, or even a complete sentence. Limitations include only peer reviewed articles and chronology. A tremendous advantage for beginners is the relatively clear toolbar with easy to understand search icons.

At the top of the screen, the user has numerous opportunities such as: refine search, find more, key word search, advanced search, options, and the like. An open page indicates if a citation can be found in full text, and there are notes as to whether or not the library has the periodical. All of this, plus numerous other features are easy to use. As a result it is one of the best series of indexes, particularly for public libraries.

Gale Group: IAC[15]

Gale Group, Farmington Hills, MI: Information Access Company, www.galegroup.com.

Online: Expanded Academic ASAP, 1980 to date, monthly. Price negotiated for all online indexes.

Online: General Reference Center, 1980 to date, monthly.
    CD: InfoTrac: Academic Index, 1976 to date, monthly. $2,700.
    CD: General Reference Center, 1976 to date, monthly.

Founded in the mid-1970s, Information Access Company (IAC) is a subsidiary of Thomson Business Information which owns Gale Group, a large reference publisher, as well as the *Peterson Guides* in education and *Primary Source Media.* IAC, as EBSCO, is its own publisher and distribu-

---

[15]As part of this service, Gale Group offers what they call "InfoTrac Web" or "InfoTrac Total Access" which is a method of organizing the indexes and other Gale services on the Net.

tor of the online index, and, again like EBSCO, offers more general databases from ERIC to PAIS.

IAC is a rival to both EBSCO and the H. W. Wilson Company in terms of the number of indexes offered libraries. The IAC's CD *InfoTrac* and online *SearchBank* indexes in total approximately 2,500 periodicals, or about 1,000 less than EBSCO. Full text is available for about 1,000 titles.

The *Expanded Academic* is impressive. It indexes 1,500 periodicals, primarily in subjects covered in most American colleges and universities as well as general news stand type magazines. Six months of *The New York Times* is included. IAC, as with its other general indexes, has a policy of offering indexes for the current year, plus three years of archives. Each month one month's of indexing is added, while another month from the previous three years is dropped. Therefore, the index never covers more than three consecutive years.

The junior partner *(Academic ASAP)* follows the same pattern, but is less expensive because there are only 550 titles indexed with 250 in full text.[16] The *General Reference Center*[17] is a comprehensive index for medium to large public and academic libraries. There are 1,100 periodicals indexed, with 700 available in full text. Most of these are popular to semi-popular titles which are most likely to be used by students and will answer the majority of reference questions concerning current events. It is no accident that here, as with competitors, the index adds relatively recent issues (past two months) of *The New York Times, The Wall Street Journal* and *The Christian Science Monitor.*

Searching Patterns

There are various levels of searching, e.g., key word, subject, relevance, advanced. All are marked clearly on a menu bar with an explanation of what a particular type of search will or will not accomplish. Depending on the subject searched, another useful feature is "view other articles linked to these subjects." For example, one may look up encyclopedias as find links to Ephraim Chambers (of the encyclopedia which carries his name), as well as related works, including dictionaries.

---

[16]As its rivals, IAC has an index for school libraries (primary, super, and super junior) with fewer titles analyzed and at much lower prices. There also is the Gale Group School Collection designed for specific grade ranges from primary through high school. Note, too, the availability of a Spanish language general index (on both CD and online), called Informe.

[17]Following the standard pattern, IAC offers this at a lower price as the General Periodicals ASAP Abridged. This translates into 150 indexed titles of which 125 are available in full text via companion CD-ROMs.

Following the pattern of other digital indexes there is the "limit the current search optional" which permits the user to call for only "articles with text" or "peer reviewed journals." Other limitations are possible. Usually there are good abstracts followed, where available, by the full text of the article.

The price for all of this varies wildly, as it does for other general indexing publishers. Much depends upon the number of users. On the other hand, in a multiple library situation, as, for example, in a large state educational system with about 300,000 potential users (and "potential" should be stressed, as only a small portion of the 300,000 are likely to find a library), the annual cost for the major IAC index is $190,000. Essentially, as pointed out before, prices depend upon negotiations and larger libraries usually do better.

Bell-Howell

Information and Learning, (ProQuest) Ann Arbor, MI: Bell Howell, www. umi.com/proquest.

Online: ProQuest Direct: Online Service, 1988 to date, daily. Annual subscription: schools $4,000; public and academic libraries, $12,370.

Online: Periodical Abstracts, 1986 to date, monthly. Price varies.[18]

Bell-Howell, formerly known as UMI, University Microfilms, is part of the Bell-Howell Information and Learning company. UMI was founded in 1938 to provide microfilm periodical backfiles, which it continues to do as well as publish and provide indexing services. The BellHowell family of general indexes is available both online and on CDROM (with the umbrella term, "ProQuest"). ProQuest claims to index and abstract articles from "over 6,000 periodicals."[19] They are divided between general and subject indexes. In addition there is full-text coverage of *The New York Times, The Wall Street Journal*[20] and several publications, such as *Barron's.* Unlike most full-text index services, UMI offers full-image coverage (i.e., the full page as it appears in the publication) of some 2,000 titles and text only (i.e., ASCII) coverage of another 1,000. Add citations to 1.5 million dissertations and this is one of the more complete general indexing services.

[18]There are several basic general Bell-Howell indexes with the usual different names.

[19]Actually libraries can choose which periodicals to index.

[20]Late in 1997 Bell-Howell and Dow Jones joined forces to share the content of their indexing services, as well as potential customers. Concentrating on corporate libraries, Dow Jones leaves the rest of the field open to Bell-Howell. The agreement allowed Bell-Howell to add the full text of *The Wall Street Journal* not for a few years, but back to the 1960s. Other financial services, such as Barron's, became a part of the Bell-Howell service.

When a citation is found which indicates the article is in full text, the user may call up several formats: the full-page image, text, and graphics, or ASCII text only.

Images tend to be much clearer than in other services, particularly as full pages are called up to read. In high resolution Bell-Howell is by far the best. The catch is the speed it takes to bring these to the average screen. It tends to be slow, and for most searches, despite excellent graphics, it is faster to ask for only the text.[21]

Periodical Abstracts (part of the ProQuest system) is the major Bell-Howell index. This covers more than 1,800 periodicals, plus current indexing of both *The New York Times* and *The Wall Street Journal.* Backfiles are to 1990, with some back to 1986. Its school companion, *Resource/One* has 180 general periodicals available in full text (both on CD and online back to 1986). The more restricted *Resource/One Select* has 60 full-text titles.

Magazine Express, available only on a CD with files from 1991 to date, is designed for small libraries and schools. It indexes 180 titles, most of which are familiar to *Readers' Guide* users. In addition, it claims to have full image (i.e., full page) articles from about 80 percent of the titles indexed. This translates into 125 of the 180 periodicals full text with coverage back to 1991. *USA Today* (from 1991) and *The New York Times Current Events Edition* (from 1998) is part of the package.

Bell-Howell makes several claims, which seem to be substantiated by use, that give it an advantage over its competitors: *(a)* There is less of a lag between publication of the magazine and the time it appears in the index—usually about one month. *(b)* There are more formats for full text, e.g., a choice of text only (i.e., ASCII), or text and illustrations, or full image of the page.

Searching Patterns

ProQuest offers the usual software for beginners and experienced searchers. There are, as in most systems of this type, various levels and types of search patterns. The most direct, easiest to use is the topic/subject search. The user enters a topic and that subject as well as surrounding subjects are shown on the screen with the number of articles for each. One may then highlight what is needed and call up one or two sample citations, usually with abstracts.

The advanced step is the use of Boolean logic where the searcher can combine terms for more sophisticated quests. An online thesaurus is useful as a guide to scroll through the terms and related terms. A link to "search wizard" will construct narrow search quests. Users can also

---

[21]"Bell-Howell Text-Only" format has color. The color is only for select titles.

search only to retrieve full-text articles, change databases at will, examine various subject headings, etc.

On several of the more popular ProQuest databases the librarian can ask for generated statistics which show over a period of set time the number of records printed, the number of searches made, the amount of time a database was used, and so forth.

Charges differ, too. Bell-Howell offers the usual price system for a package of X number of periodicals indexed and Y number of titles in full text. However, in addition it gives the library the opportunity of paying only item by item. In the latter case other options include such things as only the citation, the whole full text, the text with graphics, etc.

LEXIS-NEXIS

There is another large indexing service which is found in libraries, and while it can't be classified as "general" it often is employed in that way. LEXIS-NEXIS is a law index with a major general indexing component in NEXIS.

Reed-Elseiver, New Providence, NJ., www.lexis-nexis.com.[22]

Online: LEXIS-NEXIS. "Academic Universe" 1973 to date, daily, www.cis-pubs.com. Price varies, begins at $9,000.[23]

The NEXIS wing of LEXIS-NEXIS made its entry in 1979 as a method of augmenting the legal index. Many libraries subscribe to LEXIS-NEXIS, and use the NEXIS section as a general index. The idea then, as now, was to furnish searchers with items from newspapers, magazines, newsletters, etc. which would augment what was found on purely legal sources. There are now over 7,000 separate sources of data which are indexed, of which well over 1,000 are magazines. The primary emphasis on law with the secondary command of most of the major sources of news and business makes this a powerful aid to librarians both at the general and specialized level.

[22]Some notion of the size of the service is furnished by the publisher: "based in Dayton, Ohio [the service] employs 6,700 individuals worldwide. Today 1.3 million professionals worldwide subscribe. They perform more than 300,000 searches per day."

[23]"Academic Universe" is a version of LEXIS-NEXIS at a reduced price for libraries, e.g., (2000): $9,000 base rate. (It includes about 6,000 titles vs. the full 7,000 sources). This "provides access to a wide range of news, business, legal, and reference information" with an emphasis on business and government affairs, as well as legal matters. For a detailed evaluative description see "Database & Disc Reviews," *Library Journal,* February 15, 2000, pp. 207–208. Still another database for laypersons and those interested in business is Nexis.com (www.lexis-nexis.com).

The LEXIS service focuses on current legal information, with federal and state case laws, regulations, statutes, rulings and the like in the database. If offers, too, the familiar and widely used government indexes published by *CIS Congressional Information Service*, as well as "statistical universe." The major benefit to librarians, business, lawyers, etc. is that it not only indexes, but offers the full text of almost the entire group of publications indexed. This may mean a transcript of a radio program, an article from a journal, a full newsletter, laws, Supreme Court cases, etc.

It is expensive, but probably the best of all the groups for reliable indexing and full texts.

LEXIS-NEXIS also features what they term a "scholastic universe" edition for high school students. Obviously this is as much a public relations move as a practical way of making money. Once secondary school students learn to use the service they will go to ask for it at work and, more important, in academic libraries. This follows the pattern or other cutdown versions of the main work, but has all the major search features of the primary index. There are some 40 magazines and 65 newspapers indexed. Wire services, foreign language news sources and broadcast transcripts are a few of the other features. Also legal research, statistics and legislation (all in a limited way) may be browsed.

Searching Patterns

Searching moves from the simplified "enter search key words" system to the more sophisticated advanced types of searches. Limits may be set in standard ways as well as choosing subject areas such as news, business, legal research, medical and reference. Each broad area has subdivisions for searching. And one may limit the search to periodicals, newspapers or related information sources for the previous six months to many years. (Note: the service has a clear online explanation of search methods.)

Which?

Comparatively, it is difficult to tell the indexes apart in that they all have strong cores of periodicals indexed and each offers points not found in the other. The vital quantitative figure goes to LEXIS-NEXIS "Academic Universe" (some 7,000 titles, but not all magazines) and to EBSCO with 3,200 to 4,000 titles vs. Bell-Howell (at maximum) 1,800 vs. IAC's 1,550 vs. Wilson's *Readers' Guide* with 240. Availability of full text for each service follows a similar ranking with LEXIS-NEXIS and EBSCO first. The obvious problem with a quantitative analysis is that figures change rapidly and sheer numbers are not enough—in fact, it can be a drawback for now expert users have too many choices.

The question of price is not addressed, although by now most of the competition is about equal for X number of titles indexed and/or Y number of titles in full text.

Search practices are much the same for all of the indexes. With that, though, there are subtle differences of great importance to the librarian. IAC's *InfoTrac,* for example, offers an advanced option which allows the librarian to search over a dozen indexes for a single subject employing sophisticated truncation, nesting, etc. Conversely, EBSCO (at least in studies at the State University of New York at Albany) is the easiest to use for beginners.

A major question for many users is how current is the material indexed and the full text available. Here LEXIS-NEXIS and ProQuest is ahead with a lag period of a day or two to three weeks between appearance of the article and the index. EBSCO, IAC and Wilson are behind with the average four to eight or even ten week lag.

In terms of sophistication and need of users the Wilson group is best for schools and for laypeople. At the other end of the scale, the researcher, the professional will find LEXIS-NEXIS the most satisfactory.

The only true answer to "which?" is for the individual library to try out the individual general indexing system. The decision will depend on the library needs more than any judgment handed down here or in other review sources.

Canadian and British General Indexes

Online: Canadian Periodical Index. Foster City, CA: Information Access Company, Gale Group, www.galegroup.com, 1988 to date, monthly. Rate varies.
    CD: 1988 to date, monthly. Rate varies.
    Print: 1947 to date, monthly. Price varies.
CD: British Humanities Index Plus. New York, NY: R. R. Bowker, 1985 to date, quarterly. $1,500.
    Print: 1962 to date, quarterly. $1,150.

The best known general Canadian index is the *Canadian Periodical Index,* an expanded *Readers' Guide.* The service follows the usual pattern of indexing and analyzes 400 Canadian and about 30 American magazines which have international coverage. Both English and French language titles are included. Book reviews are by title under a single section title, as well as by author and subject throughout the index.

The *British Humanities Index* is a serviceable and general guide to about 320 British journals covering such subjects as politics, economics, history, and literature. It is of limited use in the area of current materials because it is published only quarterly with annual cumulations.

INTERNET WORLDWIDE WEB

All of the general periodical indexes discussed to this point use the Internet Worldwide Web as a carrier of their services. Unlike most information on the Web, there is a substantial charge for using these indexes. Therefore, the indexes are searched via a library, corporation, or other type of organization. Few individuals pay for the services. Because indexing on this scale is expensive, there are no comparable indexes free on the Net. In fact, nothing comes even close to the sophistication of the private for profit general indexes. The for fee indexes on the Internet are available, among others from their publishers and vendors such as DIALOG, LEXIS-NEXIS, OCLC, etc. These are preferable for serious searches because they are first and foremost reliable and they have carefully thought out search patterns. The threefold catch: *(a)* they are expensive; *(b)* they each require a different search technique; *(c)* they each have separate access points and passwords.

On the other hand, as will be seen in the next chapter, there are several subject government indexes such as ERIC, which are free. They are as skillfully produced as anything by a private publisher. Still, these are subject indexes, not general indexes.

> The free index services on the Net vs. commercial databases are summed up nicely by a working librarian: What should matter to researchers is the quality of information. It's the same old questions we've always asked. How complete is this information? How current? How reliable? How easy to retrieve? How well indexed? Experienced searchers complain that spending time on the Internet is not always a productive endeavor. They can get the answer faster from a traditional [for fee] database. It can be time-consuming to hop from one Web page to another to another… [Free] information sources on the Internet give the impression of instability. There are no guarantees that data will stay online. Information can whimsically change its shape overnight.[24]

Inexpensive Net Indexes

There are some reasonably priced indexes on the Web which lack the power of the costly commercial general indexes. These should be used only if the library-based general services are not availa
  Electric Library (www.elibrary.com), cha offers rough indexing of about 150 newspapers One can call up some 12 pages of magazine ti as well as newspapers. Searching is by key wor

[24]Marydee Ojala, "The Haze of Future Business Research,"
p. 80.

cial indexes this is fairly crude, but considering the low price, the wide range of magazines and newspapers, it is well worth numerous efforts to find a specific title.

If "for free" is required, there is some help in *FindArticles* (www.find-articles.com). About one-third the size of *Electric Library*, it indexes, from 1998, some 300 magazines. Most of these are general titles, with a particular emphasis on the current news and events. Conversely, it does include some rather esoteric health journals such as *Nature Biotechnology* and *WorldWide Biotech*. This has some distinct advantages. As it draws from a limited number of magazines, the answers, i.e., citations, are much fewer and usually more accurate and precise than found in larger indexing services. But the big plus: almost all the articles are in full text online. And, worth repeating, it is free. The catch is the advertising, although this is a minor problem compared to the quite excellent searching software. What the future of this service holds is anyone's guess, but the Gale Group is not putting it online only to serve up free information.

Note: There are other "free" approaches to indexes. As almost all of the 800 plus online newspapers can be searched free, this is a source for at least current information. (Archives are spotty). Also, some of these services include limited indexing of related periodicals, e.g., the London *Financial Times* (/www.FT.com) boasts it is the "world's largest business resource, containing 2,000 publications from around the globe and over 10 million articles, with 25,000 added every day." All of this, at least for the present, is free.

There are a few limited in scope free indexes. One example: *North Carolina Periodicals Index* (http://fringe.lib.ecu.edu/Periodicals/scope.html). A current index to some 500 magazines and newsletters published in North Carolina this is of limited value to others. It is listed here as an example of what may be available from the local public or academic library which indexes state oriented periodicals and offers the index for free to one and to all.

Note: Other free to fairly reasonably priced indexes and related library services by private companies on the Web are discussed elsewhere in this text.

CURRENT CONTENTS

Online: ContentsFirst. Dublin, OH: OCLC, 1990 to date, daily, www.oclc. org/oclc/menu/home1.html. Rate varies.

ne: ArticleFirst. Dublin, OH: OCLC, 1990 to date, daily, www.oclc. g/oclc/menu/home1.html. Rate varies. No CD-ROM or print at.

A useful method of searching a vast number of periodicals, if only in a cursory fashion, is to turn to current contents. Essentially this offers the user the opportunity to examine the table of contents, hence "current contents," of one to 17,000 or more periodicals. The collection of indexes in OCLC's "First Search" includes *ArticleFirst* and *ContentsFirst*. They are prime examples of how current contents operate.

ContentsFirst contains the table of contents of over 12,000 journals in all the disciplines, from science to the humanities.[25] Each record shows the viewer the contents of one journal issue. Aside from the specific commands, the database is searched by asking for a given journal by name (if no date is indicated, the database will show the record of the latest journal content page). "Let me see the contents of the June 2000 issue of *Library Journal.*" This appears on the screen and the user then determines which article(s) to read. Depending on the particular periodical, the journal's contents may appear a month or so behind or ahead of the printed version. There are other search possibilities by key words, subjects etc., but the primary approach is by table of contents. A handy added feature: The record shows whether your library has the journal or who has it in the immediate region. This information is not always completely accurate, so it is best to double-check in one's own catalog or regional bibliography.

While interlibrary loan information is given for these services, OCLC also provides: (1) A minimum of two document suppliers, one of which usually is the publisher, for many of (but not all) the articles. Users can order the item directly over First Search and pay with a credit card, or through a library account. Delivery can be by fax or more conventional mail. In addition there is a FastDoc option which will fax articles in an hour or less. (2) Full-text online for certain, but far from all, journals. Eventually almost all full-text online periodicals will be available online, by e-mail, or by fax.

OCLC turns the *ContentsFirst* database on its head and comes up with a first cousin, *ArticleFirst*. The same 12,000 or so journals are analyzed primarily by subject. Rather than type in a table of contents (although this is a search possibility), one asks for specific subjects or authors. The database then shows where those key words appear in a brief abstract (if the journal has such a thing) or in title(s) of articles in the database. This is hardly a precision-type search. No subject headings are used, and the success or failure depends on the appearance of the key words in an article title, journal title, or abstract. At the same time one is much more likely to find a number of citations not found by using only *ContentsFirst*. Approximately one million records a year are added.

[25]EBSCO has a similar service, Current Citations and Current Citations 2.0. These give access to tables of contents of from 10,000 to 14,000 journals and conference proceedings.

Two other services should be mentioned as they are found in numerous libraries.

CARL, a smaller for profit version of OCLC and RLIN, offers table of contents searches to over 17,000 periodicals. It is searched pretty much as the OCLC group. The searches, unlike OCLC, are free. The "catch" is that to read any contents the user (i.e., usually the library) must pay so much per article, page, etc.

A second contender is *Dawson Information Quest,* an online service by the serials vendor, Faxon. This blends information about the specific periodical with table of contents entries from some 20,000 journals and desktop delivery of full-text journal articles.

The Institute for Scientific Information, publisher of the *Science Citation Index,* offers a number of current contents titles: *Life Science: Physical, Social, and Behavioral Sciences;* and so forth. These publications reproduce the title pages of journals, usually at the time of publication or even several weeks ahead of publication. The user can then scan the current contents and indicate to the librarian what might be of particular interest, or the librarian can first check off what he or she thinks will be of value and then send the user either the citations or the hard copy of the article.

RETROSPECTIVE SEARCHES

Online: Periodicals Contents Index. Alexander, VA: Chadwyck-Healey, Inc., 1998 to date. Available via Bell-Howell, OCLC, and Chadwyck-Healey, www.chadwyck.com.

Print: Poole's Index to Periodical Literature, 1802–1906, vol. 1: 1802–1881. Boston: Houghton Mifflin Company, 1981, vols. 2 to 6, supplements 1 to 5: 1882–1907. Boston: Houghton Mifflin Company, 1888–1908, 6 vols. Reprinted in 7 vols. Gloucester, MA: Peter Smith Publisher, 1963.

Despite the miracle of the electronic index, the major problem is lack of any meaningful ability to search periodicals much before the early 1980s. If anything happened before then the usual procedure is to rely on print indexes. In time, of course, the indexes will take up this slack, but for now there is only limited access to retrospective journals.

One solution is *Periodicals Contents Index* which indexes online periodicals in the humanities and social sciences in some cases as far back as 1770. Eventually it will include retrospective indexing for over 3,500 journals. Indexing is done, though, only via the table of contents, not by individual articles. The result is that one can only hope the content page is descriptive enough to meet the needs of the searcher, e.g., as in the previously discussed *ContentsFirst* index. The database contains journals primarily in English, but there are those in French, German, and other Western languages. The system is in two parts. The first covers titles from 1770 to 1990–1991. The second, at a lower price, covers from 1960 to 1993. (After 1993 the regular electronic indexes come into play to continue the search to the present.)

Poole's was the first general magazine index, and the forerunner of the *Readers' Guide*. It was the imagination of William Frederick Poole, a pioneer in both bibliography and library science, that made the index possible. Recognizing that many older periodicals were not being used for lack of proper indexing, he set out to index 470 American and British periodicals covering the period 1802 to 1881. Having completed his work, he issued five supplements which brought the indexing to the end of 1906.

The modern user is sometimes frustrated by the fact that the cited journals do not have a date, but rather are identified only by the volume in which they appear and by the first-page number. For example, the article "Dress and Its Critics" is from *Nation*, 2:10. A "Chronological Conspectus" in each volume gives an indication of the year.

There is no author approach. Indexing is entirely by subject. The author index to the 300,000 references in the main set and to the supplements was later supplied by C. Edward Wall, *Cumulative Author Index for Poole's Index* (Ann Arbor, MI: Pierian Press, 1971, 488 pp.). The index is computer-produced and not entirely easy to follow, but it is a great help to anyone seeking an author entry in *Poole*.

With all its fault, Poole's work is still a considerable achievement and an invaluable key to nineteenth-century periodicals. The last decade of the century is better treated in *Nineteenth Century Readers' Guide to Periodical Literature*, 1890–1899, with supplementary indexing from 1900 to 1922 (New York: the H. W. Wilson Company, 1944, 2 vols.). Limited to 51 periodicals (in contrast to Poole's 470), this guide thoroughly indexes magazines by author and subject for the years 1890 to 1899. Fourteen magazines are indexed between 1900 to 1922.

Numerous projects, mentioned throughout this text, are working on the ambitious goal of putting complete runs of a periodical in electronic form. One example: *Internet Library of Early Journals* (www.bodley.ox.ac.uk/ilej/start.html) which offers a limited full text of 18th and 19th century periodicals.

GENERAL INDEXES: PRINT FORMAT

Children's Magazine Guide. New York: R. R. Bowker, 1948 to date, nine
issues per year. $45.

Popular Periodical Index. Roslyn, PA: Popular Periodical Index, 1973 to
date, quarterly. $40.

Access. Evanston, IL: Access, 1975 to date, three issues per year. $157.50.

Despite the electronic revolution, there are a number of general
indexes available only in print. The explanations vary, but the primary
reasons are because the work is no longer being updated (e.g., *Poole's
Index*) or the publisher believes the user will not have a computer (e.g.,
Children's Magazine Guide). Lack of a CDROM or online searching in no
way detracts from importance.

The only guide to children's magazines is a good example of how
specialized abstracting and indexing printed services are likely to coex-
ist with more sophisticated electronic systems for decades to come. Here,
in the *Children's Magazine Guide,* young readers, teachers, and parents are
given a reliable subject approach to the contents of close to 50 titles. It
is useful for recreational reading as well as for students (ages 5 to 14 or
so) for finding material for papers. Teachers use it not only for the index,
but for the practical suggestions of how to use children's magazines, and
for the short notes on new magazines, workshops, and so forth. There are
over 16,000 subscribers.

There are two other print indexes that serve to augment the electronic cousins. They are subscribed to by many libraries for three reasons:
(1) the cost is low, (2) they cover popular titles not found in the printed
Readers' Guide and (3) they are relatively current and accurate.

The earliest index to include the omissions from the *Readers' Guide*
is the *Popular Periodical Index,* which includes about 37 titles not found in the
Wilson index. The librarian/publisher, Robert Botorff, includes subject
headings for reviews, motion pictures, recordings, and so on. Where a title
does not describe the content, the editor often adds a word or a line or
two explaining what the article is about. While this is hardly a full abstract,
enough information is given to make the index particularly useful.

Access is another general index. It emphasizes works on popular
music, travel magazines, science fiction, and arts and crafts titles. It is
particularly strong in its coverage of city and regional magazines. Its value
to librarians is as a wide net in the indexing of really popular titles not
found in other general services. About 140 periodicals are indexed in each
issue. The index is divided into two parts. The first section is author and
the second is subject. After the paperback issues in June and October there
is a cumulative hardback issue in December to round out the year.

While technically one should classify the *Catholic Periodical and Literature Index* (Haverford, PA: Catholic Library Association, 1930 to date, bimonthly service) as a religious index, actually it is much broader in scope. It indexes by author, subject, and title approximately 160 periodicals, most of which are Catholic but vary widely as to editorial content. In fact, many of the titles could be classified as general magazines. Also, the index includes analyses of books by and about Catholics. There are sections for book reviews, movie reviews, and theater criticism. Although this is of limited value in many libraries, it might be considered for public and college libraries serving a Catholic population.

Alternatives and Minorities Indexes: Print Format

Online: Alternative Press Index. Baltimore: Alternative Press Center, 1998 to date. Information: www.nisc.com/factsheets/api.html. Rate varies. *Print:* 1969 to date, quarterly. $100.

Print: Hispanic American Periodicals Index (HAPI). Los Angeles: University of California, 1970 to date, annual. $240.

Online: International Index to Black Periodicals Full Text. Ann Arbor, MI: Bell-Howell, 1999 to date, monthly, www.umi.com. Price varies. *Print: Index to Black Periodicals.* Boston, G. K. Hall, 1950 to date, annual. $95.

Despite the impressive number of general indexes, only a few deal with magazines from the political left, the social right, and almost any place other than dead center. A library may not have such magazines in days of tight budgets and limited readership, but it is a good idea to have the indexes to indicate that there is more than one view of America.

Minority indexes should be a *first priority* if minorities are a primary or secondary audience served by the library.

The *Alternative Press Index* has been about for over 25 years, and it faithfully indexes some 380 titles. All of these are to the left of center. The right is not represented because of the editors' opinion, right or wrong, that conservatives have a voice in other indexes and other services. Be that as it may, the index serves the splendid purpose of opening new doors on new ways of looking at issues. The Internet searching mechanism is simple to follow and even a beginner can usually find what is needed. In the print version arrangement is by subject, and there are book reviews by author and title. Although issued quarterly, the index does tend to lag.

The *Hispanic American Periodicals Index* examines about 250 periodicals, most of which are published in Latin America or by Latin American groups in the United States. While popular magazines are not included, the representative group of other titles does reflect trends and ideas in Latin America and among Hispanics living in the United States.

The International Index to Black Periodicals is released by Bell-Howell, but is published by its subsidiary Chad-wyckHealey. It covers some 150 periodicals, both popular and scholarly, back to 1910 and about 30 of these, with full text, are available from 1998. The serials are primarily from English speaking countries, but there are some from Africa and Latin America as well. A most welcome index as the standard, see next paragraph, is way behind in its coverage.

The print edition of *Index to Black Periodicals* is always late. Lack of finance accounts for this delay, as it does for publications which rely on volunteer or poorly paid, part-time indexers. There are 37 popular and scholarly titles indexed in the service. While useful for retrospective indexing back to 1950, it is superseded by the online version.

Ethnic NewsWatch (Stamford, CT: Softline Information, 1991 to date, monthly, www.sofline.web.com/softlineweb/ethnicBanner.html) is available online via OCLC, for one. As the title suggests this covers stories in ethnic, minority and native newspapers and periodicals. It has the added advantage of making most of the material, sometimes otherwise difficult to obtain, available online and with links to suitable interlibrary loan sites. It has the obvious advantage of covering interests not otherwise found in most newspapers or magazines, e.g., there is good coverage of not only Africa, but African Americans as well as the Middle East, Asia, the Pacific, Eastern Europe, and the Hispanic and Jewish.

INDEXES TO MATERIALS IN COLLECTIONS

Online: The Columbia Granger's World of Poetry Online. New York: Columbia University Press, 1999 to date, irregular, www.grangers.org. Price varies.
   CD: 1991 to date, irregular. $495–$1,095.
   Print: The Columbia Granger's Index of Poetry, 11th ed., 1998, 2078 pp. $199.

Online: Essay and General Literature Index. New York: The H. W. Wilson Company, 1985 to date, semiannual, www.hwwilson.com. $34 to $50 per hour.
   CD: 1985 to date, annual. $695.
   Print: 1900 to date, semiannual. $110.

Online: Short Story Index. New York: The H. W. Wilson Company, 1995 to date, annual, www.hwwilson.com. Price varies.
   Print: 1953 to date, annual. Price varies.

Anthologies and collections are a peculiar blessing or curse for the reference librarian. Many of them are useless, others are on the borderline, and a few are worthwhile in that they bring the attention of readers to material that otherwise might be missed. Collections serve the reference librarian who is seeking a particular speech, essay, poem, or play; but the usefulness of anthologies is dependent on their adequate indexes.

This type of material is approached by the average user in one of several ways. He or she may know the author and want to identify a play, a poem, or other form by that author. The name of the work may be known, but more than likely it is not. Another approach is to want something about a certain subject in a play, poem, or short story. Consequently, the most useful indexes to items in collections are organized so that they may be approached by author, subject, and title of a specific work. Indexes of this type serve two other valuable purposes. They cover books or other materials that have been analyzed. Since the analysis tends to be selective, the librarian has a built-in buying guide to the better or outstanding books in the field. For example, the *Essay and General Literature Index* picks up selections from most of the outstanding collections of essays.

Another benefit, particularly in these days of close cooperation among libraries, is that the indexes can be used to locate books not in the library. Given a specific request for an essay and lacking the title in which the essay appears, the librarian requests the book or article by giving the specific and precise bibliographical information found in the index.

The indexes tend to favor the humanities, particularly literature. There is little need for such assistance in the social science and the sciences. Where the need does exist, it usually is met by an abstracting or indexing service. The indexes discussed in this section are the best known, but others appear each year. They include guides to science fiction, information on handicrafts, costumes, photographs, and such. Once the form is recognized, the only basic change in searching is in the topics covered and the thoroughness, or lack of it, in arrangement and depth of analysis.

The single most useful work a library can have as an entry into miscellaneous collections of articles is the *Essay and General Literature Index*. The analyzed essays cover a wide variety of topics. There are subject entries to the contents of approximately 300 collected works on every subject from art to medicine.

A typical annual edition will have close to 4,000 essays. The names of the collections from which they are drawn, with full bibliographic information for each is given at the end of the volume. A typical entry includes the name of the essay author, the title of the essay and then *"In"* with a short title and editor of the volume from which the individual essay was drawn.

The elusive short story may be tracked down in the *Short Story Index*. Now published annually, the *Index* lists stories in both book collections and periodicals. A single index identifies the story by author, title, and subject. The subject setting is a handy aid for the reference librarian attempting to find a suitable study topic for a student who may not want to read an entire book on the Civil War or about life in Alaska. The names of the books and the magazines analyzed are listed. More than 3,000 stories are included each year. A basic volume covers collections published from 1900 to 1949, and there are five-year cumulations, or with the 1984 to 1988 cumulation, a group of nine volumes to search. There is also *Short Story Index: Collections Indexed 1900–1978* which lists the 8,400 collections analyzed.

Unless heavily used (which it rarely is in most libraries) the print version of *Granger's* is a cost saver. (It's also a financial boon for Columbia University Press which reports that at the turn of the century one-quarter of its revenue comes from this book.) Granted, the electronic format includes added items, for example, full text of 14,000 poems and 3,000 poetry quotes, but neither is required for daily reference service, and both are an expensive luxury the library can do without. The familiar index follows the pattern of many previous editions. There is a full index to first lines of some 70,000 poems, a subject index with close to 3,500 categories, and the expected author and title indexes. An added feature with the tenth edition is an index to 12,500 *last* lines, which can be invaluable when searching out quotations. All of this is mined from 400 anthologies of poetry. Note, however, it does not index the collected work of individual poets. Hence Geoffrey Hill's *New and Collected Poems* is not indexed, but the *Oxford Book of Modern English Verse* includes Hill as one of the poets, and through that anthology one may locate at least some of the poems found in Hill's more extensive one-person collection.

The tremendous advantage of *Granger's* online is twofold. One may search by many paths. Also, in almost all cases the sought after poem is shown on the screen. In an instant one may run down an elusive first line, last line, author, subject, title, and most important, key word. It is a great bonus for anyone trying to locate a quotation or a poem when only a garbled version of the title or first line is known. If, for example, only a word in Wallace Steven's "Sunday Morning" is used, such as "complacencies" and "peignoir" in the first line, or one of the two title words, then, presto, the poem is at hand. Still, the greatest benefit for people who hate to move away from the computer screen is the availability of the full text of 14,000 poems. Inevitably, though, the one wanted out of the 70,000 possibilities still requires the reader to get out of the chair and find the anthology somewhere in the library.

There are free Net sources for identifying poems and poets as well as subjects of poems and words used in the poem. None is as complete as *Granger*, but all at least offer a chance to find the difficult to locate poem. These are particularly useful as all words are searched, whereas *Granger* only lists the first line of the poem. So, if someone remembers a few words from the middle of a T.S. Eliot poem it is no good to use *Granger.*

At any point one should turn to any of the Net services:

Poem Finder on the Web (www.poemfinder.com). The publisher claims this site has over 650,000 citations to poems which may be searched by any word in a title, first line, last line, author, subject and some key words. This is an index which points the user to the full poem in some 3,000 anthologies, 5,000 periodicals and 4,500 single author works. In addition there are 60,000 plus poems available in full text (and searchable by key words). Brief biographies and photos are found for some entries. There is a charge ($600+) for the use of this site which makes it imperative to evaluate it in terms of price and depth of indexing as found in the superior *Granger's* entry. Ideally, the library should have both.

British Poetry 1780–1910 (http://etext.lib.virginia.edu/britpo.html). As the title indicates this is only romantic British poetry and online primarily for study by scholars. Still, the full text permits searching.[26]

Searching Patterns

Again, as in most widely used databases, three levels of searching are possible. This is true of all the indexes to collections, and the full-text additions. Wilson, of course, follows its standard pattern, discussed earlier in the chapter. The others use a straightforward "standard" search, or a detailed approach, or simply enter a more esoteric command level for the sophisticated quest. The latter mode allows the development of complex search expressions and data-element searching. This presupposes that the user knows command syntax and data codes.

Other Sources

Handy as these specialized indexes are to find short stories, poems and articles, there are other sources at hand. Among these: (1) The online catalog which may have entries for long or well known plays, short stories, poems, etc. (2) General indexes, and particularly the IAC *Expanded Academic Index* which includes short stories and major plays which have been published in periodicals over the past four or five years. (3) The Wilson *Humanities Index* (discussed in the next chapter) has author and title access to stories, plays and some poems which appeared in magazines from 1907 to the present.

---

[26]There are, and will be numerous other full-text indexes to poetry. See, for example, a subsection of Literature Online, an ambitious effort by Chadwyck-Healey to offer all (generally not in copyright) English and American literature online. (http://lion.chadwyck.com/html/homenosub.html) The subsection is "American Poetry," at a hefty price of close to $9,000.

SUGGESTED READING

Bell, Hazel, *Indexers and Indexes in Fact & Fiction* London; British Library, 2002. The
editor of *The Indexer,* travels through several centuries of literature to show
that utility is not the only purpose of indexes. They have entertainment
value, and there is an odd beauty in the cumulative entries. From the index
to *The Golden Bough* to Thomas Carlyle and George Perec, Ms. Bell edits
an entertaining and fascinating book. Who said indexing was dull?

Herring, Susan, "Journal Literature on Digital Libraries: Publishing and Indexing Patterns," *College & Research Libraries,* January, 2000, pp. 1–39. What are
the most efficient, easy-to-understand indexing terms for online searching?
The author examines existing patterns from 1992 to 1998 and finds little
or no consistency among core journal publishers. The heretofore subject
searching for complete retrieval may be a thing of the past. Key words may
be the answer.

Humphrey, Susanne, "Automatic Indexing of Documents from Journal Descriptors," *Journal of the American Society for Information Science,* vol. 50, no. 8, 1999,
pp. 661–674. The author offers still another automated approach to indexing. It is a new approach and "does not depend on previous manual indexing of hundreds of thousands of documents." Whether or not this will work
depends on a number of variables, but the author's analysis is typical of new
ways of eliminating the individual indexer in favor of a more technically
relevant system. Take her argument, or leave it, but it is cogent. *Internet Reference Services Quarterly,* vol. 3, no. 3, 1998. The whole issue is devoted to a
discussion of Net serials and how they can be employed in reference services. Also an emphasis on how such online journals are likely to change
the roles of librarians from the cataloging section to the reference desk.

Tenopir, Carol, "Human or Automated, Indexing is Important," *Library Journal*
(LJ), November 1, 1999, pp. 34–38. The regular columnist for *LJ* explains
the differences in approaches to indexing by the major companies from
the H. W. Wilson Company to LEXIS-NEXIS. Along the way she explains
the importance of specific indexing and the importance of human intervention in determining the level of the index's accuracy.

Wiley, Deborah L., "Beyond Information Retrieval," *Database,* August/September,
1998, pp. 19–22. The author points out that the next step in indexing/
abstracting will be a more refined, sophisticated use of information on
the Web. Search machines will adopt many of the techniques of good indexing and thereby bring information to people who heretofore have waded
around in a swamp of data.

CHAPTER SIX
INDEXING AND ABSTRACTING
SERVICES: SUBJECT
AND NEWSPAPER

Many of the giant general indexes have from 1,500 to close to 2,500 periodicals indexed. These cover basic newsstand magazines and journals in all major and minor subject areas.

If coverage is this ubiquitous, why bother going to a subject index? Answer: Well, most of the time librarians don't bother.

The all embracing general index serves 99 percent of the needs of students, from the early grades through graduate school. The percentage is even higher for laypeople that do not have a special need. For them the one stop general index is enough.

Ulrich's International Periodicals Directory identifies more than 3,000 subject indexes. *Magazines for Libraries* selects close to 300 as the best, and most necessary. How do they stay in business and who, if anyone, is using them? The answer is simple. They are published because there are enough specialists about, enough people with narrow subject interests, to justify their existence. Each year as knowledge divides and subdivides, new subject indexes appear. If a general work indexes 250 to 3,000 titles, who indexes the other 120,000 or more about? The answer is in this chapter.

Often a subject work is the most efficient way to answer a question put by a student or layperson. A subject index is best when the question specifically is a subject, e.g., "What is the status of the European Ecu?" (*ABI/Inform* would be a subject index with a quick, efficient reply); or "Which modern artists illustrate books?" (*Art Index*); or "I am looking for information on third grade history plans." (*ERIC*) It is usually much easier to find material in one of the three indexes about business, art, or education, than sift through masses of extraneous data in the general index.

There are other reasons besides the subject focus of the index to use it, not only for experts but, where needed, for the general public. (1) It analyzes in more depth the journals considered in the general indexes. (2) The subject index is likely to index all articles rather than a select few. (3) The abstracts tend to be longer, more informative than in the general work. (4) Many of the subject indexes go back decades, rather than a few years. True, these versions are in print and a bit difficult to use after becoming accustomed to electronic indexes, but they do cover "lost years" not found in the general indexes.

Subject Index Scope

Once a librarian understands the average general index he or she may progress to subject indexes. When considering such indexes, three facts must be kept in mind:

1. Many are broader in coverage than is indicated by such key title words as "Art" or "Education." Related fields are often considered. Therefore, anyone doing an in-depth subject analysis should consult indexes that take in fringe-area topics.

2. Most subject indexes are not confined to magazines. They often include books, monographs, bulletins, and even government documents.

3. A great number are international in scope. They usually note anything in English, even if issued abroad.

What good is it to learn of a particular article in a specialized journal and then be unable to obtain the journal? The library should be in a position either to borrow the journal, to have a copy made of the article, or turn to full text online.

Combining Sources

Rather than offering an index to only one subject area, the trend online is to package a group of similar sources for indexing. *The Literature Resource Center* is one of a growing number of such electronic reference works. Here there is rapid access to standard Gale Group publications: *Contemporary Authors, Dictionary of Literary Biography,* and selected criticism from *Contemporary Literary Criticism* as well as *Webster's Encyclopedia of Literature.* One may search by subject, author, title, time period, etc. Coverage is of more than 90,000 writers from all countries and all periods. Add the full text of articles from 24 basic literary journals, and one can find anything here from a simple plot summary to esoteric criticism of a particular book or author.

Given this base, the publisher can continue to add reference works, links, periodicals, and whatever is necessary to eventually meet almost every question about literature put to it by both laypersons and experts.

A variation on a theme, "Gale Group InfoSuites" allows the library to build an indexing full-text system as needed. And there are more names and systems. Gale is not alone in trying to cover every base. This is to keep up with the competition. The problem is the average reference librarian tends to get lost in the barrage of names—names and descriptors which seem to change with every new manager, every new advertising agency.

HUMANITIES

Arts & Humanities Citation Index. See p. 177.

Online: Humanities Abstracts, Full Text. New York: H. W. Wilson Company, 1995 to date, weekly, www.hwwilson.com. $2,995. Also, OCLC.[1]
  CD: Humanities Abstracts, 1994 to date, monthly. $1,725.
  Print: Humanities Index, 1974 to date, quarterly. Service.

The H. W. Wilson Company issues indexes that bridge general and specific subjects. All use much the same approach. The author and subject entries are in a single alphabet. There are excellent cross-references. (Some indexes, such as the *Applied Science and Technology Index,* have only a subject approach.) Subject headings are frequently revised, and in most services, book reviews are listed in a separate section. Each index has its peculiarities, but a reading of the prefatory material in each will clarify its finer points.

Covering as it does all of the areas of the humanities, there is nothing like *Humanities Abstracts.* The index offers the average person a clear path to information about religion, the arts, literary criticism, philosophy, journalism, and many other areas under the broad umbrella of "humanities." Incidentally, this includes history, which others would put in the social sciences. Some 460 titles are indexed, of which 325 to 380 are available in any of the three major general indexes discussed in the previous chapter. The online full-text edition includes 96 titles in full text.

The print index is by subject and author, with the usual section of book reviews. It has several unique features: (1) Opera and film reviews

---

[1]Here as throughout this chapter and in the text as a whole the addresses for subscription (i.e., for a fee) online databases are that of the publisher, not of the actual database. To find for fee databases (indicated by subscription price): *(a)* Turn to your library's Web page. The database usually is listed there with a link to the website. *(b)* Try another library in your area which offers users free access to for fee databases. *(c)* Use the publisher's online address given here. You may have to search for the specific title in the publisher's online catalog or search system. Once found the publisher may offer a free hour or two for sample searches. Go directly to the address for free databases, i.e., those with "Free" shown.

are listed under appropriate subject headings, that is, "Opera reviews" and "Motion picture reviews." (2) Poems may be located both by the author's name and under the section, "Poems." (3) The same procedure is followed for short stories. (4) There is a section for theater reviews. Given these divisions, the work is valuable for checking current critical thought on a wide variety of subjects in the humanities.

Humanities Abstracts follows the same 1-2-3 search pattern as all other electronic Wilson indexes. (See the previous chapter for a discussion of this software.) The user who turns to a subject index is likely to be more informed about the topic than the person who sits down to search a general index. Usually the search should begin at the second or third level, rather than the basic first level. The searcher has the opportunity to enter key words, often known only to a particular field. With Boolean logic the results are better defined.

SOCIAL SCIENCES

Social Science Citation Index, See p. 177.

Online: Social Science Abstracts, Full Text. New York: H. W. Wilson Company, 1994 to date, monthly, www.hwwilson.com. $2,995. Also, OCLC.
CD: Social Sciences Abstracts. 1994 to date, 9/yr. $2,295.
Print: Social Science Index. 1975 to date, quarterly. Service.

Social Sciences Source. Ipswitch, MA, EBSCO, 1988 to date, monthly, www.epnet.com. Rate varies.

Online: PAIS International. New York: Public Affairs Information Service, 1972 to date, monthly, www.pais.org. DIALOG file 49. Rate varies. (Note: In 2000 PAIS and OCLC merged, but the New York office of PAIS remains...and as of mid-2000 the proper title is *OCLC Public Affairs Information Service.*)
CD: PAIS International, 1972 to date, quarterly, $1,600. *PAIS Select,* 1994 to date, semi-annual. $950.
Print: PAIS International, 1914 to date, monthly. $495.

Online: SIRS Researcher. Boca Raton, FL: Social Issues Resources Series, 1994 to date, http://ars.sirs.com. $1,350. OCLC and others.
Print: 1971 to date. Price varies.

Social Sciences Abstracts[2] covers about 550 English language periodicals. There are author and subject entries with a separate section for book reviews. *Abstracts,* an addition to the service in 1994, is a vast improvement over the much older *Social Sciences Index,* which is still available at a lower cost. The online full-text version, with 200+ titles in full text, is an even

[2] *Social Sciences Abstracts, Full Text* is online from Wilson and available from Bell-Howell as well.

more advantageous system. When possible the library should try for the full-text edition.

The EBSCO rival to the H. W. Wilson Company *Social Sciences Abstracts* is edited for the same general audience in public and high schools as well as undergraduates in colleges. *Social Sciences Source* has about 400 titles. The EBSCO entry includes the full text of about 40 of the journals indexed.

PAIS International

PAIS (Public Affairs Information Service) International offers a general source of information for both the expert and layperson. Many librarians consider it the general index of the political and social sciences. Here one turns for current information on government, legislation, economics, sociology, and political science. Periodicals, government documents, pamphlets, reports, and some books in such areas as government, public administration, international affairs, and economics are indexes. About 3,600 journals and approximately 6,000 other items (from books to reports) are indexed each year. Coverage is international. Arrangement is alphabetically, primarily by subject. A few of the entries have brief descriptive notes on both contents and purpose.

Not only a direct service for those interested in political science and related areas, PAIS is a type of fill-in, back-hoe index. It will not index every article from a particular journal found in one or more other services, but it will select articles that reflect the interest of PAIS users. PAIS also provides indexing for periodicals not found in general databases. This explains entry of such diverse titles as *Farmer Cooperatives* and *Covert Action* in any given issue of the index.

Designed for laypersons and students, *PAIS Select* is a companion to *PAIS International*. Both have an index and the full text of about 2,200 selected articles and pamphlets. Full text is taken from about 177 journals and some reports (compared to 1,200 journals and over 8,000 reports in the primary service). (The "catch" is that no piece longer than 25 pages is included, which pretty much eliminates many reports, as well as pamphlets which may be hard to find in print.)

Note: All of the full text in *Select* has been cited in *PAIS International*. This means users of the major index will find cross references to indicate articles available in full text in *PAIS Select*.

SIRS

More of a reprint service than an index, although it can be used in conjunction with a built-in index, *SIRS*, i.e., *Social Issues Resource Series*, draws its full-text material from over 1,500 American and international periodicals. The focus is on current events, and more specifically the type of events likely to be found in grades K–12, with a nod to early college. The articles are selective. This is not an index to 1,500 periodicals, but rather an index to what the editors selected from that group of magazines. The online format is preferred because the print edition is in over 30 loose-leaf notebooks.

Interestingly enough, in a survey of reference librarians this was one of the few digital (rather than print) reference titles chosen as an essential reference work in all types of libraries. Among the comments: "highly searchable," "rapid access to current information," and "adore full text."[3]

SCIENCE

Science Citation Index. See p. 178.

General Science Index Abstracts, Full Text. *New York: H. W. Wilson Company, 1995 to date, monthly, www.hwwilson.com. $2,295.*
   CD: General Science Abstracts, 1984 to date, monthly. $1,995.
   Print: General Science Index, 1979 to date, monthly. Service.

Online: Applied Science & Technology Abstracts, Full Text, 1993 to date, monthly, www.hwwilson.com. $2,495.
   CD: Applied Science & Technology Abstracts, 9/yr. $1,875.
   Print: Applied Science & Technology Index, monthly service.

There are dramatically more print and online indexes available for the sciences than for the humanities or social sciences. The reason is that there are four to five times as many periodicals in this area as in the humanities or social sciences. A common estimate is that there are 65,000 scientific and technological journals. Government and business tend to be more willing to fund science than the other disciplines. Science online databases appeared earlier than those for the other disciplines primarily because of interest and good funding. At the same time, the cost of scientific indexes and periodicals are exceptionally high compared to other areas. To cite an extreme example, a year's subscription to a nuclear physics journal published in the Netherlands is around $6,000. It has more than 11,000 pages but the price is still steep.

The *General Science Index Abstracts, Full Text* covers 220 periodicals, of which 60+ are in full text. The focus here is on "popular" in that the index is produced for public school and college libraries at the fundamental levels of science instruction. It is not for the researcher. Designed for the non-specialist it covers all of the sciences from biology

---

[3]"Field Tested Reference Titles," *Booklist,* April, 1998, pp. 1532.

and chemistry to oceanography and zoology. The other versions, in print and on CD-ROM, cover the same area, but without the benefit of full text.

Moving from the general to the specialized, *Applied Science & Technology Abstracts, Full Text* indexes some 620 titles. Of these about 200 are available in full text. The differences between this and the *General* index are not only the greater number of titles indexed, but the concentration on the basic sources for each discipline. Also there is more coverage of parts of disciplines, e.g., various sections of engineering from electrical to chemical. This would be the place to turn for the expert, or for the student who could not find what was needed in the *General Science* index.

CITATION INDEXES

The following are all published by the Institute for Scientific Information in Philadelphia (www.isinet.com).

Online: Arts & Humanities Search. 1974 to date, weekly. DIALOG file 439; DataStar and OCLC. Price varies.
   CD: Arts & Humanities Citation Index. 1990 to date, 3/yr. Price varies.
   Print: 1976 to date, s–a. $5,000.

Online: SocialSciSearch. 1972 to date, weekly. DIALOG file 7; DataStar; DIMDI. Price varies.
   CD: Social Science Citation Index with Abstract Edition, 1992 to date, monthly CD-ROM Edition, 1981 to date, quarterly. Price varies.
   Print: Social Science Citation Index, 1969 to date, 3/yr. $5,920.

Online: SciSearch. 1974 to date, weekly. DIALOG files 34, 434; DataStar; DIMDI. Price varies.
   CD: Science Citation Index with Abstracts Edition, 1991 to date, monthly. CD-ROM Edition, 1980 to date, quarterly. Price varies.
   Print: Science Citation Index, 1961 to date, bi-monthly. $11,650.

Online: ISI Basic Science Index. ISI Basic Social Sciences Index. 1999 to date, monthly. Price varies.

Citation indexes are valuable for many reasons, but the primary one is that they index more periodicals than any other service. The title indicates the scope of each index. They cover every conceivable topic under the umbrella of humanities, social sciences, and the sciences. No other service comes closer to indexing so many journals in a subject area. *Arts & Humanities:* 1,150 journals, as well as "selected" items from more than

7,000 journals in science and the social sciences. *Social Sciences:* 1,700, plus 5,600 select. *Science:* More than 3,500 (expanded version: 5,600) titles.[4]

The major drawback is cost—SciSearch (*Science Citation Index*) can run online from $72 for subscribers to the print version to $142 an hour for nonsubscribers, plus about 50 cents for each record. The CD-ROM is around $12,650, and if the subscriber wants abstracts the price jumps to $17,000. The other two services are equally costly.

Citation indexing is unique in that it employs a different approach to searching. The avenue of access is through references cited in articles, hence the name of the service. It is easier to understand when one considers the printed volumes. (Conversely, for daily searching the online version is much, much superior.) The print volumes are organized in a peculiar fashion. Each index is in three parts:

1. *The Citation Index,* which lists papers cited alphabetically by author. The title of the article appears under the author's name, and beneath each article is a list of those who have cited the author's work. Most of the material is abbreviated.

2. *The Source Index,* which gives standard bibliographical information for each of the papers in *The Citation Index.*

3. *The Permuterm Subject Index,* which indexes the articles by subject, that is, by significant words in the title.

The system expects that the searcher will be familiar with the name of an author in a particular subject field. This is true for electronic searches as well. For example, someone looking for material on Japanese volcanoes would know that the leading expert on this is Kazuo Iskiguro.

The user would then turn to Iskigruo, Kazuo in the *Citation Index.* Beneath his name appear *seven* names of people *who have cited him* (and his article or book). The fair assumption is that these seven are writing about Japanese volcanoes, too. Furthermore, by citing Iskiguro, they are familiar with both the man and the field.

One then turns to each of the seven names in the *Source Index,* and finds articles or books *by the seven.*

Clearly, the obvious "catch" is that one must know an expert in the field in which one is involved. If not, the only solution is to (1) use another index with subject headings or (2) turn to the *Permuterm Subject Index.*

The *Permuterm Subject Index* is an alphabetically arranged (key-word-in-context) chic-type index. Subjects are derived from words appearing

---

[4]Current content services such as OCLC's *ArticleFirst* actually lists more titles—up to 17,000—but these are not analytical in any sense of the word. Useful as they are, current content services fail the fine-tuned searching that is possible in most indexes and certainly with the citation indexes.

in the titles of the source articles. Each significant word is precoordinated with other terms to produce all possible permutations of terms.

The uniqueness of this system, as opposed to other retrieval schemes, is that it is a network of connections among authors citing the same papers during a current year. In other words, if, in searching for a particular subject matter, one has a key paper or review article in the field, or even an author's name, one consults the *Citation Index* by author. Beneath the author's name will be listed in chronological order *any* publications by that author cited during a particular year, together with the *citing* authors (source items) who have referred to the particular work. If one continues to check the citing authors in *the Citation Index,* a cyclical process takes place, often with mushrooming results. *The Source Index* is then used to establish the full bibliographical reference to the citing author.

A citation index has a major production advantage that makes it particularly suited for automation. Indexers do not have to be subject specialists, and there is no need to read the articles for subject headings. All the compiler must do is (1) enter the author, title, and full citation in machine-readable form and (2) list all the citations used in the primary article in order by author, title, and full citation in machine-readable form. As a consequence, a careful clerk may prepare material for the computer. This speeds up indexing and also makes it possible to index considerably more material quickly.

Disadvantages of the printed volumes are numerous, among which are the reliance on type so small that it makes classified-ad-size type look gigantic by comparison and their confusing abbreviations. The most serious drawback is the lack of controlled vocabulary. This may work well enough in science, but often fails when used in the humanities and the social sciences. The multiple volumes make this a difficult print set to use, which is all the more reason for its value as an electronic database.[5]

The publisher's "Web of Science" provides access to all of the databases in a sophisticated online search system. This is divided into "quick search" for novices and "full search" for advanced users. Particularly it is useful in cutting through the sometimes confusing print routes of the citation index. In any situation where both print and electronic indexes are available, the latter is much preferred.

Very few libraries, except for the largest, can offer all or even a good number of the periodicals indexed in these services. But they can and do

[5]The publisher, ISI, has numerous other specialized citation databases such as *Chemistry Citation Index* and *Neuroscience Citation Index.* Using the same basic data the publisher also issues *Current Book Contents* in a half dozen areas. (This shows the table of contents of periodicals in the subjects). And there are numerous other related publications, although the particular focus is in the sciences. The menu of publications will be found on the Net at the publisher's home page (www.isinet.com).

use interlibrary loan and rapid document delivery, on or offline. Also, the publisher will supply tear sheets of one or a thousand articles needed—for a price, to be sure.

In an effort to find a larger audience, to reduce the price of its online indexes, ISI offers two reduced versions of its services, e.g., the *ISI Basic Indexes* (for the social sciences and for science). Here they cut back the number of journals to 500 for the social sciences and to 800 for the sciences. Although started in 1999, the indexes cover 10 previous years and are updated monthly. An easy-to-use Web interface makes the indexes more approachable than the standard citation works.

SPECIFIC SUBJECT INDEXES

What follows are examples of the basic types of narrow subject indexes that make up the 3,000 or more indexes in this category. The ones discussed here are found in most medium to large libraries. Conversely, the indexes are only representative. Each library will have particular titles for the particular needs of the community.

Dissertations

Online: ProQuest Digital Dissertation. Ann Arbor, MI: Bell & Howell Information and Learning/UMI, 1861 to date, monthly, www.umi.com. Also: DIALOG file 35. $96 per hour, Forty cents per record. OCLC, plus other carriers.
  CD: Dissertation Abstracts. 1861 to date, monthly. $1,995. (Backfile edition, three disc set: $7,995).
  Print: Dissertation Abstracts International. 1938 to date, monthly. $140 per section.
  Print: Comprehensive Dissertation Index. 1973 to date, annual. Inquire for price.

Dissertations normally are not thought of in terms of general indexes, but since they cover so many fields, they at least deserve a hearing and a place of access when one is searching for detailed information and bibliographies about a subject.

Covering over 1.6 million doctoral dissertations (and master thesis) from American universities since the mid-nineteenth century, *Dissertation Abstracts* is an invaluable index to almost any topic. Most subject-oriented indexes include dissertations. However, only the *Dissertation Abstracts* concentrates exclusively on the form. The publisher claims that more than 3,000 subject areas are covered. In addition, since 1980 the scope has been expanded to include 200 institutions in other countries, primarily

Asia and western Europe. With an addition of some 3,500 records a month there is a virtual guarantee, whether one is seeking current or retrospective viewpoints on pets or physics, that something of interest will be revealed in a search. Dissertations are important for the reference librarian seeking specific, often unpublished, information about a given subject, place, or person.

Since dissertations contain extensive bibliographies and footnotes, they can be used as unofficial bibliographies for some relatively narrow areas. There is a good chance that a dissertation has the bibliography sought, or at least indicates other major sources.

A problem with dissertations is that some librarians will not lend them. Policy differs, but the excuses for not lending include: (1) There is only one copy and it cannot be replaced. (2) A microfilm copy may be purchased from UMI, who just happens to publish the index. Actually, most libraries obtain copies by interlibrary loan through networks such as OCLC.

How does one find the dissertation? The relatively complex print search is done much faster online. Here there are several entry points, but the less complex is to use the subject, i.e., look for keywords in the title and/or abstract. Numerous other search patterns are available, but tend to be too involved for most purposes.

If one is confined to print, the first place to go is *Comprehensive Dissertation Index*. The index set is divided into the sciences, social sciences, and humanities, and each of these broad categories has subdivisions, for example, biological sciences, chemistry, and engineering. One locates the volume(s) likely to cover the subject and then turns to the finer subject heading to find a list of dissertations by full title and name of author. Entry is possible by author too; that is, the final volumes of the main set and the supplement are author-index volumes.

After each entry there is a citation to *Dissertation Abstracts,* where the librarian then turns for the full abstract. The citation refers one to the volume and page number in *Dissertation Abstracts.* For example, in the index one finds "Defining the roles of library/media personnel..." the author's name, degree-granting university, number of pages, and then: "43/06A, p. 1733." The reference is to vol. 43, no. 06A of *Dissertation Abstracts,* on page 1733. The number system is easy enough to use when it is understood.

Dissertation Abstracts International is a separate set from the index, but is issued by the same publisher. Like the index, it appears in three parts. Until the annual index is issued, the monthly issues of *Dissertation Abstracts International* must be searched individually. Each of the three sections has its own index. It is published monthly, and the arrangement by broad subject headings and then by narrow subject areas is similar to that of the index. Each entry includes a full abstract.

Obviously, because of multiple volumes and types of searching in print, it is much, much easier to use an electronic version. Also, the bound volumes take an enormous amount of valuable space. There is little justification for maintaining the print format.

Art

Online: Art Abstracts. New York: H. W. Wilson Company, 1984 to date, monthly, www.hwwilson.com. $2,495.
    CD: 1984 to date. $2,495.
    Print: Art Index, 1929 to date, monthly service.

Art Abstracts indexes over 400 domestic and foreign periodicals. Museum bulletins, yearbooks, and reviews are included as is other material that may be of value. The abstracts have been included in the index since 1994. One of the earliest guides to art magazines, *Art Index* began in 1929. A leader in retrospective indexing, Wilson has put all of the *Art Index* in digital form. Called *Art Index Retrospective* the CD-ROM covers the whole period of the index from 1929 through 1984 when it was picked up by the current ongoing CD-ROM, *Art Abstracts.*[6]

For more detailed work in art, turn to: (1) RILA *(Repertoire International de la Litterature de l'Art).* The service is published by the Clark Art Institute in Williamstown, MA. It is online as *Art Literature International* (DIALOG file 191) and covers the same time span as the corresponding print work, 1973 to date with quarterly updates. Several thousand periodicals, books, reports, museum bulletins, and so on, are covered in each year's publication. The index boasts excellent abstract coverage from art in Europe from the fourth century to the present.

ARTbibliographies Modern (Santa Barbara, CA: ABC-CLIO, 1993 to date, annual, www.abc-clio.com). Unlike the other two indexes, this primarily is limited to twentieth- to twenty-first-century art. It indexes about 350 periodicals as well as selected books, dissertations, museum catalogs, etc. At the same time it will index and abstract articles that may cover earlier periods related to the current century. (Photography is covered from its beginnings in 1839, not just the twentieth-plus centuries.)

It should be emphasized that "art" in all of these indexes takes in a wide variety of subject materials from painting and sculpture to photography, architecture, furniture, and interior design. Also, social, scientific, and political aspects of the world are found in citations where art is at the center.

---

[6]For a brief description of this retrospective program see: Carol Tenopir, "Recapturing the Past Online," *Library Journal,* February 1, 1999, pp. 41–42.

Business

Online: ABI/Inform, Ann Arbor, MI: Bell & Howell Information and Learning/UMI, 1971 to date, weekly, www.umi.com. DIALOG file 15. $132 per hour.
CD: ABI/Inform, 1992 to date, monthly. $4,950.

Online: Business and Company Resource Center, Farmington Hills, MA; Gale Group, 1989 to 1977, monthly, www.galegroup.com.
CD: Business and Company Resource Center, 1977 to date, monthly, current four years. $4,000.

Online: PROMT, Farmington Hill, MA: Gale Group, 1970 to date, daily, www.galegroup.com. DIALOG file 16. $126 per hour.
CD: Predicasts F&S Index Plus Text. 1991 to date, monthly. $6,000 (U.S. Alone: $2,500: International alone, $3,500).
Print: Predicasts F&S Index United States, 1960 to date, monthly. $850; *International* to date, monthly.

Online: Business Source Premier, Ipswich, MA: EBSCO, 1965 to date, weekly, www.epnet.com. Rate varies.
CD: Business Source Premier. 1965 to date, monthly. Rate varies.

Dow Jones & Company, *Princeton, NJ:* Factiva *(Formerly:* Dow Jones Reuters Business Interactive*) 1990 to date, daily, www.factiva.com. Rate varies.*

Online: New York: H. W. Wilson Company, *Business Full Text,* 1995 to date, monthly, www.hwwilson.com. $2,995. Also, OCLC.
CD: Business Abstracts, 1990 to date, monthly. $2,495.
Print: Business Periodicals Index, 1958 to date, monthly service.

Interest in business runs as high in America as in any part of the world. Almost everyone is aware of the ups and downs of economic and political fortunes. Radio, television, online, Internet, and just plain talking over a cup of coffee or a glass of milk will often have something to do with business. Little wonder, then, that it is a specialized area of reference services. Many medium to large libraries have sections devoted exclusively to business, economics, and related areas. And the reference librarian who wishes to specialize in this field should study equally specialized reference sources. Here it is possible only to suggest those reference sources that are basic in most libraries.

It is worth stressing, too, that business indexes may be consulted for information on everything from psychology and art to science and prison life. In fact, for a different, broader view of many subjects, the typical business index is a good secondary source.

Most current business news is available online because it is up to the minute. And as most of the services, at a hefty fee, are available via the Internet, they are even closer to the average person today than a few years ago.

There are numerous guides to business sources, including sections in *Guide to Reference Books, American Reference Books Annual,* and so forth. One of the best, and frequently updated, is *International Business Information* (Phoenix, AZ: Oryx Press, 1998, 445 pp.). This well-arranged guide to business information references is likely to help both the generalist and the subject expert. It has a nice mix of websites, electronic sources, and print. And, it includes good descriptive notes and comments on how the sources can be used to answer queries in international business. Note that in this day "international" is another word for an expanded American interest.

Bell-Howell: ABI/Inform[7]

This business index is preferred by many librarians. ABI/Informed has earned this reputation because of the superior indexing and, most important, full, well-written descriptive abstracts for all major indexed articles. Beyond that there is the superior coverage: over 2,000 of the leading business journals, magazines, newspapers, and newsletters. These are concentrated in the United States, but there is representative indexing of the International scene. In fact, the publisher claims that some 350 English language titles from outside the U.S. are indexed.

The online version is updated daily, and there is full text online. This comes in two formats. First, a choice of the complete image of the page. Second, and sometimes preferable as the first is slow, is text plus the graphics. There are about 700 full-text titles, of the titles indexed.

Business & Company Resource Group

Gale's *Business & Company Resource Group* indexes over 3,700 business periodicals, of which 2,600 are in full text. The publisher claims: "110,000 full-text company directory listings, 50,000 full-text investment reports, and thousands of full-text PR Newswire releases" are included. This means the index is not only a good place to turn for what can be found in magazines, but for directory-type data as well. This service as all online business indexes, with some variations, includes one year of indexing of the business section of *The New York Times* and *The Wall Street Journal* as well as six months of *The Asian Wall Street Journal,* a weekly.[8]

As with all of the IAC indexes, the coverage is for four years, i.e., 3 years plus the current year. Each new month means killing off a month

---

[7]As noted elsewhere, until 1999 this was called UMI, after late 1999 the company became known as Bell-Howell, Information and Learning.

[8]In this service, as in others, the number and type of newspapers has/will increase from year to year.

four years ago. *Predicasts* is a collection of several databases, each of which serves a specific purpose. *PROMPT* is the online Net version of *Predicasts*. The various services index over 3,000 domestic and foreign trade journals, business periodicals, government documents, reports, statistical publications, bank letters, long-range forecasts, and a variety of other materials. Although the focus is on business, the subject matter covers millions of records in related areas, from agriculture to education and the social sciences. The databases are searched by using well-defined thesauruses for products, organizations, events, and geographical locations. Some files are used for both retrieval and computation; that is, it is possible to perform algebraic, statistical, and forecasting routines, as well as to enter data. Both controlled and free searching are possible, but most of the files use the Standard Industrial Classification (SIC) System. This is a numerical hierarchical system established by the United States government to classify the total economy into different industrial segments. Using specific numbers one may retrieve a "needle" from millions of records.

EBSCO *Business Source Elite* indexes about 1,500 popular business periodicals (covering finance, industry, banking, etc. worldwide). About 800 are in full text. There is selective indexing of 50 business newspapers, including *The Wall Street Journal.*

Dow Jones

The Dow Jones Company, as the publisher's name suggests, is primarily involved with up-to-date information from and about the financial markets of the world. In 1999 Dow Jones Interactive merged with the English Reuters Business Briefing to form *Factiva*. Primarily a service for trained business professionals and experienced reference librarians, it is not aimed at laypersons. News sources from North America, Europe, and Asia are in one place. The database includes: over 7,000 business sources; the archives of both the Dow Jones and the Reuters news wires; archives of *The Wall Street Journal;* and offers services in 11 languages. Pricing varies, but is based on a subscription rate.

Dow Jones, like several online vendors, both produces and networks its financial services. All databases are available only through the company's own vendor systems, Dow Jones Interactive, which became available exclusively on the Web in early 1999. Terminal access no longer is supported—a gamble the company is willing to take in the hope of luring more users to an easier to use and understand system. *Dow Jones News,* for example, reports on current news about business and finance. In 1998 Dow Jones Interactive joined with Bell-Howell which broadens the Dow Jones News search to include adding key information from Bell-Howell sources, such as ABI/Inform. Full text of much of the material is available online.

A free site for business users, and particularly those day traders playing the market online, is offered by *Dow Jones:* (www.dowjones.com). Opened in mid-1999, this includes the familiar financial sites such as stock tracking and quotations services. More than 2,000 related business sites are linked to the system. Add breaking news from the Dow Jones newswires and other company services and this is a winning combination both for laypersons and for libraries. (How long the "free" will last depends on the degree of advertising support.)

Related websites for stock mavens and day traders include: *Quicken,* the financial section of the *Yahoo!* search engine; *CBS Marketwatch;* and…well, they come online almost as quickly as people searching out hot tips on the market.

H. W. Wilson Business Business Full Text

The only print business index about is the H. W. Wilson *Business Periodicals Index* which goes back to 1958. As the digital versions, it covers 400 English language general business periodicals. The Wilson *Business Full Text* (online and on CD-ROM is the same content, but starts up with indexing in 1982, with abstracts from 1990. The online and CD-ROM *Business Abstracts, Full Text* includes *The Wall Street Journal* and the business section of *The New York Times.* The "full text" online means that of the 400 periodicals indexed some 158 are in full text back to 1995.

There are scores of other business and related indexes, e.g., see *Magazines for Libraries* and/or *Ulrich's International Periodical Directory* for titles. For example, Bell-Howell's *Business Dateline* covers close to 500 business sources (from reports to periodicals), goes back to 1985, and is online with weekly updates. A daily service, by RDS Responsive Database Services, is concerned with activities of companies and industries represented in basic magazines, newsletters, general business press, and international newspapers. This is *Business and Industry.* Both the services are available from numerous vendors, including OCLC.

On the Web

Literally there are thousands of free Web pages which are devoted to business. Most are free because the sponsor has something to advertise. Many are reliable. Many are not. Where it is a question of investment advice the user should check, check, and double-check. At the same time numerous sites are reliable and of value, and, yes, quite free. A single example:

Bizzed (www.bizzed.com) is "brought to you by Citibank," and offers numerous links and sources of special interest to small business. There are three to four featured articles and then "news to grow your business" along with "tools to power your business" and "Networking to get ahead." Each of these is a doorway to numerous Web sites as well as suggestions on where and how to find information about specific problems. The service is paid for by the bank's obvious efforts to gain new customers.

Education

Online: ERIC: U.S. Educational Resources Information Center. Washington, DC: Government Printing Office, 1966 to date, monthly. Free on Internet: www.eric.org. DIALOG file 1. Also available OCLC and others. Rates vary.

CD: 1966 to date, quarterly. $650 (Retrospective disc with current disk: $1,200).

Print: 1966 to date, monthly. $56.

Note: Current Index to Journals in Education, 1969 to date is part of ERIC above online and on CD-ROM. The print version: 1969 to date, quarterly. $199 from Oryx Press.

Online: Education Abstracts, Full Text. New York: H. W. Wilson Company, 1996 to date, twice a week, www.hwwilson.com. $2,410.

CD: 1996 to date, monthly. $2,410.

Print: Education Index. 1929 to date, monthly service.

The best buy in the library, ERIC is free, at least online. Why? Because it is a government database and by the mid-1990s a decision was made to make this, and numerous other government sources, free to libraries and to individuals who have access to a computer. It seems pointless to even consider the print or the electronic versions from private concerns as the whole database is free.[9] Some libraries have both electronic and print because they started with the system and prefer to keep it that way. Meanwhile, students, teachers and interested laypersons have free access in a library, no matter what the format. The bonus is that same free access is open to everyone no matter where they are located without benefit of a library. Ahh, but the catch is that many will be baffled by trying to use the system at home.

ERIC/IR [Educational Resources Information Center/(Clearinghouse for) Information Resources] may be consulted for both original and secondary material on education, as well as related fields from library science to numerous social science topics. The system includes (1) an index to unpublished reports *(Resources in Education)* and an index to journals *(Current Index to Journals in Education)* (both are included in a sin-

---

[9]The Department of Education Net entry to ERIC has four primary entry points. A major one is "Information & Technology." Here the database begins at 1989. For a complete search use the "Reproduction Service" database which goes back to 1966.

gle unit in the electronic version, with each issued as a separate printed index); (2) an ongoing subject vocabulary, represented in the frequently updated Thesaurus of ERIC Descriptors; (3) a dissemination system which depends primarily on reproducing the material indexed on microfiche and distributing that microfiche to libraries; and (4) a decentralized organizational structure for acquiring and processing the documents that are indexed and abstracted.

The first part of ERIC is *Resources in Education* which lists unpublished reports and associated items. Each entry has a narrative abstract of 200 or so words. The abstracts are written by the authors. Reports are submitted to ERIC each month, but at least 50 percent are rejected, often as much for lack of typing skills as for content. Selection is made at one of 16 clearinghouses, each of which considers a particular subject. Experts evaluate the submitted material.

About 15,000 items are included and indexed each year. The reports are divided nearly equally among three categories: research and technical reports; proceedings, dissertations, preprints, and papers presented at a conference; and curriculum guides, educational legislation, and lesson plans prepared for the classroom.

As indicated, most of the indexed material is rarely published. This means several things for the user: (1) The reports are an excellent source of coverage of some rather esoteric areas. The studies represent a unique point of view as well as sometimes imaginative methods of research. ERIC is an excellent point to begin to discover what is on the fringe of the subject. And some subjects are not found elsewhere. (2) The reports usually are complete with bibliographies, readings, and suggestions for further research. They are an excellent beginning for many longer reports. (3) The research techniques are so varied, and so imaginative, that many of them may be used for other types of similar, related studies. In a word, this is a vast source of original thought. Yes, of course, some of it is valueless. The fishing trip will land some fine specimens, if not always a whale.

Current Index to Journals in Education, is a separate printed work, but is an integral part of the electronic formats. It indexes about 800 periodicals in education. Although published by a commercial firm, the indexing is provided by the 16 ERIC clearinghouses. *CIJE* is searched in the same fashion as *Resources in Education.* However, by indicating that one wants only journal articles, or unpublished reports, the two indexes may be searched online as separate units. Unless requested, the search results represent a single sweep of the whole ERIC.

An outstanding feature of ERIC, although a usual one among similar documentation systems such as that developed by the National Aeronautics and Space Administration, is that approximately 80 percent of the documents abstracted in *Resources in Education* are available on microfiche. In 350 to 400 libraries, the user finds the required citation on *Resources in Education* and then, instead of having to laboriously look for the item abstracted, simply turns to the microfiche collection. The items are arranged by accession number. This is a total information system and not the normal two-step bibliographical reference quest in which one finds the abstracts or the indexed item and then must try to find the document, journal, or book that the library may not have available.[10]

Ideally, the total information system would be offered with the second ERIC finding tool, *Current Index to Journals in Education (CIJE)*, included on microfiche. It is not. Why? Because here the index and abstracts are for journal articles. The cost of putting each article on a microfiche card, not to mention copyright problems with publishers, makes the price of a total information service prohibitive, at least for now. At the same time, the publishers state "that reprints of articles included in approximately 65 percent of the journals covered in *CIJE* are available from University Microfilms." One knows whether a reprint is available, because "Reprint: UMI" is stated after each citation where the service is available. Ordering information is given in the front of each issue.

Reports are identified by "ed" and journal articles by "ej." Online, the citation types are also separated out by "journal sources" or "how to obtain this doc" for documents. The latter, if not available in a large library, may be ordered at a reasonable cost from ERIC as "microfiche, print, fax, or electronic copy—either by phone or online."

AskERIC (http://askeric.org) is a version of ERIC established to assist teachers. The virtual library has a number of lesson plans with links to related sites. Most of the plans have been submitted by working teachers and are divided by broad subjects with worksheets, grade levels, and the like. An added feature is the "question and answer" service. A question can be submitted to experts who normally return an answer within 48 hours via e-mail.[11] The site includes, too, the regular ERIC databases of reports and journal articles.

[10]A pilot project launched in the late 1990s will bring all of these reports online without charge—at least without charge to libraries. The Federal Depository Library Program and the ERIC Digital Library Pilot Project "will give participants information on managing a large, high-demand collection of full-text documents in an electronic environment." The storage systems are housed by OCLC, which make the reports available through First Search.

[11]There are numerous sources of lesson plans and related material for elementary and secondary school teachers on the Internet. See, for example, the general encyclopedia Encarta/Online. Among the better, although only a sample: The History Channel (www.historychannel.com); The Virtual English Language Center (www.comenius.com); The Geometry Center (www.geom.umn.edu); The Music Education Launch Site (www.talentz.com).

Education Abstracts

Comparatively, the H. W. Wilson Company *Education Abstracts* appears a poor second to the combined strengths of ERIC, with 800 titles analyzed as compared to only 580 (including monographs and yearbooks) in *Education Abstracts*. (Full text is available for about 200 of the indexed journals). Actually, the index and abstracting service has twice the number of articles analyzed as found in *CIJE*. The latter may cover more titles, but the Wilson entry has almost double the number of citations. Given that, it is an absolute requirement in any library and in no way is replaced by *CIJE*. In reality, most indexes should be used together.

The Wilson abstracts are from 1994 and indexing begins in 1983 with full text of about one-half the titles from 1996. Furthermore, because the printed version *(Educational Index)* has been available since 1929 it has come to be almost an institution in some libraries.

There are other indexes to educational journals. They continue to grow and develop. For example, Bell-Howell has online *ProQuest Professional Educational Collection*. Made available in 1999, this indexes 250 professional education and library media journals. The audience: "school districts looking for an effective tool to support staff development needs."

History[12]

Online: America: History and Life & Historical Abstracts. Santa Barbara, CA: American Bibliographical Center–Clio Press, 1964 to date, *Abstracts,* 1955 to date, www.abc–clio.com. $6,800+/three per year.
   CD: *1964 to date, three per year. $5,500+.*
   Print: 1964 to date, five per year. Rate varies.

Online: Historical Abstracts. Santa Barbara, CA: American Bibliographical Center–Clio Press. 1967 to date, monthly, http://abc–clio.com. $6,800+.
   CD: 1982 to date, monthly. $5,500+.
   Print: 1955 to date, three per year. Rate varies.

Any historical question, either about North America or the world, can be answered by using the two indexes issued by the American Bibliographical Center.

America: History and Life & Historical Abstracts covers the United States and Canada from prehistory to the present. Something like 2,000 historical and related journals throughout the world are indexed and abstracted. Queries about not only history, but sociology, religion, political science, and interdisciplinary studies will be answered here. The digital version is preferable.

[12]Cheryl LaGuardia and Christine Oka, "Accessing History," *Library Journal* (Net connect supplement), Fall 2000, pp. 14–19. See this excellent descriptive-evaluative article for a complete overview of the basic historical indexes, including all those listed here.

The print edition is in three sections, with an annual index. Material is gathered under broad topics of interest, and despite the subject and author index in each issue it is a bit complex to use. The index includes not only citations to articles, but book reviews and dissertations. The fifth issue is the annual cumulation.

Historical Abstracts is "your complete reference to the history of the world," or so claims the publisher. It is true, but with one major reservation—history begins with this index in 1450. The four thousand or so years before are not covered, and for that one needs specialized indexes in not only history, but also the classics. (See *Guide to Reference Books* for these indexing services.)

The index and abstracts are drawn from 2,000 journals published "worldwide in history, the social sciences, and related humanities (from more than 50 languages)." The abstracts are in English. In addition there are book reviews, dissertations, reports, etc.

An electronic search employs all the usual methods from key words and authors to Boolean logic. The print work, as the American title, is in parts with separate annual indexes. (The two sections: Part A: *Modern History 1450 to 1914*; and Part B: *Twentieth Century from 1914 to the Present*). It is much more economical time wise to use the digital version.

The publisher of these indexes, known as ABC–Clio, issues numerous other bibliographies and indexes as well as basic reference works. For a complete listing, as well as detailed information on the discussed historical works see their home page: (www.abc–clio.com).

Related sources: *History Resource Center* (see the Encyclopedia chapter); *Historical Newspapers Online,* an index to both *The Times* of London and *The New York Times* from the first issues to 1980 at (www.historynews. chadwyck.com).

Law

Online: LEXIS. New Providence, NJ: Reed-Elsevier. www.lexis–nexis.com/ lncc. Cost: varies by files.[13]

Online: WESTLAW. Eagan, MN: West Publishing Corporation. www.west law.com. Cost: varies by files.

Online: Index to Legal Periodicals & Books. New York: H. W. Wilson Company, twice weekly, 1981 to date, www.hwwilson.com. $1,495.
CD: 1981 to date, monthly. $1,495.
Print: 1955 to date, monthly. $295.

---

[13]For a discussion of LEXIS-NEXIS (the law index combined with the more general index) see Chapter 5.

Online: LegalTrac. Farmington Hills, MI: Gale Group, 1980 to date, monthly, www.gale.com. Rate varies. Also: DIALOG file 150. $130 per hour, plus other carriers.
CD: 1980 to date, monthly. $5,000 (includes hardware).

Many legal questions may be answered using the particular federal or state laws, or city codes, but this requires specialized searching knowledge. Here LEXIS and WESTLAW are of great help. In between are more general legal queries, which can often be fielded using *PAIS* or even *Readers' Guide* or *Magazine Index.*

The two major legal indexes are available only online, that is, LEXIS and *WESTLAW.* Both are made up of separate, distinct databases such as *Westlaw Admiralty Database* to *Westlaw Tax Base.* In between are over a dozen databases. The same is true of LEXIS. Both contain individual parts that are found in print. For example, LEXIS includes the H. W. Wilson Company's *Index to Legal Periodicals.* The services tend to be limited to large law libraries and medium to large law firms.

Both services are supplied directly by the publisher and not through a vendor. They have complex charges that depend on which is used and how often it is employed.[14]

LEXIS has a word-for-word duplication of cases found in print, for example, federal and state court opinions, statutes of the United States Code, or decisions of the Supreme Court. Coverage dates vary, and the whole file is continuously updated. The arrangement is "by library"; hence the New York Public Library would have *New York Reports* and *Consolidated Laws* among others. The Federal Tax Library would have the *Internal Revenue Code,* tax cases, and so forth. Searches follow the normal pattern, and the full text may be searched entirely, that is, not only by title and author, but by words found in the text of the legal material. One must limit the terminology employed, or end up with hundreds of citations to less-than-relevant data. Another difficulty with the full-text search is that in earlier days the recorders were not very careful about how names were spelled, and searches may be incomplete because of an improper spelling.

WESTLAW is similar to LEXIS in that it offers the full text of various federal statutes, decisions of federal courts, and the like. In addition it covers, as does LEXIS, the various state laws. LEXIS has an advantage with its Shepard's citation method that enjoys prestige among lawyers. West uses KeyCite, generated by computers rather than by humans as in the case of Shepard's.

---

[14]Both conglomerates employ what is known as "transactional pricing." Charges accrue with every speech, every download, indeed, virtually very click the user makes. There are flat monthly rates and monthly rates, on even a case by case basis.

The two services are obvious competitors, and although they include much of the same material, there is a decided difference in the programs. Some claim WESTLAW is easier to use; others assert that this is the case with LEXIS. Also, of course, there are subtle differences in the types of materials updated which may make one more suitable than the other for certain situations. It is primarily a matter of (1) deciding which is more convenient to use and (2) establishing the cost.

By mid-2000 the two companies were at war over prices. While both continue to give law students free access to the exorbitantly expensive databases, they now have turned to libraries. There are no more free diskettes for students. Instead, the students have to master the websites where both firms offer free information. Instruction is via the library.

For Laypersons

Turning to less technical resources, there are two indexes of law material in many academic and public libraries.

LegalTrac's records go back to 1980 and consist of: indexing for about 800 legal publications from law reviews and bar association journals to legal newspapers. Coverage is international and for most libraries about as complete as necessary for nine out of ten questions involving the law.

Wilson's *Index to Legal Periodicals & Books* covers only 940 journals and legal publications. It has the standard subject and author indexes but adds an index for law cases, and case notes are found at the end of many subject headings. While a good deal of the material is technical, the careful librarian will find material which is equally suitable for the informed layperson. It can be of considerable help in almost any field remotely connected with the law or a legal decision.

Library

Online: Library Literature & Information Science Full Text. New York: H. W. Wilson Company, 1984 to date, twice weekly, www.hwwilson.com. $1,095.
    CD: 1984 to date, quarterly. $1,095.
    Print: 1936 to date, bimonthly service. (Note: A compilation covers 77 journals from 1921-1936).

Online: Information Science Abstracts. Medford, NJ: Information Today, 1966 to date, monthly. DIALOG file 202. $132 per hour.
    CD: 1966 to date, quarterly. $1,095.
    Print: 1966 to date, monthly. $515.

Online: Library and Information Science Abstracts (LISA). East Grinstead, England: Bowker-Saur, 1969 to date, monthly. DIALOG file 61. $66 per hour.

CD: 1969 to date, monthly. Price varies.
Print: 1969 to date, monthly. $500.

Library Literature & Information Science offers subject and author entries to articles that have appeared in about 290 library-oriented periodicals. Almost one-third of the entries represent publications outside the United States. (About 30 are non-English language). Books and library school dissertations and theses are included. The online full text version offers access to the full text of 93 of the journals indexed—a service which begins in January, 1998.

As with other specialized Wilson indexes, the contents of books are analyzed as are reports and pamphlets that relate to information science. The index gives the librarian a fairly complete view of the subject field. The digital *Library Literature* (without full text) includes data only from 1984. It hardly begins to tap sources that go back in the print version to 1921. Still, for current searching either electronic format is more than adequate.

Library and Information Science Abstracts (LISA) is of added help, although rarely current. Major journals are indexed and the service abstracts selected reports, theses, and other monographs. The number of abstracts now runs to well over 4,000 each year. There is excellent coverage of U.S. government reports, primarily because the U.S. National Technical Information Service allows LISA to reprint its abstracts. There are similar arrangements with other groups. Whereas the print *Library Literature* is in the traditional alphabetical subject–author arrangement, LISA depends on a classification system for the arrangement of material. Again, of course, the order hardly matters when the service is searched online or on a CD-ROM.

An even-more-sophisticated approach is offered in *Information Science Abstracts Plus.* The emphasis is on about 450 technical periodicals, books, reports, proceedings, and similar materials. And of the some 8,000 abstracts issued each year, a vast proportion deal with aspects of automation, communication, computers, mathematics, artificial intelligence, and so on. It is a service particularly suited to the needs of the information science researcher and the librarian in a large system. The abstracts are well written and complete. Each printed issue has an author index, and there is an annual subject index.

Literature

Online: MLA International Bibliography. New York: Modern Language Association of America, 1963 to date, monthly, www.mla.org. Also: OCLC and other carriers. Rate varies.
CD: 1963 to date, quarterly. $1,495.
Print: 1922 to date, annual. $750.

Providing as it does information on literature in virtually every corner of the globe, the *MLA International Bibliography* is a general index for the imaginative searcher. As literature is concerned with all aspects of human life, the index can be employed for more than trying to find X material about an author, book, or theoretical formula. For example, anyone searching for data on the history of scientific journals will find more than enough here as well as in specific scientific sources such as *Science Citation Index*.

There are over 1.6 million citations from some 4,000 periodicals. One simply types in a subject or an author to get a complete or partial run of citations. By checking the "Subjects Covered," which comes at the end of each citation, one gets leads for additional related subjects and authors. A more specific approach is to use the thesaurus that is built into the electronic databases. Unfortunately, there are no abstracts.

The printed volumes are a nightmare to use. They are divided into five separate subvolumes with additional subheadings. The organization is so complicated that it requires an expert in the field of a given section of literature to make a search. Fortunately, with the 1981 edition, things became much easier. A subject index was added. This covers all the categories and the journal dissertations (as well as selected books) which are indexed.

Medicine, Chemistry, and Biology

Online: MEDLINE. Bethesda, MD: U.S. National Library of Medicine, 1966 to date, daily, www.nlm.nih.gov/medlineplus/medline. Also: Free on Internet, *PubMed:* www.ncbi.nlm.nih.gov/PubMed/overview. html. DIALOG File 152 to 155, 1964 to date, daily. OCLC and other carriers.[15]
    CD: 1984 to date, monthly. $3,500.
    Print: Index Medicus, 1960 to date, monthly. $250. Annual cumulations, $275.

Online: BIOSIS Previews and Biological Abstracts. Philadelphia, PA: BIOSIS, 1969 to date, weekly. DIALOG files 5 and 55. Internet: www.biosis. org/homedeluxe. Rate varies. OCLC and other carriers.
    CD: Biological Abstracts, 1985 to date, quarterly. $9,700.
    Print: 1926 to date, semimonthly. $3,650.

---

[15]As this is a free government publication, there are close to a dozen vendors of MEDLINE on CD-ROM and online, as well as from the publisher. Versions of MEDLINE, too, are numerous, for example, MEDLINE/clinical collection, MEDLINE/collection, MEDLINE/ professional, MEDLINE/standard, and so forth. Each focuses on a particular need or professional aspect of medicine. If free, why go through a bibliographic network? Because the search patterns are more sophisticated. Also most of the networks charge a minimum for this service.

Online: CA Search. Columbus, OH: Chemical Abstracts Service, 1967 to date, biweekly,www.cas.org. CDP Online, $106 per hour. Also available online through many other services. (Note: No CD-ROM version.[16])
Print: Chemical Abstracts. 1907 to date, weekly. $9,200.

Medicine and Health

MEDLINE is another government index that is free to anyone on the Internet.[17] As with the previously discussed government index ERIC, this became free in the late 1990s. The idea is to reach anyone, from doctor to layperson, who can use the service. It is a tremendous prize for libraries.

What is, then, MEDLINE?

It began in 1960 as *Index Medicus* in print, and is still being published in that format. It is the world's most comprehensive and, probably, best-known medical index. Produced by the National Library of Medicine, and sold through the Government Printing Office, it represents government at its best. Approximately 9,000 English and foreign language journals are meticulously indexed. There is, as well, a selective indexing of reports, letters, editorials, and the like. The monthly printed issues are arranged by subject and author. This, along with two other databases (Index to Dental Literature and International Nursing) comprise the electronic database MEDLINE. The database contains citations, with abstracts, to articles published in the United States and some 70 other countries.

The subject headings are of utmost importance for the medical profession. They are drawn from a special list: *Medical Subject Headings.* This usually is cited as MeSH.

One of the four or five most heavily used databases in all disciplines, MEDLINE offers users a wide variety of searching options. More important, because of the subject matter, it tends to embrace, literally, the world. It has a broad potential beyond medical literature. Thanks to a file of some 10 million citations, MEDLINE may be used to find data on such related fields as psychology, education, anthropology, sociology, technology, agriculture, and almost any other area—including politics—connected in any way with medicine.

The National Library of Medicine backs up MEDLINE with an efficient article and interlibrary loan procedure. About 2,000 requests for materials are received each day. Before requests reach the NLM they are filtered through three other possible sources of supply. The librar-

---

[16]There are retrospective CD-ROM discs, (twelfth collective index, covering 1987 to 1991 from $16,000 to $25,000).

[17]This became free to laypersons only in early 1997. The Medline website now receives a million visits a day.

ian may send the request to a local library (one which is large or has medical journals); to a resource library, usually at a medical school; or to one of 11 regional medical libraries that cover well-defined geographical regions. Finally, if none of these are possible sources, to the National Library of Medicine. In other words, the NLM serves as the final resource after requests are unsatisfied at three previous levels of processing.

The NLM library can fill from 80 to 85 percent of the requests received. The unfilled requests are transmitted by computer to the British Lending Library in Boston Spa, England, and quickly accessed by the British Lending Library, thus often making it possible to receive material more quickly from England than from another part of the United States or Canada.

Other than via a library there is a fee for document delivery to the individual. The Internet search may cost nothing, but to actually read the article the user must go to the library and/or order the item from the NLM. This will change. Most of the medical journals will soon be online in full text—although, again, for a fee. For example, EBSCO in 1998 offered its *Comprehensive MEDLINE with Full Text,* which goes back to 1997, and links the MEDLINE citations to the corresponding actual full text articles in more than 60 leading medical journals. (Some journals are available in full text back to 1990).

While most scientific databases are complex, at least for the average layperson or librarian, MEDLINE offers numerous relatively easy paths of access. The searcher can browse by key words in the abstracts, and the title, or, more likely will turn to the aforementioned MeSH (Medical Subject Headings) for assistance. Although it does require some experience, one can browse MeSH using a built-in tree hierarchy. This allows immediate access to extremely specific areas of interest. There are numerous other entry points from author to countries and ISSN or gene numbers. There is excellent documentation for the electronic and print databases and this is updated quarterly by the NLM.

The free Internet access to MEDLINE is called *PubMed.* It simplifies access to a basic health resource not only for libraries but also for all, in home and in office. In addition to either browsing or advanced searches of the primary database, the system provides innovative links and related features which keeps the data current hour by hour, day by day.[18]

There are numerous variations and links sponsored by the government which helps the layperson and librarian. Among the best and

---

[18]Medline/Plus www.nlm.nih.gov/medlineplus) not only includes the index, but an added feature or "plus": news about ongoing research in the area in which the user is searching. For example, one finds the leading, latest articles on "acne" and is then given a rundown of reports, studies, projects, etc. which are in progress or have not yet been published. This may be too much for many, but it is a blessing for anyone seeking a topic in depth.

most useful: *(a) Healthfinder* (www.healthfinder.gov). This offers some 1,500 links to various reliable health sites on the Web. The links are to publications and self-help groups as well as to websites. Sponsored by the Department of Health and Human Services. *(b) National Library of Medicine,* the sponsor of MEDLINE also offers access to its medical library, which includes news about recent medical findings.

Beyond the ubiquitous MEDLINE, the major general indexing companies offer considerably more limited medical indexes. Here, though, the almost total emphasis is on material for the layperson rather than for the doctor or medical professional.

EBSCO has the most health databases including "Comprehensive MEDLINE with Full Text" database which has links to corresponding full-text articles in more than 60 medical journals. The most useful for laypersons is *Health Source Plus* (1990 to date, daily). Available both online and on a CD-ROM the *Health Source Plus* is one of a number in the same family of indexes.[19] The Gale IAC *Health Reference Center* has different divisions. The most inclusive is the so-called "Academic" which indexes 205 titles and has 150 in full text. All of the basic, general medical journals are covered, i.e., those which are likely to be of some interest to laypeople. In addition, the basic nursing journals are indexed—but this time for nursing schools as much as for the layperson. What's interesting, and the indexing of the future which has arrived: in addition to indexing magazines, the service includes limited indexing of reference books, newsletters, newspaper articles (but not the whole paper), and related reference works, including some 500 pamphlets. Many of these are in full text. There are, too, good to excellent links to similar sites. Following IAC practice, the indexes include three years, plus the current year on CD-ROM; and four years, plus the current year online.

BIOSIS (Biological Abstracts)

BIOSIS and *Chemical Abstracts,* which follows, are highly specialized technical services that require equally specialized training to use. They are found only in large or scientific subject–area libraries. Here they are little more than mentioned, not for lack of importance but for lack of space in this text.

Aspects of medicine are an important part of the well-known *Biological Abstracts.* Here abstracts from over 5,500 journals are included, and

---

[19]Related indexes include:

Health Source—with 300 journals indexed and 55 in full text, both online and CD. Includes the 1,000 pamphlet index.

Health Start—This is from the National Library of Medicine, not EBSCO which is a carrier for the service only. Primarily for medical administrators.

among these are biomedicine as well as all the biological and life sciences. As a major indexing and abstracting service, this is as well-known in science-oriented libraries as *Index Medicus* and *Chemical Abstracts*. Often the three are worked as a unit, particularly online.

Because of its wide scope, BIOSIS is employed to answer many scientific and even social science queries. A subject index uses key words in context. Topics may be searched as well by broad subject concepts; genus, species, and organism names; broad taxonomic categories; and author. As useful as it is specialized, BIOSIS is the ideal service for online searching.

CA Search (Chemical Abstracts)

CA Search, as it is called online, or *Chemical Abstracts,* as it is titled in the print version, is one of the largest abstracting services in the world. It abstracts over 15,000 scientific and technical periodicals from over 150 countries. Of the many sections, the one devoted to patents is the one that is used most.

As in all print services, the abstracts are arranged by subject, but here over 80 subject sections are consolidated into five broad groups. Each print issue includes indexes for author, patent, and key word catch phrases from the abstract and the title. It also contains a most useful "Index Guide" in addition to the numerous other aids and sections. The system is so complicated and is divided into so many different parts that a successful search can be made only by a subject expert or by a librarian who is thoroughly familiar with the literature of chemistry and related areas.

Psychology

Online: PscyINFO (Psychological Abstracts). Washington, DC: American Psychological Association, 1967 to date, monthly, www.apa.org. Rate varies. DIALOG file 11. Also available: OCLC and other carriers.
CD: PsyLit, 1974 to date, quarterly. $4,495.
Print: Psychological Abstracts, 1927 to date, monthly. $1,350.

Psychological Abstracts is familiar to many people primarily because, as with a few other subject abstracting services (such as ERIC), it can be used in so many related areas. For example, an important section concerns communication that, in turn, includes abstracts on language, speech, literature, and even art. Anyone involved with, say, the personality of an engineer or an artist would turn to this source. The better-educated person seeking information on anything from why a companion talks in his or her sleep to why people can or cannot read will use this index.

The service analyzes over 1,900 journals from all major countries in the world, although 90 percent are in English. There is full text access (via PsycArticles) to numerous articles from 1988 to the present. In addition it analyzes the contents of from 400 to 500 books each year (1987 to the present). There are about 3,000 abstracts in each monthly issue. As in other services of this type there is a cumulative index, but the abstracts themselves are not cumulated.

Psychological Abstracts (online: PsycINFO) is available from the major vendors. It covers the years from 1967 and is updated monthly. In addition to the basic features it offers the user several advantages. First and foremost one searching for foreign language materials will find them *only* in the database, not in the printed version. Second, dissertations can be found *only* online. The result is that today the online service offers from 25 to 30 percent more material than the printed version. (There is a subset service, *PsycFIRST* which covers the same materials, but only for the current year and proceeding three years.)

The printed abstracts are arranged under 16 broad subject categories from physiological intervention to personality. This allows the busy user to glance quickly at a subject area of interest without being bothered by unrelated topics. As a guide for those with less experience, there is an author index and a brief subject index in each issue.[20] The subject approach is expanded and modified in the cumulative indexes published twice a year. (When in doubt about a subject, turn first to the cumulation, not the individual issues.) A useful aid is the *Thesaurus of Psychological Index Terms.* As with any really first-rate system, this provides the necessary terminology to aid searching.

CURRENT EVENTS: NEWSPAPERS, INDEXES, REFERENCE AIDS

Where do Americans get their news? According to a Pew Research Center for the People and the Press report the majority still prefers the daily newspaper. Beyond that the not so surprising revelation is that "Almost as many people use the Internet on a typical weekday as spend time reading a magazine. About 20 percent of American adults, or an estimated 36 million people, get news from the Internet at least once a week."[21] At the same time the percentage of Americans who get their news from television is about 40 percent. Only 38 percent described themselves as reg-

---

[20]An advantage of the print version is that it allows for retrospective searching back to 1927. But for a true retrospective search see: Historic PsycINFO, a Silver Platter CD-ROM, which takes the indexing of psychology journals back to 1887 and forward to 1966 when the current online of the index is used from 1967 to the present.

[21]"Poll shows cable news catching up," *The New York Times,* June 8, 1998, p. D7. Later polls in 1999-2000 indicate the number is growing to well over 30 percent, particularly for foreign and specialized papers.

ular viewers of the network evening news broadcast, as compared with 60 percent five years ago.

By 2000 there were some 800 United States daily newspapers on the Net. Add weekly newspapers and the number goes from 800 to 2,300. The majority are free. The exception is *The Wall Street Journal* which can charge because of its unique service. Electronic delivery of the news on the Net has accustomed millions of Americans, and particularly younger people, to look to the electronic database for the latest in current events. The catch for the individual is that while the computer screen delivers the day's events, it virtually is worthless for digging out facts and figures from several years ago, at least for free. These days all the larger newspapers offer at least some retrospective (archival) searches, but inevitably for a fee.[22]

From the point of view of a working reference librarian there are three distinct aspects of news and reference service. (1) One can read the daily paper online. This tends to be used more in a casual way by daily browsers than by reference librarians. Particularly popular: foreign online newspapers and papers from the viewer's home town. (2) One can turn to standard reference works for background material on events which have folded themselves into history, e.g., *Facts on File* or a good encyclopedia may tell the user more about last year's economic conditions in Japan than spending times cruising a newspaper index.

Why bother with print newspaper indexes? The answer is the same old by now well-known refrain: (1) No newspaper online index goes back more than 10 or 15 or, at the outside 20 years. Most began in the mid-1990s. Conversely the print edition of *The Times* of London begins in 1785. (2) The print indexes are more refined, more complete than their online brethren. (3) It is much faster to use a print index for an involved research project.

Newspapers

By circulation (2000), the top 10 American newspapers are: *The Wall Street Journal, USA Today, The New York Times, The Los Angeles Times, The Washington Post, New York Daily News, Chicago Tribune, Newsday, Houston Chronicle* and the *Chicago Sun-Times*.[23] Large libraries will have all of these available in several formats. The local daily paper will be in print for about one month's issues. After that the paper will be available as an archive

---

[22]Archives primarily go back to the mid-1990s, although some are earlier, others later. Almost all papers charge for downloading archives which are more than a few days old.

[23]The latest edition of *Magazines for Libraries* has descriptive-evaluative annotations of these and other major newspapers. Both print and electronic versions are considered.

on microfiche (still the preferred format), CD-ROM, in bound volumes (rapidly disappearing) or online. In not too many years current issues and archives of all major newspapers will be available with indexing online. CD-ROMs and microfiche will disappear.

A large library will subscribe to all of what constitutes national newspapers read from one coast to the other. Small- to medium-sized libraries will want subscriptions to four or five. If funds are extremely tight, to *The New York Times* and possibly *The Wall Street Journal.*

In addition, the library will want subscriptions to the local papers, i.e., the one in the immediate community as well as the paper considered the newspaper of record in the surrounding area. Except for the index *Newsbank*, few local papers are well indexed. The solution is twofold: *(a)* The newspaper itself will have an index that can be used from time to time by the reference librarian. *(b)* The library will index the paper. This used to be the normal thing to expect, but today it is quite rare, except in special situations.

On the Web

The library may be lulled into believing daily subscription to major newspapers is not necessary because they can be read, almost in full text, on the Internet. Two points: *(a)* Most people prefer to read the paper with a cup of coffee or a glass of milk and not on a computer screen. *(b)* More important, few of the so-called full-text newspapers really have everything online. Most advertisements are cut as are filler items and numerous pictures. Only the print paper will be acceptable for those who truly want to read a newspaper from the first to the last page.

With that, the miracle of the millennium is the availability, free, on the Internet of all major newspapers...if only in partial full text. Why, except for archives, is the service free? One reason is to protect classified advertising from competition on the Web. Another is that publishers believe the Internet is a stake in the future, even though they have yet to figure out how to make money from the Net. But primarily they are influenced by the spirit of Irving Berlin whose one song ends: "Everybody's doin' it now."

The New York Times in a print full-page ad to advertisers explains in part the attraction of the Net for newspaper publishers. "With well over 7.1 million fully registered users, nytimes.com...allows for the creating of content with highly targeted information and selling mechanisms... Advertisers can now monitor and manage response rates...Consider the case of the cosmetics company that deployed a multiple contact program on nytimes.com to build in-store traffic...With advertising messages only exposed to women working or living in the trading area, this campaign delivered a higher response than any promotion."[24]

The various online services and search engines provide their own news updates. *America Online,* for example, claims some 14 to 15 monthly visitors to a constantly updated news section which offers wire-service dispatches from major outlets including Bloomberg News and Reuters. The news TV and radio stations such as *MSNBC* (www.msnbc.com) have similar services. Useful as these are for individuals, they are of limited value for libraries as the archives are limited and the searching patterns are rough, to say the least.

There are several services, all free, which help the user organize his or her own list of favorite newspapers. In the jargon, these are known as "filtered news services" and/or "custom pages." They vary wildly in terms of reference content and organization.[25] *Crayon,* an acronym for "create your own newspaper," lets the reader select what papers to read. Links are furnished so that when one turns to the site, the day's news (from general to obituaries as selected by the user) comes up on the screen from the single, or all of the papers. Crayon is at: (www.crayon.net).

Several other websites cover a group of newspapers for specific subjects. *Moreover.com* (www.moreover.com) combs major newspapers as well as the BBC, CNN, and others. It then lists the query subject with headlines likely to match and provides links to the originating sites.

The Library of Congress has the best links to newspaper sources. See "Newspaper Indexes/Archives/Morgues" (http://lcweb.loc.gov/rr/news/oltitles.html). Among other things this superior source provides links to archive sources as well as search engines with newspaper archives. There are pragmatic hints to such things as "U.S. newspaper indexes we use often or haven't seen on other lists" as well as "U.S. Newspaper Indexes (usually older, local, sometimes specialized). In other words this is the best place to begin searching for newspapers not found either by individual name or in database groups such as in the Bell & Howell Infor-

---

[24]"As an online advertising medium" (full-page advertisement), *The New York Times,* May 3, 1999, p. C11. See, too: "Hidden in the Web," *The New York Times Magazine,* July 11, 1999, pp. 22–24. A spokesman for the paper explains further how the Times as well as other newspapers on the Web hope to make money by giving away the paper. Ads target certain groups who in turn have links to sites for immediate purchases. The catch: "Investment in the actual gathering of information by conventional journalistic means is in apparent decline, under the banner of cost control, in all but a handful of traditional news organizations...The Internet...is a wonderful place to collect raw data. But it's not, so far, a wonderful place to find reliable and original reporting, real news, except where it has been siphoned off the old."

[25]"Online Journalism," *New York Times,* June 12, 2000, pp. C1, C16. An excellent overview of what is available.

mation and Learning/ProQuest "Newsstand" or the Gale Group/IAC "National Newspaper Index" as well as its "InfoTrac Custom Newspapers." The best lists with links to specific newspapers include:

U.S. News Archives on the Web (http://metalab.unc.edu/slanews/ internet/Archiveso–w.html) from the Special Libraries Association. Here one may search both back issues (usually from about 1990 or 1995 forward) as well as current issues by phrase, word or the usual "all of the words." Papers are arranged by state with dates of the archive along with the cost to retrieve full text articles. Searching tends to be free, but the articles normally are at a fee. Some non-US newspaper archives are listed. The pages are updated regularly.

NewsLibrary (www.newslibrary.com/about) Here the reader can search archives of 65 U.S. papers, i.e., current as well as past issues with broad search terms. There is a flat rate of $1.95 per story, both current and past. Searching follows the standard broad system of "finding the words and phrases that appeared in...articles." The reader is then presented with a list of headlines from which to select what is needed.

NewsDirectory (www.newsdirectory.com/archive/press) Put up by Electric Library this lists U.S. daily papers by region, and includes fewer than the other services. As such it is recommended only when the previous news sources fail to turn up what is needed.

Group Newspaper Indexes

Online: National Newspaper Index. Farmington Hills, MI: Gale Group, current year, plus three years only, daily, www.galegroup.com. Rate varies. DIALOG file 111. $120 per hour. Available with other carriers as well.
CD: 1982 to date, monthly. $4,000.
Online: Newspaper Source. Ipswitch, MA: EBSCO. 1990 to date, daily, www.epnet.com. Rate varies.
Online: ProQuest Newsstand. Ann Arbor, MI: Bell & Howell Information and Learning (ProQuest). 1996 to date, daily, www.umi.com/ proquest. Rate varies.
Online: Newsbank InfoWeb. 1991 to date, daily, www.leeca.org/infopre/ newsbank. Rate varies.
CD: Newsbank, 1991 to date, monthly. $1,800–$3,100.

Why not go directly to a newspaper? Why use a group indexing system, i.e., one which includes not one, but several newspapers? The answer: refinement of searching. The group efforts, of which the primary examples are listed here offer sophisticated search patterns rather than words or phrases which one uses as the entrance into individual newspaper files online.

One of the most popular newspaper indexes in American libraries is IAC's *National Newspaper Index*. It offers indexing and abstracts for the leading five national newspapers: *The New York Times, The Wall Street Journal, The Christian Science Monitor, The Washington Post* and the *The Los Angeles Times*. While the index goes back several years, the full text availability of stories online usually is limited to the previous 90 days. The searching patterns are among the easiest to use. This includes the full text of three basic wire services that supply many of the business stories to the papers. As DIALOG file 649, one may search these services, which are updated daily. Most go back only to 1985. The three wire services include *Reuters Financial Report, Kyodo's Japan Economic Newswire,* and *PR Newswire*. The emphasis is on business news and so, while useful, the service is of limited value to someone hunting for typical human-interest stories.

InfoTrac Custom Newspapers (www.galegroup.com) released in 2000 adds a new dimension to Gale's newspaper service online. This includes over 50 English language newspapers, although most emphasis is on the United States with a nod to England and other countries. The company plans to increase the number of newspapers each year. The bonus here is that the full text of most articles, but with no graphics, is included as part of the indexing system.

EBSCO's *Newspaper Source* has indexing of major American newspapers, including abstracts and indexing of: *The New York Times, The Wall Street Journal, USA Today, The Christian Science Monitor, The Los Angeles Times* and *The Washington Post*. It includes, too, over a dozen international papers.

Bell-Howell

ProQuest Newsstand allows the user and/or library to designate from two to 125 newspapers (national, local and international) to be indexed and available online in full text.[26] There are 27 searchable index fields as well as a date option. A special search system is in place for those who are not familiar with Boolean logic and other basic search patterns. Each record includes a citation and an abstract. Once the user has found a citation he or she can access full text in a single operation. An advantage here is that the newspapers are updated daily, one can browse through a particular paper, and there are archives for many of the titles.

Another version of the Bell & Howell index is: *Newspaper Abstracts* (www.umi.com/proquest), here are 30 United States and regional titles, including all of the major newspapers. Indexing usually begins in 1990.

---

[26]"An Online Newsstand," *Database*, June, July 1998, pp. 42+. This is a complete discussion of the database and how it searches newspapers.

NewsBank is the answer, if only in part, to indexing some 500 smaller newspapers, and up to 200 periodicals. It does not completely index the papers, but does search for material under broad topics, with subdivisions. These are tied closely to K–12 curriculum as the service primarily is for schools and small- to medium-sized public libraries. Selecting key stories, often of interest to the local community, *NewsBank* indexes each month some 60,000 to 65,000 articles from American and Canadian newspapers, liberally salted with news stories from wire services.

And...

All of the general indexing services, from EBSCO and LEXIS-NEXIS to Gale have at least some newspaper indexing. And for most purposes it is probably enough. Vendors, too, offers indexing. DIALOG's "News" category offers both general and subject newspapers online, usually with full text for current issues and limited provision made to acquire earlier articles (i.e., usually for the past 90 days). Each tends to be a separate database and can be costly. The advantage is that it provides sophisticated search patterns not often found in other services.

Individual Newspaper Index[27]

Online: The New York Times Index. New York: New York Times Company.
   1980 to date, daily. Free on Internet: www.nytimes.com.
   CD: Ann Arbor, MI: UMI, 1992 to date, monthly. $2,450.
   Print: 1851 to date, semi-monthly (plus quarterly and annual cumulation). $1,281.

No matter what its form, the best-known newspaper index in the United States is the one published by *The New York Times.* A distinct advantage of *The New York Times Index* is its wide scope and relative completeness. The *Times* makes an effort to cover major news events, both national and international. The morning edition of the *Times* is available in all major cities. It is printed not only in New York, but also in Seattle, San Francisco, Los Angeles, Chicago, Dallas, and several northeastern cities.

The *New York Times Index* provides a wealth of information and frequently is used even without reference to the individual paper of the date cited. Each entry includes a brief abstract of the news story. Consequently, someone seeking a single fact, such as the name of an official, the date of an event, or the title of a play, may often find all that is needed in the index. Also, since all material is dated, *The New York Times Index* serves as an entry into other, unindexed newspapers and magazines. For example, if the user is uncertain of the day a certain ship sank and wishes to

---

[27]See the latest edition of *Magazines for Libraries* where major individual newspaper indexes are discussed, as well as, of course, the multiple indexing newspaper sources.

see how the disaster was covered in another newspaper or in a magazine, *The New York Times Index* will narrow the search by providing the date of the event.

Basic searches offer the usual subject, author, and title points of entry. In addition one may search by key words in the abstract and descriptors. Other search patterns are by geographical names, illustration, named people, publication date, section heading, and even the story ID number.

The print version of *The New York Times Index* (which goes back to 1851) is arranged in dictionary form with sufficient cross-references to names and related topics. Events under each of the main headings are arranged chronologically. Book and theater reviews are listed under those respective headings. Some libraries subscribe only to the annual printed cumulated *Index*. This volume serves as an index and guide to the activities of the previous year. Thanks to the rather full abstracts, maps, and charts, one may use the cumulated volume as a reference source in itself. The annual cumulation is fine, but it appears late; normally it is published from six to seven months after the end of the year.

Online *The Times* indexes issues back to 1980. Two points: Not all items are covered in the online issue of the paper or the index. When searching online, as of late 1998, the *Encyclopaedia Britannica* is included along with the full text of the previous year, i.e., the past 365 day archive. The search and summary are free, but if a full article is wanted it costs $2.50 per article regardless of length. For details see: (http://archives. nytimes.com/archives).

Note, too, that *The New York Times* is carried online as part of all the major general indexes from EBSCO to IAC. In these cases, though, the library pays for the index and coverage usually goes back no further than 1994 with full text online available only for the most recent 90 days. Without full text, but with the abstracting indexing service, LEXIS-NEXIS offers the newspaper back to 1969.

An extremely useful addition to *The New York Times Index* is: *The Personal Name Index to The New York Times, 1851–1974,* followed by supplements from 1975 (Sparks, Nevada: Roxbury Data Interface, various dates, 28 vols, plus supplements). Edited by Bryon and Valeria Falk, this contains over 5 million citations to personalities who have appeared in the newspaper from its first issue through 1999. (Supplements are issued every four years). Note the online version of *The New York Times* does not even begin to cover the vast scope of the print volumes that go back to 1851. Furthermore, as the compilers claim, "a multitude of names are buried under the many headings of a general nature, such as obituaries, missing persons, concerts, theater. Under these conditions, the use of *The New York Times Index* is no longer a matter of library science but rather of super clairvoyance."

Afterthought: For the past several years the nation's newspaper publishers have reported circulation decreases. Figures from the Audit Bureau of Circulation—which is the nonpartisan guide to such statistics—show annual drops from 1 or 2 percent to as much as 5 or 10 percent. The sharpest declines are in the nation's large urban areas. Why the steady decline? "The newspaper industry has had since the invention of television, a weakening circulation picture," an industry analyst reports.[28] Hardly surprising, but of interest to reference librarians who may be putting too much faith in the average reader's interest in newspapers as sources of information. Add to this grim picture, the decline of trust by many people in the media and there is a definite shift in reference sources away from newspapers and related media.

Current Events

Online: Facts on File. New York: Facts on File News Services, 1980 to date, weekly, www.fofweb.com. $1,350. Also available on OCLC.
CD: 1980 to date, quarterly. $795.
Print: 1940 to date, weekly. $525.

Essentially, the service gives the librarian objective summaries of the events of the past week, month, or, in the cumulation, the year. Emphasis is on news events in the United States, with international coverage related, for the most part, to American affairs. Material is gathered mainly from 100 major newspapers, magazines, and government sources. Data is then condensed into objective, short, factual reports.

The publisher notes a "few ways" the service may be used: Check dates in the index, skim the weekly issues to prepare for current affairs tests, read Supreme Court decisions in the digest, or scan the "U.S. and World Affairs" column for ideas for short papers. There are countless other uses, although the most frequent call is for specific current data.

The online *Facts on File* offers a quick route to locating precisely the time and place an event took place. The online database may be searched not only with key words and subjects, but also by primary issues, events and names of people in the news. Hence, one can enter the Kentucky Derby or Presidential Election Results to get a quick coverage over a number of years, or for a specific year. There are close to 300,000 cross references to speed matters alone. There are numerous links, including reference to *Facts on File* print volumes. The latter is useful for background information, i.e., primarily before 1980.

Facts on File, when it turns to online service, offers several content features: (1) *Facts on File* itself back about 20 years to 1981; (2) *Editorial*

[28]"Newspaper Industry Fails to Stem Circulation Drop," *The New York Times,* May 4, 1999, p. C8.

on File (a self-descriptive name) by the same publisher; (3) *Issues and Controversies on File* and *Today's Science on File;* (4) Selected contents from the *World Almanac* and *Funk & Wagnalls Encyclopedia;* (5) Plus a week of the English wire service Reuters. Given all of this and the simple descriptive paragraphs about the news in each issue of the print edition are expanded forward and backward in time. Also, related events are tied together where necessary. Incidentally, each of these various components may be searched by itself or in combinations, and there is the usual basic key word or advance type of searching patterns.

With all of that, let it be said that because there is almost too much online, it may be simpler to thumb through the print version of *Facts on File* for a direct, easy to find place of information. Online is great, but in many cases may be an overkill, particularly for the reference librarian seeking a name, date, etc.

The printed twice-monthly, blue-colored print index is arranged under four primary headings: "U.S. Affairs," "International Affairs," "World News," and "Miscellaneous." Then, under these one finds broad subject headings such as "Finance," "Economics," and so on. Every two weeks, each month, and then quarterly and annually, a detailed index is issued which covers previous issues. There is also a *Five-Year Master News Index,* published since 1950.

The subject index (which includes numerous names of people in the news) features the brief tag line name of the item, then gives reference to the date of the event, the page in the issue of *Facts on File,* as well as the margin letter and column number. For example, under Yugoslavia, one might find, "Austerity measures OK'd 5–15" (date, May 15, 1999) "367 page number G3" (the letter on the margin of page 367 and the third column).

At the end of the index is a "Corrections" section. This gives the correct information by page and column, for example: "148A1 chairman (not president)" and "358D2 Symms (not Simms)." This feature is found in every issue.

Many Western countries have similar services, although the one most used in American libraries is Keesing's (London: Longman Group Ltd., *Keesing's Contemporary Archives,* 1993 to date, monthly, price varies). It is available electronically and in print from 1931 to date, and comes out monthly as well. The emphasis differs from *Facts on File* in two important respects: (1) It covers primarily the United Kingdom, Europe, and the British Commonwealth. (2) Detailed subject reports in certain areas are frequently included (the reports are by experts and may delay the weekly publication by several days). Also, there are full texts of important speeches and documents. However, *Keesing's* does not cover in any detail many events the publisher considers "less important," such as sports, art exhibitions, and movies (all of these subjects are included in *Facts on File*).

Arrangement is by country, territory, or continent, with some broad subject subheadings, such as "Religion," "Aviation," and "Fine Arts." An index is issued which is cumulated quarterly and annually.

SUGGESTED READING

Brown, M. Suzanne et al., "A new comparison of the *Current Index to Journals in Education* and the *Education Index*: a deep analysis of indexing." *Journal of Academic Librarianship*, May, 1999, pp. 216–222. While this is a basic examination of two similar indexes, the student will find it of most interest for the research methodology employed. The approach to analysis of indexes could be used for any index or abstracting service. Not incidentally, the judges have some fascinating points to make about each of the indexes examined.

Burchinal, Lee G. "The Tale of Two ERICs," *Journal of the American Society for Information Science*, vol. 51, no. 6, 2000, pp. 567–575. A brief history of the development of ERIC from 1959 to 1967. "The history of the two ERICs illustrates how knowledge and expertise...shape the development of a major national information service."

Foust, Dean, "Go, Speed Trader," *Yahoo Internet Life*, April, 1999, pp. 107–109, 133. A quick overview of day trading and how it is done on the Net. Author suggests several reliable sites to "beat the odds." Reference librarians should be aware of the process, if not the results.

Hodge, Gail and Jessica Milstead, *Computer Support to Indexing*, Philadelphia: National Federation of Abstracting and Information Services, 1998. Drawing upon experience and interviews with database publishers and producers, the authors have drawn up a blueprint of digital indexing—including developments on the Internet. This updates a 1992 study.

Jacso, Peter, "Analyzing the Journal Coverage of Abstracting/Indexing Databases..." *Library & Information Science Research*, no. 2, 1998, pp. 133–151. A scholarly study which shows the numerous drawbacks to total reliance on standard indexing and abstracting services. Most indexing fails in that the material indexed is much later than the date of the index itself indicates; the indexing is haphazard and may or may not cover what the user needs; and there is too much duplication.

Krumenaker, Larry, "Check 'em All: The Mathematics of Online Newspapers," *Searcher*, May, 2000, pp. 38–47. Here is practical advice on how to search DIALOG and two other services to find all available newspapers online. Secrets of finding the best ones are indicated as well.

Paul, Nora, "News Archives on the Web for the "Big Five," *Searcher*, June, 1999, pp. 32. An examination of the archive online policies of the five major newspapers, from *The New York Times* to *The Wall Street Journal*, indicates few have archives which go back further than 1984 and some are only from the 1990s. The author evaluates each paper individually not only in terms of archives but ease of finding the same material in each.

Platt, Nina, "Legal Periodical Indexes on the Web," *Database*, October/November, 1998, pp. 45–50. An analysis, in detail, of four legal indexes, including the Wilson *Index to Legal Periodicals & Books*. While of interest for particulars about legal indexes, the approach, the evaluation methods might be used to judge any type of index.

Tenopir, Carol, "Getting What You Pay For?" *Library Journal*, February 1, 2000. Why is a commercial online indexing service a best bet, and what questions should the librarian ask in determining which service(s) to purchase? Here representatives from major concerns make suggestions which librarians should tell those in charge of funding the library services.

Woudhuysen, H.R. "Vandals of Colindale," *The Times Literary Supplement*, August 18, 2000, pp. 14–15. A detailed story of how old newspapers, many dating back to the 19th century, are systematically being destroyed in favor of their image on microfilm rather than in print. The focus is on the activities of the British Library. A similar piece about the destruction of papers in American libraries was described by Nicholson Baker in the July 24th issue of *The New Yorker*, pp. 42–61. (Baker earlier wrote on the destruction of card catalogs in American libraries.) Critics brand the newspaper activity a crime. Others see it as a necessity to save space. This author is on the side of the former argument.

CHAPTER SEVEN
ENCYCLOPEDIAS: GENERAL
AND SUBJECT SETS[1]

Today's general encyclopedia is the first place the student or octoge-
narian turns for concise, complete, and usually current information
about anything in the universe, and beyond. From an explanation of an
adder to geographical characteristics of Zaire, the encyclopedia is every
person's key to answering perplexing questions. In a single place the
librarian finds answers to questions which might take considerable time
to find in a random search of the Internet. The wedding of the Net with
online encyclopedias is a major commercial success. Just how useful the
marriage is for librarians will be discussed later.

There are two basic encyclopedia types, general and subject. The
first, with which this chapter begins, considers data from all branches
of knowledge. The second is specialized and narrows its focus to a single subject. The subject set is recognition of the fragmentation of knowledge, an effort to make some sense out of smaller and smaller areas of
information. A question explains the difference: "Why can't we all just
love one another?" The general encyclopedia will define and explain
"love." The subject, from a set on philosophy to religion to psychoanalysis
to literature, answers according to hierarchies of opinion and research.

[1]For an abbreviated history of encyclopedias see, naturally, any encyclopedia. See, too,
the chapter on encyclopedias in Bill Katz, *Cuneiform to Computer: a History of Reference Sources*
(Latham, MD: Scarecrow Press, 1998). For a single example of an early encyclopedia see:
Omne Bonum, a fourteenth-century encyclopedia of universal knowledge. This was made
available by Harvey Miller in two volumes in 1999.

The answer is limited to findings of a single or part of a discipline.[2] The division between general and subject encyclopedias occurred relatively late. Encyclopedia is defined as a circle of learning, or a work which has information on all branches of knowledge. This definition held from the earliest Roman set until about the end of the eighteenth century when the last person who was reported to know everything (possibly from reading or editing an encyclopedia) died. "After that encyclopedias became irreversibly specialized. The scope of human knowledge having surpassed the binder's embrace, partiality will always be an irrevocable feature of expertise."[3] And then was born the subject set where a narrow area could be covered completely. General sets then, as now, were for a quick overview, not for in-depth data.

Purpose

Any encyclopedia will usually include: *(a)* detailed survey articles, often with bibliographies, in certain fields or areas; *(b)* explanatory material that is normally shorter; *(c)* brief informational data such as the birth and death dates of famous people, geographical locations, and historical events. This scope makes the encyclopedia ideal for reference work.

At the child's level, there's a misconception: an encyclopedia, no matter how good, is not a substitute for additional reading or for a collection of supporting reference books. In their enthusiasm, some salespeople and advertising copywriters are carried away with the proposition that an encyclopedia-oriented child is an educated child.

THE ELECTRONIC VS. PRINT ENCYCLOPEDIAS

Several general encyclopedia publishers have, or are about to give up print editions.[4] Why? Because it is more economical to publish electronic versions—after all consider the number of trees saved. Also, the public is used to online or CD-ROM editions which are 10 to 20 times less costly than print.

---

[2] Can anyone give a single, complete answer to the question, "Why can't we all just love one another?" A cursory search indicates no satisfactory response from either the general or the specific set. The lesson: not all questions have answers, or at least not all queries have responses which solicit a consensus. What does the librarian do in this situation? The response: admit she can't find a definite answer, but suggest several places the user may search. And if time, credibility and patience is not a problem, the Internet is a point of departure.

[3] Frederick Raphael, "The Seduction of Reason," *Times Literary Supplement,* June 26, 1998, p. 3. This opens a long, three-page review of the subject set: *Routledge Encyclopedia of Philosophy*. It is an excellent example of how to write a detailed encyclopedia review.

[4] When the *Britannica* went online for free—supported by advertising—it was announced the print edition no longer would be published. Or at least this was the plan. Also, *Compton's*

A single or two CD's solve the problem of bookcases for bound volumes.[5] And rather than rely on yearbooks, the buyer can count on the publisher sending an update, for a minimum cost, at least once each year.

Once the encyclopedia is available electronically (either on a CD-ROM or online) all the familiar reasons for their success is evident. There is animation and video clips (150 to 250); illustrations and maps (10,000 to 25,000); sound (10 to 20 hours); and numerous bells and whistles to entertain and inform. Serious quests for information are helped by Boolean searching (no matter what it is called by the publisher) which permits finding data by keywords and related words and phrases. A complete set may be searched in seconds as compared with taking down volume by volume and cruising the index. It is a simple matter to shift a quote or a full page or two to a paper the reader is writing.

Thousands of links to related websites can turn a five-minute search for information on Haydn's string quartets into hours, if not days of expanding, overwhelming data. Links are somewhat similar to looking for a definition in a dictionary and then wandering up and down the page(s) for other discoveries.

The majority of popular, general encyclopedias are on the Web. They all suffer from the same faults and delights. The plus side: (1) Most are more current than either the print or CD-ROM. They are updated monthly or quarterly. The problem is that the updates are irregular in quality and stress leading newspaper and television news stories rather than revisions in depth of less sensational material. (2) All have links to articles and Web pages, often with illustrations. This considerably broadens the scope of the encyclopedia as well as acts as a filter. The assumption is editors pick out only the very best sites.

The pleasant surprise is that as of late 1999 the *Encyclopaedia Britannica* is free online. (The loss of the standard $50 a year fee is to be made up by anxious advertisers, or so goes the theory.) The question is how many publishers will follow the *Britannica* lead. The obvious answer: they will follow it if competition dictates and if a profit is to be made from another source other than subscribers. (Note: No matter what follows, as of early 2000 all standard sets offer a free trial period online which can be useful to students.)

---

sold its print work to another firm. *Collier's* electronic rights were purchased by Microsoft. Neither is to continue in a print format. Other companies are expected to follow this lead away from print.

[5]By 2000 all general encyclopedias on CD-ROM are in a standard (single-disc) and a deluxe (2-disc) version. The move to two discs is illustrated by *Compton's* which offers the same text on both the one- and two-disc sets, but for the latter offers twice as much in the way of photos and illustrations as well as more videos and animation. The price for the double is usually no more than $10 or $20 more for the single. The double is always a better buy.

Grove, the publisher of numerous subject encyclopedias, offers a perfect example of why the electronic encyclopedia will defeat most print editions. (1) *The New Grove Dictionary of Opera Online* (www.grove opera.com) eventually will have full music clips to illustrate major entries. Read and listen. (2) *The Grove Dictionary of Art Online* (www.groveart.com) in its 34 volumes has 15,000 images along with 750 maps. But online, thanks to links to various museums and art libraries, it makes well over 100,000 images available. (3) The electronic version is a steep $1,500 a year online, but the print work is from $6,000 to $8,800. Most large libraries have both. (4) Online searching is faster and more efficient than using the printed index and numerous cross references.

The Grove features, from audio to easy use, are features of all general and subject electronic encyclopedias these days. (True, not all subject works are available electronically, but this, too, will change in the next decade). At any rate, even a few of the features listed for Grove explains the popularity of the electronic vs. print encyclopedia.

Reviewers of the electronic works, as well as librarians, are fond of comparing how long it takes to find X or Y in a CD-ROM or in print.

Here is a typical comparison of searching with a CD-ROM and a print encyclopedia: "We set two researchers—one with the 12-volume *Encyclopedia,* and one with the *Britannica CD-ROM*—the task of seeing how long it took them to find the answers to these three questions:

1. Who led the first Roman invasion of Britain and when? (Julius Caesar in 1st century BC).

2. What are the three bones in the middle ear called and what are their functions? (Auditory ossicles: malleus/hammer, incus/anvil, stapes/stirrup.)

3. In which year was *War and Peace* published, and how old was Tolstoy? (1869 and 41.)

The book:

1. Took three references and five minutes to find.

2. Two minutes and two references to find.

3. Found on first search, six minutes.

The CD:

1. Found under 'Romans AND Britain' in three minutes.

2. Difficult to find specific details. Took 15 minutes to find.

3. Three minutes.[6]

[6]*The Independent* (London), January 13, 1998, p. 10.

Speed is guaranteed electronically when hard to find, usually not indexed words, phrases, and ideas are lost somewhere in the print volumes. The searcher enters key words and normally up comes the required data. This may take no more than a few seconds or a minute, while searching the print work may take much longer. Conversely, someone looking for a date, a brief biography of a famous person, or a short explanation of a common process, may find it easier in the print set. One simply turns to the word or words, conveniently in alphabetical order and short on main entries in the text, to find what may take more time electronically.

Some 50 percent of American homes do not have facilities to run a digital encyclopedia, i.e., lack computers. Being unfamiliar with the electronic approach they rely on the library's familiar printed volumes. Possibly a more important justification for maintaining a print set is that it is more satisfying (at least for much of the older public) to read and examine illustrations in the familiar old format.

A working librarian and media specialist sums it up:

> "I lament the demise of print...and here's why: Convenience: The book always works and never crashes! Students frequently want just facts and all the bells and whistles that entertained them when they had free time...only slow them down and get in the way when they are assigned research. One of our most frequently used CD-ROM encyclopedias is an older, text-only version of *World Book*....Management: Anyone who is responsible for monitoring 27 teenagers searching the Internet on an unfiltered network knows that curiosity and hormones play a bigger role in their lives than an assignment on the early Romans, and their searches reflect that. No matter how fantastic the online encyclopedia, it can't compete with the World Wrestling Federation or sex.com....Expense: The CD-ROM encyclopedias may be inexpensive, but maintaining, upgrading, and replacing the equipment to run better multimedia versions are not. We can't keep up.[7]

CD-ROM vs. Online

The prediction that CD-ROMs soon will go the way of much print in libraries—and in homes—is not so true for encyclopedias. Actually, more people probably use the CD-ROM encyclopedia than online. Why? Answer: (1) Only 20 to 30 percent of computer owners have access to online in their homes. They all have access to CD-ROMs, and for this reason this format often is preferred. (2) Frequently the CD has more features than online, i.e., videos, sounds, etc. as it is possible technologically to do this with a CD, but only at much expense and time online. (3) Publishers see a profit in CDs, while they are busy giving away information for free online. (4) And

---

[7]Nancy D. Swider, "Letters" to the editor, *Library Journal*, February 1, 1999, p. 8. Ms. Swider is a librarian at Goodrich H.S., Fond du Lac, WI.

there are other reasons from ease of use to low cost which ensures the prob-able life of CD encyclopedias long after print versions have disappeared. In time, to be sure, the CD will give way to online, but they may take much longer than now expected. This is to explain why more attention is given in this section to CDs than in other text sections.

Online/Internet: Warning

All of the Online/Internet standard sets are acceptable. Be warned: the majority of others (and there are scores of "encyclopedias" on the Net) are worthless, at least for reference work. Most are subject sets which claim to cover everything from art to zoology.

A cruise via any of the search engines reveals scores of sites with "encyclopedia" as part of their titles. Rarely are these either traditional works, or an expression of the true meaning of the term. More often they simply use "encyclopedia" to explain a list of related data—which is not unusual for numerous printed works. For example, the *Panic Encyclopedia* (www.freedonia.com:80/panic) is an amusing answer to "why panic?" Alphabetically one finds short entries for such things as "panic cowboy" or "panic jeans." There are hundreds of other examples, equally fun, or often simply worthless.

True, there are few reliable free encyclopedias on the Net. On the other hand, expand the Web to mean "circle of knowledge" and the whole of the Web is a vast encyclopedia.[8] In that sense (and if "encyclopedia" is ignored as a valid descriptor for most free sites), the whole Web is both a general and subject encyclopedia.

Thousands of Net sites can be considered encyclopedic in nature if not in name. Many of these are good to excellent.

One example will suffice: *NASA Homepage* (www.nasa.gov). While "encyclopedia' is nowhere about, the so-called "home page" is a true sub-ject encyclopedia of space-related information from the authoritative NASA. Here one finds everything from shuttle flight schedules to the his-tory of space and such things as lunar and planetary exploration.

EVALUATING ENCYCLOPEDIAS

Most librarians and, for that matter, laypersons will turn to one or two sources for objective evaluations of encyclopedias in both print and elec-tronic formats. These are trusted, tried, and true.

---

[8]Perhaps a better descriptive in the tradition of searching is that the Web is a vast "index." And, in fact, search engines are complicated online indexes to, yes, encyclopedic knowledge online. None of this matters, of course, but it does remind librarians that the more innovation the more déjà vu.

A basic source of reviews is the well-known "Reference Books Bulletin" in *The Booklist,* which is discussed earlier in this text. Almost every, or every other, issue has a lengthy review either of a general set or, more likely, of a subject encyclopedia. These are detailed, objective, and meticulously documented. The most useful current check for the standard sets is offered by the same service in the mid September 15th issue. "Encyclopedia Update" includes material previously published about the basic 10 to 12 general sets. There is a succinct summary of the primary points of each print and electronic title.[9]

EVALUATION POINTS[10]

Librarians make up their own minds about which are the better encyclopedias. Decision is based primarily on daily use, but there are the usual specific points about all reference works to consider in a systematic evaluation: (1) *scope,* or subject coverage, emphasis, and the intended audience; (2) *authority,* which includes accuracy and reliability; (3) *viewpoint* and objectivity; (4) *writing style;* (5) *recency,* including revision plans, if any, of the publisher; (6) arrangement and entry; (7) *index* with reference to how one gains access to information in the set; (8) *format,* including the physical format and illustrations; (9) *cost;* and (10) the presence of *bibliographies.*

Advertising dictates change, and this extends to the electronic encyclopedias. Almost every year there is a variation on a particular title. The only constant seems to be the name of the publisher, i.e., "Microsoft," "Grolier," "World Book," etc. Name variation examples from year to year: *(a) Compton's Interactive Encyclopedia* to *Compton's Encyclopedia, Deluxe Edition; (b) Microsoft Encarta Multimedia Encyclopedia* to *Microsoft Encarta Encyclopedia Deluxe; (c) New Grolier Interactive Encyclopedia* to *Grolier Multimedia Encyclopedia Deluxe.* Which is to say, by any other name an encyclopedia is an encyclopedia and the librarian soon is able to distinguish change in name (always in flux).

Scope

The scope of the specialized encyclopedia is evident in its name, and becomes even more obvious with use. The scope of the general encyclopedia is dictated primarily by two considerations, age level and emphasis.

---

[9]This is republished with additional points on the evaluation of encyclopedias, both print and electronic, as *Purchasing an Encyclopedia: 12 Points to Consider* (Chicago: American Library Association, 1990 to date, annual.

[10]These are points used to evaluate a print set, but the content in electronic format is much the same. Hence, the points are applicable to sets in other formats.

Age Level. The children's encyclopedias, such as the *World Book*, are tied to curriculum. Consequently, they include more in-depth material on subjects of general interest to grade school and high school students than does an adult encyclopedia such as the *Britannica*. Most encyclopedia publishers aim their strongest advertising at adults with children. All the standard sets claim that an audience ranging from grades 6 to 12 can understand and use their respective works. This may be true of the exceptionally bright child, but the librarian is advised to check the real age compatibility of the material before purchase, not merely advertised age level.

There are two consequences of attempting to be all things to all age levels: (1) In many adult-level encyclopedias, when the material is shortened for easier comprehension by a child, the adult loses; and (2) the effort to clarify for the lower age level frequently results in an oversimplified approach to complex issues.[11]

If age level dictates one approach to scope, the emphasis of the editor accounts for the other. At one time, there were greater variations in focus than there are today; one set may have been especially good for science, another for literature. Today, the emphasis is essentially a matter of deciding what compromise will be made between scholarship and popularity. Why, for example, is as much space given to the subject of advertising as to democracy in most adult encyclopedias? This is not to argue the merit of any particular topic, but to point out that examining emphasis is a method of determining scope.

Online CD-ROM Scope. Electronically, scope is now a question of determining how much more/less one publisher has in a given CD-ROM or online than another. Comparing it with the print is no longer applicable. The real question (discussed in more detail under "format"), is how much extraneous material should be added to the encyclopedia. In addition to the video bites, sound, etc. almost all sets for young people in the high school to college add standard reference books from dictionaries and atlases to books of quotations and almanacs. Are they needed? How well is the extra material integrated into the searching patterns?

Authority

A major question to ask about any reference book has to do with its authority. If it is authoritative, it usually follows that it will be up to date, accurate, and relatively objective.

---

[11]In 1999 the *Britannica* wrote to would-be customers: "As an intelligent adult.. .*Britannica* CD enables you to do things you never thought possible." A few paragraphs later: "Speaking of children, parents agree *Britannica* CD is an outstanding educational resource." The junk mail letter is typical. Publishers want it all ways. The set is as suitable for people in old folks' homes as kids learning to walk.

Authority is evident in the names of the scholars and experts who sign the articles or who are listed as contributors somewhere in the set. It is also associated with the names of the publishers who distribute the sets.[12] There are three quick tests for authority: (1) recognition of a prominent name, particularly the author of the best, more recent book on the subject; (2) a quick check of a field known to the reader to see whether leaders in that field are represented in the contributor list; and (3) finally, determination of whether a contributor's qualifications (as noted by position, degrees, occupation, and so on) relate to the article(s).

A reader gains an indication of the encyclopedia's revision policy and age from knowledge about the authors. Some contributors may literally be dead, and although a certain number of deceased authorities is perfectly acceptable, too many in this category would indicate either overabundant plagiarism from older sets or lack of meaningful revision.

Any encyclopedia unfortunately will contain some errors and some omissions. Most are quickly corrected when brought to the attention of a publisher. The real test, of course, is the number of such mistakes. The sets considered here, while not perfect, can rarely be faulted for more than a few errors.

Viewpoint and Objectivity

Since general encyclopedias are published as profit ventures, they aim to attract the widest audience and to insult or injure no one. Despite their sometimes pious claims of objectivity on grounds of justice for all, they are motivated by commercial reasons. Only after many years of active prodding by women did encyclopedia publishers respond to this segment of the market and make a conscious effort to curb sexual bias.

Blatant sexual and racial bias have been eliminated from standard, acceptable encyclopedias, but the slate is not completely clean or neutral. One way to check this particular area is to look up names of prominent women, and particularly from African American and Hispanic backgrounds, to see how well (if at all) they are represented. Check, too, such obvious articles as sexual harassment, homosexuality, and abortion. A similar investigation may be carried on for other controversial areas from hypnosis to euthanasia.

Another way to consider the question of viewpoints is to see what the editor chooses to include or to exclude, to emphasize or to deemphasize.

---

[12]The number of publishers, the number of sets (in print or electronic form) of general encyclopedias continues to shrink. The general set publishers approved by the American Library Association are less than a half dozen, e.g., *Grolier, Britannica, World Book, Compton's* and *Microsoft.* The latter has swallowed up both *Collier's* and *Funk & Wagnall's* electronic formats. It is likely that in time the general works will be controlled only by one or two publishers.

Nothing can date an encyclopedia faster than antiquated articles about issues and ideas either no longer acceptable or of limited interest. An encyclopedia directed at the Western reader can scarcely be expected to give as much coverage to, let us say, Egypt as to New York State. Yet, to include only a passing mention of Egypt would not be suitable either, particularly in view of ancient history and the emergence of Africa as a new world force.

Online CD-ROM Authority & Viewpoint. All of the rules above apply to the electronic formats for encyclopedias. And while there is no problem with determining authority by reputation of the publisher and authors in a print work, sometimes this is difficult for the electronic encyclopedia. Why? Because often neither the publisher nor the author's authority is visible. This is not true, of course, of sets with print counterparts; but it is a major problem for those where: *(a)* There is no indication who is the publisher or the sponsor of the encyclopedia in itself, and/or of one of the links used by the encyclopedia. Even where a name is given, often there is no way of evaluating legitimacy or authority of publisher or author. *(b)* Factual data often lacks support of citation, or, for that matter, date, author, etc. *(c)* Advertising at a site may indicate a definite bias. *(d)* And it often is difficult to ascertain whether the encyclopedia, site, Web page, or whatever is the work of someone anxious to put over a point of view (often a crank) or an honest effort to inform.

All of the methods of evaluating authority and objectivity employed for printed works should be used for electronic titles, and, as indicated, with added precautions.

Writing Style

When one considers the writing style of today's encyclopedia, one notices that none of the general sets is aimed at the expert. Recognizing that laypeople considerably outnumber scholars and therefore purchase considerably more volumes, encyclopedia firms tend to cater to their market in a relatively standard fashion: Contributors are given certain topics and outlines of what is needed and expected. Their manuscripts are then submitted to the encyclopedia's editors (editorial staffs of the larger encyclopedias range from 100 to 200 full-time persons), who revise, cut, and query—all to make the contributions understandable to the average reader. The extent of editing varies depending on each encyclopedia's audience. It can be extensive for children's works (where word difficulty and length of sentence are almost as important as content), or it can be limited for major contributors to an adult volume.

Serving as a bridge between contributor and reader, the editor strives for readability by reducing complicated vocabulary and jargon to terms understandable to the lay reader or young person. The purpose is to rephrase specialized thought into common language without diminishing the thought—or insulting an eminent contributor. In the humanities and the social sciences, this usually works. The contributing scholars must be willing to have their initials appended to a more accessible version of their work.

Recency: Continuous Revision

As most large encyclopedia companies issue new printings of their sets, or revised individual volumes each year, they also incorporate updated changes. Electronic databases make this process considerably easier; editors can enter new materials, delete, and correct without completely resetting the whole article or section.

No matter what the technological procedures employed for updating, the librarian should know: (1) Few general encyclopedias use the "edition" as an indication of the relative currency of the work. For example, the *Britannica's* 14 edition was just that from 1929 until the 15 edition in 1974. (2) The relative date of the printing will be found on the verso of the title page, but this in itself means little because there is no accurate measure of how much of any given encyclopedia is revised or how often it is done. Most large publishers claim to revise about 5 to 10 percent of the material each year. The claim to continuous revision is a major selling point for publishers involved with selling sets to libraries. They reason that no library is going to buy a new set of the same encyclopedia (loss or damage aside) unless there has been substantial revision. (3) Most encyclopedias do revise material with each printing or electronic update. A printing normally is done at least once or twice a year.

Until the advent of the electronic work, publishers relied on yearbooks to keep the sets current. This was more a psychological and sales crutch than a real effort to update. (See a later section for a brief discussion of yearbooks.)

Digital Recency. Normally the digital encyclopedia, as numerous other reference works, are updated in one of two ways: (1) The publisher simply sends, usually each year, an updated version of the CD encyclopedia. This is at a reduced cost based on the initial purchase and the agreement to continue buying the update each year or so. (2) The publisher offers daily to monthly updates via the Internet. Online updates consists of revised articles and Web links. Each month the publisher provides articles that reflect new developments in science, international affairs, etc.

It is one thing to claim that modern technologically allows rapid, efficient updates. It is another to have the human staff about to make those changes. Reviews show time after time that despite the wonders of the digital age, most publishers are no more likely to update materials than they did for the print cousins.

In the rush to be up-to-date, encyclopedia publishers make way for the new by chopping out the old. In itself this is reasonable, but it has definite disadvantages for librarians who may be seeking historical data, biographies and material the publisher believes no longer of interest to readers. Medium to large libraries, and particularly those used for research, meet the problem by maintaining older sets.[13] Yes, but how does one maintain older material which appears online and the next day or year disappears? This question is yet to be answered.

Arrangement and Entry

The traditional arrangement of a printed encyclopedia follows the familiar alphabetical approach to material, with numerous cross-references and an index. Average users are accustomed to the alphabetical order of information, or the *specific entry*. Here, the information is broken down into small, specific parts, but the data are arranged alphabetically.

Digital Arrangement. The electronic format is not concerned with arrangement *per se;* but the user is placed in the position of depending on a reliable software search program to find what he or she might discover by using cross-references, alphabetical order of an index. In this sense, "arrangement" is critical for the electronic version. There must be numerous avenues of search from Boolean logic to an actual index.

Index

Some publishers have concluded that, with suitable *see* and *see also* references, the alphabetical arrangement should serve to eliminate the index.

---

[13]The research library inevitably includes older works and particularly various editions of the *Britannica*. The 11th ed. (1911), for example, is a great assemblage of 19th-century learning not found in current sets. A working academic librarian, Ms. Susan Kraats, gives two examples of why an older work is of value: (1) Had a reference query yesterday about an author named Burmann who wrote a treatise called Anthologia Veterum Latinorum Epigrammatum et Poematum. Wanted to know full name, nationality of the author, other works, etc. So I proudly found the work on OCLC, and saw the name was Pietro Burmanni...Of course, as it turns out, it was really Pieter Burmann, (Secundus), an 18th c. Dutch scholar. But what I did not know was the information is in the 11th ed. of *Encyclopaedia Britannica.* (2) The Swiss mathematician, Leonhard Euler in the latest edition of the *Britannica* is given full credit for his many contributions to his art. Factual, informative, but lacking in any indication of his human qualities. For that turn to the longer article in the 11th edition. Here are details of his life such as "He died of apoplexy on the 18th of September 1783, while he was amusing himself at tea with one of his grandchildren." And: "He could repeat the *Aeneid* of Virgil from the beginning to the end without hesitation, and indicate the first and last line of every page of the edition which he used."

The strong argument for an index is simply that a single article may contain dozens of names and events which cannot be located unless there is a detailed, separate index volume. A detailed index is an absolute necessity.

Digital Index. Searching an electronic encyclopedia normally is done with keywords and/or Boolean logic. An index is not essential. With that, though, it can be a great help, particularly to discover terms related alphabetically to the one being sought. Also an electronic index helps to clarify spelling errors, at least if the first one or two letters is correct. Better systems have at least modified indexes as well as the traditional cross-references.

Format

A good format covers such points as appropriate type sizes, typefaces, illustrations, binding, and total arrangement. When considering format, evaluate the following:

Illustrations (Photographs, Diagrams, Charts, and Maps). Nothing will tip off the evaluator faster as to how current the encyclopedia is than a cursory glance at the illustrations. But just because the illustrations are current, they are not necessarily suitable unless they relate directly to the text and to the interests of the reader. The librarian might ask: Do the illustrations consider the age of the user, or do they consist of figures or drawings totally foreign to, say, a twelve-year-old? Do they emphasize important matters, or are they too general? Are they functional, or simply attractive? Are the captions adequate?

Maps are an important part of any encyclopedia and vary in number. Many of the maps are prepared by Rand McNally or C.S. Hammond and are generally good to excellent. In the adult sets, the major maps appear frequently in a separate volume, often with the index. The young adults and children's encyclopedias usually have the maps in the text, and if this is the case, there should be reference to them in the index and cross-references as needed. The librarian should check to see how many and what types of maps are employed to show major cities of the world, historical development, political changes, land use, weather, and so on. The actual evaluation of the maps is discussed in the chapter on geography.

Most digital editions follow a standard pattern. The *Grolier Multimedia Encyclopedia* has some 1200 maps (*Americana* about 900; *World Book* about 850, etc.). Most can be printed out in either black and white or in full color. All have a "drill down" feature which allows the reader to move from a large map of a country to a particular state, county, city, etc. There are links, as well, to political and thematic maps throughout the text. And there are numerous twists to the maps. *WorldBook*, for example, permits overlays, which show everything about a given area from population to climate and primary industries. Useful as all of this may be, a print map often is easier to use and, by and large, gives a better overview of the related areas.

Size of Type. The type size is important, as is the spacing between lines and the width of the columns. All these factors affect the readability of the work.

Binding. Encyclopedias should be bound in a fashion that is suitable for rough use, particularly in a library. Conversely, buyers should be warned that a frequent method of raising the price of an encyclopedia is to change the user for a so-called deluxe binding which is often no better, and in fact may be less durable, than the standard library binding.

Volume Size. Finally, consideration should be given to the physical size of the volume. Is it comfortable to hold? Equally important, can it be opened without strain on the binding?

Online CD-ROM Format: While binding and volume size is of no interest to the publisher of an electronic encyclopedia, everything else holds. The quality and the up-to-date features associated with good illustrations are important. Here, though, add the availability of media features from sound tracks to video clips and animation. Of course publishers are more than aware of the selling potential of such format features and these days it is not so much a matter of finding them as evaluating their quality.

Using the ubiquitous heading "deluxe" or "encyclopedia suites," publishers now add extra reference books. For example, the *Grolier Multimedia Reference Suite* includes, among other items, *Bartlett's Familiar Quotations,* the *Hammond Atlas of the World* and an almanac. How much of all this added material, this "reference suite" is valuable? Each library, each individual must ask the question themselves. But it may be more academic than a real query. Why? Because there is so much virtually given away, i.e., the CD-ROM sets are well below $40. Despite the low cost the frustration of getting from point A to point B may not be worth even the low price. A simple print encyclopedia may be much more efficient, often easier to use.

Cost

Several general sets are now free on the Internet, e.g., *Britannica, Encarta,* etc. More will follow. This may or may not be healthy for libraries depending on objective data, but it is a boon for individuals and for underfinanced libraries. Meanwhile, all libraries should have both print and digital versions available.

Not only do prices vary dramatically from printed set to set, but they can range from under $1,000 to several multiples of that figure for precisely the same work. Realizing the public relations aspect of sales to libraries, publishers of general sets usually give relatively good discounts. For example, and this is true of all major sets considered here, *The Encyclopedia Americana* is about $1,000 for libraries and schools. Retail, it is priced at $1,400. *The World Book's* retail price is from $560 to $679. For libraries it is $550.

Libraries buy only about 5 to 6 percent of all print encyclopedias sold, and only about 1 percent of electronic versions. Still, the value to a publisher is not so much in the sales as in the seal of approval. If the library has it, it must be good—and with that the individual rushes out to buy a copy of the library encyclopedia or encyclopedias.

The same green light encourages laypersons to purchase subject sets. Here, though, the library is often a key factor in the financial success or failure of a work. The more esoteric and expensive subject sets may be sold almost exclusively to libraries. Without those sales the publisher shows a loss.

There is a confusion concerning the *real* price of the for-fee CD-ROM and/or online encyclopedia, although all are much lower in cost than the print versions, i.e., when print counterparts even exist. The average cost of a CD-ROM is around $30 to $50. Most CD-ROMs have two prices, or three: one for retail, one for libraries, and one for street sales, i.e., the lowest price usually offered by computer sales sources. Also, most are sold this way, but a few are sold only directly to libraries. Online prices for the fee sets differ wildly, and should be checked carefully with other libraries.

MAJOR ENCYCLOPEDIAS COMPARED

	Articles	Illus.	Maps	Video, etc.	Links	Index Entries
ADULT						
Americana						
Print	45,000	23,000	1,300	—	—	354,000
CD-ROM	45,000	2,180	830	—	155,000	—
Online	45,000	3,000	830	—	155,000	—
Britannica						
Print	70,000	25,000	2,000	—	—	790,000
CD-ROM	83,000	6,500	1,600	40	30,000	—
Online	80,000	10,000	various	various	144,000	—
ADULT/YOUNG ADULT						
Grolier (Academic American)						
Print	30,000	18,000	2,400	—	—	205,000
CD-ROM	37,000	15,000	1,200	177	26,000	—
Online	37,000	6,000	850	150	55,000	—

(continued)

	Articles	Illus.	Maps	Video, etc.	Links	Index Entries
Encarta (No print version)						
CD-ROM	42,000	18,400	628	165	21,500	—
Online	41,000	12,200	628	115	19,000	—
Funk&Wagnalls						
Print	32,000	16,000	800	—	—	135,000
CD-ROM	32,000	16,000	653	50	—	—
Online	32,000	12,000	653	100	—	—
Collier's						
Print	23,000	14,500	—	—	—	450,000
CD-ROM	23,000	18,000	400	110	3,000	—
Online	23,000	18,000	400	—	3,000	—
CHILDREN						
World Book						
Print	17,000	28,000	2,000	—	—	173,000
CD-ROM	20,000	9,500	1,060	122	15,000	—
Online	20,000	8,100	960	—	15,000	—
Compton's						
Print	40,000	23,000	480	—	—	30,000
CD-ROM	40,000	16,000	470	600	4,000	—
Online	40,000	15,000	704	—	4,000	—

Note: The number of articles says nothing about their length or worth. Comparison is of 2000. Figures change, but the relative differences, year in and year out, tend to be the same.

ADULT ENCYCLOPEDIAS[14]

Online: Britannica Online, Chicago: Encyclopedia Inc., 1994 to date, quarterly, http://britannica.com. Charge varies. *Britannica.com.* 1999 to date, www.eb.com. Free.
  CD: Britannica CD Multimedia Edition, 1993 to date, annual. $110.
  Print: The New Encyclopedia Britannica. 15th ed. 1771 to date. 32 vols. $1,500. *Ready Reference* version, 1998 to date, 12 vols. $500.

[14]Note: Here as throughout this chapter and in the text as a whole the addresses for subscription (i.e., for fee) online databases is that of the publisher, not of the actual database. To find for fee databases (indicated by a subscription price): *(a)* Turn to your library's Web page. The database usually is listed there with a link to the Web site. *(b)* Try another library in your area which offers users free access to for-fee databases. *(c)* Use the publisher's online address given here. You may have to search for the specific title in the publisher's online catalog or search system. Once found the publisher may offer a free hour or two for sample searches. Go directly to the address of the for-fee databases, i.e., those with "Free" shown.

Online: Encyclopedia Americana Online. Danbury, CT: Grolier Incorporated, 1997 to date, annual, http://ea.grolier/com. Rate varies.
CD: The Encyclopedia Americana on CD-ROM, 1995 to date, annual $179.
Print: The Encyclopedia Americana. 1883 to date, 30 vols. $995.

In late 1999 *Britannica* was the first to announce a standard set online for no charge. The free bait is to lure enough readers to justify, in turn, luring advertisers to pay the freight for what was lost in the previous $50 a year subscription.

As of mid-2000 the company offers two online versions. The *Britannica.com* version is not as sophisticated as *Britannica Online* which offers many more features and search patterns. Conversely, the latter set may cost the library several thousand dollars. There is not that much difference to warrant the library paying a fee, particularly where other sets are available online.

The *Britannica* is the best-known encyclopedia in the Western world. First published in 1768, it underwent many revisions and changes until the triumphant ninth edition in 1889. This was the "scholar's edition," with long articles from such contributors as Arnold, Swinburne, Huxley, and other major British minds of the nineteenth century. By the end of the twentieth century it has become increasingly popular but it remains the single, best encyclopedia for librarians and laypeople.

The two disc CD-ROM boasts the most text of any work (44 million words), but is weak on illustrations (some 10,000) and has a poor record of multimedia features which lack motion, color, and are harder to use than in most works. With that, though, it is the CD for the serious question, and especially the one which will require pages, rather than a few lines to respond properly to a query. There are about 30,000 Internet links. Added, too: *Rand McNally's New Millennium World Atlas* and *Merriam-Webster's Collegiate Dictionary.*

Drawing upon the print *Yearbook,* the "analyst" gives data on some 200 nations and regions. It is current. A sophisticated timeline allows comparisons (from literature to science) of events in history from its beginnings c. 9,000 BC to the present, as the online edition offers articles by famous contributors from previous editions.

Online. Free online, *Britannica* is the "best buy" of online sets. (True, there is a more costly for fee online version, but most libraries should be more than satisfied with the for free version. Period.) Considering its rapid updating, it is a required item for most libraries who heretofore might not have considered it because of the high cost of the print volumes. Primarily it is the complete print set, plus about 3,000 articles not found in the print edition (i.e., total of about 80,000 articles). There are few of the illustrations in the print version (i.e., about 10,000) as well as the full atlas. With that add some major features. First, and foremost, the online edition seems to be updated almost daily, particularly for first page newspaper type articles. Note, though, that updates often rely on Internet links rather than material in the encyclopedia. The standard background articles on people, places, and things follow the update pattern of the print volumes which is to say about 10 to 15 percent a year are overhauled. Second, there are current ready reference data (from the *Book of the Year*) on close to the world's 200 countries. Again, this frequently is updated. Third, there is the latest edition of *Merriam Webster's Collegiate Dictionary* (the firm is owned by the *Britannica*). Fourth, add essays, some quite lengthy, from previous editions of the *Britannica* ("Britannica Classics") which were written by such as Albert Einstein and Orville Wright. Primarily of historical interest, they, nevertheless, demonstrate vividly how the content and writing style of the older sets was directed at a more sophisticated audience than imagined in today's work. Also, 144,000 links to websites which are numerous but spotty at best.

The difference between the for fee and the free work online is $5 a month for the latter, i.e., for individuals. Libraries pay more. There is little real difference between the two, but some librarians may think the searching differences worth the price. (See: www.eb.com/diff.html for the publisher's explanation of the free/fee differences.)

All of this is pleasant enough, but from the point of view of a working librarian, just how good is the Net version of the *Britannica*, or for that matter any Net encyclopedia? A university librarian points out that "while there is much to recommend *Britannica Online* and similar reference titles on the Web (ease of access and use being most notable), they nonetheless are subject to the same limitations that plague the Web. Net congestion, accessing on older PCs, slow modems, and poor server connections can all affect not only search response time but also the amount of enjoyment and enlightenment one gets from the site."[15] Still, technology moves quickly and by the time the reader gets to this point perhaps the major problems will be overcome.

Britannica/Print

The text found in the printed volumes is identical, except for updates, to what is found in the electronic version. The major difference is that the print set has more illustrations, but lacks Net links. The printed set consists of:

1. A 12-volume *Micropaedia* which has short, factual ready-reference-type material arranged in alphabetical order. This is an imitation of the specific entry found in many European works. There are approximately

---

[15]Karen Schlegl, "The Reference World Expands," *Computers in Libraries*, May, 1998, p. 63.

65,000 separate entries and close to half that number of cross-references. The average length of an entry is about 300 words. (A few—covering countries, outstanding personalities, and ideas—go as high as 3,000 words, but these are the exception.) Each serves to summarize and outline the topic. Often, too, more detail is found in the companion set or part, the *Macropaedia*.

The *Ready Reference* version of the *Britannica* is little more than a recast in print of the *Micropaedia*. It is sold in bookstores for about $500 and is marketed as a work for quick reference rather than for in depth searching. It is of some use to consumers, although a one-volume work will do almost as well, but of no real value to libraries with the whole set available.

2. The second part of the set, which like the *Micropaedia* may be used independently, is the *Macropaedia*. The 17 volumes follow the nineteenth-century tradition of offering long (20- to 100-page) detailed articles, again in alphabetical order. Each volume has about 40 articles, for a total in the full 17 volumes of only 675. In effect, the reader is offered an overview of a person, field, or idea in each of the essays.

The guide to the detailed examinations is a table of contents at the head of each essay. For example, in the survey of the West Indies, instead of breaking up the various islands alphabetically (as is done in most sets) they are treated as a single unit in the *Macropaedia*. A score of individual parts treat as many of the individual countries and islands, but always within the context of the main article. Thus the major entries have a coherence not usually found in encyclopedias.

3. Current bibliographies are found at the end of all Macropaedia articles, but only after 2,000 or so in the *Micropaedia*. There are close to 25,000 illustrations, most in the *Micropaedia*. They usually are black and white and rather small.

4. The *two sets are held together by a detailed two-volume index and the Propaedia*, which is a guide to related items within the two works. Referred to in advertisement as an "outline of knowledge," this single volume is arranged by broad subjects. The idea is to outline human knowledge, to show relationships among ideas, persons, and events. The *Propaedia* is a commendable failure because the complexity of knowledge simply does not allow such a simplistic approach. The index, on the other hand, is one of the best for any set and has about 790,000 entries.

Weak Points. Similar to many sets, the *Britannica* has a distinct failing. It updates material likely to be in the news or the classroom. Computers and the results of presidential elections, for example, are updated. The work fails to do very much with "standard" entries from the history of painting to the life of President Grant. The publisher's claim of about 12 percent revision each year is correct, although there are still many articles in need of revision.

The division of the print set into two major parts is confusing, and although the format has some benefit for ready-reference work, it is decidedly confusing for laypersons. Another real difficulty is that many of the detailed articles in the *Macropaedia* are highly technical (e.g., see "Mathematics") and beyond the comprehension of all but experts. At the same time, the very challenge makes this a refreshing counterpoint to the sometimes too easy other sets.

The small illustrations in the *Micropaedia* are fine, but the plates, while numerous enough, are not always tied to the articles. This seems particularly true in works of specific artists, architects, and others in the graphic arts. The primary article will include two or three illustrations, but others pertaining to the creators may be scattered through numerous volumes. Also, color is used sparingly.

The Americana

The Encyclopedia Americana is based on the seventh edition of the German encyclopedia *Brockhaus Koversations Lexikon*. In fact, the first published set (1829 to 1833) consisted of little more than pirated, translated articles from the German work. It was asserted in 1903 that the *Americana* was a wholly new work, but still many of the articles were carried over from *Brockhaus*. The set was reissued in 1918 with changes and additions, although still with material from *Brockhaus*. It claims to be the oldest "all-American" encyclopedia in existence.

As the title implies, the strength of this work is its emphasis on American history, geography, and biography. The *Americana* unquestionably places greater emphasis on these areas than any of the other sets, and it is particularly useful for finding out-of-the-way, little-known material about the United States. However, general coverage of the United States is matched in other major encyclopedias.

Unlike the *Britannica,* the major audience is not the college educated, but "the nonspecialist reader." The writing style is easier to follow than in the *Britannica,* and the articles tend to be more concise. On the other hand major entries, such as for Japan, can run from 100 to 150 pages. Note, too, the excellent index with 350,000 plus entries.

Americana CD-ROM

A latecomer to the CD-ROM parade (the first was in 1995), the *Americana* essentially is the electronic version of the full 30-volume print set, although with considerably fewer illustrations (about 2,000 on the CD-ROM vs. 23,000 in print). The 45,000 articles remain some of the best available, e.g., see comments on the print version.

What is missing: A low price. No sound, video or other multimedia pleasures. Here is plain text. This is for the serious student, and not the one looking for data spiced with entertaining sound or sight bites.

What is unique on the CD-ROM? Add: the *Merriam-Webster Collegiate Dictionary;* a *Chronology of World History;* and a *Dictionary of Science and Technology.* While mildly useful, none of it is really necessary and one ends up with the basic set as the heart of the matter.

There are some 155,000 hypertext links, which may be a bit hard to find on the main screen which is a jumble of icons. This opens up a mass of approaches to information, and some most useful indexes, but on the whole it is more work than it is worth for anyone except the devoted computer hack.

A definite plus is the careful selection of the Net sites. There are detailed descriptors which are a great help in deciding which of numerous choices to make.

Grolier Online

Under the umbrella title, "Grolier Online," the company offers its three major encyclopedias as a single package, *Encyclopedia Americana Online, Multimedia Encyclopedia Online, New Book of Knowledge Online,* and *Nueva Enciclopedia Cumbre en line* which the publisher claims is "the first online Spanish language encyclopedia." The package goes from $325 for schools to $695 and up for public and academic libraries. (Pricing is based on number of users as well as how many sets are chosen—two out of three minimum.) The librarian or layperson simply selects the work most likely to answer the query. It's hardly a difficult choice as the *Americana* offers data in depth while the *Multimedia* is stronger on short, quick responses with much media hoopla. The *New Book of Knowledge* is for children. One suspects other encyclopedia publishers will follow this package scheme online.

Following the usual pattern, the *Americana Online* includes all of the 45,000 articles found in the print/CD-ROM version, plus selective additions when the service is updated quarterly. The catch, not mentioned in the advertisements, is the online updates are highly selective (items in the news, major national and international events, etc.). Still, this keeps the online encyclopedia ahead of the CD-ROM and print. On the Net there are few of the illustrations (about 3,000) that are found in the standard volumes.[16]

True, the maps, tables and line art items are there, but certainly not the colorful reproductions of art, scenic spots and the like.

Americana/Print

If the *Americana* is easier to read than the *Britannica,* if there sometimes is as much emphasis on hobbies (from house plants to model railroads) as on politics, the focus is always tied to school curriculum and the interests of the average person. Baseball may be an attraction, but the articles on abortion and sex education are equally thoughtful, and, if anything, a bit more balanced and objective.

A major plus for the set is that it is fairly current. Each year all the 45,000 primary articles are updated, and new or revised illustrations are considered. Bibliographies are frequently updated.

The writing style is clear, the arrangement admirable, the index good, and the general format (including illustrations and type size) adequate. A helpful feature is the insertion of summaries, resembling a table of contents, at the beginning of multiple-page articles. The set is edited for the adult with a high school education. It is not suitable (despite the zealous efforts of copywriters) for grade school children.

The illustrations are closely associated with the text. The maps are detailed and easy to follow, although those of detailed city plans are not always the best.

The emphasis is on short, specific, ready-reference entries and is, therefore, ideal for reference work. However, it sometimes contains much longer articles, particularly those which cover states, countries, and historical events. The *Americana* is excellent for *both* the concise articles and the fewer in-depth pieces.

Weak Points. Although its performance in revising items and personalities likely to be in the news is fairly good, the same is not true in continuous revision of the basic articles. (This was helped somewhat by a two year update program (1997–1999), but it remains a problem.) This lack of timeliness in certain sections can be a major drawback, particularly in schools where curriculum is tied to basic knowledge and not the passing scene. The electronic versions are a first choice as they are considerably more current than the print work.

Artwork remains mediocre to poor. A preponderance of illustrations are in black and white and the color pictures are far from ideal. The

---

[16]To be exact (as of mid-2000): 800 maps, 1,000 tables, 1,200 line drawings and 275 flags. The rational is that the 130,000 Internet links, many of which have illustrations, compensate for the lack in the basic set. It is a poor excuse. Also, often, too often, the links lead to a blind alley, e.g., illuminated manuscripts has virtually nothing by way of illustration.

general layout follows this rather dismal attitude toward the graphic. All and all, one of the less interesting of the group in terms of appearances.

Which Is Best

Most libraries will want both of these standard adult encyclopedias. The sensible approach is to have access in digital format to both. If funds allow, one might alternate print and CD-ROM each year.

POPULAR ADULT AND HIGH SCHOOL

Online: Grolier Multimedia Encyclopedia Online. Danbury, CT: Grolier Incorporated, 1996 to date, quarterly, http://gme.grolier.com. Pricing begins at $395. Note: In 2000 both the online and CD-ROM have the added *"Year 2000 Grolier..."* By any other name, it is the same work.

CD: Grolier Multimedia Encyclopedia (also titled: *New Grolier Interactive Encyclopedia.* 1985 to date, annual. $60.

Print: Academic American Encyclopedia, 1980 to date, 21 vols. $725.

Online: Encarta Online Deluxe. Redmond, WA: Microsoft Corporation, 1996 to date, annual, http://encarta.msn.com/EncartaHome.asp. Free on the Internet.

CD and DVD: Microsoft Encarta Multimedia Deluxe Encyclopedia, *1993 to date, annual. $30. Three disc deluxe edition, $70. DVD version:* Encarta Reference Suite 200-DVD, *2000 to date, annual. $99.*

Online: Funk & Wagnalls Encyclopedia. *New York: Versaware, 1998 to date, updated daily, www.funkandwagnalls.com. Free.*

CD and DVD: Funk & Wagnalls Multimedia Encyclopedia, 1998 to date. $25. (Note: A similar version for $20 is: *Simon & Schuster New Millennium Encyclopedia.* New York: Simon & Schuster, 1999 to date.)

Print: Funk & Wagnalls New Encyclopedia. *1912 to date, 29 vols. $164.*

CD: Collier's Encyclopedia. *New York: Sierra Online (i.e., Microsoft) 1996 to date, annual. $50 to $80.*

Print: New York: Collier Newfield, 1951 to date, 24 vols. $850.

The two major competitors in the adult/young people field, *Grolier* and *Encarta Microsoft,* have excellent CD-ROMs and well-thought-out online editions. (Collier's sold its electronic rights to Microsoft, and for all intents and purposes the electronic *Collier's* is another Microsoft product.) Both have about the same amount of text and illustrations, and both are about the same price. Which is best? Neither, in that they complement one another and the wise will have both.

Grolier Multimedia/Online

Grolier (deluxe edition) has 10 million words and 37,000 articles (*Encarta* has 10.5 million); *Grolier* claims 15,000 pictures and 177 videos and animations. (*Encarta*: 12,500 pictures, 4,000 music and audiotapes, 140 videos and animations). *Grolier* has 26,000 Web links and *Encarta* has 13,500.

Statistically then, one can see where one is strong, the other is less so, and vice versa. It adds up to two excellent electronic sets.

The online *Grolier* actually has more articles than in the CD-ROM or print editions. And of the 37,000, some 5,000 are unique to the online version. As the text is updated monthly, by the end of a year there are timely items found in no other edition of *Grolier.* The usual drawbacks, though: *(a)* There are fewer illustrations, some 15,000 vs. 18,000 in print. *(b)* Unlike the CD, there are fewer interactive features or video clips and limited sound.

Following a growing notion that the more the better, the *Grolier* CD-ROM not only includes the basic encyclopedia, but: (1) Access online to the company's other major works, i.e., the *Americana* and the *New Book of Knowledge.* (2) A small hardcover book, How to Improve Your Grammar and Usage. (3) A paperback book of quizzes. (4) *Bartlett's Familiar Quotations,* the latest edition. (5) *The Hammond Atlas of the World,* again, the latest edition. (6) *The Wall Street Journal Almanac.* (7) *The New York Times Book of Science Questions.* (8) A timeline. (9) 100 to 360 degree panoramas, 163 video bites, and over 50 guided tours. (10) Atlas of 1,200 maps.

There are, too, some 26,000 links to relevant websites. These, at the "Internet index" are briefly annotated and closely aligned with the subject being searched. (There is no easy way, however, to view the whole index. One has to first turn to a subject, person, place, etc. to have the relevant index terms on the screen.)

Aside from the numerous, sometimes fascinating panoramas, videos and graphs, there are added features to encourage school work. The best is the "Research Starters" section which covers the basic courses from history to the physical sciences. Each has text, sound, videos, and whatever is likely to capture the attention of the younger reader. (This may have some value for adults, but Grolier has students more in mind.)

Question: is this an encyclopedia or a general store? Answer: the set itself is fine, but navigating through all of these extras often takes more time than it would take to simply look them up in print versions. Also, it can become confusing, especially for younger people. Still, many love the side trails and the video/sound bypaths. The magic is the integration of the sources. Is this what an encyclopedia is all about? The question depends on the user.

Academic American/Print

First published in 1980 by a Dutch firm, and then sold to Grolier, the *Academic American Encyclopedia* is prepared expressly for high school students and for less sophisticated adults. The 21 volumes feature brief 30,000 articles, numerous illustrations, (about 18,000) and a relaxed writing style that offers few challenges in terms of vocabulary or complex ideas. The printed set is updated regularly with about 10 percent of the material changed or added each year. With that, the editors carefully keep up with current events and it is among the better sets for finding what major new legislation passed Congress or who won this or that literary or sports prize during the past year. Bibliographies are updated regularly, too.

An outstanding feature of the print set is that the illustrations are bright, well selected, and appealing. They dot almost every page and include photographs, line drawings, charts, maps, and even "exploded" illustrations which show, for example, the interior of a ship or airplane. The 18,000 illustrations, according to the publisher, make up 20 percent of the space. Almost 75 percent of these are in color. In the revision process, the editors add new, color photographs each year and the general level of the illustrations is improving. The page makeup and general layout are among the best among the sets.

The set manages to eliminate any overt bias in the biographical entries and in the articles. But there could still be better coverage of prominent modern women. The coverage of minorities is not all it might be, either.

The index of over 205,000 citations is one of the best available, and extremely easy to use. Unfortunately, the publisher does not follow through with enough adequate cross-reference within the set itself—a pity because many students tend to avoid the index and rely on such references. A bibliography of over 200 pages winds up the index volume and offers approximately 12,500 titles under broad-to-narrow subject headings.

Weak Points. While most of the material is under continuous revision, and the "news" items are current, there is evidence that some basic articles are not. Although the quality of the illustrations has been improved, some are still a bit muddy and not related to the subject matter. On the whole, though, it is difficult to fault the set on any of the major criteria.

Encarta/CD-ROM[17]

The multimedia king among the CD-ROMs for general encyclopedias, *Encarta* is in the best tradition of Microsoft's innovations. The heart of

[17]In 1998 Microsoft released one of the first encyclopedias in DVD format: *The Funk & Wagnalls Unabridged Encyclopedia.* According to the publisher this is a combination of the encyclopedia, deluxe edition, the atlas and the ready-reference *Bookshelf.* The asking price was $130, but was selling for about half that in stores.

the work is the print *Funk & Wagnalls* (32,000 plus articles).[18] Beginning in 1999 Microsoft branched out to include another 3,500 articles from *Colliers*. There is a suspicion that eventually *Colliers, Funk & Wagnalls* and *Encarta* will be one, or three separate works with pretty much the same configuration and content, but possibly at different prices.

Innovations are in such things as the "virtual tours" which move the reader from the interior of Westminister Abbey to the space shuttle. There are close-up views and vantage points which permit a full-circle picture. The searching is made relatively easy, and often the videos, virtual views, etc. can be mixed with the text, or filtered out as the reader requests. See, too, the "research organizer" which helps students organize text and multimedia features for a project or paper.

Browsing offers numerous approaches from word by word to actual index terms assigned by, yes, human beings. Needless to say, the human touch makes it much easier to zero in on a given topic. Note, too, that one may browse the "index," much as one would an encyclopedia print index. One nice touch for those who hate to read more than a few lines: the "sidebars" which offer documents and summaries of what is found in the primary article.

As with the *Grolier* encyclopedias, *Encarta* constantly is expanding its CD-ROM work. It is now, in a deluxe edition, up to five discs. In addition to the set itself, there are: *(a)* the *Microsoft Bookshelf,* discussed elsewhere, but includes nine reference books from a dictionary to a book of quotations. *(b)* a text to speech engine which is more publicity than real worth, i.e., one fan can use the oral approach to questions, but only a poor typist is much faster. (This, as the winds, will change, and probably for the better.) There are other features from "research organizer," which helps the student find, organize and write a term paper, to a "virtual globe." The catch is that this is a real space hog, taking up five discs. On the other hand, it is among the easiest of the encyclopedias on CD-ROM to use. And it is almost given away.

The DVD version of *Encarta* (which flies under various names, although always with *Encarta* in the title) has the advantage of having the whole interactive package on one disc, thus eliminating the need for five discs. The DVD includes the whole of the *Encarta* reference suite family as well as the expected website links. Where the library has the DVD equipment this is strongly recommended over the CD package.

---

[18]Shorter non-news articles tend to be identical to the print edition. Longer pieces, particularly those in the news, represent new material and revisions to *F&W.* A comparison show the article on Irving Berlin is much expanded over the print set and an article on Gaza is quite different. On the other hand, briefer article, tend to slavishly follow the print version. Note, the electronic version of the life of Bill Gates (under William Henry Gates III). All hail the chief. This is a tribute not found in the print work.

An online edition of the CD-ROM, *Encarta* is nearly a full scaled-down version of the CD-ROM. The articles are much the same.

The site is of great use to teachers. In fact, it seems directed to them in that there is emphasis on teacher materials, worksheets, lesson plans, and the like. There is an impression lesson collection by subject area. The publisher claims all the material has been tested in classrooms. Monthly updates add new plans, subjects, and additions to existing lessons. The *Encarta* offers about 21,500 Web links with age and grade level, good links, worksheets, and basic directions.

Spreading its Microsoft reference wings, *Encarta* includes a "virtual globe" and other goodies such as "recent articles from over 800 magazines, newspapers, and other resources." This follows in the steps of other such endeavors, e.g,. the *Electric Library.* Begin with any encyclopedia and build an online library seems to be the way of at least larger organizations online. The catch: a charge of $9.95 per month to use the service. There is a free trial. The URL: (http://encarta.msn.com/library).

Funk & Wagnalls/Print

A familiar sight in many supermarkets, *Funk & Wagnalls New Encyclopedia* is an example of a good-to-superior set, sometimes downgraded because of the company it keeps. One of the few works approved by the American Library Association, its frequent revision, serviceable format, and low, low price makes it a bargain for almost anyone. It is the least costly of all printed multivolume encyclopedias.

Funk & Wagnalls has almost the same number of words as the much better designed *Academic American.* They are relatively close to covering about the same amount of material, and they are both quite good in their different ways.

Aside from the point of sale, *Funk & Wagnalls* confuses many by its deceptive, almost casual appearance. The two columns to a page format is no more inviting than the unappealing binding. The articles are short—averaging no more than a quarter to a half page—and the illustrations are numerous, if somewhat less than exciting. Is this the stuff of a traditional encyclopedia? Yes, in that the articles are well written, authoritative (there are close to 1,000 outside consultants), current, and often illustrated. One can go to the set for almost any item and be sure to find it offered in almost a *Readers' Digest* fashion. In this respect it is ideal for the high school student or adult who rarely uses a set. Ease of use is helped by an excellent 135,000 entry index in the last volume. Add to this a well-chosen bibliography section in the next to the final volume and one has a most useful set. While not always current, most of the choices are at least suitable for the set's target audience.

Weak Points. Perhaps the greatest fault, although built into the set by the audience scope, is the uneven treatment of material. The popular and current are often stressed at the expense of standard, historical items. Understandably, the set with the fewest words cannot hope to brag about in-depth articles—and that can be a major weakness. On the other hand, for its intended audience the short entries are possibly even more useful for a quick, easy-to-understand overview.

The thin-ice area is in the humanities and the arts. Here, for some odd reason, many of the articles are unaware of either progress in literature or development in, say, painting. Editors, from time to time, say these sections are to be improved. Illustrations are not indexed, and some relatively common controversial topics such as gun control and oil spills are not covered adequately.

The CD-ROM contains the complete text of the 29 volume print set, and adds about 50 video clips, 400 audio clips and 51 animations. There are almost the same number of illustrations as in print, i.e., about 10,000. There are monthly updates, but no Web links within the brief articles. A particular feature of this CD-ROM: the reader may purchase and download added electronic, complementary books from Merriam Webster's *Biographical Dictionary* to the *Oxford Dictionary of Art*. There is a link, too, to the online *Funk & Wagnalls Knowledge Center,* the Reuters News Service site.

The online encyclopedia surfaces on the Internet as a free, reliable, general encyclopedia. It includes most of the material in the print set with additions of multimedia capabilities like audio and video clips. (These, by the way, differ from *Encarta* which has *Funk & Wagnalls* at its heart.) Additional free delights: the *Random House Webster's College Dictionary* and hourly newsflashes from Reuters. Why free? A company spokesman explained the publisher hopes to use the site to inspire visitors to buy the CD-ROM version of the set which is much more elaborate and contains more articles.

Collier's/CD-ROM

The CD-ROM Collier's (a product of Microsoft) includes the full text of the print set, some 4,000 more illustrations (a total of 18,000) and six hours of video. In addition: a *Rand McNally* atlas, the *American Heritage* dictionary and direct links to 3,000 carefully selected websites. A single search can scan the encyclopedia, dictionary, and atlas. What's interesting here is that 95 percent of the pictures are unique to the CD-ROM and only about 5 percent are from the print version. Zooming allows the reader to close in on pictures, buildings and fine details in other photos. The result is a much more pleasing visual image on the CD-ROM. Add the usual—from simulations and time lines—as well as ease of use and the electronic set is a joy to use. For example, articles are displayed on part of the screen while options, including an outline, are available in another section. The multimedia possibilities are closely tied to text and illustrations. The work is kept current by downloading monthly additions from the Internet—not an entirely satisfactory method, but better than nothing. The movie and sound bites are short, sometimes no more than a few seconds, but they at least have a close relationship to topics searched.

There are some drawbacks: (a) no bibliographies, although, as noted numerous Web links to enhance the basic information; (b) there are a great number of videos, but most are only a few seconds to a minute in length; (c) while it is easy to find websites, the time it takes from contact to the actual site is much longer than for most works. Note: In 1998–1999 the CD-ROM was ranked by *PC Data* as the number-one-selling multimedia encyclopedia. The claim is based on the number of units sold by 42 retail and mail order chains.

Collier's/Print

The writing style may be too bland for some, but it has the advantage of clarity. The 23,000 articles are extremely well organized and the set is unusual because it stresses long, rather than short, articles that are often accompanied by biographical sketches and glossaries of terms. The longer articles often include subject glossaries, a welcome feature for many users.

Some complain that the articles in *Collier's* are too long. In fact, they can run over 40 or even 70 pages for a particular country. At the same time, there is a fine index which has over 450,000 entries—almost double those found in rival sets. Another plus for the final volume is the section on bibliographies. About 12,000 titles are arranged under 31 broad subjects and are subdivided. Most entries are current, and the reading lists offer adults and students a satisfactory choice of supplements to material found in the set.

The 14,500 illustrations, according to the publisher, make up 20 percent of the space. Almost one-half are in color. In the revision process, the editors add new, color photographs each year and the general level of the illustrations has improved. The page makeup and general layout are among the best among the sets. The set manages to eliminate any overt bias in the biographical entries and in the articles.

Weak Points: While most of the material is under continuous revision, and the "news" items are current, there is evidence that some basic articles are not. Although the quality of the illustrations has improved, some are still a bit muddy and not related to the subject matter. On the whole, though, it is difficult to fault the set on any of the major criteria.

CHILDREN AND YOUNG ADULT

Online: Chicago: World Book, 1997 to date, www.worldbook.com. Fee varies.
   CD: World Book Multimedia Encyclopedia, 1989 to date, two-disc deluxe edition. $69.95.
   Print: The World Book Encyclopedia, 1917 to date, 22 vols. $769.
   Note: *World Book,* as almost all the sets, continually adds variation to its name, e.g., by 2000 it is *The World Book Millennium 2000 Encyclopedia;* and on CD-ROM: *The World Book Millennium 2000 Deluxe CD.* No matter, just look for *World Book.*
Online: Compton's Encyclopedia Online. Redmond, WA: Microsoft Corporation, 1996 to date, annual, www.comptons.com. $30 per year.
   CD: Compton's Interactive Encyclopedia, 1989 to date. Deluxe edition, $40.
   Print: Compton's Encyclopedia, 1922 to date, 26 vols. $480.

World Book/CD-ROM

After a few false starts the *World Book* CD-ROM, with the help of IBM, emerges as one of the best in its class. There are about the same number of articles as in the print volume, with 3,200 unique to the electronic version. True, the outstanding illustrations are still at a minimum, (9,500 vs. 28,000 in print) but there are useful additions and replacements: some 800 plus videos, numerous simulations and animations and 880 or so excellent maps. The 18,000 links are carefully chosen for the child/young adult audience. A sane, easy to follow "homework wizard" is a useful feature. Here, with due consideration to the age and experience of the user, the program takes one from choosing the proper topic to finishing the final paper. A well thought out approach to a sometimes difficult problem for many readers.

   The navigational methods are easy to follow, with a filtering system which lists material in order of relative importance. The ranking system, as with online search engines, can be frustrating, but at least it is an effort to control the vast amounts of data. The so-called "virtual image" feature is found here with selected 360 degree views of major buildings and landmarks. This, by the way, includes the ceiling of the Sistine Chapel.

   The inexpensive three-disc deluxe edition includes: a speech recognition feature; the Merriam-Webster Reference Library, with definitions and words for younger people; the *Information Please Almanac,* and all of the other features found in the simpler model. As with competitive CD-ROM encyclopedias, the voice recognition hardly works at all, and the problem is the amount of space it takes to use the work. The integration of the various reference works is satisfactory, but, once again, the question arises: are all of these really needed in an encyclopedia, and would it not be more efficient to turn to individual works. On the plus side is the ability to move from one work to another with a minimum of bother.

The online version is similar to the CD-ROM, although the cost, which varies from library to library, is higher. One advantage is the day by day update of current events, i.e., "Behind the Headline." The question: yes, but how many children are involved with current events from an encyclopedia. There is a more useful monthly feature which considers everything from a major tied to a curriculum topic as well as a calendar of dates. There are the usual links as well as access to about 25,000 full text periodical articles.

Searching is relatively easy. The focus is on the main articles in the encyclopedia. With that, there are links to relevant websites as well as related cross-references. Add the usual assortment of such things as "streaming videos and animation," and this is a first rate online encyclopedia—at least for the audience envisioned.

World Book/Print

The triumph of *World Book* is that it is a planned, careful combination of many elements, not the least of which is a nice balance between timely illustrations and text. The clarity of style and the massive number of excellent illustrations put it so far ahead of the other sets that it really has no competitors. Inevitably, critics rank it highly and librarians regularly repurchase it. Its popularity makes it the best-selling single set in America. Its target audience is the student, ages ten to sixteen, give or take a year or so.

The *World Book* follows a pattern of initial ease to progressive difficulty in longer articles, which is sometimes a policy of adult encyclopedias and other reference works. For example, a detailed piece on energy begins with not only an easy vocabulary, but also careful attention to definition and explanation of unusual words and phrases. As one progresses, say past the first one or two columns, the material becomes more sophisticated, that is, more difficult. For the most part, though, the policy of short, specific entries makes this usual only for the detailed, lengthy articles. All of the brief pieces, which are the background of the set, may be easily understood by the average grade school student. The editors follow a much heralded reading-level test pattern based on curricula across the United States.

The twenty-second and last volume contains an excellent index of approximately 173,000 entries. Because the set has numerous cross-references, the index may not be needed for most students, and rarely for ready-reference work.

The most dramatic aspect of the set are the illustrations on each and every page. It has more illustrations than any set, adults' or children's, and the 28,000 plates include most in color. Illustrations take up over one-third of the total space.

While all children's sets are kept current, the degree of revision varies considerably. *World Book* is by far the best in this respect, particularly in that careful attention is given to current events, and biographical data are updated regularly.

Weak Points. Few of the sets are likely to win applause for challenging the reader to consider controversial issues. Here the publisher is more concerned with not shocking the parents than with the children. The article on human reproduction, for example, seems to avoid sexual intercourse as a necessary part of the formula. The editors, wisely or not, leave the vital act up to parents to explain. *World Book,* closely tied to the curricula of the nation's schools, assiduously avoids appearing to endorse anything that may be controversial. At the same time, it is quite objective in handling national arguments from abortion to the place of religion in education. It often fails to indicate that foreign affairs affect American policy. The advertising for *World Book* may be faulted for indicating that it is for younger children. Actually it is for someone at least nine years of age, but probably close to ten or twelve years old up through high school.

Compton's/CD-ROM

With 40,000 articles, (of which over 1,000 are not in the print set) 600 plus sound clips and over 100 video animations, *Compton's* is a lively approach to information for children and early teens. The articles are easy to follow, generally well illustrated (about one-half the number in the print set, i.e., 16,000 or so), and suited for most classroom projects and assignments.

More than one critic points out that while the number of illustrations is impressive, too often "quantity is at the expense of quality. There are still lots of mediocre pictures from an unidentified collection."[19]

Among the plus features: picture tours and slide shows of arts and communications. A planetarium which lets the user explore the heav-

---

[19]Peter Jaco, "The 1999 Editions of General-Interest Encyclopedias," *Computers in Libraries,* June, 1999, p. 31. This is an annual roundup which is brief, critical, and of great value to librarians.

ens by clicking on a constellation and then reading an article about it. There are good maps and a dictionary.

"Highlights of recent events" which is arranged chronologically, with monthly additions often downloaded from the Net, and includes brief to sometime rather full articles on current events. References are to primary articles in the complete work. Multimedia presentations are made possible as are 3-D environments.

With each annual edition the publisher updates the videos, sound, slides, etc. adding some, dropping others. The focus is on recent news stories and background material likely to interest younger readers.

There are some 7,000 links to related websites, including access to the Electric Library. Note, though, this is only a test run and after 30 days a regular fee is charged for use of this index with some full-text material from magazines.

A nice touch, "Ask the librarian" where the baffled student may pose questions and receive brief answers (often with references to articles in the encyclopedia and to websites. A two- or three-day turnaround for the e-mail response is normal.

A tremendous advantage for *Compton's* is the superior software which permits sophisticated searching as well as word-by-word approaches for beginners. (Note: there is an age filter for users below 5 years, 13 to 17 years, etc. This tends to give about the same information for each age group, though).

Again, the Net site for *Compton's* is considerably less satisfactory than the CD-ROM. Lack of detailed articles, pictures and other features makes it a poor choice. At the same time it is a great resource for finding related websites in the area(s) being researched. The sites tend to be more precise than those found in many other encyclopedia link systems. (In addition to its stand alone subscription, *Compton's* is part of the package offered by America Online.)

Compton's/Print

Compton's is unique for its "Fact Index" in the final volume. The feature serves both as an index to each volume and as a source of ready-reference data for basic queries. The publisher claims that there are over 30,000 short, up-to-date articles in the "Fact Index." These ready-reference-type entries cover a wide variety of topics, as well as people and places. There are also useful "Reading Guides," which are edited to suit current curriculum-oriented subjects and give the young reader related materials to consider.

The writing style is passable, and while far from sparkling, it is clear enough. The 40,000 articles are generally short, although major topics may cover several pages. Controversial topics are handled, but gingerly. There are some 23,000 illustrations of which about two-thirds are in color.

The set is extremely well organized for easy use. Among encyclopedias it is one of the easiest to use, particularly for the audience of upper elementary grade students and high school students. It can also be recommended for general family use.

Weak Points: Sensitive subjects are often overlooked or simply skated over. The reader may have no idea that the topic is controversial. The article on abortion includes only a few words on why someone is for or against abortion. Arrangement, with the index part of the "Fact Index," can be confusing as can the letter-by-letter rather than word-by-word arrangement in the main volumes.

The updating procedure is odd. Current events, unless of major importance, are relegated to the "Fact-Index." Where a primary article needs updating, the usual procedure is not to operate, but to simply add new material at the end of the old article.

OTHER CHILDREN'S SETS

Childcraft

World Book publishes a 15-volume set, *Childcraft,* for preschool children, which is really a luxury for both parents and a library. Perfectly suitable, and extremely well illustrated and cleverly laid out, the 750,000 words and 4,600 illustrations cost $170. Many volumes give pronunciation for new words and sentences to show how the words are used properly. Articles are arranged by topic, but each volume has its own index, with a general index in the last volume.

The topic arrangement by science, children's literature, social studies, and so forth, is reminiscent of a shelf in the library trying to appeal to all interests of young readers. Is it really an encyclopedia or a collection of nicely presented fiction, nonfiction, and activities? The latter is the real answer and as such it is of more real value to families than to libraries.

New Book of Knowledge

The New Book of Knowledge (Danbury, CT: Grolier Incorporated, 1911, to date, 21 vols. $659), edited for children from about seven to thirteen years of age, is a full-fledged set and not, as it was for many decades, a simple collection of reading materials. Thanks to extensive revision it features numerous facts and biographies as well as activity projects which neatly fit into articles, e.g., the piece on clowns has a section on how to apply clown make-up and other article feature stories or poems written by the entry subject. There are close to 85,000 entries in the index, and each volume has its own individual index.

More than one third of the space is given over to illustrations, of which more than 94 percent are in color. The 28,000 illustrations and maps are close to the number in the more elaborate *World Book* and ahead of all other children's sets except the *World Book*. Within many of the longer articles are charts, graphs, and summaries, such as "quick-reference" materials.

The articles are well written and, in fact, the writing style is better than that found in many of the pieces in *Compton's*. An effort toward clarity is made and most of the articles are short with precise definitions and explanations, usually punctuated with illustrations.

Weak Points. Considering the age group (elementary through middle school) for which this is designed, and the careful attention to their interests, there is little to fault. It is *not* appropriate, though, as some have suggested for older children with reading problems. The coverage of countries other than the United States is rather simplistic.

The New Book of Knowledge Online (http://nbk.grolier.com/login/nbk_login.html) follows the print pattern, but without most of the illustrations. However, there are new update features which offer current event coverage each week, e.g., "NBK News" which is tailored for young readers. The five to six stories will remain active for a month, and then be dropped or incorporated into the main work. Note: At $395+, this is an expensive, really not needed choice online.

Children's Britannica (Chicago: Encyclopedia Britannica, 1960 to date, 20 vols. $369) is a nondescript set which has about 4,000 articles written for children ages eight to fourteen. It is edited and published in England, but is sold here as an American set. Except for minor changes for Americans, it is directed to English school children. The 6,000 illustrations, primarily in black and white, are as inviting as the dismal layout. Although recommended by the American Library Association, it is not recommended by this author. The money is better spent on a CD-ROM or a secondhand set of the *World Book* which may be purchased for less than the new *Children's Britannica*.

First Connections: The Golden Book Encyclopedia (East Lansing, MI: Hartley Courseware, 1993 to date. $90 to $150) is the familiar Golden Book set on CD-ROM format. Given a child from ages five to ten who can function at a computer terminal, this is a possible purchase. The audio (about 60 minutes) is imaginative. The animations appeal to children from pregrade through about the sixth or seventh grade. The more than 3,000 maps and illustrations are adequate. The text is easy enough to understand.

The catch is that this is edited primarily for entertainment. Few articles go into any depth. Some basic entries are skipped over. Material is relatively current, but no always that up-to-date. As a tool to draw young children into the world of information it is a success, and as such can be used in many schools. At the same time it is not the place to turn for up-to-date answers to reference questions put by children. Considering the appealing features of the set, as well as its low price, it might be purchased for reading and browsing. It is not up to passable encyclopedia criteria.

Eyewitness Children's Encyclopedia (New York: DK Multimedia, 1998 to date. $40). On a CD-ROM, this is for the 7 to 11 age group and features animations to a mechanical voice which reads aloud anything found on the screen. The text is as lively as the numerous, CD-ROM features. Entertainment is stressed more than raw information, but it is a convenient way of introducing children to the delights of more sophisticated information sources.

On the Web

This side of the preceding general standard sets, there is no satisfactory general encyclopedia on the Net. (Note, though, that for free or for fee, all of the preceding sets are available on the Net and are recommended.)

Scores of free encyclopedias are to be found on the net. Only a few are worth the search effort. If content is not a strong point among Net only encyclopedias, at least they are free. Among the most often nonstandard sets found online, and listed in order of descending value, are:

1. *Free Internet Encyclopedia* (http://clever.net/cam/encyclopedia.html) is one of the earliest, and still best of Net only works. There is no version in print or on a CD-ROM. It stresses "free" and is operated by Cliff Davias and Margaret Fincannon. The collection of data is based on a simple principle—draw together information on a network of Web pages (which are constantly revised, added to and updated). "This is an encyclopedia composed of information available on the Internet. There are two main divisions. The "Macro Reference" contains references to large areas of knowledge...The "Micro Reference" contains short bits of information and reference to specific subjects sometimes with instructions on finding the specific subject inside a general reference. While the section titles echo the *Encyclopaedia Britannica,* there any resemblance ends. Searching, for example, is less direct.

The "Macro Reference" opens with an alphabetical listing of subjects from "Africa," "alternative," and "atheism," under "A" to five to ten under the other members of the alphabet. If one calls for "books," there are some 30 desperate links to everything from *BookWire* and online books to "Internet movie books." There is no word-for-word search mechanism. All has to be done through preassigned subject headings. Just how useful is all of this? Not much as there is little connective matter and certainly no order as one finds, for example, in the *Britannica* entry there are scores of relevant cross-references that indicate the true breadth of "book" as a subject.

2. *Encyberpedia* (www.encyberpedia.com/eindex.html). "Advertising and promotional links now available" is one of the first things on the opening page. A member of the "MonteCristo Information Services," the encyclopedia suggests the answer to financing such titles may be through advertising. The user, of course, is more involved with the material.

There are two search approaches. The first is to use the work's own search engine. Enter a key word or topic and, if there is anything, it appears. The second path is to pull up broad subject topics. These are dutifully listed in an "overview index" followed by descriptive annotations of the major links. For example, under "environment" the user is offered "hot and new links to the U.S. Environmental Protection Agency, Australian Environment on-line, Canadian Environmental Knowledge and Oceanography sites from around the world." Others are less complex, certainly with less information. Biography links to "Biography.com—New Search through 15,000 biographies of notable personalities..." The data is skimpy and not up to even the most modest print encyclopedia. Conversely Civil War (the American, of course) refers to "BullRun.com— the most complete summary of civil war reference information on the Internet." And it is full.

Within the topics are a variety of non-traditional sites which, in themselves, are of value but not associated with the encyclopedia form. Among these: Libraries with links to online libraries; Mailists; Museums; *Electric Library*, which claims to offer "the full text of over 900 magazines, 150 newspapers, 20,000 books, encyclopedias, and 20,000 photos and maps."

3. *Knowledge Adventure Encyclopedia* (www.letsfindout.com). Employing key words, phrases, or Boolean logic this allows the user to search an undefined encyclopedia. There is no statement as to purpose or scope, although the work is for the teenager or adult who wants brief facts. Under "abortion" for example, appear six different alternatives with suggestive headings. One, "right life; whose?" results in a 300 to 400 word entry which nicely sums up the pro and con arguments, as well as offers an objective view of a key issue. The problem, and one for many similar entries, is that there appears to be little data after the late 1980s. Although this does have some material for young children (primarily pictures and a bit of text from space to dinosaurs), it is not a children's work as some sources indicate.

ENCYCLOPEDIA SUPPLEMENTS: YEARBOOKS, CD-ROMS, ONLINE

Prior to the digital encyclopedia, the publisher of a standard print set assured the purchaser that the initial work could be updated each year. This was done by mailing the customer a yearbook, usually at a modest fee. The yearbook was a type of "year in review" with long pieces about economic and political and scientific trends, with shorter entries for people and places in the news over the past year. There was little direct entry by entry relationship to the main set. In fact, a separate staff, a separate group of contributors were employed by the yearbook.

The standard yearbook continues to be published in print, but along with the primary set is likely to fade away shortly. The arrangements are broad, with emphasis on large current topics from agriculture to "Latin America's new investors." These entries are connected to the main work by such notes as "This article updates in the *Britannica*, for example, the Macropaedia articles..." Most of the material is not incorporated later into the revised set.

The yearbooks do serve a useful purpose other than updating the primary works. They are excellent annuals of the year's past events, and some, such as the *Britannica*, have supplements which update and parallel much information found in almanacs and political yearbooks. For example, in the *Britannica* there is a 350 to 400 plus page section, "Britannica World Data" which is a country by country analysis found in a slightly different form in the *Statesman's Yearbook* of *Europa*. Here is current data on demography, vital statistics, national economy, foreign trade, etc. for each country. Again, though, there is little or no real connection with the primary encyclopedia. Note: by the late 1990s the *Britannica* often was adding, after each country where applicable, useful "Internet resources for further information" with addresses on the Net.

Rather than an electronic yearbook, *Encarta* offers online "monthly updates," or the "Encarta Yearbook Builder" (www.encarta.msn.com/downloads). This has data on current events as well as other features which are incorporated later into the annual CD-ROM, and more frequently into the online edition of the encyclopedia.

The electronic update is sure to replace the print version and, for the most part, has done so already. The advantage of a monthly online version is that the material is more current than when one has to wait around for the yearbook. The advantage for the annual CD-ROM is *not* that it is more current than the old form, but, as the online work, is an integrated whole. One does not have to go from main set to yearbook, for example, to find the latest federal legislation, scientific discovery, or the name of a current Pulitzer prize winner. The wedding of the yearbook data with the electronic data ensures rapid, easy to use quests for information. Little wonder they are favored by almost everyone over the now antiquated print format.[20]

Nupedia (www.nupedia.com). Supported by Bomis, an internet portal concern, this free work has a paid editor. All of the contributors work for nothing in order to be part of what the editor terms a "major information resource." Entry, too, is free to anyone interested. It is geared for high school students through older adults, although the level of sophistication is hard to judge in mid 2000 as only a few sections are complete. What makes this different from other free encyclopedias is the promise of a rigorous peer review of articles which will be signed by the contributors. (Most free works fail to indicate who wrote what.) The question is: will it work? Only time and the cooperation of creditable contributors will tell.

ONE VOLUME ENCYCLOPEDIAS

Online: The Columbia Encyclopedia, 5th ed., New York: Columbia University Press, 1997, to date, www.bartleby.com. Price varies.
    CD: 1999, $195.
    Print: The New Columbia Encyclopedia, 6th ed. 2000, 3,200 pp. $125.

Online: The Concise Columbia Electronic Encyclopedia, 3rd ed. New York: Columbia University Press, 1993 to date, www.bartleby.com. Also available in Electric Library, OCLC, and others. Rates vary.
    CD: The Concise Columbia Encyclopedia in Microsoft Bookshelf. Renton, WA: Microsoft, 1994 to date. $99.
    Print: 1994, 975 pp. $49.95.

Print: The Random House Encyclopedia, 3rd ed. New York: Random House, 1990, 3,000 pp. $95 to $130.

Print: The Cambridge Encyclopedia, 3rd ed. New York: Cambridge University Press, 1997, 1,344 pp. $55.

When was George Chapman born? (1560); What is a Rorschact test? (ink blots to indicate an individual's psychological inclinations); Where are pistachio's grown? (East Asia and the Mediterranean region); What is the population of Cyprus? (735,000). Questions like these, questions which require only a brief answer, are best found in a one-volume ency-

---

[20]Ahh, but there is a possible catch to this new technological slayer of the print yearbook. In print the reader could visibly see what was new, what, if even indirectly, was added to the initial set. Not true electronically where the actual amount of revision cannot be measured except by painstaking, fruitless examination of item after item after item. One suspects publishers, in a quest to save money, will not be as thorough with new material, certainly not offer as much electronically as they had to when it could easily be measured each year.

clopedia. Here one may make an argument, in terms of time taken, and ease of search for the one volume standard encyclopedia. It usually is faster to turn to a print work than stagger through one online or on CD-ROM. Granted, this is not always the situation, but for daily reference work it is almost a given the one volume work (or for that matter the Macropedia section of the *Britannica*) is the most efficient.

The drawback is a question which relies on the time element (e.g., the population of Cyprus query). Most print one-volume works are dated. Most CD-ROM and online are more current. Depending on which format is best in terms of up-to-date information, the golden print rule may be voided.

Columbia Encyclopedia

The *Columbia* is the best of a group of one-volume encyclopedias that embraces close to 18 various titles. Only three or four can be recommended. The sixth edition of the *Columbia* follows the pattern of the early editions. It has over 6.6 million words, or about 3 to 4 million words less than the multiple sets from *Compton's* to *Funk & Wagnalls.*

The oversized, close to 12-pound volume is equally in the top-weight quality ring. Thanks to its long history, academic publisher, and numerous advisers and contributors *The Columbia Encyclopedia* easily shoves all competitors to one side. While written for adults, the majority of high school students can cope with the relatively easy-to-follow, brief entries. Longer articles include impressive, current bibliographies. The black-and-white drawings dot the three-column pages. They lend an air of scholarship to the work, but hardly excite either the imagination or the eye.

The digital *Columbia* can be searched by word or phrase as an encyclopedia entry or in the text. It is simple to use, although, again, it may be just as fast to use the print edition. (Note: Generally this is available only via a library or a commercial service. As a result there are numerous Web addresses.)

The digital work has some 80,000 hypertext links. Again, though, if one gets to a point where more than ready reference data is needed it is much more efficient to begin with a standard set, not a one volume work, which has more relevant links.

Much the same praise and mild criticism hold for the set's junior partner, the *Concise Columbia Encyclopedia.* Here "concise" is translated into a *Reader's Digest* approach. There are 1 million words versus 6.6 million in the larger volume, and one-third the number of pages. The 150 illustrations hardly count. The smaller book has the advantage of a low, low price ($39.95, often discounted) and, for many, the delight of weighing only one-third as much. The minimal attitude is not reflected in the equally excellent text. There simply is less of it and, of course, many fewer entries. Still, for all but the most esoteric ready-reference questions, it more than meets the average need of a reader. Good as it is, it is not recommended for libraries, which should stay with the senior member.

On a CD-ROM by its lonely self, the *Concise Columbia Encyclopedia* would not be worth a notice. Aware of this, the ubiquitous Microsoft Corporation puts it on a low-priced disc along with other equally valuable reference titles. In typical Microsoft fashion, the encyclopedia section includes most of the illustrations, as well as enhanced animation, sounds, and music. Often sold for about $99 the *Bookshelf* is a best buy. The package not only includes the $50 encyclopedia, but close to $150 more in reference books, often, again, with enhanced pictures, pronunciation, and so forth. These include *The Encarta Dictionary, The American Heritage Dictionary, Roget's Thesaurus, Bartlett's Familiar Quotations, Hammond Atlas, The World Almanac,* and the *Concise Columbia Dictionary of Quotations.*[21] Thanks to well-worked-out search software, a simple point and click will usually find the precise information required. There are numerous integrated cross-references. Given all of the features and the five other basic reference works, the *Microsoft Bookshelf* is a best buy for library and individual. The *Concise* is available online through OCLC, the Electric Library, and other websites. While passable for laypersons, it is not recommended for the reference section bookmarks.

The Random House Encyclopedia

The print version of *The Random House Encyclopedia* has a distinguished history. It has 3 million words and is only about one-half the size of the *New Columbia.* Unlike the *Columbia* it stresses illustrations. In fact, the primary draw, particularly among shoppers, is the stunning, usually full-color drawings, photographs, charts, and other graphics. It has no competitors in terms of appearance. It is a better buy for younger adults. It should be found in all libraries next to the *Columbia.*

As with the previous two editions, it is in two sections. The first is called the "Alphapedia" and has short, useful entries. This is the most updated part of the new edition and may be of value for ready-reference queries concerning recent news events and personalities. ("May" because most of the data are just as readily available, at less cost, in standard works from the *World Almanac* to a basic encyclopedia yearbook.)

The second part (the "Colorpedia") is where one finds the majority of illustrations, usually in color, and longer topical essays on everything

---

[21]Each year the Microsoft people tend to update, change, and otherwise improve on the *Bookshelf.* It will have a different content in the years to come.

from the nature of things to world history. It is a visual delight and of some interest to younger readers and adults who enjoy *The National Geographic.* All and all it is a delightful set.

Not known for its strength of text, the one-volume work is imaginatively designed and packaged. Edited for all markets, not just English-speaking nations, the work compromises and cuts to satisfy everyone. Children seem to enjoy the colorful MTV-like format and if the information does not run deep, it runs with style. Parents and libraries would be better off with a CD-ROM encyclopedia, but if a relatively inexpensive print version in one volume is needed, this is the answer.

A children's *Random House* one-volume work becomes *The Random House Children's Encyclopedia* (New York: Random House, 1991, 664 pp., $50). This is *not* a revised edition of the adult *Random House Encyclopedia.* Rather it is a slightly modified version of the English *Children's Illustrated Encyclopedia,* which, like its adult counterpart, has been translated into numerous languages. It is a rare item, in that few children's encyclopedias are limited to a single volume. Also, it is the largest of its kind, with more than 3,500 attractive illustrations. Most of the 400 entries are broad in scope and limited to one to four pages, with some going to six pages.

In terms of weight, the *Cambridge* falls behind the *New Columbia* at only seven pounds. (The *Columbia* is close to 11 pounds.) While the information in both is reliable, the English one-volume work understandably has much less text: 26,000 entries, a "ready reference" section of some 130 pages, 24-page atlas and approximately 600 illustrations. Another "problem" for American readers is the English bias, understandable, of course, and the almost total reliance on experts from the United Kingdom. The English-European slant makes this a nice supplement to the *Columbia* or *Random House,* and useful in larger libraries. Still, as good as it is, a third choice.

Hardly six months goes by that some firm does not offer a general one-volume encyclopedia for adults and young people. (As noted, the single volume for children is a bit rare.) In 2000, *Books in Print* lists some 30 titles, although several might be called subject works. Be that as it may, how many are worth considering? None, other than those listed here.

FOREIGN-PUBLISHED MULTI-VOLUME ENCYCLOPEDIAS: PRINT FORMAT[22]

For Americans, most reference questions can be quickly and properly answered by an American encyclopedia. There are occasions when a for-

---

[22]The basic sets are arranged by country and language with brief annotations.

eign language work is more suitable. Obviously, a foreign encyclopedia will cover its country of origin in greater depth than an American work, including biographies of nationals, statistics, places, and events.

Even for users with the most elementary knowledge of the language, several of the foreign works are useful for their fine illustrations and maps. For example, the *Enciclopedia Italiana* boasts some of the best illustrations of any encyclopedia, particularly in the area of the fine arts. A foreign encyclopedia is equally useful for point of view: Some American readers may be surprised at the manner in which the Civil War, for example, is treated in the French and the German encyclopedias. Further, the evaluation of American writers and national heroes in these works is sometimes equally revealing about the way Europeans judge the United States. More specifically, the foreign encyclopedia is helpful for information on less-well-known figures not found in American or British works, foreign language bibliographies, detailed maps of cities and regions, and other information ranging from plots of lesser-known novels and musicals to identification of place names.

In Europe, as in America, there are only two or three major publishers (including, incidentally, the *Encyclopaedia Britannica*, which has arrangements for co-publishing with the firms). The giants include: (1) Brockhaus and Herder in Germany, (2) Larousse in France, and (3) Garzanti in Italy. When the librarian finds one of these names on a new or revised set, the odds are about 99 to 1 that the work will be of high quality.

One problem, as with most European encyclopedias, is the alphabetical arrangement. Any student who has had a brush with a foreign language realizes that although the Latin alphabet is employed, there are variations in letters; Spanish, for example, has two letters not found in English, "ch" and "ll." There are also marked differences in common names. In other languages, *John* turns up as Giovanni, Jan, Juan, Johannes, or Jehan. Consequently, before abandoning a foreign encyclopedia for lack of an entry, the user should be certain to look for the entry in terms of the language employed.

What follows is a one-sided sample of only major European sets. Actually, almost every country from Italy to China and Australia to South Africa can boast their own particular brand of encyclopedia. These are dutifully listed with short annotations in the latest edition of *Guide to Reference Books* and *Guide to Reference Materials*. Both reference works have these under the subject heading "encyclopedias." Anyone, for example, looking for a Finnish or Hebrew work will find it here. On the other hand, coverage of most of the world is limited and for any in-depth exploration of what is available one must turn to the bibliographies, the reference guides of the particular country.

The popular CD-ROM/DVD and the online (via the Internet) English language encyclopedias have more or less captured the globe—at least where English is understood. This is likely to change, if only a bit, when these new technologies become available more widely outside of the West.

French[23]

Print: Grand Dictionnaire Encyclopédique Larousse. Paris: Larousse, 1982–1989, 10 vols. $1,250 (Distributed in the United States by French and European Publications, Inc.)

The name Larousse is as familiar in France as the *Encyclopaedia Britannica* is in the United States. Pierre Larousse was the founder of a publishing house which continues to flourish and is responsible for the basic French encyclopedias. In fact, *Larousse* in French is often used as a synonym for *encyclopedia.*

Larousse continues with the policy of short, specific entries, but it does give some rather extensive treatment of major subjects. For example, the length of articles for countries and leading personalities often equals that found in American works. Returning to an older concept of encyclopedias, the *Grand Dictionnaire* is precisely what the title suggests in that it not only includes specific encyclopedia entries, but definitions of words as well. There is a strong emphasis on brilliant illustrations, usually in full color. Each page includes photographs, charts, maps, diagrams, and the like. Regardless of one's command of French, everyone will enjoy the illustrations.

Another major set is often found in American libraries: *Encyclopaedia Universalis,* 2d ed. (available in the United States from *Encyclopaedia Britannica,* 1993, 30 vols., plus a 2-vol. supplement. $1,600). This work is in the fashion of the *Macropaedia,* in that the articles are long, detailed, and scholarly and are extremely well illustrated. The 23 to 24 volumes are a type of ready-reference work with brief entries. The next two volumes called the *Symposium* consist of 180 essays, with a particular emphasis on current political and social trends. This is supplemented in two volumes. The index, with short fact-finding entries as well, is in volumes 27 to 30.

German

Print: Brockhaus Enzyklopadie, rev. 19th ed. Wiesbaden: Brockhaus, 1986, 24 vols. $4,000. Plus irregular supplements.

First issued as *Frauenzimmer Lexikon* (between 1796 and 1808), this was an encyclopedia whose content, as the title indicates, was focused pri-

---

[23]All foreign language encyclopedias are listed here only in print editions.

marily on the interests of women of the period. The original publisher, possibly because of his limited sales, gave up the financial ghost; in 1808, Friedrich Brockhaus purchased the set and issued the last volume. A wise man, Brockhaus continued to offer his volumes not as scholarly works, but as books guaranteed to give the average man (or woman) a solid education. By doing so, he was years ahead of the times, in fact, he was so far ahead of his American and British counterparts that they freely borrowed his text, if not his sales techniques. As noted earlier, the Brockhaus works were the basis for the early *Americana* and *Chambers's*.

Brockhaus developed the idea of short, easy-to-read entries. Some articles were little more than a few sentences or paragraphs in length. Consequently, all the Brockhaus encyclopedia—and there is a family of them—are an admixture of dictionary and encyclopedia. (The family includes the basic 24-volume set, the revised 12-volume set, and a 1-volume work, among others.)

As might be expected, the longer articles, some of them over 100 pages, focus on European countries. In many respects, the *Brockhaus* encyclopedia is considerably more nationalistic than the *Larousse,* and while it is an excellent source of material on German history and personalities, it can be passed by for other items.

Because of its scope, the *Brockhaus* is useful in large research libraries or where there is a German-speaking populace, but it is probably near the bottom among choices of all the foreign language encyclopedias, if for no other reason than the outrageous price of $4,000, plus the cost of supplements.

Italian

Print: Enciclopedia Europea. Milan: Garzanti, 1976–1984, 12 vols. $3,600.

This is the most modern of the Italian sets, and is updated from time to time. It is important for three reasons: (1) It has brief, specific entries that afford a marvelous overview of Italian and European history, culture, and science. (2) There are longer companion articles of considerable substance, particularly in terms of coverage of the sciences and social sciences. (3) There are excellent illustrations.

One of the major European records of the arts is the famous *Enciclopedia Italiana* (Rome: Istituto della Enciclopedia Italiana, 1929–1936, 35 vols., plus supplements 1958 to date; price varies, but in 1995 was $17,500). The basic pre-World War II set is found in almost all large libraries because of its superb illustrations and its scholarly and well-documented articles. Although the articles on the government are far from impartial, the general coverage is excellent and the set is one of the best prewar works to come out of Europe.

Japanese

Print: Kodansha Encyclopedia of Japan. New York: Kodansha International, 1983 to date, 9 vols. and supplements. $900.

This is an unusual and superior encyclopedia which analyzes, explains, and even critically assesses Japan, past and present. The all English-Japanese encyclopedia represents the work of 1,300 scholars from 27 countries, including Japan and the United States. The text was written with the average layperson in mind, although much of the material will interest the subject specialist. The style is much above average. There are about 10,000 entries and 4 million words. The largest single category of entries concerns Japanese history, followed by geography and art. These are slightly over 1,000 articles covering Japanese economics and business. The articles are quite objective, and considerable effort was made to ensure that nothing about Japan's past was glossed over or ignored.

The same publisher, in 1993, issued the widely acclaimed *Japan: An Illustrated Encyclopedia* (2 vols., 1,924 pp. $250). A shorter version of the larger work, this has the advantage of superior illustrations (the main set is weak in this respect) and current data on Japanese politics and culture. Here one will find practical advice on making sushi as well as philosophical meditations. The price is as reasonable as the set is superior.

Russian

Print: The Great Soviet Encyclopedia, 3d ed. New York: Macmillan, 1973–1983, 32 vols. $2,500. (Published in Russia from 1970 to 1980 as *Bol'shaia Sovetskaia Entisklopediia,* or *BSE.*)

With the chill of the Cold War past, this set is now primarily of value for its historical material and the static information on such things as geography, music, and the arts. Beyond that, it offers some striking examples of bias.

The *BSE* is somewhat equivalent in scholarship to the older version of the *Britannica.* The entire set has more than 21 million words and over 100,000 articles. Including both the specific-entry and the broad-entry forms, the set is a combination of routine dictionary and gazetteer items, with detailed, lengthy articles covering every aspect of Soviet interest.

Since most American readers will use the English translation, two points are worth making: (1) The index is necessary because of the unusual alphabetical arrangement of each volume, caused by differences between the Russian and Latin alphabets. For example, the first translated volume "A to Z" contains entries for "Aalen Stage" and the "Zulu War of 1879." (2) The quality of the translation is good. The American version differs from the Russian in that cost considerations made it necessary to delete the fine maps in the original Russian version.

There are numerous current books on today's Russia, and these should be turned to first for the average query. Among the best: *The Cambridge Encyclopedia of Russia and the Former Soviet Union* (New York: Cambridge University Press, 2d ed., 1993).

Spanish

Online: Nueva Enciclopedia Cumbre en Linea. Danbury, CT: Grolier Incorporated, 1999 to date, quarterly, http://grolier.com. Rate varies.
Print: Enciclopedia universal ilustrada Europeo-Americana (Espasa). Barcelona: Espasa, 1907 to 1933, 108 vols., including annual supplements, 1934 to date. $8,995. (Distributed in the United States by French and European Publications, Inc.)

A current Spanish encyclopedia for young people and adults, *Nueva* is a welcome addition to the online family of encyclopedias. It includes more than 15,000 entries and close to 8,000 illustrations, tables, maps, etc. The articles are easy to read and although they have a Latin American bias, the overall coverage is international. Using Boolean logic, the more complex searches are the best choice. The simple one to two word entries tend to be too broad. Also, coverage is uneven with some articles longer than others for no apparent reason. There are Web links, but they are far from thorough.

Despite its faults, Grolier is to be commended for taking a step in the right direction and over the years the online work is sure to improve. A must in any library with a Spanish language group of patrons.

The clear leader is the famous *Espasa.* Usually cited simply as *Espasa,* the *Enciclopedia* is a remarkable work. First, it never seems to end. Forgoing continuous revision or new editions, the publishers continue to augment the 80 volumes (actually 70 basic volumes with 10 appendixes) with annual supplements, which are arranged in large subject categories and include an index. (The term *annual* must be taken advisedly, as the supplements generally are not issued until three to five years after the period covered. For example, the 1981–1982 volume came out in 1985.)

Second, *Espasa* has the largest number of entries—the publishers claim over 1 million. Since they evidently do not count on "authority," no articles are signed, although they are signed in the supplements after 1953. Again, as in the German and French encyclopedias, the emphasis is on short entries of the dictionary type. Still, there are a number of rather long articles, particularly those dealing with Spain, Latin America, prominent writers, and so forth.

SUBJECT ENCYCLOPEDIAS

Ranging in price from $35 to close to $9,000, one-volume to multi-volume subject encyclopedias gain in importance. Their numbers increase as the society becomes more specialized. Almost every discipline, every subject, every object of curiosity can now claim recognition in a subject encyclopedia. Among the 1,200 or so in print, the range of topics is obvious from a few of the titles published in the late 1990s and early 2000: *The Mafia Encyclopedia; Encyclopedia of Animal Rights & Animal Welfare; Encyclopedia of Mental Health; The New Encyclopedia of the American West; The Cat Encyclopedia; The Encyclopedia of Mummies; The Encyclopedia of Conflict Resolution; Encyclopedia of the Consumer Movement* and *Encyclopedia of the War of 1812*. Check the annual "Outstanding Reference Sources" of the American Library Association (which usually appears in the April 15 issue of *Library Journal*. (Also in *American Libraries* around May 1 and *Booklist* for May 1). Among the 50 to 60 outstanding titles chosen for the previous year, one inevitably finds a dozen or more subject encyclopedias. Most are in print format, but a few, and particularly those published exclusively on CD-ROM, are in an electronic version.

Publishers of subject encyclopedias follow the special-audience philosophy. Generally, the result is encouraging for reference librarians, particularly when (1) a ready-reference question is so specialized or esoteric that it cannot be answered in a general encyclopedia, or (2) a user needs a more detailed overview of a subject than that found in a single article in a general encyclopedia. The more limited the library budget for both reference work and general titles, the more reason to turn to subject encyclopedias.

Such key descriptors as "companion," "handbook," or "dictionary" may indicate a subject one- to three-volume encyclopedia. For example, Oxford University Press is known for companion series such as *The Oxford Companion to American Theatre* and, in a narrower field, *The Oxford Companion to Chess*. There are dozens of these reputable works edited by well-known experts. Inevitably they are alphabetically arranged by subject. One may argue that these are not encyclopedias, but another form of an information package. No matter, the point is that the arrangement, scope, and audience for each is such that it fits the encyclopedia pattern. More important, they often serve as reference sources for quick, often in-depth answers to common questions.

Evaluation

Use the same evaluative techniques for subject sets as those used for general encyclopedias. Even with limited knowledge of the field covered,

librarians may judge a set. Using reviews or subject experts for evaluation of the expensive works is useful. Subject sets often are evaluated
in scholarly periodicals, which discuss them at greater length than in
standard reviews.

See, too: the *ARBA Guide to Subject Encyclopedias and Dictionaries*
(Englewood, CO: Libraries Unlimited, Inc., various dates). This frequently is revised and is a collection of the critical reviews which have
appeared in earlier editions of the *American Reference Books Annual.* Allan
Mirwis' *Subject Encyclopedias* (Phoenix, AZ: Oryx Press, 1999, 2 vols.)
lists with grades of importance, as well as an index to subject matter,
some 1,129 titles.

Space does not permit a full discussion of the numerous, many
quite superior, subject encyclopedias. The focus here is on works that are
best known and likely to be found in many medium to large libraries.
Most, although not all, have been published relatively recently. This
rather arbitrary approach gives at least a cursory glance at the direction
of subject encyclopedia publishing.

Africa and America

Online: Africana. New York: Time-Warner, 2000 to date. Irregular,
   www.Africana.com. Price varies.
   CD: Encarta Africana. Redmond, WA: Microsoft, 1999, annual. $39.95.
   *Print: Africana: The Encyclopedia of the African and African American
   Experience,* New York: Perseus Book Company, 2,144 pp., 1999. $99.

CD: The American Indian: A Multimedia Encyclopedia. New York: Facts on
   File, 1993. $295.
   Print: Carl Waldman, Encyclopedia of Native American Tribes. New York:
   Facts on File, 1988. $29.95.

The two-disc *Encarta Africana* is a collaborative effort between
Microsoft, the publisher and Henry Louis Gates Jr., an academic all-star,
chairman of Harvard University's African American studies and a team
of African American scholars. It includes some 2 million words, 3,000 articles and more than 2,500 multimedia entries. Among the latter: video
clips, audio recordings and maps which consider the early human ancestors in Africa millions of years ago to today. Coverage of both Africa and
African Diaspora is excellent.

Mr. Gates hopes the encyclopedia will draw more African American
children into the computer age. "Several studies have shown that African
Americans are less likely to use computers to have access to the Internet than other American children. The main reason, of course, is that

a higher proportion of African-Americans, compared with whites, live in low income families and neighborhoods."[24]

Based on Carl Waldman's popular *Encyclopedia of Native American Tribes,* the CD-ROM version adds material and comes up with coverage of more than 150 tribes of native peoples in what is now the United States. The standard illustrations (250 out of 900 in color) are coupled with the full text of documents relating to the government and the tribes. Maps, charts, time lines, and related material round out the reading matter. It boasts the usual features such as cross-references to related material and the possibility (equipment being suitable) to print out the illustrations. An added voice-over of sound bites of Native American songs is pleasant. With that, though, one wonders why the CD-ROM is considered much better than the main work by Waldman. The answer is hard to find. The librarian is wise to (1) purchase the Waldman print version (for under $30) and (2) invest in *Handbook of North American Indians* (Washington, DC: Smithsonian Institution, 1978 to date). Individual volumes are from $25 to $50 and eventually 20 will be published. As of 1995 about one-half the volumes were available. Thanks to the clear writing style, the marvelous illustrations, and the careful indexing these are both scholarly and popular. Together they may cost a bit more than the CD-ROM, but together they represent the best there is on the subject.

All of this is to illustrate the point that while electronic databases for reference works are a blessing, there are times, particularly in certain subject encyclopedias, when the librarian is wiser to consider the print version.

ART AND ARTS

Online: The Grove Dictionary of Art Online. New York: Grove, 1998 to date, www.grovereference.com/TDA/online/Index. Price varies, but about $1,500 a year.[25]

---

[24]The starters of *Africana.com* (Harvard professors Henry Louis Gates Jr. and Kwame Anthony Appiah) sold the site to Time Warner in order to keep it active. According to Gates, the site needed an inflow of cash. With a focus on cultural history to advice on general subjects from health to finance, *Africana.com* is less popular than rivals, e.g., *NetNoir* (www.netnoir.com) which has an interest in celebrities or *BlackVoices* (www.blackvoices.com) which is strong on chat rooms.

[25]Prior to this behemoth set, the standard art encyclopedia was the *Encyclopedia of World Art* (New York: McGraw Hill Book Company, 1968. 5 vols. $1,500. Two supplements, 1983 to 1987). The well-illustrated articles (plates are at the end of each volume) continues to make this a major set for research. Most of the material is covered in the *Dictionary of Art,* but here one finds different opinions and approaches. Well worth a look for more than ready reference questions.

Print: The Dictionary of Art. New York: 1996. 34 vols. $8,000.
Print: International Encyclopedia of Dance. New York: Oxford University Press, 1998. 6 vols. $1,250.

The Dictionary of Art, by the same publisher of another landmark set, *The New Grove Dictionary of Music and Musicians* is the most impressive of all subject works.[26] Statistics make the point: the 34 volumes weigh in at 168 pounds; there are 32,600 pages covering every aspect of art and artists from the earliest caves (c. 14,000 BC) to modern minimalists; the 41,000 articles are by over 6,700 expert contributors; and their work is illustrated with some 15,000 images and 750 maps. Finally, but not least, it is expensive, $8,800 as compared to about $50 for the average general CD-ROM encyclopedia.

Is it worth it? The consensus is a resounding "yes," and the set is found in any medium to large library. The articles are easy to understand and the majority are free of academic jargon. Of particular value is the emphasis on non-Western art and there is no more complete guide to both old and new cultures outside of the West. The articles all include bibliographies and often outstanding illustrations. The index is excellent. The only partial rival to this work is the still to be completed German equivalent, begun in 1907, known fondly by the name of its original editors, Thieme-Becker.[27]

The complete index, along with the total content of the print 1996 edition, went online in late 1998. The obvious advantages, cost aside, are summarized by the publisher: "Users will love having the option to search quickly and easily through the equivalent of 34 volumes with the click of a mouse." Added features online include: links to over 100,000 images at other Internet sites (includes picture libraries and collections from large museums throughout the world); quarterly updates now, but monthly by the end of 2000; and highlighted cross-references. And, to be sure, this has the usual advantages of being searched by numerous ways from keywords to article headings. It is updated, too, once a month rather than every four or five years.

Less well organized are the numerous online websites of specific art institutions. These range from the Prado in Madrid to the National Gallery in London. See, too, individual museum catalogs such as: *National Gallery Complete Illustrated Catalogue on CD-ROM* (London National Gallery, 1998, $95). Here are the images, as well as background information on the 2,300 plus works in the collection as well as data on artists.

[26]For a glowing report on the Net version, see "Art on Line," *The New York Times,* May 13, 1999, p. G1/G9.

[27]Named after Ulrich Thieme and Felix Becker, the set has reached 37 volumes, but that was in 1950 and no other volumes are announced. While superior to the *Dictionary of Art* in number of bibliographies, it has been translated into English.

Three points to make about the excellent *Encyclopedia of Dance*—points which are applicable for almost all multiple volume sets. First, it is expensive and beyond most individuals' budgets. All the more reason, then, to have in a library. Second, it is available only in print (at least as of 2000). The obvious reason is that the publisher hopes to recoup the millions it cost to edit and produce the set and does not feel this can be done by offering it at a cut-rate CD-ROM or online price. Third, it is the work of scholars from most major countries. It is not limited to a single nation, or to the work of an editorial staff.

Expensive, available only in print, and expert contributors: all three points usually may be made for giant subject sets of this type.

Specifically, this covers dance from all periods, all places, and more than 600 specialists move from anthropology to art without difficulty. They indicate that dance is not an isolated event, but part of the whole culture. They support the sometimes lengthy articles with extensive bibliographies which not only include books, but multimedia sources from videos to CDs. All of this is supported by over 2,000 illustrations, extensive cross-references and a detailed index. There are some drawbacks: the set is weak on biographies, possibly because the slack is taken up by the *International Dictionary of Ballet* (London: St. James, 1993). As in all cooperative reference works there are marked discrepancies in the contributors' knowledge and prose styles. Still, it is the ideal place to turn for any aspect of dance, and should be found in most libraries.

Folklore

Print: An Encyclopedia of Beliefs, Customs, Tales, Music and Art. Santa Barbara, CA: ABC-CLIO, 1997. 2 vols. $150.

The folklore encyclopedia is one of the few subject works which casts a broad audience net. Instead of being directed only at one group, the usual practice of subject encyclopedias, this is aimed at everyone from grade school through university and beyond. It assumes, as the subtitle indicates, that folklore covers a broad area of interests and, hence, has a wide audience. The notion is upheld by the content: 240 easy-to-follow articles, of a page to numerous pages; clear definitions and explanation of terms; a historical overview matched by the place of the entry in today's scene; and current bibliographies. There is a good index. The scope, as indicated, is broad moving from "children's folklore" (about seven pages) to folklore in Africa, India, etc. Note, though, there are no biographic entries as such, although names are found in the index. See, too, the related: *Dictionary of Chicano Folklore* (Santa Barbara, CA: ABC-CLIO, 2000, 330 pp.) is a combination of definitions and history of the subject.

History

Print: Chronicles of World History. See Subject Indexes, Chapter 6.

Print: Civilization of the Ancient Mediterranean: Greece and Rome. New York: Charles Scribner's Sons, 1988, 3 vols. $259.

Print: Dictionary of the Middle Ages. New York: Charles Scribner's Sons, 1982–1989, 13 vols. $1,300.

Scribner, or Charles Scribner's Sons (a division of Macmillan) are leaders in historical encyclopedias and related reference works. They are reliable and imaginative enough to bring out useful new titles every year or so as well as update existing, much used works. Here is a sampling only of their numerous titles.

Greece and Rome occupy considerable space in any multiple-volume general encyclopedia, but neither is treated in the depth desirable for either the expert, or the would-be expert, who needs to know, for example, how women fared in one or both of the societies during a certain time frame. It is for that type of query that one turns to a subject set such as this, or the numerous other works in the field, for example, the excellent one-volume *Oxford History of the Classical World* (New York: Oxford University Press, 1988).

The three-volume Scribner's work covers the sciences, social sciences, and of course the humanities in the two civilizations, but taking a somewhat different approach. Rather than a chronological system, there are 95 individual essays by as many experts. Organized under broad subject headings, each article considers the topic in some depth. Illustrations accompany some of the pieces, and there is a detailed index in the final volume.

Published in 1995 by Scribner's, *Civilization of the Ancient Near East* (4 vols.), complements the Greek and Roman encyclopedia. Here a group of experts, who write as well as they understand the subject, cover the cultures from the Bronze Age, circa 3,200 B.C. to the high point in Greek civilization, circa 325 B.C. No better work about for such a length of time and number of cultures.

History attracts many publishers but, as indicated, the leader in historical sets is Scribner's. For example, between 1983 and 1990 they published the first edition of the *Dictionary of the Middle Ages.* The 13-volume work (including a detailed index) moves from A.D. 500 through to the end of the period, A.D. 1500. There are over 5,000 articles by some of the world's leading historians in this area. A fascinating point about the coverage is the emphasis on daily life of average people. One moves from the monastery to the farm, not just from the castle of the king. In addition, there are biographical pieces on both famous and minor figures. There are some black-and-white and a few color illustrations, but the strength of the set is the text, not the illustrations. The articles are by 1,300 scholars from approximately 30 countries. It can be read as a history book as well as used for a reference work—an almost ideal situation. See, too, the related set by the same publisher: *Encyclopedia of the Renaissance* (1999, 6 vols. $695). This features 1,200 articles, maps, illustrations and the work of experts in the period from 1350 to 1650.

Gale Group's *History Resource Center: U.S.* (www.galenet.com) includes the Scribner family as well as basic historical indexes from ABC-CLIO and other sources. From Scribner this massive online database includes several related historical encyclopedias: the full text of *Dictionary of American History, Encyclopedia of American Social History, The Presidents: A Reference History,* and supplements 9 and 10 of *Dictionary of American Biography.* In addition, is an index to about 65 historical journals (most available online in full text). There are texts of major historic documents from the Mayflower Compact to the Warren Report. Six hundred images have been incorporated, and there are scores of other features and reference works. There are numerous ways of searching, most of which are easy to understand. With an emphasis on excellent texts and a minimum of bells and whistles, this is a fine place to begin basic research over a wide area of primarily American history.

A glance at *Books in Print* will show there are numerous history encyclopedia choices. The ones listed here are examples of the best. Note, too, for a modest sum the library may purchase a one-volume work such as *Encyclopedia of World History* (New York: Oxford University Press, 1999, 784 pp. $30) which has over 4,000 entries in alphabetical order. The descriptive paragraphs are short and move from people and places to events.

Library Science

Print: Encyclopedia of Library and Information Science. New York: Marcel Dekker, 1968 to date, 35 vols., plus supplements. $115 each.

Even though it is controversial, the *Encyclopedia of Library and Information Science* cannot be faulted for its wide coverage and its ambitious effort. Some think there is too much material; others, that areas are not always covered as well as they might be, particularly by the contributors involved. The supplements, issued approximately yearly, are an effort to keep the complete set current. Actually, the lengthy articles in the supplements tend to be better than those in the primary set, and are a good source of information on major trends in library and information work.

Ironically, this is a major subject set that is not available in electronic format. Still, it makes the point that limited readership, limited interest, and limited funding is not conducive to CD-ROM or online versions of subject encyclopedias—even when dealing with library and information science.

Taking a broader view, the English *International Encyclopedia of Information and Library Science* (London: Routledge, 1997. 235 pp.) is an alphabetically arranged compilation of data and opinion about information science. Various regions of the world are considered in the major articles from "communication" to "information management." The editors, John Feather and Paul Strangle, have experts with an ability to write as authors of the essays.

Literature

Print: *Benet's Readers' Encyclopedia, 3d ed.* New York: HarperCollins, 1987, 1091 pp. $45.

There are scores of one- and two-volume guides to literature, most of which are particularly suited for the ready-reference questions: "When was R. R. Boyd born?" "When did she die?" "What did she write?" "How important is her *Tale of Three Horses* among her other works?" And on and on. One finds answers in these guides.

There is no better-known one-volume literature reference than *Benet's Readers' Encyclopedia*. Named after its first compiler, William Rose Benet, this is an alphabetically arranged, short-entry format of the world's literature and arts. The close to 9,500 entries move from biblical personalities to best-selling authors, right up through and including most of 1987. Much of the data are in handy chart or outline form. Mentioned are not only literature, but also the other arts, from painting and opera to the military. The explanation are usually short, clear, and well written.

Benet, as it is called by librarians, deserves a place on the ready-reference shelf right next to *Bartlett* and *World Almanac*. It is a most valuable aid, and one, by the way, which can be recommended to almost anyone as the ideal birthday or holiday gift.

Music

Online: The New Grove II Dictionary of Music and Musicians Online, New York: Grove. 2000 to date, www.grovemusic.com. Price varies.
Print: 2nd ed. 2000. 28 vols. $4,250.

The 29-volume *New Grove II* is unquestionably the standard set in the field of music. Like earlier editions it is extremely reliable, drawing on the experience and skills of over 2,500 contributors. (Note: The 1980 20-volume set remains a "best buy," if it can be found in paperback for $500 or less. The bound 20-volume set in good used condition may be under $1,500. Most of the information is useful, and differs only from the new edition in amount, but not quality, of editorial material, illustrations etc.)

While of value to reference librarians, primarily for the detailed articles on pre-twentieth-century music and musicians, the latest edition now includes detailed information on modern musical life, covering not only the contemporary classical composers and performers, but also those from popular music, including the vast area of folk music.

There are some 29,000 articles with over 3,500 illustrations which, according to the publisher, occupy about 7 percent of the page space. In addition, there are several thousand musical examples. Of particular interest, in addition to the detailed material on music and the long biographical sketches, are the many bibliographies. Not only are these found at the end of articles but in numerous cases they are separate entries, for example, "Germany and Austria: Bibliography of Music to 1600." There is equal emphasis on lists of works by various composers. Still, there appears to be a consensus in many reviews of the set that the high points are the biographies. These are the best of their type to be found in any reference source, and a first choice for reference libraries.

The online version has various prices around $600 a year for a single subscription. It has all the usual advantages of an electronic work. The best probably is the link system which ties individual articles to related material on the Web. Quarterly updates are planned including biographical additions and new digital sounds. Most libraries will want both the print and online versions, but if budget dictates only one, the online is the best choice.

As with all subject encyclopedias, online sources complement music. One may find valuable to useless information on almost any composer, performer, or anyone related to music online. An expert has no trouble separating the bad from the good. The amateur had best stay with standard print-electronic encyclopedias as listed here.

The real advantage of the electronic path to information is the systematic, yet terribly slow procedure of putting heretofore difficult to locate archives online. Music is a case in point, e.g., as of mid-2000 a good many of Bach's manuscripts are at the *Bach Digital Library* (www.bachdigital.org). The project was opened with the posting of the 180 page score of the "Mass in B-Minor."

The New Grove Dictionary of American Music (1986, 4 vols. $695) is primarily an original work. One may find entries in *The New Grove Dictionary of American Music and Musicians* for the same material but nowhere in such depth as in this new work. For example, "Popular Music" is in the best set, but here it is expanded to almost 22 pages. When the ads claim that 70 percent of the material is original to this set, they are right. Its primary contribution is the stamp of approval (often in elegantly written essays) given to American music in its many forms from the classical and jazz to folk and rock. It is exceptionally useful for biographical sketches and thoughtful pieces on regional contributions. With the second edition there is for the first time an index in volume 29—a great addition.

Related, equally excellent works, again by the same publisher: *The New Grove Dictionary of Jazz* (1988, 2 vols. $350); *The Encyclopedia of Popular Music*, 3rd ed. (1998, 8 vols. $750). The latter has an index of over 350 pages with a song index of 50,000 plus titles. Coverage is complete for 20th-century nonclassical music from country to rap.

PHILOSOPHY

CD: Routledge Encyclopedia of Philosophy. London: Routledge, 1998. $2,995.
   Print: 10 vols. $2,995. (Note: Print and CD-ROM combined: $3,495).
   Concise version in one volume, 1999. $40.
Print: The Encyclopedia of Applied Ethics. Orlando, Florida, 1997. 4 vols. $625.

The *Routledge Encyclopedia of Philosophy* solves the problem of self competition by pricing the CD-ROM at the same price as the printed work. (This may work as the CD and the print combined is only $500 more.) The CD has the complete text of the set as well as the usual advantages of electronic navigation and searching. The concise version has the same number of entries as the larger works, but they are cut back severely and primarily are summaries. Not a substitute, but can be used where budgets are tight.

More important is the content of over 2,000 lengthy entries by some 1,300 contributors. Although published in England, with a Cambridge University editor, the experts are from various parts of the world. The work has two tremendous advantages: *(a)* It is up-to-date and not only covers the historical aspects of a philosophical movement or individual, but suggests current debate, if any, about the area. *(b)* It is by and large the most comprehensive approach to the subject now available in a single work.

International authority, from numerous disciplines, examine the pragmatic aspect of ethics in the multiple-volume *Encyclopedia of Applied Ethics.* The some 282 subjects are analyzed in detail. Most articles are from 4,000 to 7,000 words. Literature, for example, is considered along with the more obvious ethic problems connected with modern medicine and science. Sex education, for example, covers the pros and cons of the subject and, as all articles, includes a glossary and a current bibliography. Numerous cross-references, as well as an extensive index, connect the contributions. Note: the Internet website: (www.academicpress.com/ethics) is an effort to keep the information current, particularly by adding additional readings and news items.) It does not, however, have the text of the set.[28]

A related title, although it covers more than philosophy, is what the *Reference Books Bulletin* called "an immediate reference classic."[29] This is the *Encyclopedia of Aesthetics* (New York: Oxford University Press, 1998, 4 vols.). Here are some 600 lengthy articles on individuals, theories, movements, etc. Coverage is international, and the work is for both the expert and interested layperson.

Psychology

Print: Encyclopedia of Psychology, 2d ed. New York: Wiley Interscience, 1994, 4 vols. $475.

An award-winning set, this encyclopedia has a basic approach to psychology and related areas. It is found in most medium to large libraries. Coverage is broad from excellent history and background articles to specific material, and articles on therapy and research, which vary from region to region, country to country. All the disagreements among the experts are found here, as is the occasional broadside from the lay press.

As psychology touches so many human areas, one will find numerous articles on music, sociology, art, science, business, law, and so on. Whenever there is a call for a profile of the people involved in the human comedy/tragedy something is to be found in the four volumes. The quest for bits and pieces is helped tremendously by an excellent name and subject index. (Also, the fourth volume has an up-to-date bibliography, as well as biographical sketches of leading psychologists.)

About 400 contributors, who sign their work, account for the approximate 2,500 articles. Many of these boast charts, graphs, and other helpful illustrations. The purpose is to cover the subject in depth and there is little or no effort to simplify sometimes dense material. Jargon is limited, though, and a careful reading (sometimes with a good dictionary) will be worth the work.

The publisher offers a one-volume abridgment of the set, the *Concise Encyclopedia of Psychology*, for $100. The catch is that this is based on the first edition and is dated. Apparently a new edition is planned in the next year or so.

---

[28]For more specialized situations, as is the case with almost all broad subject sets, there are individual volumes covering particular aspects of philosophy. Most of these are mentioned in the Routledge. For example: *Encyclopedia of Classical Philosophy* (Westport, CT, Greenwood, 1997, 614 pp.) which covers Greek and Roman philosophy from the 6th-century BC to the 6th-century AD.

[29]February 1, 1999, p. 989.

Meanwhile, for libraries with the budget and the patron interest, the more current work in this area is *The Encyclopedia of Psychology* (Oxford: Oxford University Press, 2000, 8 vols. $995). Twice as large as its competitor (and twice as expensive), it covers much the same material as the earlier work. The advantage, obviously, is that it is up-to-date, although one may prefer its competitor for somewhat better written and documented articles. At any rate, a luxury, but a pleasant one for large libraries.

Religion[30]

Print: The Encyclopedia of Religion. New York: Macmillan Company, 1986, 16 vols. $1,400. (In 1993 the set was reissued in 8 volumes for $750.)

Print: The Encyclopedia of Christianity. New York: Eerdmans, 1999 to date, vol. 1 (A–D). $100.

CD: Encyclopedia Judaica. Shaker Heights, OH: Judaica Multimedia, 1997. $595.
Print: 1972. 16 vols. $. Yearbooks, irregular, 1974 to date.

Entries in the *Encyclopedia of Religion* are current and arranged in alphabetical order with cross-references and an excellent index. There are superior bibliographies. Coverage is international and the authorities move with ease and clarity from Jewish and Muslim history and rites to the beliefs of the Hindus. There are superior entries for related areas from the occult and alchemy to atheism. Particularly noteworthy is the fine style of writing and editing which opens up the set not only to students of religion, but also to casual readers.

Expected to be completed by about 2004, *The Encyclopedia of Christianity* is a translation of a German work, *Evangelisches Kirchenlexikon*. Coverage is international and includes all major Christian denominations and sects. Note, too, the related articles from ethics and politics to birth control and colonialism. The scholarly entries are objective and present various sides of any debatable issue. An essential purchase for any reference library with a strong interest in the subject.

The *Encyclopedia Judaica* is the standard work in the field, and thanks to CD-ROMs it is now more current than before. Published in 16 volumes in 1972, it soon became dated (except, of course, for the basic historical information which one could argue makes up a good three quarters of the set). The yearbooks and decennial collections were employed as updates, but only the CD brings them together in one place

---

[30]There are hundreds of works which cover religion in an encyclopedic fashion, without the term "encyclopedia" in the title, e.g., *America's Religion* for one. See *Guide to Reference Books* for a definitive listing as well as "Reference Sources for Non-Christian Religions," *Booklist,* October 1, 1997, pp. 345–349.

for efficient searching. This is made even better by the addition of the print index which may be browsed as well as, of course, the standard key words and use of Boolean logic. The result is the definitive specialized religious encyclopedia which boasts over 25,000 articles by some 2,200 experts. The CD has added film clips, sound recordings, slide shows, and the standard links. Still, the basic set remains as it was in print with authoritative articles back to the first Jew in Biblical history to modern political confrontations in the Middle East. Thanks to its broad scope it, as other such sets (e.g., the *Catholic Encyclopedia*, for one) it offers multiple resources for the individual seeking historical and biographical data throughout the ages.

A more current set is the *Encyclopedia of Judaism* (New York: The Museum of Jewish Heritage. Distributed by Continuum Publishing, 1999, 3 vols. $250). This has about 120 subject areas, all written by scholars. Areas move from the Dead Sea scrolls to the holocaust and modern Israel. Unfortunately, it has a rather poor index.

Science

Online: Access Science. New York: McGraw-Hill, 2000 to date, daily, www.accessscience.com. Price varies.
   CD: McGraw-Hill Multimedia Encyclopedia of Science and Technology. 1995 to date. $795.
   Print: McGraw-Hill Encyclopedia of Science and Technology, 9th ed. New York: McGraw-Hill, Inc., 2002, 20 vols. $2,495.
CD: Science Navigator. New York: McGraw Hill, 1977 to date, annual. $150.
   Print: McGraw Hill Concise Encyclopedia of Science & Technology. 1994 to date, annual. $150.
CD: Mammals: A Multimedia Encyclopedia. Washington, DC: National Geographic Society, 1990 to date. $99–$150.
   Print: Book of Mammals. National Geographic Society, 2 vols., various dates. Price varies.
CD: Eyewitness Encyclopedia of Nature. New York: DK Multimedia, 1998. $39.95.

Scientific encyclopedias particularly are important in libraries. Both academic and public librarians in a *Library Journal* survey, "when asked which books libraries found in greatest demand, books in the sciences ranked at the top."[31]

The leading science and technology encyclopedia, *The McGraw Hill Encyclopedia of Science & Technology* claims that position because: *(a)* it has exceptionally easy-to-understand text for laypersons as well as students; *(b)* it has some 13,000 superior illustrations, primarily in color,

[31]"Science at Your Fingertips," *Library Journal,* April 1, 1999, p. 86.

which complement and explain the text; and *(c)* it has an excellent index. There are about 7,500 entries in the twenty volumes, and with each new edition (every five years), 15 to 20 percent of the articles are updated. The index is in two parts. The first has over 170,000 entries while the second is divided into about 80 disciplines.

The online and CD-ROM encyclopedia includes all of the text found in the 20-volume print set, but the number of illustrations are cut from slightly over 13,000 to about 2,000. This allows space for the publisher to add 60 minutes of audio narration and another hour or so of animation sequences. In addition, there is space left over for the 115,000 term *McGraw-Hill Dictionary of Scientific and Technical Terms* (6th ed., 1999, 2,300 pp. $150). Updated every five years, this includes definitions based on what is found primarily in the encyclopedia. If possible, the library should have both the print and the CD-ROM because each has a distinctive use in reference work. Where frequently used, the online version—even if expensive—is preferable as it is regularly updated via the weekly *Science News* and "research updates" which eventually find their way into the set's yearbook.

The single volume *McGraw-Hill Concise Encyclopedia of Science & Technology* (available both in print and on CD-ROM as *Science Navigator*) is a boiled down version of the 20-volume set. It is ideal for home and the library with the major work which only wants to update it every four or five years. (The historical material does not date, and the one volume title acts as a type of yearbook for the larger work.) The concise version has more than 8,000 articles—about the same number as in the larger work, but drastically cut back. At the same time there are hundreds of new entries and illustrations which update the basic set.

Popular science encyclopedias with self defining titles are found in most middle- to large-sized libraries: *The Facts on File Encyclopedia of Science, Technology and Society* (New York: *Facts on File,* 1999, 3 vols.) and *The International Encyclopedia of Science and Technology* (New York: Oxford University Press, 1999, 471 pp.).

A familiar work in most libraries is the *Van Nostrand's Scientific Encyclopedia* (New York: J.W. Wiley, 8th ed. 1999, 2 vols.). This is ideal for quick ready-reference work as entries are written for the beginner. The information is short and easy to understand. The 7,000 articles plus is available on a CD-ROM. This is regularly updated and has all the usual search advantages. One catch: the price is $350.

Produced by the National Geographic Society for children from about ten to sixteen years of age, *Mammals: A Multimedia Encyclopedia* has the familiar full-screen photograph with brief captions. But that, of course, is only the beginning. The user can call up the animal information and then (1) see 45 full-motion clips of the mammals in action, (2) listen to 155 digitized vocalizations, (3) play a game, (4) locate definitions, (5) hear a narrator pronounce animal names, and so forth. Many of the film clips are from the well-known television features from the Society. The children control the presentation by using graphical icons. The CD-ROM is taken from the Society's two-volume set, *Book of Mammals.*

On the same topic, yet at another extreme, is the CD-ROM *McGraw-Hill Multimedia Encyclopedia of Mammalian Biology* (1992. $495). Based on the almost legendary set, Grimzek's *Encyclopedia of Mammals,* the electronic version has the entire text of that work, as well as its numerous illustrations. The reason for purchase is the addition of hypertext features from sound and video clips to graphics. This work is primarily for advanced high school students and adults.

Science seems particularly suited to hypertext and there are scores of other possibilities for adults, children, and a mix of the audiences. For example: *Multimedia Audubon's Birds* (Portland, OR: CMC Research. $49.95) and the same company's *Multimedia Audubon's Mammals* ($49.95). All have sound, motion, and delights for the user, no matter what age.

DK Multimedia has gained a place for itself in the production of popular, easy-to-understand scientific CD-ROMs. The audience generally is from middle school through adult. The point is to consider various aspects of science for the layperson, not the expert. Typical, the *Eyewitness Encyclopedia of Nature* moves from ants to robins to salmon. Typical questions from how ants build ant hills to how bats sleep are explained in text, panoramas, videos, and recreations of nature at her best. While this is hardly the place to find in-depth information, it does offer a solid overview for mildly involved readers.

Among other recommended, usually found in libraries DK Multimedia discs are: *Eyewitness Encyclopedia of Science* (a more general work which covers mathematics, chemistry, the life sciences, etc.), and also "Eyewitness" of space.

On the Web

There are at least a dozen or more subject "encyclopedias" free on the Web. The majority are not only of questionable authority, but are dated, and are of no real value. Some are simply electronic versions of turn-of-the-century sets, e.g., *Catholic Encyclopedia* (www.newadvent.org/cathen). This, one should hasten to add, is not the current print set which is an outstanding work.

The presence of "edu" in the address is the key usually to the online set being worthy of notice. Here there are only a few. Examples of outstanding works:

Stanford Encyclopedia of Philosophy (http://plato.stanford.edu). Maintained by Stanford University's Center for the Study of Language and

Information the sponsors claim, it is "an authoritative reference work suitable for use by professionals and students." It is not for the average layperson. Although the work is free, there is a copyright notice that authors retain rights to the articles as does Stanford University and nothing may be reproduced except for "fair use," i.e., individual information. Unlike many general sets, "contributions...are normally solicited by invitation from a member of the Board of Editors." The work will be comprehensive. It not only gives background information, but serves to update current print encyclopedias in philosophy. The search mechanism is sophisticated and offers numerous approaches to entering single terms, strings of words, names, etc. It has been devised by the editors to serve scholars. It serves its purpose well. Note: Of 766 commissioned articles, in 2003 there were about 380 online. The site is widely used. The first 100 articles are in *Google* and in 95 instances the relevant article was among the top 10 search results for the topic involved. As one critic put it: "Not bad for a work in progress."

Perseus Project (www.perseus.tufts.edu). The prototype (i.e., a sampling, not the complete work) of an encyclopedia covering the ancient Greek world. Roman materials are planned. Supported by Tufts, Yale, the National Science Foundation, and Harvard, this is available both online and on CD-ROM. The Yale University Press CD-Rom version, at $350, is complete. Eventually the whole of this format will be transferred to online.

Encyclopedia Smithsonian (www.si.edu/resource/faq/start). Primarily this is a series of answers to frequently asked questions. It is arranged under broad subject headings: armed forces, anthropology, mineral sciences, music, physical sciences, services, textiles, conservation, transportation, history and vertebrate zoology. There is no word by word search allowed, and one must go to the main headings and subheadings for topics which are extremely limited. A piece on Egyptian mummies, one of only three subheadings under Anthropology, is short, well written and directed to the average high school student or layperson. Much more detailed entries will be found in other encyclopedias. While this is suitable for browsing, it is a poor substitute for a general or specialized encyclopedia in any format with adequate search patterns.

Equally this is true for other subjects from music to zoology. The problem: time. It may take much more time to locate an item on the Web

[32]Almost any issue of the *Web Guide Monthly* or *Yahoo! Internet Life,* as well as reviews in *Choice, Library Journal* and *Booklist* will reveal encyclopedia type sites. See, for example: "Surfing History," *Booklist,* February 1, 2000, p. 1040; "Arts & Literature" *Web Guide Monthly,* July 1998, pp. 32+ for dozens of informative sites. Try, too, "Web Watch," *Library Journal,* May 1, 1998, p. 28+ for additional art sites.

than in a specific printed/CD-ROM/online encyclopedia. When used properly the Web site nicely augments information found in standard sets.[32]

SUGGESTED READING

Auchter, Dorothy, "The Evolution of the *Encyclopedia Britannica:* From the Macropaedia to Britannica Online," *Reference Services Review,* no. 3, 1999, pp. 291–299. The author examines the trials and tribulations of the *Britannica* as it first failed to take advantage of online services, almost went under, and then turned to the Net. The end result has been a welcome rebirth of the major work in libraries throughout the world. Much of what is reported here is applicable to the switch from print to online for other reference works.

Dahlin, Robert, "You're As Good Ad Your Word," *Publishers Weekly,* November 15, 1999, pp. 33–7. How can you make an encyclopedia appeal to a mass audience while maintaining its authority? The author gives the answers of publishers, at least to the editing of single-volume encyclopedias. Much of the article, too, concerns how dictionaries are updated by complete overhaul of content and format.

Inglis, Kari, "A Comparison of the Online Encyclopedia," *Ohio Media Spectrum,* Winter 2000, pp. 42–3. A brief, yet thorough analysis of the *Britannica* online, this offers hints on how to evaluate such encyclopedias.

Nauman, Matt, "Grove Dictionaries," *Against the Grain,* April 1999, p. 56. A brief summary of the history and future plans of a major subject encyclopedia publisher.

Shneidman, Edwin, "Suicide on My Mind, *Britannica* on My Table," *American Scholar,* Autumn, 1998, pp. 93–104. A professor of thanatology covers how suicide is treated in over 220 years of the *Britannica.* He points our there might be something to learn from similar *Britannica* surveys of other socially sensitive tag words. Also he suggests, "why not take a look at the word in dictionaries of the past?" Both a thoughtful and imaginative guide to how reference works may be used to trace cultural history.

CHAPTER EIGHT
READY-REFERENCE SOURCES: ALMANACS, YEARBOOKS, HANDBOOKS, DIRECTORIES

Librarians call them "ready-reference" questions. They are queries answered by a simple fact. Answers are found quickly in one or two easy-to-identify, "ready" at hand reference works—online or in print.

People ask ready-reference questions for many reasons. The query can be easy: "What's the population of New York City?" (8 million). They can be relatively difficult: "How did the life span of George Washington (67 years) compare with the average life expectancy in the late-eighteenth-century? (about 35 years). Questions can be almost impossible: "How much does smoking cost the nation?" (The answer depends on so many variables that it slips from a ready-reference query to a research question.) And then there is the etiquette type, which often border on the humorous and the wise: "How does one politely indicate to a religious advocate to depart from one's door?" (T. H. White, the eminent author with a long white beard, gave this response. Tell them "Splendid. I am Jehovah. How are we doing?")

The who, what, when, where, and why questions are the typical ready reference type. Who is my Congress person? What is the current cost of living? When did the second World War end? Where is Seattle? Why do cats stalk birds? Note that none require more than a brief, straightforward answer. Rarely does more than one source have to be consulted.

This is the major type of query in public libraries, and is often heard in school and academic libraries. No wonder experienced reference librarians agree a handful of ready-reference aids (both print and digital) are the major building blocks in a reference collection.

Answers are quickly found because of a well-organized, well understood group of reference works. Most, even today, are used as much in

STATISTICAL ABSTRACT OF THE U.S.

WORLD ALMANAC

print as in an electronic format. The top two preferred reference titles (from all areas and disciplines) are: *The Statistical Abstract of the United States,* and *The World Almanac*—both ready reference works and available online. Close behind is the work horse of all reference: *World Book Encyclopedia.*

Why these three? Because "they cover what people want to know," one reference librarian responded. She was speaking for all when asked for the top most-often-mentioned reference works. Other factors which determine heavy usage include: *(a)* Age. "Most of the titles have been part of library reference collections for a long time." *(b)* Consistency. "The titles that cluster around the top of the list came from all types of libraries. (*c*) Print. Although there are "a number of electronic titles on the list, only one, *SIRS Researcher* was mentioned with the same frequency as standard print resources." [Other lists, other guesses about what is most popular are published regularly. It is comforting that there is agreement that at least 30 to 50 titles are absolutely basic.[1]

Libraries long recognized this situation and in almost every library there is a small collection of print sources, usually near the reference desk, which can be labeled ready-reference works.

In answering fact questions, the most efficient approach is to match the query with one familiar source. An almanac, for example, is a quick way to find the world's 10 largest cities. A directory will give the address of X or Y company. A quotation source will be the place go find who said what. All of this presupposes the librarian is familiar with the reference family, if not necessarily the specific site or title.

When standard sources (many of which are discussed in this chapter) fail, then there are emergency escapes: (1) Call a library near you, particularly where you have a friend. (2) Put the query to an expert—or do it directly by Internet. (3) Countless directories help you find the names of experts, organizations, and havens where the ready-reference query can be put to rest, for example, *The Encyclopedia of Associations,* to name only one.

Every question is important, even trivia, e.g., "Where is Santa Claus?" and "How can I win at the track? (the stock market, in love, etc."[2] Other

---

[1]"Field Tested Reference Titles," *Booklist,* April 1998, pp. 1532–1534. This is based on an informal survey, over a year, of reference librarians from the largest to the smallest library, from academic to public and school. See, too, Brian Coutts and John B. Richard, "50 Sources for the Millennium," *Library Journal,* November 15, 1999, p. 8. A one-page listing "of the 50 best reference sources of the past millennium still in use today." No. 1: *Webster's Third New International Dictionary,* followed by the *World Almanac, Times Atlas of the World, Statistical Abstract of the United States* and the *Oxford English Dictionary.* All are available in digital and print format. Most are discussed in this text. See Chapter One for more on basic reference works.

[2]These type of questions are matched by hundreds of Web pages with answers—well, answers of sorts. Many sites offer answers peculiar enough to make one wonder about the authority of the Net.

typical trivia questions include: (1) Who was the head of state interviewed in his pajamas on a 1959 Edward R. Murrow TV show? (Answer: Fidel Castro) (2) Who was first American to hit a golf shot on the moon? (Answer: Alan Shepard) (3) What English word contains all five vowels in alphabetical order? (Answer: Facetious)[3]

The librarian is urged to treat each question seriously—unless in residence at the Vatican Library, where the print library guide carries a warning that any reader who asks more than three "senseless" questions will be expelled. (Just who evaluates what is *senseless* is not explained.)

At the same time, one person's trivia is another starting point for a talk, paper, or friendly conversation. One may ask about the meaning of "Albany doctor" (a Western Australia sea breeze) to field a crossword puzzle query or to solve a pressing problem about Australia's weather. Someone else may need information on the population of central Borneo (955,000) to determine the wisdom of opening a business there, or a high school student may use the same data to make a point about Indonesian government.

The ready-reference question may develop into an involved query when (1) one cannot immediately locate the source of the answer and must spend much time and effort seeking it out, or (2) the question becomes a search or research topic because the person asking it is really in need of more data than the query implies. Someone who wants the address of a corporation may actually want not only that address, but also information on how to apply for a position with that firm, lodge a complaint, find data to prepare a paper, or make an investment. The ready-reference question may be only an opening gambit for the person who uses it to start the interview dialogue.

It is this latter development—the possibility that a ready-reference question may become more complex—which supports the view that professional librarians should be on duty at the reference desk. Although it is true that someone with a minimum of training is able to find a book or website to answer a question about a title or an address, it requires an expert to know when the query is really an opener for a complex series of other questions on the same or a related topic.

Print or Digital?

When is it best to use a digital or a printed ready-reference source?

Answer: Use the source where the answer may be found quickly. Also, turn to a place where the information is accurate and current.

[3]"Trivia Challenge. Quick to the Library" *The Christian Science Monitor*, March 4, 1997, p. 17. This is a report on a California high school's annual problem-solving contest from which the questions—and answers—were taken.

Beyond speed, accuracy, currency, and availability, there are scores of variables that determine the best medium. Online may be more up-to-date. A print volume may not have a digital cousin. Searching online may be too time consuming. The Net may offer numerous sites, none of which is dependable and so on, and so on.

On balance, though, most reference librarians turn to print to answer the quick fact query. Nowhere is the advantage of a print reference work more visible than in ready-reference titles. Most print fact books are easy to use. Needed data may be found in a matter of seconds. Conversely, finding information on the Internet "can be a nightmare," explains Barbara Berliner, coordinator of NYPL-Express, a fee-based research service of the New York Public Library. "With a print almanac it's quicker, easier, and more accurate."[4]

Library Web Pages and Ready-Reference

Without exception, large academic and public library Internet home pages feature sections devoted to reference in general and ready-reference in particular. For example, the State University of New York at Albany has a "virtual library" (www.albany.edu/library) that is subdivided. A major division is a "reference collection" which offers links to "desk reference," i.e., ready-reference which offers links to basic sets from "acronyms and abbreviations" and "Bartlett's Quotations" to zip codes. The two dozen or so links primarily are directories. On a broader scale Albany, as other libraries, then moves to "research a subject" and dutifully offers links to basic sites from the arts and humanities to social welfare.

If the local Web page is of limited use, other libraries suggest solutions to difficult problems. They may list reference works the librarian has not considered. More helpful yet are the major reference centers on the Net which not only give the source, but where possible, provide links to the actual text. Among the best for ready-reference:

1. *Michigan Electronic Library. The Reference Desk.* (www.mel.lib.mi.us). This all-around winner for reference services offers an alphabetical menu of specific and general ready reference places. Major sites with direct links to the sources are highlighted. There are about 30 of these. Among the primarily ready-reference sites: almanacs, associations, legal, medical, occupations, etiquette, grants, population, statistics and demographics, quotations, style sheets, telephones, weather, weights and measures. Under each are links to five to twenty or more Net sources that usually afford quick search methods to find answers.

[4]"The Old Fashioned Almanac Thrives in the Age of the Internet," *The New York Times,* December 22, 1997, p. D10.

There are, too, well over 100 other minor and major sources from a ham radio call book to video terms and definitions. A quick glance down the screen often will remind the user of a probable place to find a fast answer to a fact query.

Other reference centers offer similar services, but few are so consistently in tune with the needs of the average person or librarian.

2. *The Internet Public Library. Ready-Reference Collection.* (www.ipl.org). This library has a special page turned over to nothing but reference questions, many of which may be classified as fact queries. There is even provision for answering individual reference queries by e-mail. Describing the ready-reference collection, the site explains this "is not intended to be a comprehensive hotlist to all sites on every subject, but rather an annotated collection, chosen to help answer specific questions quickly and efficiently." Sources are selected according to ease of use, quality and quantity of information, frequency of updating, and authoritativeness.

Searches may be conducted under medium groups or by individual titles.

While this has many of the same titles found in the *Michigan Electronic Library*, it is not as detailed. Divisions, with specific titles to search, include: almanacs, census data, news, and telephone. The real strength here is not so much in fact sources as in quite fine tuning of reference works in larger areas from arts and humanities to the sciences. The experienced reference librarian is everywhere. This is another way of saluting the human element in constructing and monitoring such major aids as this one.

There are scores of ready-reference commercial sites on the Web, but the most general and sometimes useful one is: *Reference: Best Sources for Facts on the Net* (http://refdesk.com). This is a mix of current information from weather and headlines to stock quotes. It is backed by standard almanac and encyclopedia data both by title (*Encyclopaedia Brittanica, Merck Manual, American Heritage Dictionary*, etc.) and by subject (exchange rates, find a college, tax preparation, etc.). There are links to the standard search engines. While this is passable for a teenager or layperson, the searching patterns are much too broad for a standard ready-reference search.

EVALUATION

The general rules for evaluating a reference work, from audience to cost, are applicable to ready-reference titles. Some works have specific points to evaluate, and these will be considered as the chapter moves along.

1. *Arrangement.* Is the print work easy to consult for quick facts? An index is an absolute necessity. The only exception is if dictionary order with brief entries is used, as in the classic *Brewer's Dictionary of Phrase &*

Fable (London: Cassell, 1870 to date). This work has gone through numerous editions and is a core item for checking out odd facts, particularly of a literary nature.

In digital form arrangement has a natural substitute in the availability of navigational tools which serve as an index.

2. *Current information.* This problem is overcome by almanacs, yearbooks, and titles that are updated once each year. Others have semiannual or more frequent additions.

Where data must be minute by minute and up to date, there is nothing to compare with the online databases.

3. *Illustrations.* Whereas most ready-reference queries are verbal and can be answered the same way, there does come a time when one illustration is well worth the proverbial thousand words. Therefore, where appropriate, one should test the ready-reference work for adequate illustrations.

4. *Authority.* Most standard reference works, and particularly those found in libraries year after year, have proven to be authoritative. A fact is a fact in print or online. This is due to a conscientious publisher and compiler, as well as frequent fact check editing. On the other hand, even with the most esteemed publisher, the best known work can have flaws. For example, the second edition of *The Cambridge Biographical Encyclopedia* (Cambridge University Press, 1998) points out that the American novelist Sara Orne Jewett was the first president of Vassar College. Oh? The dates are from 1862 to 1865 when the author was between 13 to 15 years of age. A check of *The World Almanac* shows the college was founded in 1861, not 1862. A check of the *Britannica* indicates Ms. Jewett was at home at age 12 or 13 where she was educated by her father.

Which makes the point when the "fact" is of major importance, say to a biographer of Sara, or a student preparing a brief talk, it may pay to double check.

To some extent we all rely on what reference works say a fact is, but these should be tested regularly. Is it a fact, or an opinion? Is the fact no longer true, that is, has it been bypassed by new findings? For example, what is one to make of the book, which states categorically that "babies should be handled as little as possible." A common notion (or fact) in the nineteenth century, this belief has been canceled out by experiment and common sense in the twentieth.

An invaluable way to quickly check a fact is to see its original source. *World Almanac*, like most ready-reference works, clearly indicates where information is obtained.

If a reference work does not show a fact source, one should be doubly cautious. This is particularly true when one cruises the Internet. As pointed out previously, the great catch online is just who is saying what.

If the fact comes from a reliable source (i.e., one known by the librarian to be trustworthy), there is not a problem. Conversely, on the Net few this side of the well-known titles discussed here give enough information about their sources to warrant anything but skepticism.

GENERAL FACT BOOKS

The titles discussed are considered "basic" by reference librarians, although any given library, librarian, or situation may have a different list. Thousands of fact books are published throughout the world each year. When one goes out of print two more rush in. All of these, or at least those published by a reliable firm, can be used in a library. As with books of quotations, there can't be too many about. There is always an odd query, a peculiar fact that can be dug out of one of these less-well-known titles.

Although there are numerous specialized ready-reference sources, the librarian should not forget the general places to turn for answers. Encyclopedias, particularly, are good for isolating ready-reference facts. One immediately thinks of the *Micropaedia* of the *Britannica* or the short, fact entries in the *World Book*. In another form these can be quickly read online. All too often the librarian may be so anxious to match the specific answer to the specific question that the obvious encyclopedia is overlooked. Then, too, for current data, there are no better places to turn than the numerous newspaper indexes, and particularly *The New York Times Index* or *Newspaper Abstracts*. The *Abstracts* alone may provide the needed answer. *Facts on File* is another excellent source.

Facts Together

CD: Microsoft Bookshelf. (Note: In 2001 augmented by *Encarta Reference Suite*) Renton, WA: Microsoft, 1994 to date, annual, www.encarta. msn.com/products/info/RefSuite.asp. $54.95.

One approach to quick inexpensive access to ready-reference works is to package many on a single CD-ROM. This has the advantage for a library over online in that payment is only for the disc, not for continual use by scores of people of the much more costly online service.

Microsoft Bookshelf is an annual CD with ten reference works, of which about one-half are ready-reference titles and the others are used often to answer that type of question. The reference titles on the disc: *The Encarta Dictionary; The American Heritage Dictionary of the English Language; The Microsoft Bookshelf Internet Directory; The People's Chronology; The Columbia Dictionary of Quotations; The World Almanac and Book of Facts; The Original Roget's Thesaurus of English Words and Phrases; The Encarta Desk World Atlas; The Encarta Desk Encyclopedia; The National Five-Digit Zip Code and*

Postal Office Directory; and *The Microsoft Bookshelf Computer and Internet Dictionary.* (Note: Specific titles change from year to year but the type of material covered, from dictionary to fact book, remains pretty much the same.) In 2001 this was augmented by the *Encarta Reference Suite* with fewer sources, i.e., the *Encarta Encyclopedia;* Interactive World Atlas; World English Dictionary; Africana; timeliness. Also, archives with articles from 1938 to 2000. Each update features new search techniques. A single click can bring up any of the individual reference works and there are added touches from creating automatic footnotes to links to more than 40,000 websites. As the dean of CD-ROM critics, Cheryl LaGuardia, puts it: "This is probably the single most useful desktop ready-reference tool available for the money today. If you own no other CD-ROM, you should own this one."[5]

Today other publishers offer matching packages, e.g., *Gale Ready Reference Handbooks* (Farmington Hills, MI: Gale Group, 1999, 4 vols. $500). In print and digital form this includes: *Fast Answers to Common Questions; Fast Help for Major Medical Conditions; First Stop for Jobs and Industries; Where to Go and Who to Ask.* Actually, much of the material is found in other Gale publications, but is conveniently gathered here.

The Odd Fact

CD: Guinness Multimedia Disc of Records. New York: Facts on File, 1993 to date, annual. $99. (Annual update, $49.)
Print: The Guinness Book of Records, New York: Sterling, 1955 to date, annual. $26.00

Online: *Kane, Joseph,* Famous First Facts, *5th ed., New York: H. W. Wilson Co., 1999 to date, www.hwwilson.com. Price varies.*
CD: WilsonDisc, 1999 to date. $150.
Print: 1998, 1,122 pp. $95.

"The trouble with most reference books is that they never seem to give you quite the information you are looking for. I wanted to know, for example, how many ducks there were in the world....try looking it up in any encyclopedia. It won't be there."[6]

Many of the things considered of less than importance by encyclopedia editors are found in what may be called "odd reference works." At the head of the list is *The Guinness Book of Records* which needs no intro-

---

[5] *Library Journal,* October 15, 1997, p. 103.

[6] "Odd Books of the Week," *The Independent* (of London), November 1, 1997, p. 12. Actually, the answer may be in an encyclopedia, but not one used by the author of the article. The point is that "odd reference books" are a great help in reference work for equally odd queries.

duction—it is among the top-10 best-selling books of all time, and known to almost all readers. Divided into broad sections, it includes everything from the final scores of soccer and baseball contests to those of football and tennis. There are illustrations, some of them in color. Also, it features much trivia from the fastest wedding to the record speed for pushing a baby carriage. For example, Bozo Miller ate 27 two-pound chickens at one sitting; Alan Peterson holds the record for eating 20 standard hamburgers in 30 minutes. It is a place to find information on almost any winner, and the quest is aided by an excellent index.

The title is updated each year, and past editions are useful for sometimes out-of-the-way facts. A good part of every edition of *Guinness* consists of records set by swimmers, climbers, pilots, runners, and others determined to establish a new test for ultimate endurance and adventure. As there are no physical frontiers this side of space, adventuring today means doing old things in a new way.

The CD-ROM adds data from several Guinness works. The hypertext approach is as much for facts as for fun. There are, in addition to the close to 4,000 records, approximately 600 pictures, video clips of record breakers in action, and many, many sounds of grunts, groans, and applause.

Note: As is the fashion these days, titles of ready-reference works change slightly from year to year. Guinness, for example, chose the millennium to call its 2000 dated issue: *Guinness World Records 2000, Millennium Edition.* Next year?

Famous First Facts, simply called "Kane" after the compiler, is primarily concerned with American "firsts" in everything from the first toothbrush to a first major discovery. It has been published since 1933 and, according to the publisher there are more than 150,000 copies in print. "The reference has served generations of researchers." It is arranged chronologically in such a way that one may find a subject area and either browse or seek out the essential first fact. For example, under "Library" one finds the *first* library catalog (Library of Congress); first library chair endowed in a library school (Columbia University); first library periodical *(Library Journal)*; first library building (Philadelphia); and so on. With the fifth edition, a new subject index was introduced. One can trace an event by year, month, and day of occurrence, names of persons involved, and state and municipality where the event took place. Electronic versions have the usual convenience of adding many more points of entrance to the facts, e.g., the electronic version permits a user to find the first night baseball game by using a Boolean search. While a bit more than the print version, the CD-ROM generally is preferable, as is the online edition.

This work has proved such a success that there are over a dozen offshoots from *Facts About American Wars* and *Facts About the Presidents* to *Facts About China* and *Facts About the World Languages.*

With the 5th edition (1999) Steven Anzovin and Janet Podell updated and edited Kane. They will continue to do so with future editions. They, too, are editors of a related work: *Famous First Facts International Edition* (New York: H.W. Wilson Co., 2000). This follows much the same pattern as Kane but expands coverage past the U.S. borders.

Fact reference books have become a cottage publishing industry. At any one time there are scores of them in print. The library has them all, or at least all which are considered authoritative.

Among relatively current titles one finds such "odd" works as:

The Book of Mosts (New York: St. Martin's, 1997). Answers to what is the highest, lowest and other queries dealing with facts and figures are organized here under 22 broad subject headings from "automobiles" to "movies." Each fact is documented, (although sometimes too briefly) and the numerous lists and tables are easy to follow. A major drawback: no index.

The World in One Day (London: Dorling Kindersley, 1998). This is a splendid collection about "an average 24 hours in the earth's life." What happens, for example, every day? Answer: 26,000 Chinese couples get married, 101,000 washing machines are made and two people are killed by snakes in Shri Lanka.

ALMANACS AND YEARBOOKS

Although almanacs and yearbooks are distinctive types or forms of reference work, they are closely enough related in both use and scope to be treated here as a single class of ready-reference aids.

Almanac. An almanac is a compendium of useful data and statistics relating to countries, personalities, events, subjects, and the like. It is a type of specific-entry encyclopedia stripped of adjectives and adverbs and limited to a skeleton of information.

Yearbook/Annual. A yearbook is an annual compendium of the data and statistics. The yearbook's fundamental purpose is to record the year's activities by country, subject, or specialized area. In ready-reference work, the type that is most often used is usually confined to special areas of interest.

Compendium. A compendium is a brief summary of a larger work or of a field of knowledge. For example, the *Statistical Abstract of the United States* is a compendium in that it is a summary of the massive data in the files of the U.S. Bureau of the Census.

Purpose

These types of works serve several definite purposes in the average library. This is true whether in print or digital format. What follows generally is true for all formats. Among the more important:

Recency. Regardless of form and presentation, the user turns to a yearbook or an almanac for relatively recent information on a subject or personality. The purpose of many of these works is to update standard texts that may be issued or totally revised only infrequently. An encyclopedia yearbook, for example, is a compromise—even an excuse—for not rewriting all articles in the encyclopedia each year.

Although most almanacs and yearbooks are dated 2000, 2001, and so forth, the actual coverage is for the previous year. The 2000 almanac or yearbook probably has a cutoff date of late 1999. The built-in time lag must be understood. If, in middle or late 2000, one is looking for 2000 data it simply will not be there. The digital equivalent can boast it is updated regularly, and for that reason may be preferable to print. The real question, though, is the online version really that much more recent? The answer: it depends on the publisher.

Brief Facts. Where a single figure or a fact is required, normally without benefit of explanation, the almanac is useful. A yearbook will be more useful if the reader wishes a limited amount of background information on a recent development or seeks a fact not found in a standard almanac.

Trends. Because of their recency, almanacs and yearbooks, either directly or by implication, indicate trends in the development or, if you will, the regression of civilization. Scientific advances are chronicled, as are the events, persons, and places of importance over the previous year. One reason for maintaining a run of certain almanacs and yearbooks is to indicate such trends. In the 1908 *World Almanac,* there were 22 pages devoted to railroads. The 2000 issue contains about one page, while television performers has close to 16 pages. The Internet, computers, and related items are now entries. The obvious shift in interest of Americans over the past fifty years is reflected in collections of yearbooks and almanacs.

Informal Index. Most of the reliable yearbooks and almanacs cite sources of information, and thus can be used as informal indexes. A patron interested in retail sales will find general information in any good almanac or yearbook. These publications in turn will cite sources such as *Fortune, Business Week,* or *Moody's Industrials,* which will provide additional keys to information. Specific citations to government sources of statistics may quickly guide the reader to primary material otherwise difficult to locate.

Directory and Biographical Information. Many yearbooks and almanacs include material also found in a directory. For example, a yearbook in a special field may well include the names of the principal leaders in that field, along with their addresses and perhaps short biographical sketches. The *World Almanac,* among others, lists associations and societies, with addresses.

Browsing. Crammed into the odd corners of almost any yearbook or almanac are masses of unrelated, frequently fascinating bits of information. The true lover of facts—and the United States is a country of such lovers—delights in merely thumbing through many of these works. From the point of view of the dedicated reference librarian, this purpose may seem inconsequential, but it is fascinating to observers of human behavior.

Almanacs

Online: World Almanac and Book of Facts. Mahwah, NJ: Primedia: 1997 to date, www.facts.com/k3ref.htm. Price varies. Available on OCLC, and from numerous vendors.
CD: In Microsoft Bookshelf (see p. 238).
Print: 1868 to date. $29.95; paper, $10.95.

Online: Information Please Almanac. Boston: Houghton Mifflin Company, 1997 to date, www.infoplease.com. Free.
Print: Time Almanac (formerly *Information Please Almanac),* 1999 to date. Price varies.

Print: Whitaker's Almanac. London: J. Whitaker & Sons, Ltd., 1869 to date. $92. (Distributed in United States by Gale Research, Inc.).

The titles listed here are basic, general almanacs found in most American libraries. For use and importance, they are ranked as follows: (1) *World Almanac,* (2) *Information Please Almanac,* and (3) *Whitaker's Almanac.* The order of preference is based on familiarity. Sales of the *World Almanac* (over 2 million copies) now exceed the combined sales of its two principal competitors.

With the exception of *Whitaker's,* all are primarily concerned with data of interest to American readers. To varying degrees, they cover the same basic subject matter, and although there is much duplication, their low cost makes it possible to have at least two or three at the reference desk. The best one is the one that answers the specific question of the moment. Today, it may be the *World Almanac,* tomorrow, *Whitaker's.* In terms of searching, though, it is usually preferable to begin with the *World Almanac* and work through the order of preference stated above.

All almanacs have several points in common: (1) They enjoy healthy sales and are found in many homes. (2) They depend heavily on government sources for statistics. Readers will frequently find the same sources (when given) quoted in all the almanacs. (3) Except for updating and revising, much of the same basic material is carried year after year.

Publishers love almanacs and yearbooks because they can bring out a new book each year at a relatively low cost and high profit margin. While each year new material is added and updated, essentially the almanac is recycled from year to year without change. Moreover, there are no royalties to pay authors.

World Almanac

The *World Almanac* will tell the reader everything he or she wants to know about efficient driving, the literacy rate in Zimbabwe, and the elevation of Albany, New York. It provides brief, accurate essay pieces on topics of current interest. For example, there are sections on diet and a part devoted to forecasting the future. Still, the real strength of the work is in facts, facts, and more facts. A quick reference index, with 60 to 75 broad subject headings from actors to zip codes, provides access to the work. There is a 16- to 20-page section on maps and flags in color.

The online version has the usual advantage of being updated more regularly, but as the print comes out once each year, it is the rare fact that needs to be verified as being more current online than in print.

The publisher, since 1995, cuts back the same 1,050 page adult edition to around 340 pages. This becomes *The World Almanac for Kids.* Much of the same data is offered, but with additional easy to follow graphs, charts, and illustrations. It is an ideal reference work for the early grades. The senior edition is advised for high schools.

Information Please

The cousin of the *World Almanac* features discursive, larger units on such subjects as the lively arts, science, education, and medicine. *Information Please Almanac* expanded its contents to include medicine, the economy, and political and world developments. It's primary claim for the reference librarian's attention is the detailed index. This is more complete than in the *World Almanac* as well as much more precise. It has several pages of colored maps. *Information Please* gravitates more to the methods of encyclopedia yearbooks than to the standard form set by traditional almanacs. *Yearbook* in the subtitle emphasizes this focus, as does the advertising, which stresses that it is the "most complete, up-to-date, easiest-to-use reference book for home, school, and office." While "most" is Houghton Mifflin's claim, it is certainly excellent. Its makeup is considerably more attractive with its larger type and spacing than the *World Almanac.*

On the free website (www.infoplease.com) the *Information Please Almanac* has the advantage of including all its cousins and aunts from editions for sports and entertainment to the *Infoplease Dictionary* and the shorter edition of *The Columbia Encyclopedia.* Maps and much of the politician information is taken from the government reference works. In addition to key word searches, a menu offers basic choices from people to business. Also, the site has consistent updating: see "Spotlight" and "Daily Almanac" which has brief notes on events and people.[7]

Again, though, as with the *World Almanac,* when the librarian is looking for a specific fact (and particularly one which is not likely to have changed drastically between annual editions) it is much more efficient to consult the detailed index in the print version.

Whitaker's

Whitaker's Almanac, as one English reporter puts it, "offers a magisterial guide to the Establishment to projected high tides, recent sporting records and the pay of Field Marshals."[8] *Whitaker's* some 1,300 pages is distinctive in that, as might be expected, it places considerable emphasis on Great Britain and on European governments. For example, the edition has an almost complete directory of British royalty and peer age, with another 150 pages devoted to government and public offices. Other features include an education directory, lists of leading newspapers and periodicals, and legislative data. Each year the almanac includes special sections on items in the news. Usually from 60 to 75 pages are devoted to this "events of the year" section. There are from 250 to 300 pages in Commonwealth nations and their activities, as well as major foreign countries. Other unique features include the only easily accessible list of salaries of the upper civil service, including Church of England stipends for dignitaries.

No almanac offers so much up-to-date, reliable data on Great Britain and Europe...a claim not lost on Bram Stoker's *Dracula.* Jonathan Harker, who arranges for passage to England for Dracula, is astonished to discover Dracula's library is similar to the reference section in a Lon-

---

[7]An added feature: *Ask Jeeves* (wwwask.com). Here one can put questions and hope for answers not found in the almanac. Also, the link serves to update basic information in the almanac.

[8]*The Weekend Telegraph,* November 27, 1983, p. 28.

don library. It contains a London directory, the Army and Navy lists and, yes, *Whitaker's Almanac*. Before invading England Dracula studies these books in detail.

Other Almanacs[9]

Trading on its slogan "newspaper of record," *The New York Times Almanac* (New York: Penguin Reference Books, 1997 to date, annual) refers to itself as "almanac of record." Aside from the rhetoric, what does this mean? Answer: a concentration on United States and international data that is considered basic. Divided into six parts—from science and technology to sports—the focus is on current, major news items for the previous year. Data is built on the usual base of standard facts such as zip codes and association addresses. There is, except sports, little trivia included. There are no pictures, with the maps being the only illustrations. There are no essays or efforts to attract the casual reader. This is for facts, and only facts. Note, too, the detailed index. At $10.95 an ideal reference aid. This augments rather than replaces the standard almanacs.

The Old Farmer's Almanac (Dublin, NH: Yankee Publishing, 1792 to date, annual. $3.95) is not only the oldest almanac in the United States, but thanks to its distribution of some 4 million copies in supermarkets and drugstores, one of the best known. The familiar yellow covers are found on the free Net site (www.almanac.com), although most of the Web content is an advertisement rather than a full almanac. Both formats feature folksy charm with an emphasis on crops (gardening), weather (the online version allows for personalized weather forecasts), and trivia such as what happened on this or that day.

It is neither an almanac of nostalgia nor one turned over completely to weather reports. The former misconceptions are due to its 18th-century founding, while the weather notion is based on its sometimes outstanding predictions. There is no "secret formula" for that, but there is a good meteorologist about.

REPRESENTATIVE YEARBOOKS

There are two types of yearbooks. The first, and probably best known, is the general work that covers, as the title suggests, the past year's activities. The type found in most libraries is the annual encyclopedia year-

---

[9]If one turns to a search machine on the Internet with simply "almanac" there will be from 1,500 to over 2,000 matches. None qualifies as a standard general almanac. The majority are so narrow in scope as to be of use only to specialists, e.g., *Astronomy Almanac, Nautical Almanac, Hawaiian Almanac* and the like.

book that is used to check names, dates, statistics, events, and almost anything else that might have been noticed in the past year. Newspaper indexes, from the *National Newspaper Index* to *The New York Times Index*, often serve the same purpose, as does the weekly *Facts on File.*

Almost every area of human interest has its own subject compendium, or yearbook. It is beyond the scope of this text to enumerate the literally hundreds of titles. What follows, then, is a representative group and, more particularly, those "basic" or "classic" works that cross many disciplines and are used in some libraries as often as the familiar index, encyclopedia, or general almanac.

Yearbooks are used to find data and background material on places, peoples and things that changed or made the news in the previous year. Types of questions answered: What is the current population of Austria? How much is spent on education in Ireland? Who is the chief of state in France? What are the primary imports/exports of the United States?

Yearbooks serve to give detailed information on, for example, social, economic, and political details of a given country. Yearbooks tend to supplement older articles that are standard in any reputable encyclopedia. For example, the history of France will be found in an encyclopedia, but where one wants to check the current population of Paris a yearbook would be best. Most encyclopedias are updated with a print yearbook online, and to a greater extent with digital additions.

As the stress is being current, the yearbook ideally is suited for digital format. Or is it? Again, as with almanacs, the average print yearbook is easier to consult than the one online—at least for particular facts when what is wanted is known and quite specific. On the other hand when the user has only a vague idea of what is required, the digital version is faster to use.

Government: International

Print: Europa World Yearbook. London: Europa Publications, Ltd., 1926 to date, 2 vols., annual. $815.

Print: Stateman's Year-Book. New York: St. Martin's Press, Inc., 1864 to date. $120.

CD: World Country Analysis. Farmington Hills, MI: Gale Group, 1997 to date, annual. $425.

Note: As of late 2000 none of the above is online. In the next few years it is likely all will be available in digital format.

Published for over a century, the *Statesman's Year-Book* provides current background information on 166 nations. Along with a general encyclopedia and an almanac, it is a cornerstone for reference work in almost any type of library. It has a distinct advantage for ready-reference work:

It is up-to-date and can be relied on for timeliness. It has a superior index. The indexes include a name, place, and product category.

Information is arranged systematically. Typical subheadings for almost every entry concern heads of government, area and population, constitution and government, religion, education, railways, aviation, and weights and measures. There are excellent brief bibliographies for locating further statistical and general information and numerous maps showing such things as time zones and distributions of natural resources.

Europa

The Europa World Yearbook covers much of the same territory as its competitor, but it has several advantages. (1) The work is almost as timely as the *Statesman's Year-Book.* (2) It leads in the number of words and amount of information. (3) The first volume covers the United Nations and over 1,650 special agencies and international organizations by subject and European countries. (4) The second volume covers non-European countries, for a total of 250 nations and territories. There is a uniform format throughout. Each country begins with a short introductory survey, followed by a statistical profile, the constitution, government, political parties, diplomatic representatives, judicial system, religion, the press, publishers, radio and television, trade and industry, transportation, higher education, and miscellaneous facts peculiar to that country. This wider coverage, particularly of the media, gives it a substantial lead for ready-reference queries over the other two works. The balance among countries is good.

There are scores of titles covering much the same territory, although always in a somewhat different way. *Europa,* for example, publishes six related titles, which simply expand on the data found in the basic work, for example, *Africa South of the Sahara, The Middle East and North Africa,* and *Western Europe.* See, for another example, the data section of *Britannica Yearbook.*

World Country Analyst

Specifically targeting business interests, the *World Country Analyst* differs from general profiles of countries, as found in the *Statesman's Year-Book.* It focuses on key issues for investors abroad. The search may be conducted by subject, by country, and by any key word(s) of interest. Some 200 countries are analyzed in great depth. The information is garnered by reliable, relatively current United States government sources. One may move from the general, i.e., background information on France, to specifics such as wine and restaurants, each of which is divided and subdivided. There are numerous maps and charts that follow the mainline of the query.

The wise reference librarians will make a cost-effective end run around the Gale publication. How? By asking the U.S. Department of Commerce for the free disc (No. 1), called the *National Trade Bank*. This has much the same data as the *World Country Analyst.*[10]

Gale issues numerous companions to *World Country Analyst*. Particularly suited for schools and public libraries: CD-ROM: *Discovering Nations, States & Cultures*. This links the standard data about countries with cultural information from living conditions to cultural heritage. *Worldmark Encyclopedia of Nations* is updated about every four years and is used more for background than current information. There is data on more than 200 countries, with entries ranging from four to 30 pages and more. One volume is given over to the United Nations. A cousin, by the same publisher, is the *Worldmark Encyclopedia of Cultures and Daily Life*. Divided into four geographic regions it discusses such areas as language, religion, folklore, family life, recreation, etc.

And…[11]

Background information on countries is available in standard encyclopedias. Beyond the basic encyclopedias are even more specialized works that concentrate only on countries of the world. While not designated as yearbooks, they nicely complement the annual statistical publications. The best:

1. *Lands and People.* (Danbury, CT: Grolier Incorporated, 1997. 6 vols. $259). An impressive set in that it covers the countries of the world in objective detail. While this has to be supplemented by the yearbooks for current information, it is excellent for background data. Numerous well-chosen illustrations as well. Suitable for both young people and adults.

2. Tailored for about the fifth grade through high school, *The World Book Encyclopedia of People and Places* (Chicago: World Book, 1998. 6 vols. $160) covers about 200 nations in language the average reader can understand. Countries are in alphabetical order. Visually much the same as *Lands and People,* with reproductions in full color, plus graphs, charts and

[10]For a detailed comparison of the two CD-ROMs, see a perceptive review by Nancy Van Atta in the Winter, 1997 issue of *Reference & User Services Quarterly,* (p. 208–209).

[11]"See "References on the Web: Countries and Cultures Online" *Booklist,* June 1 & 15, 2000, pp. 1936+ for yearbooks and related reference works listed and annotated by major countries. The two Gale series are only a hint of what is offered. Some other Gale titles, equally useful where the budget is large and the need is there: *Worldmark Encyclopedia of the States and Countries of the World and Their Leaders Yearbook; Handbook of the Nations.*

highlights, this still has more appeal for younger readers. In terms of age groups, the two sets nicely complement and overlap one another.

3. *Culturegrams: The Nations Around Us.* (Provo, UT: Bringham Young University/Kennedy Center Publishers, 1985 to date, annual. $80 set). Primarily for middle grades through high school, this covers major countries. Many minor ones are not included. Cultural activities from music and art to food and friendship customs are covered in detail. Out-of-the-way types of information seem to delight students and are a savior for many ready-reference questions regardless of age group. Note: *Culturgrams* is incorporated into the *Microsoft Virtual Globe,* a CD-ROM, which is updated annually.

On the Web

Specific facts, such as the population of X or Y city, may be found quickly online by simply typing in the name of the city in the search engine box. Conversely, where a great deal of data is sought presented in an orderly fashion, the print works are faster as they are easier to browse. China's current demography, national economy, education, transportation and the like are summarized quickly in a print yearbook, whereas it might take hours to find this data on the Net. Ideally, the Net and the print sources are combined for detailed searches.

One of the best general free sites on the Net is brought to you by the Central Intelligence Agency; *World Factbook* (www.odci.gov/cia/publicatons/factbook). This has basic data about countries as found in such standard works as the *Statesman's Year-Book* but with a difference—the data is gathered not only by the CIA but by a dozen or more government agencies. Coverage is worldwide and the data for each country is extensive, although, surprisingly enough, not always up-to-date. Searches are by country or by such categories as government, communication, geography, etc. Note: *The World Factbook* is available in print as well as on a CD-ROM.[12]

Annual Events, Book of Days, Chronologies

Online: Chase's Calendar of Events Online. Chicago: NTC/Contemporary Publishing Group, 2000 to date, annual (www.chases.com/buy/buy.html. $150.

[12]Two of the Central Intelligence Agency's references are available from NTIS on a single CD-ROM, or in print: *World Fact Book and Handbook of International Economic Statistics.* The price is $59 plus $5 shipping from: National Technical Information Service, U.S. Department of Commerce, Springfield, VA, 800/553-6847.

Print: Chase's Calendar of Events. 1957 to date, annual, 752 pp. $60.

Print: American Book of Days. New York: H. W. Wilson Company, 1978, 1212 pp. $75.

Print: Timelines of The Arts and Literature. New York: Harper Collins, 1994, 712 pp. $30.

Print: Chronology of World History. Santa Barbara: ABC-CLIO, 1999, 4 vols. $375.

Questions such as "What happened on November 23?" or "I am doing a paper on George Washington. Who else was born on his birthday?" "What are the appropriate ways to celebrate Ground Hog Day?" are answered in numerous sources. The most often used is the chronology, which lists events by days and/or years.

A good example is *Chase's Calendar of Events Online.* Published each winter, and frequently updated, it traces the events of the previous year, as well as marks the upcoming year's day-by-day celebrations. For every celebration or event, it gives the name of the sponsor(s). Of special interest is the attention to trivia. For example, January 1 marks a turn in events, but also is the time when there is the "announcement of the ten best puns of the year" and it opens "National Hobby Month." *Chase's* also includes more substantial information, for example, a good, short biography of E. M. Forster and an accurate account of the anniversary of the Emancipation Proclamation. The online version duplicates the print work, but with the obvious advantage of offering numerous points of entry not found in print.

The American Book of Days is a classic that is updated infrequently. It is among a few ready-reference aids that really need little revision. The basic material—how and why to celebrate holidays—changes little from year to year, generation to generation. Beneath each day of the year the guide lists major and minor events. Most of these are explained in detailed essays that indicate, too, the traditional method of celebration. Particularly useful in schools, it puts most of the emphasis on the major days of celebration.

Numerous titles in this area range from *Anniversaries and Holidays* (Chicago: American Library Association, 2000), which offers succinct data and additional readings; to *Holidays and Anniversaries of the World,* 2d ed. (Detroit, MI: Gale Group, 1990); and the classic *The Book of Days* (London: W. R. Chambers, 1864), which is reissued from time to time. This is the earliest of the genre and of value today as much as a curiosity as a profile of Victorian historical and cultural views. See, too: *Let's Celebrate Today* (Englewood, CO: Libraries Unlimited, 1998) a listing of holidays and events specially designed for students in grades K–12.

Timelines of the Arts

Chronologies, one of the oldest reference book forms, essentially tell the reader what was going on where at any given time in the history of the world. Two examples are cited here. There are scores.[13]

The first entry in *Timelines* is headed "Literature" and reads: "The markings on bones indicate probable use of numbering systems in northwestern and north central Europe (c. 30,000 BC)." Visual arts, performing arts and world events follow as major categories, as they do throughout the chronology with the addition in later centuries of "Theater and Variety," "Music and Dance," and from 1920, "Film and Broadcasting." The information is in broad bands of time until 1500 when it is listed year by year.

How is a book like this used? Several examples will suffice. An author writing a historical novel wants to know what was going on in the arts, and in the world, in 1893 when his characters reach a crisis. When Andrew Jackson was elected president (1828) who was reading what in America? In the year Bach composed his St. Matthews Passion was there any comparable work in art? The weaving back and forth in time, the counterpoint of one event with another is covered in a superior reference work—made even more so by a detailed index.

Chronology of World History, is the most detailed general chronology now available and moves from "Prehistory" to 1491 AD to "The Modern World," i.e., from 1901 to 1998. A drawback: there is a detailed index for each volume, but not an overall guide to what the publisher claims to be a record of 70,000 events. While a splendid reference work with entries grouped by year under subjects, i.e., "arts and ideas—music" etc., it has a major drawback: price. As Ken Kister points out in his review, one should consider other alternatives. To quote him: "This is the largest—and by far the most expensive—general history chronology currently on the North American market. Most librarians that have the smaller but much less pricey single-volume *Encyclopedia of World Facts and Dates* (New York: Harper Collins, 1993, o.p.) which covers 50,000 events will find it adequate for their needs."[14]

---

[13]Try, too: *Chronology of World History* (Santa Barbara: ABC-CLIO, 1996) which is a cutback version of the four volumes at around $50.

[14]Most subject areas have their own chronologies, e.g., *Timeliness of African American History* (Berkeley, CA: Berkeley, 1994) covers five centuries of African American history year by year. On the aforementioned Microsoft Bookshelf there is *The People's Chronology*. Another CD-ROM is considerably more detailed, e.g., *Chronicle Encyclopedia of History* (New York: DK Multimedia, 1998, $39.95). This is a chronology written as a series of news events over a standard time line. Access is by key words, events, personalities, etc. Includes audiovisual and illustrations. Another example: *A Handbook of Dates.* (Cambridge: Cambridge University Press, 2000. 200 pp. paper, $19.95). For a select list of chronologies, see: "What Happened When," *Booklist,* January 1, 2000, pp. 966–67.

HANDBOOKS AND MANUALS

Handbooks and manuals are the "how-to-do-it" side of ready-reference questions. A manual can range from how to hold a wedding (etiquette) to how to get a job (occupational guide). A handbook, which is much the same as a manual, but presupposes readers know the field well and turn to it to refresh memory will move from medicine *(The Merck Manual)* to summaries of law.

How-to-do-it guides are among the oldest in the reference repertoire. They gained instant acceptance where the printed book became widely available. Some 500 years on and the purpose, if not always the advice, remains much the same. Whereas a 16th-century reader in quest of good manners would turn to Castliglione's *The Book of the Courtier* (1528, with countless editions), today the answer can be found in Emily Post. Dr. Spock or Dr. Miriam Stoppard guide today's parents. The 15th-century parent would consult Dr. Michele Savonarola's ...*Of Newborns to their Seventh Year,* who warned father's not to push their children too hard in early schoolwork. Taken together, the manuals from century to century give the reader a rich picture of everyday culture of at least the middle ranks. (Hence, the interest by large research libraries to keep numerous editions of manuals and handbooks.)

There are almost as many manuals and handbooks as fields of interest. New ones appear each year, while some old ones disappear or undergo a name change. It is obviously impossible to remember them all. In practice, based on ease of arrangement, or amount of use, librarians adopt favorites. With some exceptions, most handbooks and manuals have one thing in common—a limited scope. They zero in on a specific area of interest. In fact, their particular value is their depth of information in a narrow field.

What follows are a few select examples chosen as much for the number of times they are likely to be called for in a library, as for the familiar sound of many of their titles.

Etiquette

Print: Emily Post's Etiquette, 16th ed. New York: HarperCollins, 1997. $35.

"Whatever happened to good manners...Bemoaning the collapse of civility has become a bipartisan cottage industry."[15] In *Civility* (New Haven: Yale University Press, 1998) Yale law professor Stephen Carter explains the current crisis in American morals and manners. Half a dozen other books and scores of articles make the point. Etiquette books sell at a rapid pace, and not just to libraries. Note, too, the number of mag-

---

[15]"Polite Society," *Lingua Franca,* March, 1998, p. 11.

azine and newspaper advice columns. All of this adds up to more civility, not less.

Etiquette books take a neutral stand, declaring good manners and rules of decorum change, but there are standards to which everyone should strive. If, for example, few are worried anymore about how to eat chicken, etiquette books stress the importance of environmental manners such as not throwing empty cans on the grass, but saving them for the recycling bins.

What etiquette manuals should be found in the library? The library has the standards from Emily Post to Amy Vanderbilt to Judith Martin (Miss Manners) to Letitia Baldrige.

While the modern genealogy of etiquette began in the sixteenth century, today its primary ruler, if only a ghost, is Emily Post. She realized that a new, affluent group of middle-class people needed help on where to put the second fork. And in 1922 she brought out the first edition of a major work that is known throughout the world. Her success continues, carried on by her publisher and family. (She died, close to 90 years of age, in 1960.)

Today's etiquette book pretty much follows the Post pattern, piloted by Emily's great-granddaughter, Peggy Post. It is directed to Mary and Joe average, not to aristocrats or those who head the Fortune 500. As such the guide is a great leveler, a democratic force. Needless to add, generation after generation claim that manners have deteriorated. Perhaps, but the sales of etiquette books increase. Every library should have the standards and backups when a few are stolen.

There are now numerous basic books of etiquette, but the only traditional rival to Emily Post is the familiar *Amy Vanderbilt Complete Book of Etiquette* (New York: Doubleday, 1995). The author, or course, is dead but each new edition has another compiler. In this 1995 edition (the last was in 1978) the compilers are Nancy Tuckerman and Nancy Dunnan. Be that as it may, this follows the usual pattern of practical advice on everything from cellular phones (it is bad form to pop one out at the dinner table) to tipping, weddings, and funerals.

Librarians find the three most common concerns involving manners and form are (1) the arrangement of weddings, funerals, and special events; (2) the proper way to address someone in office, whether it be a politicians or a priest; (3) rules of personal behavior at meals, in conversation, and in the working environment.

On the Web

There is nothing on the Net that even comes close to the standard etiquette books and while eventually Post and company will be on the Web, for now the print volumes are only available. The one close exception:

Good Housekeeping (http://goodhousekeeping.women.com/gh/advice/etiquette/00post21.html). Here is advice by Peggy Post, on the basics from weddings and business questions to father's day. The commands are short but practical and based on current practice. If further advice is required there is an e-mail "ask Peggy Post" which will come back with an answer within days.

Literature and Term Papers

CD: Masterplots Complete. Hackensack, NJ: Salem Press, date varies. $650.
   Print: (All Salem Press). *American Fiction Series,* 1986; *Short Story Series,* 1986; *British and Commonwealth Fiction Series,* 1987; *World Fiction Series,* 1988; *Nonfiction Series,* 1989; *Drama Series,* 1990; *Juvenile and Young Adult Fiction Series,* 1991; *Cyclopedia of World Authors,* 1989; *Cyclopedia of Literary Characters,* 1990. Note: All have various numbers of volumes in a set, and all have supplements.

Online: Monarch Notes online as part of: *Study World.* Oakwood Management, www.studyworld.com. Free.
   CD: Monarch Notes. Parsippany, NJ: Bureau of Electronic Publishing, 1992, no updates. $99.
   Print: More than 200 separate pamphlets. Various prices.

Online: Barron's Book Notes. Hauppauge, NY: Barron's Educational Series, 1993 to date, www.cheatbooks.com, available on America Online. Price per hour varies.

Students often request plot summaries and other shortcuts to reading. As far back as the Middle Ages, there were so-called cribs to assist students studying for an examination or working on a paper. There is nothing new about the medium and, in its place, it is a valuable reference form. A librarian may have mixed reviews about the desirability of such works for students, but that is a problem which students, teachers, and parents must work out together. It is an error to deny a place on the reference shelf to "crib" sources, regardless of how they may be used or misused.

By far the most famous name in this area is Frank N. Magill's *Masterplots,* a condensation of almost every important classic in the English language. Not only are the main characters well explained, but there is also a critique of the plot's highlights and its good and bad points. There are numerous stepchildren, cousins, and aunts to the main volumes of *Masterplots,* which are found in many libraries under various main titles and subtitles.

The Masterplots Complete on a CD-ROM (first issued in 1997) includes 7,500 titles and 12,000 essays about the books. These are drawn from the 100 volumes which make up the basic print set of *Masterplots.* The CD has revised, updated and edited the set which first appeared in the early

1940s. There are major entries from other related works such as the *Cyclopedia of World Authors,* but essentially the CD is an electronic twin of the print work(s).

Masterplots on a CD-ROM is much less expensive than the collected volumes. As it is used often, it is a good purchase for most libraries. The software allows for the standard type of searching patterns, and it is easy to use. Author, title, genre, and subject are the common access points. The directions on the screen can lead the reader to even more sophisticated searches such as "fiction of manners" or "roman à clef."

Under the rubric, "Magill's Choice" the publisher offers such titles as *Explorers, Notable Poets, Notable Novelists, Civil Rights,* etc. Within each volume (and some titles are multi-volume) one finds biographical sketches, critical studies, articles, etc. Many, if not most of the figures are found in *Masterplots* and cousins. The separate "Choice" sets run from $55 to $175. A perfect example of the necessity for the librarian to check carefully for redundant information, for too much of a good thing at too high a cost.

Book Notes

The print *Monarch Notes* series 35- to 80-page pamphlets are familiar to almost any senior high school or college student. As a crib, *Notes* is useful for a summary of plot or content, character analyses, commentary on the text, author background data, and so forth. Closely related to senior high school and college English courses, the relatively inexpensive CD-ROM, which includes all the guides, is too useful to pass over. Searching follows standard paths by author, title, subject, or a combination. And while Boolean logic is possible, it is much too involved for most situations where title or author alone is the usual navigational tool. Again, because the price is low the search patterns are rudimentary and sometimes require numerous tries. For example, some entries can be located with punctuation, others cannot.

As part of the consumer online service, American Online, *Barron's Book Notes* offers the complete text of 100 cribs published by Barrons. Most are the classics from Beowulf to Shakespeare and Hemingway. The approach is similar to *Monarch Notes,* and while not a consideration for libraries, is a useful enough work for students at home. *Barron's* is available, as well, in a print format.

Cliff Notes (Lincoln, NE: Cliff Notes, 1980 to date) contains even more familiar study aids. The firm was founded by Cliff Hillegass who mastered the art of condensing books into 70 to 90 easy-to-read pages. About five million paperback black-and-yellow copies are sold each year. The greatest audience for the notes are tenth, eleventh, and twelfth graders. Freshmen and sophomores are heavy users in college, but usually break the habit by their senior year. The 10 best sellers, in no

ticular order, include *The Odyssey, Hamlet, Great Expectations, The Grapes of Wrath, Huckleberry Finn, The Great Gatsby, Julius Caesar, Macbeth, A Tale of Two Cities,* and *The Scarlet Letter. Notes* is not available in any electronic format, possibly because it does so well in print.

On the Web

The dark side to the Internet Worldwide Web has several aspects. Consider the prewritten term paper.

The term paper mill is known to many high school and college students as well as alert teachers. Advertisements for the prewritten papers appear in magazines such as *Rolling Stone.* Word of mouth has been the best advertisement, at least until recently when the Net took over.

The ready-to-hand-in prewritten term papers are available on the Net at scores of sites. Simply enter "term paper" in almost any search engine box and the possibilities are everywhere. Even more possibilities will be found in news groups, e.g., try *Deja News* (www.dejanews.com). Type in "term papers" and over 1,000 comments, sources of term papers, and general news about the subject is offered. Most companies charge a fee (from $6 to $10 a page). A few sites offer free papers sent in by high school to graduate students.

Quality of the papers differ from paper to paper, not so much from company to company. A few will actually write the paper to order, instead of reaching into a bin of much used papers. These tend to be somewhat better in quality.

None, and absolutely none will get past the alert teacher, particularly if the assignment is more than general. For example, a professor might ask a student to write a general paper on Conrad's *Heart of Darkness* (general and suitable grist for the term paper houses). The wise teacher is more specific, e.g., the author's experiences and how they influenced Conrad's view of civilization as reflected in the *Heart of Darkness* is a much more difficult task for the standard term paper.

Teachers automatically would flunk a student who attempted to pass using a ready made paper purchased, or found free, from one of scores of term paper sites. Many institutions go further and dismiss the student for cheating.

The use of prewritten term papers is not strictly illegal. Therefore, ... n they are issuing papers as aids, not as works to be present's own. One example: *n File* (www.termpapers-on-file.com) makes a finer dish papers. "The intended purpose of our term papers l as models to assist you in the preparation of your own. h NJ Statutes 2A:17-77.16-18 and similar statutes that exist in other states, neither [we] nor any subdivision…will ever sell a model paper to any student giving us any reason to believe that (s)he will submit our work, either in whole or in part, for academic credit at any institution in their own name."

Despite the jargon and legal efforts, the prewritten term paper is a bold form of cheating. Students know it, teachers know it, and even the most modest of term paper mills know it.

Occupations and Careers

Online: Occupational Outlook. Washington, DC: U. S. Department of Labor, Government Printing Office, 1994 to date, quarterly, http:// stats.bls.gov/ocohome.html. Free.
   Print: Occupational Outlook Handbook, 1929 to date, biennial. $25.

CD: In Discovering Careers & Jobs. Farmington Hills, MI: Gale Group, 1994 to date, annual. $495.
   Print: 1929 to date, biennial. $22.

Online: So You Want to Get a Career. Princeton, NJ: The Princeton Review, online, www.review.com. Free.
   Print: Princeton Review Guide to Your Career. New York: Random House, 1996 to date.

Print: Encyclopedia of Careers and Vocational Guidance, 10th ed. Chicago: J.G. Ferguson, 1987, 4 vols. $150.

In larger libraries vocational guidance is not usually a part of the reference service, but it is very much so in medium-sized and small libraries, and certainly in schools. When occupational and professional advice is given to students by trained counselors, inevitably there is a fallout of young men and women seeking further materials, either for personal reasons or in the preparation of class papers. The rush has grown so that even the smallest library is likely to include a considerable amount of vocational material in the vertical file.

Anyone looking for employment will bow down not once, but three times to the Internet. Here, for the first time one may literally do two things: (1) Determine type of employment and what the opportunities for the long run are in that particular job or profession. This via *Occupational Outlook, Discovering Careers & Jobs,* or *So You Want to Get a Career.* (2) Immediate employment classified advertisement opportunities are available across the country in several Internet sites. The websites are updated frequently.

The *Occupational Outlook Handbook* is especially useful. This is a United States government publication. Close to 700 occupations are discussed in terms that can be understood by anyone. Each of the essays indicates what a job is likely to offer in advancement, employment, location, earnings, and working conditions. Trends and outlook are emphasized to give the reader some notion of the growth possibilities of a given line of work. Unfortunately, the writers are often no more accurate in their predictions than economists and racehorse touts. The title is updated more frequently online and in print via a quarterly: *Occupational Outlook Quarterly* (Washington: Government Printing Office, 1957 to date, quarterly). The periodical contains information on employment trends and opportunities.

Occupational Outlook is in company with other useful print companions. Among these: (1) The *U.S. Dictionary of Occupational Titles* (Washington: Government Printing Office, various dates), which lists all of the legitimate working careers recognized by the government. It is as much a mnemonic device as a reminder that there are thousands of occupations out there in addition to airline pilot and model. (2) Gale's *Career Advisor Series* (Farmington, MI: Gale Group, various dates) is a six-volume set of books which is frequently updated. Each volume features a full description of the work, as well as how to prepare for the occupation. In addition there is good advice on interviewing, résumés, and the like. The series is of equal use to high school graduates and university students in quest of a career. Gale's *Career Advisor Series* on a CD-ROM incorporates the *Occupational Outlook Handbook* and the print series as: *DISCovering Careers & Jobs,* has most of the information people need as well as specific advice on the careers and occupations to which students are drawn. A simple menu allows the user of *DISCovering* to search for a career by subject, that is, "career category"; by employer, with 30,000 firms at the user's fingertips; and by job title, from librarian to mechanic. Current literature offers information from about 1,000 articles, with abstracts and full text.

So You Want to Get a Career is a commercial website that invites the high school senior or college student to search the *Princeton Review Guide to Your Career* by a career. There are several hundred choices that average about three to four print-out pages. Each covers: daily life, educational requirements, and the future of the position for two, five and ten years out. Usually there is a handy profile of basics, i.e., for *librarian* this includes the number of people in the profession (141,000); the percentage of males and females, 35% and 65%; average starting salary, etc. There even are a few titles of films, books and TV shows where librarians figure as characters. Major associations and employers end the sketch. The data is current and reliable.

Jobs On the Web

Beyond background information on careers is the real question of where to find an actual job. Here the Internet Worldwide Web excels. It may not land you employment, but it certainly gives you the opportunity to scan the wide field of possibilities each and every day. There literally are scores of such services online, but the two best, particularly for libraries:

CareerPath (www.careerpath.com). Classified job advertisements from some two dozen of the country's leading newspapers. (*The New York Times* to the *Sacramento Bee*) offers an immediate overview of what is available as well as pay scales. Some 100,000 ads are featured which cover everything from highly professional positions to service spots in offices or fast food places. Easy to use, the search can be done by desired job, region, or key words. One can pick a wide field, such as law and browse what is available throughout the United States, or simply focus on a narrow area. Added features include advice on writing résumés, interview techniques, statistics on employment, etc. Unfortunately there are no e-mail addresses to would-be employers, but box or phone numbers are given.

The Monster Board (www.monster.com). Lists around 397,000 jobs posted by the individual employers, not through newspapers. This narrows the field, but in some ways has the advantage of being more specific, particularly in terms of just who is doing the hiring. Searching is relatively simple, and permits requests by region, level of experience (from beginner to expert) and other features such as opportunities for work outside of the United States. See, too, such things as employer and company profiles, discussion groups and studies, and a sign-up which tips the user to his or her particular talents when a job opens.

The Internet has approximately 30,000 job boards similar in purpose, if not scope, to the *Monster Board*. The majority are highly specialized, i.e., directed to a particular profession or area such as Accounting.com or Utah-Jobs.com. The sites offer more than listings. Many, including *Monster Board* have individual résumés which can be sent to the employer. The job seekers can often apply for several jobs by pressing a button which instantly sends their résumés to prospective employers. Other services actually administer employment tests on line to help the employer. Despite all of this the newspaper help-wanted ads continue to flourish because they tend to be local and, more important, not all that number of job seekers are aware of what is available online—a fact which might be remedied in part by libraries.

In order of relative use (as of mid-2000) *Monster Board* is the most popular, followed by: *Jobsonline.com; Careerpath.com; Headhunter.net; HotJobs.com; Careerbuilder.com; Jobs.com; Dice.com*. All are sites worth exploration for librarians working in this field. (All URLs preceded by the usual www., e.g., www.jobsonline.com.)

With all of the help offered online, the best single and immediate place to find work in a community is, to be sure, the classifieds in the local online or print newspaper. "For sheer volume of job openings, your local paper's website probably beats the leading nationwide job listings sites for finding openings in your area."[16] Here "local" should be interpreted first by community, then by state and finally by region.

Quotations

Online: Familiar Quotations. New York: Columbia University Press, 1997 to date, irregular, www.bartleby.com/100/. Free.

Bartlett's Familiar Quotations, 17th ed. Boston: Little, Brown and Company, 2002, 1,432 pp., indexes, $50.
Print: 16th ed. 1992, 1,405 pp. $49.

CD: The Oxford Dictionary of Quotations, 5th ed. New York: Oxford University Press, 1999. $40.
Print: 5th ed. 1999, 1,061 pp. $45.

Print: Chambers Dictionary of Quotations. New York: Larousse, 1997. 1527 pp. $40.

Online: Gale's Quotations: Who Said What. Farmington Hills, MI: Gale Group, 1994, www.gale.com, no update. $400.

Quotations are beloved by everyone, and they pop up everywhere. They may salt an after-dinner speaker's delivery, get a laugh on a late television show, or be enshrined in literature. It is true that the love of the quotation is disappearing. What is worse, quoting can be dangerous because these days few realize that the speaker or writer is quoting at all. Still, let's quote on.

If one wishes to find the precise source of a quotation, it is necessary to search a book of quotations. The librarian would hope (1) that it was an actual quotation, and not one made up or slightly changed by the seeker; (2) that the wording was approximately, if not precisely, correct; (3) and that the primary actors involved in the quotation were accurately named.

The good quotation book will indicate the source, usually a printed work. Lacking a source, one is left in doubt, particularly when there may be a question about when and just who did say "You dirty rat" or "Eternal vigilance is the price of liberty."

In addition to the standard, general quotation titles, there are from 250 to 300 specialized quotation books. Normally these are limited to a given subject area such as Quotations for dentists or doctors or teachers or, yes, librarians, etc. Most of these can be passed, but there are some

---

[16]*Yahoo! Internet Life,* May, 1998, p. 121. See, too, "Career Sites" *The New York Times,* October 4, 1999, p. C5.

certainly worthwhile. One excellent example: *African American Quotations,* (Phoenix, AZ: Oryx, 1998).

How does a phrase or a few sentences become a memorable quotation? There are two or three rules governing compilers. First, if it is well known and memorable the quotation is automatically included. Shakespeare's "What's in a name? That which we call a rose by any other name would smell as sweet" is found in almost all books of quotations. Second, the quotation may reflect current feeling and policy. Third, it may drive home a point about morals, homespun wisdom, and so forth.

While the first two rules are applicable to almost all works, the third should be kept in mind as well. For example, Civil War general John Sedgwick's last words fit nicely into a work of last words or "black" humor but not into a book celebrating the skill of generals. This quotation is supposedly the general's last comment as he raised his head above the parapet in the Battle of the Wilderness: "Nonsense, they couldn't hit an elephant at this dist..."

Librarians and readers who want to save precious time and frustration turn to the printed quotation books. Easy to use, easy to understand, the print quote source is used without the intermediary computer.

A rule of the profession: turn to *Bartlett* or *Oxford* first, then try the secondary line of books such as *Chambers*. If these fail, turn to the electronic Gale's *Quotations*. If not there, the real delight begins. Now one searches, book by book, virtually every title in the library. (One might dismiss, of course, those already captured by the Gale database.)

Bartlett's Familiar Quotations is the best known in the world. It is one of the oldest. Compiled by a bookman, John Bartlett, in 1855 it originally had quotes by 169 authors. The present edition has over 2,500 authors with over 20,000 quotations arranged chronologically. (The first quote is from the Egyptian Song of the Harper c. 2600 B.C. The last, fittingly enough, is from "anonymous" a Spanish proverb). Easy to use, almost one-third of the volume is given over to a detailed index.

Avoid the free Net version of *Bartlett*.[17] Although sponsored by Columbia University, this is a waste of time. It has only about 12,000 quotes, none of which is dated after 1919. Columbia is drawing upon

---

[17]There is no satisfactory free online general quotation book, despite the fact the Bartlett's is often featured as a useful Web source. Even a second hand copy of a 20th century print edition of Bartlett is better.

On the other hand, for specialized quotes, the Net is useful. See, for example: Mother of All Quotes (http://users.erols.com/dboger/html/movies.hmtl). Pop culture on a major scale, this consists of quotes lifted from television, movies, congress, presidential soundbites and anywhere else a quote is floundering about for recognition. The arrangement, the spelling, the quotes themselves can be terrible, but it is a useful site for locating hard to find media messages.

the 9th edition (1901) and the tenth edition (1919). This is totally worthless for anything of note since 1919.

The Oxford Dictionary of Quotations is a popular book found in many libraries. The fifth edition represents substantial revision. According to the admirably written preface, selection is based on what is most familiar to a majority of people and, in this case, while the bias is British, most of the 17,000 quotations (from 2,500 men and women) represent a considerable international tone and will be equally well known to educated Americans. Here, too, are "famous last words" (from King George V to convicted killer Garry Gilmore who hastened his demise with "Let's do it.") The CD-ROM edition includes *The Oxford Dictionary of Modern Quotations* (1984, 384 pp. $45). The latter has 6,000 selections from 20th century figures.

A useful supplement (some would say a replacement) to the *Oxford Dictionary of Quotations* is the *Chambers Dictionary*. The focus here is on English and European and world notables, with the quotes arranged alphabetically by the individual's name (and within each section chronologically). Comparisons show *Chambers* tends to have more quotes by well known figures than found in *Oxford*. A spot check indicates considerably more modern authors from various parts of the globe. Of course, given time, *Oxford* and all the other rivals will incorporate most of the personages into their next edition. *Chambers* underlines the importance for librarians to have as many current, as well as standard historical quotation sources, about as budget and space permits.

The Oxford Dictionary of Literary Quotations (Oxford: Oxford University Press, 1997. 479 pp. $30) is an example of subject quotation books. In two parts, the first section consists of some 3,500 quotations dealing with literature in general (from writer's block to the canon). The second sections are quotes from about 600 authors, British and foreign, arranged alphabetically from Kingsley Amis to Yeats. Most emphasis is on English speaking writers from Chaucer to the present. Under "originality," for example, is the famous Sam Goldwyn quote: "Let's have some more clichés."

If available to the library online, the single best place for quotations, and the first place to turn is *Gale's Quotations* which has over 117,000 common quotations primarily drawn from out of copyright sources. This is about the number of quotations found in four to five standard reference works. Usually, if only because of the number of quotes, what is needed can be found here.

Gale's Quotations may be searched, as one would expect, by the name of the author or speaker, by a key word or phrase, and by year of origin of the quotation. This latter feature is useful when someone is quoted at length, such as American presidents and celebrities; but as there are few such people it is of little practical value. It is one thing to limit a search for words by John F. Kennedy, and quite another to use it for Shakespeare, the Bible, or for Dr. Johnson when most users have not the faintest notion of years involved.

Why isn't there one online gigantic quotation database? Answer: Each copyrighted quotation book is from a different publisher. Each represents the work of a different compiler or team of compilers. Each wishes to be paid. Each believes an electronic wedding with 100 or 1000 other quotation books would cut back substantially on potential income. One might circumvent this by using out-of-copyright titles as Gale has done, but this would eliminate the magic words for the past fifty years. Eventually the copyright problem will be resolved, but until then one has *Gale*, which is at least an impressive beginning.

ADVICE AND INFORMATION

A common question in reference service is when to give information, when to give advice, and when to give neither. Normally, the emphasis is on information, not advice. The distinction is important, because advice and information are confused when medicine, law, or consumer help is sought by the layperson. Most librarians are willing to give consumer data, even advice (as this author believes they should about reference books and related materials), but some hesitate to give out data on medicine and law.

There is no reason not to give information about law or medicine. This does not mean the librarian is offering guidance. The trend today is to welcome legal and medical queries. Still, doubts may arise:

1. "I feel that I am practicing law (medicine) without a license." In no case has a library been named defendant in a legal suit on this ground. Of course, the librarian should not try to diagnose the situation or offer treatment (legal or medical), but simply provide the information required, no matter how much or in what form.

2. "I don't know enough about law (medicine) to find required information." There are now numerous books, articles, pamphlets, and television and radio tapes available for the layperson. These are reviewed in most of the standard reference review media. Furthermore, as with any subject area, the librarian soon becomes familiar with ways to evaluate a title for reliability, currency, or style of writing.

Thanks to thousands of medical websites, all of this is academic. People really don't care about the librarian's possible ethical worries. And if the librarian does not help them, they can turn to the Net on their own.

The sections that follow, on medicine, law, and consumer advice, point out specific problems and reference works. It is wise to remember that many basic legal or medical questions may be answered by consulting equally basic periodical indexes.

Health and Medicine

MEDLINE. See Chapter 6.[18]

Online: Mayo Health Oasis. Minneapolis, MN: IVI Publishing Inc. 1997 to date, daily, www.mayohealth.org. Free.
CD: Mayo Clinic Family Health Book. 1993 to date. $69.95-$99.95.
Print: New York: William Morrow, 1990. $34.95.

Online: Scientific American Medicine. New York: Scientific American, 1990 to date, monthly, www.samed.com. Free.
CD: Scientific American Medicine on CD-ROM. 1990 to date, quarterly. $645 (Individual CDs, $395).
Print: Scientific American Medicine. 1978 to date, monthly. $245.

Online: Complete Home Medical Guide. New York: Columbia University College of Physicians and Surgeons, 1997 to date, irregular, www.cpmcnet.columbia.edu/texts/guide. Free.

Online: The Merck Manual of Diagnosis and Therapy. Rahway, NJ: Merck and Company, 1996 to date, www.merck.com. Free.
CD: The Merck Manual in Physician's Desk Reference Library on CD-ROM. 1990 to date, quarterly. Price varies.
Print: The Merck Manual of Diagnosis and Therapy. 1899 to date. $45; paper, $24.

Online: PDR Net. Montvale, NJ: Medical Economics Company, 1999 to date, irregular, www.pdr.net. Free.
CD: Physicians' Desk Reference Electronic Library, 1990 to date, quarterly. $595-$895.
Print: PDR/Physicians' Desk Reference to Pharmaceutical Specialties and Biologicals. 1947 to date, annual. $82.95.

Visit any large local bookstore. Go to the medical/health section. Here are hundreds of current titles for laypersons arranged by "general" and then by every conceivable problem from acne to xenophobia. On the Internet the amount of health information is overwhelming. The sheer volume of the data indicates the wide interest in health matters.

Libraries follow much the same pattern, at least where the book budget allows. There is no place on the shelves for casual medical or

---

[18]For any in depth medical questions, the librarian turns to the index MEDLINE and its various configurations. What is listed here primarily are more general aids.

health books. This fact should be widely publicized. The library is an invaluable filter which saves laypersons worries about whether X or Y source is reliable—an obvious major consideration for anyone with a medical question. The acquisitions filter gives the library a considerable edge over even the brightest display in the bookstore where everything in print is available.

The librarian should be scrupulous about medical reference sources purchased and providing information on the Web. The user must be able to understand the books (website) concerning consumer health information. This can be ensured by (1) purchasing books written for laypersons; (2) purchasing medical dictionaries which give solid, clear definitions; and (3) purchasing or providing Web access to technical information which is not beyond the understanding of the better-educated or the more involved layperson.[19] The reference interview should ascertain precisely what information is required and at what level of sophistication. Many librarians feel slightly uncomfortable because they think the type of information required is more personal than usual. Then, too, there are other problems that range from offering "bad news" about a particular disease to the user who wishes to talk at great length about a personal difficulty. Nevertheless, the librarian is morally bound to remain objective, to give the right information, and to refrain from making judgments either about the patron or the advice given in a particular source.

Dictionaries

In addition to the volume listed at the beginning of this section as being appropriate for a library, there are a number of standard medical dictionaries; among those most often found in libraries is *Dorland's Illustrated Medical Dictionary* (Philadelphia: W. B. Saunders Co., 1900 to date). Frequently revised, this is the work of over 80 consultants, who review all entries and the numerous illustrations. *Stedman's Medical Dictionary* (Baltimore: Williams & Wilkins: 1911 to date) is another often-revised work that has some of the more up-to-date entries.[20]

---

[19]There is no shortage of guides to best and better medical books. All the standard reviews, from *Library Journal* to *Choice,* carry health-medical sections. See, too: *Doody's Rating Service: A Buyer's Guide to the Best Health Science Books* (New York: Doody, 1996 to date, annual) is a collection of opinions from reviewers, librarians and publishers on the best medical books for laypersons. Each title is briefly annotated and the choices seem reliable.

[20] Stedman's is available, for $69 to $99, on CD-ROM from the publisher of the print version. It adds some 85,000 definitions from a *Merriam-Websters Tenth New Collegiate Dictionary.* It is updated "as needed" but has no particular advantage over the print version.

Indexes

This is a good place to recall the excellent medical indexes discussed in the chapter on subject indexes. In particular the reference librarian will want to call on The National Library of Medicine's *MEDLINE* for sophisticated searches and for topics not covered in depth in standard medical reference sources. *PubMed* (www.ncbi.nim.nih.gov/PubMed) includes MEDLINE.

Internet

Hospitals, medical schools and commercial health firms (as well as individuals who may or may not be trusted) are reaching out to laypersons on the Net. While most online medical information is reliable, the same rules apply for evaluating these sites as are applicable for any reference work. Sometimes the source fails the test, e.g., according to one study of nearly 400 Web pages it was found that at least six percent contained wrong information and more than one-third had not been subject to peer review. In all cases of more than minor bits of advice doctors warn that patients should see them. "Anybody can put information on the Internet about any medical condition," and it may or may not be reliable.[21]

Mayo

The Internet *Mayo Health Oasis* is a combination of what is found in the print *Health Book* and current journal articles as well as other Mayo-sponsored reference materials. The website has a dozen full-time editorial workers who publish medical news daily. Three physicians review each story and it gives both technical and easy-to-understand medical advice to people who are not able to visit the clinic—about 40,000 visitors a month. This site covers almost all health topics of interest to the average individual. "Newsstand," has the full text of current articles. "Resources," covers the material from the *Mayo Clinic Health Letter*, medical terms, childcare, etc. A special feature: a question/answer section that invites queries from readers.

Essentially, it may be searched by causes, symptoms and treatment as well as broad subject headings (diet & nutrition; heart center, pregnancy & children, etc.). There is an exhaustive medication database with more than 8,000 prescriptions and nonprescription drugs described along with much the same material found in the PDR. Effects are clearly described. According to the site, some 1.5 million people visit there each month.

[21]"On Line Medical Information Does Poorly on Accuracy Exam," *The New York Times*, August 3, 1999, p. G2. See, too: "The Health Hazards of Point and Click Medicine." Ibid, August 31, 1999, p. F1, F6.

While lacking the daily updates, the print and CD-ROM versions have definite advantages. The CD-ROM has added delights such as 500 color illustrations, 45 animations, and close to two hours of audio. Questions may be targeted by using key words and phrases as well as Boolean logic. The text is clear and precise. For those with more time there are the usual menus and five large areas of discussions: modern medical care, human disease, life cycles, the world around us, and keeping fit. The medical care section gives diagnosis, care, and treatment tips. Generic and brand name drugs are covered as well as a splendid atlas of the human body. A nice feature is a type of cross-reference in the form of sidebars that refer the user to parallel topics of interest. All and all this is a first-rate CD-ROM for any library and, for that matter, many homes.

The print version of the Mayo title is precisely the same in content as the CD-ROM. While it lacks animation and sound, it makes this up with a low price and ease of use. Also, the illustrations are a trifle more well defined than on a computer screen.[22]

Scientific American

On a CD-ROM, in print, or online the *Scientific American Medicine* service is much the same. The only real difference is the ability to quickly search in the electronic form, although cross-references and indexing in the print version are equally good.

The loose-leaf *Scientific American Medicine* is updated monthly, making it one of the more current print ready-reference health services. (The online version is on the same schedule. The CD-ROM comes out only every quarter.) Prepared and written by medical researchers and doctors, the service is divided into 15 sections from dermatology to rheumatology. Within each part one finds illustrations, charts, tables, and other graphics to help explain the sometimes technical details. The writing style is generally easy to follow, although it does presuppose a reader who is a college graduate or equivalent.

Columbia

One of the best medical sites on the Net is the *Columbia University Complete Home Medical Guide*. Best because it gives virtually the whole content of the printed volume, and not just bits and pieces. Best because it covers most complaints in easy to understand language. Best because of a few, but excellent illustrations. And best because it is easy to navigate— and it is free.

---

[22]Mayo Clinic is a section on the Mayo Web site. It gives background on the world famous clinic.

These general guides are only examples. There are at least a score of other works which equally are as good and/or excel in a particular area. The reference librarian will keep the collection current by judiciously adding recommended titles (e.g., favorably reviewed in *Choice, Library Journal, Booklist,* etc.). Two examples: the *John Hopkins Family Health Book* (New York: Harper Resource, 1999, 1,680 pp. $50) from the hospital ranked No. 1 by *U.S. News & World Report* (1999). *The Gale Encyclopedia of Medicine* (Farmington Hills, MI: Gale Group, 1999, 5 vols. $499) has the advantage of being more comprehensive than the other general guides, and the drawback of being about ten times as expensive. *The Harvard Medical School Family Health Guide* (New York: Simon & Schuster, 1999, 1,192 pp. $40) is relatively unique in that it links the printed text to the school's website. Also, while content is much the same as found in other guides, many articles have more depth and are easier to find and use.

Sooner or later, and better sooner than later for those who want to live a long life, the doctor shakes his/her head and suggests a medical test, "just to see if that tick is significant." Ahh, but what does the test involve? Will it prove I am on the way to the mortuary? The answer is found usually in the *Yale University School of Medicine Patient's Guide to Medical Tests* (New York: Houghton, 1997, 620 pp. $40). Subtitled "detailed descriptions of the most common diagnostic procedures" this has 29 chapters that detail every conceivable test. Full details are included along with anatomical drawings and the likely amount of pain involved.

The Merck Manual

A much-used technical work, although suitable for certain library situations, is the *Merck Manual of Diagnosis and Therapy.* Published for many years as a manual for physicians, it is clear to laypersons with a medical dictionary at hand. Illnesses and diseases are described in relatively technical language, symptoms and signs are indicated, and diagnoses and treatments are suggested. Updated about every five years, the 1999 seventeenth edition includes numerous new topics since the sixteenth edition of 1992: drug therapy for the elderly, the problems with smoking cessation, chronic fatigue syndrome, etc.

The online version, it is important to note, tends to be more of an advertisement for the print and CD-ROM editions. The Web manual is two or more years out-of-date, and while still useful, it's not the best place to turn for other than background information.

Reaching out for a wider public, Merck published in 1998 a cutdown, rewritten version of the regular manual as *The Merck Manual of Medical Information, Home Edition.* This covers some of the same material as the larger work, but is tailored for the layperson. The 24 sections consider every conceivable problem, and are written in easy-to-understand terms. A good index and numerous other features make this a required item in most libraries, although it no way replaces the more detailed original *Merck Manual.* (Available, as well on a CD-ROM, from McGraw-Hill at $40, but with animation, audios and some 1,800 audio pronounciations of medical terms).

PDR

The best known and most often found pharmacology work in a library is the *Physicians' Desk Reference.* Frequently referred to as the *PDR,* it provides information on close to 4,000 drugs by generic and product name. The publisher notes that "the information is supplied by the manufacturers." At the same time, the Food and Drug Administration has approved the material sent by the manufacturer. With a little experience, one can easily check the content of this or that drug. (A generic and chemical name index is a major finding device.) For each item, the composition is given, as well as such data as side effects, dosage, and contraindications. One section pictures over 1,000 tablets and capsules, with product identification. The neatly divided six sections are arranged for easy use.

Online the *PDR Net* is a version of the print/CD-ROM version, but with added materials aimed primarily at doctors and nurses. A smaller section is directed to "consumers." While no more easy to understand at times than the CD-ROM or print versions, it is somewhat easier to use.

The CD-ROM *Physicians' Desk Reference Electronic Library* picks up the printed version. It adds related titles: the *Physicians' Desk Reference for Nonprescription Drugs, The PDR for Herbal Medicines* and the *Physicians' Desk Reference for Ophthalmology.* The complete text of *The Merck Manual,* and the *Stedman's Medical Dictionary* are optional add-ons for another $300. It can be searched independently, or one can cross-search all titles. In addition to ease of searching, it has the advantage over the print format in that the CD-ROM is updated each quarter, rather than annually.

The *Physicians' Desk Reference for Nonprescription Drugs* on the CD-ROM considers some 1,000 over-the-counter products. Arrangement and content are much like the basic title, including a section with photographs of actual tablets and packages. It is particularly useful for an objective analysis not only of what the drugs promise, but also of any bad side effects. The printed volume (1980 to date) is issued once a year from the publisher of the *PDR.*

A free website offers considerable information on drugs. This is *RxList* (www.rxlist.com) which has much of the same data found in the

PDR, although in an abbreviated form. A real plus here: the librarian can search for a drug not only by name but by the imprint codes, i.e., the numbers engraved on pills or capsules.

There are several other reliable sites to check out pills: *Food and Drug Administration* (www.fda.gov/cder/drug.html) puts emphasis on drug safety records and any government reprimands. *CenterWatch* (www.centerwatch.com) is a good place to turn for information on more than 7,000 clinical trials of drugs. Trustworthy data, although from a commercial site. *IMS Health* (www.ims-health.com) tallies sales of all prescription drugs in the United States. Valuable for investors, and more important for people searching to identify the most popular drug for a given condition.

The pharmacy online, which sells drugs, is outside reference services, but librarians who work with medical sources should understand such digital drugstores exist. They can save the user money, but pose a danger: How vigilant are the sites about warning of possibly harmful interactions? Reliable sites call the doctor reference given by the user. Others do not.[23]

On the Web

In addition to the previous sources mentioned on the Web, there are thousands of sites that cover every aspect of medicine and health. Unfortunately, the majority represents a commercial interest more involved with selling pills than good advice. When using the Web, be sure as a cautionary measure to closely examine commercial sites and/or stick to "org," "edu," or "gov" as at least a relatively good sign of reliability. Numerous commercial (.com) sites are excellent, but it is best to realize they can be a disaster. Aside from the usual advantages of being online, health and medical resources on the Net are valuable primarily because they are current and follow, sometimes on a daily basis, medical developments. Also, the Net has an expanding interest in multimedia sites that stress both visual and oral information in an easy-to-understand fashion. On the minus side, sites are not patrolled and there can be a good deal of misleading information. The student or librarian should always check on the source of the data. Also, there are close to 50 or more *reliable* health/medical databases available through major online vendors from DIALOG and EBSCO to IAC and LEXIS-NEXIS.

Medscape (www.medscape.com). Some believe this is the single best medical site on the Web. Why? Because: *(a)* It boasts a highly talented editorial board led by the former editor of the *Journal of the American Medical Association*. *(b)* It is an ongoing source of coverage of current medical news from articles to conference summaries. *(c)* Most important: it offers

---

[23]For a discussion of such sites see: Yahoo! *Internet Life*, August, 1999, pp. 139–142.

doctors up-to-date coverage, i.e., the articles can be brief summaries or supported with technical data usually available only to the medical profession. *(d)* Equally of value: the search process is easy to use and takes in everything from MEDLINE to searches for various drugs, treatments and even specialized areas from cardiology to respiratory care. The catch is that the site is for professional medics, not for laypersons. In fact, registration is required to indicate a professional status, albeit libraries can go online without difficulty. Given that, the more dedicated, better educated layperson will find it invaluable precisely for its professional approach to medicine. Used wisely and it becomes a first stop for medical questions.

Among other trustworthy Internet sources of medical information which originate with commercial firms are: The team effort of John Hopkins and Aetna U.S. Healthcare: *IntelHealth* (www.aetnaushc.com). This is continuously updated and claims to have over two million pages of data. Particularly noteworthy for its design and its effort to appeal to average users. (2) *Medcast Networks* (www.medcast.com) is sponsored by the Greenberg News Networks. While directed primarily to physicians, the "daily news broadcasts" are suitable for readers with an interest in medical problems. (3) *Medicine Net* (www.medicinenet.com) which is put together by physicians for laypeople. Covers procedures, diseases and drugs with links to related sites. (4) *Health Central* (www.healthcentral.com) is one of the best commercial sites, and equally reliable. It particularly is good for current opinion and data, e.g., the menu begins with "news" from prominent columnists, moves on to the popular "Dr. Dean show," the "people's pharmacy," "my health" and various related sites. The links from here to the world are superior. Note, too, there are links to discussion groups, usually involved with specific medical and health problems, to reviews of the best current books. (5) *Emergency Medicine* (www.Emedicine.com). Two physicians from the Chicago Medical School and the Boston General Hospital are behind this extensive free medical database. While it began only for professionals in an emergency room situation, it now is a much broader database with general as well as specific medical information. It is updated by over 400 doctors who keep the encyclopedia running. The sponsors claim they have over 400,000 hits a day for the text which includes video clips and illustrations. The textbook is technical, but can be understood by anyone who feels at home with Merck. It is free as it is sponsored primarily by drug companies and the two founding doctors.

Several other impressive, reliable health links to sites include:

Healthfinder (www.healthfinder.gov) One of the most popular websites, *Healthfinder* is sponsored by the Federal Department of Health and Human Services. This is invaluable in that: *(a)* it covers current news about medical matters; *(b)* has regular sections on major illnesses from cancer to diabetes; and *(c)* of probably most importance for reference librarians, it provides links to information from Government health agencies, public health and professional groups, universities, support groups, and medical journals. It may be searched by simple key words and by subject, as well as full-text searching. Note: This site is expanded regularly to offer improved consumer access. It adds resources frequently. Of all medical sources this should be at the top of the librarian's list.

Medical Matrix (www.medmatrix.org/index.asp) This provides links to scores of medical/health resources, and has the primary advantage of reliable rankings of sites as well as being updated regularly. The sources are nicely annotated and this usually is enough to steer the user in the right direction. Other data on the site includes electronic journals and medical news, as well as information particularly for physicians.

American Medical Association Physician Select (www.ama-assn.org) Supported by the AMA this serves two or three purposes. First, it will give biographical information, including training, on a doctor. Second, it will help you find a doctor in a given area of medicine. Third, it covers such details as whether the doctor accepts new patients as well as hours, phone number, and often a map to pinpoint his or her location.

Law

LEXIS-NEXIS. See Chapter 6.

Online: FindLaw. Mt. View, CA: FindLaw, 1999 to date, daily, www.findlaw. com. Free.

Legal questions are similar to medical queries in that they require more than an average knowledge of the field. This side of a professional law library, most librarians consult general works as well as specific laws of the state, city, and region. The discussion of indexes earlier in this text indicates the basic places (such as LEXIS-NEXIS) to turn to for current data, both specific and general.

Who asks what? In one survey of public libraries it was found that the people asking legal questions are primarily students and business people. Others want to know about divorce, wills, tax laws, and immigration procedures. Three points should be kept in mind in purchasing a legal guide: (1) Is it current? (2) Is it written for nonlawyers? At the same time it should not be oversimplified. (3) Do the works clearly indicate when a lawyer should be consulted?

There are several much-used guides to legal research, but they are for the librarian. The average layperson wants the information, not a book on how to find it. The best guide for non-lawyers is Stephen Elias's *Legal Research* (Berkeley, CA: Nolo Press, various editions and dates). It gives step-by-step instructions, is frequently updated, and is reliable.

On the Web

Supported by Northern California Law Librarians, the free *FindLaw* on the Web offers links to a variety of sites that will answer most questions—both by practicing lawyers and law librarians, as well as, to a lesser extent, laypeople. One enters key words or terms to find information that concentrates on law schools, law firms, consultants and legal directories. Actual information on the law is found under "Laws: Cases and Codes" as well as what is found under a "Legal Subject Index."

Consumer Aids

Online; Consumer Reports Full Text. Yonkers, NY: Consumers Union, 1982 to date, monthly, www.consumerreports.org. Free. DIALOG file 646, $60 per hour. Also available on other carriers.
   CD: Palo Alto, CA: DIALOG Information Systems, 1984 to date, quarterly. $375; annual updates, $235.
   Print: 1936 to date, monthly. $24.

The reference librarian is usually asked one of three questions about products and consumer protection: (1) "What is the best product for my needs?" (2) "To whom can I complain, or to whom can I turn for information about a product or service?" (3) "How can I protect myself from poor-quality products or services?" No one reference source answers all queries, although several are of particular value in locating possible sources. The best product answer may be found in numerous places, including articles indexed in *Readers' Guide* and other general digital indexes.

Consumer rip-offs, according to the National White-Collar Crime Center, are reported by about 40 percent of Americans. Most complained of unnecessary auto repairs and similar scams, but many who replied in the survey "said they had lost money through Internet schemes, credit card fraud and investment swindles."[24] With this there is enough reason that libraries, along with groups and government agencies, help crime victims as well as those likely to be stung.

Given the popularity of consumer-type information, and the various reference works it crosses and recrosses, many public and school libraries meet the problem by establishing special consumer collections or sections. These may include the whole range of Dewey numbers and everything from websites to books to magazines and video. The collection is used both for reference and for circulation, particularly when there is more than enough material to cover popular topics.

---

[24]"As Swindlers Branch Out…" *The New York Times,* May 25, 1999, p. C25.

A practical, reliable source of information on products is found in the well-known *Consumer Reports*. The electronic version goes back to 1982, and includes: *Consumer Reports Travel Letter* and *Consumer Reports on Health*. Complete text is included for all articles.

On the Internet, *Consumer Reports* is free to browse. This is only for the current issue. For past numbers, subscribers pay a modest $2.95 a month to search the archives back to 1982. A more extensive search, at a considerably higher price is found at other places, e.g., DIALOG, for one.[25] The question "To whom can I complain?" may be answered in many ways. At the local level, a call to the Better Business Bureau may serve the purpose. When one is trying to contact the manufacturer of the product, often a careful look at the container will give the address. If this fails, or if more information is needed, then a guide is helpful.

One of the best places to turn to find a company's address and personnel is: *Thomas Register* (New York: Thomas Publishing Company, 1905 to date, annual). The oversized multivolume print edition (33 volumes) has for most libraries been superseded by the less expensive electronic version. Online or via the eight CD-ROM set, one can locate data on 5,100 American companies via their catalogs which are the heart of the Register. In addition the indexing allows a search of 156,000 sources of supply under 58,000 product and service headings. Brand names are included. The CD-ROM set is $210 while online (DIALOG file 535) the cost is only $15 per hour, plus $1.70 per full record. There is an abbreviated free online service at: (www.thomasregister.com).

Note: A free, less than complete, but useful service on the Internet: *Online Guide to Companies* (www.companiesonline.com). Some 100,000 public and private companies are listed, but with a minimum of information. Phone numbers and addresses are included. For detailed information: *Standard & Poor's Register* (www.standardpoor.com). This is the electronic version of the well-known print guide to 75,000+ leading corporations as well as names of over 40,000 executives with brief biographies of 70,000. For costs (high) see S&P's website.

On the Web

The Web is an ideal place to turn for information on almost any product, or company. Simply enter the company name and/or the type of product or the specific trade name of the item in the search engine box and one usually is inundated with information.

---

[25]Nonevaluative information about products can be found with *Consumer Index* (Ann Arbor, MI: Pierian Press, 1973 to date, quarterly, with annual cumulations). This covers product reports in some 100 periodicals with brief annotations. Available, too, online (via OCLC and others) as well as on CD-ROM.

The catch—and an important one—most of the information about X or Y product originates with the manufacturer. It tends to be biased, although specific design information is accurate. There are countless possibilities to find consumer help, but begin with:

Consumer World (www.consumerworld.org). A private consultant for the U.S. Federal Trade Commission, with an excellent record for consumer protection, is behind this site which offers links to more than 1600 consumer oriented sites. A simple searching system, with detailed subject suggestions, allows the patient searcher to find specific products as well as more general information on money and credit, various consumer agencies and developments in travel.

U.S. Consumer Gateway (www.consumer.gov) has the advantage of being an objective source of free information—including a section devoted to "scam alerts." Some 40 federal agencies feed material into this government site which covers everything from health to products.[26]

DIRECTORIES

Directory information is among the most called for in libraries, particularly public libraries. People often try to locate other people, experts, and organizations through addresses, phone numbers, zip codes, titles, names, and so on.

Staff-produced directories are found in almost all libraries. These days they are a part of the library website, but some still maintain typed/handwritten/print sources. The directory made by the local library includes such items as frequently requested phone numbers, the names of individuals and agencies in the community, sources of help for difficult questions, often-requested names of state and federal officials, and a wealth of other miscellany. The Chicago Public Library reference staff, for example, lists the staff-produced files as the most useful source of data for daily reference work, matched only by the *World Book Encyclopedia* and the *World Almanac*.

Definitions

The *ALA Glossary of Library Terms* defines a directory as "a list of persons or organizations, systematically arranged, usually in alphabetical or classed order, giving addresses, affiliations, and so forth, for individuals, and addresses, officers, functions, and similar data for organizations."

---

[26]For other consumer sites see "Consumer Protection," *Yahoo!*, March, 1999, p. 126.

The purpose of directories is implicit in the definition, but among the most frequent uses is to find out (1) an individual's or a firm's address (including e-mail) or telephone number; (2) the full name of an individual, a firm, or an organization; (3) a description of a particular manufacturer's product or a service; or (4) the name of the president of a particular firm, or the head of a school, or the person responsible for, say, advertising or buying manuscripts.

Less obvious uses of directories include obtaining (1) limited, but up-to-date, biographical information on an individual, whether still president, chairperson, or with this or that company or organization; (2) historical and current data about an institution, a firm, or a political group, such as when it was founded, how many members it had; (3) data for commercial use, such as selecting a list of individuals, companies, or organizations for a mailing in a particular area, for example, a directory of doctors and dentists serves as the basic list for a medical supply house or a dealer in medical books; and (4) random or selective samplings in a social or commercial survey, for which they are basic sources. Directories are frequently employed by social scientists to isolate certain desired groups for study. Because directories are intimately concerned with human beings and their organizations, they serve almost as many uses as the imagination can bring to bear on the data.

Scope

Directories are easier to use than any other reference tool, chiefly because the scope is normally indicated in the title and the type of information is limited and usually presented in an orderly, clear fashion. There are many ways to categorize directories, but they can be broadly divided as follows:

Local Directories. There are primarily two types: telephone books and city directories. However, also included in this category may be all other types issued for a particular locality, for example, directories of local schools, garden clubs, department stores, theaters, and social groups.

Governmental Directories. This group includes guides to post offices, army and navy posts, and the thousand and one different services offered by federal, state, and city governments. These directories may also include guides to international agencies.

Institutional Directories. These are lists of schools, foundations, libraries, hospitals, museums, and similar organizations.

Investment Services. Closely related to trade and business directories, these services give detailed reports on public and private corporations and companies.

Professional Directories. These are largely lists of professional organizations such as those relating to law, medicine, and librarianship.

Trade and Business Directories. These are mainly lists of manufacturers' information about companies, industries, and services.

Additional Directory-Type Sources

The almanac and the yearbook often include directory-type information, as do numerous other sources of directory information:

1. Encyclopedias frequently identify various organizations, particularly the more general ones that deal with political or fraternal activities.

2. Gazetteers, guidebooks, and atlases often give information on principal industries, historical sites, museums, and the like.

3. A wide variety of government publications either are entirely devoted to or include directory-type information. Also, some works are directories in name (*Ulrich's International Periodicals Directory,* for example) but are so closely associated with other forms (periodicals and newspapers) that they are usually thought of as guides rather than as directories.

Formats

By definition and use the directory is best suited to an electronic format. As an online service, the directory can be updated frequently, while in print it is usually only every year, or, at best, half a year. The electronic version takes little space, thus clearing library reference shelves of sometimes multi-volume printed editions over numerous years. And, finally, it is easier to search in one sweep rather than consulting multiple indexes. Today most standard directories are in electronic format. And there is no question this is what the library should buy.

Directories of Directories

Online: Directories in Print in Gale Database of Publications and Broadcast Media, Farmington Hills, MI: Gale Group, 1990 to date, semiannual, www.galegroup.com. DIALOG file 469, $84 per hour.
Print: 1977 to date, annual. 2 vols. $315; supplement, $185.

The basic listing of directories is the *Directories in Print.* The publication lists more than 16,000 new or revised titles under about 26 broad subject categories from business to professional and scientific. There are a detailed subject index and a title index. Information for each entry includes the name of the directory, the publisher, address and phone number, and full description of the work. A separate section lists over 8,000 publishers of directories with necessary information from address to telephone number. There is a geographical approach to states, and there are other helpful indexes. An "alternative format index" primarily lists those directories available in electronic versions. Also, it includes mailing-list information. The supplement adds about 1000 new and revised titles each half-year.

Gale Ready Reference Shelf consists entirely of Gale publications and, more particularly, its 11 basic directories. (The title is hardly descriptive of real content). In addition to *Directories in Print* as well as *Gale Directory of Publications and Broadcast Media* there are over 300,000 listings from such works as the *Encyclopedia of Associations* to *Government Research Centers*. Searches may be done directory by directory, or across the whole field of entries. Prices vary, but depend primarily on how many are using the online service—and there are other plans as well.

A less expensive, although only in print directory of directories is the *Guide to American Directories* (New York: Todd Publications, 1985 to date, annual. $95). Here is succinct data on nearly 10,000 directories arranged alphabetically by subject. In some situations the subject areas are arranged geographically by state.

Association Central (Bethesda, MD: Association Central, www.associationcentral.com, 2000 to date. Rate varies.) is an online search engine limited entirely to finding information about some 15,000 trade and professional organizations primarily in the United States. Search may be done by key words and/or by limited searches under broad topics from arts and humanities to entertainment to science and society and culture. Arts & Humanities—Museums gives about 30 associations with full addresses and other basic data. One may then search the group or a specific association.

City Directories

The two most obvious, and probably the most-used, local directories are the telephone book and the city directory. Although separate printed works, they are more and more being combined online. The city directory is particularly valuable for locating information about an individual when only the street name or the approximate street address is known. Part of the city directory includes an alphabetical list of streets and roads in the area, giving names of residents (except for an apartment building, when names may or may not be included). The resident is usually identified by occupation and whether she or he owns the home. Some city directories, but not all, have reverse telephone number services, that is, a "Numerical Telephone Directory." If you know the phone number, you can trace the name and address of the person who has the phone.

The classified section of the directory is a complete list of businesses and professions, differing from the yellow pages of the telephone book in that the latter is a paid service that may not include all firms. Like the telephone book, city directories are usually issued yearly or twice yearly.

Most city directories are published by the R. L. Polk Company of Detroit, founded in 1870, which issues over 800 publications. In addition to its city directories, it publishes a directory for banks and direct-mail concerns.[27]

A number of ethical questions arise regarding the compilation and use of the city directories. For example, bill collectors frequently call large public libraries for information which can be found only in the city directory, such as reverse phone numbers and addresses and names of "nearbys," that is, the telephone numbers of people living next door to the collector's target. Some librarians believe such information should not be given over the telephone. They argue that this helps the collectors in an antisocial activity and promotes invasion of privacy.

This policy may be commendable in spirit, although questionable in practice, as it simply makes it more difficult, but not impossible, to use the directories. The author of this text would say that the librarian is there to supply information, not to question how or by whom it is used. Most large urban libraries give the information over the phone.

Much of the same information found in city directories will be available on the Web via online phonebooks, e-mail guides, etc. (These are discussed in the next section). Searches who require more information can find it at a growing number of commercial charge sites. Two examples: *Knowx* (www.knowx.com). Here the for fee service will search for everything from personal bankruptcy filings to such public documents as records of marriages, real estate purchases, etc. Similar searches via LEXIS-NEXIS, and West Publishing (legal databases discussed in the indexing chapter) range from free to $65. *Peoplefinder* (www.peoplefinder.com) has access to over two billion public records. If a match is found, the service charges $40.

The obvious question: what happens to an individual's privacy with city directories and online commercial services? The answer: very little. Most personal information about you can be made public, either online or in print, quite legally. Even unlisted phone numbers can be traced via utility companies who may have the number for billing purposes or,

---

[27]City Directories of the United States (www.citydirectories.psmedia.com) is on the Internet—but at a fee which varies. All historic major directories are included from 1859–1898. This is for serious genealogical searching.

more likely, through an old directory before the individual called for an unlisted number. Individuals can search out the people finder databases, and directories to have their names removed. But this is an almost impossible task.

Telephone Directories and E-mail Directories

CD: Business Phone Book USA: The National Directory of Addresses and Telephone Numbers. Detroit: Omnigraphics, 1985 to date, annual. Rate varies. *Print:* 1985 to date, annual, 2 vols. $165.

CD: Direct Phone. Marblehead, MD: ProCD Incorporated, 1994 to date, quarterly. $149. Includes 72 million white-page listings, plus 7.5 million business white-page listings.

CD: PhoneDisc. Bethesda, MD: Digital Directory Assistance Incorporated, 1993 to date, quarterly. $249. Five disks: Western, Central, Middlewest, Northeast, Southeast states. Includes 90 million residential and business listings.

Online: The Ultimates. Infoseek, 1997 to date, daily, www.theultimates.com. Free on the Internet

The day when libraries might have shelf after shelf of telephone books is past. Today the average library will have a CD-ROM and online service that can pick a single number of series of names and numbers from almost any part of the United States, Canada, and the world. To be sure the local phone book, as well as phone books of major cities in the area are retained as much for ease of use as for constant demand for information. And from the point of view of a historian or genealogist, a long run of telephone books is a magic key to finding data on elusive individuals.

Depending on the sophistication of the software, the various electronic approaches to phone numbers generally have much in common. The CD-ROMs are used much like a regular phone book. If the user knows a name, this is typed in and the phone number and address appear. But unlike the printed version, the searchers have numerous paths: (1) They can look up the known phone number and find (in reverse) the name of the person or business and address. (2) If they know the address, then up pops the phone number and name. They can narrow the quest by zip code, area code, city, state, or a combination. All the people who live on a given street can be traced, as well as businesses. The business section may be searched, too, by Standard Industrial Classification, again for the nation, or by zip code, and so forth. Generally, the electronic data is accurate, but from time to time one finds the wrong phone number, the wrong name, the wrong zip code, and so on. This seems to be as much the fault of the phone companies as the directory publishers.

A tremendous advantage of the electronic CD systems is that they are updated quarterly and one subscribes, usually at reduced rates, for the various updates. Many of the services offer variations on a theme at different prices. Thanks to the competition, most prices are reasonable.

This side of the local phone book, another print volume is a favorite of reference librarians. "Kept next to the phone for a variety of ready- reference answers,"[28] is the consensus. *The Business Phone Book USA* has three claims to much use in almost any library: (1) It lists, under a variety of broad topics, the type of phone numbers nationwide that people are most likely to request. The first volume is a listing by organizational name. The second or "yellow pages" lists the same names by subject. (2) The subjects include everything from associations and universities to hotels and hospitals in major and some minor centers across the country. (3) There are the added touches from fax numbers, e-mail addresses, zip codes to toll free numbers. There are close to 140,000 listings, including nearly 1500 major foreign concerns as well as all major business and government numbers. To top it off—it is extremely easy to use. So easy, in fact, that there is little reason to consider the CD-ROM, published by the same firm. It is only called into play when there may be a complex search, say, for all the hotels with 800 numbers in the Northeast. Note: The same publisher has a stable of related titles: *Toll-Free Phone Book USA; WebSite Source Book; FaxUSA; Government Phone Book* with annual updates and print versions running from $145 to $230.

The people who publish *PhoneDisc* offer half a dozen other versions from *PhoneDisc QuickRef* (with 100,000 of the most frequently dialed business, educational, government, etc., numbers for $69) to *PhoneDisc California*. The *DirectPhone* people bring up *SelectPhone*, a $300 four-disc package covering various sections of the United States. The least expensive discs (under $300) are easiest to use because they have less information and fewer access points. Normally one simply types in the required name and the number appears. Problems arise when there are hundreds of John Smiths without proper indication of location, or when a name pops up without a phone number.

On the Web

None of the for free net databases used to locate phone numbers, e-mail addresses, street addresses, etc. is perfect, but the ones listed here are very close—and besides that they can be used efficiently by both librarian and layperson. Supported by advertising revenue most of these have minor flaws. Actually, in most cases it is faster, more efficient and

[28]"Field Tested Reference Titles," *Booklist*, May 1, 1998, p. 1532.

much easier simply to use the old fashion method of calling the operator for help.[29]

1. *Infospace* (www.infospace.com). With modesty, the publisher calls this "the ultimate directory" and claims to have over 100 million listings in the United States as well as many more for Europe. It is close to the truth. Among other things the user can quickly find personal phone numbers and addresses across the United States. Ditto e-mail addresses. There is a section for yellow pages, along with 800 numbers. Reverse phone numbers are identified. There is a group of numbers for "international," but these are far from complete. Other services, primarily supported by advertising, move from finding an apartment to e-shopping and government phone numbers. Easy to navigate, this is by way of an ideal free service for librarians and laypersons. (Note: for $5 the user can order a fairly complete profile of any business which is located on this site.)

2. *Big Yellow.* Bell Atlantic (Verizon) Electronics/Database America (www.bigyellow.com) has the advantage of backing from Verizon (formerly Bell Atlantic). Here the focus is some 17 million business listings, arranged under the familiar phonebook subject headings with suggestions of other subject headings to use as well as related sites. The information includes the phone number as well as links to maps and helpful cousins and aunts. One of the best "yellow page" sections on the Net, but of no value to someone looking for a specific name.

3. Switchboard (www.switchboard.com). An AltaVista guide, this claims to have more than 120 million listings. It follows the same patterns as its competitors, e.g., e-mail addresses, telephone numbers, etc. An added feature is a "knock-knock button" which indicates if those with e-mail addresses wish to receive mail from searchers.

At least once a year the magazine, *Yahoo!* offers suggestions about locating people on the Net, e.g., in their February, 1999 issue (p. 127) they cover many of the sites listed above. Also, they recommend: *Bigfoot* (www.bigfoot.com); and understandably, *Yahoo! People Search* (http://people.yahoo.com).

E-Mail

Finding an e-mail address on the Web is relatively easy and often is a feature of the Web guides to telephone numbers. The addresses are drawn from sources such as those involved in chat groups, online bulletin boards, etc. People often change e-mail addresses, but it is worth a try.

---

[29]It takes less than a minute to find an area code by contacting an operator (although there usually is a charge). On the Net it can take from 3 minutes to 10 or 15 minutes as one has to scroll through long lists first.

Sponsored by the search engine Infoseek, *The Ultimates* are a family, in this case a family of 25 Net service directories. These include the white pages of the majority of phone books across the U.S. Access is by name to find the phone number and address. Yellow pages are added. The most useful is the "Ultimate E-Mail Directory." This finds e-mail addresses of individuals across the whole of the Net. The latter has six different e-mail directories including *Infospace*. If one does not work, try another. It is the most rewarding of all the e-mail address sites and a good 95 percent of the time comes up with the address. Note: one does have to have an approximate idea of location as there may be dozens of similar names. There is a "reverse" in two of the search engines. One can enter the e-mail address and up comes the name of the person or institution with said URL. There are scores of other paths to e-mail addresses. Some are highly specialized, e.g., *WhoWhere?* (www.whowhere.lycos.com) has a wide range of difficult, arcane addresses not found in most other places.

Associations and Foundations

Online: Associations Unlimited. Farmington Hills, MI: Gale Group, 1986 to date, semiannual, www.galegroup.com. Rate varies. DIALOG file 114. $102 per hour. Also available on OCLC and other carriers.
   CD: 1995 to date, annual. $725.
   Print: Encyclopedias of Associations. 1956 to date, annual, 3 vols. $380 to $490 each.

Online: Foundation Directory. New York: Foundation Center, 1987 to date, annual, www.fconline.fdncenter.org. Rate varies. DIALOG file 26. $60 per hour.
   Print: 1960 to date, annual, 3 vols. $435.

Directory searching is not the most scintillating reference work. Still, given a bit of imagination, it has promise. Consider the print version of the *Encyclopedia of Associations* under "National Organizations of the U.S." one finds over 23,000 groups. Divided by broad subjects, with detailed indexes, this is a profile of American realities and dreams. It goes from the "American Association of Aardvark Aficionados" (600 members who love the animals) to the "Zippy Collectors Club" ("philatelists interested in the collecting of zip code and other marginally marked material"). This catalog of organizations brings the often arid landscape of American commerce to multifarious life. The same inventory that includes the "Financial Accounting Federation" also yields up the "Electrical Women's Round Table" and the "Pressure Sensitive Tape Council."

A typical print entry covers 15 to 20 basic points about the organization, whether it has a half dozen members or many thousand, whether it be deadly serious or just deadly, for example, see "The Flying Funeral

Directors of America" (who "create and further a common interest in flying and funeral service"). Information for each entry includes the group's name, address, chief executive, phone number, purpose and activities, membership, and publications (which are often directories issued by the individual associations). There is a key word alphabetical index, but the second volume is really an index to the first in that it lists all the executives mentioned in the basic volume, again with complete addresses and phone numbers. Another section rearranges the associations by geographical location. The third volume is issued between editions and keeps the main set up to date by reporting on approximately 3,000 changes in the primary set.

A habit of directory publishers is to develop "spin-offs." A case in point: *Encyclopedia of Associations: Regional, State and Local* (Detroit, MI: Gale Research Inc., 1988 to date). First published in 1988, with promises of frequent updates, this follows the pattern of the major set, but is limited to 113,000 local, state, and regional associations. There are five volumes (at $570). If there is humor and pathos in the directory of national organizations, one can only imagine what can be found in the entries arranged here alphabetically: first by state, then by city and town, and finally by the association name. The subject index is little more than a key word approach, that is, it lifts the key words from the title, and if these are not explanatory of the subject matter, one is lost. True, the editors do add subjects, but not enough.

In the online format, *Associations Unlimited,* the same text is included, but there are additions which include (1) the aforementioned regional, state, and local directories; and (2) *International Organizations,* with coverage of over 30,000 organizations. There are a total of over 450,000 entries which can be searched online via 22 different fields from title and keywords to subject. The online version has the advantage of being more current than the print work in that it is updated semiannually. (Note: The entire work of *Encyclopedia of Associations* is available, too, in the much larger package of directories—*Gale's Ready Reference Shelf,* discussed earlier in this chapter.)

There are countless methods of searching the online version from subject and name of a group to address and geographical location. Through Boolean logic, the quest might limit hits to Oklahoma associations with a membership of more than 3,000 and with budgets in excess of $4,000. It is helpful too when the patron knows only a few key words such as "bowling" and "restaurants." A search may turn up organizations that deal with bowling alley food requirements.

If one adds up the cost of all the electronic services, the total cost—particularly online for infrequent searches—is actually less, for a change, than the print volumes. The online or CD-ROM directories show the tremendous advantage of electronic databases over print.

Foundations and Grants[30]

Updated each year, the *Foundation Directory* online includes added works by the same publisher, such as the *National Directory of Corporate Giving*. The database describes some 12,000 sources of potential grant funds. Private as well as business and community organizations are included. Full information is given regarding the amount of money involved, and there is considerable detail available on what must be filed by whom. Most important: addresses, phone numbers, names of personnel, and so on, make it possible to gain further information where and when needed. The initial printed volume includes only foundations with assets of at least $2 million. There are close to 7,000 listings. The second volume includes another 4,000 "mid-sized foundations." The third volume is a supplement issued about six months after the initial two volumes. By now it is redundant to add that the online version is preferable for complex searches, but the print edition is probably a better buy when the guide is often consulted.

The *International Foundations Directory* (New York: Europa, 1974 to date, irregular) lists about 1500 foundations from 107 countries in its eighth edition (1998). It follows much the same pattern as the Foundation Directory.

Trying to find grants is the primary use of both these guides. Other help comes from the Oryx Press (Phoenix, AZ). *GrantSelect* (1999 to date, annually, www.grantselect.com. $1,500. Here are 10,000 possibilities from 3,400 nonprofit organizations—most of which are listed in the printed sources. The advantage of this work, of course, is that it is updated daily and can be searched by numerous paths not open to print users. The search patterns are less than satisfactory, but with a little patience....

On the Web

While nothing free on the Net is as comprehensive as *Association Unlimited* there are at least links to association data:

Associations on the Net. Internet Public Library (www.ipl.org). An alphabetical list of over 500 Internet sites which provide information on professional and trade associations. Also includes listings of cultural and art organizations, political parties, labor unions, academic societies, etc. There are two search approaches. The first is by subject which is broken down into links to subcategories, e.g., Arts, Humanities and Culture

---

[30]See the July 1998 issue (pp. 1900+) of the "Reference Books Bulletin," in *Booklist* for a basic guide to "sources on grants, funding and financial aid." Each entry has a descriptive, evaluative annotation and all aspects of foundations and related areas are covered.

includes: arts, ethnic, historical, libraries, literature, media, museums, philosophy and religion. The second approach is to browse by title.

Unless one wants to spend hours of time searching by type of information or name of foundation on the Net, there is nothing as sophisticated as the for-a-fee titles available.

Education

Online: Peterson's College Database. Princeton, NJ: Peterson's, 1997 to date, annual. DIALOG file 214, $30 per hour. Available on other carriers. *CD:* 1987 to date, annual. $595.
  Print: Peterson's "Core Library Set." Various dates, annual, 15 vols.

CD: Lovejoy's College Counselor. Philadelphia: Intermedia Active Software, 1994 to date, annual. $99; professional/profile edition, $199.
  Print: Lovejoy's College Guide, New York: Monarch Press, 1949 to date, semiannual. Paper, $14.95.

The Peterson guides are the most exhaustive and informative of scores of college, university, and trade schools throughout the United States and Canada. As they are much the same in content, the best place to begin is with the print set. (These volumes may be purchased individually). The core is the four volume set: *Scholarships, Grants and Prizes, College Money Handbook, Four Year Colleges* and *Two Year Colleges.* Another valuable part of the set is the six volume Guides to Graduate Study. Detailed information is given for over 2,000 four year institutions and 1,500 two year colleges. There are nearly 800,000 scholarships described with a fine section on how to apply for such grants. Financial aid for 1,600 colleges is outlined in the money book. In addition the set includes six books which analyze graduate programs in major disciplines as well as six volumes given over to job opportunities.

The most thorough and extensive listing of universities and colleges is in the for-a-fee electronic Peterson series. All the nation's institutions of higher education are in the printed *Guide to Two Year Colleges* and *Guide to Four Year Colleges* which make up the electronic databases. Searches may be made with Boolean logic and one can limit the quest to a given institution, subject, area, cost estimate, and the like. Full and current data are given from graduate requirements to special programs and number of students and teachers.

Peterson's does have a free website. One can turn to: (www.petersons. com) for partial free searches, but most of it is at a charge. It is worth considering by libraries who don't choose to have the more expensive commercial online carrier. See, too, the commercial competitor with Petersons, i.e., College Board, who also issues numerous educational guidebooks. Their products often are used by high school guidance people. For a view of their offerings see: (www.collegeboard.com).

A similar service called Peterson's GRADLINE (available online and on CD-ROM) offers detailed descriptions of the more than 30,000 graduate and professional programs in about 1,500 accredited colleges and universities. Updated annually, the CD-ROM is $695 and the online search on DIALOG file 273 is $60 per hour. Most libraries will want the first of these services. Universities will want both.

The frequently revised printed *Comparative Guide to American Colleges* (New York: HarperCollins) explains the best school for the person looking for the best in social activities or academic excellence, or both. Everything from admission requirements and the racial composition of the student body to the amount of social life is considered in a standard form of each institution. It answers such questions as how many full-time men and women are on the campus or what percentage of students go on to graduate work. Many students have found it to be remarkably accurate over the years. The listings are by the name of the academic center, and at the end of the book there is an index by subject from accounting to library science and zoology.

A standard work in the field, *American Universities and Colleges,* (New York: Walter deGruyter, 1928 to date) gives detailed information on over 1,900 institutions. One finds answers to questions ranging from what is taught by whom, to the number of students, to the shape of various graduate and professional education programs. Schools are listed by state and by city, and there are a detailed index and several appendices that list ROTC schools, dress codes, and so forth. Among hundreds of such single-volume printed guides, it provides the details most students and parents are seeking. Consider, for example, the faculty, shown here by number as well as by sex and rank. Valuable background information on the history and current status of U.S. higher education is in each edition. But there is a drawback. Usually the statistical data are three to four years behind the date of the latest edition, and editions come out only every four or five years. (The 15th edition was published in 1997 at $199.95).

Detailed information on colleges, universities, trade schools, graduate degrees, and other aspects of advanced education are found in scores of directories.[31] The majority are in various electronic formats as well as in print. One envisions the time when scores of numerous and varied print guides to education will find a home in a single electronic database.

---

[31]Peterson and Lovejoy are selected here because they are typical. But this is not a recommendation of only two out of numerous excellent titles. They are representative, not definitive. For example, almost as many librarians favor the *College Blue Book* (New York: Macmillan, 27th ed., 1999, 5 vols.) which is a superior guide to thousands of colleges and universities in the United States and Canada. Available both in print and on a CD-ROM— at the same $250. Note: This work frequently is updated.

On the Web[32]

Virtually every college, university, and trade school in the United States
and Canada, as well as throughout much of the world, has a home page
or related sites on the Web. Type in the name of a given school in a search
engine box and, zap, up comes more information than you probably wish
to know. There are filters. While a good place to start, the college Web
page is little more than a public relations brochure online, often matched
with the more detailed college catalog. And don't forget college newspapers. *The College Press Network* (www.cpnet.com) has links to over 300
such papers.

The best, and a first choice, are the aforementioned pay-as-you-go
electronic and print guides. Beyond these, as much for odd details or
more current data, are the links to the academic sites.

Some of the more representative free websites include:

College Net (www.collegenet.com). Primarily this links the user to
university and college websites throughout the United States and Canada.
Depending on the local website the viewer can do everything from find
out the number of programs in X or Y study to available scholarships and
entrance requirements. Some allow you even to file applications online.
Thanks to a refined searching program one can look for colleges in terms
of type, state, tuition levels, and enrollment. The system is updated
regularly and one of the best designed on the Web.

Money Magazine (www.money.com/money) which puts out an
annual print issue on colleges and universities, has transported this same
data to the Net. Now the student may search for the best college using
42 different factors from cost of tuition and room to number of sunny
days in the location of the college. *U.S. News and World Report,* both in
print and online, offers a similar service with specific rankings of the
top 25 schools: (www.usnews.com). A more objective site: *College Rankings*
(www.library.uiuc.edu/edx/rankings.htm). Here are rankings as
determined by Daniel Burgard, librarian at the University of Illinois.
Drawn from reliable sources with numerous entry points.

Pure Advice (www.pureadvice.com) is a for-a-fee service which offers
one-on-one counseling sessions to help high school students decide which
college is most appropriate for their needs—and income. The charge is
about $75 for a 45-minute chat with experienced counselors. This is

---

[32]For a discussion of these and numerous other websites see *Yahoo! Internet Life,* February,
1999, p. 126, "Preparing for College," sites to help with the college board exams. See, too:
"Site Seeing—College Searches," *The New York Times,* September 28, 2000, p. G7. A dozen
sites "for students who are starting their college searches."

followed up with a written summary of the session. The service seems to be reliable. Note: part of it is for free, i.e., extensive data on individual United States colleges and universities. A rival organization, *Achieva* (www.achieva.com) does much the same thing at about the same costs. In addition they assist students in preparing for tests, applications, strategies, résumés, etc.

LIBRARIES

See Chapter 4, Bibliographies.

STATISTICS

Online: CIS Statistical Universe, Bethesda, MD: Congressional Information Service, 1973 to date, www.lexis-nexis.com. Rate varies.
CD: Statistical Masterfile, Bethesda, MD: Congressional Information Service, Incorporated, mid-1960s to date, quarterly. Rates vary.
Print: American Statistics Index. 1973 to date, monthly. *Statistical Reference Index.* 1980 to date, monthly. *Index to International Statistics.* 1983 to date, monthly. Note: Rates vary, but about $2,000 per year for each.

Online: Statistical Abstract of the United States, Washington, DC: Bureau of the Census, 1995 to date, annual, www.census.gov/statab/www. Free.
CD: 1993 to date, annual. $50.
Print: 1879 to date, annual, 980 pp. $30; paperback, $25.

Statistics are the ultimate labyrinth. It takes a sophisticated modern day Theseus to navigate the labyrinth, more or less meet head on the crafty statistician known by the Greeks as the Minotaur. Skip a few thousand years and the Scottish poet Andrew Lang summed it all up: "One uses statistics as a drunken man uses a lamp post—for support rather than illumination."

Of course, this side of Theseus few understand the statistical labyrinth. They hide their lack of confidence, if not downright distrust, in clever jokes. This seems true among many librarians who prefer humanistic delights rather than pages of columns and figures. The reference librarian's most difficult problem remains one of identifying a source for an answer to the esoteric, specialized statistical query; almost as hard is translating the query into the terminology of the statistical source. Given the numerous sources it is no wonder that in larger libraries the expert in statistics is as important as the subject bibliographer. Normally, this librarian is located in the government documents or the business section.

A statistical reference work is highly specialized. This text indicates only the basic general sources with which the beginner should be familiar. The federal government, followed by state and local governments, provide the greatest number of statistical documents. A number of agencies issue them regularly, and they are an important source of forecasting in the private sector.

Statistics Sources (Farmington Hills, MI: Gale Group, 1962 to date, annual) in the 2000 edition, it lists more than 3,000 sources of statistics under 20,000 subject headings. To be sure, not all of these are issued by the government, but the major American government sources are listed, as are sources for 200 nations of the world.

How reliable are the statistical data? If they come from standard federal and major state agencies, they are likely to be quite reliable, although there are always exceptions. Most errors are caught, but international data are likely to be more error-prone because, among other things, there are legal constraints imposed on the collection agencies. The parent organizations of the agencies that collect and disseminate international statistics heavily influence the accuracy and validity of the data presented for consumption. They may be less than ideal because of political constraints or because the governments simply do not have the funds for extensive statistical data.

It is one thing to gather statistics, quite another to understand and interpret them. Is there anyone who has not heard the saying, "Statistics lie"? Statistics are as much an art as a science. Numbers mean little unless they are interpreted properly. And that is precisely what makes many of the statistical works published by the government so baffling. Rarely is proper guidance given to help interpret what they mean.

Indexes

Anyone who feels uncomfortable with statistics will bless the three indexes published by the Congressional Information Service which is part of the behemoth LEXIS-NEXIS publishing group. Almost any question dealing with statistical data can be answered using this service. If the answer is not found, there usually is an indication of where to turn next. Thanks to the excellent abstracts one rarely has to go to the complete document, at least for most ready-reference queries.

The print indexes, as well as the electronic cousins, follow a basic pattern: (1) Issued monthly, they have a quarterly index and are cumulated, with an index, annually. When searching the print volumes one should begin with the annual index to get a sense of subject headings and general arrangement. (2) The index, a separate section or volume, refers the user to the document in the main work. Material is indexed by subject, title, issuing agency, primary individuals involved with the document, and so forth. Each document or series is abstracted, and there is complete information about the issuing agency and the necessary background about the statistics. The entries in the main section are arranged by accession number. Almost all the documents are available, as with ERIC and similar services, in microfiche. The abstract is keyed to the proper microfiche item. In addition there is a Superintendent of Documents classification number to help locate the hard copy. Given this type of detailed support system, the librarian has a marvelous set of tools for answering almost any statistical question.

The indexes, in print or online, are extremely easy to use, particularly as they have such detailed abstracts. There is no problem in locating the documents themselves. Actually, the abstracts are often sufficient to answer many research questions other than the most involved.

The three cover distinct areas. The *American Statistics Index* indexes and abstracts almost every statistical source—some 500—issued by the federal government. This includes the contents of over 800 periodicals. It provides entry to close to 10,000 different reports, studies, articles, and the like. Its twin, *Statistical Reference Index,* indexes and abstracts state documents. It does *not* include federal materials. It *does* include many nongovernmental statistics as well. These range from those issued by private concerns and businesses to nonprofit organizations and associations. The *Index to International Statistics* includes major governmental statistics from around the world. There is particular emphasis on western European countries, including the European Community. It is an excellent source of United Nations statistical data. As in the other indexes, periodicals are analyzed (in this case about 100). Almost all the publications are in English, albeit there are some in Spanish and other languages when there is no English equivalent.[33]

Searching the various indexes is simple enough. Look for the subject or name. Note the accession number(s) for relevant documents. Turn to said number(s) in the front part of the volume. Here one will find an abstract of the document's contents.

The online version, *Statistical Universe,* as the CD-ROM, *Masterfile,* have the advantage of allowing a single search. The searches may be performed in various ways, although the basic title, agency or subject approach is the more direct. Online has the tremendous advantage of allowing the user to search three services at once. Then, too, there is

[33]For a detailed explanation of what is available in print and online see the home page for the CIS Statistical Universe via (:www.lexis-nexis.com/cispubs).

an invaluable "category" index that analyzes the data in terms of age, income, states, type of legislation, and so forth. All and all, the online version is superior to the printed format and much easier for the layperson to master.

Yearbook

Statistical Abstract of the United States is the basic source of American statistical data in any library. Filled with 1500 tables and charts, the work serves to summarize social and economic trends. The guide is divided into 34 major sections—from education and population to public lands—with a detailed 40- to 50-page index that takes the reader from abortion to zoology. Note, too, the concluding section which covers basic statistics of the states. Despite the good index, the over 500,000 statistics are not always easy to understand. There is, for example, need for clearer explanations of the figures. Reference librarians should study each edition with care.[34]As a profile of America, the *Statistical Abstract* attracts much journalistic attention. Each annual volume brings a group of stories in magazines and newspapers about the many strange facts and statistical data. A typical, although better written than most, example is a story by an English author. The *Abstract* reports "in one year nearly 400,000 Americans suffered injuries involving beds, mattresses, or pillows...My point in raising this is not to suggest that we are somehow more inept than the rest of the world when it comes to lying down for the night (though certainly there are thousands of us who could do with some additional practice), but rather to observe that there is scarcely a statistic in this vast nation that doesn't give one pause."[35]

There are numerous other statistical reference works with equally alarming reports for the general public. A good example, and one worthy of a place in most reference collections: *Statistical Handbook on the American Family* (Phoenix, AZ: Oryx Press, 1999, $62.50).

Two valuable titles cover American historical statistics. They are *Historical Statistics of States of the United States* (Westport, CT: Greenwood Press, 1994, 478 pp.) and *Historical Statistics of the United States* (Washington: Government Printing Office, 1976, CD-ROM, 1997. $195). The first has 18

---

[34]The Statistical Abstract as the majority of government reference works and documents are in the public domain, i.e., is not copyrighted. As a result publishers often pick it up, add a few features and reissue—usually at a higher price. Example: *The Statistical Abstract of the United States, Library Edition* (Lanham, MD: Bernan, 1998, $50). This is identical to, but twice as much as the government paperback, but has two advantages: "the type is a full 25% bigger," according to the publisher and "our large format...has a sturdy...binding."

[35]Bill Bryson, "You See, Doctor, My Pillow Hit Me," *The New York Times*, May 20, 1999, p. 26.

data items, for each decade from 1790 to 1990, for each of the then existing states. Territories are considered as well. The latter considers historical data from 1790 to 1970, but this time for the nation as a whole. Here one finds comparative figures for wages, production, agriculture, and the like. Note: The 1997 CD-ROM has no additional data after the printed volumes, i.e., 1970.

The majority of Western nations follow the pattern established by the American government in issuing equivalents of the *Statistical Abstract* and specialized statistical information. For example, England has *Annual Abstracts of Statistics* (London: Her Majesty's Stationery Office, 1854 to date). On an international level the best-known equivalent is the United Nations *Statistical Yearbook* (New York: The United Nations Publications, 1949 to date, annual) which covers basic data from over 150 areas of the world. The information is broken down under broad subject headings.

Statistical information is hardly limited to these sources. Other valuable data will be found in the basic indexes such as *Public Affairs Information Service Bulletin, ABI/INFORM, Business Periodicals Index,* and any service which regularly reports on the activities of government and business such as Predicasts. *Facts on File* contains statistics, and as explained previously, is a good launching pad to find more about a particular matter. A related work, available online as well as in print is *A Matter of Fact* (Ann Arbor, MI: Pierian Press, 1984 to date, annual). This draws facts and statistical data from approximately 300 newspapers and periodicals, and various government documents. OCLC offers it online under the name of Fact Search.

Most professions have their own handbooks for statistical amateurs. In the library world, for example, the best guide is *Descriptive Statistical Techniques for Librarians* (2nd ed. Chicago: American Library Association, 1997. 497 pp. $55). Edited by Arthur Hafner, this is an easy to understand text on how to use statistics in evaluating and presenting library services. Most of the information is applicable to all types of statistical data.

On the Web[36]

There are not that many statistical sites on the Web. As in numerous other reference works, statistics are too valuable to publishers to make them free on the Web. Fortunately, the government has another philosophy. Aside from the free *Statistical Abstract,* there is the valuable government

[36]Paula Bernstein, *Finding Statistics Online.* (Medford, NJ: Information Today, 1998.) This is a how-to manual of statistical resources which can be used freely by laypersons and librarians via the Internet. There are numerous website addresses as well as an overview of those who compile statistical data. In a latter section the author takes the reader through the various steps of gathering statistics with numerous case studies.

database *FedStats* (www.fedstats.gov). Drawing upon the statistics of more than 70 United States government agencies, this site is the single best place to turn for quick, accurate statistical data generated by the government. Searching is by key words, subjects and agencies. For example, "middle class income" results in eight citations with annotations and, if needed, access to the full document's text. By beginning with environmental "spills" and the Environmental Protection Agency the search is limited to a specific group of statistics which show, among other things, the 10 largest hazardous substance spills. Easy to use for both beginner and statistician.

See, too: *U.S. Census Bureau* (www.census.gov). The ultimate statistical profile of the nation is found in the easy-to-follow subject categories, nicely indexed from A to Z. While primarily for experts (the heart of the statistics are found in Statistical Abstract), this can be useful for anyone seeking current data. It is updated regularly and with a mass of material, including access to the census. Topics are well defined and normally cover the query at hand. Note, too, there are links to other relevant websites.

The European Community appears to follow the same pattern set by the United States government—many valuable websites are free. In statistics this means turning to the *Organization for Economic Cooperation and Development* (www.oecd.org). Here are comparative statistics from not only European community countries, but from at least a dozen or more Western nations. A first place to turn for relatively easy to follow data on every statistical query dealing with countries outside of the United States—although the latter is included in many of the configurations.

A broader source of business and economic news will be found at the U.S. Department of Commerce site: *Stat-USA Internet* (www.stat-usa.gov). This is a "one stop Internet browsing for business, trade and economic information." It is in two major parts: "State of the Nation" which offers access to economic and financial releases such as Federal Housing Finance Board, State and Government Bond Rates, etc. The second part "Globus and NTDB (National Trade Data Bank) has information on current and historical trade related releases in international markets. The system is updated hour on the hour.

The Dismal Scientist (www.dismal.com) is an excellent source of current information on business statistics and related areas. The free service boasts all the latest statistical data from both government and private agencies. Often the data are fully explained in easy to follow terms. In terms of strictly business use the figures give current economic activity indicators from employment to inflation. While not for investment, it certainly can be used by sophisticated stock market types. Note, too, that there are numerous statistics and information of concern to demographers, social scientists and almost anyone working with statistics. There are countless other advantages to turning to this site first, including non-partisan reports on major economic trends and developments. Note, too, the excellent links to similar sites. Although most know, the website name comes from the old saw: "The dismal science: economics" or, if you will, use "social science," "political science" etc.

SUGGESTED READING

Arant, Wendi and Brian Carpenter, "Where is the Line," *Reference & User Services Quarterly*, Spring, 1999, pp. 235–240. Where does the librarian "draw the line" in giving out legal data, particularly to people who are trying to act as their own lawyer? The authors offer numerous guides which will help in solving this problem, as well as give some practical advice on how to meet the challenge of the legal advice question.

Baker, Lynda M. et al., "The Provision of Consumer Health Information..." *Public Libraries*, July/August, 1998, pp. 250–255. A report on what Michigan public libraries do about furnishing medical information to users. Includes a survey and literature review. Generally, most librarians approve of such service, although with some reservations about how it is done.

Barnes, Julian, "Most Modernism: Adventures in Etiquette," *The New Yorker*, April 12, 1999, pp. 102–109. The English novelist explains the difference between American and British etiquette as outlined in the latest edition of Emily Post. He discovers the book requires much attention to authority and endangers spontaneity, e.g., Americans "need to loosen up a little."

Bell, Rudolph, *How to Do It: Guides to Good Living for Renaissance Italians*. Chicago: University of Chicago Press, 1999. A survey of much-used manuals and guides in Renaissance Italy, this is both informative and amusing. Even the illiterate enjoyed the "wisdom" of the guides as they often were read by the one literate member of the community to all its citizens. Advice runs from childcare to the art of growing older. As one reviewer put it, "What's the Italian for 'plus ca change...'" See, too, a related title: Mark Caldwell, *A Short History of Rudeness*, New York: Picador, 1999. This concentrates on "manners, morals, and misbehavior in modern America."

Di Su, "Quick Access: Find Statistical Data on the Internet," *Information Outlook*, May, 1999, pp. 35+. A research librarian offers a basic guide to reliable, easy-to-follow statistical sites on the Internet. Most of them are free. Di Su's analysis and explanation of the sites is such that the article is a fine beginning point for anyone and a refresher for those who have been working with statistics.

Freudenheim, Milt, "Medical Web Sites Transforming Visits to Doctors," *The New York Times*, May 20, 2000, pp. 1 & 14. Both doctors and laypersons are finding distinct advantages in medical websites. The sites significantly improve medical care for patients who live far from leading medical centers. Individuals, too, can find information on minor aches and pains, thus saving at least some visits to the doctor. The article lists sites primarily used by doctors.

Goldberg, Matt, "To Crib or Not to Crib?" *Yahoo!*, February 2000, p. 162. A brief, informative note on another variety of the online term paper—paid for class notes on the Web.

Janes, Joseph and Charles McClure, "The Web as a Reference Tool," *Public Libraries*, January/February, 1999, p. 30. How well are ready-reference queries answered by using the Internet? It depends. If the librarians are looking up the questions it may be faster to use print, although the level of accuracy, etc. is much the same. And the Web offers many more possibilities than found in print. What is totally apparent—the libraries need faster Internet access and reference librarians need additional training.

Murdock, Theresa, "Revising Ready Reference Sites," *Reference & User Services Quarterly*, Winter 2002, pp. 155–163. The Net is the ubiquitous ready reference site. The abundance of possibilities calls for careful selection when creating "a more user centered ready reference Web site." Using the University of Washington experience, the author offers a methodology, based on usage, for constructing and/or revising a library ready reference Web site.

Pagell, Ruth, "Information," *Database*, February/March, 1999, pp. 34+. A clear explanation of how government statistics are repackaged and offered to the public (i.e., libraries). Specific sources are given and evaluated, including basic online sites. Particularly important: the suggestions on how to evaluate statistical data as well as a profile of the major repackager of said data.

Poovey, Mary, *A History of The Modern Fact*. Chicago: University of Chicago Press, 1998. Subtitled, "problems of knowledge in the sciences of wealth and society," this is considerably more than a glance at ready reference sources. The author is deeply concerned on why one kind of representation (i.e., facts and numbers) has come to seem to be immune from interpretation. A fascinating study which illustrates the fallacy that most people simply want a fact. They probably need considerably more than librarians are used to giving.

White, Marilyn, "Historical Statistics of the United States..." *Reference Services Review*, Spring, 1998, pp. 15. Covers the historical development of the work over three editions and two supplements. The problems, primarily financial, have kept this valuable work from being updated more frequently. The author shows, too, the issues involved in the compilation.

Zuger, Abigail, "Takes Some Strychnine and Call Me in the Morning," *The New York Times*, April 20, 1999, pp. F1, F9. On the 100th anniversary of the *Merck Manual*, a working doctor explains how it developed over the years and why it is of such value today to both doctors and laypersons. Optimists may take heart in the fact medicine has made more than a few advances since the first edition, e.g., note the suggested cure in the title of this article. And it is not a joke.

CHAPTER NINE
BIOGRAPHICAL SOURCES

What does the Sunday newspaper supplement *Parade* have in common with *Who's Who in America, The Dictionary of National Biography,* and *Stipple, Wink & Gusset: Men and Women Who Gave Their Names to History?* The answer—all tell the reader what the "folks" have done and are doing. They are sources of gossip, fact, and pictures of everyday life. They are gems of biographical information.

In a library, bookstore, and home the biographical sketch or book is extremely popular. The ephemeral *Parade* explains the status of the Spice Girls. *Who's Who in America* lists the activities of eminent men and women as well as the address where Madonna may be contacted. And the *Dictionary of National Biography,* whose major requirement for entry is that the person be dead, will afford hours of leisurely reading about such people as Guy Burgess, Soviet spy; multimurderer John Christie; as well as Queen Victoria, and painter Gwen John.

In reference work the primary use of biography is: (1) To locate people who are famous in a given occupation, career, or profession. (2) To locate supporting material about an individual for any number of reasons from a paper on the fall of Rome to a study of the modern automobile's brake system; and, not the least (3) to locate a possible name for the baby.[1]

---

[1] The are scores of works from *The Perfect Name of the Perfect Baby* to *What Shall We Call the Baby?* At a somewhat less mundane level, but for the same purpose, Oxford University Press covers the field with two titles: *A Dictionary of First Names* (1996) contains more than 7,000 names from the whole of Europe and North America with supplements on the Arab world and the Indian subcontinent. The 480 pages look at the rise and fall in popularity of certain first names. At another level of query, *A Dictionary of Surnames* (1997) has over 70,000 entries

SEARCHING BIOGRAPHICAL SOURCES

In determining which biographical sources to search, the librarian will want to know how much of the history of an individual life does the user require and what types of data are required. The data type of question is by far the most common in the ready-reference situation. Typical queries: "What is the address and phone number of X?" "How does one spell Y's name?" "What is the age of R?" "When did Beethoven die?" Answers will be found in the familiar who's who directory-biographical dictionary sources. Approach varies with each title, but all are consistent in listing names alphabetically and, at a minimum, in giving the profession and position (with or without claim-to-fame attributes) of the individual. At a maximum, these sources will give full background on the entry from birth and death dates to publications, names of children, and so on. The information is usually, although not necessarily, in outline form. It is rarely discursive or critical.

The second major type of biographical question comes from the person who wants partial or relatively complete information on an individual. The questioner may be writing a paper, preparing a speech, or seeking critical background material. Typical queries: "How can I write a paper on Herman Melville?" "What do you have on [X], a prominent American scientist?" "Is there a book about George Washington and the cherry tree?" Answers will be found in biographical reference sources which emphasize essays (i.e., entries of 300 words to several pages in length).

How many biographical reference works would one find in the average medium to large public or academic library? There will be a dozen or so digital indexes, and 20 to 500 print sources, depending on need. Actually, today's library requires fewer print works. Most print biography reference works have migrated to electronic formats. Online they are easier to search as well as to keep current.

Discussion here is limited to reference titles. If the librarian moves from the reference section to the reading area, there will be thousands of individual biographies and autobiographies. The person who wants biographical information will use the general collection as well as the reference section.

------

with meanings, origins, and variants given for every name. While there are numerous baby name books to be found in any library, a fast overview on the Net is at the *Michigan Electronic Library* (http://mel.lib.mi.us). Here one finds about a dozen links to "names" from *Baby Names* and *Baby Names Online* (for the person who never gets enough of a good thing) to *Baby Names in Michigan*. A wider use of the page is suggested by the inclusion of such links as: *Nom de Guerre Pseudonyms* used by well-known people to an all-time favorite—*The Pet Name Pages*.

EVALUATION

The quest for information about the living and the dead has made numerous publishers, compilers, and biographers (not to mention living celebrities penning their autobiographies) richer. Whether the massive numbers of biographies issued each year has made the reader or the librarian richer is another question.

How does the librarian know if a biographical reference printed source or electronic database is legitimate, authoritative and based on accurate material? A rule of thumb will do in most cases: The title should be listed in basic bibliographies such as *Guide to Reference Books* and Walford, *American Reference Books Annual,* or the current reviewing services. Note: A useful compilation of reviews taken from the ARBA from 1986–1997 is the *ARBA Guide to Biographical Sources* (Englewood, CO: Libraries Unlimited, 1998, 400 pp.).

The publisher's name is another indication of authority. Four publishers are responsible for a large number of available biography reference titles. They are the Gale Group, the H. W. Wilson Company, St. Martin's Press, and Reed/Reference publishing. If the librarian does not recognize the publisher, and particularly if it is not one of the major four, then the warning flag should be out to do further checking. (Trade publishers, from Random House to Harper & Row, publish popular biographical sources, but few reference titles.)

Beware

Dealing as much with individual ego and pride as with accomplishment and fact, early biographical reference sources were great sources of income for what some call the "tin cup" brigades. These were people who literally moved into a community, established a biographical book of that community, and then charged individuals for an entry. These "mug books" are a far cry from the legitimate works. Yet, ironically enough, historians are grateful for the information they provide of Americans, particularly in the nineteenth and the early twentieth century.

Even today vanity biographical schemes abound. Take, for example, a biographical publisher in North Carolina. The firm, in early 1998, wrote a Brighton, England resident informing him he could become an entry in the "distinguished biography of the Millennium Hall of Fame book." The Hall "showcases the lives of men and women who have made the century great." The invaluable reference title, in deluxe leather, is $375. For another $750 the individual will receive a plaque and a statue. In reporting this, the "famous" person noted "I've been racking my brains to recall my many contributions to humankind. It's true I had a letter published in your newspaper column not long ago..."[2] In this type of biographical source, anyone is fair game who will pay for the "honor."

Bells and red lights should flash when the publisher insists the "famous" person buy the book(s) before an entry is possible. This is a sure signal of a rip-off. Of course, even the most legitimate source will often suggest that the individual buy the book; but there is a great difference between "suggest" and "insist." For example, the Reed *Who's Who in America* will include a name without requiring that the individual purchase anything. At the same time a series of letters will urge the purchase of one of "several distinctive items especially for you." These represent the "lasting symbol of your achievements," and range from a $65 paperweight to a $150 mantel clock. As silly as it seems, it is lucrative for the company. All of this is perfectly legitimate. The purchase of the book or wall plaque has nothing to do with acceptance or rejection in *Who's Who in America*.

Other Evaluative Points

Beyond the publisher how does the librarian know whether a biographical source is reliable? The key questions are as valid for print sources as for electronic databases. There are a number of tests.

Selection. Why is a name selected (or rejected) for the various biographical reference aids? The process is relatively easy to describe. The compiler includes all the names that qualify for the scope of the work, as in *American Men and Women of Science* or *World Authors*. In both cases, the widest net is cast to include figures and authors likely to be of interest. There are limitations, but they are so broad as to cause little difficulty for the compiler.

A publisher may apply automatic standards of selection or rejection in a biographical source. Briefly, (1) the person must be living or dead; (2) The individual must be a citizen of a given country, region, or city; (3) the person must be employed in a specific profession or type of work. One or more of these measurements may be employed in any given reference work.

Editors of reputable works establish some other objective guidelines for inclusion. *Who's Who in America* features many people "arbitrarily on account of official position." This means that a member of Congress, a governor, an admiral, a general, or a Nobel Prize winner, is automatically included; and people in numerous other categories as well are assured of a place in the volume because of the positions they hold. The *International Who's Who* is certain to give data on members of all reigning royal

[2]"Letters," *The Times* (of London), February 6, 1998, p. 21.

families. The *Dictionary of American Biography* takes a more restrictive approach: One must first be dead to be included; after that requirement is met, the editor begins making selections.

There are levels of exclusiveness. It is more difficult to get into *Who's Who in America* than *Who's Who in American Art.* For the former listing, it is a matter of "Don't call us, we'll call you," and inclusion depends on some public achievement. Being listed in other reference sources may depend only on membership in a group or profession. It is difficult to stay out of such titles as *Who's Who in the United Nations* if one happens to work there, or *Who's Who in Golf* should one be a professional or a well-known amateur. A listing in a given biographical title depends on whether one responds to the publisher's request to fill out an entry form. Failure to answer may mean failure to be included unless one is such a famous UN employee or golfer that the editor digs up the information without the help of the to be listed person.

Then, too, there are some automatic exclusions. In the case of subject biographical reference works, the exclusion is usually evident in the title: One does not look for poets in *Who's Who in American Art* or *American Men and Women of Science.* Although the *Dictionary of National Biography* now includes a few outstanding criminals, some biographical sources restrict selections of everyone from popular entertainers to sports figures. Others counter that any person of importance, acceptable, respectable or not, should be included. In the past, admission to a biographical reference book was seen as a sign of moral approval, and this is still true for a few works today. A more mature editorial policy would include everyone the broad public wants to know about—a policy now followed by *The New York Times Biographical Services* as well as *Current Biography.*

A typical reaction to selection practices in a who's who directory is captured by a critic: "It is hard not to feel in some eerie way that these [in the biographical source] are the Beautiful and the rest of us are the Damned... *Who's Who* is a slightly more jaunty Raft of the Medusa, everyone on it frantically waving their CVs in the direction of the ship of immortality as it sails away over the horizon...We must all await our turn, and I'm afraid to say that, for this particular raft, it is definitely not women and children first."[3]

Audience. The majority of reference works in biography are published for adults, although there are some (particularly concerning books and writers) for younger people. For the adult searcher, works can then be divided by purpose, education level of the user, and so forth.

---

[3] *The Spectator,* February 4, 1995, p. 28. In 2001 the same summary is true, although now more women are chosen than only a few years ago.

Length of Entry. Once a name is selected, a question is: How much space does the figure warrant, five or six lines a page? The purpose and scope of the work may dictate a partial answer. The who's who data calls for a relatively brief outline or collection of facts. The biographical dictionary may be more discursive; the essay type of work will approach the same entry in a way particular to its form. Regardless of approach, the editor still has to make decisions about balance and length.

Authority. Biography began as an accepted form of approbation. *Ecclesiasticus* (44:1) has the famous line, "Let us now praise famous men"; and this was the purpose of biography until well into the seventeenth century. After a period of relative candor, including Boswell's famous *Life of Johnson* and Johnson's own *Lives of the Poets,* the form returned to uniform panegyric in Victorian nineteenth century. With the Freudian influence in the twentieth century, unabashed praise once more gave way to reality. The fashion today is for truth in biography, at least of historical figures. Living people who are more in the publicity spotlight than in the realm of fact often will hire a professional writer to doctor their biography—particularly if it is an essay, or a book. Still, it hardly takes a trained librarian to determine glitter from fact.

Lack of total veracity on the part of those listed, coupled with less than perfect copy editing sometimes results in bizarre entries. Shirley Povich, one of the country's best male sports columnists, said the strangest acknowledgment he received was being listed in *Who's Who in American Women* in 1958. "The editors had lifted a paragraph on him from *Who's Who in America,* although it plainly said he was married to Ethyl. The next year, he recalled, they dropped me, like they used to do in the New York Social Register if you had married a stripper—the snobs."[4]

Sources of Information. Today the question about authority must begin with another question: Who wrote the biographical entry—an editor, the subject, an authority in the field, a secretary?

Some think the biographical directory approach is critically flawed in that the subject supplies the material. He or she is asked to fill out the publishers' standard form and return it to the publisher. Questions range from age and education to accomplishments and address. Accuracy or the entry, then, depends almost entirely on the thoroughness, the honesty of the individual who filled out the form. *Who's Who* (for example) is not so much a biographical reference work as an autobiographi-

[4] *The New York Times,* June 7, 1998, p. 35. Note: the name "Shirley" for a boy was not uncommon in Maine where Mr. Povich was born in 1906.

cal one—a crucial distinction. This may not automatically lead to the telling of outright untruths, but it does promote the suppression of facts embarrassing to the author.

In preparing almost any material except statistical information, the person who penned the entry will have had either conscious or subconscious biases. Even in a straightforward presentation of data, if the biographical subject supplied the information (the usual case with most current biographies), there may be slight understatements or exaggerations concerning age (men more often than women lie about this), education, or experience. Biographical sources relying almost entirely on individual honesty cannot be completely trusted. This leads to the next query: Have sources of information other than the subjects' own questionnaires been cited? The preface should make these two points clear.

It is useful to know whether the biography was prepared completely by the publisher's editorial staff, whether it was simply slightly edited by that same staff from the form received from the subject, and whether it includes sketches written by outside experts. The last is the usual procedure for essay-length biographies.

When the biographical reference work is questionable, it should be verified in one or more other biography titles. If a serious conflict remains that cannot be resolved, what should be done? The only solution is to attempt to trace the information through primary source material, such as newspapers, contemporary biographies, or articles about the individual, or through his or her family or friends. This undertaking involves historical research. An excellent example can be found in the recurrent arguments concerning the details of Shakespeare's life and times or the famous attempt to straighten out the facts in the life of Sir Thomas Malory, author of the stories of King Arthur and his knights.

Frequency. Most biographical reference sources are on a regular publishing schedule. Some are issued each year, or even every month, while others are regularly updated every three or four years. With celebrities coming and going rapidly, it is obviously important to know the range of time covered by the parent work and its supplements. Many (although not all) biographical reference books are less than satisfactory because of no regular updated procedure. This problem is solved, if only in part, by electronic databases.

Other Points. Are there photographs? Are there bibliographies containing material both by and about the subject? Is the work adequately indexed or furnished with sufficient cross-references? (This is important when seeking individuals connected with a major figure who may be mentioned only as part of a larger biographical sketch.) Is the work arranged logically? The alphabetical approach is usual, although some works may be arranged chronically by events, birth dates, historical periods, or areas of subject interest. If in digital format, the navigational aids should be checked for much the same points.

Actually, in practice, few of these evaluative tests are employed. If a person is well known, the problem is not so much one of a source but of screening out the many sources for pertinent details. If the individual is obscure, usually any source is welcome.

On the Web

There are two potential major drawbacks to for free Web biographical sources: (1) The first, and one stressed over and over again in this text, is the lack of authority of many sites. Just who says, for example, President Kennedy was killed by the Mafia, or by the FBI, or by the Communists, or by (you name it, and/or the person). Gossip about current figures should not be taken as fact, nor should conjecture about historical leaders be based on a website's sponsor who may have had no more than a course or two in history. Again, where the key identifiers such as "edu," "org," or "gov" appear in the address there is a good indication it is reliable. If it is an individual or commercial, further investigation should be made of the site—at least if the information is for more than passing entertainment. (2) The Web will not always give answers immediately to biographical questions. Often a digital search is a much more tedious, longer route than consulting a standard reference source.

The Web works best for lesser known individuals such as Ernest Shepard (illustrator of A. A. Milne's Winnie the Pooh) In fact, the Web often can turn up information not found elsewhere. The system tends to overload, though, for well-known people. Look up any American president, or well-known actor, composer or artist and you will be swamped with excellent to indifferent material that may take hours to go through. A regular reference source filters out the extraneous, thus saving the reader much time.

The *Michigan Electronic Library* offers a good cross section of the thousands of free biographical sources available on the Net. Turn to (http:mel.lib.mi.us) where the page "biography" begins with *4,000 Years of Women in Science* and ends some 30 sites later with a *TV Guide Motion Picture Database* which includes biographies of actors, directors, producers, and other filmmakers. These vary wildly in terms of length of entries and timeliness. Again, the better to best sites tend to charge for the information.

INDEXES TO BIOGRAPHY

Online: Biography Master Index. Farmington Hills, MI: Gale Group, 1991 to date, annual, www.galegroup.com). DIALOG file 287, $30 per hour.
   CD: Biography and Genealogy Master Index. 1993 to date, annual. $1,250. Annual update, $565.
   Print: 1980, 8 vols., out of print; 1981–1985 cumulation, 5 vols. 1986-1990 cumulation, 3 vols. $810; 1991–1995 cumulation, 3 vols. $900. Annual supplements, 1996 to date. $348 each.
   Print: Abridged Biography and Genealogy Master Index. 1995, 3 vols. $432.
   Print: Almanac of Famous People, 6th ed. 1994, 2 vols. $115.

Online: Biography Index. New York: H. W. Wilson Company, 1994 to date, semiweekly, www.hwwilson.com). $25 to $40 per hour. Also available on OCLC.
   CD: 1984 to date, quarterly. $1,095.
   Print: 1947 to date, quarterly with annual cumulations. $135.

Online: World Biographical Index. New York: K. G. Saur North America. 1998 to date, www.saur-wb1.de). Price varies.

   There are two types of indexes to biography. The first, represented by *Biography and Genealogy Master Index,* is a key to over 11 million entries with about 450,000 added each year. As entries are duplicated, the actual number of people covered is about 4 million found in more than 900 biographical dictionaries and directories such as *Who's Who in America.* The purpose is to reduce tedious searching of basic, generally current guides.

   The second type of index, represented by *Biography Index* includes citations to biographies appearing in periodicals and selected books. The purpose is to offer a key to biographical information about persons living and dead from a wide variety of periodical sources.

   The first type would be employed for ready reference when the data type of information is required. The second would more likely be used to seek detailed information for a paper, research project, speech, or other presentation. For example, a user who wishes to find the address of Mary Doe would turn to the *Biography and Genealogy Master Index* for sources of short data entries in the various biographical dictionaries indexed. The user who wishes to write a paper on the achievements of Doe would need a fuller entry and would turn to biographical information in periodicals as indicated in *Biography Index.*

   In an opening search, where not much is known about an individual, the *Master Index* is preferred. If the person is well known to the searcher and the essential facts are in hand, one would go first to *Biography Index.* The two basic reference works may be used separately or together, but they are the first steps in any biographical search.

The publisher of *Biography and Genealogy Master Index* issues a new volume each year, and cumulates the annual volumes every five years. (The CD-ROM and online are updated once a year.) The work is arranged in a single alphabet by the last name of the individual. After the name are the birth and death dates, and then a key to one or more sources in which there is a short entry or essay about the individual. Famous people may have up to a dozen or more citations, but for the most part the citations usually number no more than two to three.

Among the 900 biographical works indexed are both data type *(Who's Who variety)* and essay type *(Dictionary of National Biography)*. In the early years the focus was almost entirely on the data variety, but this changed as the publisher indexed more and more biographical sources. Most of the standard works published by the five largest biographical reference publishers are indexed in the *Master Index*.

As useful as all of this may be for the librarian, the index is far from perfect. The publisher simply prints names as found in the sources. If, for example, Joe Doaks cites his name in this form in *Who's Who in America*, but prefers Joe Vincent Doaks in *Who's Who in American Rat Catchers* and Joseph V. P. Doaks in *American Businesspersons*, his name will be alphabetically arranged in three different ways. Of course, it could be three different Doaks, but the date of birth indicates that it is probably the same person. Just to make things confusing, the date of birth for the same person may vary, depending on which sources were indexed. Also, there may be a simple listing of the same name, albeit with reference to four or five different sources. With all of those possible misunderstandings, a poem shows how this misunderstanding may arise: "Dewey took Manila/and soon after invented the decimal system/that keeps libraries from collapsing even unto this day. A lot of mothers immediately started naming their male offspring "Dewey," which made him queasy...In his dreams he saw library books with milky numbers/on their spine floating in Manila Bay."[5]

There are several versions of the print *Master Index*.

1. *Abridged Biography and Genealogy Master Index.* This includes the basic set, plus the supplementary volumes, cut from 11 million to about 2.2 million entries. Some 226 current and much-used basic sources are analyzed. According to the publisher, the selection of biographical source material is based upon a nationwide survey of holdings of small- and medium-sized libraries, for example, only standard biographical sources are indexed. Updates are planned every five years.

---

[5]John Ashbery, "Memories of Imperialism, *The Times Literary Supplement*, April 30, 1999, p. 29. Ashbery, to be sure, knows the differences in his Deweys, but used the two names in the service of poetic license.

2. *Almanac of Famous People.* In an effort to bring the set within the financial means of libraries. This work has data on about 30,000 people.

How long Gale will keep these works in print format is not known, but chances are the print will give way entirely to the single database online, i.e., *Biography Master Index.* At any rate, the online version is much faster and easier to use.

There are several arguments for an electronic database search: (1) A search may be done by birth or death year. This will bring up all people who died or were born within the given time frame. (2) A search may be by the source year, that is, a librarian may ask for a listing of all the biographical dictionaries published in a specific year. (3) The search may be limited to entries with a portrait. (4) And possibly most important, a search may be made by profession or occupation, a luxury not afforded by the Gale print volumes.

At times, even the *Biography and Genealogy Master Index* fails—the name cannot be found. There may be many reasons to explain the omission. One may not be so obvious; that is, the name may be of a literary character, and such names are not found in standard biographical guides of real people. (An exception, although limited to major characters based on real people, are listings in *Biography Index*). If one suspects this to be the situation, numerous literary guides, as well as general encyclopedias, carry entries for everyone from Simon Legree to Holden Caulfield. Two examples: *Dictionary of American Literary Characters* (New York: Facts on File, 1990) has brief notes on over 11,000 personalities from American novels published between 1789 and 1980. *Characters in 20ᵗʰ Century Literature* (Gale Group, 1990) is another source that considers characters from 250 novels. *Masterplots,* and its numerous spin-offs, is a third good place to seek literary character.

Saur's *World Biographical Index* includes roughly 3 million biographical articles on about 2.5 million individuals from North and South America as well as Europe. The biographies are short. It has the advantage of having material on the subject available online without any further searching. Also it includes archives of early biographical sources from the United States to England and most of Europe. This is useful when looking for lesser known people who make their mark, say, in the 1750s. But it covers less than one-fourth of the people found in the Gale work.

Biographies in Periodicals

Where information from periodical articles is required for more details than found in standard directory type sources indexes in the *Biography Master Index* is the first choice. *Biography Index* has more than 3,000 different magazines and newspapers which are analyzed for biographical material, as well as 1,800 books, including individual biographies. This gives the user an extremely wide range of sources, which move from the popular to the esoteric. The end result is rarely disappointing. When searched over several years, inevitably something turns up, and often that "something" may be quite detailed. Arrangement in print is by name of the person. An added bonus is that birth and death dates, nationality, profession and, of course, the citation to the periodical are given.

Another useful feature is the index by profession or occupation. Someone looking for material on an architect simply turns here, as would another individual looking for biographical data about dentists or zookeepers. Note: Unlike the *Biography and Genealogy Master Index,* where profession can be searched only in the digital version, *Biography Index* allows the same search in both digital and print. As many libraries are confined to the print edition, this is a major point to consider.

The index makes particular note of individual print biographies and autobiographies, as well as collections. A nice touch is the inclusion of some, but certainly not all, fiction that has a well-known real figure at the center of the novel. The same is true of poetry, drama, and so forth. Obituaries are indexed, including those from *The New York Times.* Also it is a handy index to *The New York Times Biographical Service.*

On the Web

There is no free central index of biographical entries on the Internet. For example, if one is looking for data on John Ridley, a less than famous nineteenth century American artist, one might go to a number of sources. The fastest way is to first consult the for fee index to millions of names in the *Biography and Genealogy Master Index,* which is likely to cite one or more sources about Ridley. On the Net one might put his name in the box of a search engine, just in case he is the subject of a free home page discussion group of whatever. Still, this will not ferret out individual entries in various biographical sources. Unless the individual is a well-known historical figure, or a current celebrity, the search engine road is a tedious one and likely to turn up too much or too little.

UNIVERSAL AND CURRENT BIOGRAPHICAL SOURCES

Universal biographical sources include entries from all parts of the world, or at least those parts selected by the editors. Normally they list both living and dead personalities. The result is a compendium of relatively well-known individuals from all periods, and places.

Biographical Dictionaries

Print: Webster's Biographical Dictionary, Springfield, MA: G. & C. Merriam Company, 1995, 1,170 pp. $27.95.

Print: Chambers Biographical Dictionary, 6th ed., London: Chambers, 1997, 2,008 pp. $55.

Online: Biography. A and E History Channel (www.biography.com). Free.
Print: The Cambridge Biographical Encyclopedia, 2nd ed., Cambridge: Cambridge University Press, 1998, 1,179 pp. $55.

Before the advent of the *Biography and Genealogy Master Index,* the biographical dictionary was a first place to turn to identify, qualify, and generally discover basic facts about an individual. The biographical dictionary today is excellent for a birth or death date, occupation, claim to fame, and so on. By far the best known and most used of the biographical dictionaries, *Webster's* gives brief biographies for about 30,000 people from the beginning of history through the early 1990s. The individual's primary contribution is noted, along with nationality, birth and death dates, and pronunciation of name. The entries are all safely dead. Its primary value is for checking on lesser known persons. The breadth of coverage makes this a first choice, but as with most reference works, it needs help, i.e., for living personalities, for a good number of famous women and for minority names.

The sixth edition of *Chambers Biographical Dictionary* marks its 100th birthday. As a standard biographical guide it is found in most English language libraries from here to Australia. The 17,500 entries, for both living and dead, cover major figures from the beginning of history to the mid 1990s. The alphabetically arranged listing includes the nationality, occupation, year of birth (death), brief career data, bibliographic information and where pertinent, film and discography. Major figures are set off in boxed, longer entries.

The *Cambridge Biographical Encyclopedia* has some 26,000 names. Entries average 250 to 300 words of text for each biography. These cover all nationalities and time periods in alphabetical order by last name. Living people are included. In addition, there is a "ready-reference" section in the back which lists the majority of entries by broad subjects from "political leaders and rulers" to "competitive sports and games."

The website *Biography* is an outgrowth of the A&E television program "Biography." Basically it is the electronic version of the *Cambridge Biographical Encyclopedia.* There is, too, a useful alphabetical listing of names in the news. Material is added weekly to the online work. Also, it is updated by material in *Biography Magazine.* While helpful for standard historical personalities, it is stronger on recent names. There are, too, a list of the month's ten best-selling biographies; "Born on this day"; and a schedule of A&E related topics.[6]

Using the *Cambridge* on the Web is useful if the individual or the library does not have the print edition—which it should. Otherwise it is considerably faster to simply turn to the print volume.

A similar cross-over from television to biography is found at the *CNN Chat* (www.cnn.com/chat). Primarily world leaders from political to sports are highlighted here. The material is taken from the CNN files used in television. They tend to be short and more involved with entertainment than the straight facts. Note: biography is only a small part of *Chat* which covers numerous areas of interest.

Pseudonyms

Print: Pseudonyms and Nicknames Dictionary, 3rd ed. Detroit, MI: Gale Research Company, 1987, 2 vols. $143.

Covering all periods and most of the world, this is a listing of about 55,000 pseudonyms and nicknames from Johnny Appleseed (John Chapman) to Mark Twain (Samuel Clemens). Information includes birth and death dates, nationality, and occupation. When one looks up the pseudonym or nickname, there is a reference to the original name and the primary information. Cited sources are included, and these amount to over 200 basic biographical works. Arranged in a single alphabet, the guide is extremely easy to use. It is updated by two supplements which are issued between editions of the primary work.

DIRECTORY: THE WHO'S WHO FORM

Online: Marquis Who's Who. New Providence, NJ: Reed Reference Publishing, 1992 to date, www.marquiswhoswho.com. LEXIS-NEXIS rates vary. DIALOG file 234, $90 per hour. Also available through other carriers. *CD: The Complete Marquis Who's Who.* New Providence, NJ: Reed Reference Publishing, 1992 to date, quarterly. Price varies. *Print: Who's Who in America.* 1899 to date, annual, 3 vols. $575.

CD: Who's Who, London: A & C Black, 1849 to date, annual, 1897–1999. Price varies. *Print: Who's Who.* Price varies (Distributed in the United States by St Martin's Press, Inc.).

---

[6]Another website *Lives, the Biography Resource* (www.amillionlives.com) is a poor source for standard figures and biographies, but excellent for out-of-the-way figures. Only the dead are listed. Also superior links to both basic and odd biographical sites.

CD: The International Who's Who 2000 CD-ROM. London (US: Florence, KY): Europa Publications Ltd., 2000 to date, annual. $560.
Print: International Who's Who. 1935 to date, annual. $365.

The "who's who" hieratical structure began with a single *Who's Who* in England, spread to a single similar title in America, and then to points east and west.[7] By the end of the Second World War it became apparent to publishers that everyone wants, or appears to want, a part of the fame bestowed when listed in a biographical source. From this developed the geographic series of who's who from *Who's Who in the West* to *Who's Who in California*. Next came the who's who professions explosion with self-explanatory titles such as *Who's Who Among Artists*.

The who's who aids may be classified by scope as international, national, local, professional or business, religious or racial, and so on, and are usually indicated in the title. The who's who directories vary in scope, and often in accuracy and timeliness, but their essential purpose is the same: to present objective, usually non-controversial facts about an individual. The approach and style are monotonous. Most are arranged alphabetically by the name of the person. The paragraph of vital statistics normally concludes with the person's address and phone number.

Information is normally compiled by sending a questionnaire to the candidate, who is then free to provide as much or as little of the requested information as he or she wishes. The better publishers check the returns for flaws or downright lies. Other publishers may be content to rely on the honesty of the individual, who normally has little reason not to tell the truth, although—and this is a large "although"—some candidates for inclusion may construct complete fabrications.

The directories are among the most frequently used of the biographical sources. Common questions they answer: (1) Where does X live, or receive his or her mail? (2) What is X's age and position? (3) What has X written? (4) What honors does X claim? These are just a few of the typical queries. The who's who directory forms list only the living, and, for that matter, only those in some outstanding position. Again, most of the who's who are indexed in the *Biography and Genealogy Master Index.*

---

[7]The English *Who's Who* was an effort at democracy, but not the earliest work of its kind in modern Europe. Almost a century earlier appeared the *Almanach de Gotha*, published in the Saxon city of Gotha annually from 1763 to 1943. The Soviet army occupied the town and called a halt to the work that contained genealogies of the sovereign and chief princely houses of Europe. By 1771, the editor added encyclopedia-type articles on everything from mathematics to how to keep hamsters as pets. In 1998 a revised edition, by another publisher in London, was brought out. It has a much different, broader editorial policy.

America: Who's Who

Who's Who in America has a long history of reliability. It is a source of about 128,000 names of prominent American men and women, as well as a few foreigners with some influence in the United States. As the nation's current population is close to 270 million, how do the editors determine who is, or who is not, to be included? The answer is complex, usually based on the person's outstanding achievement or perceived excellence. The natural question is one of legitimacy. Is the selection of Y based on Y's desire to be included (supported by willingness to buy the volume in question or, in a few cases, literally to pay for a place in the volume), or is it based on the editor's notion of eminence, where no amount of persuasion of cash will ensure selection? All works listed here are indeed legitimate. One's way to fame cannot be bought. This is not to say there is no room for criticism.

No one will entirely agree on all names selected or rejected in, say, *Who's Who in America.* On balance, the selection is adequate, if not brilliant. In the 1990s there appeared to be more a drive to include people who might buy the volumes than necessarily those completely qualified as entrants. Aside from automatic selection (from presidents to heads of large corporations) the inclusion process is not all that clear. Some even believe it is clouded by poor choices.

The data for entrants varies in length but not in style, as each fills out a standard form requesting basic information, including date of birth, education, achievements, and address. The form is used to compose the entry, and a proof of the entry is sent to the individual for double checking.

The set also includes a list of those who died and those who retired since the last edition, and a feature "Thoughts on My Life" is included in some entries. This is blatant commercialism to appeal to egos. Here entrants are asked to reflect on principles and philosophies that have guided them through life. This can be downright foolish, but it is an always-fascinating facet to otherwise straight directory-type information.

Cashing further in on ego, the publisher offers everyone—notable or not—"family information" and/or "enhanced professional information" at a "pre-paid fee of $75 per Enhancement." If selected, this appears in *Who's Who in America* and "any other Marquis publication for which you are selected." The comments are limited to 100 words each. This is of no value other than a Marquis.

Searching the printed volumes is a matter of simply looking up the name(s), which are arranged in alphabetical order. A third printed volume allows searching by geographical area and professional interests. Subject headings in the latter category are too broad, but the solution is to use, where available, the online version. Here, as usual in electronic formats, the searcher may have over 40 different points of entry, from the person's name to his or her address, company, or other affiliation. The geographic possibilities are even more rewarding; for example, the number of prominent Americans who are women living in Chicago or the ratio of successful attorneys in Los Angeles and San Francisco compared to the total number in the guide or those not found in the guide. Another advantage is that new names may be added each quarter.

The online service (with some 800,000 entries) and the CD-ROM includes 15 numerous other related titles originally initiated by Marquis as part of the "who's who" cycle, including *Who Was Who in America*. Many of these individual print titles are found in libraries. The regional titles: *Who's Who in the East*, *Who's Who in the Midwest*, *Who's Who in the South and Southeast*, and *Who's Who in the West*. Topical titles: *Who's Who in the World*, *Who's Who of American Women*, *Who's Who in Finance and Industry*, *Who's Who in American Law*, *Who's Who in Entertainment*, *Who's Who in Advertising*. The databases may be searched collectively or individually.[8]

British Who's Who

The British *Who's Who* is the only one that does not have a qualifier, that is, Who's Who in *Siberia*, Who's Who in *America*, and so forth. Why? The not too subtle point is that there is no need to go beyond *Who's Who*. It must be a select group of British, or it would not be the genuine thing.

Who's Who was first published in Britain on January 15, 1849, fifty years before there were enough prominent Americans to make a volume possible here. During its first forty-seven years, *Who's Who* was a slim book of about 250 pages which listed members of the titled and official classes. In 1897, it became a biographical dictionary. The 2003 edition is over 2,500 pages. Selection is no longer based on nobility but on "personal achievement or prominence." Most entries are British, but the volume does include some notables from other countries. And in the past decade, it has put more and more emphasis on prominent entertainers, professional people and political and industrial leaders among well over 32,000 entries.

The digital *Who's Who* not only allows a search of the most famous British entries for almost a century, but permits numerous search patterns. In addition to name, one may call up professions, colleges attended, books written and so forth. For example, one may type in the school Eton, and below that appears about 1,400 names. Double click and the who's who entry for a given name is on the screen.

[8]Online, via NEXIS, there are two more related databases: *Marquis Who's Who Regional Library*, which included *Who's Who in America*, but only the regional titles in addition. *Marquis Who's Who Topical Library* is limited to subject areas and does not include the *Who's Who in America*.

The first "select" guide, and one often found in British libraries as well as genealogical collections elsewhere, is *Burke's Peerage and Baronetage* (London: 1826 to date, irregular. In U.S.: Chicago: Fitzroy Dearborn, 2 vols. $395). Temporarily discontinued in 1970, it began publishing again in 1998. Here are over 12,000 hereditary titled British families with sometimes lengthy notes on where claim to this or that title began. In addition, thanks to the aid of a computer, there are 100,000 names in an index which is over 200 pages long. Note, too, the fascinating essays on royalty which lead off the first volume. Jane Austin paid the ultimate tribute to the guide in *Persuasion* where Sir Walter Elliot "who for his own amusement" never took up any book but *The Baronetage*. Here he found "occupation for an idle hour, and consolation in a distressed one." The remark is applicable to most of the biographies in this chapter.

International Who's Who

Depending on size and type of audience served, most American public, university, and college libraries will have *Who's Who in America* and possibly *Who's Who*—"possibly" because the better-known figures apt to be objects of inquiry in *Who's Who* are covered in the *International Who's Who,* which opens with a section of names of "reigning royal families," then moves to the alphabetic listing of some 20,000 brief biographies of the outstanding men and women of our time. The range is wide and takes in those who are prominent in international affairs, government, administration, diplomacy, science, medicine, law, finance, business, education, religion, literature, music, art, and entertainment. Note: The first edition on CD-ROM (2000) lacks the sophisticated search abilities of most CD-ROMs. Under the circumstances it is best to save money and purchase the print edition.

Thanks to its world coverage, the guide is a much livelier read than a standard *Who's Who*. Most of the data, as usual, is supplied by the entrants. Human vanity is strong. Lesser known figures may contribute up to 100 lines, where as Lady Thatcher, former Prime Minister, does well with a modest 29.

Almost every country in the world has a similar set of who's who directories, that is, a basic work for the living famous and a set for the famous who have died. Most of these are published by reputable firms listed in the standard bibliographies such as *Guide to Reference Books* and *Guide to Reference Materials*. For example, there is *Canadian Who's Who* (Toronto: University of Toronto Press, 1910 to date, every 3 years). This includes a wide variety of biographical sketches from all walks of life, including businesspeople, authors, performers, and teachers.

By Sex and By Race

Who's Who of American Women (Chicago: Marquis Who's Who, Inc., 1959 to date biennial) is a dictionary of notable living American women. It follows the same general pattern as all the Marquis works. The average edition includes 30,000 women's names. The editor's breakdown of 1,000 sketches indicates that, according to occupation, a woman's chances to earn an entry are best if she is a club, civic, or religious leader (9.6 percent of all biographies).

There are separate multicultural directories. One example is *Who's Who among Black Americans* (Farmington Hills, MI: Gale Group, 1976 to date, about every 2 years). This lists 20,000 people from all fields of endeavor. Entries include the standard type of material, and there are cross-references when needed. The "Occupational Index" lists most, although not all, of the names under 150 categories. There is a "Geographical Index" which needs to be improved.

Unquestionably, biographical dictionaries that focus on occupations and professions are valuable reference aids and, as such, serve a real purpose. Turn from the professional and subject titles to the multicultural and women's listings and the territory becomes foggy. A serious case might be made in opposition to multicultural separate titles as well as those for women. If people in these groups are truly a success they belong first and foremost in the who's who where it all began. At best they might be in geographical who's who or by subject and professional interest. But to divide these books by culture and by sex is at least questionable, and in some ways insulting.

On the Web

There is nothing free on the Net which is close to the *Who's Who* series in terms of limiting entry to the "best" in the field. The discrimination may not be great, but at least there are a number of good websites for "who's who" type of data. Among the best:

Biographical Dictionary. Notable Citizens of Planet Earth (www.tiac.net/ users/parallax). Under the jurisdiction of Eric Tentarelli of Cornell University, this offers short, factual biographical data on some 18,000 "notable people from ancient times to the present day." Searchers are by name, key words and, if needed, by date.

The Obituary Page (http://catless.ncl.ac.uk/obituary). Out of England and put together by a lecturer in computer science at the University of

Newcastle, this is an eccentric listing of famous people who have died. The name, birth and death dates, and a few words about claim to fame are given. It opens with the latest death and moves chronologically to the first (in 1994) when the work began. Entry points vary, but essentially it is a matter of reading down the list.

ESSAY FORM OF BIOGRAPHICAL SOURCES

Online: Current Biography: New York: H. W. Wilson Company, 1940 to date, monthly, www.hwwilson.com. $545; annual renewal, $175 (1983 to date, monthly, $295; annual renewal, $175).
  CD: 1995 to date, annual. $189.
  Print: 1940 to date, monthly except August. $58.

Online: The New York Times Biographical Service. New York: *The New York Times.* 1990 to date, daily. This is part of the newspaper online at (http://nytimes.com).
  Print: 1970 to date, monthly, loose-leaf. $120.

CD: Encyclopedia of World Biography, Farmington Hills, MI: Gale Group, 1999. $975.
  Print: 2nd ed., 1998, 17 vols. $975.

Current Biography is the single most popular essay-length biographical aid in all types of libraries. Issued monthly, it is cumulated, often with revised sketches, into annual volumes with excellent cumulative indexing. Thanks to the format and catchy photographs on the cover, *Current Biography* resembles a magazine which can be read cover to cover.

Annual emphasis is on around 200 international personalities, primarily those in some way influencing the American scene. Articles are long enough to include all vital information about the person, but not so long to disturb the short attention span of many students. They usually are objective. A special staff prepares the sketches that draws information from other biographical sources and from the person covered in the article. Subjects are given the opportunity to check the copy before it is published and, presumably, to approve the photograph which accompanies each sketch. There is an increasing focus on popular culture. It is getting close to a student version of *People Magazine.* Still, the major public figures, from publications to authors and scientists are included.

Source references are cited. Obituary notices, with due reference to *The New York Times Obituaries Index,* are listed for those who at one time have appeared in the work. Each issue includes a cumulative index to past issues of the year, and with the twelfth number, the title is published as a hardbound yearbook. The yearbook adds a subject index by profession, useful for looking for leaders in various fields.

The online database includes more than 15,000 full text biographies and about 9,500 obituaries from the first issue in 1940 to the present. Both are searchable by name, profession, gender, and date of birth, etc. Note that the CD-ROM is updated once a year, while online it is every month—a distinct advantage for the online version.

The New York Times Biographical Service serves the same purpose, and usually the same audience, as *Current Biography*. The essential difference is that *Current Biography* is staff-written with source references. *The New York Times* biographies are usually written by reporters who do not cite sources. Published online it is part of the daily newspaper, and updated daily. One must search the archives for previous biographies in this series. In print it is published each month in loose-leaf form. In print it is a first choice for any medium-size or large library. It includes obituaries, the "man in the news," and features stories from the drama, book, sports, and Sunday magazine sections. The sketches are often reports on controversial, less-than-admirable, individuals. Most of the reporting is objective. Each sheet is a reprint of biographical material that has appeared in *The New York Times*. The monthly print section has its own index, cumulated every six months and annually.

The lack of online current indexing is a real headache. The efficient way to search for names is to turn to where *The New York Times* is indexed, e.g., *Newspaper Index* or *Newspaper Abstracts*. Given the lack of a special section online for the service, it is far easier to search the print version.

The target audience for the *Encyclopedia of World Biography* is the student from grades 6 to 12, the general public and some less demanding college undergraduates. The prose is easy to follow, there are numerous good to excellent illustrations, and—for all reference purposes—it includes people found in no other standard essay biographical reference works. The added names tend to be of current cultural stars from movies to television and music.

There are about 7,500 entries of both living and dead men and women from all parts of the globe, although the focus is on the West. Most of the essays are short, about 1200 words and many are accompanied by printable portraits. Longer entries are found for the better known, both current and historical. On the CD-ROM there are links to jump to online related sketches. The compilers are truly democratic with Madonna and Madeline Albright sharing about the same space. The last print volume is an extensive index by subjects, nationalities, occupations, characteristics, etc.

RETROSPECTIVE ESSAY BIOGRAPHY

Online: American National Biography Online (formerly *Dictionary of American Biography,* see below). New York: Oxford University Press, www.anb.org. Price varies, $550 for single user.
Print: 1999, 24 vols. $2,500.
CD: Dictionary of American Biography on CD-ROM. New York: Charles Scribner's Sons, 1997. $600.
Print: 1974, 10 vols. Eight supplements, 1977 to date, irregular. Price: the set, $1,400.
CD: Dictionary of National Biography on CD-ROM. London: Oxford University Press, 1997. $550.
Print: Stephen, Leslie, and Sidney Less, eds. *Dictionary of National Biography.* 1885–1901; reissue, 1938, 22 vols, with supplements. $2,250 including supplements.

The listing in *ANB,* the *DAB* or *DNB* is a way of making certain that a person's reputation lives forever. Usually a candidate for inclusion has been dead at least 10 to 20 years before his or her name is considered for the honor. The judgment of the work is the yardstick whereby everyone from historians to politicians measures the importance of an individual. Posthumous celebrity is the final accolade, although it often is bestowed on somewhat obscure, and dimly remembered people.

Both the *Dictionary of American Biography* and the new *American National Biography* are concerned with prominent, quite dead, Americans. It is not certain the older work will continue to publish supplements, more or less a new edition. Meanwhile, the library has the advantage of two marvelous reference works covering many of the same people, but in different ways. Both sets are recommended highly.

The Dictionary of American Biography (or the *DAB,* as it is usually called), with its supplements, covers 19,200 figures who have made a major contribution to American life.[9] Almost all are Americans, but there are a few foreigners who significantly contributed to our history. (In this case, they had to have lived in the United States for some considerable length of time.) Furthermore, no British officers "serving in America after the colonies declared their independence" are included.

---

[9] *The Concise Dictionary of American Biography,* 5th ed. (New York: Charles Schribner's Sons, 1997, 2 vols. $235) includes all of the entries in the main set, but at considerably reduced length per entry. Includes indexes to birthplace, occupation, etc. An excellent ready-reference work if the library can't afford the set. Watch this space. Eventually the rival *American National Biography* will offer a similar cut-back, less expensive version, for the libraries and laypersons.

About 3,000 scholarly contributors add their distinctive styles and viewpoints to the compilation. As a consequence, most of the entries, which vary from several paragraphs to several pages, can be read as essays rather than as a list of connected but dry facts. The original set and the supplements are indexed in a single volume, published in 1990 as *Dictionary of American Biography: Comprehensive Index*. The index is in six sections: subjects of the biographies, their birthplaces, schools and colleges attended, occupations, topics discussed within the biographical entry, and names of contributors to the biographical essays. The occupations index (with politician to mercenary to racketeer to mystic) reflects the Americans at their best and most kinky. There are numerous cross-references in each section, which makes the index easy to use. It is a required item for any library with the basic set and supplements.

The Scribner Encyclopedia of American Lives is a reduced version of the publisher's larger set, *The Dictionary of American Biography*. Volumes are issued to cover people who died recently. In 2003 the sixth volume covers 350 Americans who died in the previous two years. It has two advantages: the text is cut back for readers who do not want all the details or the biographies found in the larger set; and it is less expensive. As a result it is found in many public and school reference collections in place of the DAB.

The CD-ROM version has the advantage of being a little less than one-half the cost of the printed volumes, plus the convenience of searching for 19,000 entries at one computer. One may search by name, occupation, birth year, death date, and occupation across the whole set of printed volumes.

American National Biography

The *American National Biography* (ANB) is completely new work which overlaps and in a sense competes with the better known *Dictionary of American Biography*. New work is supported by the American Council of Learned Societies (a federation of 61 scholarly societies).

The two sets differ in at least four ways: (1) Here there are some 17,500 biographical entries as compared with over 19,000 in the DAB. (2) There are numerous figures not found in the DAB. There are more women, minorities and pre-colonial figures than found in the older set. Representative Americans, i.e., other than politicians, clergy, businesspeople, etc. is evident. The ANB has nearly 40 percent of the biographies which do not appear in the DAB. This represents 6,802 new biographies which vary in length from 750 to 7,500 words. Entrants (for the 1999 edition) must have died before 1996. (3) "Collective" entries include people who functioned as a group in exploration, science, etc. Some 6,000 experts contributed to the set and placed particular emphasis on the social and political aspects of the entries. Also, the newer work includes more current information. (The DAB's coverage ends in 1980). (4) Unlike the original DAB, the new ANB includes foreigners who affected the development of the United States, e.g., Columbus, General John Burgoyne, Antonin Dvorak, etc. A beginning and final section summarizes the person's contributions. All entries are signed.

Navigation of the 24 volumes is provided by four major indexes: subject, contributors, place of birth and "occupations and realms of renown." The latter is the most fascinating. There are the usual headings from presidents to explorers and inventors. And there are the more unusual: chanters, fluegelhorn players, smugglers, gangsters, murder victims and adventuresses, to name only a few of the more fascinating headings. The Duchess of Windsor has a place under adventuresses, and Sally Stanford (eventually a mayor of Sausalito, California) is listed under brothel keepers. Hetty Green, the richest woman in America who lived in poverty is a member of the eccentrics group and Ida Lewis is under lighthouse keepers. Many people are under a number of such headings. John Jacob Astor 4th, for example, is under real estate business leader as well as shipwreck victim—Titanic.

The online version has all the usual advantages from searching keywords in the text to finding a person quickly by birth date, birthplace, deathdate, occupation, etc. Also there are links to other subjects within the ANB, as well as basic biographical sources on the Web.

Does the library need both sets? Yes and no. The large research library does as there are many people in the DAB not found in the ANB—and inevitably they have the older work on the shelves. Smaller libraries, and those serving the general public may hesitate at the $2,500 price tag for the new work. For them it is more reasonable to continue with the DAB and its supplements. The new work can be purchased when *(a)* the price is cut and/or *(b)* the online version is more reasonable than the print edition.

The DNB[10]

The *Dictionary of National Biography* includes entries on over 40,000 deceased "men and women of British or Irish race who have achieved any reasonable measure of distinction in any walk of life." It also lists early set-

---

[10] *The Concise Dictionary of National Biography* (New York: Oxford University Press, 1992, 3 vols., 3,334 pp. $195) is a substitute title for libraries that do not have the funds, or the space, for the primary set. The *Concise* covers every major entry in the main set up until 1981. The problem is that most of the biographical sketches have been cut back so drastically that little is left of the wit and intellectual challenge of the full entries. Shakespeare receives five columns (as compared to 49 pages in the main set) while Jane Austin is limited to nine lines. On the whole, the *Concise* is dependable for essential facts, but not for critical comments. (Much the same can be said about the aforementioned *Concise Dictionary of American Biography.*)

tlers in America and "persons of foreign birth who have gained eminence in this country." The 1986-1990 supplement was published in 1996 and includes 450 individuals prominent in British life for that period.

A *Chronological and Occupational Index to the Dictionary of National Biography* (New York: Oxford University Press, 1985) is primarily an index which divides the entries into 20 basic professional and occupational categories. There is a separate chronological listing for each category. This is a massive index (close to 1000 pages) to both the basic set and the supplements.

An unusual out-of-phase supplemental volume was published in 1993 with the subtitle *Missing Persons.* Oxford University Press had experts go back over the *DNB* volumes and suggest who should be added in the "missing persons" category. The suggestions resulted in 1,086 entries from Thomas Tuberville (d. 1295), the first person in England to be executed for spying, to Julian Maclaren-Ross (1912–1964), a bohemian writer on an heroic scale.

Employing Boolean logic or searching word by word, the CD-ROM version of the *DNB* is a rapid route to finding isolated data difficult to locate through the standard index. Here are the lives of nearly 40,000 people as found in the print edition, but they can be located via a great number of points from occupation to birth date. The search follows pretty much the same pattern as the CD-ROM for *Dictionary of American Biography.*

Beginning in the mid-1990s, the publisher launched a complete new edition program. Estimated dates for the work (to be called *The New Dictionary of National Biography*) is from 2004 to 2010. The number of entries will go from about 40,000 to 50,000, and all of the old biographical material will be revised, even rewritten as necessary. The idea is to move away from the original opinions of the Victorian contributors and into the new age. Along the way there will be added group entries and a stress on social contributions rather than simply being born to fame. An added 10,000 likenesses, taken from the National Portrait Gallery, will be added. It is scheduled to be both in print and digital form.

The biographical form that honors the dead and the worthy is found in almost all countries. A single example close to home is the *Dictionary of Canadian Biography* (Toronto: University of Toronto Press, 1966–1990, 12 vols.). About every five or six years, a new volume that covers a particular time period is issued. For example, the twelfth came out in 1990 and features people from 1891 to 1900. The set has biographical sketches of educators, military figures, craftspeople, and so forth. Published in French as well as English, this is considered a definitive source of biography in Canada. A cumulative index to the first part of the series was published in 1991, which solved the problem of multiple indexing. Note, especially, the useful bibliographies. Subsequent volumes are in progress.

Newspaper indexes offer an excellent key to retrospective biography of both the famous and the infamous. Some newspaper obituary columns, such as *The Times* of London and to a lesser extent *The New York Times*, have distinctive points of view about people who may not quite make the *DAB* or the *DNB*.

On the Web

Substantial retrospective biographies are rare on the Net. The exceptions are primarily found in standard online encyclopedias—for free or for a fee. Example:

Britannica's Lives (www.eb.com/people/). Each day this list of names, with a 50 to 75 word outline of their lives, changes. The list, which may run from three to four pages to over a dozen, represents important people born on the particular day of the search. All are abbreviated versions of what may be found in the latest edition of the *Encyclopaedia Britannica* either in print or in digital format. Arrangement is by the latest year of birth. For example, April 17 opens with a German immunologist born on April 17, 1946 and ends—6 pages later—with Maximilian I born on the same day in 1573. One can jump to the day of one's own birthday for a similar list.

PROFESSIONAL AND SUBJECT BIOGRAPHIES

Almost every publisher's list will include biographical works, from individual biographies to collective works to special listings for individuals engaged in a profession. The increase in the number of professions (nearly every American claims to be a professional of sorts), coupled with the growth in education, has resulted in a proliferation of specialized biographical sources.

What was stated about general biographies applies here: The reliability of some works is questionable, primarily because almost all (and sometimes all) the information is supplied directly to the editor or publisher by the subject. Little or no checking is involved except when there is a definite question or the biographical sketch is evaluative. Entries tend to be brief, normally giving the name, birth date, place of birth, education, particular "claim to fame," and address.

The primary value of the specialized biographical work is as a:

1. Source of address
2. Source of correct spelling of names and titles

3. Source of miscellaneous information for those considering the person for employment or as an employer or as a guest speaker

4. Valuable aid to the historian or genealogist seeking retrospective information, (if the work has been maintained for a number of years).

Following are only representative examples of professional and subject sources. There are hundreds more. When conducting a search for a specific individual, it is usually much faster to begin with the *Biography and Genealogy Master Index* or one of its spin-offs. The exception is when the profession of the individual is known and it is obvious that he or she will be listed in one of the basic professional and subject biographical sources.

Literature

Online: Contemporary Authors. Farmington Hills, MI: Gale Group, 1994 to date, semi-annual, www.galegroup.com. Rate varies.
CD: Contemporary Authors on CD, 1960 to date, semiannual. $4,197, plus $914 for annual and semiannual updates.
Print: Contemporary Authors, 1960 to date, approximately 110 volumes, updated annually. $120 per volume.

Online: Literature Resource Center. Farmington Hills, MI: Gale Group, 1998 to date, monthly, www.galegroup.com. Rates vary.

Online: WorldAuthors: 800 B.C.–Present. H. W. Wilson Company, 1997 to present, www.hwwilson.com. Rate varies. Also available on OCLC.
CD: 1997 to date. Price varies.
Print: World Authors, 1980–1985. New York: H. W. Wilson Company, 1990, 1000 pp. $80. Supplements: *World Authors 1975–1980,* 1985, 831 pp. $68; *World Authors 1970–1975,* 1979, 893 pp. $73; *World Authors 1950–1970,* 1975, 1340 pp. $90. *World Authors 1990–1995,* 1999, 863 pp. $95.

Almost any published American writer is included in the *Contemporary Authors.* The qualifications according to a publicity release by the publisher are that: "The author must have had at least one book published by a commercial, risk publisher, or a university press within the last three or four years...Novelists, poets, dramatists, juvenile writers, writers of nonfiction in the social sciences or the humanities are all covered." In fact, just about anyone who has published anything (this side of a vanity or a technical book) is listed. Newspaper and television reporters, columnists, editors, syndicated cartoonists, and screenwriters are included. The information is gathered from questionnaires sent to the authors and arranged in data from personal facts; career data; writings; and "sidelights," which include discursive remarks about the author and his or her work. As of 2000, the service included about 100,000 writers. This makes *Contemporary Authors* the most comprehensive biographical source of its type.

While the multiple print volumes are a headache—there are well over 100—it is easy to turn to either the online or CD-ROM version.[11] In print, one must cruise through a confusing index or several indexes. At the computer it is a simple matter of entering a name, title of work, or various background key words such as awards or nationality.[12]

A better single source for *Contemporary Authors* is the second online database from Gale: *Literature Resource Center* (www.galenet.com). This not only includes *Contemporary Authors,* but other Gale related databases from *Black Writers* and *Children's Literature Review* to *World Literature Criticism* and *Yesterday's Authors of Books for Children.* It amounts to a one-step search for what most people would require concerning criticism of an author's work, plus information on both the author and the literary effort. There are close to 130,000 authors who have in-depth entries. Others are more sketchy. In the future the database will incorporate several Macmillan works such as the Twayne's author series discussed below. One can search, too, by title of a work. There are over 140,000 title entries.

World Authors is one of the best-known series on authors, and includes not only essential biographical information but also bibliographies of works by and about the author. The source of much of the material is the author, if living; or careful research by consultants, if the author is deceased. Some of the entries are printed almost verbatim as written by the author and are entertaining reading in their own right. Most biographical works devoted to a subject or profession have mercifully short entries.

An example of the series is *World Authors 1950–1970,* edited by John Wakeman, with Stanley Kunitz as a consultant. International in scope, there are long, discursive essays.

And...

The two large databases, and series of printed volumes, are only the major sources of literary biography. There are scores of competitors—none as comprehensive or as easy to use—online and on CD-ROMs.

---

[11]But don't abandon the print columns. Unfortunately, the online version does not include all material found in print.

[12]Gale publishes two related heavily used reference titles—at least by students and graduate students. They are: *Contemporary Literary Criticism,* 1973 to date, irregular; and *Dictionary of Literary Biography,* 1978 to date, irregular. Both are available in print, and online at $850 and $2,100 respectively. See, too, somewhat similar works on CD-ROM such as *DISCovering Authors* and *DISCovering Poetry.*

Major differences arise in availability of full text. Here are two examples:

1. *Twayne's World Authors* (New York: Simon & Schuster, 1998. CD-ROM. $995). This includes the text of 190 books, with particular focus on out of copyright 19th and early 20th century authors. One can search by key words, by name, time period, nationality, etc. The user can search across the full text of all the books, or limit to one or two. Most of the books will be found in any library. The standard *Twayne's Author Series,* in print, offers a detailed background of a given writer's work from a chronology of the author's life, to criticism of major works, to a thorough bibliography. The volumes, one to an author, are compiled by experts. Probably not necessary, except for large research libraries.

2. *Major Authors on CD-ROM* (New York: Primary SourceMedia, 1998. CD-ROM. $2,395). Each disc has a particular author, as, for example, The Brontes, Walt Whitman, Cervantes, or Virginia Woolf. Strictly for research, these include full text of the novels and other writings, manuscript material, letters, painting, commentary, and anything at all to do with the author and worth from about $2,000 to $2,400 per disc. Unlike the Twayne set this is a truly landmark project with extreme value for scholars and graduate students.

On the Web

Anyone looking for specific information, or, more likely fan club data on authors should turn to various Web pages and newsgroups. The former may be found simply by entering the name of the author, in quotations, in the search engine box. A cursory sampling, for example, shows over 300 author sites, and there are probably many more.

The Literary Menagerie (http://sunset.backbone.olemiss.edu/~egcas). Here is the ideal author site for someone who has to do an extensive paper or an in-depth study of a given writer, usually one with an international reputation. After a brief biographical outline there follows a well-chosen bibliography of articles and books about the writer as well as about his or her works. Almost any of these will give the necessary background and in depth material for the student or interested reader. There are no links from the individual author references to other sites on the Net. The menagerie is the work of English PhDs and would-be professors.

Yahoo! Authors (www.yahoo.com/arts/humanities/literature/authors). This is a useful listing of author sites via *Yahoo!*. Searches may be made by individual names of authors as well as in genre categories such as authors of mysteries, science fiction, romance, etc. The actual sites vary wildly in both reliability and quantity of data. Best used for hard to find authors not available in standard print or CD-ROM biographical sources.

Catharton: Authors (www.catharton.com/authors). A search engine which makes a special point of running down material on the Web about authors who are better known for their style than for their relationship to Star Trek. Enter a name and, among other things, the site offers links to websites, message boards, mailing lists, and even chat rooms. There follows a list of the author's work with, again, links to reviews and comments. Numerous other aspects of *Catharton* are useful from book reviews to "budding writers."

Genealogy[13]

Print: Printed Sources: A Guide to Published Genealogical Records, Salt Lake City: Ancestry, 1998, 840 pp. $50.

Print: Raymond Wright. *The Genealogist's Handbook.* Chicago: American Library Association, 1995, 280 pp. $40.

A major interest of many library clients is genealogy. The quest for family history fascinates and confuses. As a result it tends to be the province of experts, but there are numerous basic handbooks and guides that may be used by the librarian (and layperson) to launch and complete a genealogical project.

A guide to the maze of published records, *Printed Sources* is for the beginner and the expert. The first chapter gives the necessary background information on research. This is followed by four sections and chapters that outline key concepts and give basic data on where to look for information. Outstanding for the accurate detail, this is a first stop for anyone seeking genealogical information.

The Genealogist's Handbook spells out the steps necessary to fill out the family tree. The author explains the basics and then indicates the various paths, highways, and accidents that may help or hinder along the way. There is even a chapter on how to write about ancestors. A useful guide for almost any library. For an update of this volume, plus added material see another American Library Association work: Dahrl Moore, *The Librarian's Genealogy Notebook* (1998, 160 pp. $32). Also, this is a more concise explanation suitable for smaller libraries.

---

[13]Thomas Kemp, "The Roots of Genealogy Collections," *Library Journal,* April 1, 1999, p. 57. An annotated listing of basic guides by one of the nation's leading experts. See, too: "Genealogy Bookmarks" plus several other pages on genealogy reference sources in *Booklist,* May 1, 1999, pp. 1,618+; *Yahoo!* magazine, July 10, 1997, p. 10 for a list of websites.

On the Web

There are hundreds of places on the Net to find genealogical information. The difficulty is they are not all that reliable and many overlap. Others focus on such a narrow area of interest to be of value to only a few. A grape shot approach is to enter the name of the city or state historical society in the search engine box. Almost all have some genealogical files that may be open for online searching.

Stripped to essentials, the best sites in order of widest use and accuracy are:

Family Search (www.familysearch.org) is the Mormon Church's genealogy website which gives millions of users access to the world's largest genealogy library. This is for non-church members as well as Mormons, and can be used to find data for almost any name. It is supported by hundreds of thousands of documents, and according to professional genealogists it is the premier site for such research. Actual documents may not be online and will have to be ordered from the library in Salt Lake City.

Genealogy Home Page (www.genhomepage.com) offers links to sources, with the focus on "how-to-do-it" rather than actual data. Particularly useful is the links to genealogy collections in libraries and to commercial sources. Also there are keys to major newsgroups and FAQs. A Roots surname list of close to 85,000 surnames puts the searcher in line with others working on the same name(s). Maintained by a reliable private source, i.e., Stephen A. Wood.

Cyndi's List of Genealogy Sites on the Internet (www.cyndislist.com). This individual effort claims to have close to 20,000 links to genealogy sites. Links are in alphabetical categories.

GROUP SUBJECT BIOGRAPHIES

Online: Gale Biography Resource Center. Farmington Hills, MI: Gale Group, 1999 to date, library, www.galegroup.com. $3,000+, price varies.

Online: Wilson Biographies Plus Illustrated. New York: H. W. Wilson Company, 1999 to date, http://hwwilson.com. $1,500; annual renewal, $395. *CD:* 1999 to date, annual. $945, single user.

Online: Bowker Biographical Directory. New York: R. R. Bowker, 1993 to date, updates vary. DIALOG file 236, $90 per hour.

In a trend which is sure to grow, the H. W. Wilson Company takes not one, but all close to 100 print biographical references and makes

them available as a single unit online. The obvious convenience, time saving and cost cutting means that this type of venture is likely to continue.
It is nothing but gold for librarians, although the failure to "blend" the
scores of sources often ends in faulty searches.

The *Gale Biography Resource Center* will serve up various amounts of
information for some 250,000 individuals. The data is taken from over 85
Gale publications, including *Contemporary Authors*. Drawing, too, from
its cousin's general index (i.e., IAC), it makes available current biographical data drawn from periodicals and newspapers.

The problem, as with almost all group efforts of this type which
draw data from numerous sources, is that there is no consistent approach
to entry. Here, for example, some biographies include name, occupation
and dates. Others forget the occupation and even, sometime, the dates.
Also there is a careless encoding of names which produces less than perfect lists by subject. There is a general misapplication of subject headings over the large group of sources.

Here, as in all of the discussed group biographies, one may search
online at various points from birth and death dates to occupations, gender,
ethnicity, etc. As there are numerous full text articles, not just directory type
information, the whole process of finding a biography can be shortened.

As usual, there are various levels of searches from the simple keywords to sophisticated Boolean logic. Because entries tend to differ, i.e.,
a name may be presented first name last, last name first (or vice versa)
and the nickname may or may not be used as a main entry, some searches
are less than perfect. Still, on balance the overall result is good and one
can, after all, go back and try again.

Note: Libraries may receive the various Marquis *Who's Who* databases
in this system—but at an added charge. The additional cost covers 20
Who's Who titles and about 900,000 entries, many of which are found
anyway in the basic sweep of biographical data.

Wilson

Wilson Biographies claims "comprehensive coverage of over 72,000 figures
from antiquity to the present." About 1,000 new names are added annually.
Searches can be done online or on the equivalent CD-ROM by name, place
of origin, profession, date of birth and other key words. Among the volumes that have migrated to the online or CD-ROM format: *Current Biography Yearbooks* from 1940 to the present. (This makes up 59 of the some
100 volumes claimed for the system.) *World Authors Series*, 800 B.C.–Present
(another 14 volumes), and then single volumes from *World Artist and Popular American Composers* to *Nobel Prize Winners* and *American Songwriters*.

The system includes 27,000 photographs (and growing) of the subjects. Searching allows one to seek out a prominent artist or zebra trainer

without knowing his or her name. Other points available move from keywords to place of birth.

While Wilson does not have as many biographies as found in Gale, it does have the advantage of more lengthy entries, almost always with a picture. If a library must choose, the Wilson is preferable. Larger libraries should have the Gale as well.

Bowker

Combining three of their biographical dictionaries, the R. R. Bowker Company published the online *Bowker Biographical Directory.* The listings contain the standard who's who type of information and are primarily used for addresses, titles, and brief background data on an individual for a total of 160,000 entries. Quantitatively: there are 11,500 biographies in *Who's Who in American Art;* 26,000 in *Who's Who in American Politics;* and 120,000 in *American Men and Women of Science.*[14] (Despite the title, contents of the arts and sciences services include Canadians as well as Americans.) Updated every two to three years, the numbers change, but content primarily remains much the same. Few new people enter or leave the fields.

The online version wins over the individual print volumes of which the digital database is composed. For example, the print *Who's Who in American Art,* as its cousins, is in alphabetical order. There are discipline indexes from librarians to critics in art. The online service allows the same type of access, as well as by gender, date and place of birth, research interests and the like.

Except for special situations, such as an art museum library, most of the services are used only infrequently. In view of their print cost, it is much more economical to rely on the online approach.

SUGGESTED READING

Carlson, Tucker, "The Hall of Lame," *Forbes FYI,* Spring, 1999, pp. 63–66. The author questions the selection process of *Who's Who in America,* and makes several points which confirm his idea that the publisher is more interested in profit than in careful selection. Good points made, too, about how the publisher ties "schlocky products" to its entrants. (Note: *Forbes FYI* is a special issue given over primarily to advertising.)

---

[14]*American Men and Women of Science* (1906 to date, every three years. $900) of the three in the electronic service is found in most libraries. The print eight-volume set adds and drops about 4,000 to 5,000 names with each edition, thus keeping a balance of some 120,000. The data for each person is of the *Who's Who* type. Of particular value is the index that covers 190 disciplines in 10 major areas of study. For other major scientific biographical sources, see the December 1, 1998 *Booklist,* p. 694, "Reference Books Bulletin" page on "Lives in Science."

Conway, Jill, *When Memory Speaks*. New York: Alfred A. Knopf, 1998. 205 pp. A popular history attempt to explain how autobiography became a respected literary genre. From St. Augustine to modern day works, the history "seeks to explain how conventions of gender have historically dictated the archetypes that men and women summon when writing their lives." The premise is not really proved, but the roll call of leading autobiographies makes this worthwhile.

Lane, Anthony, "True Lives," *The New Yorker,* July 27, 1998, pp. 68–76. Why are English newspaper obituaries so fascinating, particularly in comparison with the more methodical American types? An English writer explains in this witty survey of obituaries and how they both entertain and inform. "It was not until the late nineteen eighties that I became fully conscious of the rich, wicked talents of obituaries." With that he launches an explanation that should turn almost anyone to similar reading.

McCullough, David, "The Art of Biography," *The Paris Review,* Fall, 1999, pp. 35–43. The well-known American biographer discusses what it takes to write and to research a prize-winning biography. The author is familiar with the skills required to write biography and he passes along hints, if only indirectly, on how to evaluate a biographical reference work. Besides that, it is a splendid read.

Morgan, Edmund and Marie Morgan, "Who's Really Who," *The New York Review of Books,* March 9, 2000, pp. 38–43. A lengthy and highly favorable review of the *American National Biography,* this is a joy to read on three counts. First, the authors demonstrate the delights of this type of reference work. Second, they show the plus and minuses of the new edition. Third, and most important for librarians, they offer a model of a detailed reference review. Oh, and in the process they give a unique view of American life.

Morrison, Susan, "The Use of Biography in Medieval Literary Criticism," *The Chaucer Review,* vol. 34, no. 1, 1999, pp. 1–69. A scholarly article which demonstrates how biography is used in literary theory. The author outlines the details of such research. The article does point out that biography in libraries is sometimes linked to matters other than recreational or a two-page school paper.

Watson, H., "Constructing American Lives: Biography and Culture," *Reviews in American History,* March, 2000, pp. 45–49. In this book review the author explains the basic ingredients of refined, reliable biography. It serves as not only a model for reviewing biography, but a useful scale for librarians faced with the buy or not buy decision.

Woody, Donna. "African American Biographies," *Journal of Youth Services in Libraries,* no. 1, 2000, pp. 5–9. A discussion of what is needed to build a collection of black literature and biographies in the standard school library. Suggestions are given as to what to look for in acceptable biographies, as well as how to find them.

CHAPTER TEN
DICTIONARIES

The power of words is demonstrated in a national newspaper contest. People were asked to select 20 words that best summed up the 20th century. Television came first followed by: technology, communication, and computer. Global and globalism were taken together for the fifth most popular choice. The top 20, after globalization include: silicon chip, holocaust, automation, bikini, innovation, Internet, progress, speed, microchip, global village, media, butterfly effect (an example of the chaos theory in mathematics and science), change, genocide, and penicillin.[1] Interestingly enough, the only phrase which may need some explanation is the butterfly effect.

Definition of words and spelling are the primary use of the dictionary. The dictionary indicates the reader's own, sometimes deplorable knowledge of his or her native language. The nonprofit organization Books to Prisoners reports that dictionaries top the reading list requests of inmates. Publishers claim dictionaries equally are popular with people outside of prison. Now for the rest of the story.

Dictionaries are far more effective instruments for inculcating linguistic humility than prayer books are for inculcating the spiritual variety. One may turn to the dictionary for the last word not only for definitions and spelling, but for pronunciation, meaning, syllabication (word division), and other points. Hardly a day goes by that the average

---

[1]"The book that sums up the spirit of the age," *The Times* (of London) March 14, 1998, p. 7. Among words that did not make the 20 were: landfill site, myself, rollercoaster, and sliced bread.

person does not have need of a dictionary, if only to assist (on the sly) with a crossword puzzle.

A common misunderstanding concerns the nonappearance of a word. Many think there is *no* such word. In a fast-changing world this is as sad a commentary on education as on the temerity of lexicographers to drop words they believe are too esoteric, racially insulting, sexually vulgar, and so forth. Another error is to assume that the order of a definition or spelling or pronunciation represents preference. An earlier spelling may be seen as preferable to a later one. Finally, most do not understand labels such as "colloquial." Students often think this means "regional" or "sloppy" rather than the true meaning of "conversational."

Scope

Dictionaries cover every interest. There are eight generally accepted categories in print or digital: (1) General English language dictionaries, which include unabridged titles (i.e., those with over 265,000 entries) and desk or collegiate dictionaries (from 139,000 to 180,000 entries). These are for adults and children. (2) Paperback dictionaries which may have no more than 30,000 to 55,000 words and are often used because they are inexpensive and convenient to carry. (3) Historical dictionaries that show the history of a word from date of introduction to the present. (4) Period or scholarly specialized titles that focus on a given time period or place, such as a dictionary of Old English. (5) Etymological dictionaries that are like historical dictionaries, but tend to put more emphasis on analysis of components and cognates in other languages. (6) Foreign language titles, which are bilingual in that they give the meanings of the words of one language in another language. (7) Subject works which concentrate on the definition of words in a given area, such as science and technology. (8) "Other" dictionaries include everything from abbreviation to slang and proper usage.

Compilation

How is a dictionary compiled from the written and spoken words which are its source? Today the larger publishers, from Houghton Mifflin to Merriam-Webster, and Random House, have substantial staffs and freelance lexicographers.

England's dictionary companies, as well as those in America profit from the British National Corpus (BNC) which makes over 300 million words computer accessible: (http://info.ox.ac.uk/bnc/). The word bank helps to show how a given word or phrase is employed in speech and writing. For example, "transpire" pops up around 25 percent of the time in the sense of "occur," whereas most use the term to mean "to become known or apparent." It remains a grammarian's pet argument, but for most people the "occur" definition seems more useful. Hence this is an example of the "rule" that says words mean whatever they appear to mean in context, that every definition is as valid as any other, that the descriptive school reigns.

The word bank process differs from firm to firm, but essentially it is in two stages. Freelance readers send in new or unusual use of words taken from magazines, newspapers, and other sources. The newly coined words, or the variations on an older word (as for example the use of "hardware" in relationship to computers) are dutifully recorded on 3- by 5-inch cards, or, these days, entered in a computer's memory. At a later stage they are considered for inclusion based on their probable "lasting" power.[2]

EVALUATION

For those who seek to evaluate dictionaries, the first rule is not to expect any dictionary to be perfect. Dr. Johnson said, "Dictionaries are like watches: the worst is better than none, and the best cannot be expected to go quite true." There is no perfect dictionary, and there never will be one until such time as the language of a country has become completely static—an event as unlikely as the discovery of a perpetual-motion mechanism. Language is always evolving because of the coining of new words and the change in meaning of older words.

Published in mid-1999, the much heralded (by the company) *Encarta World English Dictionary* boasts an earnest photograph of William H. Gates on page 738. The note on the cofounder of Microsoft (publisher of the dictionary) is understandable, although why no picture of President John F. Kennedy? Rivals soon made gleeful sport of errors in the print-digital newcomer. A few examples illustrate the need for careful evaluation of a dictionary: (1) Sensitive warning labels warn the use of "lady friend," or "hard of hearing" as potentially offensive. One well-known expletive, favored by soldiers, movie tough people, and many others, is labeled offensive some 20 times in a single passage. (2) The pronunciation of Niagara Falls is "nigra falwz." (3) George Gordon

---

[2]Case in point: "misandry," a dislike of men, is not found in many dictionaries before the women's movement. The opposite of "misogny," dislike of women, misandry appeared around 1946. On the other hand, and understandably so, misogyny appeared as early as the 17th century. For a history of these words, how they find a place in a dictionary, and, for that matter, literature and speech, see: "In the Battle of The Sexes, This Word is a Weapon," *The New York Times*, July 25, 1999, p. 2.

Meade is a general during the Revolutionary War. Actually, it was the Civil War. (4) A picture of a sedan has the label "saloon." In later editions errors were corrected and modified.

No single dictionary is sufficient. Each has its good points, each its defects.

This is true of the digital versions, which normally are no more than the print text in an electronic format. The evaluation of a digital dictionary is much the same for the print version.

The basic evaluation rule should be self-evident, but is rarely followed: Consult the preface and explanatory notes at the beginning of a dictionary. The art of successfully using a dictionary, or any other reference book, requires an understanding of how it is put together. This is important because of the dictionary's constant use of shortcuts in the form of abbreviations, various methods of indicating pronunciation, and grammatical notations.

Points of Evaluation

Beyond recognizing no dictionary is perfect and reading the preface there are points to check in deciding whether to purchase or avoid a dictionary:

Authority. There are only a limited number of publishers of dictionaries. The reputable ones include Merriam-Webster; Oxford University Press; Random House; Scott-Foresman; Doubleday; Macmillan; Simon & Schuster; and Houghton Mifflin—to name the larger, better-known publishers. [In England the four leading publishers are Oxford, Collins, Longman and the Edinburg based Chambers.] The clear leader is Merriam-Webster. Their college dictionary goes through five or six printings each year and sells over a million copies annually. In specialized fields and other areas where dictionaries are employed, there are additional reputable publishers. The reason that there are comparatively few general dictionary publishers is the same as that used to explain why there are so few working on general encyclopedias—cost. A dictionary is an expensive matter.

"Webster" in the title of a dictionary may be a sign of reassurance, and it frequently is found as the principal name of a number of dictionaries. G. & C. Merriam Company, which bought out the unsold copies of Noah Webster's dictionary at the time of his death in the nineteenth century, had the original claim to the name. For years the use of Webster's name was the subject of litigation. Merriam-Webster finally lost its case when the copyright on the name lapsed. It is now common property and may be used by any publisher. Hence the name "Webster's" in the title may or may not have anything to do with the original work which bore the name. Unless the publisher's name is recognized, "Webster" *per se* means nothing.

Vocabulary. Vocabulary can be evaluated in terms of the period of the language covered, as well as in the number of words or entries. Other special vocabulary features may include slang, dialect, obsolete forms, and scientific or technical terms.

In the United States the field is divided between the *unabridged* (over 265,000 words) and the *abridged* (from 50,000 to 265,000 words) type of dictionary. Most dictionaries are abridged or limited to a given subject or topic. The two unabridged dictionaries vary from about 460,000 entries for *Webster's* to 315,000 for *Random House.* The *Oxford English Dictionary* has 500,000 words but is not considered a general dictionary. Most desk dictionaries, such as the much-used *Merriam-Webster's Collegiate Dictionary,* or the *American Heritage,* have about 150,000 to 170,000 words, and are considered more than sufficient for average use.

LS Language. Dictionaries now include most basic slang. There is controversy over this editorial decision, and particularly when the dictionary fails to stress the given word is not to be used in "polite" company, or is a slur, etc. as one opponent to such inclusions puts it: "It should be becoming clear...that this sort of populism isn't particularly democratic...It may be that what the public wants from a dictionary is correctness. They can make up slang on their own."[3]

Despite the wish of a minority to delete slang from the vocabulary found in a dictionary, most publishers include such words. Why? Because while slang may not be socially acceptable, it is used widely. Various publishers have many ways to indicate the less than acceptable use of such words, e.g. label them "usually offensive," "not used in polite company," "slang," etc.

With the inclusion of slang and those numerous "four-letter words," not a year goes by without a problem. In 1999 America Online withdrew the Merriam-Webster electronic version of Merriam's college thesaurus "for revisions" after it was found a word list for "homosexual" included slang synonyms without due warning that the words were slurs. It is now back online with those designations clearly given. The 2000 version of the *Random House Webster's College Dictionary* has "reader beware" features. Some 300 words are flagged as offensive, e.g., "probably the most offensive word in English" is given for a particular racial slur. Even before a definition, "holy roller" is labeled: "A slur and must be avoided. It is

---

[3]"Too Many Words to the Street Wise" *The Guardian Weekly,* September 6, 1998, p. 26.

perceived as insulting." Bolder "politically incorrect" words come with milder warnings. "Babe" is defined with the politically incorrect signal. At the same time it is noted that babe is "an affectionate term of address used by a man or woman to a sweetheart."

Up-to-Date. Dictionary revision is a never-ending affair. New editions are usually issued every seven to ten years, but hundreds of changes are usually made in each printing, online and CD-ROM version. These include adding new words, revising definitions of older words that have taken on new meaning, and dropping a few technical terms that are no longer used. A quick check of a desk or unabridged dictionary that claims to be up-to-date should include the words introduced into the language by television, radio, and film.

Supplements are a tried method of keeping dictionaries up-to-date without thoroughly revising the primary work.[4] An example: *Dictionary of New Words* (2nd ed. New York: Oxford University Press, 1997. 366 pp. $30). As the title indicates, this is a dictionary of 2,000 new words, most of which are not found in the numerous current dictionaries. If they last a generation or so, they will become enshrined, most of the new verbal challenges are more fashionable than lasting. *The Dictionary of New Words,* as its cousins and aunts, is of value primarily as a reflection of popular words during a brief span of time.[5]

The obvious advantage of a digital dictionary is that it can be updated rapidly by simply adding words and definitions. Still, someone has to make the additions. Simply because a dictionary is in an electronic format does not necessary mean it is any more current than its print equivalent.

Format. A major consideration of print format is the binding of the dictionary. Both individuals and libraries should purchase hardcover editions because the hard binding will withstand frequent use. Another consideration is how the words are arranged. Most dictionaries now divide the words among a great number of separate headwords. If a dictionary does not do this, and crams many items under a single entry such as *lay,* one must look for *lay* to find such words as *layout* or *lay-by.*

Other important factors to be evaluated are print size and how readability is affected by spacing between words and lines of type, the use of boldface type, and the differences in type families. With the exception of

---

[4]See David Isaacson, "New Word Sources..." *Reference Services Review,* Summer, 1997, pp. 53–64, 72. This is a descriptive, annotated listing of the basic "new word" dictionaries. The author lists well over a dozen entries, including the Oxford title.

[5]For an amusing discussion of this and other works which update dictionaries see Jenny Diski "Diary" *The London Review of Books,* January 1, 1998, p. 33.

some colored plates, most dictionary illustrations are black-and-white line drawings...exception the 2000 edition of the *American Heritage Dictionary*. The average desk dictionary has from 600 to 1,500 illustrations, the unabridged from 7,000 to 12,000. Online dictionaries and those wedded to word processing rarely boast illustrations, but where they do pop up one must expect both black and white and color.

Encyclopedia material. Some dictionaries are a combination of facts found in an encyclopedia and a dictionary. For example, the *New Oxford Dictionary of English* (Oxford: Oxford University Press, 1998) has a section with more than 4,500 place names and 4,000 biographical entries. The section "claims to include all those terms forming part of the enduring common knowledge of English speakers." The problem is it is too small, too selective. And as one critic put it, "If I wanted encyclopaedic knowledge, I'd use an encyclopaedia."[6] Generally a dictionary is better off eliminating encyclopedia type information.

Spelling. Where there are several forms of spelling, they should be clearly indicated. *Webster's* identifies the British spelling by the label "Brit."; other dictionaries normally indicate this variant by simply giving the American spelling first, e.g., *analyze, analyses* or *theater, theatre*. Frequently two different spellings are given, either of which is acceptable. The user must determine the form to use. For example, *addable* or *addible, lollipop* or *lollypop*. (It is worth reminding both librarians and laypersons that explanations of such refinements are found in the preface.) Some other points of disagreement: *eye-opener* or *eye opener; dumfound* or *dumbfound; gladiolus* (plural), or *gladioli*, or *gladiolus's*.

An *Oxford English Dictionary* survey found that the most difficult words to spell are either of nonEnglish origin *(nil dessperandum:* do not despair; *hoi-polloi:* the rabble); very obscure *(poetaster:* an inferior poet); or simply defy common sense. Words which sound the same or have a similar meaning are another source of confusion.

Etymologies. All large dictionaries indicate the etymology of a word by a shorthand system in brackets. The normal procedure is to show the root word in Latin, Greek, French, German, Old English, or some other language. Useful as this feature is, the student of etymology will be satisfied only with historical studies.

The history of words and how they develop is not purely academic. Such a study can clarify odd notions and downright falsehoods

[6]"Mind Your Language," *The Spectator,* August 29, 1998, p. 16. There are numerous checks here of what the encyclopaedia section has and does not have. It fails on most counts.

linked to words. One example: How many words do the Eskimos have for snow? A typical answer is that there are scores, if not hundreds of such words. In English the number is limited to a half dozen or so. The idea began with Frank Boaz, a prominent anthropologist, who in 1911 explained languages other than English may describe things from a single root. The Eskimos use the distinct roots "aput" for snow on the ground; or "qana" for falling snow; or "qimuqsuq" for snowdrift and so on. In 1940 an amateur linguist used this root system to claim the Eskimos have numerous words for snow. This was picked up by a magazine writer, and *The New York Times* by 1988 claimed "four dozen" Eskimo words for snow. Actually there are only two possible relevant roots: "quanik" meaning snow in the air or snowflake and "aput".[7]

Definitions. Dictionaries usually give the modern meaning of words first. Exceptions include most older British-based dictionaries as well as the Merriam-Webster publications and *Webster's New World*. Without understanding the definition ladder, an unsuspecting reader (who has not read the preface) will leave the dictionary with an antiquated meaning. Also, the meaning may be precise, but it can lead to "circularity" in which words of similar difficulty and meaning are employed to define one another. The quality of the definition depends on several factors. Separate and distinct meanings of words should be indicated clearly. This usually is done by numbering the various definitions. The perfect definition is precise and clear, but in more technical, more abstract situations this is not always possible. What, for example, is the true definition of *love?*

Then there are the definitions which may slip in by mistake, or simply represent someone's way of relieving the tedium of assigning definitions by adding a dash of humor and irony. In *Chambers Dictionary* (London: Chambers, 1998) under sea serpent—"an enormous animal of serpent-like form, frequently seen and described by credulous sailors, imaginative landsmen, and common liars." (Serpent-like form? Is this a definition of serpent?) Try eclair—"a cake long in shape, but short in duration." (What?) Or Japanese cedar—"a very tall Japanese conifer...often dwarfed by Japanese gardeners." (Are all Japanese conifers under, say, five feet 10 inches?) Picture restorer—"someone who cleans and restores and sometimes ruins old pictures." Then there is the *Macmillan Dictionary of Psychology* (London: Macmillan, 1989). Under psychoanalyst appears the definition "a person who takes money from another on the pretense that it is for the other's own good." (No comment.)

---

[7]"Outwitted by Inuit" *Independent,* January 15, 1998, p. 10. The ultimate source of the correct information: C. W. Shultz-Lorentzen's *Dictionary of the West Greenlandic Eskimo Language* (1927).

Pronunciation. In print there are several different methods of indicating pronunciation, but most American publishers employ the diacritical one. In *Merriam-Webster's Collegiate Dictionary,* the pronunciation system tends to be quite detailed and, except for the expert, equally confusing. In the *American Heritage Dictionary* the process is much easier to understand.

All dictionaries employ the simple phonetic use of the familiar, that is, a person looking up *lark* finds the "r" is pronounced as in *park.* Regardless of what the person's accent may be, the transferred sound will be the same as that in *park.* Regional accents do make a difference in that *park* may be pronounced as "pock," "pawk," or even "pack." At the same time, the phoneticists consider variations such as the pronouncing of *tomato, potato,* and *economics* which differ from region to region, even person to person. In these cases, more than one pronunciation is noted as correct.

An advantage of online and the CD-ROM is that here one often can hear the pronunciation of up to one-third or more of the words. Usually this is done using both men's and women's voices. Almost all standard online dictionaries now feature voice pronunciation. One example: *Encarta World English Dictionary* website (www.encarta.com) has about 60,000 words of 100,000 in the dictionary which one can hear pronounced.

Syllabication. All dictionaries indicate, usually by a centered period or hyphen, how a word is to be divided into syllables. The information is mainly to help writers, editors, and secretaries divide words at the ends of lines. There are special, short desk dictionaries that simply indicate syllabication of more common words without benefit of definition or pronunciation.

Synonyms. The average user does not turn to a general dictionary for synonyms, but their inclusion helps to differentiate between similar words. Some desk dictionaries indicate the differentiation and shades of meaning by short essays at the conclusion of many definitions.

Grammatical Information. The most generally useful grammatical help a dictionary renders is to indicate parts of speech. All single entries are classified as nouns, adjectives, verbs, and so on. Aside from this major division, dictionaries vary in method of showing adverbs, adjectives, plurals, and principal parts of a verb, particularly the past tense of irregular verbs. Usually the method is clearly ascertainable; but, again, the prefatory remarks should be studied in order to understand any particular presentation.

Usage. The most controversial aspect of evaluation concerns how proper usage is or is not indicated. Today there is division between those who wish a dictionary to be *prescriptive* (i.e., to clearly and categorically indicate what is or is not good, approved usage) or *descriptive* (i.e., simply describe the language as it is spoken and written without any judgment as to whether it is acceptable by the common culture). Dictionaries vary on how they handle usage. At one extreme is the work that says almost anything goes as long as it is popular (e.g., most of the Merriam-Webster dictionaries). At the other is the dictionary which is critical and gives rules of good usage (for example, *Webster's New World Dictionary* from Simon & Schuster). In between is the "it depends" school which is more pragmatic than prescriptive or descriptive (for example, *The American Heritage Dictionary*). Most people believe that dictionaries should be both descriptive and prescriptive, setting rules about right and wrong usage, yet including words as they are used by a majority.

What makes anyone's English "correct"? Some say an answer is impossible. There are too many variables from a definition of correctness to the meaning of semantic competence. Usage has become the foundation of not only descriptive linguistic, but much grammar. The study of spoken English has become more important than written English. Different social and cultural situations offer their own rules. Bound up with belief in traditional grammar is a conviction that modern English is worse than that of previous generations because of a failure to teach grammar.

Guide to Dictionaries: Print

Print: Kister, Kenneth. *Kister's Best Dictionaries for Adults & Young People: A Comparative Guide.* Phoenix, AZ: Oryx Press, 1992, 448 pp. $39.50.

Print: Loughridge, Brendan. *Which Dictionary?* London: Library Association Publishing, 1990. 177 pp. $26.

Both of these "best" dictionary titles are dated, but useful in that while new editions of dictionaries appear regularly the basic patterns and differences pretty much remain the same. Kister's *Best Dictionaries,* is the leading guide to English language dictionaries. There are over 132 entries for general adult works, from the *Oxford English Dictionary* to inexpensive paperbacks. Some 168 children's dictionaries are evaluated. An excellent preface sets the stage on how to evaluate a dictionary. Necessary background information is given about publishers, publishing and the electronic dictionary. For each of the titles there is a thorough analysis, often over several pages. Helpful charts and graphs with forthright grading of A to failure, are extremely useful. While dated, it remains useful.

In England, Loughridge's *Which Dictionary?* is an approach similar to that employed by Kister. Here there are seven divisions of dictionaries from standard to pocket to a group of works that defy categorization.

Unlike Kister, Loughridge includes many "odd" titles from those covering crossword puzzles to subject dictionaries. Not as thorough as its American cousin, but casting a wider web, the Library Association publication is a nice addition for larger libraries. It in no way replaces Kister.

The best review of current dictionaries will be found in the "Reference Books Bulletin" of *The Booklist*.

On the Web

The dictionary was one of the earliest print reference family members to migrate to digital format, particularly as part of word processing software (from spelling checks to built–in definition banks). On CD-ROM the print dictionary becomes a talking dictionary. On the Internet equally there is a vast number of standard titles, subject works, and translation aids. Manuals of style and thesaurus also are at the command of the mouse.

The searcher knows instinctively when to call up an electronic dictionary and when to turn to the print edition. In almost all cases where it is a matter of checking a single word for spelling, pronunciation, meaning, word division and definition, the print volume is the easiest, most efficient route. On the Web there are dozens of free dictionaries, some of which will be described later, but, again, it seems pointless to look up a word online when it can be done more efficiently with a print dictionary.

When trouble looms, i.e., trying to find a word to fit a preconceived definition or testing various spellings, the digital dictionary is best. The use of key words, of course, is the key to success—a methodology which cannot be employed in the print alphabetically arranged volume. On a more ambitious scale, one can search for quotes, hard to find definitions, history of words and the like much easier in the digital dictionary.

Even a casual Web surfer soon discovers there are numerous digital dictionaries from the big four publishers online. All, too, come in CD-ROMs. Why so many? It is called digital licensing, a new source of revenue. At Houghton Mifflin *(American Heritage Dictionary)* digital licensing accounted for more than $1 million in profit in 2000, or more than 10 percent of the earnings from the company's trade and reference division. Similar figures, similar enthusiasm to go digital will be found among all major dictionary publishers.

Links to numerous dictionaries, both English, foreign and special will be found on most library home pages. See, for example, the *Michigan Electronic Library* (http://mel.lib.mi.us) where there are two dozen general dictionaries and again that many "specific language" titles. The latter begins with links to "Afrikaans-English," goes through the standard English and European languages and ends with a link to "Urdu-English." This single page will more than meet the needs of 99 percent of students and researchers. If more is needed, see: *A Web of On-Line Dictionaries* (http://www.bucknell.edu/rbeard/diction.html). Developed by an individual via Bucknell University, this has links to dictionaries and wordbooks in some 100 languages as well as English.

Other recommended sites—and these are only a sample, include: (1) *OneLook Dictionaries* (www.onelook.com). This commercial site offers definitions from close to 500 dictionaries, both general and specialized. The user may enter specific words, and/or call up a particular dictionary, and/or call up a subject area(s) covered by dictionaries. (2) *Vocabulary* (www.vocabulary.com). The perfect thesaurus in that one simply clicks on a word and the site looks up the meaning and synonyms as well as the same word in some 10 other languages. (This latter feature works sometimes in reverse, too.) (3) *The Word Detective* (www.word-detective.com). Here one finds the history and roots of words as well as salty comments by Evan Morris who has a series of books and columns on words.

UNABRIDGED DICTIONARIES

CD: Random House Webster's Unabridged Dictionary. New York: Random House, 2000, irregular update. $28.
   Print: Random House Unabridged Dictionary, 1993, 2510 pp. $89.95.

CD: Webster's Third New International Dictionary. Springfield, MA: Merriam-Webster Inc., 2000, irregular update. $69.95.

Print: 1961. 2752 pp. $119. Supplements, 1976 to 1988, various paging, each $10.95.

In 1988 it was called *The Random House Dictionary of the English Language.* By the early 1990s the marketing department saw the advantage of a switch to "unabridged." The question is, then, Is it truly unabridged? The answer is "yes," in that the publisher claims 315,000 entries and 2,500 maps and mediocre illustrations. It is well over the average 130,000 to 265,000 words found in smaller works. The answer is "no" if it is compared with its competitor. *Webster's* claims 450,000 entries or some 135,000 more than in *Random House.*

Today there is only one true unabridged dictionary of the English language. This is *Webster's Third New International.* One may count *The Oxford English Dictionary (OED)* in this category, but it really is more concerned with etymology than definitions, and is not meant to be an everyday working dictionary.

Essentially, then, "unabridged" is what the publisher cares to define. As long as it is within reason, which the *Random House* is, few will argue, or for that matter, care. Where does this leave libraries? Most libraries should have the *Webster's* (which does have more words) *and* the *Random House* (which is more current.)

The *Random House* dictionary, no matter what the publisher wishes to call it, has a solid reputation. There is no argument that this is one of the best "big" dictionaries. There are added features, such as concise, yet quite practical, bilingual dictionaries in French, German, Spanish and Italian; almost 30 pages of full-color maps; and the usual style manual. Although not as large as *Webster's,* the *Random House* has the distinct advantage of being relatively current. Approximately 50,000 new words were added or revised for the second edition. Expletives are in more common use, and many four-letter words were added. These are normally identified as "vulgar."

The dictionary is descriptive. One looks, without much help, for some guidance in the use of the word *hope* as a modifier. Disputes about *hopefully* are noted, and other embattled terms are described as such. It accepts the word, *infer* in its general meaning "to draw a conclusion" and also as a synonym "to imply" or "to suggest," but adds that the distinction between the two words is "widely observed."

Definitions are clear, and uses words likely to be understood by the average person. Many entries conclude with helpful synonyms and antonyms.

The CD-ROM version of the *Random House Unabridged Dictionary* (with "Webster's" added to the title) consists of the last edition of the printed version, with new entries added each year. So while the CD-ROM is updated it remains primarily the print work with its 315,000 entries. On the other hand it eliminates many of the added features of the print work such as the style manual.

The *Random House CD-ROM* has all the usual advantages. Its real value is the ability to search words in the definition. One may search for related words, for quotations, synonyms, and the like by a click or a key. In a library it is available for everyone as a supplementary aid to searching at a computer. And, finally, it has the usual plus of taking up little or no space.

Webster's

Despite the publishing date (1961), *Webster's* is essential. Each new CD-ROM or printing includes new words, or variations on definitions of older words. See, for example, recent computer, political, and sociological terms. Most will be included, if not in the main work, at least in the print supplements and CD-ROM which add about 22,000 words to the basic 450,000 in the primary volume. *Webster's* on CD-ROM has the same advantages as *Random House,* as well as other CD-ROMs for ease of searching.

But there are some particular additions such as typing out a word and then entering "rhymes with" or "quoted author is" etc.

Noah Webster had been involved with publishing dictionaries through the early nineteenth century. It is important to stress that 1909 was the date of the first current series of *unabridged* titles. A second edition came out in 1934 and a third in 1961. A 2000 print dictionary has several copyright dates: 1961, the date of the original revision, and later dates—usually every five years—which imply some revisions since 1961. However, the work is primarily the original 1961 work. The publisher has given no indication when the next edition will be available, although this is expected by 2003. Until then the library must have *Webster's* as the only true unabridged dictionary, along with the much more current *Random House.*

Since it is a recognized authority, many claim *Webster's* should be prescriptive and lay down the verbal law. It does not. It is descriptive, and sometimes it is difficult, despite labels, to pinpoint the good, the bad, or the indifferent use of a word. Also, it has such an involved scheme of indicating pronunciation that most people are helpless to understand how to pronounce anything.

DESK (COLLEGE) DICTIONARIES[8]

Online: Merriam-Webster's Collegiate Dictionary, Springfield, MA: Merriam-Webster Inc. 2000 to date. (www.m-w.com). Free. Also on other websites.

CD: *Merriam-Webster's Collegiate Dictionary and Thesaurus.* 2000. $199.

Print: Merriam-Webster's Collegiate Dictionary, 10th ed. 2000, 1,559 pp. $24.95. *Online: The American Heritage Dictionary.* Somerville, MA: Houghton Mifflin Interactive, 2000. Price varies. Available on other websites.
　　CD: The American Heritage Talking Dictionary. 4th edition, Boston: Houghton Mifflin Company, 2000, $42.95.
　　Print: 4th ed. 2000, 2,074 pp. $75.

CD: The Random House Webster's Dictionary and Thesaurus College Edition. New York: Random House, 2000. $99.
　　Print: The Random House Webster's College Dictionary, 2000, 1,600 pp. $24.95.

CD: Webster's New World Dictionary of American English, in *The Software Toolworks Reference.* Novato, CA: Software Toolworks, Inc., 1991 to date, annual. $99.

[8]Typically, the publishers offer numerous price variations on the basic college or desk dictionary. For example, Random House begins with its college dictionary and then adds: *Webster's American Family Dictionary ($24); Random House Large Print Dictionary ($40); Random House Webster's Large Print Thesaurus ($40).*

Print: Webster's New World Dictionary of American English, 4th ed. New York: IDG Books Worldwide, 1999. 1,574 pp. $18. 1,600 pp. $17.95.

The four dictionaries listed are the four best, and most often found in the library and, for that matter, in the home. All are available in digital format. A careful watch should be kept for new editions, for updates of the four. The standard publisher's dictionaries are periodically revised, and all are authoritative. The four account for sales of about 2.5 million hardcover copies each and every year. Shorter paperback versions of some are available. The digital versions are popular. In the home and in the office they usually are part of a larger reference system, such as *Microsoft Bookshelf.* It is doubtful the digital dictionary will replace the familiar printed volume.

The core of the dictionary publishing business is the familiar desk or college version. The definitions are written for those with a college education, although they can be used by almost all age groups and by anyone who has basic literacy. It normally includes from about 139,000 to 180,000 words, has illustrations, and offers added material such as short biographical and geographical notes. Digital dictionaries tend to add such things as a thesaurus, style manual, etc.

Differences are essentially those of format, arrangement, systems of indicating pronunciation, and length of definitions. All include synonyms, antonyms, and etymologies. Price variations are minimal. The natural question is which is best, and the answer depends primarily on personal need. All have about the same number of words, and all meet the evaluative tests of excellence.

Webster's Collegiate

Free on the Internet, the *Merriam-Webster* online has the advantage of virtually combining the dictionary with a thesaurus. There are additions such as the transcripts of the radio show "Word for the Wise" which traces word histories. As with all the major collegiate dictionaries, a version of this is to be found at numerous websites, usually in combination with other reference sources. Also, it is used in word processing systems. Be that as it may, the user normally is better off going directly to the publisher's Web site for most purposes. Still, as with other dictionaries, for most it is much easier to simply pick up the print version. The online Net version is simplicity itself: one can "look up a definition, pronunciation, etymology, spelling, or usage points in the...online version of *Merriam-Webster's Collegiate Dictionary.*" Generally most people enter a word and find pronunciation, part of speech, etymology and a short definition, i.e., everything found in the desk edition. There is a thesaurus/synonyms section which follows the same pattern. Type in the wanted word and the synonyms and antonyms appear, often with enough definition to indicate subtle differences.

Merriam-Webster's Collegiate Dictionary is based on the unabridged Third. It has about 160,000 words and 700 illustrations. It reflects the philosophy of the larger work and places considerable emphasis on contemporary pronunciation and definitions. As in the primary dictionary, the philosophy is descriptive, although there is more emphasis on usage notes (fully explained in the explanatory preface). "Nonstandard" is the warning for the use of *ain't,* and this is followed by a short paragraph that discusses the current use of the word. In this case it is noted that "although disapproved as nonstandard and more common in the habitual speech of the less educated, *ain't...*is flourishing in American English." When the four-letter words are explained, and major ones are included, the usage note is "considered obscene" or "considered vulgar." In that latest edition (i.e., 2000) about 200 words have a notation that they are racial, religious or sexual slurs. Groups petition the dictionary to remove the words entirely, but the publisher refuses pointing out the dictionary records usage and does not censor.

There are passable line drawings, although in number they do not come close to those found in the *American Heritage Dictionary.* The history of words is usually shown, along with a date when the word first appeared in the language. The pronunciation system remains a problem. The symbols employed are listed in full inside the back cover, and a shorter version appears at the bottom of each right-hand page. The whole is extremely complicated and it takes a special section, "Guide to Pronunciation," to try to explain the process to readers. The overall result is less than satisfactory.

Although the maze of pronunciation symbols may be puzzling, the definitions are improved. Derived from the unabridged version, the definitions are considerably more lucid and simplified. They are still given in chronological order, with the modern meaning last. For example, *explode* begins with the labeled archaic definition "to drive from the stage by noisy disapproval."

The 12,000 geographical and 6,500 personal names are not included in the main alphabet, but are separate features in the appendixes, a habit now followed by other dictionaries. The appendices also include foreign words and phrases.

American Heritage

Another standard dictionary available online is the *American Heritage.* Here it comes as a bonus with numerous commercial online carriers. The online version contains the complete print text, and can be searched in the usual fashion for definitions, quotations, etc.

The famous *American Heritage Dictionary* is transformed digitally. The digital versions contain all the information in the print volume, with a distinct plus. The CD version, with "talking" in the title, reveals a strong selling point. Many of the words are pronounced for the viewer. Other than that, it adds *Roget's II: The New Thesaurus*. The search patterns are clear and one may move from the simple definition of a single word to matching it with synonyms, parts of speech, correct or incorrect usage and the like. The linkages are good to excellent and the disk may be used as much for a history of the language as for a definition of a single word.

American Heritage stresses prescriptive entries. The usage notes are useful to help guide the average person seeking to find whether this or that word may be used in polite society. This is determined by a panel, and the collective result is a valuable guide for laypersons. The notes summarize the sometimes differing views of the panel and are well worth reading.

On the middle ground between the standard desk or college dictionary and the unabridged dictionary, the *American Heritage* has more words, about 200,000 versus some 160,000 entries in the nearest competitor. There are, or so the publisher claims, over 10,000 new words in the 2000 edition from computer terms such as "laptop" and "pixel" to socially new expressions from "birthparent" to "slam dunk." The fourth edition carries on the tradition of a superior format. The entries are in boldface. The 40,000 illustrations, (with many in color) typography and general layout is quite superior to competitors. There are 30,000 or so examples of how the words are properly used. These are made up by the staff, and sometimes the examples are silly. On the other hand, they are easy to understand and fortified with historical quotations. The *American Heritage* is the best single desk dictionary for etymology and gives details on the linguistic sources of most words.

Webster's New World Dictionary

As part of a larger unit, *Webster's New World Dictionary* is on a CD-ROM with numerous reference publications by Simon & Schuster, for example, *Webster's New World Thesaurus, Webster's New World Guide to Concise Writing*, and five other related titles. It is searched in the usual fashion, although, because the disk has so many other units, it is employed primarily for spelling and definition of words. This hardly discounts the value of the CD-ROM, particularly as the annual updates do include new materials and are one-half the price of the original disk.

Again, though, one would be better off simply using the printed work for most questions, and the print version is quite superior. *Webster's New World Dictionary of American English* is not from Merriam-Webster, and the two works are often confused.

The publisher claims that there are 170,000 entries, and about 800 black-and-white illustrations. The *New World* is aptly named because its primary focus is on American English as it is spoken and written. There are particularly good definitions which are closely related to current speech. The definitions are in historical order, not by the most common current understanding of the word.

A star preceding an entry indicates an American word or expression. There are some 11,000 of these. Meaning is illustrated with made-up sentences and phrases. Pronunciation is clear, and a key is found in the lower corner of every right-hand page. There are only a few—about 800—illustrations, but these are at least adequate.

Of the three, it is by now the most prescriptive, even more so than the *American Heritage*. It is favored by *The New York Times,* as well as by various press services. Given this type of recommendation, it has won many readers.

Random House

The Random House Webster's College Dictionary offers some of the best treatment of modern American words and phrases. It rightfully takes pride in including in each new revision the difficult and unusual words that work their way into American vocabulary. Also it has more words and definitions than any of its desk competitors. The revised 2000 edition, for example, includes the majority of Internet terms as well as some current television slang (for example, cyberpunk, politically correct, e-mail, and secondhand smoke). It is a close runner with the other desk or college dictionaries and should be found in most libraries.

The print *Random House* is, like *Merriam Webster's*, modeled after the parent company's larger work, that is, *The Random House Unabridged Dictionary*. It has a fine "User's Guide" in the introduction, and one librarians might consult for general information on dictionaries. Unfortunately, not one person in a thousand is likely to read the introductory material. The entries are the same as in the larger volume. As with the parent work, the dictionary can be considered "best" in several areas: its commonsense treatment of slang; the concise, clear definitions; and a descriptive approach to words.

The Random House CD-ROM includes the text from the printed version with 180,000 words as well as biographical and geographical data. The thesaurus has the total text of the *Random House Thesaurus* with more than 275,000 synonyms and antonyms. The CD-ROM version has many advantages, most of which are found on other CD-ROM dictionaries. Among these: (1) The ability to move back and forth from the words in the dictionary to needed synonyms in the thesaurus. If, for example, the user needs another word for "sarcastic," a key will bring up "acerbic," "caustic," and so forth. If not sure of the meanings, another key defines "acerbic." And so it goes for words as needed. (2) Boolean logic allows one to find the word for an uncertain phrase.

And...

There are numerous dictionaries other than those published by the four publishers just examined. Many of them are good to excellent. The big three publishers are: Oxford University Press, Chambers and Collins. Closer to home, see the *Canadian Oxford Dictionary* (2000) which claims to have 2,000 "distinctly Canadian words and meanings," out of the 130,000 entries. This is not to say only the four have a hammarlock on the best dictionaries published in England and other English language countries. Other firms compete so it is a matter of carefully reading before selecting any desk dictionary.

Even the standard desk dictionary can be modified, e.g., *Encarta World Dictionary* (New York: St. Martin's Press, 1999, 2,078 pp. $50). After a rocky start (as explained earlier in this chapter) and after additions and corrections it emerges more as a curiosity than a working dictionary. Published in England and available in the United States in print, as well as a CD-ROM and online, this has only about 100,000 main entries. The difference is that of these over 3,000 are non-American terms from such areas as the Caribbean, Africa, South Asia and, in fact, most of the world. All are in English. Another selling point: lots of new words and slang, although each is so modified by politically correct warnings about use that it is hardly worth the effort. Finally: the inclusion of *Roget's Thesaurus*, a computer dictionary, style guide and an almanac as well as a book of quotations turns this into a bit of an encyclopedia as well as a dictionary. Is it worth it? No, as standard works have most of the same words, better definitions and, yes, some 50,000 or more added words at about half the cost. At the same time, larger libraries will want it to augment the linguistics collection. A more serious charge leveled against *Encarta* is made by critics. They point out the politically correct warnings are as excessive as the definitions are repetitious and inconsistent.

Reduced-Word Dictionaries

Many dictionaries are limited to under 60,000 words. Some of these are available in paperback and from the same publishers of the standard desk works. Others are from equally reliable firms. For example, the *Oxford American Dictionary* (New York and London: Oxford University Press) has only

30,000 words. *The Concise Oxford Dictionary of Current English* from the same publisher has 50,000 words, and there are other versions from Oxford.

CHILDREN'S DICTIONARIES

CD: Macmillan Dictionary for Children. New York: The Macmillan Company, 2000 to date, irregular update. $60.
    Print: 2000, 900 pp. $15.

CD: The World Book Dictionary in *The World Book Multimedia Encyclopedia.* Chicago, IL: World Book Publishing, 1992 to date, annual. $395.

Print: 2000, 2 vols. $79. *Print: Scott, Foresman Beginning Dictionary.* Glenview, IL: Scott, Foresman, 2000, 832 pp. $17.95.

CD: Merriam-Webster's Dictionary for Kids. Springfield, MA: Merriam-Webster, Inc., 2000. $59.95.
    Print: Webster's Elementary Dictionary, 2000, 607 pp. $12.95.

There are as many, if not more, dictionaries for children as for adults. (See: "Children's Dictionaries," *Booklist: Reference Books Bulletin,* October 15, 2000, pp. 475+ where all major titles are briefly reviewed.) The reason is easy to see: There are many school libraries and all of them require not just one dictionary, but different ones to fit different grade levels. It is, in a word, a lucrative market for publishers.

Are they of equal worth? It is the same story as for adult works. A few publishers are responsible for the accepted titles. And these few are generally the same publishers who issue the adult dictionaries. World Book; Scott Foresman; and Macmillan are exceptions in that they concentrate on children and young people's dictionaries rather than adult titles.

The works are usually graded for preschool through elementary grades, for junior high school or equivalent, and for high school. The rub is that by junior high school, students should be able to use adult desk dictionaries and not need special works for their age group. Obviously, some teachers (and librarians) do not agree. If they did, there would not be the specialized dictionaries for younger people. A case can be made for elementary grades, and most would agree that at this level at least, the younger dictionary is preferable to the adult work.

The four listed here are the ones most often found in school and public libraries along with the standard adult works for beyond elementary grades. They are four out of almost 50 possibilities. Many of the 50 are spin-offs of the basic four titles from the publishers. For example, Macmillan has about 10 related works. On the other hand, World Book has only the single title. The CD-ROM *Macmillan Dictionary* is typical of what is likely to be a developing group. It has the complete text of the printed volume (i.e., 12,000 words and approximately 1,000 illustrations) plus the necessary animation and sound effects to make looking up words much fun. There are several word games as well. In addition to the careful, easy-to-understand definitions, the dictionary offers word histories and language notes. The animated character "Zac" provides a guided tour showing the beginner how to get started. From time to time Zac pops up with comments about this or that word. The whole is for the reader who is from seven to twelve years old, although it may be used by younger and older children. While a bit crude, it is at least a beginning.

Librarians often favor the print *Macmillan Dictionary* over all the others because: (1) It has 35,000 entries for grades 2 through 6, although it may be used by younger or older students. (2) It has 1,000 illustrations in color. (3) It uses simple easy-to-understand definitions with numerous illustrative phrases and sentences. (4) Its pronunciations, given at the end of the definition, are clear. (5) It contains added materials such as maps, lists of presidents, and so forth.

All this adds up to a work a trifle too elementary for some, and it lags in including new words which may be used regularly on, say, MTV. Nevertheless, because it is so easy to use and so easy to understand, librarians have found many children prefer it.

The *World Book Dictionary* has 225,000 entries. It has from 125,000 to 200,000 more words than its rivals. This makes it the "unabridged" dictionary for children and young people. The dictionary follows the familiar Thorndike-Barnhart system of using definition words which are within the grasp of the reader. One does not have to turn to other entries to find the meaning of words used in a definition. The definitions are models of clarity, although a sophisticated adult is likely to find many of them much too simple. The format is good, and the illustrations, although not up to the number in the *American Heritage,* are at least clear and placed properly. The *World Book Dictionary* is available on CD-ROM as part of the digital version of the fine encyclopedia. The dictionary has the advantage of being closely tied to the information work. Words can be called up for definition and explanation as found in the text of the encyclopedia, or separately.

Scott, Foresman publishes a series of dictionaries that include titles for the elementary grades through high school. The beginning version for elementary grades 1 to 5 is typical, and is based on the Thorndike-Barnhart system, which relies heavily on illustrations. About 75 percent of the pictures are in color. Some words have histories set off in a different-colored ink. The whole is in a pleasing format, but is as much for instruction as for definitions.

Equally an opinion winner among librarians is *Webster's Elementary Dictionary.* It is somewhat similar to the Macmillan entry in terms of number of entries, (33,000) care of definitions used, and so forth. On the other hand, and this is a major difference, the publisher relies on quality rather than appeal to a special age group. The result is a true junior type of adult work rather than a specialized dictionary for children. The CD-ROM version, based on the printed work, has a new name *Merriam-Webster's Dictionary for Kids* and is distributed in the United States by Mindscape. It appeared first in 1994 and contains the same number of words and definitions as the printed work. The digital version has phonetic pronunciations for 20,000 of the 33,000 entries, 200 animations, 500 color illustrations, word games, and approximately 200 sound effects.

Which is best among the numerous children's dictionaries? To reach consensus much depends on whether the work is used in a classroom, in home, or in a library. Among the titles listed here one could not go wrong in selecting any depending on purpose and age of the prospective user. Considering the basic works for preschool through high school, and the numerous spin-offs (for grade levels), any of the dictionaries by the firms listed will be good to excellent.

THESAURUS/SYNONYMS AND ANTONYMS

Online and CD-ROM: See "Desk (College) Dictionaries" section. Most of the basic college dictionaries are not only online and on CD-ROM, but include a built-in thesaurus. Also part of *Microsoft Bookshelf.*
Print: Roget's Thesaurus of English Words and Phrases. New York: Penguin Books, 1998, 1,381 pp. $19.

A book of synonyms often is among the most popular books in the private or public library. It offers a key to crossword puzzles, and it serves almost everyone who wishes to increase his or her command of English. There are some 50 dictionaries giving both synonyms and antonyms in English, but the titles listed above appear more often in libraries. Certainly, the best known is the work of Peter Mark Roget (1779-1869), a doctor in an English mental asylum. He began the work at age 71 and by his ninetieth birthday had seen it through 20 editions. (The term *thesaurus* means a "treasury," a "store," a "hoard"; and *Roget's* is precisely that.)

His optimistic aim was to classify all human thought under a series of verbal categories, and his book is so arranged. There are approximately 1,000 classifications. Within each section, headed by a key word, are listed, by parts of speech, the words and phrases from which the reader may select the proper synonym. Antonyms are usually placed immediately after the main listing; thus, "possibility/impossibility," "pride/humility."

> The advantage of *Roget's* is that like ideas are placed together. The distinct disadvantage is that *Roget's* offers no guidance or annotations; and an overzealous user may select a synonym or an antonym which looks and

sounds good but is far from expressing what is meant. Even though Roget's is often misused and abused by those desperately in search of a style, the book remains one of the English language's greatest achievements. Every language has a dictionary, but not everyone needs a thesaurus. Where a dictionary offers definitions, the thesaurus suggests associations; while the dictionary works from word to thing, the thesaurus works in reverse; while a dictionary is a book of bare reason, the thesaurus is a work of conjecture and imagination; dictionaries seize words, and make them static, the thesaurus frees them and makes them mobile; dictionaries are for grammarians, the thesaurus is for dreamers. Most brilliant of all, the thesaurus contains no history, suggests no tradition, and makes no attempt to clarify, justify or explain its inclusions. It is pure poetry.[9]

There are at least a dozen titles which freely use Roget's name. Like Webster's, the name Roget cannot be copyrighted and is free to any publisher. Many of the dozen titles are little more than poor, dated copies of the master's original work.

The Penguin edition, edited by Betty Kirkpatrick, follows the traditional pattern, but with 5,000 modern words and phrases added, for example "air kissing" with "salutation" and "Le Shuttle" with the "Orient Express." It is the first revision for ten years.

The various online and CD-ROM versions of Roget pretty much follow the master's original plan. The advantage, at least for some, is that often the words are called up in alphabetical order.

On the Web

With numerous print thesaurus about, as well as combined on the Web with standard dictionaries, there is little reason to turn to a specific thesaurus on the Web. (Also, of course, standard word processing programs include a thesaurus). Still, if one wishes there are numerous thesaurus on the Net. Among the best:

Synonym Dictionary (http://vacouver-Webpages.com/synonyms.html). "Please enter an English word, usually a singular noun such as car or ladder." And that's about all there is to it. The synonym then appears. More subtle searches can be done by entering one or more alternate spellings or single word close synonyms, e.g., "automobile for car." Classes of words may be entered as well. Thanks to these added features this university Web page particularly is useful for more extensive searches for synonyms.

[9]Ian Sansom, "Midwife and undertaker to the imagination," *Guardian Weekly*, August 23,1998, p. 29.

Roget's Internet Thesaurus (www.thesaurus.com). This is about as simple to use as any online dictionary. Type in the wanted word, and the synonyms and antonyms appear. ("Help" resulted in 14 entries.) If a definition is needed for any of the words, it can be clicked on for the complete definition.

Usage and Manuscript Style

CD: The Chicago Manual of Style, 14th ed. Chicago: University of Chicago Press, 1993, in *Microsoft Bookshelf.*
Print: 936 pp. $40.

Print: The Columbia Guide to Online Style. New York: Columbia University Press, 1998, 224 pp. $34; paper, $17.50. *Print:* Turabian, Kate. *A Manual for Writers of Term Papers, Theses, and Dissertations,* 4th ed. Chicago: University of Chicago Press, 1987, 300 pp. $20. Paperback, $7.95.

Print: Webster's Dictionary of English Usage. Springfield, MA: Merriam-Webster, Inc., 1989, 980 pp. $18.95.

"Who uses language guidebooks?" asks author John Updike. "Editors, seeking to impose order and clarity on the torrents of prose that flow through their publications, have recourse to them."[10] And much the same might be said for laypersons and students seeking "to impose order and clarity" on their own writing. That is what style manuals are all about.

The Chicago Manual of Style is the standard guide to good English. First and foremost, the *Manual* is an aid for preparation of papers, either for publication or for a class. Second, these days it shows how to employ electronic databases for everything from indexing to footnotes. Third, it has significant, accepted advice on nitty-gritty matters from the proper use of authors' initials to arrangement of citations as references, footnotes, additional readings, and the like. There are sections, too, with definitions of book and paper terms, copyright information, and related areas. It is a standard for all libraries and for many individuals.

The electronic databases pose a problem for traditional rules of style. Most standard titles listed here have sections on how to cite, for example, a full text article online. There are a growing number of manuals given over almost entirely to the electronic media. The *Columbia Guide,* by Janice Walker and Todd Taylor, is one of the best. It gives over the first part to examples of citations that are based on the Modern Lan-

---

[10]John Updike, "Fine Points: Why we should still care about Fowler seventy years on," *The New Yorker,* December 20/30, 1996, p. 148.

guage Association form. This is enough for most readers. The more advanced scholars and those directly involved with online publications will use the second part that describes online document styles. For style form for the basic citations online, as well as for updates from time to time, turn to: (www.columbia.edu/cu/cup/cgos). This is not the whole book, only updates.

The MLA Style Manual (2nd ed. New York: Modern Language Association, 1998, 350 pp. $25) is a standard guide for college students, teachers and scholars. It moves from the publication process, and what is involved from the original idea to the finished book. A second chapter is on legal issues, including copyright. Still, the major part of the guide sets the rules for stylistic conventions and how to prepare papers or theses or dissertations. The second edition includes aids on how to cite online works as well as material found on a CD-ROM. Note: A variation on this manual is the *MLA Handbook for Writing Research Papers,* which is updated frequently. This is specifically for undergraduates and high school students preparing papers.

Turabian, as *A Manual For Writers* is often called, is an even more specific work for students. It is updated regularly and is, in a real sense, a shorter version of the *Chicago Manual.* Here one finds specific rules for everything from grammar and footnotes to the type of paper to employ. It also discusses rules concerning punctuation, spacing, and indexing. There are discussions of how to cite computer sources, nonprint material, the meaning of cataloging in publications, and even how an author should phrase a letter when sending a publisher a manuscript.

Webster's Dictionary of English Usage offers direct advice and clear instructions as to proper usage. It is highly recommended for all libraries as an up-to-date, easy-to-follow guide. Arranged alphabetically from "a, an" to "zoom" it is extremely easy to use. The editors tend to follow the prescriptive school, as does the publisher, but there is a discussion of different points of view. See, for example, the ubiquitous "ain't" and some 10 columns of discourse with scores of illustrative quotes. There are 20,000 such quotations used throughout to emphasize this or that point of usage. See, too: *A Dictionary of Modern American Usage* (New York: Oxford, 1998) which is narrower in scope, but useful for its emphasis on ordinary speech.

The New Fowler's Modern English Usage (Oxford: Oxford University Press, 1996) is a revision of H. W. Fowler's famous revised reference work of 1926. The older guide remains a revered name among those who believe in the prescriptive rules of grammar. There appeared some major cracks, even chasms, in this traditional approach in the new edition, edited by R.W. Burchfield. The latest editor takes strong exception to the rules set down for the "King's English" descriptive school. Libraries are advised to have both the latest and the earlier editions, as there is considerable difference between each.[11]

On the Web

There is little on the Net that compares with the scope of the print and grammar manuals. The nearest to acceptance is the *Guide to Grammar and Writing* sponsored by a Hartford Connecticut college (http://webster. comment.edu/grammar/index/html). This is primarily, though, a guide to basic grammar for students, and while good enough, it is hardly useful for more sophisticated readers. Excellent links to related sites.

The Slot (www.theslot.com). A copy editor for *The Washington Post*, Bill Walsh, runs this website which concentrates on the finer points of good English. The basic section, "The Curmudgeon's Stylebook" is divided by eight categories (word choice to use of punctuation) and there is a word by word index of 20 or so pages. The index begins with the proper use of acronyms and the use of "about." It follows the same pattern throughout so the puzzled student or layperson can find almost all answers to style questions in this excellent source—a source, by the way, which is constantly being updated. Note: The editor follows the *Associated Press Stylebook*.

MLA-Style Citations of Electronic Sources. University of South Florida (www.cas.usf.edu/english/walker/mla.html). Using specific examples of common student papers, Janice Walker, a member of the University of South Florida English Department, demonstrates the Modern Language Association's rules for citing material which appears on the Net and in other electronic sources. An excellent, easy-to-follow style sheet that is the first place to turn when the student is using Net citations.

Note: For complex citation problems see *The Internet Public Library Citing Electronic Resources* (www.ipl.org). This has a dozen links to citation rules as well as a half dozen print sources.

---

[11]See Updike, *op. cit.*, pp. 142–49 for an extensive review of the new Fowler. Online Fowler is available free (www.barleby.com/116) but only the 1908 first edition. Over the years this has been drastically rewritten and updated. As a consequence many of the "rules" are antiquated.

HISTORICAL DICTIONARIES

Online: Oxford English Dictionary (OED) Online, New York: Oxford University Press, 2000 to date, www.oed.com. Library: $795+. Individuals: $550.
CD: The Oxford English Dictionary (OED) 2nd Edition on CD-ROM. 1992 to date, not updated. $895.
Print: 1989, 20 vols. $2500. (On sale 1998–1999: $995). Additional series: vol. 1 (234 pp.); vol. 2 (234 pp.), vol. 3 (234 pp.) $35 each.

CD: The New Shorter Oxford English Dictionary on CD-ROM, New York: Oxford University Press, 1998. $75.
Print: The New Shorter Oxford English Dictionary, 1998, 2 vols. 3,776 pp. $100.

Of all the dictionaries of the English language, the *Oxford English Dictionary* (begun as the *New English Dictionary on Historical Principles*) is the most magnificent, and it is with some justification that H. L. Mencken called it "the emperor of dictionaries." The purpose of the dictionary is to trace the history of the English language. This is done through definitions and quotations that illustrate the variations in the meaning and use of words.

Author and critic Hugh Kenner ranks the *OED* as the single "epic" of reference works, or, for that matter, the one epic of the nineteenth century. If *Paradise Lost* is the epic of the seventeenth century, *Gibbon's Decline and Fall* of the eighteenth, and Joyce's *Ulysses* of the twentieth, then the *OED* is the nineteenth century's unparalleled achievement. The *OED's* first fascicle was published when the Irish author of *Ulysses* was two years old, and the last when *Ulysses* itself was six. Work on the great dictionary began about the middle of Victoria's and Tennyson's century.

The dictionary defines 616,500 words and supports the definitions and usage with some 2.5 million quotations. In *Webster's New World Dictionary* the etymology of *black* takes 5 lines, whereas in the *OED* it takes 23 lines. The entry on "set" alone is 60,000 words long. By comparison, Milton's *Paradise Lost* has just under 80,000 words. The word *point* in the *OED* consumes 18 columns and *put* accounts for 30 columns. (This is an observation of fact, not a criticism. After all *Webster's* is in one volume, while the *OED* is in 20.)

The online *OED* searching system is simplicity itself. One enters in a word for a quick search and the full entry of the print dictionary appears. There are numerous methods of narrowing or making the search wider, e.g., one may choose words from the vulgate Bible to twentieth century texts (1900–1941). Success of the system is based on a careful analysis of the software by teachers and librarians. Based on such research the company itself, rather than a vendor, as is usual, supervised the online edition.

The digital *OED* is a best buy for libraries paying under $800, but for most (i.e., large libraries) the cost runs to $8,500 plus. This may give pause, particularly if there are not that many people about using the online edition. It is more compact than the printed set and most important, it gives the user access points impossible to find in print. Just what can one do with the digital besides checking out the history, definition, spelling and so forth, of a single word? Many things: (1) Search for quotes with key words from among the 2.5 million possibilities in the work. Quotations may be isolated by date, author, title of work and the text. One can, for example, find every quotation with the word "football." (2) Find words from the definitions, that is if one only knows "conspicuously bad" the computer will turn up "egregious" as one possible word. (3) Filter headwords by part of speech or date. (4) Follow the close to 600,000 cross-references to pursue a given word or idea in its multiple forms. (5) List all the words that have entered the language from French, German, and so forth. (6) List every word ending in "q" and identify every adverb that does not end in "ly." (7) Select entries according to the earliest quotation cited. And much, much more.

Thanks to sometimes pages of variations and quotes about a single word, phrase or concept, the *OED* is an excellent sophisticated thesaurus. For example, how many words are there for muddy and muddy places? Here one might turn to a thesaurus, but if a complete record is wanted, at least in the English language, an even better choice is the CD-ROM version of the *OED*. Ask for all the words including mud in their definition and the results are astonishing. In all there are over 111 words with muddy in their definitions, and 313 whose definitions include the word mud. The next time a synonym is wanted why not try: dub: a muddy pool or puddle; or riley: thick turbid mud; or limicolous: living in mud. If you fall into the latter category you are a person besmotted (splattered with mud) or someone bymodered (smeared with mud).[12]

Editors keep a running file on new words and neologisms. For example, the OED is considering "fashionista," a noun which has crept into the fashion world and means a dedicated follower of fashion; in extreme cases a fashion victim. This is keeping company with "meatspace," which is the opposite of cyberspace and refers to real people in the flesh and blood world.

Work on the third edition began in the early 1990s, and by 2000 the publisher had issued, in print, several volumes of the third that will become part of the proposed revision, that is, identified as *Oxford Eng-*

---

[12]"Weather wise," *The Independent*, March 9, 1998, p. 2.

lish Dictionary Additional Series. Volume 2 appeared in late 1997 and is typical. There are 18,000 examples of "sage" which came to Oxford each month from some 60 readers around the world. Quotes float in from not only books, but newspapers, magazines, manuals, television and even other dictionaries. Among the new words and phrases: "bungee-jump-ing," "feelgood," "post structuralism," and "virtual reality." Each of the first two volumes contains about 3,000 words, meanings, or earlier cita-tions for words. Actually, these serve as supplements to the main set until a third edition is published. And when will that be? According to Oxford University Press, it will be around 2010. (The digital edition, though, will absorb new words and additions as they are passed for the print edi-tion. As a result the online will, as usual, be considerably more current than print.) Today thousands of volunteers are helping gather revisions, new items, new etymological and bibliographical information from the ever-growing body of scholarly literature as well as popular material. All of this will be part of the new edition.[13] The real question: "Is a print edition needed, if the whole of the revised *OED* is available digitally,?" The answer for most libraries is the digital edition, particularly online. Only large research centers will need the print version as well.

Shorter OED

The CD-ROM version of the *Shorter Oxford English Dictionary* features: pre-cisely what is found in the print edition. For a simple definition almost any print dictionary will do as well, but for in depth searching the CD, as usual, is a winner. Beyond the simple search for a word one may search an index for abbreviations, phrases, headwords, etc. If this is not enough, there is a full text search available (seeking, for example, all quotations with pears and apples in the quotes). Special search patterns allow run-ning down rhymes, phonetics, etc. There are only about 170,000 entries under 100,000 headwords. Actually, one has more definitions in the aver-age desk dictionary, but the reader will not find better history, better examples, and, often, more current words. It is an excellent source for tracing the history of words, but here that history begins only at 1700. Anything earlier requires using the full *OED.*

---

[13]The project cost of the project in 2000: $50 million. The next edition will be a minimum of 30 volumes as contrasted with 20 volumes in the present work. For a fascinating article on the revisions see "The Oxford English Dictionary Revision Program" on the *OED's* website at (www.oed.com). See, too: David Tyckoson, "What Were They Thinking," *Against the Grain,* September, 2000, pp. 38–42. The reference expert gives an excellent presentation on the high online cost of the work and what might be done to bring the price down. "The OED Adds the Web to its Lexicon," *The New York Times,* November 5, 1998, p. G1+. The online edition appeared in England in early 2000. For detailed reviews see: *The Times,* March 7, 2000, p. 13; *The Times,* March 16, 2000, p. 19.

American Regional Dictionaries

Print: Dictionary of American Regional English (DARE). Cambridge, MA: Harvard University Press, 5 vols.; in progress. Price varies.

While the *OED* remains the "Bible" of the linguist or the layperson tracing the history and various meanings of a word, it is not the best place to go for correct usage, at least for Americans. English-speaking Americans and English-speaking Britons actually come close to using two different languages, the latter, of course, being recorded in the *OED*. A decision was made that in the *OED* supplements more attention would be paid to American words, particularly as most of these are now familiar to Europeans or to viewers of American television and films and readers of American magazines. In fact, since 1970, the *OED* is better than many American dictionaries at providing careful definitions and the history of new and slang American words.

The *Dictionary of American Regional English* assembles colloquial expressions and their meanings from 50 states. The monumental project began in 1965, and specially trained workers spent five years interviewing nearly 3,000 Native Americans in over 1,000 communities. In addition to the interviews, material for the *Dictionary of American Regional English,* often referred to as *DARE,* has been gathered from countless printed sources including regional novels, folklore journals, newspapers, and diaries.

Aside from curiosity, what practical value does a dictionary like *DARE* have for laypersons? An example: suppose you are a medical school graduate who grew up in Seattle. Your first job is in the Appalachians. How could you diagnose complaints such as "ground itch" or "dew poison" or "sore leaders" or "pones" unless you had *DARE* on hand to translate the local ailments into medical jargon. Then there is the Unabomber who was traced in part by his use of language—language found in various dictionaries including DARE. Obviously, the work is equally of value to all libraries. And what about words not found in the dictionary. In that case the editors plead for help, e.g., contact them online at (http://polyglot.lss.wisc.edu/dare/dare/html). Note: the dictionary itself as of 2000 is not online, but may be by the time this page is read.

In any discussion of the history of the American language, there is one outstanding work which many have enjoyed reading, literally from cover to cover. This is Henry Mencken's *The American Language* (New York: Alfred A. Knopf, Inc., 1919 to 1948). In three volumes, the sage of Baltimore examines a very large proportion of all American words in a style and manner that are extremely pleasing and always entertaining and informative. The initial one-volume work of 1919 was supplemented with two additional volumes. All are easy to use as each volume has a detailed index.

Speaking Freely: A Guided Tour of American English From Plymouth Rock to Silicon Valley (New York: Oxford University Press, 1997). Originally edited by Stuart Flexner as *Listening to America and I Hear America Talking*, this version is by Ann Soukhanov. No matter. The purpose is the same— to list in alphabetical order the words and phrases which often puzzle and amuse readers. It is filled with history and gossip. Benjamin Franklin, for example, had more than 200 synonyms of drunk. Among them were nimptopiscal, cherry-merry and oiled.

In tracing the history of words the *OED* goes back only to the Norman Conquest (1066). With that event, "modern English" began to form and was completed by about 1500. Earlier English, earlier history will be found in the *Dictionary of Old English,* a sprawling 30-year project by the University of Toronto. (By 1999 the staff was only on the letter G, but with luck and finance the work should be completed by 2012.) The dictionary will map approximately 35,000 words of English in use between the years 600 AD, when Christianity came to Britain, and 1100 AD, just after the Norman Conquest.

Slang

Print: Random House Historical Dictionary of American Slang. New York: Random House, 1994 to date, 3 vols. Price varies.

In the past most of the vulgar, four-letter words simply were not included in dictionaries. Today even the desk dictionary includes the common words and expressions. Most are labeled, usually as "offensive."

The common desk dictionaries also list and define words that describe people who are physically or mentally lacking *(loony, fatty)*; slang terms for religious or ethnic groups (from *WASP to wop*); designations for women *(doll, tomato)*; slang terms for homosexuals, and so forth. All of these terms should be clearly labeled to show that they are far from acceptable. Today the committee of the "Reference Books Bulletin" considers a dictionary remiss if it refuses to include such words—carefully labeled, to be sure, as "vulgarisms" or "unacceptable." Other reviewers, aside from those evaluating children's works, take much the same attitude.

The library needs dictionaries of slang because: (1) Most dictionaries do not indicate the variations of meaning given slang terms or words. Few trace their history, which is a part of the history of a nation's popular culture. (2) Readers come across expressions that are not defined well in an ordinary dictionary. (3) Authors look for words to convey the background, class, or occupation of a given character, and the slang dictionary is a fine place to double check such words. (4) Readers indicate just plain curiosity and interest in the language.

A fascinating aspect of slang is that as a concept it appears to be relatively recent. Chaucer and Shakespeare used ribald language, but there is no indication either author, or their audience, considered the words in a special category. The point is obvious. Before you can have slang you must have a public awareness of standard language from which deviants spring. Only with mass education in the nineteenth century did the awareness of slang become widespread.

The first volume of the *Random House Dictionary of American Slang* appeared in 1994 and the third and final volume is to be published in late 2000. The over 300,000 entries are the work of J. E. Lighter, an English instructor at the University of Tennessee who spent more than two decades tracking down the history of unusual words. When complete the dictionary will record lexicographic information on all major slang words and phrases coined in the United States from Colonial times to the present. As with the larger historical dictionaries, the word is defined and then its development in chronological order of first use is shown. Quotations are used as supporting evidence. In fact, this "has to be the only guide to the English language ever published to quote 'Public Enemy' and 'The Valley Girl Handbook' more often than Henry James or the Bible."

Words and phrases are drawn equally from Shakespeare to *Penthouse*, Beckett to Butt-head, and from numerous television shows. Dates are given for the first appearance. In the 1997 volume, for example, "out to lunch" dates to 1955 while "longhair" (an intellectual) goes back to 1920. The 1997 volume (H–O) opens with "happy camper" and "hairhopper" (someone who frequently changes hair styles) to "ootchima-gootchi" (love-making) and "out of sight."

The editor of the *Random House Historical Dictionary of American Slang* points out that "slang tends to flourish in subcultures that employ a particular vocabulary as a sign of status, solidarity or inclusion: among, for instance, teenagers, drug users, athletes, ethnic groups and military personnel. The aspect of human behavior that seems to have produced the most slang is sex.[14] In the last few decades, mass communications have vastly accelerated the dissemination of slang, and recent shifts in political, racial and cultural attitudes have been rapidly reflected in slang usage as well, in both the entry of new expressions in mainstream speech and in changing meanings for old phrases."[15]

---

[14] The word with the most variations—and accordingly the most pages (12) in the first volume was a vulgarism beginning with F.

[15] *Books of the Times*, November 18, 1997, p. E6. Anyone who wishes to study slang in a cultural, historical way is advised to turn to the excellent *Swearing: A Social History of Foul Language, Oaths and Profanity in English* (New York: Penguin, 1998).

There are numerous less expensive dictionaries of slang, most of which are found in *Guide to Reference Books*. And they are published each year. *The Cassell Dictionary of Slang* (London: Cassell, 1999) is an example. This has over 70,000 words and expressions from the 16th century to the present in the English speaking world. Note, too, the *Cassell Dictionary* list of slang websites.

FOREIGN LANGUAGE DICTIONARIES (BILINGUAL)

Print: The HarperCollins Series, all published by HarperCollins of New York and London. Different editions, different dates, various pagination, and so forth. *HarperCollins-Robert French Dictionary, HarperCollins Spanish Dictionary, HarperCollins German Dictionary,* and so on. Price range: $7.99 paperback to $55.00 hardbound.

Readers are familiar with the typical bilingual print dictionary which offers the foreign word and the equivalent English word. The process is then reversed with the English word first, followed by the equivalent foreign word. For other than large public, academic, and special libraries, the print bilingual dictionary is quite enough. The HarperCollins entries are standard, familiar desk dictionaries. Most have gone through numerous editions and revisions by many editors. Pronunciation is given clearly enough for even the amateur to follow, and the equivalent words are accurate. All the dictionaries usually include slang words, colloquialisms, idioms, and more common terms from various subject areas. The number of main entries varies from 40,000 in paperback to 120,000 to 130,000 in hardback.

There are several other reputable publishers of basic print foreign language dictionaries. Cassell (by Sterling Publishing in the United States), Random House, Charles Scribner's Sons, Simon and Schuster, and Oxford University Press, as well as Cambridge University Press, are only a few of the better-known, reliable publishers of works which range from French to Swahili.

Larger and specialized libraries will have dictionaries of other countries. Larousse is the venerable French publisher of dictionaries (and encyclopedias). University libraries are likely to have several of the Larousse bi-lingual dictionaries such as *Larousse French Dictionary* or the *Petit Larousse en Couleurs,* a common title found in most French homes. Equally basic dictionaries from other countries will be purchased.

The person who simply seeks a common foreign word or phrase is likely to find the answer in almost any desk dictionary as either part of the main dictionary or set off in a special edition. When it comes to more sophisticated, specialized words, the choice is to turn to a bilingual dictionary. Even those who have no idea of mastering Spanish, for example, turn to a Spanish dictionary for more detailed entries than found in the standard bilingual edition. And this type of person is increasing in numbers as travel increases. This same individual is more likely than not to wonder about slang and street terms rarely found in the bilingual work. Here HarperCollins, for one, marks such words with little stars. In the *Harper-Collins Spanish Dictionary* the user finds one star means "the expression, while not forming part of standard language, is used by all educated speakers in a relaxed situation." Three stars, though, indicates "words liable to offend in any situation." Note: There are numerous guides and encyclopedias which consider various languages. One of the best: *Encyclopedia of the Languages of Europe* (Oxford: Blackwell, 1998) which is a guide to nearly 300 languages, both in current use and no longer spoken. See, too, the related: *Dictionary of Languages* (New York: Columbia University Press, 1999), an encyclopedic guide to 400 living and extinct languages.

There are bilingual and foreign language digital dictionaries, translation aids, and language lessons. Digital is useful in three situations: (1) Hear the foreign word pronounced correctly. (2) When one wants to compare or find words in more than a single language, and (3) when the user wants to retrieve simple translations of a specified word in business, technology, science, and so on. These and other translation programs are available for as little as $60.

Numerous CD-ROMs will help the beginner take first steps towards mastering a language. Typical, inexpensive and recommended: *Berlitz Passport to 31 Languages* (New York: Learning Corporation, 1999 to date, $30 for three disks). This is ideal for reference work, if not for individuals who only need one or two languages on a CD. For each language there are 2,500 key words shown on screen and pronounced. To this are added 300 phrases for ordering a meal to finding a bathroom. And all of this can be mastered from Arabic and Chinese to Turkish and Vietnamese. Learning to ask for a glass of water in 31 languages will be useful, of course, for anyone trying to bring conversation to a standstill at a dinner party.

Ideally the day may come when the traveler can carry a simple recorder that will receive a foreign language, translate it, and feed it back as English to the user. This is a long, long way off. "Not one translator is ever going to lose their job because of machine translation, not in the foreseeable future, says an expert at a computer systems and consulting company."[16] Meanwhile, the computer can help the layperson where a machine translation is a rough guide and not a final translation.

[16] *The New York Times,* April 30, 1998, p. G7. As the story points out even advertisements often do not fare well with translation software. For example, the M&Ms ad "Melts in your mouth, not in your hands" becomes in French "Funtes dans votre bouche, pas dans des vos mains," which ends up as "Pig iron and cast iron in your mouth, not in your hands."

On the Web

There are an impressive number of English-foreign language or foreign anguage-English dictionaries available on the Internet. Most of these are the work of scholars and they are reliable. In fact, an advantage of the Net is that there are numerous bilingual dictionaries in scores of narrow language areas as well as the standard French, German, English, etc. types.

The *Michigan Electronic Library*. Dictionaries by Specific Language (http://mel.lib.mi.us/reference/REF-dict.html) is the number one place to turn for a foreign language-English dictionary on the Net. About two dozen are listed in alphabetical order and links are provided to each. As new dictionaries become available they are added to the list. While searching varies from title to title, the majority require little more than typing in the word (in English or in the foreign language). The definition and the word in the second language is given. A particularly useful site for out-of-the-way languages from Belarusian to Swahili.

Note: Related sites include: *Language Dictionaries and Translators* (http://rivendel.com/?ric/resources/dict.html) is a good listing of online dictionaries with links to translators. These are as varied as the Icelandic Translation Centre work as a dictionary which lists 202 German words and their Austrian equivalent. While a trifle messy and not well organized, it can be of help to the patient.

The best place to turn for foreign language dictionaries on the Net, *Eurodicautom* (www2.echo.lu/edic). ECHO, the European Commission Host Organization and branch of the European Community, offers a unique dictionary. Billed as "a translator's best friend on the Web" this offers to find the match for one word in the language of another country. One establishes the "source language," say English, and then the "target language" say German. The entry is the English "book" and the response is "buchen." Some ten languages may be checked. One can go from "book" in French to "book" in Spanish to "book" in English, etc. The system handles abbreviations, phrases, key words, etc. There are auxiliary services from the usual FAQs to "discussion forums."

Wordbot. Washington University (www.cs.washington.edu/homes/kgolden/wordbot.html). The term "wordbot" means "a robot assistant for looking up translations, definitions, synonyms, antonyms, references, etc. of words appearing in a document." Here the focus is on looking up words in basic European languages from Italian to Spanish. One may look up definitions as well as words from English to German to German to Spanish, etc. The system does much more, but for the average user its translations and definitions usually will be enough.

Now ePals.com is an educational website at (www.epals.com). This has an approach of special interest to e-mail fans. Here one may type in a message in English and then switch to French, German, Japanese, Italian, Spanish or Portuguese to convert the English to the other language. The sponsor claims this is the Internet's first e-mail service with language translations available. Note, too, other features: names of schools with foreign language programs in 182 countries and with an interest in pen pals; and materials from Scholastic which relate to translation and cultures abroad.

AltaVista translation services (www.babelfish.altavista.digital.com) has a similar program. One can write a letter, note or novel in English and then covert it to a foreign language. Nothing more to do than write what one wants translated. All basic languages are covered. For example, one may move from a French phrase to English, or from an English sentence to German, etc. Beware of some odd translations, though. And at all cost avoid idiomatic expressions or words and phrases with more than a single meaning.

A related site: *E-Lingo* (www.e-lingo.com) which is not as good as the *WebTranslator,* or even *AltaVista,* but can be useful as a double check for difficult words.

The Human-Languages Page (www.june29.com/hlp). This is a link to scores of historical and language dictionaries both modern and ancient. While primarily for linguists, the site offers open doors to out-of-the-way foreign language dictionaries, translations and information on some 50 different languages.[17]

SUBJECT DICTIONARIES

Subject dictionaries explain particular meanings of particular words in terms of professions, occupations, or areas of subject interest. Otherwise, of course, most of the material might be found in the unabridged dictionary, or desk dictionaries which are regularly updated and show an interest in adding new terms.

While all evaluative checks for the other dictionaries apply, there are also some special points to watch. The major question to ask when determining subject dictionary selection is: Does this title offer anything which cannot be found in a standard work now in the library? It is surprising, particularly in the humanities and social sciences, how

[17]Note: For further sites see the magazine *Yahoo!* (April, 1999, p. 129).

much of the needed information is readily available in a general English dictionary. Also:

1. Are the illustrations pertinent and helpful to either the specialist or the layperson? Where a technical work is directed to a lay audience, there should be a number of diagrams, photographs, or other forms of graphic art, which will make it easier for the uninitiated to understand the terms.

2. Are the definitions simply brief word equivalents, or is some effort made to give a real explanation of the word in the context of the subject?

3. Is the dictionary international in scope or limited chiefly to an American audience? This is a particularly valuable question for the sciences. Several publishers have met this need by offering bilingual scientific dictionaries.

4. Are the terms up-to-date? Again, this is a necessity in a scientific work, somewhat less in a social science dictionary, and perhaps of relatively little importance in a humanistic study.

Many of the subject dictionaries are virtually encyclopedic in terms of information and presentation. They use the specific-entry form, but the entry may run to much more than a simple definition.

There are several hundred English language subject dictionaries. These range from the *Microsoft Press Computer Dictionary* (Renton, WA: Microsoft, 1990 to date. Frequently updated) to *The Oxford Classical Dictionary* (3rd ed. Oxford: Oxford University Press, 1997). Descriptive annotations will be found in the latest *Guide to Reference Books* and *Guide to Reference Materials*. Name a trade, profession or hobby and there is a subject dictionary about.

On the Web

The Web normally features standard dictionaries, but in keeping with its own special vocabulary the student might want to begin with the *Ultimate Silicon Slang Page* (www.sabram.com/site/slang.html) which defines such cyberslang as "idea hamsters," i.e., people whose ideas move as fast as hamsters: "That guy or gal is a real idea hamster." A more conventional, print dictionary in this area is the third edition of *The New Hacker's Dictionary* (Cambridge: MIT Press, 2000) an excellent source of geek-speak.

What follows are other dictionaries available free on the Net. To find others type in "dictionary-[subject]" in the box of a search engine and usually several possibilities present themselves. Note, though, that too many of these possibilities are either unreliable in that they are put up by individuals with mixed training or are, which is more the case, early editions of out of copyright works.

Two examples are listed, but they are typical of many more:

OneLook Dictionaries (www.onelook.com). This commercial site offers a wide variety of subject dictionaries (about 300 with some 1.75 million words) from sports to religion. The use is easy enough. Pick a subject, and under it are found the dictionaries—if any. When the area of interest is located, type in the word or words and the service indicates the quantity of matches in the various subject dictionaries. The definitions are brief, but accurate and cover all of the dictionaries that included the word. Most of these dictionaries originate online and few are in print or on a CD-ROM. As a result numerous titles may have no more than 98 to under 1,000 words.

Free On-line Dictionary of Computing. Dennis Howe (http://foldoc. doc.ic.ac.uk/foldoc/index.html). A dictionary built by contributors, this follows the normal pattern of the user typing in a needed word. Note, though, it is limited to computing terms and is not a general work. A definition and related entry material appears. Where there is a problem, "all entries whose headings start with your search string" appear. This is maintained in the United Kingdom and some of the words and definitions, by over 700 contributors to FOLDOC, may not always meet North American needs.

Abbreviations and Acronyms

Print: Acronyms Initialisms, and Abbreviations Dictionary, Farmington Hills, MI: Gale Group. Regularly updated. 3 vols. Price varies.

The basic guide in this field is the Gale publication. It is in three volumes. The first volume has over 520,000 entries for acronyms, initialisms, and related matters. These are listed alphabetically, and the full meaning of the term is then given. Most of the focus is on the United States, but acronyms from western Europe are included. The second volume is really two softbound supplements issued between editions. They provide about 15,000 new acronyms in two sequences, by acronym and by meaning. The third volume is a "backward," or "reverse," companion to the first volume, that is, one looks up one of the 520,000 entries to find the acronym. For example, one would turn here to find the acronym for the *Dictionary of American Regional English (DARE)*.

A smaller version is DeSola's *Abbreviations Dictionary* (New York: Elsevier, various editions) which has 180,000 entries and is about $65.

Crossword

CD: Webster's Official Crossword Puzzle Dictionary. Springfield, MA: Merriam-Webster, Inc., 1992, irregular update. $29.95.
Print: 1992. Paperback. $4.99.

The CD-ROM version of the typical crossword puzzle dictionary allows entry by either: (1) the phrase or definition that is used in the puzzle or (2) the individual words. Actually, given the power of the CD-ROM it seems almost pointless to do a crossword puzzle. In fact, crossword purists say it is not fair to consult a dictionary. Still, when one is stuck and frustrated, the crossword puzzle can be solved by turning to dictionaries for synonyms and antonyms, or to this guide. The clues, that is, the typical entries, are listed in alphabetical order in print works with the key words to fill in the boxes. Little is left to chance, and an experiment indicates that from 50 to 70 percent of the queries put to the reader in a typical crossword puzzle can be answered here.

SUGGESTED READING

Appleyard, Bryan, "e-English Rules the Waves" *The Sunday Times,* March 19, 2000, pp. 47–49. A detailed review of the *Oxford English Dictionary* online gives both a history and a current appraisal of the work.

Arnold, Martin, "Loved Strictures in a Lenient Age," *The New York Times,* June 24, 1999, E3. Here is a review and history of one of the most famous guides to proper use of the American language: William Strunk and E.B. White *The Elements of Style* (New York: Allyn & Bacon, 1999). The fourth edition is based on the original 1919 work. Popular? Well, as of late 1999 some 10 million copies have been sold—primarily to college and high school students.

Dean, Paul, "Opening the Billgates," *The Times Literary Supplement,* October 1, 1999, pp. 3–4. "*Encarta* makes some grand claims." And most of them, according to this critic, are inflated. Dean believes it fails as a dictionary and as a confusing encyclopedia. "Neither as dictionary nor encyclopedia is it wholly reliable." The review is of value not so much for the judgment of the dictionary but for the methodology employed—a methodology which could be used to evaluate any dictionary.

Hullen, Werner. *English Dictionaries 800–1700.* Oxford: Clarendon Press, 1999. 525 pp. A history, this covers every major and minor development in English language dictionaries from the first through the early 18th century. The style is a bit pedestrian, and the detail is overwhelming, but no other source covers so much material.

"In the Dictionary Game," *The New York Times,* August 22, 1999, p. WK7. How do dictionary publishers decide what new words are to go into their work? Staying power and a long history helps, but there are other rules. These are explained, with numerous examples, by the publishers of five basic desk dictionaries.

Johnson, Paul, "Want to Know Us? Watch Our Lips," *The Spectator,* April 1, 2000, pp. 43–44. What makes an English person English, asks the historian? Answer: The language which has made its point by becoming global rather than limited to English speaking countries. Johnson traces the development of the language through its writers and dictionaries.

Willinsky, John, *Empire of Words: The Reign of the O.E.D.,* Princeton, NJ: Princeton University Press, 1995. The thesis of this fascinating history of the *OED* is that it was more than a catalog of the English language. It was part of a whole nation-building process. "It appeared in the age of empire, a period in which Great Britain was having all sorts of impacts on the world."

Winchester, Simon, *The Professor and the Madman: A Tale of Murder, Insanity and the Making of the Oxford English Dictionary.* New York: Viking, 1998. A fascinating true story about a paranoid murderer and lexicographer who spent 40 years in jail. A good deal of his time was given over to completing his personal library in his two cells and working on derivations, history and intricate definitions of words for the *Oxford English Dictionary.* The best-selling biography reinforces awe for the driven scholars who saw the first edition of the dictionary through 70 years to its publication.

CHAPTER ELEVEN
GEOGRAPHICAL SOURCES

Geographers call it the "geographic renaissance." Supported by new advances in science and computers, geography has become not only a discipline in itself, but a bridge among disciplines. An understanding of what can be done with maps, surveys, studies and automation "compels people to put together ideas they might not otherwise," points out a Harvard professor.[1]

The academic ascent of geography in the late 1990s came after some 50 years of neglect. Many universities had eliminated geography departments, and students educated after the 1960s rarely were exposed to geographical principles. "Geography was fine if you worked at Rand McNally or played Jeopardy. But when American scholars tackled persistent questions like why industrialization first took root in Europe instead of China or India, geography was played down."[2]

In response to such queries one may draw upon epidemiology, sociology, zoology, anthropology, botany, and history, but inevitably geography is the key to the puzzle. One may claim that Western culture based on Judeo-Christian and Enlightenment values is the major reason for the economic success of the West. At the same time the student must factor in a nation's geography, such as its rainfall which guarantees year round crops. Scholars argue which geographical factor is the most important, which accident of history a consideration. The fact remains that geography is now front and center stage in such discussions.

---

[1]David Landes, quoted in *The New York Times*, March 21, 1998, p. B7.
[2]*Ibid.*

Geography is very much a part of the library reference collection. Aside from the shelves of books in the general collection dealing with the subject, the reference section has a particular focus on maps and atlases. Other items in the collection, from indexes and travel books to magazines also will be employed.

Geographical Information Management

Geographic digital information programs are now relatively common. Software allows one to analyze data and link it to a specific location. This permits someone to find the right neighborhood to open a pizza outlet factory, or an opera house. Government census information, plugged into a geographic program, helps companies determine sales opportunities. Census software allows one to zoom in on a continent, country, state, city, and small section of a city right down to a particular block or point. It can be used to keep track of everything from population trends to the number of manhole covers.

The formal and informal collaboration between cartographers and the world of data has introduced a new type of librarian, the one in charge of the "geographical information management" center who may be running a "geographical information system" (GIS). Both policy and technology involve this librarian. She has the ability to give current, first-hand information on everything from a complete list of recorded plants in the San Francisco area to suggestions for easing traffic problems in New York City. The ability both to create maps at a computer terminal as well as target high-income groups within a city or region who might be interested in purchasing X or Y goods gives a new dimension to the graph, written report, and map. One may also map out educational, medical, and occupational needs for an area, city, or complete region.

Dark Side

There is another side to this optimistic view of maps. "The Disaster of Gallipoli, the first world war military campaign in which 42,000 allied troops lost their lives, was caused largely by the poor quality of the maps used by officers...troops had no idea of the terrain of the layout of the Turkish positions. Officers relied on maps from tourist guidebooks...which were at least 10 years out of date.[3]

The Russian government policy of publishing deliberately false maps (with wrong roads, cities placed in wrong places and even wrong names) is said to have done much to baffle the invading German armies in World War II.

[3] *The Sunday Times,* (of London) March 21, 1999, p. 12.

Coming up to date, in 1999 the Director of the Central Intelligence Agency revealed the CIA had targeted by mistake the Chinese Embassy in the air war over Yugoslavia. The accident was caused for lack of current maps. "Two Yugoslav commercial maps from 1989 and 1996, and a United States Government map produced in 1997 were used. None showed the current location of the Chinese Embassy, which was built in 1996. Only after the disaster did the CIA turn up in its files two maps that accurately placed the embassy."[4]

And Yet...

The previous marvels of geographic excitement rarely reach the general librarian. In most libraries geographical questions are more ordinary: "Where can I find a map of [this or that state, city, county, etc.]" or "Where is Albany, Oregon located?" or "How far is it between London, Ontario and Hamilton?" Standard atlases, road maps and similar basic reference works offer ready answers.

Geographical sources may be used at the mundane level ("Where is it?"), or in a more sophisticated way to help clarify linkages between human societies. Reference librarians are familiar with both approaches. The first, and the more common, is the typical question about where this or that town is located, the distance between points X and Y, and what type of clothing will be needed to travel in Italy in December. Moving away from the ready-reference query, one becomes involved with relationships concerning climate, environment, commodities, political boundaries, history, and everything with which geographers are deeply interested.

When she is asked to quickly identify a city or a country, the reference librarian has little difficulty matching the question with a source. Usually, the correct answer is in an atlas, an individual map, or a compilation of geographical data, which may be readily available on a CD-ROM or in an online database. Asked to establish the elements common to the Philippines and Ethiopia, the librarian must turn to both geographical sources and related works which, in this case, might range from the *Statesman's Yearbook* and an encyclopedia to the periodical and newspaper indexes for current events. Then, too, the librarian would wish to search the geographical texts and individual economic and political historical studies.

If the reference librarian thinks of the typical atlas or map as the center of a pool with ripples that may wash over scores of reference works, then geographical sources assume their true importance. Granted this type of use is limited to larger libraries, to a smaller group of people than those asking for help on finding a hotel in Paris or Peoria, but its impor-

[4]"In a Fatal Error..." *The New York Times,* July 23, 1999, p. A10.

tance and scope are likely to increase as the world shrinks, as trade and travel become increasingly widespread.

Mary Larsgaard, comfortable in both the technical and the day-by-day area of geographical queries, sums it up:

> Determining what references to collect depends on your patrons' interests and needs. Public libraries, serving a broader clientele, will want more basic atlases, dictionaries, and other print and nonprint resources as well as recreational maps, state and local maps, and street guides for major metropolitan areas, often issued by local commercial firms. Academic libraries will require more specialized materials that will support both their schools' curricula and the research demands of their faculty. With few exceptions—and that mainly in atlases (where names such as National Geographic, Rand McNally, and Times/Bartholomew predominate)—most of the publications in this field are produced by federal, state, and local governments.[5]

GEOGRAPHICAL SOURCES

No matter what format, geographical titles used in ready reference may be subdivided into three large categories: maps and atlases, gazetteers, and guidebooks.

Map and Atlases. A map is, among other things, a representation of certain boundaries of the earth (or the moon and planets as well) and we generally think of them as on a flat surface. Maps may be divided into charts, collections of maps in atlas form, globes, and so forth. Cartographers refer to these as *general* maps, that is, for general reference purposes.

A physical map traces the various features of the land, from the rivers and valleys to the mountains and hills. A route map shows roads, railroads, bridges, and the like. A political map normally limits itself to boundaries (e.g., towns, cities, counties, states) but may include topographical and route features. Either separately or together, these three types make up a large number of maps found in general atlases.

Cartography is the art of mapmaking, and a major headache of cartographers is achieving an accurate representation of the features of the earth. This task has resulted in various projections, that is, the method used to display the surface of a sphere upon a plane without undue distortion. Mercator and his forerunners devised a system, still the best known today, based on parallel lines; that is, latitude (the lines measur-

---

[5]Mary Larsgaard, "The World at Your Fingertips: Map Resources," *Library Journal,* July, 1999, p. 57. This annotated bibliography of basic sources usually appears in the *Library Journal* each year about the same time.

ing the "width" of the globe, or angular distance north or south from the equator) and longitude (the lines measuring the "length" of the globe, or angular distance east or west on the earth's surface). This system works well enough except at the polar regions, where it distorts the facts. Hence on any Mercator projection, Greenland is completely out of proportion to the United States. Since Mercator, hundreds of projections have been designed; but distortion is always evident—if not in one section, in another. For example, the much-praised azimuthal equidistant projection, with the North Pole at the center of the map, indicates directions and distances more accurately, but in other respects it gives a peculiar stretched and pulled appearance to much of the globe.

The only relatively accurate graphic representation of the earth is a globe. The need for a globe in a reference situation is probably questionable. The reference librarian who has had occasion to use a globe instead of a map to answer particular reference questions is rare indeed.

The average general map gives an enormous amount of information for the area(s) covered. Cities, roads, railroads, political boundaries, and other cultural elements are indicated. The physical features, from mountain ranges to lakes, are depicted. Relief is usually indicated by shading and contrast or color.

Libraries will primarily purchase *atlases,* or collections of maps. Libraries with larger holdings will include flat or sheet maps such as those distributed by the National Geographic Society or the traditional state and regional road maps.

Another large group of maps are termed *thematic,* in that they usually focus on a particular aspect of geographical interest. Reference here is usually to historical, economic, political, and related matters that may be shown graphically on a map. An example: *The Times Atlas of World History.*

Note: When speaking of flat maps, atlases, relief maps, and even globes it is assumed the reader appreciates that many, if not most of these are available in electronic format. Still, the content, no matter what the format, remains much the same.

Gazetteers. Gazetteers are geographical dictionaries, usually of place names. Here one turns to find out where a city, mountain, river, or other physical feature is located. Detailed gazetteers will give additional information on population and possibly leading economic characteristics of the area.

Guidebooks. Guidebooks hardly need a definition or introduction; they furnish information on everything from the price of a motel room in Paris or Kansas to the primary sights of interest in New York or London.

Government And Local Maps

Conservatively, at least 90 percent of maps published each year originate from government sources. They provide details of almost every area of the world, with particular emphasis on the United States. The "best buy" department for maps are those free on the Internet, brought to you by the United States Government. (These are detailed in the pages that follow.) For an overall view of what is available turn to the *Manual of Federal Geographic Data Products* (http://www.fgdc.gov/fgpd/title.html). This includes information from various agencies such as the Department of Commerce and the Department of Defense.

The U.S. Geological Survey (USGS) has a continuing publishing program whereby many librarians routinely receive maps as issued. The maps are detailed, covering elevation, vegetation, and cultural features. The National Mapping Division of the USGS provides mapping information to the library as does the National Cartographic Information Center for the USGS. Libraries may learn about these various publications through the *USGS's New Publications of the Geological Survey and A Guide to Obtaining Information from the USGS. The Monthly Catalog of United States Government Publications* is another source, and, from time to time, maps appear in *U.S. Government Books,* a quarterly listing of more popular publications.

Of all the USGS series, the topographic maps are the best known, the most often used. The maps show in detail the physical features of an area, from streams and mountains to the various works of humankind, and are of particular value to the growing number of hikers and others who enjoy outdoor activities. Libraries have a separate collection of these maps and take particular pride in offering them to the public. They are sold by map dealers throughout the United States and are available directly from the USGS, National Mapping Program at Reston, Virginia.

Digital Geographical Sources

The magic of CD-ROMs and online geographical references is undeniable. There is much information, such as the ready location of geographic names, which may be lacking in a standard atlas. At the same time the ability, for example, to print out maps and to hear one speak in the dialect of a country is more of the "bells and whistles" which may be fun, even instructional, but time consuming for a rushed librarian.

Working reference people point out the sometimes overlooked factor of speed and ease when checking out a typical geographic query. It often is, as with a dictionary and most ready reference works, easier to turn to a printed source than to navigate the sometimes treacherous time consuming waters of the electronic geographical source. The digital geographical sources are best for in depth sophisticated searches.

Two experts on maps, libraries and geographical collections make a point that remains true for many (too many) basic reference works:

> Even though data in digital form are increasingly available, paper maps will still be around for a long time; presently, approximately 90 percent of all spatial data are available only in hardcopy. The new materials are presented in digital forms; older materials...generally remain in hardcopy until someone is willing to pay to convert them to digital form. Also, hardcopy is simply more convenient for many users. This is true of maps that are larger than a computer terminal screen.[6]

On the other hand, current geographical sources in digital form are plentiful and there is no reason a student or layperson cannot find an answer online to common questions about geographical problems, whether these be how to get from point Y to point Z or measuring the rainfall in a given part of the earth.

There are a myriad of related sources which give detailed information on the peoples of this globe. One can find masses of current, usually reliable information to assist in world understanding.

> "Maps are never neutral: they have political implications. When in Moscow...I visited the Exhibition of Economic Achievements...Most touching was the brisk sale of maps of Moscow—large-scale, detailed town plans of a sort which were simply unobtainable before...Good maps are precious; they represent freedom. But they can also be an instrument of power— by the state or its agents, the town planners, or the road engineer."[7]

Innovations, from the user's ability to draw a map at the computer to locating one of some 1.7 million geographic names has elevated the importance of digital atlases and maps. Today the digital versions are not only inexpensive, but rival their print counterparts in that they have more information, more points of access, and splendid multimedia features. The maps themselves are excellent.

On the Web

Maps are everywhere on the Web. Map categories are a standard feature of search engines. These cover everything from back roads and main highways to subways and bus routes. Add thematic and historical maps and virtually every type of map is somewhere on the Net.

---

[6]Katherine L. Tankin and Mary L. Larsgaard. "Helpful Hints for Small Library Collections," *Public Libraries,* May/June, 1996, p. 176. Note: For nonbook cartographic material, as well as maps and atlases, globes, etc. see the *Library of Congress National Union Catalog,* via OCLC, RLIN, etc.

[7]Gavin Stamp, "Map Culture" *The Spectator,* December 6, 1997, p. 58.

In addition, the by now fairly high quality maps may be personalized. Routes from home to the concert hall, a favorite aunt or the local sin castle may be plotted and printed out.

The major key to geographical sources will be found at the *WWW Virtual Library: Geography* (http://geography.pinetree.org). Here are links to major departments of geography in educational institutions as well as numerous links to all types of geographical areas and countries. There even is a FAQ, i.e., frequently asked questions section on geography.

For an in-depth appreciation of what sophisticated geographical and cartography means see: *The Alexandria Project* (http:alexandria. sdc.ucsb.edu). This is a consortium of researchers, developers, and educators, spanning the academic, public, and private sectors, exploring a variety of problems related to a distributed digital library for geographically referenced information. There are numerous links to other digital libraries involved with similar work.

EVALUATION

Geographic CD-ROMs and online maps have their own individual evaluative problems, although content, as always, remains the most important and this is covered in the general evaluation below. There are several major points to consider in map evaluation that differ from book evaluation. Because maps and atlases depend on graphic arts and mathematics for presentation and compilation, a librarian is called on to judge them with a type of knowledge not usually important in book evaluation. From time to time, the "Reference Books Bulletin" in *The Booklist* offer reviews of just-published atlases. The Geography and Map Division, Special Libraries Association, issues a bulletin which frequently has articles of interest to librarians. Contributors cover new atlases, books, and related material in each issue.

Publishers. As with dictionaries and encyclopedias, there are no more than a half dozen competent cartographic firms. In the United States, the leading publishers are Rand McNally & Company, C. S. Hammond & Company, and the National Geographical Society. In Great Britain, the leaders are John G. Bartholomew (Edinburgh) and the cartographic department of the Oxford University Press. When the cartographic publisher's reputation is not known, it is advisable to check through other works it may have issued, or in a buying guide. The mapmaker may differ from the publisher, and in the case of an atlas both should be checked. All of this particularly is true of digital maps where the vendor or even the publisher may differ from the standard companies of print atlases.

Scope and Audience. As with all reference works, the library geography section must represent a wide variety of titles for many purposes and, in a public or school library, for the appropriate age groups. Essentially, it is a matter of scope. Some atlases are universal; others are limited to a single country, or even a region. Other maps, even within a general work, may be unevenly distributed so that 50 percent or more of the work may give undue attention to the United States or Canada, ignoring the weight of the rest of the world.

Scale. Maps often are classed according to scale. One unit on a map equals a certain number of units on the ground, that is 1 inch on the map may equal 10 or 100 miles on the ground. The detailed map will have a larger scale. The scale is indicated, usually at the bottom of the map, by a line or bar that shows distances in kilometers or miles, or both.

Geographers use map scale to refer to the size of the representation on the map. A scale of 1:63,360 is 1 inch to the mile (63,360 inches). The larger the second figure (scale denominator), the smaller the scale of the map. For example, on a map which shows the entire United States, the scale may be 1:16 million (1 inch being equal to about 250 miles). This is a small-scale map. A large-scale map of a section of the United States, say of the Northwest, would have a scale of 1:4 million. In the same atlas, the scale for Europe (and part of Russia) is 1:16 million; but for France (and the Alps) it is 1:4 million.

The scale from map to map in a given atlas may vary considerably, although better atlases attempt to standardize their work. The standardization is determined both by the size of the page on which the map appears as well as the effort of the publisher to use the same basic scales throughout.

Currency. World tension, as for example in the former Yugoslavia, China and North Korea results in a plus for map publishers. New maps are required almost every week or month, if only for consumption by newspapers, television and other visual forms of communication. New maps of course are necessary for libraries and for travelers. Virtually every library must update its world map collection at least once each year. The task has been made considerably easier (and less expensive) thanks to digital maps.

As it is not practical to make a new atlas every time a place changes name or a border shifts, publishers have reached two solutions. The first, as Rand McNally offers with some of its more expensive atlases (such as *Atlas of Today's World*), is to provide a free world print map showing changes since the atlas was published. A more favored approach is to use an online update that is considerably easier to edit than the printed work. Hammond, for example, has its own Digital Cartographic Database which contains constantly updated information on the state of the world. The database allows the publisher to transform the new or revised data into new maps almost within seconds. With that one can then print a map quickly.

It should be noted that the date of publication for almost all geographic maps and atlases is the latest year on the calendar. At the same time, it may not be a new edition. (i.e., an atlas with 2000 on the title page may not have been thoroughly revised since 1995.) A new edition, that is when the title is completely overhauled and developed from possibly another point of view, normally takes place every 10 years. Why 10 years? It is obvious. That is the time span between the American census. Librarians turning to this text, or any other guide to geographical sources, should insist on a valid date of 2000 or, better yet, 2001 which means the maps have incorporated the latest United States census. Thanks to digital maps current trends and changes can be made without completely editing the older edition—online or in print.

The Index. A comprehensive index is as important in an atlas as the maps themselves. Online or on a CD-ROM the software should make it easy to find a name, place, or by-product, say, of mining. A good index clearly lists all place names that appear on the map. In addition, there should be a reference to the exact map, and latitude, longitude, and grid information. A page number alone is never enough, as anyone who has sought an elusive town or city on a map lacking such information will testify. The index in many atlases is really an excellent gazetteer; that is, in addition to basic information, each entry includes data on population and country. A check: Try to find four or five names listed in the index on the maps. How long did it take, and how difficult was the task? Reverse this test by finding names on the maps and trying to locate them in the index. Difficulty at either test spells trouble.

Format. When one considers print format, the basic question is simply: Can I find what I want easily on the map, and is it as clear as it is legible? The obvious problem is to print a map in such a way that it is easy to read a mass of names that cover a densely populated area. It is one thing to clearly print maps of the north and south polar regions, and quite another to be able to arrange type and symbols so that one can find a path from point to point in a map of the areas around New York City, Paris, and London. Maps with fewer items of information will be clearer and easier to read. The actual number of points represented on the map is a major editorial decision.

The digital format is not the best source of clear, easy-to-read maps. The resolution on a computer screen normally is less satisfactory than in a printed book. Still, the advantages, particularly of being able to zoom in on a given section, more than make up for the loss of color sharpness.

Cost. Atlases and maps run the cost course from free to thousands of dollars. In most libraries, though, the cost is relatively low. Standard print atlases are from $30 to $150, and individual maps, unless historical, rarely are expensive. Digital versions are either free or moderately priced.

Commercial atlases and maps are widely used by business, and they tend to be costly. The more detail, the higher the price. One example: *ArcView GIS/Version 3.0* Redlands, CA: ArcView, 1997 to date (www.esri. com/software/arcview/avsoftware). This, as similar expensive digital formats of this type ($1,195 to $1,500) have a set pattern. First the map of the country, state, community, city, etc. is shown and on that is laid down various sets of data. Using a census tract, for example, one can set up a color coded thematic map that explores everything from population to income. The strength of these costly digital maps is the amount of data supplied and the ability to manipulate it in relationship to the maps.

GEOGRAPHICAL ENCYCLOPEDIAS AND DICTIONARIES

Print: World Geographical Encyclopedia. New York: McGraw-Hill Companies, Inc., 1995. 5 vols., translated from the Italian edition. $500.

An expansion of political yearbooks, a series of atlases, and a number of subject encyclopedias, the *World Geographic Encyclopedia* casts a wide geographical net. The five volumes, translated from the Italian edition, includes the expected maps, and adds statistics, history, and cultural background for continents and individual countries. The advertisement claims the ambitious work "creates a living tapestry out of the accurate and up-to-date geographic facts." No one can argue with that claim. Each of the five well-documented volumes include over 1,000 illustrations, the majority in color. The text is geared for the average high school student and adult. The volumes cover: Africa, The Americas, Asia, Europe, and Oceania. There is a detailed index.

Merriam-Webster's New Geographical Dictionary (Springfield, MA: Merriam-Webster, Inc., various dates) is typical of a series of geographical dictionaries that list, alphabetically, geographical names. It has some 48,000 entries with over 200 maps. After each comes a variety of information from brief descriptive notes to major features from famous people born there or the first to reach the top of the given mountain.

Locations and definitions are given as well as other data which is invaluable to reference librarians.

ATLASES AND MAPS

Today maps are as common on CD-ROMs and the Net as in print. Also, they gradually are making their way into automobiles as active dashboard guides to help the driver move from place to place. A major benefit of the digital map is the use of spatial layouts which give a much better idea, for example, about the height of a mountain than a normal printed map. Another plus is the ability to move and shape data. The key feature of digital maps is the amount of data that can be called up, mixed and matched and moved to a specific map location. Everything from underground telephone wires to property boundaries and roads can be shown with dimensional data. The only thing which stops finer and more refined digital maps is the amount of time and money taken to feed the computer the raw data.

Here is a single example of how modern digital maps and data may be used to solve a problem:

> Back in 1854 cartographers used a map of London to study outbreaks of cholera and locate the site of the infected water pumps that caused them. But, with [digital maps], the overlays of information can be much more complex. By taking information from vets about dogs that tested positive for exposure to Lyme disease and layering the map that resulted across a satellite photograph showing the vegetation of Westchester County in New York, cartographers determined that heavily planted yards located immediately alongside forest edge were the key locations of exposure. Now, health officials know precisely where to take precaution.[8]

Digital atlases and individual maps have another important dimension not found in the older printed versions. They usually add sound and motion, i.e., one can hear a waterfall, see a video clip of people swarming in New York's Times Square. Also, there are configurations that clarify statistical data. On the other hand, if one is simply seeking to locate X or Y city or mountain, it may be much simpler to use the average print atlas or map.

Possibly even more direct is to turn to any general encyclopedia for geographical information. This side of the articles, general digital encyclopedias have similar geographic features. All have maps and educational videos relating to the environment and weather, as well as photographs.

[8]Jack Hitt, "Atlas Shrugged" *Lingua Franca,* July/August, 1995, p. 30.

All of the print atlases listed here pride themselves on front matter which some may consider extraneous, but others find a value. For example, in the *Oxford Atlas of the World* there are some 50 pages of text, including charts, photographs, climate bars, population figures, etc. *The Hammond Atlas of the World* opens with photographs taken from space, as does *The National Geographic Atlas of the World*. Digital atlases, even more than their print cousins, include the hum of bees to video clips of erupting volcanoes. Is this necessary? No, but it helps to sell digital atlases.

Atlases

Print: Times Atlas of the World: Comprehensive Edition. London: Harper-Collins, (Distributed in U. S. by Random House) 2000, 220 pp. $250.

Print: The New York Times Atlas of the World, 4th rev. ed. New York: Times Books, 2000, 288 pp. $75.

CD: Encarta Interactive World Atlas (formerly: *Encarta Virtual Globe*). Redmond, WA: Microsoft, 2000. $50.

Millennium World Atlas, *Skokie, IL: Rand McNally & Company, 2000. $59.95.*
Print: The New International Atlas, 2000, 560 pp. $99.
Print: Rand McNally Premier World Atlas, 2000, 248 pp. $24.95.

Online: National Geographic Map Machine. Washington, DC: National Geographic Society, 1997 to date, www.nationalgeographic.com/resources/ngo/maps. Free.
Print: National Geographic Atlas of the World, 7th ed., New York: Washington: National Geographic, 1999, 280 pp. $125.

CD: Hammond World Atlas, 2000. $49.95. (With print atlas, below: $85).
Print: Hammond World Atlas, 312 pp. $70.

Online: World Atlas Online. New York: Faces on File News Service. 2000 to date, www.fofweb.com. Price varies.

This side of the familiar map that fits into the car glove compartment, (or in some cases an electronic dashboard moving atlas), the most used and best known series of maps is the ubiquitous atlas. This collection of maps, usually on a global scale, come in all formats, shapes and sizes as well as in price ranges from a few dollars to several thousand dollars. The print 350 to 550 page, $50 to $175 atlas, is typical of the one found in libraries, along with, to be sure, less costly items. Most libraries, too, have CD-ROM versions as well as access to maps online.

The atlases listed here have three to four things in common, besides price and relative size. They are by reputable publishers and the text can be trusted. They are well designed and the maps are of high graphic quality. All offer additional information from population and climate data to profiles of cities, states, and so forth. And, finally, all have adequate to excellent indexes, varying from 70,000 to 200,000 plus entries. (Generally, the size generally is in direct ratio to the price.)

Given the similarity among reputable publishers of atlases, the question is which one(s) to pick? The answer: Which covers what in most depth, and the "what" is of greatest interest to people using the library. For example, one would turn to the Hammond entry for a greater coverage of North American countries, cities and places. A close contender for the same area of the world, and equally good in other areas, the Rand McNally would be a Hammond rival. Oxford would be the choice for in-depth European treatment.

Thematic maps are the added strength, the added reason for purchasing several atlases. These are particularly useful in secondary schools and universities and colleges. Here one finds excellent graphics to bring home the importance of such things as food, energy, overpopulation (or under population). At a glance one may see where the primary oil-producing areas of the world are to be found. It is also a winner in terms of vivid comparisons between places of the world, that is, would you really like to live in X or in Y?

Times Atlas

The *Times Atlas of the World* is the best single-volume atlas available. That it happens to be the most expensive is chiefly because such meticulous care has been taken, with emphasis on large-scale, multiple maps for several countries and attention to detail and color rarely rivaled by other American atlases.

The print volume consists of three basic parts. The first section is a conspectus of world minerals, sources of energy and food, and a variety of diagrams and star charts. The atlas proper comprises 123 double-page eight-color maps, the work of the Edinburgh house of Bartholomew. This is the vital part, and it is perfect in both typography and color. The clear typeface enables the reader to easily make out each of the enormous number of names. A variety of colors is used with skill and taste to show physical features, railways, rivers, political boundaries, and so on. A remarkable thing about this atlas is that it shows almost every noteworthy geographical feature from lighthouses and tunnels to mangrove swamps—all by the use of carefully explained symbols.

The *Times Atlas* is suited for American libraries because, unlike many other atlases, it gives a large amount of space to non-European countries. No other atlas matches it for the detailed coverage of the Soviet

Union, China, Africa, and Southeast Asia, lands not overlooked in other atlases, but usually covered in much less detail. A uniform scale of 1:2,500,000 is employed for most maps, but is changed to 1:850,000 for the United Kingdom. Maps of the larger landmasses are supplemented with smaller, detailed maps that range from maps of urban centers to maps of the environs of Mt. Everest.

The final section is an index of over 210,000 place names, which, for most purposes, serves as an excellent gazetteer. After each name, the country is given with an exact reference to a map.

About half the size and about half the price of the *Times Atlas of the World, The New York Times Atlas* is a close cousin of the larger work. While the format is a bit smaller, the maps are much the same, and all are from the firm of John C. Bartholomew & Son in Edinburgh. The atlas scales are in keeping with the reduced format. There is a well-balanced coverage of the world. The index is smaller (100,000 entries) and the introductory matter more concise, but essentially this is a moderately priced version of the larger title and an excellent choice for library or home where the original atlas is not found.

Encarta Interactive World Atlas

With no print edition, Microsoft is outside the traditional circle of map publishers. No matter, the *CD-ROM Encarta Interactive World Atlas* is typical of the best in electronic format. All digital atlases and maps share most of *Encarta* characteristics, and it is used here as an example, not necessarily as a library requirement.

From the point of view of a reference librarian the leading feature is the ability to locate not 200,000 to 300,000 geographical locations, but some 1.2 million geographic names—all of which are located on a map. (A "sound like" search technique allows someone to find a difficult name by using only the approximate spelling.) Impressive, but Rand McNally boasts 1.7 million geographic names. Both publishers keep the lists updated to reflect constant name changes, and there are cross-references from older and less common names.

Encarta has other usual features associated with digital atlases and maps. One can zoom and pan to find a place. There are a variety of maps from historical to topographical. One can save a ⌐¹ ⌐ ⌐ bol or pushpin and this is useful when deciding j out. Statistical data such as literacy rate in a coun listed. (It has the usual problem, though: does mean in the thousands, hundreds or what? Someti times it is a major puzzle).

Added features: A mass of textual information which is more than found in most print works. Pronunciation of common sentences by native speakers to illustrate characteristics of dialect, language, etc. Links to websites also helps.

Rand McNally

Suitably named, the *Rand McNally Millennium World Atlas* saw in the millennium and beyond. It has several claims that make it ideal for reference work: (1) There are 1.7 million geographic names which can be located on the maps. As with the *Encarta* work, these are constantly being updated and are considerably more current than either the print or online versions. (2) There are a series of subject areas from population and climate to disasters that can be matched to offer such information as the number and place of cyclones in the central United States. (3) One can tailor a map to fit, e.g., the reader can specify map styles from outline to political and there are numerous menus which allow such things as displaying cities by size or major national parks. (4) There are numerous statistical features that allow gathering data such as the number of television sets in the United States. (5) There is a mass of text, with animated features, which covers all the major points found in a print atlas. (6) And there are thousands of links from X or Y place to facts to Internet sites. Thanks to its popularity, many libraries have several copies of the CD-ROM for circulation and another at the reference desk.

The New International has 160,000 entries in the index and 300 good to excellent maps. A team effort of international cartographers, the atlas strikes a good balance between the needs of American readers and those in other countries. The scales are large with most countries at 1:6 million to 1:3 million. The maps tend to be double-paged and are models of legibility. The atlas' "birthday-cake-icing" material (from essays on the climate to thematic maps) is mercifully missing. The main focus is on maps of extraordinary quality.

With a political map for each continent followed by detailed country by country maps, the *Rand McNally Premier World Atlas* is an inexpensive workhorse for individuals and librarians. It has all the detail needed for most questions, e.g., close to 60 pages of maps for U.S. states and Canadian provinces as well as similar detailed maps for other parts of the globe. There are some 45,000 place names in the index—a bonus as few atlases at this price range offer such indexing. Within the usual finely detailed maps of other Rand McNally atlases, the only major failure, particularly for reference work, is lack of geographical data for individual countries. Related atlases are published by Hammond, i.e., the concise n of the *Hammond Atlas of the World*.

National Geographic[9]

The *National Geographic Atlas of The World* has much in addition to maps. It is by way of an encyclopedia as well. Also it has the advantage of complete revision in 1999. It is quite attractive, at least to many people and school children. Here one finds numerous thematic maps and discussions of world resources. Divided by continent, the 172 maps are introduced in each section by an encyclopedic–like article on the various countries. (There are more than 75 large format color maps). The maps are clear and easy enough to read. There is a 140,000-entry index. There is much emphasis on American interests, but rarely to the neglect of third-world countries. The atlas has other strong points, including large scales, good-sized pages, and the aforementioned extensive index. It is favored by many who want something more than just an atlas.

Based on the *National Geographic Atlas* the *National Geographic Map Machine* site offers about the same number and type of maps as found in the print edition. The online system, too, keeps the printed atlas current. There is considerable front matter as well, e.g., flags, environmental conditions, industrial developments, etc. "Map Resources" has links to numerous other map Web sites, including the major Perry-Castaneda Library Map Collection. The drawbacks are twofold: *(a)* the maps are not as detailed or as refined on the Net as in print; and *(b)* because of the size of the computer screen some maps are not shown in a size large enough to give a notion of the country's real boundaries.

A true bargain: *National Geographic Maps* which includes over 500 of the famous foldout maps on eight CD-ROMs. And all for only $60.

Hammond

Hammond maps and atlases are among the most reliable in the world, and the firm has numerous individual atlases. One of the standards is the *World Atlas*. This has 167 pages of oversized maps, with slightly under one-

[9]See, too, *The National Geographic Desk Reference* (Washington: National Geographic, 1999. 700 pp. $40). Here about one page is dedicated to each of the world's nations with basic geographical data from climate to religion. Also: the CD-ROM: *The Complete National Geographic.* This includes nearly 200,000 pages of all the articles, illustrations, and features in the magazine from the first 1888 issue to 1999. (Updates will be available). The whole is on 31 CD-ROMs for a modest $130 or on four DVDs, at near the same price. This fits in a small box compared to the 90 feet of linear shelf space it takes for the print volumes. (One catch: each time you load a disc it is necessary to listen/see a two-minute ad for the magazine. Shame.) A reduced version of this, although kept current, is on the Web at (www.nationalgeographic.com).

half on double pages. The average scale is 1:3 million, with particular emphasis on North America. Thanks to imaginative use of the computer, the maps follow a new projection that is good in showing relative size of areas. There are 62 U.S. urban centers (at 1.1 million) along with numerous smaller insert, blowup maps. Thematic maps showing global relationships are well designed and there are several text sections on such things as the environment and the development of cartography. There is a 110,000-entry name index.

Ease of use makes this an ideal atlas for most reference situations. It equally is true of other Hammond maps and atlases. As a result Hammond publications are found in all libraries.

The Hammond CD-ROM follows the usual pattern of linking the print maps to Net sites and adding editorial material as well as multimedia features such as zooming in on places—although this feature is much more limited than on other CD-ROMs. While passable, it is much less satisfactory than other such atlases on CD-ROM, and is not a necessary purchase for a library.

Larger libraries will want all these atlases. If a choice has to be made, *The Times Atlas* (or *The New York Times Atlas of the World*) would be first; although the *International* would be a close second. *The Times* has the reputation and is expected to be found in major libraries.

The Book of the World (New York: Macmillan, 1999, 560 pp. $465) is the most expensive of the giant atlases. It is not worth it for most libraries. At the same time the 18 pound *Book of the World* boasts the famous Bertelsmann maps, an index of 100,000 plus entries and impressive (though, is it really necessary) front matter, including full page satellite photographs. One suspects, despite its scholarly support, that it is meant more to impress the neighbors than to be actively used in a reference section.

The advantage of *World Atlas Online* is the ease of printing out the maps, and particularly the unmarked outline format. This shows the outline of a state, country or continent, but without designations of name or physical areas. Also one may get a clear, colored map with details in under four minutes for two or more pages. Another plus: the numerous search patterns which permit the user to find cities, lakes, archipelagoes, etc. by simply entering in the requested form. The forms are listed so one does not have to remember either spelling of form designation. There is the usual method of enlarging the map on the screen for more detail. A third bonus, and one of particular value to reference librarians: data for individual countries from history and forms of government to vital statistics. Note that all data, including the maps, is dated. Finally, there are useful links to everything from the census to an "earth and moon viewer."

Desk/School Atlases: Print Format

Print: Goode's World Atlas. Chicago: Rand McNally Company, 1999. 384 pp. $35.

Low price, reasonable size, and ease of use are the three basic reasons many people prefer a school or desk-type atlas at home. And they are used in numerous elementary school geography classes. The problems are three-fold: the format requires small-scale maps which result in tremendous distortions; the gazetteer or index, where it exists, is limited to 20,000 to 36,000 names; and the maps while adequate lack the refinement of larger works.

The inexpensive atlas found in most libraries, and particularly small public and almost all school libraries, is the familiar *Goode's.* This is revised every three or four years, and is as much of most people's memory of geography as any other single item in elementary schools. It is typical of the small, inexpensive works. It has a serviceable index (36,000 entries) and close to 400 (sometimes less than astonishing) maps. As it is used in schools, from the late elementary grades through colleges, there is a particular emphasis on thematic elements from population data to environmental problems.

There are countless variations of intermediate to small atlases. Take, for example, the *Desk Reference World Atlas* (Chicago: Rand McNally). This sells for a modest $20, it has 350 pages of good maps and an index of some 30,000 place names. Between the sections is a modest encyclopedia of 200 pages filled with tables and facts pertaining to geographical queries.

Check, too, the large bookstores for atlas bargains. Barnes & Noble, for example, lists the $50 *Rand McNally New Universal World Atlas* for $20. This is a current edition with 11-inch by 14-inch maps. Particular focus is on Canada and the United States. There is a modest, but useful 39,000 entry index/gazetteer.

Rand McNally publishes a series of atlases for children from *Rand McNally Children's Atlas* (7 vols.) and *Rand McNally Picture Atlas of Prehistoric Life* to *The Rand McNally Children's World Atlas.* Hammond offers *Discovering Maps: A Children's World Atlas.*

On the Web[10]

This side of the websites previously mentioned, there are several which are of interest to the librarian working with atlases and maps:

Perry-Castaneda Library Map Collection. University of Texas (www.lib.utexas.edu/Libs/PCL/Map_collection/Map_collection). Here are about

[10]"Maps," *Web Guide Magazine,* March/April 1998, pp. 69–71. This gives the address and a brief explanation of the major historical map libraries. They range from the *Library of Congress Geography and Map Reading Room* (http://lcweb.loc.gov/rr/geogmap/gmpage3.html) to Oxford's Bodleian Library Map Room (www.bodley.ox.ac.uk.nnj).

3,000 digital maps that amount to a good sized world atlas. Its particular value is that it has maps of current geographical places in the news, e.g. Bosnia, Gaza, the West Bank, detailed maps of Africa, etc. The maps cover all points of the globe, although there is a heavy emphasis on domestic maps. They are drawn from files of the U.S. Department of State, Bureau of the Census, etc. One clicks on a number of entry points for: cartographic reference, general maps, city maps, county maps, state maps, weather maps, and historical maps.

National Atlas of the United States (www.nationalatlas.gov). While limited to the United States, the United States Geodetic Service atlas features numerous topographical maps of the country as a whole and of individual states. One simply clicks on the state and the map appears. There are numerous links to other map sites as well.

GAZETTEERS

Print: The Columbia Gazetteer of the World. New York: Columbia University Press, 1998. 3 vols. $750.

Online: U.S. Gazetteer. Washington, DC: United States Census Bureau, 1997 to date, www.census.gov/cgi-bin/gazetteer. Free.

A gazetteer answers the question "Where is X or Y area, town or physical feature?" Generally, a gazetteer is an alphabetical listing of names from under 100,000 to over 3 million that gives the longitude and latitude of X as a key to finding it on a map. Also the key may be the familiar letters and numbers on a map which help to narrow the area in which the place is located.

The problem of simply locating a geographical name is solved to a great extent by using one of the two CD-ROM atlases, e.g., *Encarta Virtual Globe* (with 1.2 million names) or the *Rand McNally Millennium Atlas* (1.7 million names). On the other hand, where more information is wanted about the place, a gazetteer is in order.

While there are smaller works,[11] the best general gazetteer is the three volume *Columbia Gazetteer.* Here in alphabetical order are more than 160,000 places. This may seem small compared to the numbers on the CD-ROM atlases, but there is considerably more than a name. So much more that it is an ideal reference aid. Among the points in each entry: *(a)* Physical description of the named place. *(b)* Background on the economic, political and historical aspects of the site—similar to an abbreviated *Statesman's Yearbook. (c)* Pronunciation(s). *(d)* Longitude-latitude-

---

[11]The standard smaller gazetteer is the *Merriam-Webster's Geographical Dictionary* discussed earlier in this chapter.

elevation measurements. *(e)* Cross-references from older forms of place names to the latest name. Note: *The Columbia Gazetteer of North America* by the same publisher was issued in 2000 but at only $250. This has 50,000 entries all drawn from the primary volume.

An atlas, map service and gazetteer, the *U.S. Gazetteer* is free and has detailed information on American communities. Detail is the key word as it is overkill to use this for simple questions about where is this or that place. Anyone looking for census data via the Web need only type in the name of the area or the town. The screen then displays a relatively detailed map. This can be "drawn" by the user to include railroad lines, main highways, boundaries within the city or county, parts, etc. Once the map is on the screen one may "click on the image to zoom in...or zoom out...place maker," etc. In addition the database gives brief information on the community that follows standard pattern: population, location, zip codes and where to look for more details in the census.

The ultimate gazetteer lacks the data found in the Columbia work, but beats all sources, the two CD-ROM atlases included, for the number of geographic names. This is the *GEOnet Names Server.* (http://164.214.2.59/gns/html). Here is the ideal gazetteer for finding longitude and latitude of any place in the world, i.e., outside of the United States. "The GEOnet Names Server (GNS) provides access to the National Imagery and Mapping Agency's database of foreign geographic feature names. Approximately 12,000 of the databases 3.3 million features are updated monthly with names and information approved by the U.S. Board of Geographic Names." This allows the user to search for any name out of 3.3 million possibilities on the face of the globe. The site provides information by coordinate, by name, by feature designation and several other points. It does not have a link to maps.

An unlikely Web source of a gazetteer is a world famous museum. The sponsor is the J. Paul Getty Trust, and the site includes, too, an art and architecture thesaurus as well as a union list of artist names. The *Getty Thesaurus of Geographic Names* (http://shiva.pub.getty.edu/tgn_browser), referred to on the site as the TGN, allows the user to enter a key word or full names. The latitude and longitude are given as well as data on which continent, country and state, province, etc, it is located. The place records are sparse, but at least they indicate where to find such spots as Little Heaven.

THEMATIC ATLASES AND MAPS

Print: Atlas of World History. New York: Oxford University Press, 2000, 368 pp. $85.

Print: Atlas of Exploration. London: Oxford University Press, 1997, 248 pp. $40.

Print: The Times Atlas of World History. New York: HarperCollins, 1993, 380 pp. $65.

Print: Rand McNally Commercial Atlas Marketing Guide. Chicago: Rand McNally & Company, 1976 to date, annual. $300+, rate varies.

The thematic or subject map is usually limited to a specific topic or related topics. Almost anything with a geographic focus may be the subject of such a map. Those listed here are representative of a much larger number which can be located by consulting the *Guide to Reference Books, American Reference Books Annual,* and, of course, geographical bibliographies.

Historical maps may settle more than one argument. *In The Two Gentlemen of Verona,* Shakespeare has Proteus travel from Verona to Milan by boat. A modern-day map indicates this is impossible. But a map of the 1483 to 1499 period shows a series of canals, once designed by Leonardo da Vinci. Even though the two Italian cities are not connected by water, the canals come quite close—within 40 miles of each other—so a substantial part of the trip could have been by boat as Shakespeare claims.

Subtitled, "from the origins of humanity to the Year 2000," the *Atlas of World History* is the latest of the breed and boasts superior editing as well as focus on the whole world, rather than simply the Western nations. There are 450 color maps with accompanying illustrations and easy to follow text. Sections follow the chronology approach from the ancient world through to a final section on a multicultural, modern time line. Basic, and along with the *Times* entry should be found in all libraries.

Supported by 100 maps and over 300 photographs and illustrations, the *Atlas of Exploration* covers 5,000 years of discoveries from the earliest across Africa, Europe and Asia to James Cook in Antarctica. The primary routes are depicted on the graphic relief maps. Maps from various historical periods add to the gradual development of cartography. The volume closes with an index and biographical sketches of the major explorers and cartographers.

Updated every five to six years, *The Times Atlas of World History* shows parallel historical events, cultural activities, and social movements in parallel development in Europe, Asia, Africa, and the Americas. The maps are large, easy to read, and placed in such a way that one may trace the history of an event, individual, or, more likely, a movement that is developing. The atlas has an excellent index and a useful glossary of unusual historic terms. A $40 companion by the same publisher, *The Times Atlas of European History* (1994), covers Europe from about 900 B.C. to 1994. A brief text accompanies the maps.

The value of the *Rand McNally Commercial Atlas* is that it is revised every year. The library that can afford to subscribe to the *Atlas* solves the problem of adequate United States and Canadian coverage. All information is the most up-to-date of any single atlas or, for that matter, any print reference work of this type. It is an excellent source for current statistical data. The first 120 pages or so offer (1) regional and metropolitan area maps, (2) transportation and communication data, (3) economic data, and (4) population data. Most of this is listed by state and then by major cities with codes that clearly indicate the figures.

The largest single section is devoted to "state maps and United States index of statistics and places by states." Here one finds the large-scale state maps. The statistical data, arranged by state, follow. This includes such details as principal cities and towns in order of population, counties, basic business data, transportation, banks, and post offices by town, and are followed by briefer data for Canada and the world. The MSAs (Metropolitan Statistical Areas) and the BTAs (Business Trading Areas) are used to bring order to the massive statistics. The approximately 128,000 locations are analyzed with easy-to-use tables that summarize such things as population, economic data and 2000 to 2005 projections. One can quickly find data on the per capita, median household as well as help patrons find a hard-to-locate place. The details and maps make this a necessity in almost any library.

There are subject area historical atlases as well as general works. For example: *The Atlas of Literature* (London: DeAgostin, 1996. 362 pp.). Edited by author Malcolm Bradbury this covers the subject from the Middle Ages to World War II and "The World Today." In each of the eight sections there are sketches of authors, background material on their time, photographs and numerous full color maps which pinpoint such things as Don Quixote's ride as pictured by Cervantes. An invaluable reference work for avid readers and students. More discursive: Franco Moretti, *An Atlas of the European Novel 1800–1900* (London: Verson, 1998, 206 pp.). Punctuating the text are about one hundred maps to support the charming narrative. And as much for the kids as the adults *Atlas of the Prehistoric World* (New York: Random House/Discovery Books, 1999, 224 pp.) takes the reader over 500 million years of time with particular focus on the dinosaurs period before 65 million B.C. Photographs, line drawings, maps, and text add to both the thrill and accuracy of the presentations. And there are many more, but these three are representative of the best in a single subject.

STREET MAPS[12]

Digital street and highway maps have become a "cottage industry." There are scores of them, with new ones coming out each month. The titles noted here are the best, but only representative of a much larger group

---

[12]The digital city maps multiply by the day. For a good overall view, at least as of 1999, see "Most Wired City Guides" *Yahoo!* magazine, April, 1999, pp. 103–108.

that may have particular points of interest to the individual who is likely to travel a great deal. DeLorme, Microsoft and Rand McNally are among the major publishers.

The online city maps are roughly the same in that they all contain a nationwide database of road maps, including parks, hotels and other points that can be shown on a map. In order to plan a trip, the user enters the beginning town and the concluding point, as well as any stopovers. The software then calculates various routes, i.e., the fastest, the most scenic and so forth. The routes are displayed on the computer screen with estimates of driving time and suggested attractions along the way.

A definite problem with some digital maps: there are too many "bells and whistles" from pantographic photographs of major cities to videos. This interferes with the primary goal of getting from X to Y and can be more of a headache than a help.

There are a number of free good to excellent street and highway maps on the Internet. Two good examples:

Maps on US (www.mapsonus.com). Here the focus is on mapping specific routes from place to place, whether within an American city or between cities. It is simple to use and there is a detailed "user guide: what next" to help the beginner. One enters the home address, then the point of destination. A map and directions are then offered. As with many systems of this type there are numerous options such as selecting the fastest route, or the most scenic or selecting sites of interest. There are individual maps for each section of a distant trip. Within the city or town the route maps often show so much detail they are hard to read.

MapQuest (http://mapquest.com). This is "door-to-door" maps similar to the trip planning of the American Automobile Association, only here the traveler maps out his or her own personal journey. There is an online interactive American atlas which provides specific directions to get from point X to point Y, and, in some cases, even street by street. The user can type in a street address or a landmark site and a map is immediately shown of the address or site with the surrounding area. Routine travel information is part of the free package, i.e., everything from museums and parks to restaurants are located. Points of interest are first shown as icons. One clicks them on for an address, phone number, name of the site, etc.

An added, valuable and rare feature for this type of site is the inclusion of an interactive world atlas. This includes all of the major cities on every part of the globe. While the detail is not as great as for the United States, there is enough to be able to set a route within London or Paris, as well as from Paris to Berlin.

An added feature of the street maps online is the information available on the cost of flights from point Y to Z. Some are worldwide. Others are for North America. Sites particularly are helpful for showing the latest low fare from point X to Y. The favored sites (in August 2000): *Mapquest.com* with 7.5 million visitors; *Travelocity.com* with 6.94 million visitors; *Priceline.com,* 6.91; *Expedia.com,* 6.72. Others in the 2.5 million number of visits: *AA.com; ITN.net; Delta.com.* Scheduled to join this group in mid-2001: *Orbitz.com* which will represent its airline owners, American Airlines, Continental, Delta, Northwest and United.

Other[13]

Print: Michelin "City Streets, " Paris: Michelin, 1998 to date, annual. $12.95.

CD: Rand McNally Trip Maker, Skokie, IL: Rand McNally & Company, 1994 to date, annual. Price varies.

CD: Street Atlas USA. (also titled: *AAA Map'NGo*) Yarmouth, ME: DeLorme Mapping, 1992 to date, monthly. $34.95.

CD: Compass 3800. Lemont, IL: Chicago Map Corporation, 1997 to date, annual. Price varies.

The travel guide publisher, Michelin, is a good example of print city street maps. They issue numerous series of street maps covering most of the world. They are small enough to fit into a pocket and are ideal for walking. The scales range from 1:10,000 (Rome and Lyons) to 1:17,500 (Brussels). On a scale of 1:12,000 about 31/2 inches covers slightly over one-half mile. All the maps fold into 13 or more panels with a booklet inside the front cover that has an index to streets.

Among the more familiar general road maps and atlases the best for libraries, in no particular order: *Rand McNally Road Atlas* (Chicago: Rand McNally, annual. $17); *AAA North American Road Atlas* (Washington, DC: AAA, annual. $11); National Geographic Road Atlas (Washington, DC: National Geographic Society. Annual. $17).

There are numerous variations on this theme of easy to carry and great detailed pedestrian maps of major cities. Then there are the free maps issued at major subway and bus stations. The American Automobile Association (AAA) pioneered the travel maps that in bright red or yellow over a printed map crayon trace a desired route for the careful driver. The "TripTik" remains a popular, personalized map booklet for millions of drivers.

---

[13]Another aspect of travel and street/highway planning is the maze of car navigation systems. Eventually these will be found in all cars, but for now are a luxury item and outside the library reference section.

Published primarily for travelers, and more particularly for drivers, these maps and built–in travel plans can equally be useful for libraries. The obvious first point is that they offer a handy, easy to read map of a given area (town, county, or state). Second, many have overlays that give vast amounts of information from climatic conditions to locations of parks and museums and major business areas. All of this will be of use to the student or layperson attempting to understand conditions in a given part of the United States. (Note: Almost all of the CD-ROMs and online street and highway maps described are for America. However, they are available, as well, for Canada, Latin and Central America, Europe and many other parts of the world.)

One of the best CD-ROM road maps is produced by Rand McNally. It has some 650,000 miles of road and 125,000 cities in its database. The driver seeking the shortest route from Seattle to Washington, DC simply turns to the *Rand McNally TripMaker.* By typing in the point of origin and the point of destination, the route is drawn on the map. One may qualify this with cities, parks, historical sites, and so on that one wishes to visit along the way. It can be manipulated to show how much distance is covered in day 1, day 2 and so forth. And for each community there is a fine breakdown of streets and major sites

With *Street Atlas USA* (or the similar *DeLorme AAA Map'n'Go)* the user has a chance to investigate literally every marked street in the United States. The user can view the whole country on a screen and then zoom down to his or her own city, street, or road. Put in the beginning and ending points, and a route is established. Prompts help if the driver gets lost in the process. There are AAA evaluations of hotels and motels as well as restaurants with a multimedia show of major attractions. The publisher says the CD-ROM has more than 5 million streets and 1.1 million geographical and man-made features. In addition to the street name, the projected map will give data on physical features and prominent crossroads and buildings. By zooming in and out of Y town, for example, the user can find the necessary street or streets by name, or even by the zip code for the area or an individual phone number. One can make up maps as needed. Simple to use and relatively inexpensive, this is a sure winner in many school and public libraries.

Mapping all streets in the United States, *Compass* is typical of the CD-ROM street map reference work. Easy steps show street level information on all places or regions within the United States. One zooms in and out using the mouse or the computer keys. There are 16 zoom levels that move from a scale of 500 miles to .05 miles.

Searching can be done in a variety of ways, but primarily by city, place name and street address. Other possibilities include latitude and longitude as well as zip code and area codes. The software allows the user to customize the maps by adding material, inserting lines and various markers. The program includes standard cartographic symbols that may be moved about on the map.

TRAVEL GUIDES

Online: Fodor's World View. New York: Fodor's Travel Publications, 1997 to date, irregular, www.fodors.com. Free on the Internet.
   Print: Fodor's... New York: Publisher varies, 1953 to date, annual.

Print: Guides Michelin. Paris: Service de Tourisme Michelin, 1905 to date, annual.

Print: Birnbaum... New York: Houghton Mifflin, various dates.

Travel guidebooks are a popular item in libraries—and bookstores. Many bookstores have large sections of current guides that, particularly in the spring and summer, attract browsers. One of those browsers might be the librarian in quest for new editions and new approaches to current travel tips. The library collection should have a nice blend of the standard guides along with popular works on geography and picture travelogues. Picture books particularly are a useful mix with the guides.

Two questions must be answered by the reference librarian. The first concerns the countries that are popular among library users. Inevitably the first choices are guides of the United States and Canada. Next comes the Caribbean for East Coast residents, and the Pacific regions for those on the Pacific Rim. Turning to Europe, as might be expected, England is the most popular European country, followed by Western Europe. Of course, none of this is pertinent when an individual wants a particular title on some unexpected section of the world. On the other hand, the consensus on points of interest does help shape the collection.

The second question concerns which guides are best. Given that the points of travel are more or less settled, then the reference librarian turns to well known publishers and ongoing reviews of new titles. Usually only prices change from year to year so one can get along on a series for three to four years without much updating. Provided, that is, that another series or two purchased in alternative years does have the latest information. An ordering schedule that assures this year's updated guides are available, if only from one or two standard publishers, is desirable.

Publisher series tend to emphasize the same basic data such as location and price of hotels, hours of opening of museums and points of interest, and background information on places and people. Beyond that each specializes.

The first standard is *Fodor's* (there are over 300, under various names such as *Fodor's Europe*) which covers both the highlights to see and hotels and restaurants. The *Michelin* guides are among the oldest in the world, and the most reliable. One volume considers places to stay in X or Y country, while a companion book lists every major and many minor sites to view with sometimes quite detailed explanations. The *Birnbaum* guides provide the standard information on places to see and to stay. The dozen or so guides are updated regularly, and are particularly good for points in the USA.

Fodor's is typical of the guides which have a website. The Web page is primarily a method of advertising numerous books. There is some rather shallow online aids. There are "miniguides" to vacations that give vital information on travel, lodgings, attractions, etc. Also one can "create your own miniguide," but this tends to be slow and it is much faster to look through a travel book, or, for that matter, contact a travel agent.

The "new traveler" appeared in the 1990s, and is catered to by a series of guidebooks that thrive on difficulty and danger. For example, the otherwise middle class, middle of the road *Fielding* aids now have a branch for the adventurer.

Fielding's guides are similar to *Fodor's*, although tend to be a bit more up-market.) Borneo (1998) describes itself as one of "a series of guides on remote regions for adventurers by adventurers." The narrator points out that "I am happy here; soaked to the bone, a steaming rank animal in the middle of primitive jungle." Most might want to stay at home after the first few pages of *Borneo*. Those who thrive on discomfort will find much assistance in similar *Fielding* guides such as *The World's Most Dangerous Places* or *Asia's Top Dive Sites* (primarily deep diving places for danger and excitement). Other travel publishers, from *Lonely Planet* to the aptly names *Rough Guides*, offer similar solace for those seeking adrenaline highs.

On the Web[14]

The librarian who wants *current* material about anything from new plays and museum hours to daily weather reports and the fluctuation of the dollar should use the Net. The simple search is the best. Type in the name of the city or area in the search engine and watch the results. Paris or London, for example, will bring up hundreds of sites, as will any well-known tourist area around the world.

[14]Geared as it is to interests of laypersons, *Yahoo!* magazine at least once a year, and sometimes more often, reports on major travel sites. The informative annotations are evaluative and comparisons are made between sites, e.g., "Gold Star Travel Sites," *Yahoo!*, June, 1999, pp. 128+. Here they give Biztravel.com (www.biztravel.com) the distinction of being the best site for booking trips. See, too, a similar type of comparison in *The New York Times* (May 13, 1999, G1/G6) of "travel agent or travel site?"

Students and laypersons seeking information about a city or country can often find much useful data by playing the role of Net tourist.[15] Many of the sites give in-depth information about historical places as well as biographical sketches of important personalities from politics to sports. Here it is pretty much a "hit-and-miss" type of search, entering the name of the city first, but with patience, a good deal of information usually is forthcoming.

Representative sites:

Citysearch (www.sidewalk.citysearch.com). Current arts and entertainment, weather, local news, best places to eat and sleep, etc. are found here for a dozen major American cities: New York, San Francisco, Los Angeles, Portland, Oregon, Washington and so on. Addresses, phone numbers, travel directions and even a map is furnished. The only problem here is that there is almost too much detail, but for an overall view of today's events in a single city this is tops.[16]

Excite. Your Guide to the World (www.excite.com/travel). A geographical resource page with links to "top cities," "maps," and trip information. Key word search is possible and maps "to 25 U.S. cities" and "top 25 international cities." Tips on hotels, etc. Heavy on promotional advertising, but useful.

Adventure Online (www.adventureonline.com). While this is filled with advertisements about outdoor gear, it is a valuable site for anyone who wants to rough it on the road from New York to the Amazon. Information varies from on the spot e-mail reports to background information on various geographical areas as well as reports on current archaeological activities around the globe. Thanks to vast amounts of geographical and even political data, it is by way of a winding road for the student or layperson looking for information about various parts of the globe. A bit untidy for this kind of search, but if time is no problem, well worth the effort.

---

[15]Sites that will help the traveler in specific parts of the world are numerous. The sites tend to come and go, and new sites appear almost monthly. They all give information on travel questions from hotels to climate as well as historical places to visit. For assortments, see "Around the World in 80 Clicks," *Yahoo!*, July, 1999, pp. 109–111. Beyond countries, every state in the United States has some kind of website, usually of interest to the would–be tourist. Type in the name of the state in the search engine box.

[16]With a bit of diligence and careful searching there are countless breakdowns of this type of information, i.e., separate websites for everything from weather in a particular city to when the zoo is open. See, for example, City Rail Transit (http://pavel.physics. sunysb.edu/RR/metro.html). This shows subway maps for every major, and not a few minor cities from Paris to Hoboken, New Jersey's PATH trains.

Expedia (www.expedia.com) is one of the better examples of travel
sites which are tailored to help the individual do everything from book
flights to reserve hotel rooms. It boasts such features as "Fare Compare"
where the screen shows the lowest fares from point X to point Y. There
are other favorable bits such as "family friendly" travel savings.

SUGGESTED READING

Black, Jeremy, *Maps and History.* New Haven, CT: Yale University Press, 1997. More
than a history, this excellent guide shows the relationship of maps and geography to daily living, economics and culture. From Ortelius' historical atlas
of 1570 to the latest moment, Black traces the fascinating story of maps. See,
too, the estimate on what we are likely to see in maps in coming decades.

Giles, Barbara, "The English-Language Guidebooks to Europe up to 1870" in
Robin Myers *Journeys Through the Market.* New Castle, 1999, pp. 93–106. A
clever, original sketch of the birth of the guidebook, and how it was
employed by the typical English person in the eighteenth and nineteenth
centuries. Little has changed. People today are pretty much interested in
the same points.

Larsgaard, Mary, *Map Librarianship,* 3rd ed. Englewood, CO: Libraries Unlimited,
1998. This is the standard guide to the subject with detailed information
on all aspects of map librarianship from selection to how maps are used
in reference services.

Lewis, G. M. and J.B. Harley, and David Woodward, eds., *The History of Cartography.* Chicago: University of Chicago Press, 1987 to date. This definitive history has seen the death of one of the coeditors, J. B. Harley, and by 2000
had published only five volumes. The first covers ancient and medieval
Europe (1987), while others discuss cartography in non-Western countries.
An infinitely valuable source for any medium to large library. Eventually
there will be 7 to 10 volumes.

Sobel, Dave, *Longitude,* New York: Walker, 1995. 184 pp. The fascinating story
of how to "read" longitude (i.e., the distance east or west on the earth measured in degrees along any latitude line). The puzzle was solved for
mariners by John Harrison, an Englishman with no formal education. The
solution, which took the inventor 46 years to perfect, was a motion-proof
sea-clock. Sobel's book became a best seller.

Tenner, Elka and Katherine Weimer, "Reference Service for Maps," *Reference &
User Services Quarterly,* vol. 38, no. 2, 1998, pp. 181–186. How does the reference librarian find the necessary maps? No problem if one has a sophisticated catalog with detailed bibliographic records. The two university
librarians explain the importance of such records and how they must be
modified for today's needs.

Wilford, John, "Redrawing the World," *The New York Times,* February 6, 2000, Arts
section. Various pages. Celebrating the new edition of the *National Geographic Atlas,* this detailed review not only points out the merits of the
work but moves on to various approaches to judging atlases.

CHAPTER TWELVE
GOVERNMENT DOCUMENTS

What do these diverse publications have in common: *Atlas of United States Mortality, Flights of Discovery, Judaic at the Smithsonian, Revelations From the Russian Archives, Coming to Grips With Your Finances, The North Dakota Tree Book* and, finally, *Be a Super Snooper Sleuth at Your Library?*[1]

They are all government documents, i.e., any publication that is printed at government expense or published by authority of a governmental body. The United States Government Printing Office is responsible for the publication of documents, but more than 70 percent of all government printing is contracted out to private firms. Most of the contracts are based on the lowest, suitable bid.

Publications touch every interest from cosmetics and gardening to international intrigue and centennial celebrations. Here there is something for everyone. In a mid-1990s decision, the United States government joined the Internet Worldwide Web.[2] Free access to almost all public documents is available.

The stamp of reliability and authenticity is guaranteed in a government document. One may disagree with what is written, but this is not

---

[1]"Notable Government Documents," *Library Journal,* May 15, 1998. The titles were chosen as "winners" in this annual evaluation of the best federal, state and local, and international government documents by librarians. The article appears each year around May 15th.

[2]This was an act of the 104th Congress (1995) to make Federal information available free to the Internet public. The decision to put government generated information on the Internet has resulted in a fierce debate between public interest advocates who believe such data should be made available free and companies that purchase the data from government agencies to resell.

to question the accuracy of the source. The parallel factors of reliability and a vast range of information, and information which is free makes the government site (i.e., usually identified in the address by "gov") an ideal place to turn for current information.

Masses of paperwork are ideally suited to digital formats. The U S. Government Printing Office has switched to digital databases, although it maintains the print format as well for popular, general titles. The trend is becoming international. The North Atlantic Treaty Organization in Belgium, for example, offers citations to close to 45,000 papers in its NATO-PCO Database, published each year since 1973. Most of the basic works with this chapter are available online. They represent only a sampling of the overwhelming number of titles that range from *Toxic Release Inventory* from the Superintendent of Documents to the *National Economic–Social and Environmental Database* from the U.S. Department of Commerce.

There are some drawbacks to digital government documents. (1) The Net data is from the late 1980s or the early 1990s. There is little earlier digital information. (2) A considerable amount of repetition exists among the various government departments and agencies. (3) Finally, there is the problem of information overload. All government sites offer a mass of detail beyond the needs of even the specialist, more or less the innocent student or layperson. The situation for the average individual cruising the government sites on the Net is summed up nicely by an expert on such matters:

> Finding U.S. Government information on the Internet is often like walking into a strange house. The house has new, different, and interesting items that you never expect to see even if you know the inhabitants of the house well. Sometimes you find whole rooms in the house that are incredibly surprising, like an art gallery on the second floor.[3]

---

[3]Sydney Pierce, a veteran reference services professor, points out that "things are being added so rapidly on the GPO (Government Printing Office) site that the only thing one can do is keep checking in: (www.gpo.gov)." See, too:

Infomine. University of California (http://lib-www.ucr.edu). This university website offers links to over 5,000 Net sources, including a wide variety of government databases which may be searched by key word, subject, title or various other combinations. The site particularly is useful as it includes not only federal, but state and some local government agencies as well as an excellent selection of foreign and international governments and organizations. Brief annotations indicate the content, scope and purpose of the link. There is a "table of contents" which is another easy to follow lead to information. Also there is a "what's new" section which indicates new material added in the past 20 to 30 days.

Federal Web Locator (www.infoctr.edu/fwl/). Published by the Villanova University Center for Information Law and Policy, this offers links to major government websites. The search mechanism is easy to use, and the organization is equally easy to understand.

Document Forms

Government documents come in many different forms. They do have one thing in common, and that is numbers: In 2000, the Superintendent of Documents sold over 100 million copies of its publications. In the early 2000s the federal government was spending from $6 to $7 billion each year on information sources.

Documents may be considered in terms of issuing agencies: the congressional, judiciary, and executive branches, which include many departments and subdivisions. The documents are classified as: (1) records of government administrations, (2) research documents for specialists, including a considerable number of statistics and data of value to science and business, and (3) popular sources of information.

While this discussion mainly concerns federal documents, state, county, and municipal governing bodies issue publications. Space and scope permits only mention of local documents here, but they are of importance in all libraries.

Some of the mystery surrounding government documents will be dispelled if one compares the government with the average private publisher. The publishing process is much the same, although normally the commercial publication will be expressed in somewhat more felicitous prose.

ORGANIZATION AND SELECTION

Bibliographical control and daily use of documents in reference work are often difficult and requires expertise beyond the average experience of the reference librarian. Nevertheless, there are certain basic guides and approaches which should be familiar to all librarians.

The organization and selection of government documents in all but the largest of libraries is relatively simple. Librarians purchase (or receive free) a limited number of print documents, usually in terms of subjects of interest to users or standard titles, such as the *Statistical Abstract of the United States*.[4] If they are pamphlets, they usually are deposited by subject in a vertical file. If books, they are cataloged and shelved as such. In digital format, they are part of the CD-ROM and online reference service.

---

[4]Throughout this text individual government documents and publications have been described where they fit into a chapter, such as "Ready Reference" or "Bibliography." In this chapter the focus is *only* on the document as a document and not as part of a larger reference unit.

The Superintendent of Document's goal is to turn from print to an electronic format. Eventually the majority of print documents will disappear. They will be replaced by electronic formats, and particularly online. When this happens organization will be another type of problem. Until provisions are made electronically for retrospective items (particularly before the 1990s), the standard print/organizational patterns will remain in place.

Normally, the reference librarian will be responsible for the acquisition of documents. Confusion is minimal because government documents are rightly treated like any other information source and shelved, filed, or clipped like other media. Digitally, guides, bookmarks and memory help the librarian locate the same documents, often with updates, online.

When one moves to the large or specialized libraries, the organizational pattern is either a separate government documents collection or, as in the smaller libraries, an integration of the documents into the general collection.

Even the large libraries tend to partially integrate government documents with the general collection, although complete integration is rare. About one-third of large libraries have total separate collections. The justification for separate collections is that the volume of publications swamps the library and necessitates special considerations of organization and classification. There are other reasons, but on the whole, the decision is the librarian's in seeking the simplest and best method of making the documents available. The separate document collection isolates the materials from the main reference collection. The reference librarians are inclined to think of it as a thing apart and may answer questions with materials at hand rather than attempt to fathom the depths of the documents department.

The wide use of digital reference services has brought the document collection closer to the daily life of the average reference librarian. Still, when it comes down to actually locating the needed material (print or online) it often is left up to a specialist.

Public vs. Private

Now that most current government documents are available free on the Web, why do private carriers, such as DIALOG, continue to offer those same documents online, but at a fee? The answer is service. Some claim the private firms offer more sophisticated searching, more rapid document delivery (either online or via fax and the mails).

In comparing a private service (CIS's *Congressional Universe*) with government services, the "Reference Books Bulletin" sounds a general conclusion when private vs. public are reviewed: Compared to government databases," *Congressional Universe* provides superior indexing and abstracting and more full text covering a greater number of years."[5] One wonders how long private companies can serve up documents at a price when the government is offering them for free on the Web? No one knows the answer.[6]

A single example of how a private company takes over government information and sets a fee for its use can be found in the search engine *Northern Lights*. (It is to be stressed, this is only one example. It may change tomorrow. Still it illustrates the general approach of turning "free" to "fee.") What does the library receive for a fee that it can't get for free? *Northern Lights,* as others who succeed in this field, has a ready answer: complete, faster service.

The service is called *Usgovsearch* (www.usgovsearch.com). It is a search engine which covers all possibilities in one sweep, thus eliminating the necessity to search website by website. The machine claims it indexes approximately 22,000 government and military websites. Here one finds over 4 million pages...and growing. *Northern Lights* says only about one-quarter of the government sites can be found via other search machines. They assert they cover almost 100 percent of such sites. Charges vary for otherwise free sites. *Northern Light* has subscription rates from $5 per day to over $1,000 per year.

Evaluation

There are no problems with evaluation of government documents. There are no choices. One either accepts or rejects, say, *The Statistical Abstract of the United States.* The government has no competitors, and evaluating such a document in terms of acquisitions is as fruitless as commanding the seas to dry up. Government documents are unique and no one, but no one, is going to challenge them with another publication. These days evaluation is more in terms of how the information is delivered rather than the information itself. What, for example, is the best print or digital software for the text of the *Congressional Record?*

Depository Libraries[7]

In order to ensure that the documents are freely available, the government establishes places where they may be examined. These are called

---

[5] *Booklist,* June 15, 1998, p. 1800.

[6] This is an involved puzzle which lines up different notions about public vs. private. For example, one idea is to have the government simply transfer ownership or copyright of agency documents to a private sector publisher. That will solve "free" on the Net, but at what cost to the public?

[7] When all government documents become available online, the depository library may disappear. A few depository libraries will be retained to house retrospective documents, but

depository libraries. There are some 1,400 depository libraries in the United States, with at least one in every Congressional District. The purpose is to have centers with relatively complete runs of government documents located throughout the country. In 1995 the Federal Depository Library Program (DLP) celebrated its hundredth birthday.

Federal agencies are not mandated to disseminate material through the program. Much information has been and is lost. A central system to ensure deposits of all, not just select government information sources is needed and this is rapidly happening via the Net. The catch so far: lack of earlier government documents and still no way of insisting all agencies make documents they consider "sensitive" available to the public.

The depositories receive print publications free of charge from the Superintendent of Documents. In each of the 50 states there is one or more depository library that accepts *every* unclassified government publication. Few other libraries take all the government documents (the average is about 54 percent of what is published). About two-thirds of the depository libraries are academic, whereas public libraries account for about 20 percent of the total.

The remaining (less than 14 percent) consists of federal, state agency, court law, historical society, medical and private membership libraries.

The basic problem faced by all but the largest of the depository libraries is the volume of material. Much of it is of limited use, and a good deal is nothing but raw data and statistics employed to support arguments or gathered more for the sake of gathering than for any specific purpose. The volume problem will be solved by putting most, if not all, of the documents in digital formats.

Acquisition[8]

Depository libraries have a peculiar set of problems, but for the average library, the acquisitions process is much simpler. Once a print or CD-ROM document has been selected for purchase its acquisition is no more difficult—indeed, often somewhat easier—than that of a book or periodical.

Few libraries want to depend totally for basic government documents (or, for that matter more esoteric ones) completely in a digital format. Until that changes, the following steps are the rule.

---

not for current titles which may be available only in electronic form. In order to reach a select group of federal depository libraries, on the Web, turn to: *Federal Depository Library Gateways.* Superintendent of Documents. (www.access.gpo.gov/su_docs/aces/aaces004.html). This offers links to about 20 geographically scattered libraries from California to Maryland. Each carries instructions for using the library gateway document service.

[8]Again, where all documents are available online, the acquisitions picture will change. It may be then easier to access digital formats, but complications are guaranteed.

1. Payment may be made in advance by purchase of coupons from the Superintendent of Documents. In the case of extensive purchases, deposit accounts may be established.

2. Some documents may be obtained free from members of Congress. However, as the supply of documents is limited, the member of Congress should be notified of need in advance. It is particularly advisable to get on the regular mailing list of one's representative or senator to receive publications.

Issuing agencies often have a stock of publications that must be ordered directly from the agency. These frequently include valuable specialized materials, from ERIC documents to scientific reports.

3. There are government bookstores that sell documents. In addition, some larger private bookstores sell the documents, or at least government published books dealing with popular subjects from space to gardening.

Many citizens purchase government documents each day, primarily for "how-to-do-it" type information, as well as for hobbies and personal interests. *The U.S. Consumer Information Center* (www.pueblo.gsa.gov) is a source of a wide variety of government documents, most of which are considered of interest and value to laypeople. Full bibliographic information is given and one may order directly online as the source of the particular document is given along with its price. Arrangement is by broad subject categories that are then subdivided. Note: Some, but hardly all of the documents may be read or downloaded by the individual at his or her computer.

GUIDES

Print: Morehead, Joe. *Introduction to United States Government Information Sources,* 6th ed. Englewood, CO: Libraries Unlimited, Inc., 1999, 440 pp. $65.

Print: Schwarzkopf, Leroy. Government Reference Books. Englewood, CO: Libraries Unlimited, Inc., 1972 to date, biennial. $67.50.

The basic textbook in the field is the Morehead volume, which is revised about every four years. It is a nice combination of facts about individual reference works and a clear, concise explanation of how the government manages to publish documents. Thanks to the superior organization and fine writing style, the textbook is easy to read. Both the beginner and the expert will find considerable assistance here. It is the first place to turn when puzzled about some mysterious aspect of the acquisition, organization, and selection of government documents. The sixth edition puts particular emphasis on how digital information has drastically changed access to government publications. See particularly the eleventh chapter which is a clear explanation of various departments and agencies.

Government Reference Books is published every two years and is a roundup of basic reference books, many of which are not familiar to either the layperson or the expert. Here they are arranged by broad subject, that is, general, social sciences, science and technology, and humanities. The documents are then indexed by author, title, and subject. Each is fully described. About 1,200 titles are annotated every two years. Carefully edited and easy to use, the Schwarzkopf bibliography augments the standard sources.

The best, selective list of government documents for small- to medium-sized libraries is published each year by the American Library Association's Government Documents Round Table or GODORT. The annotated list of 50 to 75 publications includes federal, state and local efforts as well as those published by international groups. Usually the list appears each May in *Library Journal*. Frank Hoffman's *Guide to Popular U.S. Government Publications* (5th ed. Englewood, CO: Libraries Unlimited, 1998, 300 pp.). The 1998 edition—and this frequently is updated, covers publications issued from 1995–1996. The 1,600 titles are organized by broad topics.

On the Web

There are a half-dozen or so guides to Internet access to government information sources. The three best which are updated regularly: Peter Hernon et al., *U.S. Government on the Web* (Englewood, CO: Libraries Unlimited). The first edition of this came out in 1999 and is a clear guide to about 1,000 reliable government websites. It is directed as much to the average user (including high school students) as the researcher. A first choice for most libraries.

Two worthwhile often updated supporting volumes include: Bruce Maxwell, *How To Access the Federal Government on the Internet* (Washington, DC: Congressional Quarterly) and Greg Notess, *Government Information on the Internet* (Lanham, Maryland: Bernan Press). Maxwell includes descriptions of close to 500 federal Internet sites. The entries are fully annotated with basic instructions on how to find the Net site. There are good introductory chapters on the use of government documents for study and research. Notess is less selective, but more inclusive, with virtually every site listed and annotated.

Searching On the Web

Understandably, government websites pretty well follow a standard format. They inevitably include, although not necessarily in this order, the following data: (1) Background and history of the agency or branch. (2) The key personnel, often with Net addresses as well as e-mail addresses. (3) A description of what the agency is now doing, often in some detail. (4) Publication lists and catalogs that can be ordered or sometimes accessed on the Net. (5) Links to similar organizations as well as subordinate agencies and divisions.

There are several ways of searching a particular government document on the Net. Once a specific site is located most follow the standard patterns, i.e., the use of Boolean logic, key words, phrases and the name of a document or its author.

There are some key differences from the norm. With documents one may find a specific title by using the Superintendent of Documents classification number. This is assigned by the Superintendent, just as the Library of Congress, the individual libraries, assign Dewey Decimal classifications or Library of Congress classifications. The SDCN is in a different form, but follows the same classification pattern.

Where a general approach seems best, then turn to one of the overview Web sites such as *GPO Access* that have links to various government branches and departments and agencies. Here luck and a bit of knowledge may help the user focus almost immediately on what is needed. Conversely, because these sites take in so much, it is unlikely to be productive unless one has at least a basic knowledge of government.

Another method, and potentially the least rewarding of all is to call up the broad sites for the three primary parts of government, i.e., the executive branch (and its departments), the legislative branch and the judicial branch. For example, the media has generated a good deal of publicity about how easy it is to reach the *White House* by clicking on: (www.whitehouse.gov). This is fine if one wants to take a virtual tour of the White House, view historical documents or, for that matter, get the full text of current press releases. Most of this is entertaining, and a bit educational, but it is so broad as to leave the average student lost when trying to apply the mass of material to a paper or talk. At the same time if the librarian is looking for the full text of today's President's meeting with the press, and knows that is what he or she wants, then this would be a prime site. It would fulfill the suggestion in (1) above where the best approach is to go to the precise government site.

Note: The difficulty with regulating pornography on the Web is apparent when one realizes the small difference between the government White House URL and one offering humor or rated-X movies at:

(htwww.whitehouse.com). The only difference in the URLs is the critical "gov" and "com."

On the Web—Search

The importance of having specific sites to search for government documents and information about government can be illustrated briefly. The
question is "Who contributed X number of dollars to Y congressional candidate?" The answer might be found in any of the online newspapers or the
online magazine indexes, but it is unlikely it would be in the detail required.

A best bet here is to know where to find sites that specifically are
involved with finance elections and government. Knowledge of the work
of the *Federal Election Commission* would be a good beginning. That in turn
would lead to related sites.

Here are three specific sites for specific answers to the question of
who gave what.

Federal Election Commission (www.fec.gov). This shows contributions
by individuals to political campaigns as well as data concerning election
finance in general. Here one can find financial reports on all candidates
in considerable detail, and links to related sites.

FECInfo (www.tray.com/fecinfo). A commercial site, although free
to Net users, this offers a wide selection of government statistics and
data on elections and donations of funds to candidates. The joy for the
average user is that one simply types in a phrase, key words or a name
to find out what is available. The response will be brief, but accurate. A
typical question concerns what X or Y donated to a political candidate.

Common Cause (www.commoncause.org). This public interest group
studies how money influences legislation. It is well known and often is in the
news. The material behind its research is free to the public on the Net.

This is a single example of how to trace sometimes difficult data
in government documents and related websites. Note that the quest
begins with knowledge of a government agency, moves on to a related private information source and closes with an even more general approach
to the whole problem of money and government.

GOVERNMENT ORGANIZATION

Online: In GPO Access (see p. 460).
CD: U.S. Government Organization Manual. Alexandria, VA: Government
   Counseling, Ltd., 1993 to date, annual. $99.

Print: United States Government Manual, Washington: Government Printing Office, 1935 to date, annual, 904 pp., paperback. $30.

Print: U.S. Congress Joint Committee on Printing, *Official Congressional Directory.* Washington, DC: U.S. Government Printing Office, 1809 to date, biennial, 1625 pp., paperback. $15.

Normally, federal documents tend to be divided by the source of the document. As everyone knows the primary divisions of government are the legislative, judicial and executive. Each branch issues masses of material.

1. *President/Executive.* Here are many documents, although the most used are the executive orders and presidential proclamations. Under the executive branch one finds the various departments and agencies.

2. *Departments and agencies of government.* These have their own special interests and if one knows what type of publication can be found, say, NASA, it is much easier to narrow the search either in print/CD-ROM or on the Net.

3. *Legislative.* Congress, i.e., the House of Representatives and the Senate, are sources of ongoing debates about laws, budget, and almost anything else of interest to the American public. Between action on the floor and hundreds of hearings and investigations there is a constant flow of information.

4. *Judiciary.* This includes decisions of the courts from the Supreme Court down to the individual federal courts throughout the United States.

United States Government Manual

The basic purpose of the *Manual* is to give in detail the organization, activities, and chief officers of all government agencies within the legislative, judicial, and executive branches. Each of the agencies is discussed separately, and the units within each organizational pattern are clearly defined. Occasionally, charts and diagrams are employed. The style is factual, yet discursive enough to hold the interest of anyone remotely involved with such matters.

Directory data is published for each agency, as well as telephone numbers, addresses, names of officials, and addresses of regional offices for the major departments. There are several indexes, including one by subject. A useful feature of each year's issue is the list of agencies transferred, terminated, or abolished. Full particulars are given. This, by the way, is a justification for holding several years of the *Manual* on the shelves. All too often, someone will want information on a certain agency that can be found only in earlier editions.

Historical queries may be fielded in another useful work: *A Historical Guide to the U.S. Government* (New York: Oxford University Press, 1997. 704 pp. $95). An alphabetically arranged guide, this covers all of the major departments and agencies of government as well as the other divisions. Such things as branch. Such subjects as the budget, lighthouse service and the freedom of information act are covered in detail. A good index helps.

A quick, although relatively expensive way to find information on more than 200,000 individuals working in office type positions for federal, state, county and local governments is via *Carroll's Government Directory Online* (www.carrollpub.com). At about $1,300 a year the library is given the power to search for names in dozens of ways from the name itself to titles and functions.

Congress

Issued every two years, *The Congressional Directory* includes biographies of members of Congress. The sections include data, too, on Supreme Court justices, names of foreign representatives and consular offices in the United States, and the chief officers of departments and independent agencies. It is a type of "who's who" of government, along with the essential addresses, phone numbers, and even maps of congressional districts. The drawback: Matters change quickly in Washington and the *Directory* comes out biennially. It cannot be trusted, for example, to have the latest information on committee assignments or members of the press corps, both of which are included. One might think it would be current when first issued, but it can be up to six months behind the official publication date. The problem will be solved when the reference work goes online and is updated when needed.

There are numerous more current directories. An example is *Staff Directories* (Mt. Vernon, VA: Staff Directories, 1990 to date, semiannual. $395) which is on CD-ROM and includes three directory files covering the congressional staff, the judicial staff, and the federal staff (about 30,000 executives and military people). All three have a limited number of short biographies, as well as the standard data from telephone numbers and titles to addresses. The bulk of the volume is an alphabetically arranged entry of members of Congress, as well as resident commissioners, delegates, and vice presidents. A short "who's-who" type of entry is used for each name.

Among the most-used directories and biographical sources for members of government, at both the national and local levels, is *Who's Who in American Politics* (New York: R. R. Bowker Company, 1967 to date, biennial). This work gives information on 25,000 individuals at the federal, state, and local level. The "who's-who" data include office held and current address as well as basic biographical facts.

Where does one find information on former members of Congress no longer listed in the *Congressional Directory?* They will be listed in such sources as the *American National Biography* (if deceased) or in a good encyclopedia. But for short, objectives sketches of all senators and representatives who served from 1774 to the present, the best single source is *Biographical Directory of the American Congress, 1774–Present* (Washington: Government Printing Office, various dates, prices). There is a handy first section which includes officers of the executive branch. Note: A free online version is at the website: (http://bioguide.congress.gov). Useful for current updated material which may not be in the current print edition.

Executive and Judiciary

CD: U.S. Presidents. Minneapolis, MN: Quanta Press, Inc., 1990 to date, updated as needed. $69.95.

Print: Kane, Joseph. *Facts About the Presidents,* 6th ed. New York: H. W. Wilson Company, 1993, 432 pp. $75.

Print: Encyclopedia of the American Presidency. New York: Simon & Schuster, 1994, 4 vols. $355.

Questions concerning the presidents are answered in considerable detail in almost any encyclopedia as well as in the basic guides to government discussed in this chapter. The two titles listed here are easier to use because they offer facts in a consistent, well-organized fashion. Also, of course, they are both limited to the presidents.

Everything that anyone wants to know about a president will be found on the CD-ROM *U.S. Presidents.* The disc even includes pictures of the gentlemen, from the first to the immediate occupant of the White House. While the data is available in any good encyclopedia, it has the advantage of having supporting statistical comparisons as well as historical sketches of the first ladies.

The first section of Kane has a chapter on each of the presidents, including family life. A bibliography is included. Possibly of more use, at least for ready-reference purposes, is the second part, which is a comparative guide of all the presidents. Here one finds everything from the number of children each had to their last words. Also, there are facts on the office itself from legal problems to the cabinet officials.

The definitive work on the subject is the four-volume *Encyclopedia of the American Presidency.* It is a scholar's dream. There is little that is not covered, from the dentistry of George Washington to the romances of some of the other gentlemen who filled the office. Thanks to an excellent index one might add that it is a place of last resort for puzzled reference librarians unable to find, for example, a clue as to the fate of President Cleveland's home after he left office. And there are other gems.

CATALOGS

Online: GPO Access. Washington, DC: U.S. Government Printing Office, 1994 to date, monthly, www.access.gpo.gov/su_docs/dbsearch.[9] Free.

Online: Catalog of U.S. Government Publications. Washington, DC: U.S. Government Printing Office (GPO), 1994 to date, monthly, www.access. gpo.gov/su_docs/locators/cgp/). Free. DIALOG file 66, $15 per hour. Also on OCLC and other carriers.

CD: GPO, plus various publishers. 1895 to date, monthly. Price varies.

Print: Monthly Catalog of the United States Government Publications. 1895 to date, monthly. $199.

GPO Access is subtitled "keeping America informed electronically."[10] Put online by the Government Printing Office, it casts a wide net. It has links and offers access to every major and not a few minor Web government document sites. It has numerous full text, basic government documents, online Congressional bills, laws and other documents may be called up through this site. In addition it includes: (1) Links to collections in about a dozen designated university libraries. (2) Links to online databases in the Federal Depository Libraries. (3) A "History of Bills" keeps track of what is going on in Congress. Searching ease varies with each set of documents, but Boolean logic may be used in the majority of cases, as well as key word searching.[11] (4) Links are furnished to most government agencies and departments. A few examples will indicate the wealth of data available:

Department of Education (www.ed.gov). The source of information on American education, from-two page reports to the impressive *Digest*

---

[9]Links to the *Access* site are available on many university Web pages. One of the best, because it offers a simple search interface: *GPO Gate* (www.gpo.ucop.edu). This is put up by the University of California, San Diego and offers numerous methods of searching not found in the government database.

[10]For a good explanation of *Access*, see "GPO Access: Government at its Best?" *Database*, April/May, 1998, pp. 41+.

[11]Information and links to foreign government documents is found at *Governments on the WWW* (www.gksoft.com/govt/en/). Includes parliaments, ministries, offices, law courts, embassies, and city councils from over 200 countries. (Considered a "best reference site" in the 1998 *Library Journal* runoff, e.g., April 15, 1998 issue, p. 48).

of Education Statistics. Thanks to an excellent search software it is relatively easy to find what is needed by subject, name, etc. Much of the material available in full text online.

Department of Health and Human Services (www.os.dhhs.gov). With health as a main interest of both government and laypeople, this is a perfect site to find the latest information on subjects from specific diseases to the number of dollars being spent or cut from the health budget. Note: there is a link to the *Consumer Information Center* so one can download full texts.

Department of the Interior (www.doi.gov). For most laypeople the primary interest here is the profuse data on the National Park Service as well as the U.S. Fish and Wildlife service. There is loads of information and much of the material can be used as much for school work as for vacations. Note: this site includes information on American Indian affairs.

Department of Justice (www.usdoj.gov). Here is the place to turn for massive statistics on crime. Numerous full text reports and studies are available online. A related site: *Federal Bureau of Investigation* (www.fbi.gov). While this site is for law enforcement officers, it does have general information of use to students, e.g., there is background data on the general problems of law enforcement, information on investigations (specific and general), and statistics on crime. See, too, the ten most wanted fugitives.

U.S. Department of Commerce's National Trade Data Bank (www.stat-usa.gov/) is a superior economic-trade source. It has data from more than 20 different government agencies and has some 400,000 plus documents. Data moves from agriculture and export financing to import and export statistics by both commodity and country. OCLC says this is "the most widely held computer file in the WorldCat database." The closest runner up is the *Statistical Abstract of the United States.*[12]

Catalog of U.S. Government Publications

The *Catalog of U.S. Government Publications* (also titled: *Monthly Catalog of the U.S. Government Publications*) is a record of publications of U.S. government agencies, a type of *National Union Catalog* for the government. The electronic *Catalog* offers a relatively inexpensive way of searching and is familiar to almost every reference librarian. Where there is a significant collection of separately filed documents libraries tend to rely on the *Cat-*

[12]"Top 100 computer files in WorldCat," *OCLC Newsletter,* July/August, 1998, p. 16.

alog both as a finding device and catalog, as well as a source of information for purchase.

Arrangement in the print *Catalog* is by the classification number of the Superintendent of Documents. This amounts to arrangement by issuing agency; that is, most documents issued by the Library of Congress will be listed under that agency name—most, but not all. Special classification situations arise when documents are arranged under a main entry other than the organization that issued the document. Hence, it is always wise to check the indexes and not assume that the document will be under the likely agency, department, and so on. There are four major indexes: author, title, subject, and series and reports. For reference, the subject and title indexes are the most useful. The subject and title indexes list the documents by their full title. There are about 400,000 citations to government publications, and an estimated 2,000 records each month are added to the catalog.

With that, the print version has rapidly fallen out of favor because of the searching problems. In digital form, and particularly with Boolean logic, the experienced librarian can normally find what is wanted, if only by searching by key words.

CONGRESS[13]

Online: CIS. Bethesda, MD: Congressional Information Service Inc., 1970 to date, monthly, www.cispubs.com. DIALOG file 101, $60 per hour. Also LEXIS-NEXIS and other carriers.
CD: Congressional Masterfile, 1970 to date, quarterly. Price varies.
Print: CIS/Index to Publications of the U.S. Congress, 1970 to date, monthly. Service.

Online: Congressional Universe. Bethesda, MD: Congressional Information Service Inc., 1998 to date, daily, www.cispubs.com. Rate varies. LEXIS-NEXIS and other carriers.

Online: CQ Weekly Report. Washington, DC: Congressional Quarterly Inc., 1983 to date, weekly, http://library.cq.com. Rate varies.
Print: 1945 to date, weekly. Rates vary.

---

[13]The best guide to Congress and its numerous documents is the two volume: *CQ's Guide to Congress.* (Washington, DC: Congressional Quarterly, 2000 edition, 1200 pp. $295). The two largest commercial government information firms, CIS and CQ offer their own online services. As CIS is a wholly owned subsidiary of LEXIS-NEXIS, it is no surprise CIS indexes are available there as well.

Online: CQ Researcher. *Washington, DC: Congressional Quarterly Inc., 1991 to date, weekly, http://library.cq.com. Rate varies.*
CD: 1992 to date, quarterly. $695.
Print: 1923 to date, quarterly. $340.

Online: Thomas. Legislative Information on the Internet. Washington, DC: Library of Congress, 1989 to date, daily, http://thomas.loc.gov. Free.

All of the indexes listed here, with the exception of *Thomas* are published by commercial firms. All, except *Thomas,* have high subscription costs. All inevitably are employed in libraries, business, government, etc. where the high price of the index is absorbed by the organizations.

With close to 300,000 citations, and about one thousand added each month, the commercial Congressional Information Service online, CD-ROM and print indexes are the place to turn to find congressional publications. These are records, with abstracts, of hearings, reports, House and Senate documents as well as bill prints and Executive and treaty publications. As the publisher points out: "Records of hearings comprise several subrecords, each of that contents abstracts of testimony given by individual witnesses or groups of witnesses."

The *CIS/Index* is a blessing for the reference librarian seeking information on the progress of a bill through Congress. Popular names of bills, laws, and reports are given, as well as the subject matter of those materials. In addition, an index covers the same material by bill number, report number, and so on.

As Congress is almost as ubiquitous in its interests as the Government Printing Office (and, for that matter, *Books in Print*), there is little subject matter that can't be found in the *CIS* indexes. Broad areas of commerce, economics and technology are considered as are health, education and the finer points of foreign affairs. Thanks to a detailed subject index in the print volumes, as well as word, phrases, key words, etc. search possibilities in the electronic versions, it is relatively easy to locate an answer to almost any question concerning government.

Online searching is made easy through a clear menu system that leads the user through various paths to the documents. The user may search by standard index terms, congressional session and data, the name of a witness, the title of a hearing, committee prints, serial set, and so on. A considerable amount of information—as in the printed work—is given on the screen. Often it is enough so the user does not have to turn to the actual document.

There is a complete system for the library that can afford to purchase all the indexed materials. *CIS/Congressional Bills, Resolutions & Laws on Microfiche* offers the full-text collection in one place. The user locates the desired item in the index and, through a simple keyword system, finds the microfiche copy. Eventually most full text will be online. The Index is in two parts: (1) The index section offers access by subject, author, and title. This section is cumulated quarterly, and there is an annual. (2) The summary section gives the full title of the document and includes an abstract of most of the items indexed.

Congressional Universe

"Congressional Universe is a document librarian's dream,"[14] claims the Reference Books Bulletin. Why? Because of its online ease of use and careful organization. Possibly more important, one section offers the full text of bills from the 10th Congress on. Also available are the full text of laws, the majority of hearings and many of the committee prints as well as three quarters of the House and Senate documents. Most of this is from 1994 to 1995 to date.There are a total of eight broad research areas, most of which are supported by full text online. These cover the above as well as current topics in Congress and Washington. They move from "Congressional Publications" to "Bills, Laws, Regulations." Another valuable feature: links to similar services.

"*Congressional Universe* has sped light years forward to provide access to a tremendous amount of material. The best news is that *Congressional Universe* should be affordable to public and academic libraries."[15] The online price (2000) varies with number of users, but begins around $2,500 per year.

CQ Weekly Report

The best day-by-day coverage of U.S. Congressional activity is carried in the *CQ (Congressional Quarterly) Weekly Report.* Here are summaries of all major, and some minor congressional activity from hearings and debates to reports of votes and floor action. As with the *CIS* series, every conceivable subject can be located in either the print or online publication.

The Report, as well as other services in the series, has two distinct advantages: *(a)* It is updated weekly. *(b)* Almost all documents are online in full text, via other CQ services. The *Report* is by another private publisher and it supplements its rival, the *CIS/Index.* It, too, focuses primarily on congressional activity.

The *Report,* a much-used reference aid, is similar in some ways to a congressional version of *Facts on File.* It is not an index but a summary of the week's past events, a summary which is often sufficient to either (1)

[14]*Booklist,* June 15, 1998, p. 1800.
[15]*Ibid.*

identify a government document to be later found in a specialized work, or (2) answer, in one step, a reference query. Each issue analyzes in detail both congressional and general political activity of the week. The major bills are followed from the time they are introduced until they are passed and enacted into law (or killed along the way). A handy table of legislation shows at a glance where the bills are in the Congress. Cross-references to previous weekly reports allow easy access to material until the quarterly index is issued and cumulated throughout the year.

Trying to keep track of a piece of legislation, from its formation to its final passage (or death) is difficult. The process is made relatively easy through a series of online services offered by the publisher of *CQ Weekly Report* under the umbrella term "CQ Washington Alert Service." The base of the system is the *CQ Bill Tracking* (1983 to date, daily) which chronicles all bills and resolutions introduced into Congress since the 98th Congress. There are cross-references to the *CQ Weekly Report* and *Congressional Record*. The full bibliographical information helps find the piece of legislation. Also the online system has summaries of the bills and resolutions beginning with the 101st Congress. The user may find background on members of Congress, research current issues, and so on. The service offers, too, the full text of bills and major documents. The main menu lists all of the databases that may be searched individually or across as required.

The *Congressional Quarterly Almanac,* by the same publisher (1945 to date, annual. $195) is a handy reference work for almost all libraries. The annual divides the work of Congress into 11 subject areas (from environment and health to transportation and law). Summaries are given of each bill in the various subject categories. Most of the material is analyzed objectively. In addition, there is a handy summary of Supreme Court decisions and data on Presidential messages. Thanks to a splendid index, it is the ideal reference work in the area it covers.

CQ Researcher

In an effort to reach libraries with limited budgets, *The Report* publisher has issued the much used *CQ Researcher* since the early 1920s. As of the 1990s it became available electronically. The Reference Books Bulletin highly praises the service and points out it is "long noted for its accuracy, objectivity, and almost uncanny timeliness." It serves a wide range of users "from a high school student preparing a speech or term paper to a journalism graduate student writing an editorial to practitioners in such fields as mass media, political science, health sciences and education."[16]

[16]Mary Ellis, "Another look at the CQ Researcher" *Booklist,* January 1 & 15, 1999, p. 928.

The weekly analysis offers objective, well researched comments on key current political, social and international issues that have been part of the federal-international scene over the previous week. Thanks to its organization and careful coverage it is an excellent source of information.

While expensive, it is relatively less costly than the other commercial services. On the other hand *Thomas*—see below—is free and serves much the same purpose, although it is not arranged as well as the *Research*.

Thomas

Unlike commercial services, *Thomas* is a government database and has the delight of being free. It is stripped to essentials and is easy to use. *Thomas* is for laypersons and overworked reference librarians. It's many advantages include daily update, the text of many documents online and a summary of congressional activity.

The *Thomas* homepage, as conceived by The Library of Congress, is a model of its type. It includes these helpful features: (1) A "quick search text of bills" that can be searched by bill number or by word/phrase. (2) Frequently asked questions. (3) A House and Senate directory. (4) Links to Congressional Internet services as well as Library of Congress Web links.

The main information page is divided into six parts: Congress Now; Bills; Congressional Record; Committee Information; The legislative process (an essay on how laws are made and enacted); and Historical documents. There is a clear, easy to read eight–page summary "About Thomas" which should be examined by anyone who plans to use this site for more than a single search.

Legislative Questions and Answers

Print federal documents could fill every shelf in the largest library. Given the vast amount of material, it is a good idea to know what precisely is needed before beginning a government documents search. So, first and foremost, have a specific idea of: *(a)* the subject matter required as well as the time frame and the amount needed; and/or *(b)* the author or name of the document required. It is likely in nine cases out of ten the jumping off point will be by subject.

With a subject there is one basic approach to finding information in government documents: know where to go. This means an understanding of the various branches and departments of agencies of government. With that one can pinpoint which agency, for example, is likely to have information on the environment problems of the Pacific Northwest. The *United States Government Manual* will explain the different parts of the federal government and their responsibilities. The *Monthly Catalog of U.S. Government Publications* will show precisely what each division of government publishes.

Typical legislative questions may be answered in most of the afore-mentioned reference works. For nonexperts *Thomas* is by far the best place to turn. Those with more detailed searches will use the commercial services. The basic steps, though, are much the same:

1. "I am looking for information about a congressional hearing."[17] Turn to the *CIS/Index* which covers subjects and titles as well as other points of access such as the name of the committee. (This can be done via *Thomas* but the *CIS* is more precise.)

a. Lacking the *Index*, or for hearings of several years ago, turn to the *Monthly Catalog* where the subject, title, and committee involved offer access.

b. *PAIS* (Public Affairs Information Service) offers a subject approach to most major hearings, but not all, and it is highly selective. Note, too, that *PAIS* will index periodicals and some books and reports about the hearings, and so for background information this is most useful.

c. Other sources include current newspapers (usually online) such as *The New York Times* or online periodicals in the subject area.

2. "What is happening to the bill which guarantees three little pigs for every family in America?" Here one again might turn to the *CIS/Index*, but a more current, somewhat easier-to-follow approach is offered by the *CQ Weekly Report*. This traces the development of the bill into a law. See sections "On the Floor" and "In Committee." See, too, the excellent status tables of important legislation that includes the votes as well.

3. "Where can I find a current law?[18] It just became law." Laws are cumulated at the end of each session of Congress in volumes called

---

[17]When someone desires a new law, normally a "hearing" is held before Congress (either/or both House and Senate) to determine the wisdom of the proposed law. Expert testimony is given. Also, hearings are heard to clarify a public issue such as the budget hearings; examine the appointment of officials; and so forth. Hearings are familiar to an estimated 30 million people who watch C-Span (the cable television network). This channel often gives full television coverage of Senate and House hearings about a given issue and debates about new proposed laws.

A *report* is the result of the hearing and the recommendations of the legislative body. This accompanies the proposed new law, that is, the *bill* as it goes to the full House and/or Senate.

[18]When the bill is passed either by both houses of Congress or by one (as procedure dictates), it becomes a "law." Of course, many hearings do not result in either a report or a bill or a law; and numerous bills are killed or vetoed by the President before they become law. Actually, if it really did "just" become law, it probably would appear only in what is called "slip law" form, that is, an unbound pamphlet which has not been cumulated and bound as part of the *Statutes at Large*. These are normally identified by a public law number and filed as such according to their reference government document section. See: *FedLaw Easy Search* (Phoenix, AZ: Oryx, 1998). This CD-ROM provides quick searches of *Statutes at Large* and the *United States Code*, plus related data.

Statutes at Large (1789 to date). Later the laws are organized in a more detailed fashion and become part of the *U.S. Code*. Current laws are in the *Statutes* and those of some standing are in the *Code*. While the full law may not be given, the content is reported, often with its implications, in the *CIS/Index, CQ Weekly Report* and the other reference works listed above.

These steps will result in finding 90 to 95 percent of the answers to questions put to the reference librarian about ongoing federal legislative activities.

Periodical Index

CD: U.S. Government Periodicals Index. Washington, DC: Congressional Information Service, 1994 to date, quarterly. $795.
Print: 1994 to date, quarterly. $795.

The *U.S. Government Periodicals Index* gives access to 180 government published periodicals.[19] The index follows the usual place, subject, corporate name, and the like, as entry points. Although expensive, the index has a definite place in large research libraries. Much of the information found in the federal journals and magazines is found nowhere else. Subjects range from economics and business to satellites and ethics. And while it is true most of the emphasis is on science and technology, there is a great deal of information on social sciences and politics.

INDEXES AND THE CENSUS

Online: CENDATA. (Census Data) Washington, DC: U.S. Bureau of the Census, 1980 to date, daily. Free on the Internet (www.census.gov).[20]
Print: Current Population Reports, various dates and prices.

Online: Tiger Map Server Browser. Current data only, irregular. Free on the Internet (http://tiger.census.gov/cgi-bin/mapbrowse-tbl).
CD: TIGER/Line Files. Current data only, irregular. Price varies.

Data collected by the U.S. Bureau of the Census are the statistical backbone of many of the statistical works considered in this text. Often

[19]There are about 2,000 periodicals and serials currently available from the federal government and probably several times that number from agencies and sections not found in Washington.

[20]This URL is not CENDATA *per se* but is divided into eleven parts, one of which, "Uncle Sam's Reference Shelf," gives popular statistics on everything from climatic conditions to rankings of state by income, i.e., essentially the material found in the *Statistical Abstract of the United States.* Beyond that there are links to more refined statistical data, including CENDATA.

the secondary statistical sources (such as *Statistical Abstract of The United States*) are enough, but where primary material is required the librarian turns to the U.S. Bureau of the Census. Before discussing the basic sources, consider other excellent places to go for both statistical data and for Census Bureau information. First, one should turn to *Fed Stats* (www.fedstats.gov), discussed in the statistics section of the chapter on Ready Reference Sources as is *American Statistics Index*. Second, other business and related indexes (from *Predicasts* to the *CIS/Index*) will analyze census material. Third, for a detailed description of the various files and reports there is the *Bureau of the Census Catalog* (Washington, DC: Government Printing Office, 1946 to date, annual). Essentially it arranges news and information about statistical data by subject, from agriculture to trade. There is a detailed index that allows one to locate material by a specific area. Most of the statistical data found in reference works, including those considered in this chapter, are based on the last *Census of Population*. The 10-year overview is the single best and most expansive source of information of its type in the world.

CENDATA

CENDATA (i.e., Census Data) draws its data from the most recent census (2000) as well as from previous surveys. Online its primary advantage is the daily update that takes into consideration everything from economic and demographic reports on agriculture and business to housing and durable goods manufacturing. The database also includes information on all U.S. counties and most of the small to large cities.

In other words this is a statistician's dream. The delight of the expert, though, is matched by the confusion for the casual visitor. It is a difficult database to search, despite helpful menus and other aids. Nothing is quite like it for current data. Note, too, it includes statistics for more than 200 countries outside of the United States on such things as life expectancy, literacy, agriculture, and so forth.

TIGER Map

Tiger Map Server Browser. TIGER (Topographical Integrated Geographic Encoding and Referencing), from the U.S. Census Bureau, is employed by a majority of commercial Net map sites. It has the advantage of providing detailed street maps for every American community as well as a considerable amount of census data about the area covered by the particular map. In order to use, the searcher must have the city, state and zip code. (Easiest access is by the zip code.) The street map then provides overlays about everything from income to population density. For example, to learn about Seattle, Washington one types in the city name. A map will show where Seattle is located. If the user wants to see Seattle in relation to state boundaries and/or Tacoma, Washington as well as airports, etc, one simply goes to the "on boxes" for the overlay information. A "redraw" will then show all of the features on a new map. A particularly valuable site for someone doing an in-depth study of a given part of a city. [Note: A somewhat similar site for Canada will be found at: *National Atlas Information Service* (www-nais.ccm.emr.ca)]

Stressing as it does the geographical and economic facets of the United States, TIGER may be searched by itself or in conjunction with CENDATA and other Bureau publications, in print or online. At any rate, the medium- to large-sized libraries with these two databases available will be able to respond to most questions concerning the census and statistical matters.

TECHNICAL—SCIENTIFIC REPORTS[21]

Online: NTIS Order Now. Springfield, VA: U.S. National Technical Information Service, 1964 to date, monthly, www.ntis.gov. Free. DIALOG file 6, $60 per hour and other carriers.
CD: NTIS, 1980 to date, quarterly. Various publishers, $2,350 current and previous 4 years.
Print: Government Reports Announcements & Index, 1965 to date, semimonthly. Rate varies.

Librarians familiar with the unpublished reports indexed in ERIC may not be as well acquainted with unpublished studies available through the U.S. National Technical Information Service. ERIC is concerned primarily with education. NTIS turns to technical reports from U.S. and non-U.S.-government-sponsored research. As of the late 1990s there were some three million such reports available. About 750,000 new reports are added each year. (Note: the online versions cover only the most recent four to eight years and include about 500,000 reports.)

Major areas: the biological, social and physical sciences; engineering, mathematics, and business information regarding technology and science. The projects are explained in various length abstracts.

Produced by local, state, and federal government agencies, as well as by individuals and private and for-profit groups, the reports cover a

[21]By 2000 there was talk that the NTIS (National Technical Information Service) would close down and shift its archives to the Library of Congress. Why? Because they no longer can charge for materials which are free on the Internet. Unable to charge they have lost revenues used in operation. Congress refuses to make up for those lost revenues. Result: operation curtailed, and officials think it best to simply close down. See *Library Journal,* September 15, 1999, pp. 16-18.

wide spectrum of interests, including much material in the social sciences. In fact, NTIS and ERIC interchange some report information and there is a limited amount of duplication.

The *Index* includes subject, personal and corporate author, contact number, and access/report number. Annual cumulations may be purchased separately. In print there are two distinct services, the *Government Reports Announcement* and the *Government Reports Index.* Both are joined in digital formats, and become one. The announcement section includes abstracts of about 70,000 reports each year. They are divided into 26 major subject areas and then subdivided. NTIS is backed up by documents on microfiche, print and online.

STATE AND LOCAL DOCUMENTS

CD: The USA State Factbook. Minneapolis, MN: Quanta Press, Inc., 1990 to date, annual. $49.95.
Print: Book of the States. Chicago: Council of State Governments, 1935 to date, biennial, 500 pp. $79.

CD: County-City Plus. Washington, DC: Slater Hall Information Products, 1990 to date, annual. $195.
Print: County and City Data Book. Washington, DC: U.S. Bureau of the Census, 1952 to date, updated irregularly. Price varies.

Print: U.S. Library of Congress, *Monthly Checklist of State Publications,* 1910 to date, monthly. $26.

Built on material from the U.S. Bureau of the Census, *The USA State Factbook* allows the user to search a single CD-ROM for masses of information on the individual states. Territories are included, back to 1776 when the statistical data began. Still, most of the information relates to current rather than historical situations. Here one may check, for example, the size of major cities in Nevada or who is governor of Oregon, or how much is manufactured in Maine. There is little of a political, geographic or economic interest not covered in this single, easy-to-search source. As a virtual almanac of the states, this includes, too, numerous maps, state seals, and helpful graphs and illustrations.

The aptly named *Book of the States* is valuable on three counts. First, there are standard articles on issues such as reapportionment, consumer protection, rights for women, and the like. These are updated with each new volume. Second, there are reviews of trends, statistics, and developments at both the local and federal level which have, or will have, a strong influence on state government. Third, it has relatively current information on names of principal state officers. The wealth of data makes it an invaluable print reference work for almost any type or size of library.

Demographic data on all United States counties, as well as statistical data on cities of more than 10,000, is offered in the *County-City Plus* CD-ROM. With an easy-to-use menu system, the comparisons, say, between housing costs in one major city and/or county and another can be made in seconds. In fact, the primary use of this database is for comparative purposes and, of course, to answer specific questions about any area of the country as well. It is based in part, but with additions, on the *U.S. County and City Data Book*. Unlike the print book from the government, the commercial CD-ROM is updated each year and the information on everything from banking and crime to education and health care is relatively current.

At the state level, there is no entirely satisfactory bibliographical tool that lists the majority of publications of all states. Individual states tend to have their own bibliographies and listings. The *Monthly Checklist of State Publications,* prepared by the Library of Congress, represents only those state publications received by the Library. Arrangement is alphabetical by state and then by issuing agency. Entries are usually complete enough for ordering, although prices are not always given. There is an annual, but not a monthly, subject and author index. The indexes are not cumulative. Periodicals are listed in the June and December issues.

On the Web

There are numerous ways of finding state and local community government information on the Web. All states have websites. At the minimum the site provides: the names and addresses (including e-mail) for all major and many minor state officials; information on how the government operates as well as a listing of major agencies; sometimes historical data; and almost always business, industrial and occupational background material.

State pages, too, are useful for tourist information such as the location of museums, state parks and other sites of interest to travelers. Weather, transportation links, major economic developments, etc. are part of the pattern. One can locate links to state documents and legislative bills. Usually this is as extensive as for the federal government. Full texts of meetings, hearings and the like, as well as the bills, are available on most, but not all of the state sites.

To locate a specific state homepage, simply type in the address, i.e., (www.state.[state abbreviation].us). For example, for New York State this would translate into (www.state.ny.us).

Where more than one state is required there are several overview Net sites. Two examples:

State and Local Governments. Library of Congress. (http://lcweb.loc. gov/global/state/stategov.html). This provides links to virtually all of the state websites as well as to major cities. There are links as well to the

National Conference of State Legislatures and Public Technology. The site is extremely easy to use and should be the first place to turn for more than a single state.

State & Local Government on the Net (www.piperinfo.com/state/index.cfm). Here are links to both state and local governments. However, the major benefit is links to related areas such as tribal government as well as U.S. Commonwealth and Territories. See, too, the lists of national organizations which serve the needs of cities and states. Easy to use, particularly the "quick search" feature.

Final Words

Ahh, but how does the librarian remember all of this? Two answers: Memory. This develops after practice. An experienced government documents person can find answers in seconds. Those less well trained may take many minutes, hours, or never find the right answer.

In searching the Net and the "old way" of going to a library, *Yahoo!* finds that asking a librarian for census data (the number of young people 15 to 19 in America) is much faster than trying to find it the "net way." Mucking around on the Net without a real clue how to find such government statistics, the writer took close to 47 minutes to discover what a librarian did in less than half the time.[22]

The second approach is first to turn to the guide books discussed earlier in this chapter, e.g., *U.S. Government on the Web,* for one. This will take time. It will save many moments of grief later on.

A third method, and one not recommended, is to point the person with the question to the computer, suggest a URL for a general site, and then disappear in the stacks.

The purpose of the present volume of this guide, which now ends, is to give the librarian the confidence and the will to stay with the person who asks the question. If you are not up to this, leave for a less demanding position in the White House.

SUGGESTED READING

Bouwman, Harry and John Nouwens, "Government Electronic Publishers? The Dutch Case," *Government Information Quarterly,* vol. 16, no. 1, 1999, pp. 29–45. An explanation of how one government uses the Internet to make information available to its citizens. This is hardly news to Americans, but the article moves from the Net to "how the Dutch government has tried

---

[22]"Researching census info.," *Yahoo! Internet Life,* November, 1999, p. 108.

to improve accessibility to six particular cases of electronic publishing." The "feasible options" will be of interest to anyone involved with electronic data and government information. This periodical, *Government Information Quarterly* is an excellent source of government/library activities.

Byerly, Greg, "Government Documents on the Web," *School Library Media Activities Monthly,* no. 5, 1999, pp. 34–36. Too often it is forgotten how useful government documents can be in schools. The author reminds readers of their value and how they can be found and used on the Net.

Clark, Cynthia and Judy Horn. *Organization of Document Collections and Services.* Washington, DC: Association of Research Libraries, 1998. A survey of ARL libraries reveals the cold winds blowing through the documents collection are limited budgets, digital developments and countless plans for reorganization. The authors point out that more and more libraries are integrating the documents within the general reference collection—particularly digital documents.

"Government," *Forbes,* September 13, 1999, p. 110. This issue of *Forbes* is given over to the Internet. In this short piece the role of government documents and information on the Net are explored. A list of websites from the government is given.

Morehead, Joe, "Sites for Sore Eyes: A Melange," *The Serials Librarian,* vol. 27, no. 4, 2000. A study of the census, past and future. Most of the focus, though, is on the 2000 census with its numerous problems. With that the author moves to related areas from copyright to a website for federal periodicals. This is, after all, a "melange."

Newlen, Robert, "Fifty Years of Silent Service," *American Libraries* 29 (4), 1998, pp. 62-64. Subtitled: "A Peek Inside the CIA Library," this is an entertaining and only somewhat informative article about the Central Intelligence Agency library and why it is held in such high esteem by the agency. Often the librarian serves as a major source of information on problems faced by CIA agents.

Risen, James, "CIA Director Emphasizes Differences in Security Cases," *The New York Times,* February 3, 2000, p. A22. The CIA director explains to Congress that his predecessor had no intention of placing classified government documents at the disposal of foreign agents. This brings up the whole question of secrecy and the need to make government documents public. There is a vast amount of literature on this, and more each day. See, for example, James Thurman, "Limiting What Bureaucrats Rubber-Stamp Top Secret," *The Christian Science Monitor,* November 17, 1999, p. 2+; and Lucy Komisar, "Documented Complicity," *The Progressive,* September, 1999, pp. 1–24.

Shill, Harold and Lisa Stimatz, "Government Information in Academic Libraries: New Options for the Electronic Age," *The Journal of Academic Librarianship,* no. 2, 1999, pp. 94–104. In view of the government decision to put almost all government documents in a digital format, the librarian must use new strategies for collection and searching of said documents. The article "explores the implications of this change and describes the initiative of one medium-sized non-depository library to become a government information center."

INDEX